EIGHTH EDITION

Gapenski's

Understanding Healthcare Financial Management

EIGHTH EDITION

Gapenski's

Understanding Healthcare Financial Management

GEORGE H. PINK | PAULA H. SONG

HAP

AUPHA

Health Administration Press, Chicago, Illinois

Association of University Programs in Health Administration, Washington, DC

Your board, staff, or clients may also benefit from this book's insight. For information on quantity discounts, contact the Health Administration Press Marketing Manager at (312) 424-9450.

24 23 22 21 20 5 4 3 2 1

Library of Congress Cataloging-in-Publication Data
Names: Pink, George H., author. | Song, Paula H., author.
Title: Gapenski's understanding healthcare financial management / George H. Pink, PhD, Paula H. Song, PhD.
Other titles: Understanding healthcare financial management
Description: Eighth edition. | Chicago, Illinois : Health Administration Press ; Washington, DC : Association of University Programs in Health Administration, [2019] | Revised edition of: Understanding healthcare financial management. Louis C. Gapenski, George H. Pink. 2015. | Includes bibliographical references and index.
Identifiers: LCCN 2019026834 (print) | LCCN 2019026835 (ebook) | ISBN 9781640551091 (hardback) | ISBN 9781640551107 (ebook) | ISBN 9781640551114 (xml) | ISBN 9781640551145 (epub) | ISBN 9781640551138 (mobi)
Subjects: LCSH: Health facilities--Business management. | Health facilities--United States--Business management. | Medical care--United States--Finance. | Health services administration--Economic aspects--United States.
Classification: LCC RA971.3 .G37 2019 (print) | LCC RA971.3 (ebook) | DDC 362.1068/1--dc23
LC record available at https://lccn.loc.gov/2019026834
LC ebook record available at https://lccn.loc.gov/2019026835

The paper used in this publication meets the minimum requirements of American National Standard for Information Sciences—Permanence of Paper for Printed Library Materials, ANSI Z39.48-1984. ♾™

Acquisitions editor: Janet Davis; Manuscript editor: Theresa Rothschadl; Cover designer: James Slate; Layout: PerfecType

Found an error or a typo? We want to know! Please email it to hapbooks@ache.org, mentioning the book's title and putting "Book Error" in the subject line.

Health Administration Press
A division of the Foundation of the American College of Healthcare Executives
300 S. Riverside Plaza, Suite 1900
Chicago, IL 60606-6698
(312) 424-2800

Association of University Programs in Health Administration
1730 M Street, NW
Suite 407
Washington, DC 20036
(202) 763-7283

BRIEF CONTENTS

DETAILED CONTENTS

PREFACE

It has been 26 years since *Understanding Healthcare Financial Management* was first published, and it is now in its eighth edition. The original concepts of the book included (1) a broad definition of the health services sector that recognized that many of today's health services management students are seeking careers outside the hospital field and (2) a focus on the environmental factors that are unique to health services and hence make healthcare financial management different from generic corporate financial management. Although the book remains grounded in these original concepts, we have made many updates and improvements along the way and have tried very hard to ensure that the book continues to be of maximum value to both students and instructors. In today's healthcare environment, financial issues are of paramount importance, and future managers must be prepared to deal with these issues as they strive to improve the delivery of health services to all Americans.

Concept of the Textbook

Our goal in creating this edition, like all previous editions, is to produce a textbook that provides health services management students with (1) an operational knowledge of healthcare financial management theory and concepts and, even more important, (2) the ability to apply this knowledge to real-world decision-making. In addition, we want the textbook to be useful as a reference during internships and residencies as well as after graduation. Finally, we want a textbook that students find user friendly, meaning one that they enjoy reading and could learn from on their own. If students do not find a textbook interesting, understandable, and useful, they will not read it!

The book begins with basic concepts pertaining to health services and financial management. It then progresses to illustrate how managers of healthcare businesses can apply financial management theory and concepts to make better decisions—that is, decisions that promote the financial well-being of the organization.

Intended Market and Use

The book is designed primarily for use in graduate-level courses for students whose primary interest is the management of health services organizations. The book can be used for other student clienteles, but the absence of explicit accounting content, the amount of theory, and the nature of the ancillaries make the book most suitable for master of health administration, master of business administration (healthcare concentration), and master of public health (management concentration) programs. Also, because *Understanding Healthcare Financial Management* is designed to provide students with a higher level of cognition according to Bloom's taxonomy, the end-of-chapter problems are provided on spreadsheets rather than printed in the textbook. Finally, student knowledge, skills, and abilities are maximized when the textbook is paired with cases.

Alternative Course Formats

There is no best approach to teaching a healthcare financial management course. The approach varies with students' backgrounds, instructors' interests, class contact hours, and the role of the course in the overall curriculum. Because these factors change, most instructors vary their approaches over time.

Financial management courses are generally taught as a theoretically based lecture course, as a pragmatically based pure case course, or as a blend of theory and practice that combines lectures with some cases. Over time, we have used all three approaches, and the one that we have found best is a blend of theory and practice, but with a strong bias toward practice. Thus, we lecture occasionally but use a large number of cases, minicases, and problems to provide insights into the complex financial decisions faced by practicing healthcare managers.

Understanding Healthcare Financial Management provides the theory and concepts behind financial decision-making in health services and the nuts-and-bolts tools required to implement the theory and concepts. Students learn the ideas underlying healthcare financial management from the textbook and periodic lectures and then implement the concepts by working cases.

Although the textbook is designed primarily for use in a more advanced course in financial management, a great deal of introductory material has been included. Even when students have already completed one or more finance courses, we have found that many do not have a good grasp of the basic fundamentals of financial management. Thus, they appreciate that the book reviews basic concepts in addition to presenting new material. After all, repetition is the key to learning.

Changes in the Eighth Edition

The most substantial change to the textbook involves authorship. The seventh edition was authored by Louis Gapenski and George Pink; however, Dr. Gapenski passed away in 2016 (see tribute in the "About the Authors" section). Fortunately, Dr. Paula Song, associate professor of healthcare finance at the University of North Carolina at Chapel Hill, agreed to step in as coauthor. Since the seventh edition was published, we have used the textbook several times and have received many comments from users at other universities. Furthermore, Health Administration Press has solicited and received a number of thoughtful reviews. The reaction of students, other professors, and the market in general has been overwhelmingly positive; every comment indicates that the basic concept of the textbook is sound. Even so, nothing is perfect, and the health services sector is evolving at a dizzying pace. These circumstances have prompted a number of changes to the textbook.

We have two primary goals for the eighth edition: (1) to update the book by incorporating changes such as tax reform and leasing reporting requirements and (2) to make the book even more reader friendly. In addition, we have two primary goals related to the ancillary material: (1) to create in-class problems that instructors can use to illustrate theory and calculations and (2) to improve the user-friendliness of the chapter models by directly linking examples and calculations to textbook content. Many revisions were made to accomplish these and other goals; following is a list of the most important. (Please note that **some** of the healthcare organizations used as examples in this and previous editions are fictitious. Any similarities in organizational name and characteristics are unintentional. Real organizations are typically accompanied by the address of their home page.)

New and Revised Material

- Chapter 1: Introduction to Healthcare Financial Management has been revised to reflect the major changes of the December 2017 tax reform bill. Federal tax rates have been updated and the ranges of state tax rates are included.
- Chapter 5: Financial Risk and Required Return has been extensively rewritten to better differentiate risk measures of realized and expected return distributions, to incorporate actual return data for calculation of beta, and to lay out how the capital asset pricing model is used to make investment decisions more explicitly.

- Chapter 8: Lease Financing has been revised to reflect the recent changes in Financial Accounting Standards Board reporting requirements.
- Throughout the textbook, illustrative tax rates have been changed from 40 percent to 30 percent based on an assumption of a 21 percent federal tax rate and a 9 percent state tax rate.
- Chapter supplements have been removed from the textbook and can now be found online at ache.org/HAP/PinkSong8e.

Ancillary Changes

- An in-class problem for each chapter has been created that instructors can use to illustrate concepts and calculations.
- Content in chapter models is now directly linked to chapter content. For example, exhibit x.x in the textbook is clearly identified as exhibit x.x in the chapter model. This allows students to see exactly how the textbook numbers are calculated. In addition, the chapter models now include the calculations for the Integrative Application at the end of each chapter.

Miscellaneous Changes

All aspects of the text discussion, as well as the references, have been updated and clarified as needed. We have taken particular care to include content reflective of the changed healthcare financial environment after the passage of tax reform in 2017. In addition, contemporary real-world examples have been added throughout the text.

Ancillary Materials

Several ancillary materials have been designed to enhance the learning experience.

Materials for Students

Six useful ancillaries are available to students (as well as instructors) who use this text. All student ancillary materials can be accessed online at ache.org/HAP/PinkSong8e. A section called Chapter Models, Problems, and Minicases at the end of most chapters indicates whether models, end-of-chapter problems, and minicases are available.

1. **Text models.** Most of the chapters have accompanying Excel models that illustrate the text calculations and additional calculations relevant to the chapter material. The purpose of these spreadsheet models

is twofold. First, students' learning is enhanced because they can more easily visualize how various input factors influence a particular calculation. For example, the spreadsheet model for capital budgeting allows students to change input values (such as volume and average reimbursement) and immediately see the effects these changes have on profitability. Second, the spreadsheets enable students to learn the mechanics of spreadsheet analysis in a less challenging context than the minicases (discussed later) because these models typically are not part of a graded assignment. Note that sections of the text that have accompanying models are designated by a web icon (see margin).

On the web at: *ache.org/HAP/PinkSong8e*

2. **End-of-chapter problems.** A set of problems in spreadsheet format is available for most chapters. The instructor may assign the problems as homework, or students can work them on their own to gain a deeper understanding of the topics in the chapter.
3. **Minicases.** A minicase in spreadsheet format is available for most chapters. The minicases are more complicated than the end-of-chapter problems. Again, the instructor may assign the minicases as homework, or students can work them on their own to gain a deeper understanding of the topics in the chapter.
4. **In-class problems.** A short problem in spreadsheet format is available for most chapters. Instructors may use these to illustrate concepts and calculations during class.
5. **Calculation videos.** New 5–10 minute videos are included at ache.org/HAP/PinkSong8e.
6. **Online chapters.** Two chapters are available online at ache.org/HAP/PinkSong8e. These can be used by instructors in class or by students for independent learning. Chapter supplements are also on the same page.

Materials for Instructors

In addition to the materials for students, five useful ancillaries are available to instructors who adopt this text. Instructor ancillaries are contained in a secure part of the Health Administration Press website and are available only to adopters of this text. For access information, email hapbooks@ache.org. A section called Chapter Models, Problems, and Minicases at the end of most chapters indicates whether end-of-chapter problems and minicases are available.

1. **Slideshow.** Sets of PowerPoint slides that cover essential topics are available for each chapter. Each presentation contains approximately 40 slides featuring concepts, graphs, tables, lists, and calculations. Copies of the slides can be provided to students for use as lecture notes. Many instructors will find these slides useful, either without modification or customized to meet unique course and student requirements.

2. **End-of-chapter problem solutions.** A set of problems in spreadsheet format is available for most chapters. Solutions to these problem sets, which are available only to instructors, can be used to grade homework or can be provided to students for self-study.
3. **Minicase solutions.** A minicase in spreadsheet format is available for most chapters. Solutions to the minicases, which are available only to instructors, can be used to grade homework, to help students prepare for a case, or in other ways the instructor deems appropriate.
4. **Test bank.** A multiple-choice test bank that consists of roughly 20 questions or problems per chapter is available to instructors. Most instructors use problems and cases to evaluate student knowledge, skills, and abilities; however, a test bank often is useful for in-class quizzes or other purposes.
5. **In-class problem solutions.** A short problem in spreadsheet format is available for most chapters. Solutions to the in-class problems, which are available only to instructors, can be used to illustrate concepts and calculations during class.

The Casebook

In addition to the free ancillaries, many adopters pair this textbook with its accompanying casebook, *Cases in Healthcare Finance*, sixth edition. The most realistic application of healthcare finance occurs in health services organizations, and there is no substitute for on-the-job experience. The next best thing—and the only real option for the classroom—is to use cases to simulate, to the extent possible, the environment in which finance decisions are made. Cases provide students with an opportunity to bridge the gap between learning concepts in a lecture setting and applying them on the job. By working cases, students can be better prepared to deal with the multitude of problems that arise in the practice of healthcare financial management.

The latest edition of *Cases in Healthcare Finance* contains 32 cases that focus on the practice of healthcare finance, including accounting, in provider organizations. In general, each case addresses a single financial issue, such as a capital investment decision. The uncertainty of the input data, along with the presence of relevant nonfinancial factors, makes each case interesting and challenging. The case settings include a variety of provider organizations, including hospitals, medical practices, integrated delivery systems, and managed care organizations.

In general, cases may be classified as "directed" or "nondirected." **Directed** cases include a specific set of questions that students must answer to complete the case, while **nondirected** cases (as we use the term) contain only general guidance to point students in the right direction. The cases in the casebook are nondirected, because such cases closely simulate how real-world managers confront financial decision-making. However, students who stray from the key issues of the cases often do not obtain full value from their effort.

We have found that students with more advanced finance skills gain the most from nondirected cases, while students who have had less finance exposure gain most from directed cases. The online instructors' material for the casebook contains sets of questions that can be used to convert each of the cases to directed cases. Thus, instructors can use the cases in either way, depending on the experience of the students, the objectives of the course, and the extent to which cases will be used.

Spreadsheet analysis has become extremely important in all aspects of healthcare finance. Students must be given an opportunity to hone computer skills and be allowed, or required, to use spreadsheet programs to assist in financial analyses. Furthermore, spreadsheet models can reduce the amount of busywork required to perform the required calculations and hence leave students with more time to focus on financial management issues. Because of these factors, we developed well-structured, user-friendly spreadsheet models for every case to enable students to perform more efficient analyses. In addition, spreadsheet models enable students to easily create graphics and other computer outputs that will enhance the quality of the analyses and any required presentations.

The student version of each case model is complete in that no modeling is required to obtain a base case solution. However, zeros have been entered for all input data, so students must identify and enter the appropriate input values. The model then calculates the base case solution automatically. However, the models do not contain risk analyses or other extensions, such as graphics, so students must modify the models as necessary to make them most useful in completing the cases.

Acknowledgments

This book reflects the efforts of many people. The following individuals reviewed previous editions of the textbook and provided many valuable comments and suggestions for improvement:

Doug Conrad of the University of Washington
Tom Getzen of Temple University
Pinar Karaca-Mandic of the University of Minnesota
Mike McCue of Virginia Commonwealth University
Kristin Reiter of the University of North Carolina at Chapel Hill
Dean Smith of Louisiana State University
Jack Wheeler of the University of Michigan

Special thanks are also due to Michael Lindsay, who helped us revise the eighth edition.

Colleagues, students, and staff at the University of North Carolina at Chapel Hill provided inspirational as well as tangible support during the development and testing of this edition. And last, but certainly not least, we thank the staff at Health Administration Press; they were instrumental in ensuring the quality and usefulness of the textbook.

Errors in the Textbook

Despite the significant effort that has been expended on this edition, it is safe to say that some errors exist. To create the most error-free and useful textbook possible, we strongly encourage students and instructors to write or email us with comments and suggestions for improvement. We welcome and value your input!

Conclusion

Good financial management is vital to the economic well-being of the health services sector. Because of its importance, financial management theory and concepts should be thoroughly understood and correctly applied—but this feat is easier said than done. We hope that *Understanding Healthcare Financial Management* will help you better appreciate the financial management problems faced by health services today and provide guidance on how best to solve them.

George H. Pink, PhD
1105-D McGavran-Greenberg Hall
Department of Health Policy and Management
University of North Carolina at Chapel Hill
Chapel Hill, NC 27599–7411
gpink@ad.unc.edu

Paula H. Song, PhD
1105-A McGavran-Greenberg Hall
Department of Health Policy and Management
University of North Carolina at Chapel Hill
Chapel Hill, NC 27599–7411
psong@unc.edu

PART

I

THE HEALTHCARE ENVIRONMENT

Two factors make the provision of health services different from the provision of other services. First, many providers are organized as not-for-profit corporations—they are not investor owned. Second, payment for services typically is made by third parties rather than by patients, the people who receive the services. By focusing on these differences, part I of the text provides students with unique background information that creates the framework for financial decision-making in healthcare organizations.

Chapter 1 discusses the institutional setting for the delivery of healthcare services. Topics covered include the role of financial management, organizational goals, tax laws, and the implications of the major changes facing healthcare delivery for healthcare financial management. The chapter supplement reviews alternative forms of organization and ownership.

Chapter 2 focuses on insurance concepts and the third-party payer system. The chapter includes a discussion of consumer-directed health plans and the implications of health reform for health insurance.

Chapter 3 describes the primary methods that public and private insurers use to pay healthcare providers for their services. Healthcare managers must understand who the payers are and the payment methods they use because these external factors have a profound influence on financial decision-making. The chapter includes a discussion of value-based purchasing and the implications of health reform for payments to providers.

CHAPTER

1

INTRODUCTION TO HEALTHCARE FINANCIAL MANAGEMENT

Learning Objectives

After studying this chapter, readers should be able to

- explain the difference between accounting and financial management;
- discuss the role of financial management in health services organizations;
- explain how the goals of investor-owned and not-for-profit businesses differ;
- describe, in general terms, the tax laws that apply both to individuals and to healthcare businesses; and
- assess the implications of the major changes facing healthcare delivery for the financial management of healthcare organizations.

Introduction

The study of healthcare financial management is fascinating and rewarding. It is fascinating because so many of the concepts involved have implications for both professional and personal behavior. It is rewarding because the healthcare environment today, and in the foreseeable future, is forcing managers to place increasing emphasis on financial implications when making operating decisions.

First and foremost, financial management is a *decision science*. Whereas accounting provides decision-makers with a rational means by which to budget for and measure a business's financial performance, financial management provides the theory, concepts, and tools necessary to make better decisions. Thus, the primary purpose of this textbook is to help healthcare managers and students become better decision-makers. The text is designed primarily for nonfinancial managers, although financial specialists—especially those with accounting rather than finance backgrounds or those moving into the health services sector from other industries—will also find the text useful.

The major difference between this text and corporate finance texts is that we focus on factors unique to the health services sector. For example, the provision of health services is dominated by ***not-for-profit*** or ***nonprofit*** organizations (private and governmental), which are inherently different from ***investor-owned*** businesses.[1] Also, the majority of payments made to healthcare providers for services are not made by patients—the consumers of the services—but rather by some third-party payer (e.g., a commercial insurance company, a government program). This text emphasizes ways in which the unique features of the health services sector affect financial management decisions.

Although *Understanding Healthcare Financial Management* contains some theory and a great number of financial management concepts, its primary emphasis is on how managers can apply the theory and concepts; thus, it does not contain the traditional end-of-chapter questions and problems. (Note, however, that end-of-chapter problems in spreadsheet format are available as ancillary materials.) Rather, the text is designed to be used with the book *Cases in Healthcare Finance*, sixth edition, which contains cases based on real-life decisions faced by practicing healthcare managers. The cases are designed to enable students to apply the skills learned in this text's chapters in a realistic context, where judgment is just as critical to good decision-making as numerical analysis. Furthermore, the cases are not directed, which means that although students receive some guidance, they must formulate their own approach to the analyses, just as real-world decision-makers must do.[2]

This text and the casebook are oriented toward the use of spreadsheets that can help managers make better decisions. This text has accompanying spreadsheet models that illustrate the key concepts presented in many of the chapters. The casebook has spreadsheet models that make the quantitative portion of the case analyses easier to do and more complete.

It is impossible to create a text that includes everything that a manager needs to know about healthcare financial management. It would be foolish even to try because the field is so vast and is changing so rapidly that many of the details needed to become completely knowledgeable in the field can be learned only through contemporary experience. Nevertheless, this text provides the core competencies readers need to (1) judge the validity of analyses performed by others, usually financial staff specialists or consultants; and (2) incorporate sound financial management theory and concepts in their own managerial and personal decision-making.

How to Use This Book

The overriding goal in creating this text was to provide an easy-to-read, content-filled book on healthcare financial management. The text contains several features designed to assist in learning the material.

First, pay particular attention to the learning objectives listed at the beginning of each chapter. These objectives give readers a feel for the most important topics in each chapter and set learning goals for that chapter. After each major section, except the introduction, one or more self-test questions are listed. Answers to these questions are not provided. When you finish reading each major section, try to provide reasonable answers to these questions. Your responses do not have to be perfect, but if you are not satisfied with your answer, reread that section before proceeding.

In the book, italics and boldface are used to indicate special terms. *Italics* are used whenever a key term is introduced; thus, italics alert readers that a new or important concept is being presented. **Boldface** is used solely for emphasis; thus, the meaning of a boldface word or phrase has unusual significance to the point being discussed. Boxes are used to highlight key formulae or equations. As indicated in the preface, the book has accompanying spreadsheet models that match—and sometimes expand on—selected calculations in the text. The sections of the text that have accompanying models are indicated by a web icon (see the margin).

On the web at: *ache.org/HAP/PinkSong8e*

In addition to in-chapter learning aids (e.g., sidebars, time lines, solutions), materials designed to help readers learn healthcare financial management are included at the end of each chapter. First, many chapters contain an integrative application section that shows how a method covered in the chapter can be used to solve a practical problem. Second, a feature called Chapter Supplement can be found online at ache.org/HAP/PinkSong8e for many chapters; this includes materials that are important but not essential to the concepts discussed. Third, a summary section titled Chapter Key Concepts briefly reviews the most important topics covered in the chapter. If the meaning of a key concept is not apparent, you may want to review the applicable section. Fourth, a section called Chapter Models, Problems, and Minicases indicates whether spreadsheet models, problem sets, and minicases are available for that chapter. (See the preface for more information on these ancillaries.) Finally, each chapter includes a selected bibliography and list of selected websites. The books and articles listed in the bibliography can provide a more in-depth understanding of the material covered in the chapter, while the list of websites is designed just to scratch the surface of relevant material available online.

Taken together, the pedagogic structure of the book is designed to make the learning of healthcare financial management as easy and efficient as possible.

SELF-TEST QUESTION

1. Briefly describe the key features of the text designed to enhance the learning experience.

The Role of Financial Management in the Health Services Sector

The primary role of financial management is to plan for, acquire, and use funds (capital) to maximize the efficiency and value of the enterprise. Because of this role, financial management is known also as *capital finance*. The specific goals of financial management depend on the nature of the business, so we will postpone that discussion until later in the chapter. In larger organizations, financial management and accounting are separate functions, although the accounting function typically is carried out under the direction of the organization's chief financial officer and hence falls under the overall category of "finance."

In general, the financial management function includes the following activities:

- **Evaluation and planning**. First and foremost, financial management involves evaluating the financial effectiveness of current operations and planning for the future.
- **Long-term investment decisions**. Although these decisions are more important to senior management, managers at all levels must be concerned with the capital investment decision process. Such decisions focus on the acquisition of new facilities and equipment (fixed assets) and are the primary means by which businesses implement strategic plans; hence, they play a key role in a business's financial future.
- **Financing decisions**. All organizations must raise funds to buy the assets necessary to support operations. Such decisions involve the choice between the use of internal versus external funds, the use of debt versus equity capital, and the use of long-term versus short-term debt. Although senior managers typically make financing decisions, these choices have ramifications for managers at all levels.
- **Working capital management**. An organization's current, or short-term, assets—such as cash, marketable securities, receivables,

and inventories—must be properly managed to ensure operational effectiveness and reduce costs. Generally, managers at all levels are involved, to some extent, in short-term asset management, which is often called *working capital management*.

- **Contract management**. Health services organizations must negotiate, sign, and monitor contracts with managed care organizations and third-party payers. The financial staff typically has primary responsibility for these tasks, but managers at all levels are involved in these activities and must be aware of their effect on operating decisions.
- **Financial risk management**. Many financial transactions that take place to support the operations of a business can increase a business's risk. Thus, an important financial management activity is to control financial risk.

In times of high profitability and abundant financial resources, the finance function tends to decline in importance. Thus, when most healthcare providers were reimbursed on the basis of costs incurred, the role of finance was minimal. At that time, the most critical finance function was cost accounting because it was more important to account for costs than to control them. Today, however, healthcare providers are facing an increasingly hostile financial environment, and any business that ignores the finance function runs the risk of financial deterioration, which ultimately can lead to bankruptcy and closure.

In recent years, providers have been redesigning their finance functions to recognize the changes that have been occurring in the health services sector. Historically, the practice of finance had been driven by the Medicare program, which demanded that providers (primarily hospitals) churn out a multitude of reports to comply with regulations and maximize Medicare revenues. Third-party reimbursement complexities meant that a large amount of time had to be spent on cumbersome accounting, billing, and collection procedures. Thus, instead of focusing on value-adding activities, most finance work focused on bureaucratic functions. Today, to be of maximum value to the enterprise, the finance function must support cost-containment efforts, managed care and other payer contract negotiations, joint venture decisions, and participation in accountable care organizations and integrated delivery systems. Finance must help lead organizations into the future rather than merely record what has happened in the past.

In this text, the emphasis is on financial management, but there are no unimportant functions in health services organizations. Managers must understand a multitude of functions, such as marketing, accounting, and human resource management, in addition to financial management. Still, all business decisions have financial implications, so all managers—whether in operations, marketing, personnel, or facilities—must know enough about financial management to incorporate financial implications in decisions about their own specialized areas. An understanding of the theory and principles of financial management will make them even more effective at their own specialized work.

SELF-TEST QUESTIONS

1. What is the role of financial management in today's health services organizations?
2. How has this role changed over time?

Current Challenges

In February 2019, the American College of Healthcare Executives (ACHE) announced the top issues confronting hospitals. Responses to a 2018 survey of 355 community hospital CEOs were used to determine these issues. The top five concerns identified by respondents are as follows:

1. Financial challenges
2. Governmental mandates
3. Patient safety and quality
4. Personnel shortages
5. Behavioral health and addiction issues

The specific financial challenges facing hospitals, as reported by the CEOs, are as follows (ACHE 2019):

- Increasing costs for staff, supplies, and so on
- Medicaid reimbursement
- Reducing operating costs
- Bad debt
- Competition from other providers
- Managed care and other commercial insurance payments
- Medicare reimbursement
- Government funding cuts
- Transition from volume to value
- Revenue cycle management (converting charges to cash)
- Inadequate funding for capital improvements

- Emergency department overuse
- Moving away from fee-for-service care
- Pricing and price transparency

Financial challenges were at the top of the list of hospital CEOs' concerns in 2018, just as they had been for the past ten years. As such, financial issues are of primary importance to today's healthcare managers. The remainder of this book is dedicated to helping you confront and solve these issues.

SELF-TEST QUESTION

1. What are some important issues confronting hospitals today?

Organizational Goals

This text focuses on business finance. Because most healthcare managers work for corporations and because not-for-profit businesses are organized as corporations, this text emphasizes this form of organization. The other forms of business organization and alternative forms of ownership are described in the chapter supplement ache.org/HAP/PinkSong8e.

Financial decisions are not made in a vacuum but with an objective in mind. An organization's financial management goals must be consistent with and support the overall goals of the business. Thus, by discussing organizational goals, health services organizations develop a framework for financial decision-making.

In a proprietorship, partnership, or small, privately owned corporation, the owners of the business generally are also its managers. In theory, the business can be operated for the exclusive benefit of the owners. If the owners want to work hard to maximize wealth, they can. On the other hand, if every Wednesday is devoted to golf, no one is hurt. (Of course, the business still has to cater to its customers or else it will not survive.) It is in large publicly owned corporations, in which owners and managers are separate parties, that organizational goals become most important.

Large, Investor-Owned Corporations

From a financial management perspective, the primary goal of investor-owned corporations is generally assumed to be *shareholder wealth maximization*, which translates to stock price maximization. Investor-owned corporations do, of course, have other goals. Managers, who make the decisions, are interested in their own personal welfare, in their employees' welfare, and in the good of the community and society at large. Still, the goal of stock price maximization is a reasonable operating objective on which to build financial decision rules.

The primary obstacle to shareholder wealth maximization as the goal of investor-owned corporations is the *agency problem*. An agency problem exists when one or more individuals (the *principals*) hire another individual or group of individuals (the *agents*) to perform a service on their behalf and then delegate a decision-making authority to those agents. In a healthcare financial management framework, the agency problem exists between stockholders and managers and between debtholders and stockholders.

The agency problem between stockholders and managers occurs because the managers of large, investor-owned corporations hold only a small proportion of the firm's stock, so they benefit little from stock price increases. On the other hand, managers often benefit substantially from actions detrimental to stockholders' wealth, such as increasing the size of the firm to justify higher salaries and more fringe benefits; awarding themselves generous retirement plans; and spending too much on such items as office space, personal staff, and travel. Clearly, many situations can arise in which managers are motivated to take actions that are in their own best interests, rather than in the best interests of stockholders.

However, stockholders recognize the agency problem and counter it by creating the following mechanisms to keep managers focused on shareholder wealth maximization:

- **The creation of managerial incentives**. More and more firms are creating *incentive compensation plans* that tie managers' compensation to the firm's performance. One tool often used is *stock options*, which allow managers to purchase stock at some time in the future at a given price. Because the options are valuable only if the stock price climbs above the *exercise price* (the price that the managers must pay to buy the stock), managers are motivated to take actions to increase the stock price. However, because a firm's stock price is a function of both managers' actions and the general state of the economy, a firm's managers could be doing a superlative job for shareholders but the options could still be worthless. To overcome the inherent shortcoming of stock options, many firms use *performance shares* as the managerial incentive. Performance shares are given to managers on the basis of the firm's performance as indicated by objective measures, such as earnings per share, return on equity, and so on. Not only do managers receive more shares when targets are met—the value of the shares is also enhanced if the firm's stock price rises. Finally, many businesses use the concept of *economic value added (EVA)* to structure managerial compensation. (EVA is discussed in chapter 13.) All incentive compensation plans—stock options, performance shares, profit-based bonuses, and so forth—are designed with two purposes in mind. First, they offer managers incentives to act on factors under their control in a way that will contribute to stock price maximization. Second, such plans help firms attract and retain top-quality managers.

- **The threat of firing**. Until the 1980s, the probability of a large firm's stockholders ousting its management was so remote that it posed little threat. Ownership of most firms was so widely held, and management's control over the proxy (voting) mechanism was so strong, that it was almost impossible for dissident stockholders to fire a firm's managers. Today, however, about 70 percent of the stock of an average large corporation, such as pension funds and mutual funds, is held by institutional investors rather than individual investors. These institutional money managers have the clout, if they choose to use it, to exercise considerable influence over a firm's managers and, if necessary, to remove the current management team by voting it off the board.
- **The threat of takeover**. A *hostile takeover*—the purchase of a firm against its management's wishes—is most likely to occur when a firm's stock is undervalued relative to its potential because of poor management. In a hostile takeover, a potential acquirer makes a direct appeal to the shareholders of the target firm to tender, or sell, their shares at some stated price. If 51 percent of the shareholders agree to tender their shares, the acquirer gains control. When a hostile takeover occurs, the managers of the acquired firm often lose their jobs, and any managers permitted to stay generally lose the autonomy they had prior to the acquisition. Thus, managers have a strong incentive to take actions to maximize stock price. In the words of the president of a major drug manufacturer, "If you want to keep control, don't let your company's stock sell at a bargain price."

In summary, managers of investor-owned firms can have motivations that are inconsistent with shareholder wealth maximization. Still, sufficient mechanisms are at work to force managers to view shareholder wealth maximization as an important, if not primary, goal. Thus, shareholder wealth maximization is a reasonable goal for investor-owned firms.

Not-for-Profit Corporations

Because not-for-profit corporations do not have shareholders, shareholder wealth maximization is not an appropriate goal for such organizations. Not-for-profit firms consist of a number of classes of *stakeholders* who are directly affected by the organization. Stakeholders include all parties who have an interest—usually financial—in the organization. For example, a not-for-profit hospital's stakeholders include the board of trustees, managers, employees, physicians, creditors, suppliers, patients, and even potential patients (who may include the entire community). An investor-owned hospital has the same set of stakeholders, plus one additional class—stockholders. While managers of investor-owned firms have to please only one class of stakeholders—the shareholders—managers of not-for-profit firms face a different situation. They have to please all of the organization's stakeholders because no single, well-defined group exercises control.

Many people argue that managers of not-for-profit firms do not have to please anyone because they tend to dominate the board of trustees, who are supposed to exercise oversight. Others argue that managers of not-for-profit firms have to please all of the firm's stakeholders because all are necessary to the successful performance of the business. Of course, even managers of investor-owned firms should not attempt to enhance shareholder wealth by treating any of their firm's other stakeholders unfairly because such actions ultimately will be detrimental to shareholders. Typically, the goal of not-for-profit firms is stated in terms of a mission. An example is the mission statement of Bayside Memorial Hospital, a 450-bed, not-for-profit, acute care hospital: "Bayside Memorial Hospital, along with its medical staff, is a recognized, innovative healthcare leader dedicated to meeting the needs of the community. We strive to be the best comprehensive healthcare provider through our commitment to excellence."

Although this mission statement provides Bayside's managers and employees with a framework for developing specific goals and objectives, it does not provide much insight into the goals of the hospital's finance function. For Bayside to accomplish its mission, its managers have identified five financial goals:

1. The hospital must maintain its financial viability.
2. The hospital must generate sufficient profits to continue to provide its current range of healthcare services to the community. Buildings and equipment must be replaced as they become obsolete.
3. The hospital must generate sufficient profits to invest in new medical technologies and services as they are developed and needed.
4. The hospital should not rely on its philanthropy program or government grants to fund its operations and growth, although it will aggressively seek such funding.
5. The hospital will strive to provide services to the community as inexpensively as possible, given these financial requirements.

In effect, Bayside's managers are saying that to achieve the hospital's commitment to excellence as described in its mission statement, the hospital must remain financially strong and profitable. Financially weak organizations cannot continue to accomplish their stated missions over the long run. What is interesting is that Bayside's five financial goals are probably not much different from the financial goals of Jefferson Community Medical Center (JCMC), a for-profit competitor. Of course, JCMC has to worry about providing a return to its shareholders, and it receives only a small amount of contributions and grants. To maximize shareholder wealth, JCMC also must retain its financial viability and have the financial resources necessary to offer new services and technologies. Furthermore, competition in the market for hospital services will not permit JCMC to charge appreciably more for services than its not-for-profit competitors.

SELF-TEST QUESTIONS

1. What is the difference between the goals of investor-owned and not-for-profit firms?
2. What is the agency problem, and how does it apply to investor-owned firms?
3. What factors tend to reduce the agency problem?

Tax Laws

The value of any financial asset such as a share of stock issued by Tenet Healthcare (www.tenethealth.com) or a municipal bond issued by the Alachua County Health Facilities Authority (http://advisoryboards.alachuacounty.us/boards/info.aspx) on behalf of UF Health Shands Hospital (https://ufhealth.org/shands-university-florida) and the value of many real assets (e.g., MRI [magnetic resonance imaging] machines, medical office buildings, hospitals) depend on the stream of usable cash flows that the asset is expected to produce. Because taxes reduce the cash flows that are usable to the business, financial analyses must include the impact of local, state, and federal taxes. Local and state tax laws vary widely, so we do not attempt to cover them in this text. Rather, we focus on the federal income tax system because these taxes dominate the taxation of business income. In our examples, we typically increase the effective tax rate to approximate the effects of state and local taxes.

Congress can change tax laws, and major changes have occurred every three to four years, on average, since 1913, when the federal tax system was initiated. Furthermore, certain aspects of the tax code are tied to inflation, so changes based on the previous year's inflation rate automatically occur each year. Therefore, although this section gives you an understanding of the basic nature of our federal tax system, **it is not intended to be a guide for application**. Tax laws are so complicated that many law and business schools offer a master's degree in taxation, and many who hold this degree are also certified public accountants. Managers and investors should rely on tax experts rather than trust their own limited knowledge. Still, it is important to know the basic elements of the tax system as a starting point for discussions with tax specialists. In a field complicated enough to warrant such detailed study, we can cover only the highlights.

Current (2019) federal income tax rates on **personal income** go up to 37 percent, and when state and local income taxes are added, the marginal rate can approach 52 percent. **Business income** is also taxed heavily. The income from partnerships and proprietorships is reported by the individual owners as personal income and, consequently, is taxed at rates of up to 53 percent. However, such income can now qualify for pass-through tax deductions of up to 20 percent. Corporate income, in addition to state and local income taxes, is taxed by the federal government at 21 percent. Because of the magnitude of the tax bite, taxes play an important role in most financial management decisions made by individuals and by for-profit organizations.

Individual (Personal) Income Taxes

Individuals pay personal taxes on wages and salaries; on investment income such as dividends, interest, and profits from the sale of securities; and on the profits of sole proprietorships, partnerships, and S corporations (S corporations are ordinary business corporations that elect to pass corporate income, losses, deductions, and credits through to their shareholders for federal tax purposes). For tax purposes, investors receive two types of income: (1) ordinary and (2) dividends and capital gains. *Ordinary income* includes wages and salaries and interest income. *Dividend income* (which arises from stock ownership) and *capital gains* (which arise from the sale of assets, including stocks) generally are taxed at lower rates than is ordinary income.

Taxes on Wages and Salaries

Federal income taxes on ordinary income are **progressive**—that is, the higher one's income, the larger the *marginal tax rate*, which is the rate applied to the last dollar of earnings. Marginal rates on ordinary income begin at 10 percent; then rise to 12, 22, 24, 32, and 35 percent; and finally top out at 37 percent. Because the levels of income for each bracket are adjusted for inflation annually, and because the brackets are different for single individuals and married couples who file a joint return, we do not provide a complete discussion here. In brief, in 2019, it takes a taxable income of $600,000 for married couples to be in the highest (37 percent) bracket, so most people fall into the lower brackets.

Taxes on Interest Income

Individuals can receive *interest income* on savings accounts, certificates of deposit, bonds, and the like. Like wages and salaries, interest income is taxed as ordinary income and hence is taxed at federal rates of up to 37 percent, in addition to applicable state and local income taxes.

Note, however, that under federal tax laws, interest on most state and local government bonds, called *municipals* or *munis*, is not subject to federal income taxes. Such bonds include those issued by municipal healthcare authorities on behalf of not-for-profit healthcare providers. Thus, investors get to keep all of the interest received from municipal bonds but only a proportion of the interest received from bonds issued by the federal government or by corporations. Therefore, a lower interest rate muni bond can provide the same or higher after-tax return as a higher yielding corporate or Treasury bond. For example, consider an individual in the 32 percent federal tax bracket who can buy a taxable corporate bond that pays a 10 percent interest rate. What rate would a similar-risk muni bond have to offer to balance out its appeal with that of a corporate bond?

Here is a way to think about this problem:

$$\begin{aligned}\text{After-tax rate on corporate bond} &= \text{Pretax rate} - \text{Yield lost to taxes}\\ &= \text{Pretax rate} - \text{Pretax rate} \times \text{Tax rate}\\ &= \text{Pretax rate} \times (1 - \text{T})\\ &= 10\% \times (1 - 0.32) = 10\% \times 0.68 = 6.8\%.\end{aligned}$$

Here, *T* is the investor's marginal tax rate. Thus, the investor would be indifferent to the choice between a corporate bond with a 10 percent interest rate and a municipal bond with a 6.8 percent rate.

If the investor wants to know what yield on a taxable bond is equivalent to, say, an 8.0 percent interest rate on a muni bond, they would follow this procedure:

$$\begin{aligned}\text{Equivalent rate on taxable bond} &= \text{Rate on municipal bond} \div (1 - \text{T})\\ &= 8.0\% \div (1 - 0.32) = 8.0\% \div 0.68 = 11.76\%.\end{aligned}$$

The exemption of municipal bonds from federal taxes stems from the separation of power between the federal government and state and local governments, and its primary effect is to allow state and local governments (as well as not-for-profit healthcare providers) to borrow at lower interest rates than otherwise would be possible.

Dividend Income

In addition to interest income on securities, investors can receive dividend income from securities (stocks). Because investor-owned corporations pay dividends out of earnings that have already been taxed, there is double taxation on corporate income. Given that taxes have already been paid on these earnings, dividend income is taxed at the same rates as long-term capital gains income; these rates are lower than those on ordinary and interest income. If an individual is in the 35 percent or higher tax bracket, dividends are taxed at 20 percent. If an individual is in the 12 to 32 percent tax bracket, dividends are taxed at only 15 percent. To see the advantage, consider an individual in the 35 percent tax bracket who receives both $100 in interest income and $100 in dividend income. The taxes on the interest income would be 0.35 × $100 = $35, while the taxes on the dividend income would be only 0.20 × $100 = $20, a difference of $15.[3]

Capital Gains Income

Assets such as stocks, bonds, real estate, and property and equipment (e.g., land, buildings, X-ray machines) are defined as ***capital assets.*** If an individual buys a capital asset and later sells it at a profit—that is, if the individual sells it for more than the purchase price—the profit is called a ***capital gain.*** If the individual sells it for less than the purchase price, the loss is called a ***capital loss.*** An asset sold within one year of the time it was purchased produces a short-term capital gain or loss, whereas an asset held for more than one year produces a long-term capital gain or loss. For example, if you buy 100 shares of Tenet Healthcare for $10 per share and sell the stock later for $15 per share, you will realize a capital gain of 100 × ($15 – $10) = 100 × $5 = $500. However, if you sell the stock for $5 per share, you will incur a capital loss of $500. If you hold the stock for one year or less, the gain or loss is short term; otherwise, it is a long-term gain or loss. Note that if you sell the stock for $10 a share, you will realize neither a capital gain nor loss; you will simply get your $1,000 back, and no taxes will be due on the transaction.

Short-term capital gains are taxed as ordinary income at the same rates as wages and interest. However, long-term capital gains are taxed at the same rates as dividends; these rates are lower than those on ordinary income. For an illustration of the effect of this tax benefit on long-term capital gains, consider an investor in the top 35 percent tax bracket who makes a $500 long-term capital gain on the sale of Tenet Healthcare stock. If the $500 were ordinary income, she would have to pay federal income taxes of 0.35 ×

\$500 = \$175. However, as a long-term capital gain, the tax would be only 0.20 × \$500 = \$100, for a savings of \$75 in taxes. There are many nuances to capital gains taxes, especially regarding the effect of losses on taxes. Our purpose is merely to introduce the concept. The purpose of the reduced tax rate on dividends and long-term capital gains is to encourage individuals to invest in assets that contribute most to economic growth.

Corporate Income Taxes

The corporate tax structure has a flat rate of 21 percent. For example, if Midwest Home Health Services, an investor-owned home health care business, had \$80,000 of taxable income, its federal income tax bill would be \$16,800:

$$\text{Corporate taxes} = [0.21 \times \$80{,}000] = \$16{,}800.$$

While the corporate tax rate is flat, there is variability based on the state in which the corporation operates. Exhibit 1.1 outlines the difference in tax rates by state. For the remainder of this book, calculations will assume that **corporations face a combined federal and state income tax of 30 percent**.

Unrelated Business Income

Though tax-exempt holding companies can be created with both tax-exempt and taxable subsidiaries, tax-exempt corporations can have taxable income, which is usually referred to as *unrelated business income (UBI)*. UBI is created when a tax-exempt corporation has income from a trade or business that

EXHIBIT 1.1
2019 State Tax Rates

State	*Tax Rate*
NV, OH, SD, TX, WA, WY	0–1.99%
NC	2–3.99%
AZ, CO, FL, MS, NM, ND, SC, UT	4–5.99%
AL, GA, HI, ID, IN, KS, KY, MI, MO, MT, NE, NY, OK, OR, RI, TN, VA, WV, WI	6–7.99%
AK, AR, CA, CT, DE, IL, LA, ME, MD, MA, MN, NH, NJ, PA, VT, DC	8–9.99%
IA	10–12%

Source: Data from Tax-Rates.org.

(1) is not substantially related to the charitable goal of the organization and (2) is carried on with the frequency and regularity of comparable for-profit commercial businesses.

As an example of UBI, consider Bayside Memorial Hospital's pharmacy sales. In addition to its services to the hospital's patients, the not-for-profit hospital's pharmacy has a second location, adjacent to the parking garage, which sells drugs and supplies to the general public. In general, the Internal Revenue Service (IRS) views the charitable purpose of a hospital as providing healthcare services to its patients, so the income from Bayside's sales of drugs and supplies to nonpatients is taxable. The fact that the profits from the sales are used for charitable purposes is immaterial. Note, however, that if the trade or business in which a not-for-profit entity is engaged (1) is run by volunteers, (2) is run for the convenience of its employees, or (3) involves the sale of merchandise contributed to the organization, the income generated remains tax exempt. Thus, the profits on Bayside's sales of drugs and supplies to its employees, as well as the profits on the sale of items in its gift shop run by volunteers, are exempt from taxation.

Not-for-profit organizations must file UBI tax returns with the IRS annually if their gross income from unrelated business activity exceeds $1,000. Taxable income is determined by deducting expenses related to UBI income production from gross income. Then, taxes are calculated as if the income were earned by a taxable corporation.

Interest and Dividend Income Received by an Investor-Owned Corporation

Interest income received by a taxable corporation is taxed as ordinary income at the regular federal tax rate of 21 percent, plus the applicable state tax rate. However, a portion of the dividends received by one corporation from another is excluded from taxable income. As we mention in our discussion of holding companies, the size of the dividend exclusion depends on degree of ownership. In general, we assume that corporations that receive dividends have only nominal ownership in the dividend-paying corporations, so 30 percent of the dividends received are taxable. The purpose of the dividend exclusion is to lessen the impact of triple taxation. Triple taxation occurs when the earnings of firm A are taxed; then dividends are paid to firm B, which must pay partial taxes on the income; and then firm B pays out dividends to individual C, who must pay personal taxes on the income.

To see the effect of the dividend exclusion, consider the following example. A corporation that earns $500,000 and pays a 21 percent federal tax plus 9 percent state tax would have an *effective tax rate* of only $0.30 \times 0.30 = 0.09 = 9.0\%$ on its dividend income. If this firm had $10,000 in pretax dividend income, its after-tax dividend income would be $9,100:

$$\begin{aligned}\text{After-tax income} &= \text{Pretax income} - \text{Taxes}\\ &= \text{Pretax income} - (\text{Pretax income} \times \text{Effective tax rate})\\ &= \text{Pretax income} \times (1 - \text{Effective tax rate})\\ &= \$10{,}000 \times \{1 - [0.30 \times (0.21 + 0.09)]\}\\ &= \$10{,}000 \times (1 - 0.09) = \$10{,}000 \times 0.91 = \$9{,}100.\end{aligned}$$

If a taxable corporation has surplus funds that can be temporarily invested in securities, the tax laws favor investment in stocks (which pay dividends) rather than in bonds (which pay interest). For example, suppose Midwest Home Health Services has $100,000 to invest temporarily, and it can buy either bonds that pay interest of $8,000 per year or preferred stock that pays dividends of $7,000 per year. Because Midwest is taxed at 30 percent, its tax on the interest if it bought the bonds would be 0.30 × $8,000 = $2,400, and its after-tax income would be $8,000 − $2,400 = $5,600. If it bought the preferred stock, its tax would be (0.21 + .09) × (0.30 × $7,000) = $630, and its after-tax income would be $5,600. Other factors might lead Midwest to invest in the bonds or other securities, but the tax laws favor stock investments when the investor is a corporation.

Interest and Dividend Income Received by a Not-for-Profit Corporation

Interest income and dividend income received from securities purchased by not-for-profit corporations with **temporary surplus** cash are not taxable. However, note that not-for-profit firms are prohibited from issuing tax-exempt bonds for the sole purpose of reinvesting the proceeds in other securities, although they can temporarily invest the proceeds from a tax-exempt issue in taxable securities while waiting for the planned expenditures to occur. If not-for-profit firms could engage in such tax arbitrage operations, they could also, in theory, generate an unlimited amount of income by issuing tax-exempt bonds for the sole purpose of investing in higher-yield securities that are taxable to most investors. For example, a not-for-profit firm might sell tax-exempt bonds with an interest rate of 5 percent and use the proceeds to invest in US Treasury bonds that yield 6 percent.

Interest and Dividends Paid by an Investor-Owned Corporation

A firm's assets can be financed with either debt or equity capital. If it uses debt financing, it must pay interest on that debt, whereas if an investor-owned firm uses equity financing, normally it will pay dividends to its stockholders. The interest paid by a taxable corporation is deducted from the corporation's operating income to obtain its taxable income, but dividends are not deductible. Put another way, dividends are paid from after-tax income. Therefore,

Midwest, which is taxed at 30 percent, needs only $1 of pretax earnings to pay $1 of interest expense, but it needs $1.43 of pretax earnings to pay $1 in dividends:

$$\text{Dollars of pretax income required} = \frac{\$1}{(1 - \text{Tax rate})}$$
$$= \frac{\$1}{0.70} = \$1.43.$$

The fact that interest is a tax-deductible expense, while dividends are not, has a profound impact on the way taxable businesses are financed. The US tax system favors debt financing over equity financing. This point is discussed in detail in chapter 10.

Corporate Capital Gains

At one time, corporate long-term capital gains were taxed at lower rates than were ordinary income. However, under current law, corporate capital gains are taxed at the same rate as operating income.

Corporate Loss Carryback and Carryforward

Corporate operating losses that occur in any year can be used to offset taxable income in other years. In general, such losses can be carried back to each of the preceding 2 years and forward for the next 20 years. For example, an operating loss by Midwest Home Health Services in 2019 would be applied first to 2017. If Midwest had taxable income in 2017 and hence paid taxes, the loss would be used to reduce 2017's taxable income, so the firm would receive a refund on taxes paid for that year. If the 2019 loss exceeded the taxable income for 2017, the remainder would be applied to reduce taxable income for 2018. If Midwest did not have to use the 2019 loss to offset 2018 or 2017 profits, the loss for 2019 would be carried forward to 2020, 2021, and so on—up to 2039. Note that losses that are carried back provide immediate tax benefits, but the tax benefits of losses that are carried forward are delayed until some time in the future. The tax benefits of losses that cannot be used to offset taxable income in 20 years or fewer are lost to the firm. The purpose of this provision in the tax laws is to avoid penalizing corporations whose incomes fluctuate substantially from year to year.

Consolidated Tax Returns

As we mention later, if a corporation owns 80 percent or more of another corporation's stock, it can aggregate income and expenses and file a single consolidated tax return. Thus, the losses of one firm can be used to offset the profits of another. No business wants to incur losses (it can go broke losing

$1 to save 30 cents in taxes), but tax offsets do make it more feasible for large multicompany businesses to undertake risky new ventures that might suffer start-up losses.

SELF-TEST QUESTIONS

1. Briefly explain the individual (personal) and corporate income tax systems.
2. What is the difference in individual tax treatment between interest and dividend income?
3. What are capital gains and losses, and how are they differentiated from ordinary income?
4. What is unrelated business income?
5. How do federal income taxes treat dividends received by corporations compared to dividends received by individuals?
6. With regard to investor-owned businesses, do tax laws favor financing by debt or by equity? Explain your answer.

Depreciation

A fundamental accounting concept is the ***matching principle***, which requires expenses to be recognized in the same period as the related revenue is earned. Suppose Upside Family Practice buys an X-ray machine for $100,000 and uses it for ten years, after which time the machine becomes obsolete. The cost of the services provided by the machine must include a charge for the cost of the machine; this charge is called ***depreciation***. Depreciation reduces profit (net income) as calculated by accountants, so the higher a business's depreciation charge, the lower its reported profit. However, depreciation is a noncash charge—it is an allocation of previous cash expenditures—so higher depreciation expense does not reduce cash flow. In fact, higher depreciation increases cash flow for taxable businesses because the greater a business's depreciation expense in any year, the lower its tax bill.

To see more clearly how depreciation expense affects cash flow, consider exhibit 1.2. Here, we examine the impact of depreciation on two investor-owned hospitals that are alike in all regards except for the amount of depreciation expense each hospital has. Hospital A has $100,000 of depreciation expense, holds $200,000 of taxable income, pays $80,000 in taxes, and has an after-tax income of $120,000. Hospital B has $200,000 of depreciation expense, holds $100,000 of taxable income, pays $40,000 in taxes, and has an after-tax income of $60,000.

EXHIBIT 1.2
The Effect of Depreciation on Cash Flow

	Hospital A	*Hospital B*
Revenue	$1,000,000	$1,000,000
Costs except depreciation	700,000	700,000
Depreciation	100,000	200,000
Taxable income	$ 200,000	$ 100,000
Federal plus state taxes (assumed to be 30%)	60,000	30,000
After-tax income	$ 140,000	$ 70,000
Add back depreciation	100,000	200,000
Net cash flow	$ 240,000	$ 270,000

Depreciation is a noncash expense, whereas we assume that all other entries in exhibit 1.2 represent actual cash flows. To determine each hospital's cash flow, depreciation must be added back to after-tax income. When this is done, hospital B, with the larger depreciation expense, has the larger cash flow. In fact, hospital B's cash flow is larger by $270,000 – $240,000 = $30,000, which represents the tax savings, or *tax shield*, on its additional $100,000 in depreciation expense:

$$\text{Tax shield} = \text{Tax rate} \times \text{Depreciation expense} = 0.30 \times \$100{,}000 = \$30{,}000.$$

Because a business's financial condition depends on the actual amount of cash it earns, as opposed to some arbitrarily determined accounting profit, owners and managers should be more concerned with cash flow than with reported profit. Note that if the hospitals in exhibit 1.2 were **not-for-profit hospitals**, taxes would be zero for both, and they would have $300,000 in net cash flow. However, hospital A would report $200,000 in earnings, while hospital B would report $100,000 in earnings.

For-profit businesses generally calculate depreciation one way for tax returns and another way when reporting income on their financial statements. For *tax depreciation*, businesses must follow the depreciation guidelines laid down by tax laws, but for other purposes, businesses usually use *accounting*, or *book*, *depreciation guidelines.*

The most common method of determining **book depreciation** is the *straight-line method*. To apply the straight-line method, (1) start with the *capitalized cost* of the asset (generally, price plus shipping plus installation); (2) subtract the asset's *salvage value*, which, for book purposes, is the estimated value of the asset at the end of its useful life; and (3) divide the net amount by the asset's useful life. For example, consider Upside's X-ray machine, which cost $100,000 and has a ten-year useful life. Furthermore, assume that it cost $10,000 to deliver and install the machine and that its estimated salvage value after ten years of use is $5,000. In this case, the capitalized cost, or ***basis***, of the machine is $100,000 + $10,000 = $110,000, and the annual depreciation expense is ($110,000 – $5,000) ÷ 10 = $10,500. Thus, the depreciation expense reported on Upside's income statement would include a $10,500 charge for wear and tear on the X-ray machine. The name "straight line" comes from the fact that the annual depreciation under this method is constant. The ***book value*** of the asset, which is the cost minus the accumulated depreciation to date, declines evenly (follows a straight line) over time.

For **tax purposes**, depreciation is calculated according to the ***Modified Accelerated Cost Recovery System (MACRS)***. MACRS spells out two procedures for calculating tax depreciation: (1) the ***standard (accelerated) method***, which is faster than the straight-line method because it allows businesses to depreciate assets on an accelerated basis, and (2) an ***alternative straight-line method***, which is optional for some assets but mandatory for others. Because taxable businesses want to gain the tax shields from depreciation as quickly as possible, they normally use the standard (accelerated) MACRS method when it is allowed.

The calculation of MACRS depreciation uses three components: (1) the depreciable basis of the asset, which is the total amount to be depreciated; (2) a recovery period that defines the length of time over which the asset is depreciated; and (3) a set of allowance percentages for each recovery period, which, when multiplied by the basis, gives each year's depreciation expense.

Depreciable Basis

The ***depreciable basis*** is a critical element of the depreciation calculation because each year's recovery allowance depends on the asset's depreciable basis and its recovery period. The depreciable basis under MACRS generally is equal to the purchase price of the asset plus any transportation and installation costs. Unlike the calculation of book depreciation, the basis for MACRS depreciation is **not** adjusted for salvage value regardless of whether the standard accelerated method or alternative straight-line method is used.

Modified Accelerated Cost Recovery System Recovery Periods

Exhibit 1.3 describes the general types of property that fit into each ***recovery period***. Property in the 27.5- and 39-year classes (real estate) must be depreciated using the alternate straight-line method, but 3-, 5-, 7-, and 10-year property (personal property) can be depreciated by either the standard accelerated method or the alternative straight-line method.

EXHIBIT 1.3
MACRS Recovery Periods

Period	*Type of Property*
3 years	Tractor units and certain equipment used in research
5 years	Automobiles, trucks, computers, and certain special manufacturing tools
7 years	Most equipment, office furniture, and fixtures
10 years	Certain longer-lived types of equipment
27.5 years	Residential rental property, such as apartment buildings
39 years	All nonresidential property, such as commercial and industrial buildings

Note: Land cannot be depreciated.

Modified Accelerated Cost Recovery System Recovery Allowances

Once the property is placed in the correct recovery period, the yearly recovery allowance, or depreciation expense, is determined by multiplying the asset's depreciable basis by the appropriate recovery percentage shown in exhibit 1.4. The calculation is discussed in the following sections.

Under MACRS, it is generally assumed that an asset is placed in service in the middle of the first year. Thus, for three-year recovery period property, depreciation begins in the middle of the year the asset is placed in service and ends three years later. The effect of the ***half-year convention*** is to extend the recovery period one more year, so three-year property is depreciated over four calendar years, five-year property is depreciated over six calendar years, and so on. This convention is incorporated in the values listed in exhibit 1.4.

Modified Accelerated Cost Recovery System Depreciation Illustration

Assume that the $100,000 X-ray machine is purchased by Upside Family Practice and placed in service in 2019. Furthermore, assume that Upside paid another $10,000 to ship and install the machine and that the machine falls into the MACRS 5-year class. Because salvage value does not play a part in tax depreciation, and because delivery and installation charges are included (are capitalized) in the basis rather than expensed in the year incurred, the machine's depreciable basis is $110,000.

Each year's recovery allowance (tax depreciation expense) is determined by multiplying the depreciable basis by the applicable recovery percentage. Thus, the depreciation expense for 2019 is 0.20 × $110,000 = $22,000, and for 2020 it is 0.32 × $110,000 = $35,200. Similarly, the

EXHIBIT 1.4 MACRS Recovery Allowances

Ownership	*Recovery Period*			
Year	Three Years (%)	Five Years (%)	Seven Years (%)	Ten Years (%)
1	33	20	14	10
2	45	32	25	18
3	15	19	17	14
4	7	12	13	12
5		11	9	9
6		6	9	7
7			9	7
8			4	7
9				7
10				6
11	100%	100%	100%	100%

Note: The tax tables carry the recovery allowances to two decimal places, but for ease of illustration, we will use the rounded allowances shown in this table throughout this text.

depreciation expense is $20,900 for 2021, $13,200 for 2022, $12,100 for 2023, and $6,600 for 2024. The total depreciation expense over the six-year recovery period is $110,000, which equals the depreciable basis of the X-ray machine. Note that the depreciation expense reported for tax purposes each year is different from the book depreciation reported on Upside's income statement, which we calculated earlier.

The *book value* of a depreciable asset at any point in time is its depreciable basis minus the depreciation accumulated to date. Thus, at the end of 2019, the X-ray machine's tax book value is $110,000 – $22,000 = $88,000; at the end of 2020, the machine's tax book value is $110,000 – $22,000 – $35,200 = $52,800 (or $88,000 – $35,200 = $52,800); and so on. Again, note that the book value for accounting purposes is different from the book value for tax purposes.

According to the IRS, the value of a depreciable asset at any point in time is its tax book value. If a business sells an asset for more than its tax book value, the implication is that the firm took too much depreciation, and the IRS will want to recover the excess tax benefit. Conversely, if an asset is sold for less than its book value, the implication is that the firm did not take sufficient depreciation, and it can take additional depreciation on the sale of the asset. For example, suppose Upside sells the X-ray machine in early 2021 for $60,000. Because the machine's tax book value is $52,800 at the time,

$60,000 – $52,800 = $7,200 is added to Upside's operating income and taxed. Conversely, if Upside received only $40,000 for the machine, it would be able to deduct $52,800 – $40,000 = $12,800 from taxable income and hence reduce its taxes in 2021.

SELF-TEST QUESTIONS

1. Briefly describe the MACRS tax depreciation system.
2. What is the effect of the sale of a depreciable asset on a firm's taxes?

Health Reform and Financial Management

The *Patient Protection and Affordable Care Act (ACA)* of 2010 has been called the most significant healthcare legislation since Medicare and Medicaid in 1965. The new law was enacted on March 23, 2010, and was designed to provide all US citizens and legal residents with access to affordable health insurance, to reduce healthcare costs, and to improve care and quality. This legislation puts in place comprehensive health insurance changes to expand coverage, hold insurance companies accountable, lower costs, guarantee more choices, and enhance the quality of care—all of which are intended to transform and make the US healthcare system more sustainable.

The ACA has numerous major aims. However, the central goal is to expand healthcare coverage through shared responsibility between government, individuals, and employers. Employers are required to offer direct coverage to employees or indirect coverage through the provision of tax credits. Public programs such as Medicare and Medicaid have expanded eligibility requirements to cover qualified individuals and families with incomes less than 133 percent of the federal poverty level. These changes are intended to reduce the number of uninsured by half and provide coverage for about 94 percent of Americans. In addition, these reforms are intended to reduce healthcare expenditures by $100 billion in the next ten years by controlling overspending, waste, fraud, and abuse.

Some of the benefits of the ACA include free preventive care, no preexisting-condition limitation, prescription discounts for seniors, protection against healthcare fraud, small-business tax credits, extended coverage for young adults, lifetime coverage on most benefits, prevention of coverage cancellation, transparency on increases in insurance premium rates, and patient selection of primary care doctors from network.

The 2016 election brought about the possibility of further change in health reform. This was indicated by the passage of the American Healthcare Act of 2017 (AHCA) in the House. The major impacts of this reform are intended to be as follows:

- Change the income tax credit to an age-based rate instead of an income-adjusted rate
- Enable states to seek waivers for essential health benefits and out-of-pocket limits
- Remove the mandate that employers provide health insurance
- Allow insurers to charge older adults more than under the ACA
- Make health savings accounts more lucrative
- Create a state-stabilization fund to allow states to help control the cost of insurance
- Change Medicaid funding to a block grant or per capita model beginning in 2020

The major implications of health reform for health insurance and provider payments are addressed in chapters 2 and 3, respectively. The major implications of health reform for the institutional setting and the delivery of healthcare services are discussed in this section.

Accountable Care Organizations

Accountable care organizations (ACOs), one of the cornerstones of health reform, integrate local physicians with other members of the healthcare community and reward them for controlling costs and improving quality. While ACOs are not radically different from other attempts to improve the delivery of healthcare services, their uniqueness lies in the flexibility of their structures and payment methodologies and their ability to assume risk while meeting quality targets. Similar to some managed care organizations and integrated healthcare systems such as the Mayo Clinic, ACOs are responsible for the health outcomes of a specific population and are tasked with collaboratively improving care to reach cost and quality targets set by Medicare. To help achieve cost control and quality goals, ACOs can distribute bonuses when targets are met and impose penalties when targets are missed.

One feature of health reform is a shared savings program in which Medicare pays a fixed (global) payment to ACOs that covers the full cost of care of an entire population. In this program, cost and quality targets are established. Any cost savings (costs that are below target) are shared between Medicare and the ACO, as long as the ACO also meets its quality targets. If an ACO is unable to save money, it could be liable for the costs of the investments made to improve care; it also may have to pay a penalty if it does not meet performance and savings benchmarks.

To be effective, an ACO should include, at a minimum, primary care physicians, specialists, and a hospital, although some ACOs are being established solely by physician groups. For example, 30 percent of the Medicare ACOs that exist today are run by physicians and do not include a hospital partner.

An ACO can take on many forms, such as the following:

- An integrated delivery system that has common ownership of hospitals and physician practices and has electronic health records (EHRs), team-based care, and resources to support cost-effective care
- A multispecialty group practice that has strong affiliations with hospitals and contracts with multiple health plans
- A physician–hospital organization that is a subset of a hospital's medical staff and that functions like a multispecialty group practice
- An independent practice association comprising individual physician practices that come together to contract with health plans
- A virtual physician organization that sometimes includes physicians in rural areas

ACOs should have managerial systems in place to administer payments, set benchmarks, measure performance, and distribute shared savings. A variety of federal, regional, state, and academic hospital initiatives are investigating how best to implement ACOs. Although the concept shows potential, many legal and managerial hurdles must be overcome for ACOs to live up to their initial promise.

Sector Consolidation

Health reform is driving the consolidation of healthcare organizations. The ACA has accelerated health systems' acquisition of hospitals and hospitals' acquisition of physician practices, and that is likely to continue over the next several years. With the greater focus on clinical integration, quality patient care, and changing reimbursement, healthcare organizations are seeking to restructure healthcare delivery to operate more efficiently and improve coordination between patients and providers. Healthcare organizations are looking to gain a competitive advantage from combining assets, staff, and resources. Consolidation not only provides organizations access to capital, economies of scale, negotiating power with payers, and market share but may also lead to improvement in patient care by making it easier to share patient information, adhere to clinical practice guidelines (thus reducing variations in care), and access high-quality specialist physicians.

Population Health

Health reform is moving providers toward the population health management approach. The goal of population health management is to shift from focusing on treating illness to maintaining or improving health to prevent costly avoidable illness and unnecessary care. This approach is supported by new reimbursement models such as capitation, payment bundling, and shared savings. Instead of just providing preventive and chronic care when patients come in for acute problems, practices track and monitor the health status of the entire patient population, requiring greater use of health information technology (IT). The key to success in population health management will be greater awareness of the health status of the population and proactive intervention to reduce use of the health system and to achieve the best population outcomes.

Clinical Integration

A fundamental component to achieving the goals of health reform is clinical integration. Clinical integration aims to coordinate patient care across conditions, providers, settings, and time to achieve care that is safe, timely, effective, efficient, and patient focused. New payment models and advances in health information systems are used to facilitate the transition to the clinical integration model and to manage the continuum of care for patients. Provider payments are tied to results for quality, access, and efficiency with the objective of better coordination between hospitals and physicians. Health IT aims to capture patient information and make it accessible to authorized providers at the point of care. Complete patient information facilitates optimal treatment strategies and reduces the chance of medication errors and conflicting treatment plans. There will be requirements for new and more comprehensive policies and procedures that protect patient privacy and that guarantee secure data that are transferred among patients, caregivers, and organizations.

Technology

Technology has a major impact on the delivery and financial management of healthcare, as shown by the adoption of EMR systems starting in the 2000s; however, healthcare as a field is slow to adopt new technology because of privacy and safety concerns. A new technology, blockchain, has the potential to drastically change the way healthcare providers protect their data and communicate with each other. Blockchain is a system of securing data by linking them together in chains and causing a change in one part of the chain to update the rest of the chain. While this technology has the potential to revolutionize how electronic health data are shared, there are still some concerns about ensuring the privacy of the chains.

While electronic health data are still hard to share between providers, increasing emphasis on collaboration between clinicians and on quality patient care are making it necessary for healthcare organizations to invest in integrated information systems technology to collect large quantities of patient and provider data (so-called *big data*). Data analytic systems are capable of analyzing large amounts of patient data to better understand clinical processes and to identify problems and opportunities for improvement in the provision of healthcare services. Complex new IT will facilitate analysis of care coordination, patient safety, and utilization.

Staffing Shortages

Health reform has increased the number of patients who can access the healthcare system. Healthcare organizations have seen an influx of formerly uninsured patients now seeking care because they have insurance or better coverage. As a result, the demand for healthcare professionals—especially physicians, nurse practitioners, and physician assistants—will likely increase.

Health reform is also driving changes in hospital staffing by emphasizing prevention and value-based care, creating demand for primary care providers, emergency physicians, clinical pharmacists, social workers and care coordinators, and health IT and data specialists. Some professional and industry associations are predicting that current shortages of various healthcare staff will worsen in the face of this growing demand. Several strategies may increase the supply of health professionals (including primary care physicians); scholarships, flexible loan repayment programs, and debt forgiveness have been identified as ways to increase the number of providers. However, many healthcare organizations likely will face great competition for some healthcare staff.

SELF-TEST QUESTIONS

1. Briefly describe the major changes under the ACA.
2. What are the major implications of health reform for the financial management of healthcare organizations?

Chapter Key Concepts

This chapter presented some background information on business organization, ownership, goals, and taxes. Here are its key concepts:

- Financial management is a *decision science*, so the primary objective of this text is to provide students and practicing healthcare managers with the theory, concepts, and tools necessary to make effective decisions. The text is structured to support this goal.
- The *primary role of financial management* is to plan for, acquire, and use funds to maximize the efficiency and value of an enterprise.
- Financial management functions include (1) *evaluation and planning*, (2) *long-term investment decisions*, (3) *financing decisions*, (4) *working capital management*, (5) *contract management*, and (6) *financial risk management*.
- Although each form of organization has unique advantages and disadvantages, most large organizations and all not-for-profit entities are organized as *corporations*.
- From a financial management perspective, the goal of investor-owned firms is *shareholder wealth maximization*, which translates to stock price maximization. For not-for-profit firms, a reasonable goal for financial management is to *ensure the organization can fulfill its mission*, which translates to *maintaining the organization's financial viability*.
- The value of any income stream depends on the amount of *usable*, or *after-tax*, *income*. Thus, tax laws play an important role in financial management decisions.
- Separate tax laws apply to *personal* income and *corporate* income.
- For the remainder of this book, calculations will assume that corporations face a *combined federal and state income tax of 30 percent*.
- Fixed assets are *depreciated* over time to reflect the decline in their values. Depreciation is a deductible, but noncash, expense.

(continued)

(continued from previous page)

Thus, for a taxable entity, the higher its depreciation, the lower its taxes and hence the higher its cash flow, with other things held constant.

- Current laws specify that the *Modified Accelerated Cost Recovery System (MACRS)* be used to depreciate assets for tax purposes.
- The *Patient Protection and Affordable Care Act (ACA)* of 2010 aims to provide all US citizens and legal residents with access to affordable health insurance options and to transform the healthcare system to reduce costs.
- *Accountable care organizations (ACOs)* are one of the methods used to reduce healthcare costs. This type of organization integrates physicians and other healthcare providers with the goal of controlling costs and improving quality.

Although this chapter provides a great deal of background information relevant to healthcare financial management and the changes associated with health reform, it is necessary for healthcare management professionals to have a more thorough understanding of the reimbursement system. This important topic is covered in chapter 2.

Chapter Models, Problems, and Minicases

This chapter does not have an accompanying spreadsheet model. However, the chapter has five problems in spreadsheet format that focus on tax issues.

The problem spreadsheets can be accessed online at ache.org/HAP/PinkSong8e.

References

American College of Healthcare Executives. 2019. "Survey: Healthcare Finance, Governmental Mandates, Personnel Shortages Cited by CEOs as Top Issues Confronting Hospitals in 2018." Published January 25. www.ache.org/about-ache/news-and-awards/news-releases/top-issues-confronting-hospitals-in-2018.

Tax-Rates.org. 2019. "Corporate Income Tax by State." Accessed April 23. www.tax-rates.org/taxtables/corporate-income-tax-by-state.

Selected Bibliography

Ackerman, K., W. E. Kibler Jr., G. D. Steele Jr., R. L. Van Horn, and K. Swartz. 2005. "Executive Compensation in Nonprofit Health Care Organizations." *Inquiry* 42 (2): 110–17.

Arduino, K. 2018. "Healthcare Capital Markets Outlook: Short-Term Opportunities Versus Long-Term Uncertainty." *Healthcare Financial Management* 72 (5): 36–43.

Bell, C. 2018. "Tax Reform Implications for Healthcare Organizations." *Healthcare Financial Management* 72 (3): 26–28.

Fields, C. 2018. "Optimizing Physician Referrals a Key to Successful Population Health Management." *Healthcare Financial Management* 72 (7): 38–43.

Hush, T. 2018. "How Provider-Led ACOs Can Generate Long-Term Savings." *Healthcare Financial Management* 72 (5): 78–79.

Lalangas, E., D. Kroll, and A. Carlson. 2018. "The Tax Cuts and Jobs Act Takeaways for Healthcare Finance Leaders." *Healthcare Financial Management* 72 (4): 28–31.

Mayeda, E., and A. Gerland. 2018. "Using Analytics to Design Provider Networks for Value-Based Contracts." *Healthcare Financial Management* 72 (3): 36–43.

Mosrie, N. C. 2018. "Healthcare Transformational Landscape." *Healthcare Financial Management* 72 (6): 30–33.

Selected Websites

The following websites pertain to the content of this chapter:

- For more information on taxes, go to www.taxfoundation.org.
- Two of the largest integrated health systems in the United States are Kaiser Permanente and the Henry Ford Health System. To gain a better idea of what constitutes such systems, visit www.kaiserpermanente.org or www.henryfordhealth.org.
- For more information on the Affordable Care Act and accountable care organizations, go tohttp://accountablecaredoctors.org/.

Notes

1. Not-for-profit organizations are also called *nonprofit* organizations, but the former designation is becoming dominant in the health services sector. Investor-owned businesses are sometimes called *proprietary*, or *for-profit*, businesses.

2. There is a set of questions for each case in the online Instructor's Resources that accompany the casebook. Instructors who want to provide more guidance to students than that given in the case itself can distribute these questions to their students.
3. Tax rates are constantly changing, so it is important to ensure that the tax rates used for real-world financial decision-making are current.

CHAPTER

2

HEALTH INSURANCE

Learning Objectives

After studying this chapter, readers should be able to

- describe the key features of insurance,
- describe the major private and public insurers,
- demonstrate how insurers set premium rates for buyers, and
- assess the implications of health reform for the health insurance industry.

Introduction

In general, businesses in the healthcare sector that do not provide products or services directly to patients have the same operating environment as businesses in any other field. For example, Milacron (www.milacron.com), a machine tool manufacturer, and GE Healthcare Systems (www.gehealthcare.com/en/about/about-ge-healthcare-systems) sell their products in roughly the same way. Milacron sells its machines directly to manufacturers that use the machines to produce other goods, and GE Healthcare Systems sells its diagnostic equipment directly to hospitals, medical practices, and other organizations that use the equipment for diagnostic testing. The prices that the two firms charge for their products are set in the competitive marketplace, and it is relatively easy for buyers to distinguish among competing products. In general, the more expensive the product is, the better the performance, where performance can be judged on the basis of objective measures. Thus, in some fields in the healthcare sector, and in most other sectors of the economy, the consumer of the product or service (1) has a choice among many suppliers, (2) can distinguish the quality of competing goods or services, (3) makes a (presumably) rational decision regarding the purchase on the basis of quality and price, and (4) pays the full cost of the purchase.

For the most part, the provision of healthcare services takes place in a unique way. First, often only a few providers of a particular service exist in a given area. Next, it is difficult, if not impossible, to judge the quality of competing services. Then, the decision about which services to purchase is usually not made by the consumer but by a physician or some other clinician.

Also, payment to the provider is not normally made by the user of the services but by a *third-party payer*. Finally, for most individuals, health insurance from third-party payers is totally paid for or heavily subsidized by employers or government agencies, so patients are mostly insulated from the costs of healthcare.

This highly unusual marketplace for healthcare services has a profound effect on the supply of, and demand for, such services. In this chapter, we discuss elements of health insurance that directly affect financial management decisions in health services organizations.

Insurance Concepts

The third-party payer system is an insurance system comprising a wide variety of insurers of all types and sizes. Some are investor-owned, while others are not-for-profit or sponsored by the government. Some insurers require their policyholders, who may or may not be the beneficiaries of the insurance, to make the policy payments, while other insurers collect partial or total payments from society at large. Because insurance is the cornerstone of the third-party payer system, an appreciation of the nature of insurance will help you better understand the marketplace for healthcare services.[1]

A Simple Illustration

To better understand insurance concepts, consider a simple example. Assume that no health insurance exists and you face only two medical outcomes in the coming year:

Outcome	*Probability*	*Cost*
Stay healthy	0.99	$ 0
Get sick	0.01	20,000
	1.00	

Furthermore, assume that everyone else faces the same medical outcomes and the same odds and costs associated with healthcare. What is your expected healthcare cost—written as E(Cost)—for the coming year? To find the answer, we multiply the cost of each outcome by its probability of occurrence and then sum the products:

$$\begin{aligned} \text{E(Cost)} &= (\text{Probability of outcome 1} \times \text{Cost of outcome 1}) \\ &\quad + (\text{Probability of outcome 2} \times \text{Cost of outcome 2}) \\ &= (0.99 \times \$0) + (0.01 \times \$20{,}000) \\ &= \$0 + \$200 = \$200. \end{aligned}$$

Now, assume that you, and everyone else, make \$20,000 a year. With this salary, you can easily afford the \$200 "expected" healthcare cost. The problem is, however, that no one's actual bill will be \$200. If you stay healthy, your bill will be zero, but if you are unlucky and get sick, your bill will be \$20,000. This cost will force you, and most people who get sick, into personal bankruptcy.

Now, suppose an insurance policy that pays all of your healthcare costs for the coming year is available for \$250. Would you purchase the policy, though it costs \$50 more than your expected healthcare costs? Most people would. In general, individuals are risk averse, so they would be willing to pay a \$50 premium over their expected costs to eliminate the risk of financial ruin. In effect, policyholders are passing to the insurer the costs associated with the risk of getting sick.

Would an insurer be willing to offer the policy for \$250? If the insurer can sell enough policies, it can take advantage of the ***law of large numbers***. We know that it is impossible to predict the healthcare costs for the coming year for any one individual with any certainty because the cost will be either \$0 or \$20,000, and we will not know for sure until the year is over. For any individual, the expected cost of healthcare is \$200, but the standard deviation is a whopping \$1,990, so there is significant uncertainty about each individual's required expenditure.

However, if an insurance company sells a million policies, its expected total policy payout is one million times the expected payout for each policy, or 1 million × \$200 = \$200 million. Furthermore, the law of large numbers tells us that the standard deviation of costs to an insurer with a large number of policyholders is $\sigma \div \sqrt{n}$, where σ is the standard deviation for one individual and n is the number of individuals insured. Thus, payout uncertainty for the insurer, as measured by standard deviation, is only \$1,990 = \$1.99 per subscriber, or \$1.99 million in total. Given these data, we see that if there were no uncertainty about the \$20,000 estimated medical cost per claim, the insurer could forecast its total claims precisely. It would collect 1 million × \$250 = \$250 million in health insurance premiums; pay out roughly \$200 million in claims; and hence have about \$50 million to cover administrative costs, create a reserve in case realized claims are greater than predicted by its actuaries, and make a profit. Clearly, with a standard deviation of claims of about \$2 million, the \$50 million "cushion" should be sufficient to carry out a successful business. The problem for real-world insurers is their inability to forecast the cost of each claim.

Basic Characteristics of Insurance

The simple example of health insurance we just provided illustrates why individuals would seek health insurance and why insurance companies would be formed to provide such insurance. Needless to say, the concept of insurance becomes much more complicated in the real world. Insurance is typically defined as having four distinct characteristics:

1. **Pooling of losses**. The *pooling*, or *sharing*, *of losses* is the heart of insurance. *Pooling* means that losses are spread over a large group of individuals, so that each individual realizes the average loss of the pool (plus administrative expenses) rather than the actual loss incurred. In addition, pooling involves the grouping of a large number of homogeneous *exposure units* (people or things having the same risk characteristics) so that the law of large numbers can apply. Thus, pooling implies (1) the sharing of losses by the entire group and (2) the prediction of future losses with some accuracy, based on the law of large numbers.
2. **Payment only for random losses**. A *random loss* is one that is unforeseen and unexpected and occurs as a result of chance. Insurance is based on the premise that payments are made only for losses that are random. We discuss the moral hazard problem, which concerns losses that are not random, in a later section.
3. **Risk transfer**. An insurance plan almost always involves risk transfer. The sole exception to the element of risk transfer is *self-insurance*, which is assumption of a risk by a business (or individual) itself rather than by an insurance company. (Self-insurance is discussed in a later section.) *Risk transfer* is transfer of a risk from an insured to an insurer, which typically is in a better financial position to bear the risk than the insured because of the law of large numbers.
4. **Indemnification**. The final characteristic of insurance is *indemnification* for losses—that is, the reimbursement of the insured if a loss occurs. In the context of health insurance, indemnification occurs when the insurer pays the insured, or the provider, in whole or in part for the expenses related to an insured illness or injury.

Adverse Selection

One of the major problems facing insurers is adverse selection. Adverse selection occurs because individuals and businesses that are more likely to have claims are more inclined to purchase insurance than those that are less likely to have claims. For example, an individual without insurance who needs a costly surgical procedure will likely seek health insurance if she can afford it, whereas an individual who does not need surgery is much less likely to purchase insurance. Similarly, consider the likelihood of a 20-year-old to seek health insurance versus the likelihood of a 60-year-old. The older individual, with much greater health risk as a result of age, is more likely to seek insurance.

If this tendency toward adverse selection goes unchecked, a disproportionate number of sick people, or those most likely to become sick, will seek health insurance, and the insurer will experience higher-than-expected claims. This increase in claims will trigger a premium increase, which only worsens the problem, because the healthier members of the plan will seek insurance from other firms at a lower cost or may totally forgo insurance. The adverse-selection problem exists because of *asymmetric information*, which occurs when individual buyers of health insurance know more about their health status than do insurers.

Insurance companies attempt to control the adverse selection problem by underwriting provisions. *Underwriting* refers to the selection and classification of candidates for insurance. From a health insurance perspective, insurers can take two extreme positions regarding underwriting. First, if we assume that insurers offer insurance in all 50 states, insurers can base premiums on national average statistics without regard to individual characteristics. Thus, each individual (or employer) would pay the same health insurance premium regardless of age, gender, geographic location, line of work, smoking habits, genetic disposition, and so on. The premium charged for each individual would be sufficient in the aggregate to cover all expected outlays, plus administrative expenses, and the insurer would still earn a profit. In this situation, cross-subsidies clearly exist because young, healthy nonsmokers in relatively safe jobs would pay the same premiums as older, sickly smokers in relatively hazardous jobs. Thus, after taking administrative costs out of the insurance premium, healthy individuals would pay premiums that exceed their expected healthcare costs, while the sicker individuals would pay premiums that are lower than their expected costs.

At the other extreme, if no information asymmetries existed and perfect information were available, insurers could charge a premium to each subscriber on the basis of that subscriber's expected healthcare costs, as was done in the illustration presented previously. Individuals who are expected to have higher costs would be charged higher premiums, and those with lower expected costs would be charged lower premiums. Of course, neither individuals nor insurers have perfect foresight, so charging an insured individual on the basis of his expected healthcare costs is not feasible. However, insurers can take into account all factors that are proven to affect health status (and hence costs)—such as smoking habits, weight, cholesterol level, and hereditary factors—when setting insurance rates.

What approach do health insurers take in practice? When health insurance first became popular following World War II, most insurers used *community ratings*. They offered a single set of premiums, or rates, to all members of a community without regard to age, gender, health status, and so on. The rates represented an average of high-risk and low-risk individuals in that community. Thus, rates reflected geographic differences and sometimes ethnic and cultural differences if the community was dominated by a single ethnic or cultural group. Over time, some insurers (particularly commercial insurers) started to offer *experience ratings*—meaning they set rates on the basis of the claims experience of the group being insured.

For example, the Boeing Company might contract with a health insurer to insure all of Boeing's employees in the Seattle area. If Boeing's employees—who as a group tend to be younger and more educated—have lower healthcare costs than the community in general, insurers that use experience ratings can offer Boeing lower rates than those offered by competitors that use community ratings. As more and more employers with low-risk employees seek health insurance based on experience ratings, the least costly groups are skimmed from the insurance pool, and those that remain are charged higher-than-average costs. Because the healthcare costs for those remaining are above the community average, insurers serving that population have no choice but to apply experience ratings, so higher premiums will be charged to the remaining groups. The trend over time, then, has been toward the use of experience ratings and away from the use of community ratings, although community ratings are still used.

Another way health insurers used to protect themselves against adverse selection was by including *preexisting conditions* clauses in contracts. A preexisting condition is a physical or mental condition of the insured individual that existed before the policy was issued. A typical clause stated that preexisting conditions were not covered until the policy had been in force for a certain period—say, one or two years. Preexisting conditions were a problem for the health insurance industry. As we discussed earlier, one of the key elements of insurance is randomness—that is, payouts on a policy should be made in response to random events. If an individual had a preexisting condition, this key feature of insurance was violated, as the insurer no longer bore random risk but rather assumed the role of payer for the treatment of a known condition.

Actions taken by insurers that are considered to be unfair to policyholders (including preexisting condition clauses) have been the subject of much recent congressional legislation. First, Congress passed the Health Insurance Portability and Accountability Act (HIPAA) in 1996. Among other things, HIPAA established national standards regarding what provisions can be included in health insurance policies. For example, under a group health policy, individuals cannot be denied coverage or receive limited coverage, nor can they be required to pay more because of their health status. Although preexisting condition clauses were not banned by HIPAA, it established limits to what counts as a preexisting condition and to the amount of time that must pass before coverage begins. Many of the provisions of HIPAA are strengthened by the Patient Protection and Affordable Care Act (ACA) of

2010, which prohibits insurers from denying coverage because of a preexisting condition. The ACA, along with the Health Care and Education Reconciliation Act of 2010, included a large number of provisions that have (save for a few) taken effect over the past several years to help uninsured Americans obtain health insurance, improve healthcare quality and access, and reduce costs. These changes are described in the last section of this chapter.

Moral Hazard

Insurance is based on the premise that payments are made only for random losses, and from this premise stems the problem of ***moral hazard***. The most common case of moral hazard in a casualty insurance setting is the owner who deliberately sets a failing business on fire to collect the insurance. Moral hazard is also present in health insurance, but it typically takes a less dramatic form; few people are willing to voluntarily sustain injury or illness for the purpose of collecting health insurance. However, undoubtedly there are people who purposely use healthcare services that are not medically required. For example, some people might visit a physician or a walk-in clinic for the social value of human companionship rather than to address a medical necessity. Also, some hospital discharges might be delayed for the convenience of the patient rather than for medical purposes. Finally, when insurance covers the full cost or most of the cost of healthcare services, individuals often are quick to agree to a $2,000 MRI (magnetic resonance imaging) scan or other high-cost procedure that may not be necessary. If the same test required total out-of-pocket payment, individuals would think twice before agreeing to such an expensive procedure unless they clearly understood the medical necessity involved. All in all, when somebody else is paying the costs, patients consume more healthcare services.

Even more insidious is the impact of insurance on individual behavior. Individuals are more likely to forgo preventive actions and embrace unhealthy behaviors when the costs of not taking those actions will be borne by insurers. Why stop smoking if the monetary costs associated with cancer treatment are borne by the insurer, or why lose weight if others will pay for the adverse health consequences likely to result?

Insurers generally attempt to protect themselves from moral hazard claims by paying less than the full amount of healthcare costs borne by the insured. By making insured individuals bear some of the cost, insurers discourage them from consuming unneeded services or engaging in unhealthy behaviors. One way of doing this is to require a deductible. Medical policies usually contain some dollar amount that must be satisfied before benefits are paid. Although deductibles have a positive effect on the moral hazard problem, their primary purpose is to eliminate the payment of small claims because the administrative cost of processing the claim may be larger than the claim itself. Although several types of deductibles exist, the most common form is the calendar-year deductible. Here, the insured individual pays the first $1,000 (or more) of medical expenses she incurs each year. Once the deductible is met, the insurer pays all eligible medical expenses (less any copayments) for the remainder of the year.

The primary weapon that insurers have against the moral hazard problem is the coinsurance, which requires insured individuals to pay a certain percentage of eligible medical expenses—say, 20 percent—in excess of the deductible amount. For example, assume that Maria Ruiz, who has employer-provided medical insurance that pays 80 percent of eligible expenses after the $1,000 deductible is satisfied, incurs $10,000 in medical expenses during the year. The insurer will pay 0.80 × ($10,000 – $1,000) = 0.80 × $9,000 = $7,200, so Maria's responsibility is $10,000 – $7,200 = $2,800.

The purposes of coinsurance are to reduce premiums to employers and to prevent overutilization of healthcare services. Because insured individuals pay part of the cost, premiums can be reduced. In addition, insured individuals will presumably seek fewer and more cost-effective treatments and embrace a healthier lifestyle by being forced to pay some of the costs.

Some health insurance policies contain *stop-loss limits*, also called *out-of-pocket maximums*. After the insured individual pays a certain amount of coinsurance costs—say, $4,000—the insurer pays all covered costs, including coinsurance. Thus, if Maria had $50,000 of covered expenses above the deductible amount, her coinsurance share would be $10,000 if there were no stop-loss provision. If her policy contained a stop-loss amount of $4,000, Maria would only have to pay $4,000 and her insurer would pay the remaining $46,000 of costs. Of course, health insurance policies with stop-loss provisions are more costly than those without such features.

SELF-TEST QUESTIONS

1. Briefly explain the following characteristics of insurance:
   a. Pooling of losses
   b. Payment only for random losses
   c. Risk transfer
   d. Indemnification
2. What is adverse selection, and how do insurers deal with the problem?
3. What is the moral hazard problem?

Major Health Insurers (Third-Party Payers)

Up to this point, we have discussed basic concepts of insurance, some key elements of health insurance, and general types of reimbursement methodologies. Now we provide a brief background of the major health insurers (third-party payers) and, more important, discuss some of the specific reimbursement methods they use to pay healthcare providers.

Health insurance originated in Europe in the early 1800s, when mutual benefit societies were formed to reduce the financial burden associated with illness or injury. Today, health insurers can be divided into two broad categories: (1) private insurers and (2) public programs.

SELF-TEST QUESTION

1. What are the two major classifications of health insurers?

Private Insurers

In the United States, the concept of public, or government, health insurance is relatively new, while private health insurance has been in existence since the turn of the twentieth century. In this section, we discuss the major private insurers—Blue Cross and Blue Shield, commercial insurers, and self-insurers.

Blue Cross and Blue Shield

Blue Cross and Blue Shield organizations trace their roots to the Great Depression, when hospitals and physicians were concerned about their patients' ability to pay healthcare bills.

Blue Cross originated as a group of separate insurance programs offered by individual hospitals. At the time, many patients were unable to pay their hospital bills, but most individuals, except the poorest, could afford to purchase some type of hospitalization insurance. Thus, the programs were initially designed to benefit hospitals as well as patients. The programs were similar in structure. Hospitals agreed to provide a certain amount of services to program members who made periodic payments of fixed amounts to the hospitals whether services were used or not. In a short time, these programs were expanded from single hospital programs to community-wide multihospital plans called *hospital service plans.* The American Hospital Association (AHA) recognized the benefits of these plans to hospitals, so AHA and the organizations that offered hospital service plans formed close relationships.

In the early years, several states ruled that the sale of hospital services by prepayment did **not** constitute insurance, so the plans were exempt from regulations that govern the insurance industry. However, it was clear that the legal status of hospital service plans would be subject to scrutiny unless their status was formalized, so one by one the states passed enabling legislation that provided for the founding of not-for-profit hospital service corporations that were exempt from taxes and from the capital requirements mandated for other insurers. However, state insurance departments had, and continue to have, oversight over most aspects of the plans' operations. The Blue Cross name was officially adopted by most of these plans in 1939.

Blue Shield plans developed in a manner similar to that of the Blue Cross plans, except that the providers were physicians instead of hospitals and the professional organization was the American Medical Association (AMA) instead of the AHA. In 2019, there were 36 Blue Cross and Blue Shield member organizations (Blue Cross Blue Shield 2019); some offer only one of the two plans, but most offer both plans. Member organizations are independent corporations that operate locally or statewide under license from a single national association that sets standards that must be met to use the Blue Cross and Blue Shield name. Collectively, the "Blues" provide healthcare coverage for more than 100 million people in all 50 states, the District of Columbia, and Puerto Rico.

Because the Blue Cross and Blue Shield corporations operate independently, they do not all use the same reimbursement method. For example, some of the Blues use hospital reimbursement methods that are similar to Medicare's prospective payment system based on diagnosis-related groups, while other Blues use a two-tier system that pays a per diem rate for routine hospitalizations and negotiated charge-based rates for nonroutine services. In addition, virtually all of the Blues now offer managed care plans along with more traditional indemnity insurance, and many plans are contracting exclusively with integrated delivery systems in certain service areas. In these situations, capitation often is the method of payment to providers.

Commercial Insurance

Commercial health insurance is issued by life insurance companies, by casualty insurance companies, and by businesses formed exclusively to write health insurance. Commercial insurance companies can be organized either as stock or mutual businesses. *Stock businesses* are shareholder owned and can raise equity capital just like any other for-profit business can. Furthermore, the stockholders assume the risks and responsibilities of ownership and management. *Mutual businesses* have no shareholders; their management is controlled by a board of directors elected by the firm's policyholders. Regardless of the form of ownership, commercial insurance businesses are taxable entities.

Health insurance experienced an influx of commercial insurers following World War II. At that time, the United Auto Workers negotiated the first contract with employers, of which fringe benefits for employees were a major part. The majority of individuals with commercial health insurance are covered under group policies with employers, professional and other associations, or labor unions. Group health coverage has the following advantages over individual coverage:

- Group coverage has low administrative costs because many individuals are insured under a single contract. This type of coverage lowers the costs associated with sales and administration of the contract. The group contract holder—for example, the employer or labor union—usually subsidizes the premium in part or in full. Note, though, that employers that have costly employee health programs are usually forced by competitive pressures to offset higher healthcare costs with lower wages or reductions in other fringe benefits. Also, the competitive labor market forces employers to offer competitive aggregate benefits, although the benefit mix may differ.
- Typically, eligibility for a group plan does not depend on the insured individual's health status. The insurer bases its premiums on the overall health status of the group. Note, however, that the premiums paid by groups that have a small number of members can be adversely affected by the poor health of one individual.
- In general, an individual's coverage cannot be canceled unless the individual leaves the group or the plan is terminated.

Historically, commercial insurers reimbursed healthcare providers on the basis of billed charges. However, with the dramatic increase in healthcare costs that has occurred over the past 20 years, the traditional providers of health insurance—employers and unions—have seen their healthcare premiums skyrocket. Clearly, this trend cannot continue, so the major purchasers of group health insurance have put pressure on the insurance companies to trim costs. This pressure, in turn, has forced commercial insurers to offer other reimbursement methods and delivery systems, including managed care plans, that give them a better chance of controlling costs than reimbursement on the basis of billed charges allows.

Self-Insurance

The third major form of private insurance is *self-insurance*. One might think that all individuals who do not have any other form of health insurance are self-insurers, but this is not technically correct. Self-insurers make a conscious decision to bear the risks associated with healthcare costs and then set aside (or have available) funds to pay costs as they occur. Except for the wealthy, individuals are not good candidates for self-insurance because they face too much uncertainty concerning future healthcare expenses. On the other hand, large groups, especially employers, are good candidates for self-insurance. Indeed, most large groups today are self-insured. For example, employees of the state of Florida are covered by health insurance administered by Blue Cross and Blue Shield of Florida, but the actual benefits to plan members are paid by the state. Blue Cross and Blue Shield is paid for administering the plan, but the state bears all risks associated with utilization and cost uncertainty.

Many firms today are going one step further in their self-insurance programs and bypassing third-party payers. For example, Walmart, self-insures and has taken self-insurance one step further by creating a Centers of Excellence program that partners with the best programs for specific care. For example, they partner with the Mayo Clinic and send any covered employees with breast, lung, colon, or rectal cancer there, which ensures quality and controls costs. Others companies, such as Amazon, JP Morgan Chase, and Berkshire Hathaway, have announced plans to evaluate how major firms insure employees and how this can be improved through corporate initiatives. For the most part, these firms use the same techniques that managed care organizations use, but they try to do things better and at lower cost by applying the kind of management attention to healthcare that they apply to their core businesses.

SELF-TEST QUESTION

1. Briefly describe some different types of private insurers.

Public Insurers

The government is a major insurer and direct provider of healthcare services. For example, the government provides healthcare services directly to eligible individuals through the US Department of Veterans Affairs, Department of Defense, and Public Health Service medical facilities. In addition, the government either provides or mandates a variety of insurance programs, such as workers' compensation and TRICARE. In this section, we focus on the two major government insurance programs: Medicare and Medicaid.

Medicare

Medicare was established by Congress in 1965 primarily to provide medical benefits to individuals aged 65 or older. About 50 million people have Medicare coverage, which pays for about 17 percent of all US healthcare services.

Over the decades, Medicare has evolved to include four major coverages: (1) Part A, which provides hospital and some skilled nursing home coverage; (2) Part B, which covers physician services, ambulatory surgical services, outpatient services, and other miscellaneous services; (3) Part C, which is managed care coverage that can be selected in lieu of Parts A and B; and (4) Part D, which covers prescription drugs. In addition, Medicare covers healthcare costs associated with selected disabilities and illnesses (such as kidney failure), regardless of age.

Part A coverage is free to all individuals eligible for Social Security benefits. Elderly individuals who are not eligible for Social Security benefits can obtain Part A medical benefits by paying premiums of $437 per month (for 2019). Part B is optional to individuals who have Part A coverage. Most enrollees must pay a monthly premium of between $135.50 and $460.50 (for 2019), depending on income. About 93 percent of Part A participants purchase Part B coverage. Because of deductibles, copayments, coinsurance, and coverage limits, Medicare Parts A and B coverage can still require beneficiaries to bear significant out-of-pocket costs. Thus, many Medicare participants purchase additional coverage from private insurers to help cover the "gaps" in Medicare coverage. Such coverage is called *Medigap insurance.*

Part C coverage is an alternative to coverage under Parts A and B. It is offered by private insurance companies but paid for by Medicare. These plans, called *Medicare Advantage plans*, generally provide Parts A and B coverage along with many of the same benefits that a Medigap policy would include, so additional insurance is not required. (Some plans also include prescription drug [Part D] coverage.) However, because the plans are essentially managed care plans (which we discuss shortly), they typically have more restrictions on access than does standard coverage under Parts A and B. Also, some Medicare Advantage plans charge members a small premium above the amount paid by Medicare.

Part D, which was implemented in 2006, offers prescription drug coverage through plans offered by more than 70 private companies. Each plan may offer somewhat different coverage, so the benefits and costs of Part D coverage vary widely, depending on the plan.

The Medicare program is the purview of the US Department of Health and Human Services (HHS), which creates the specific rules of the program on the basis of federal legislation. Medicare is administered by an agency in HHS called the *Centers for Medicare & Medicaid Services (CMS).* CMS has regional offices that oversee the Medicare program and ensure that regulations are followed. Medicare payments to providers are not made directly by CMS but by contractors for 16 Medicare Administrative Contractor (or MAC) jurisdictions.

The *Medicare Payment Advisory Commission (MedPAC)* is an independent organization that advises Congress on issues affecting Medicare. MedPAC's primary work is to prepare two reports annually—(1) one that focuses on payment policies, including specific reimbursement amounts, and (2) one that addresses other issues. Because MedPAC is the principal "independent" advisor to Congress on Medicare payment issues, its influence over the program is significant.

Medicaid

Medicaid was established in 1966 as a modest program to be jointly funded and run by the states and the federal government to provide a medical safety net for low-income mothers and children and for elderly, blind, and disabled individuals who receive benefits from the Supplemental Security Income program. Congress mandated that Medicaid cover hospital and physician care, but states were encouraged to expand on the basic package of benefits by either increasing the range of benefits or extending the program to the near poor (i.e., people who are not destitute but whose earnings cover only basic daily needs) through optional eligibility. A mandatory nursing home benefit was added in 1972.

States with large tax bases were quick to expand coverage to many of the optional groups, while states with limited ability to raise funds for Medicaid were forced to construct limited programs. In 2017, Medicaid spending, including federal and state expenditures, totaled $576.6 billion. The federal government picks up about 62 percent of these expenditures and the states pay for the remainder (Kaiser Family Foundation 2019).

Because Medicaid is administered by the states, each state establishes its own reimbursement system. Although Medicaid historically reimbursed providers on a cost basis, more and more states are shifting to reimbursement based on per diem and fixed-fee prospective rates similar to those instituted by Medicare or contracting with managed care organizations. As Medicaid expenditures continue to rise, policymakers are continuously looking for cost-effective ways to reduce expenditures, maintain access, improve quality, and modify reimbursement systems.

Hospitals recently have been vocal in their claims that Medicaid reimbursement does not cover the costs of service, and some have even sued their state governments for increased payments on the grounds that Medicaid laws call for "fair market" rate reimbursement. Physicians have also fared badly under Medicaid because states have tried to cut Medicaid costs by freezing physicians' fees. Citing excess paperwork, high risks, and low fees, many physicians—particularly obstetricians and pediatricians—have either stopped taking Medicaid patients or are limiting the numbers they serve.

SELF-TEST QUESTIONS

1. Briefly describe the origins and purpose of Medicare.
2. What is Medicaid, and how is it administered?

Development of Premium Rates

One of the primary financial management functions of health insurance companies is the development of premium rates for healthcare buyers, typically employers. This process involves estimating the total costs of providing healthcare services to the covered population. In this section, we discuss several methodologies for estimating provider payments, which are aggregated to estimate total costs, the basis for the premium rate. Although premium rates typically are developed by health insurers, some integrated health systems contract with insurers to provide all covered services at a fixed per-member rate. In these situations, the health system acts as an insurer because it assumes utilization risk. Thus, the material in this section is relevant to those circumstances. Finally, it is useful for managers at all healthcare providers to understand how health insurers set premiums because the premiums collected by insurers establish the dollars available to pay for provider services.

Allocating Premium Dollars

Insurers collect premium dollars from employers and other purchasers of healthcare and then use those dollars to pay providers, cover administrative expenses, and earn profits. To better understand how insurers set their premium rates, consider exhibit 2.1, which is a sample illustration of how a health maintenance organization (HMO) spends a typical premium dollar.

First, HMOs have the same types of management and marketing expenses as any other business, so the premium dollar must cover such costs.

EXHIBIT 2.1 Sample Allocation of the HMO Premium Dollar

Total Premium Dollar	100%
HMO administration/profit	15%
Paid to in-system physicians	
Primary care	12%
Specialists	16
Ancillary services	5
Administration/profit	4
Total to in-system physicians	37%
Paid to in-system hospitals/institutions	33%
Paid for prescription drugs	10%
Paid to out-of-system providers	5%

Also, HMOs must earn profits, both to create reserves for contingencies and for distribution to stockholders (if the HMO is investor owned). About 15 percent of the premium dollar goes toward the HMO's administrative costs and profit, and the remaining 85 percent is paid out to providers. The largest payout is typically for physician services—at 36 percent of the premium dollar. Of this amount, approximately 12 percent is spent on primary care, 16 percent on specialist care, 5 percent on ancillary services, and 4 percent on administration and profit of the physician group. (Often, physician services are contracted through a large medical group practice, which itself has administration costs and profit requirements.)

The next major item is payments for hospital and other institutional care provided in the HMO's network (the HMO's provider panel), which totals 33 percent of the premium dollar. In addition to medical services, patients are consuming a larger and larger amount of prescription drugs, which amount to about 10 percent of the premium dollar. Finally, HMO members sometimes require services from providers that are out of the HMO's network, either because there are no in-network providers for that service or the services are required outside the geographic area served by the HMO. Payments to out-of-network providers, including physicians and hospitals or institutions, average 5 percent of the premium dollar.

Note that the percentages in exhibit 2.1 are averages, and there are wide variations among HMOs as to how they allocate their premium dollars. Healthcare purchasers want a high percentage of the premium dollar to go to providers to encourage them to provide needed services in a timely manner. Conversely, HMOs have an incentive to lower the amount paid to providers, both to increase reserves and profits and to ensure competitive pricing for buyers in an increasingly hostile marketplace. Finally, note that health reform legislation places restrictions on the proportion of premiums spent on administration. The purpose of such restrictions is to ensure that premium dollars go to healthcare services rather than to bloated administrative expenses and profits.

Developing Premium Rates: An Illustration

In this section, we illustrate several methods that an HMO or integrated delivery system can use to estimate the payments it must make to its providers to provide services to a defined population.[2] Rates are developed as if all providers were capitated because, at least initially, the premium rate will be calculated on a per member per month (PMPM) basis. When the rate is quoted to purchasers of health insurance, it may be quoted on a PMPM basis or some other basis, such as per individual or per family. Note, however, that providers can be reimbursed through capitation, discounted fee-for-service, or any other method.

Assume that BetterCare, Inc., must develop a premium bid to submit to Big Business, a major employer in BetterCare's service area. For purposes of simplicity, assume that all medically necessary in-area services can be provided by a single hospital that offers both inpatient and outpatient services, including emergency department services, a single nursing home, a panel of primary care physicians, and a panel of specialist physicians. In addition, BetterCare must budget for covered care to be delivered out of area when its members are traveling. Thus, to develop its bid, BetterCare has to estimate the amount of payments it will make to this set of providers for the covered population, plus allow for administrative expenses and profits. To keep the illustration manageable, we are excluding pharmacy and ancillary services benefits. (If you like, assume that they are *carved out* and hence provided under a separate contract.)

The *fee-for-service* method is often used to set the in-network hospital inpatient capitation rate. This method is based on expected utilization and negotiated charges rather than underlying costs, although clearly there should be a link between charges and costs. For example, assume that BetterCare targets 350 inpatient days for each 1,000 members, or 0.350 inpatient days per member. Furthermore, BetterCare believes that a fair fee-for-service charge in a competitive environment is \$1,783 per inpatient day. Note that the values chosen for utilization and payment are not based on conventional reimbursement experience. Rather, the number of inpatient days reflects a highly managed working-age population, and the fee-for-service charge is designed to cover all hospital costs, including profits, in an efficiently run hospital that operates in a highly competitive environment. The inpatient cost PMPM is calculated as follows:

$$\text{Inpatient cost PMPM} = \frac{\text{Per member utilization rate} \times \text{Fee-for-service rate}}{12}\text{, so}$$

$$= \frac{0.350 \times \$1{,}783}{12} = \$52.00\ \text{PMPM.}$$

Thus, using the fee-for-service method, BetterCare estimates inpatient costs for Big Business's HMO enrollees at \$52.00 PMPM.

Other Institutional Rates

The rates for out-of-network hospital usage, hospital outpatient surgeries, and emergency department visits, as well as for skilled nursing home stays, were developed using the fee-for-service equivalent method just discussed. The following table is a summary of BetterCare's estimates for these services.

Service	*Annual Utilization per 1,000 Members*	*Fee-for-Service Rate*	*Capitation Rate PMPM*
Out-of-area inpatient days	25	$2,375	$ 4.95
Outpatient surgeries	50	1,703	7.10
Emergency department visits	125	658	6.85
Skilled nursing home days	5	325	0.14
			$19.04

Here, each PMPM capitation rate was calculated by multiplying annual utilization by the fee-for-service rate and then dividing the resulting product first by 1,000 to obtain a per-member amount and then by 12 to get the PMPM rate. The end result is a capitation estimate of $19.04 PMPM for the services listed. Of course, actual payments to these providers typically would be made on a discounted fee-for-service basis.

Primary Care Rate

We use the *cost approach* to estimate primary physicians' costs for Big Business's enrollees. This approach is the most commonly used method for setting physicians' payments, and it is based on utilization and underlying costs, as opposed to charges. The starting point is expected patient demand, by specialty, for physicians' services. This demand is then translated into the number of full-time equivalent (FTE) physicians required per member (enrollee), which depends on physician productivity. Finally, the cost for physician services is estimated by multiplying staffing requirements by the average cost per FTE, including base compensation, fringe benefits, and malpractice premiums. In addition, an amount—usually some dollar amount per member—is added for clinical and administrative support for physicians.

In developing its capitation rate for primary care physicians, BetterCare made the following assumptions:

- On average, each enrollee makes three visits to a primary care physician per year.
- Each primary care physician can handle 4,000 patient visits per year.
- Total compensation per primary care physician is $195,000 per year.

Under these assumptions, each enrollee will require 3 ÷ 4,000 = 0.00075 primary care physicians; hence, each enrollee will require 0.00075 × $195,000 = $146.75 in primary care services annually . Finally, the cost PMPM = $146.75

÷ 12 = $12.19. Thus, the rate that BetterCare will propose to Big Business will include $12.19 PMPM for primary care physician compensation. In practice, these calculations usually are first done per 1,000 members then translated into a PMPM basis. For ease, we have simplified the calculations.

Specialty Care Rate

The capitation rate for specialists' care is developed using the cost approach in a similar manner to that used for primary care. Here are BetterCare's assumptions:

- On average, each enrollee is referred for 1.2 visits to specialty care physicians per year.
- Each specialty physician can handle 2,000 patient visits per year.
- Total compensation per specialist is $284,000 per year.

Under these assumptions, each enrollee will require 1.2 ÷ 2,000 = 0.0006 specialists; hence, each enrollee will require 0.0006 × $284,000 = $170.40 in specialists' services. Finally, the cost PMPM = $170.40 ÷ 12 = $14.20. Thus, the rate that BetterCare will propose to Big Business will include $14.20 PMPM for specialist physician compensation.

Other Physician-Related Costs Rate

Thus far, we have estimated the capitation rate for physicians' compensation, but we have not accounted for other costs associated with physicians' practices. First, Better-Care physicians require, on average, 1.7 FTEs for clinical and administrative support, and each supporting staff member receives an average of $35,000 per year in total compensation. Because the physician requirement to support each member is 0.00075 primary care plus 0.0006 specialists (for a total of 0.00135 physicians), each member will require 0.00135 × 1.7 × $35,000 = $80.33 of staff support annually, or $80.33 ÷ 12 = $6.69 PMPM.

Next, expenditures on supplies—including administrative, medical, and diagnostic supplies—average $10 per visit, and each member is expected to make a total of 4.2 visits per year to primary and specialty care physicians. Thus, the annual cost per member is $42, and the cost PMPM is estimated to be $42 ÷ 12 = $3.50 PMPM. Finally, overhead expenses, including depreciation, rent, utilities, and so on, are estimated at $6.00 PMPM.

Total Physician Rate

BetterCare has estimated numerous categories of costs related solely to physicians. For ease, assume now that BetterCare plans to (1) contract with a single medical group practice to provide all physicians' services and (2) pay the group a capitated rate. The total capitation rate for the medical group would be as follows:

Primary care	$12.19 PMPM
Specialist care	14.20
Support staff	6.69
Supplies	3.50
Overhead	6.00
Subtotal	$42.58 PMPM
Profit (10%)	4.26
In-area total	$46.84 PMPM
Outside referrals	3.70
Total	$50.54 PMPM

The $50.54 PMPM total capitation rate for the medical group is the aggregate of the rates previously developed for physicians' services, plus two additional elements. First, BetterCare believes that a fair profit margin on group practice businesses is 10 percent, so $4.26 PMPM is allowed for profit on the in-network physician subtotal of $42.58 PMPM. Second, $3.70 PMPM is allocated to cover referrals outside the group practice when needed because either a particular specialty is not available in the group or the member is outside the service area. Finally, note that the group might not capitate all its physicians, though it receives a capitated rate from BetterCare. In general, physician costs, and hence rates, include adjustments for age and gender. An alternative method of developing physician costs—the *demographic approach*—starts with utilization data already broken down by these categories. Thus, when physician payments are being determined, it is easy to make the payment amount consistent with each physician's specific patient age–gender mix.

Remember that our goal is to set a premium rate that BetterCare can use to make a bid to cover Big Business's employees. Thus far, we have estimated the PMPM rates required to pay all the providers needed to serve the population, both in and out of network. In addition, we are assuming that pharmacy benefits will be carved out and that the cost of these benefits will be $10.00 PMPM. After all costs have been considered, BetterCare concludes that it can submit a bid of $164.43 PMPM.[3] Note that if BetterCare wins the contract from Big Business, the monthly revenue to providers will be somewhat higher (usually about 5 percent) than the embedded PMPM rates because enrollees will be required to make copayments for selected services.

Medical costs	
Hospital inpatient	$ 52.00 PMPM
Other institutional	19.04
Outpatient prescription drugs	10.00
Physician care	50.54
Total medical costs	$ 131.58 PMPM
HMO costs	
Administration	$ 24.66 PMPM
Contribution to reserves/profits	4.94
Total HMO costs	$ 29.60 PMPM
Total premium	$ 161.18 PMPM

Setting the Premium Rates

Although we have developed the total PMPM required to cover the medical and administrative costs associated with Big Business's health plan, this aggregate amount now must be converted into employee premiums. Premium rates generally are categorized and quoted on a *tier basis*—each tier defines the number of premium categories offered. The following are examples of premium tiers:

- **One-tier (composite) rates**. A single premium is applied regardless of whether the subscriber is single or has any number of eligible dependents.
- **Two-tier rates**. There are two premium categories—one for single individuals and one for subscribers with dependents (families).
- **Three-tier rates**. There are three premium categories—one for single individuals; one for subscriber and spouse; and one for a family, which is defined as all other dependent situations.
- **Four-tier rates**. This tier is similar to the three-tier category, but a fourth premium category is added—subscriber with children but no spouse.

The lower the number of premium categories, the more cross-subsidization takes place. For example, with only one tier, with single subscribers paying the same premium as employees with dependents, single employees are subsidizing the healthcare costs of employees with dependents. Even in higher tiers, it is typical that a family with, say, two children would pay the same premium as a family with, say, five children.

Once the tier is decided on, the next step is to convert the aggregate PMPM into premium rates for each category in the tier. This conversion is accomplished by using a *rate ratio*, which is the markup factor applied to the single premium rate to obtain each other category rate. For example, in a three-tier plan, the rate ratios might be 2.0 for a subscriber and spouse and 2.7 for a family. In this situation, the single rate would be multiplied by 2.0 to get the subscriber and spouse rate and by 2.7 to get the family rate. The base (single) rate is a function of the premium category composition of the employee population. It must be set so that the premiums collected from all premium rate categories equal the PMPM multiplied by the number of covered lives.

Note that the rate ratios are somewhat arbitrary. Although they typically do consider family size, they often are based primarily on competitive factors and what the plan sponsor (employer) requests. In general, rate ratios are set so that some cross-subsidization exists, for reasons having to do with employer contributions and coordination of employee benefits. For example, some employers pay 100 percent of the premium for single employees but contribute only a portion for other premium categories. In this situation, subsidization makes family rates more appealing, which increases the number of covered dependents. Also, some subscribers with families choose single coverage and let their spouse include all dependents on the spouse's health plan. A higher single rate raises revenues for the health plan that enrolls only the subscriber.

In closing, note that BetterCare's bid will likely be subject to market forces—that is, there will be multiple bidders for Big Business's health contract. For BetterCare's bid to be accepted, it must offer the right combination of price and quality. If BetterCare's costs, and hence bid, are too high or its quality too low, it will not secure the contract and will have to reassess its cost and quality structure to ensure that it is competitive on future bids.

SELF-TEST QUESTIONS

1. Roughly, what is the allocation of an HMO premium dollar?
2. Briefly describe the following three methods for developing capitation rates:
   a. Fee-for-service method
   b. Cost approach
   c. Demographic approach
3. Of the three approaches, which one do you think would be the most accurate? The easiest to apply in practice?
4. Explain the difference between the total PMPM and a premium rate.

Consumer-Directed Health Plans

Consumer-directed health plans (CDHPs) use financial incentives to influence patient behavior. CDHPs were devised primarily to reduce unnecessary healthcare use and, subsequently, overall healthcare spending. Their approach is to couple incentives to save money that would otherwise be spent on higher premiums and elective healthcare services with financing arrangements that make patients responsible for purchasing more of their healthcare.

CDHPs have been available since 2003, and their prevalence is increasing. According to the Kaiser Employee Health Benefits Survey in 2018, 29 percent of workers are now enrolled in CDHPs, up from 13 percent in 2010 (Kaiser Family Foundation 2018). Rising healthcare costs, which continue to be a vexing problem in healthcare, have largely prompted this increase. Changes in behavior by patients who rely on CDHPs have important implications for providers.

Features of Consumer-Directed Health Plans

CDHPs have two components: a *high-deductible health plan (HDHP)* and a *personal health financing account*. A HDHP typically has a lower premium but higher annual deductible ($1,350 for an individual for 2019). Once a patient has paid the deductible amount out of pocket, the insurance kicks in and provides coverage for the remaining expenses through the end of the year. As a result of concerns that high deductibles will encourage patients to forgo preventive services, the majority of CDHPs pay for some preventive services before patients reach the deductible.

There are two types of personal health financing accounts (Internal Revenue Service 2019): *health savings accounts (HSAs)* and *health reimbursement arrangements (HRAs)*. Authorized by the Medicare Modernization Act of 2003, HSAs are established with a trustee (custodian) and can be used only to pay for eligible healthcare expenses. Such accounts must be used in conjunction with qualified HDHPs, which in 2019 required a minimum deductible of $1,350 for individuals and $2,700 for families. The details of HDHPs and their costs vary widely by plan. For example, one insurer might offer two different HDHP alternatives for individual coverage: (1) Plan A, with a $1,350 deductible, a 20 percent copayment, and a $5,800 out-of-pocket maximum and (2) Plan B, with a $2,500 deductible, no copayment, and a $3,300 maximum. Contributions to HSAs can be made by both the employer and the employee, although employer contributions are capped by federal law at the level of the deductible. Contributions from both parties are tax exempt.

In 2019, contributions to HSAs, which are deductible for federal income taxes, were limited to $3,500 for individual coverage and $7,000 for family coverage. HSAs are sponsored by financial institutions and health insurers that pay interest on the accounts. Money in HSAs can be used to pay for any qualified medical expense, including the cost of dental and vision care and over-the-counter drugs. Interest paid on these accounts, and all amounts used to pay for healthcare services, are not subject to taxes. In addition, the account can be rolled over from year to year with no tax consequences until the account is closed, at which time withdrawals are taxable. Employees exercise ownership of their accounts, which are maintained even when employees change employers. This design allows and encourages the use of HSAs as retirement savings accounts, although accrued savings are taxed when they are used for nonmedical expenses.

In contrast, HRAs have limited use as long-term saving mechanisms. Their primary purpose is to reimburse employees for medical expenses. The employer owns and is the sole contributor to this account. There are no federal limits on employer contributions to HRAs. HRA contributions are also tax exempt, but unlike HSAs, unused funds remain with the employer when the employee changes jobs. Nonmedical expenses are not reimbursed through HRA accounts.

The Rationale for Consumer-Directed Health Plans

Under the first-dollar coverage typical of traditional comprehensive insurance plans, patients may not consider the cost of a procedure or doctor visit when making healthcare decisions. Patients may use more healthcare services than they would if they were responsible for paying for each service directly. To pay for higher utilization by patients who are insulated from full costs, traditional insurance plans raise premiums. In the end, employers that pay all or part of employees' premiums are responsible for all healthcare costs, including those that may be higher than necessary.

There is some evidence that many patients respond to higher cost sharing with lower utilization. The RAND Health Insurance Experiment, the largest controlled study of healthcare utilization, found that patients consume fewer services when subject to higher cost sharing. To better align demand for healthcare with the costs of providing those services, purchasers and insurers designed CDHPs, which apply the RAND experiment findings to the healthcare market.

Another rationale for CDHPs is that putting the onus of paying for care on the patient may make patients more likely to engage in comparative shopping and to focus on obtaining value for their healthcare dollar. Purchasers and policymakers hope that comparative shopping among patients will lead to competition among providers that will increase quality and lower costs. Improvements in quality driven by competition for patients depend on establishment of uniform quality metrics that are publicly reported. Patients who pay directly for their healthcare may also follow care regimens prescribed by their doctors more conscientiously to prevent having to pay the costs of further health complications.

Financial Implications for Providers

Because CDHPs are relatively new, published evidence of patient and provider outcomes is limited. Initial comparisons of traditional insurance and CDHPs show lower utilization and spending. The largest study of high-deductible health plans found that families enrolled in CDHPs spent 14 percent less on care compared to families in traditional health plans and had moderate reductions in preventative care (Buntin et al. 2011).

Though research on CDHPs is ongoing, economists and policy analysts predict that there could be a number of intended and unintended consequences associated with increasing use of CDHPs. The following list discusses a few.

1. **If the dynamics observed in the RAND experiment hold true, patients will demand fewer services unrelated to serious health conditions**. Demand for preventive care and prescription drugs may decrease. To prevent this harmful result, many plans exclude preventive care and necessary prescription drugs from the deductible. CDHPs may also reduce demand for imaging and elective surgeries. Providers that have a substantial number of patients who use CDHPs may experience reduced volume and reimbursement as a consequence.
2. **CDHPs may compel providers in a given geographic area to increase their competitive efforts to attract patients**. Patients shopping for value for their healthcare dollar may seek care from providers that convince them that their deductible dollars will be well spent. They may charge lower prices, publicly report higher-quality care, or offer perks to the patient, such as access to electronic health records. Providers may have to be more transparent about their prices and quality to attract patients.
3. **Increased availability of CDHPs may change the demographics of some providers' patients**. The low monthly premium charged by HDHPs may attract younger people who seldom get sick and thus need minimal health coverage. Providers may also notice that a higher proportion of patients with traditional insurance have more severe health conditions. These demographic shifts could change insurer risk pools and might strain health insurance companies' ability to maintain existing benefit levels.
4. **Some providers may experience higher bad-debt expense as some people exhaust their CDHPs and have no way of paying for**

additional expenses. Providers incur much greater bad-debt loss as a result of healthcare utilization by self-payers than by commercial payers. Furthermore, a healthcare receivable is often difficult and expensive to collect when it becomes a consumer debt.

The Future of Consumer-Directed Health Plans

Banks, credit unions, and insurance companies are making HSAs increasingly attractive by letting plan holders invest their unused deposits in mutual funds (Optum 2014). Many employers, such as Walmart, are routing their employees into CDHPs. In addition to growth in private sector employers, public health plans are increasingly using the CDHP option. Private plans contracted to provide service to Medicare beneficiaries had the option of offering a Medicare medical savings account as of 1997. However, benefit and enrollment restrictions on these plans were limiting participation. The establishment of a demonstration medical savings account plan in 2006 created an alternative consumer-directed option that operated more like HSAs in the non-Medicare market. While these plans are heavily adapted to low-income populations, their increasing popularity shows that there is broad interest in increasing the patient's role in paying for healthcare services.

Consumer-directed healthcare continues to evolve as the published evidence weighs in on whether the health plans are best able to realize lower costs, more patient choice, and higher quality. It may also reveal the circumstances under which the plans yield the greatest societal benefit. Benefit design and eligibility are highly regulated, but as the evidence emerges, employers and health insurance companies in many markets will likely attempt to enroll more patients in these plans. Whether patients take to these plans will depend in large part on how well the plans work for them.

SELF-TEST QUESTIONS

1. What are the two components of CDHPs, and how do they work together?
2. What are some advantages of HSAs over HRAs?
3. What perverse healthcare market incentives are created by traditional indemnity insurance?
4. What is the main finding from the RAND experiment, and how do CDHPs apply it?
5. What rationales are used to promote CDHP use?
6. How could CDHPs affect providers?

Value-Based Benefit and Insurance Design

Value-based benefit design (VBBD) is the explicit use of plan incentives to encourage enrollee adoption of one or more of the following: (1) appropriate use of high health-value services, including certain prescription drugs and preventive services; (2) adoption of healthy lifestyles, such as smoking cessation or increased physical activity; and (3) use of high-performance providers who adhere to evidence-based treatment guidelines.

Value-based insurance design (VBID) is a system that bases patients' copayments on the relative value—not the cost—of the clinical intervention. The principal tenets of a VBID program are (1) medical services differ in the clinical benefit achieved, and (2) the value of a specific intervention likely varies across patient groups. VBID design concentrates primarily on the financial incentives and disincentives directed at health plan enrollees. The idea is to align insurance incentives (e.g., favorable copays and deductibles) with the goals of consumer health behavior (e.g., adhering to wellness and prevention guidelines, properly managing chronic conditions).

SELF-TEST QUESTIONS

1. Briefly describe VBBD and VBID.
2. What are the goals of these insurance designs?

Health Reform and Health Insurance

The ACA introduced a number of provisions to expand insurance coverage and improve insurance affordability and access. These provisions include minimal standards for health insurance policies, a mandate that all individuals possess coverage, the creation of insurance exchanges, price transparency, and Medicaid expansion.

A number of new insurance standards have been specified in the ACA. In terms of coverage, these include the following:

- Children under the age of 19 cannot be denied benefits or coverage because the child has a preexisting condition.
- Children and dependents are permitted to remain on their parents' insurance plans until their twenty-sixth birthday.

- Insurance companies are prohibited from dropping policyholders if they become sick and from denying coverage to individuals as a result of preexisting conditions.
- Individuals have a right to appeal and request a review of denial of payment.

In terms of costs, the standards include the following:

- Insurers are required to charge the same premium rate to all applicants of the same age and geographic location, regardless of preexisting conditions or sex.
- Insurers are required to spend at least 80–85 percent of premium dollars on health costs and claims instead of on administrative costs and profits. If this is violated, rebates will be issued to policyholders.
- Lifetime limits on most benefits are prohibited for all new health insurance plans. In terms of care, the standards include the following:
  - All plans must now include essential benefits, such as ambulatory patient services; emergency services; hospitalization; maternity and newborn care; mental health and substance use disorder services; prescription drugs; laboratory services; preventive and wellness services; and chronic disease management and pediatric services, including oral and vision care.
  - Preventive services, childhood immunizations, and adult vaccinations and medical screenings are available free of charge to the patient.
  - Individuals are permitted to choose a primary care doctor outside the plan's network.
  - Individuals can seek emergency care at a hospital outside the health plan's network.

The implications of health reform for financial management and payments to providers are addressed in chapters 1 and 3, respectively. The implications for health insurance are discussed in this section.

Individual Mandate

The individual mandate of the ACA went into effect in January 2014. All eligible individuals (i.e., US citizens and legal residents) who were not covered by an employer-sponsored health plan, Medicaid, or Medicare were required to have a health insurance policy or face tax penalties. In 2017, the passage of the Tax Cuts and Jobs Act repealed the individual mandate (effective January 1, 2019). The Congressional Budget Office (2017) estimates that repeal of the individual health insurance mandate will increase the number of uninsured people by 4 million in 2019 and 13 million in 2027.

Health Insurance Exchanges

Health insurance exchanges (HIEs) are an important part of ensuring healthcare access is available to all Americans and legal immigrants. People who are unable to receive health insurance through their employer, the unemployed, or the self-employed can purchase coverage through an exchange. HIEs are online marketplaces, where people can research and review their options and purchase health insurance. As of 2018, roughly 12 million people used public HIEs to buy coverage.

There are different types of HIEs. Public exchanges are created by state or federal government and are open to both individuals seeking insurance for themselves and to small-group employers seeking insurance for their workers. All plans listed on an HIE are required to offer core benefits—called *essential health benefits*—such as preventive and wellness services, prescription drugs, and hospital stays. Private exchanges, on the other hand, are created by private-sector firms, such as a health insurance company. The number of private HIEs may rise as more corporations consider private exchanges as a way for their employees to buy health insurance using a defined contribution. For example, IBM operates a private exchange for Medicare coverage called OneExchange, where retired employees can choose different Medicare plans based on their needs.

Medicaid Expansion

One of the key provisions of the ACA was the expansion of Medicaid to all citizens and legal residents between the ages of 19 and 64 who have household incomes below 138 percent of the federal poverty level. Medicaid expansion primarily benefits childless adults who previously did not qualify for Medicaid regardless of their income level, as well as low-income parents who previously did not qualify even if their children did qualify. As a result, if every state expanded Medicaid, it was estimated that an additional 16 million people would receive coverage.

Originally, under the ACA, Medicaid expansion was mandatory for all states; states that did not comply were to be penalized by the federal government. However, the US Supreme Court ruled that states can opt out of the Medicaid expansion, leaving this decision to participate in the hands of the state's leaders. In 2012, the court further ruled that the federal government could not penalize states through denial of federal funding if they did not expand Medicaid. Despite these rulings, 37 states and the District of Columbia expanded Medicaid eligibility as of 2019.

Price Transparency

To allow for price transparency, all insurance companies are required to post the rates for their various health insurance plans on HIEs. This will permit individuals and businesses shopping for insurance to compare all plans and rates side by side and select plans that are affordable and meet their needs.

High-Deductible Health Plans

Many of those who choose their coverage are opting for HDHPs. HDHPs are growing in popularity because they are among the least expensive options on the insurance exchanges. In fact, the rate of enrollment in HDHPs has more than doubled since 2009. These plans have low premiums and high deductibles, and some are linked with HSAs or HRAs, as we described earlier. HDHPs aim to provide individuals with control over their healthcare expenditures. As mentioned, individuals enrolled in an HDHP are required to meet minimum deductibles before the plans starts to cover healthcare expenses.

New Insurance Markets

Before health reform, the health insurance industry focused on selling group plans to employers. Now it must recreate itself to cater to a huge, entirely new market of individual consumers. Many insurers have little idea how costly it is to provide coverage to the new customers, many of whom are not working and have not been insured for a long time (or ever). One of the biggest challenges that insurance companies face is attempting to accurately price and run plans without dramatic premium increases. Another implication is that the newly insured often need education about how to use their health plan effectively and how to access different types of care.

Focus on Chronic Care

As insurers and providers continue to partner in new accountable care organizations (ACOs), the shared savings programs focus on consumers with chronic conditions. That means implementing more patient-centered medical homes that aim to manage chronic conditions with specific care pathways that address behavioral health needs and decrease hospital admissions and emergency department visits. ACOs and medical homes will also increasingly make use of personal health coaches, who motivate patients on a one-on-one basis and help coordinate patient care with all caregivers.

SELF-TEST QUESTION

1. Briefly describe the impact of the ACA on health insurance.

Chapter Key Concepts

This chapter presented information on the insurance function, the third-party payer system, and the reimbursement methodologies used by payers. Here are its key concepts:

- Health insurance is widely used in the United States because individuals are risk averse and insurance firms can take advantage of the *law of large numbers.*
- Insurance is based on four key characteristics: (1) *pooling of losses*, (2) *payment for random losses*, (3) *risk transfer*, and (4) *indemnification.*
- *Adverse selection* occurs when individuals most likely to have claims purchase insurance, while those least likely to have claims do not.
- *Moral hazard* occurs when an insured individual purposely sustains a loss, as opposed to a random loss. In a health insurance setting, moral hazard is more subtle, producing such behaviors as seeking more services than needed and engaging in unhealthy behavior because the costs of the potential consequences are borne by the insurer.
- The major private insurers are *Blue Cross and Blue Shield*, *commercial insurers*, and *self-insurers.*
- The government is a major insurer and direct provider of healthcare services. The two major forms of government health insurance are *Medicare* and *Medicaid.*
- Several methods are used by insurers to set premium rates, including the (1) *fee-for-service method*, (2) the *cost approach*, and (3) the *demographic approach.*
- *Consumer-directed health plans (CDHPs)* aim to influence patient behavior rather than provider behavior.
- *CDHPs* reduce the amount of care paid for by insurance companies and increase the amount of care paid for by patients. The plans combine a high-deductible health plan with one of two kinds of accounts from which consumers can draw to pay for care until the deductible is satisfied.
- *Value-based benefit design (VBBD)* and *value-based insurance design (VBID)* focus on improving healthcare quality and decreasing costs. They encourage the use of services when the

(continued)

(continued from previous page)

clinical benefits exceed the costs, and they discourage the use of services when the benefits do not justify the cost.

- The *Patient Protection and Affordable Care Act (ACA)* introduced a number of provisions that made health insurance more accessible. The provisions focused on expanding insurance coverage and improving insurance affordability and access.
- ACA provisions, including health insurance exchanges, Medicaid expansion, price transparency, high-deductible health plans, new insurance markets, and focus on chronic care—have many implications for health insurance companies and healthcare providers.

The information in this chapter plays a vital role in financial decision-making in health services organizations. Thus, it will be used repeatedly in future chapters.

Selected Case

One case in *Cases in Healthcare Finance*, fifth edition, is applicable to this chapter: "Case 1: New England Healthcare," which focuses on premium development by a healthcare insurer.

References

Blue Cross Blue Shield. 2019. "BCBS Companies and Licensees." Accessed April 11. www.bcbs.com/bcbs-companies-and-licensees.

Buntin, M. B., A. Haviland, R. McDevitt, and N. Sood. 2011. "Healthcare Spending and Preventive Care in High-Deductible and Consumer-Directed Health Plans." *American Journal of Managed Care* 17 (3): 222–30.

Congressional Budget Office. 2017. "Repealing the Individual Health Insurance Mandate: An Updated Estimate." Published November 8. www.cbo.gov/publication/53300.

Internal Revenue Service. 2019. "Publication 969 (2018), Health Savings Accounts, and Other Tax-Favored Health Plans." Published March 6. www.irs.gov/publications/p969.

Kaiser Family Foundation. 2019. "Total Medicaid Spending." Accessed April 10. www.kff.org/medicaid/state-indicator/total-medicaid-spending/?currentTimeframe=0&sortModel=%7B%22colId%22:%22Location%22,%22sort%22:%22asc%22%7D.

———. 2018. *Employer Health Benefits: 2018 Annual Survey.* Published October. http://files.kff.org/attachment/Report-Employer-Health-Benefits-Annual-Survey-2018.

Optum. 2014. *How Are Consumer-Driven Health Plans Impacting Drug Spending?* Accessed April 10, 2019. https://cdn-aem.optum.com/content/dam/optum3/optum/en/resources/white-papers/Consumer-Driven-Health-Plans-White-Paper.pdf.

Selected Bibliography

Bell, C. 2018. "Tax Reform Implications for Healthcare Organizations." *Healthcare Financial Management* 72 (3): 26–28.

Daly, R. 2018a. "Blues Pursue Different Approaches to Changing the Healthcare Model." *Healthcare Financial Management* 72 (7): 7–9.

———. 2018b. "Health Insurance: Pilot to Offer APM Bonuses to Physicians in Medicare Advantage." *Healthcare Financial Management* 72 (8): 7–9.

———. 2018c. "Individual Health Insurance: Short-Term Plans Advance Despite Insurer Concerns." *Healthcare Financial Management* 72 (4): 9–11.

Kotecki, L. 2018. "Reaping the Benefits of an Actuarial Mindset." *Healthcare Financial Management* 72 (4): 50–54.

Lalangas, E., D. Kroll, and A. Carlson. 2018. "The Tax Cuts and Jobs Act Takeaways for Healthcare Finance Leaders." *Healthcare Financial Management* 72 (4): 28–31.

Morrisey, M. A. 2014. *Health Insurance*, 2nd ed. Chicago: Health Administration Press.

Perez, K. 2018. "What the TCJA Means for Health Care." *Healthcare Financial Management* 72 (3): 66–67.

Rejda, G. E., and M. McNamara. 2017. *Principles of Risk Management and Insurance.* Upper Saddle River, NJ: Prentice-Hall.

Vaughan, E. J., and T. M. Vaughan. 2013. *Fundamentals of Risk and Insurance.* New York: Wiley.

Selected Websites

The following websites pertain to the content of this chapter:

- For an extensive source of information on the Medicare program for both patients and providers, see the CMS website at www.cms.gov.
- The Blue Cross and Blue Shield national organization website contains a great deal of information on the enterprise and its licensed health plans; see www.bcbs.com.

- The health insurance industry provides generic information on healthcare plans at www.ahip.org.
- To learn more about MedPAC and read some of the reports they have prepared for Congress, see www.medpac.gov.
- To obtain more information on health insurance under the ACA, see www.healthcare.gov.

Notes

1. For more information on the basics of insurance, see one of the many excellent insurance textbooks, such as *Principles of Risk Management and Insurance* by George E. Rejda and Michael McNamara (Prentice-Hall, 2017) and *Fundamentals of Risk and Insurance* by Emmett J. Vaughan and Therese M. Vaughan (Wiley, 2013). For more information on health insurance, see *Health Insurance*, 2nd ed., by Michael A. Morrisey (Health Administration Press, 2014).
2. Note that the utilization, charge, and cost data used in this section to develop capitation rates are for illustration only and do not necessarily reflect values being used today.
3. According to the 2018 Employer Health Benefits survey undertaken by the Kaiser Family Foundation and Health Research and Educational Trust, the average annual HMO premium for single coverage was $6,896. The average annual HMO premium for family coverage was $19,616. See www.kff.org/health-costs/report/2018-employer-health-benefits-survey/.

CHAPTER

3

PAYMENTS TO PROVIDERS

Learning Objectives

After studying this chapter, readers should be able to

- briefly describe medical coding and its relationship to fee-for-service reimbursement;
- describe generic payment methods used to pay providers and the incentives and risks they create for providers;
- discuss the reimbursement methods used by Medicare;
- explain the rationale, design, and incentives of value-based purchasing systems; and
- assess the implications of health reform for payments to providers of healthcare services.

Introduction

There are various payment methods used to reimburse providers. For instance, providers that are reimbursed on the basis of each patient encounter receive *fee-for-service*, the term often used to describe conventional reimbursement. In this chapter, we present alternative reimbursement methods, including capitation and pay for performance. We also consider risk-sharing arrangements, which often accompany capitation. New payment methods have emerged that focus on quality of services and are intended to reduce costs. Throughout the chapter, we discuss the incentives to providers created by these systems.

Coding: The Foundation of Fee-for-Service Reimbursement

In practice, the basis for most fee-for-service reimbursement is the patient's diagnosis (in the case of hospitals) or the procedures performed on the patient (in the case of physicians). Clinicians indicate diagnoses and procedures by codes, so a brief background on clinical coding will enhance your understanding of reimbursement.

Diagnosis Codes

The *International Classification of Diseases* (most commonly known by the abbreviation *ICD*) is the standard for designating diseases plus a wide variety of signs, symptoms, and external causes of injury. Published by the World Health Organization (WHO), *ICD codes* are used internationally to record many types of health events, including hospital inpatient stays causes of death. (ICD codes were first used in 1893 to report death statistics.) The WHO periodically revises the diagnostics codes in ICD, which is now in the tenth version (ICD-10).

The United States has used ICD-10-CM since October 1, 2015. This national variant of ICD-10 was provided by the Centers for Medicare & Medicaid Services (CMS) and the National Center for Health Statistics, and the use of ICD-10-CM codes is now mandated for all inpatient medical reporting. There are more than 70,000 ICD-10-CM procedure codes and more than 69,000 diagnosis codes, compared to about 3,800 procedure codes and roughly 14,000 diagnosis codes found in the ICD-9-CM.

ICD-10-CM codes are three to seven categories in length. The first three characters refer to the category; characters four to six refer to etiology, anatomic site, severity, or other clinical detail; and character seven refers to extension (additional information such as "subsequent encounter"). For example, S52 describes a fracture of the forearm, while S52.521A describes a torus fracture of the lower end of the right radius, initial encounter for closed fracture.

In practice, the application of ICD codes to diagnoses is complicated and technical. Hospital coders have to understand the coding system and the medical terminology and abbreviations used by clinicians. Because of this complexity, and because proper coding can mean higher reimbursement from third-party payers, ICD coders require a great deal of training and experience to be most effective.

Procedure Codes

While ICD codes are used to specify diseases and conditions, *Current Procedural Terminology (CPT)* codes are used to specify medical procedures (treatments). *CPT codes* were developed and are copyrighted by the American Medical Association. The purpose of CPT is to create a uniform language (set of descriptive terms and codes) that accurately describes medical, surgical, and diagnostic procedures. CPT terminology and codes are revised periodically to reflect current trends in clinical treatments. To increase standardization and the use of electronic health records (EHRs), federal law requires that physicians and other clinical providers, including laboratory and diagnostic services, use CPT for the coding and transfer of healthcare information. (The same law also requires that ICD-10-CM codes be used for hospital inpatient services.)

For example, there are ten CPT codes for physician office visits. Five of the codes apply to new patients, while the other five apply to established patients (repeat visits). The differences among the five codes in each category are based on the complexity of the visit, as indicated by three components: (1) extent of patient history review, (2) extent of examination, and (3) difficulty of medical decision-making. For repeat patients, the least complex (typically shortest) office visit is coded 99211, while the most complex (typically longest) is coded 99215.

Because Medicare and Medicaid and other insurers require additional information from providers beyond that contained in CPT codes, CMS developed an enhanced code set, the *Healthcare Common Procedure Coding System* (HCPCS) (commonly pronounced "hick picks"). The system expands the set of CPT codes to include nonphysician services (e.g., ambulance transportation) and durable medical equipment (e.g., prosthetic devices).

Although CPT and HCPCS codes are not as complex as the ICD codes, coders still must have a high level of training and experience to use them correctly. As in ICD coding, correct CPT coding ensures correct reimbursement. Coding is so important that many businesses offer services—such as books, software, education, and consulting—to hospitals and medical practices to improve coding efficiency.

SELF-TEST QUESTIONS

1. Briefly describe the coding system used in hospitals (ICD codes) and medical practices (CPT codes).
2. What is the link between coding and reimbursement?

Generic Reimbursement Methods

Regardless of the payer, only a limited number of payment methods are used to reimburse providers. Payment methods can be categorized into two broad classifications: (1) fee-for-service and (2) capitation. Under fee-for-service, of which many variations exist, the greater the amount of services provided, the higher the amount of reimbursement. Under *capitation*, a fixed payment is made to providers for each covered life, regardless of the number of services provided. In this section, we consider the mechanics, incentives to providers, and financial risk of these reimbursement methods.

Fee-for-Service Methods

The three primary fee-for-service methods are (1) cost-based reimbursement, (2) charge-based reimbursement, and (3) prospective payment.

Cost-Based Reimbursement

Under *cost-based reimbursement*, the payer agrees to reimburse the provider for the costs incurred in providing services to the insured population. Reimbursement is limited to *allowable costs*, usually defined as costs directly related to the provision of healthcare services. Nevertheless, for all practical purposes, cost-based reimbursement guarantees that a provider's total costs will be covered by payments from payers. Typically, the payer makes *periodic interim payments (PIPs)* to the provider, and a final reconciliation is made after the contract period expires and all costs have been processed through the provider's accounting system.

During its early years (1966–1982), Medicare reimbursed providers on the basis of costs incurred. Now most hospitals are reimbursed by Medicare, and by other payers, using a per diagnosis prospective payment system (see section titled Prospective Payment). An exception is *critical-access hospitals (CAHs)*, which are 1,346 small, rural hospitals that provide services to remote populations without easy access to other hospitals. CAHs receive cost-based reimbursement for the services provided to Medicare beneficiaries (and Medicaid beneficiaries in some states).

Charge-Based Reimbursement

When payers pay *billed charges*, they pay according to a rate schedule established by the provider, called a *chargemaster*. To a certain extent, this reimbursement system places payers at the mercy of providers in regard to the cost of healthcare services, especially in markets where competition is limited. In the early days of health insurance, all payers reimbursed providers on the basis of billed charges.

Some insurers still reimburse providers according to billed charges, but the trend is toward other, less generous reimbursement methods. As this trend continues, the only payers expected to pay billed charges are self-pay, or private-pay, patients. Even then, low-income patients often are billed at rates less than charges. Some payers that historically reimbursed providers on the basis of billed charges now pay by *negotiated*, or *discounted*, *charges*. This is especially true for insurers that have established managed care plans such as health maintenance organizations (HMOs) and preferred-provider organizations (PPOs). HMOs and PPOs, as well as some conventional insurers, have bargaining power because of the large number of patients that they bring to a provider. This power allows them to negotiate discounts from billed charges. Such discounts generally range from 20 percent to 50 percent, or even more, of billed charges. Sometimes *sliding-scale discounts* are used, the amount of which is tied to the volume generated by the payer—the greater the volume, the higher the discount.

Prospective Payment

In a *prospective payment system*, the rates paid by payers are determined by the payer before the services are provided. Furthermore, payments are not directly related to reimbursable costs or chargemaster rates. Here are some common units of payment used in prospective payment systems:

1. **Per procedure**. Under *per procedure* reimbursement, a separate payment is made for each procedure performed on a patient. Because of high administrative costs associated with this method when applied to complex diagnoses, per procedure reimbursement is more commonly used in outpatient than inpatient settings.
2. **Per diagnosis**. In *per diagnosis* reimbursement, the provider is paid a rate that depends on the patient's diagnosis. Diagnoses that require higher resource usage and hence are more costly to treat have higher reimbursement rates. Medicare pioneered this basis of payment in its *diagnosis-related group (DRG)* system, which it first used for hospital reimbursement in 1983. (Reimbursement on the basis of DRG is discussed in detail in the section on Medicare.)
3. **Per diem (per day)**. If reimbursement is based on a *per diem* rate, the provider is paid a fixed amount for each day service is provided, regardless of the nature of the services. This type of reimbursement is applicable only to inpatient settings. Note that per diem rates can be stratified. For example, a hospital may be paid one rate for a medical/surgical day, a higher rate for a critical care unit day, and yet a different rate for an obstetric day. Stratified per diems recognize that providers incur different daily costs for providing different types of care.
4. **Bundled (global) pricing**. Under *bundled pricing*, payers make a single prospective payment that covers all services delivered in a single episode, whether they were rendered by one provider or multiple providers. For example, a bundled payment may be made for all obstetric services associated with a pregnancy provided by a single physician, including all prenatal and postnatal visits, as well as the delivery. For another example, a bundled payment may be made for

all physician and hospital services associated with a cardiac bypass operation. Finally, note that, at the extreme, a global payment may cover an entire population, which, in effect, is a capitation payment (as described in the next section).

Capitation

Under **capitation**, providers receive a fixed fee for each patient enrolled in the capitated plan. This fee is the same for all patients, regardless of the amount or intensity of care a patient seeks. This reimbursement methodology requires a different approach to financial management decision-making than that used under conventional reimbursement. The basic cornerstones of finance—such as discounted cash flow analysis, risk and return, and opportunity costs—remain unchanged, but the environment in which these concepts are applied is altered under a capitated system.

Formally defined, capitation is a flat periodic payment per enrollee to a healthcare provider; it is the sole reimbursement for services provided to a defined population. The word *capitation* is derived from the term *per capita*, which means per person (literally, per head). Often, capitation payments are expressed as some dollar amount *per member per month (PMPM)*. Here, the word *member* typically means an enrollee in a managed care plan—usually an HMO.

For example, a primary care physician may receive a capitated payment of $20 PMPM for attending to the healthcare needs of 250 members of BetterCare, a regional HMO. Under this contract, the physician would receive $20 × 250 × 12 = $60,000 in total capitation payments over the year. The physician then would have to cover all primary care services offered to patients specified in the contract, as well as all administrative and other practice costs associated with providing that care.

Capitated payments are adjusted for age and gender, so unlike the example here, PMPM payments would not be exactly the same for all 250 members of the health plan. Payments can also be *risk-adjusted*, an actuarial process that incorporates health status into the PMPM amount. This process attempts to match the capitated rate to the expected healthcare needs, and hence costs, of the patient.

The widespread use of capitation began in the late 1980s among managed care organizations, which adopted the system as one tool of many designed to reduce healthcare costs. By changing the unit of payment from per service to per member, capitation removed the incentive to increase revenues by increasing service volume. Although the use of capitation did reduce the growth rate of healthcare costs for a few years, cost increases ultimately returned to the old pattern of being about twice that of general inflation.

Thus, payer enthusiasm for capitated payments waned, and the prediction that capitation would dominate the payment landscape never came true. However, under health reform, some accountable care organizations (ACOs) are paying providers a capitated rate that is tied to quality of care. The theory is that fixed payments would discourage the provision of unnecessary care, and quality-based bonuses would ensure that needed services are provided. Although the ACO model is still evolving, one possible structure would be an organization composed of both hospitals and physicians who would be paid to care for all the needs of a large group of patients—at least 5,000. In ACOs, doctors and hospitals would be paid on the basis of their ability to manage costs yet meet established quality-of-care indicators. In effect, their pay would be based on improving patient health rather than on the amount of care provided. If an ACO failed to meet certain quality and cost-savings targets, its providers would receive lower payments. On the flip side, an ACO would be rewarded for keeping patients satisfied and meeting national quality standards, such as ensuring that patients with diabetes are monitored and women obtain mammograms as suggested for age and risk factors. In the next section, we discuss more fully the implications of a capitation system and the incentives it creates for providers.

Capitation offers several financial benefits to providers. Capitation revenues are more predictable and timely than revenues from conventional payment methodologies based on volume. These factors facilitate financial management and budgeting processes in the organization. Capitation payments are received before services are rendered, so, in effect, payers are extending credit to providers rather than vice versa, as under conventional reimbursement. This arrangement will improve some financial ratios, such as time (days) in accounts receivable, and may help an organization's bond rating. Finally, capitation typically reduces the burden of reimbursement paperwork and hence lowers administrative costs.

Three other implications of capitated payment systems are worth mentioning. First, capitation encourages wellness and prevention as opposed to treatment. This emphasis may require changes to staff mix because physician extenders—such as nurse practitioners and physician assistants—may be more cost-effective than physicians in delivering wellness and prevention services. Second, historical utilization rates based on conventional reimbursement methodologies are not good predictors of future utilization when the payment system is capitation or some other system that encourages aggressive utilization control. Third, a fixed payment system means that the administrative overhead costs associated with traditional payment models will be significantly lower because the need for prior authorizations, patient billing, and collections will be greatly reduced.

SELF-TEST QUESTIONS

1. Briefly describe the following reimbursement methods:
   a. Cost based
   b. Charge based and discounted charges
   c. Per procedure
   d. Per diagnosis
   e. Per diem
   f. Bundled (global)
   g. Capitation
2. What is the major difference between fee-for-service and capitation?

Financial Incentives to Providers

Incentives Under Fee-for-Service Reimbursement

Providers, like individuals and other businesses, react to the incentives created by the financial environment. For example, individuals can deduct mortgage interest from income for tax purposes, but they cannot deduct interest payments on personal loans. Loan companies have responded by offering home equity loans that are a type of second mortgage. The tax laws assumed that these loans would be used to make home ownership more accessible, but in reality they are generally used for other purposes, including financing vacations, cars, and appliances. In this situation, tax laws created incentives for consumers to have mortgage debt rather than personal debt, and the mortgage loan industry responded accordingly.

In the same vein, the incentives offered by alternative reimbursement methods influence provider behavior. Under cost-based reimbursement, providers are given a "blank check." If payers reimburse providers for all costs, the incentive is to incur costs. Facilities will be lavish and conveniently located, and staff will be available to ensure that patients are given deluxe treatment. Furthermore, as in billed-charges reimbursement, nonnecessary services will be provided because more services lead to higher costs, which translate to higher revenues.

Under charge-based reimbursement, providers have an incentive to set high chargemaster rates, which leads to high revenues. However, in competitive markets, there is a constraint on how high providers can go, and insurers with negotiating power will demand discounts. Because billed charges is a fee-for-service type of reimbursement, under which more services result in higher revenue, there is a strong incentive to provide the largest possible amount of services. In essence, providers can increase volume, and hence revenues, by *churning*—creating more visits, ordering more tests, extending inpatient stays, and so on. Although charge-based reimbursement encourages providers to contain costs, the incentive is weak because, typically, charges can be increased more easily than costs can be reduced. Note, however, that discounted-charge reimbursement places additional pressure on profitability and hence creates increased incentive for providers to lower costs.

Under prospective payment reimbursement, provider incentives are altered. First, under per procedure reimbursement, the profitability of individual procedures varies depending on the relationship between the actual costs incurred and the payment for that procedure. Providers, usually physicians, have an incentive to perform procedures that have the highest profit potential. Furthermore, the more procedures performed, the better, because each procedure typically generates additional profit. The incentives under per diagnosis reimbursement are similar. Providers, usually hospitals, seek patients with diagnoses that have the greatest profit potential and discourage (even discontinue) services that have the least profit potential. Furthermore, to the extent that providers have some flexibility in assigning diagnoses to patients, an incentive exists to *upcode* diagnoses from the actual one to another that receives greater reimbursement.

Under all prospective payment methods, providers have an incentive to reduce costs because the amount of reimbursement is fixed and independent of the costs actually incurred. When per diem reimbursement is used, particularly at hospitals, providers have an incentive to increase length of stay. Because the early days of a hospitalization are typically more costly to the provider than the later days, the later days are more profitable. However, as mentioned previously, hospitals have an incentive to reduce costs during each day of a patient's stay.

Under bundled (global) pricing, providers are not reimbursed for a series of separate services, which is called *unbundling*. For example, a physician's treatment of a fracture can be bundled and billed as one episode, or it can be unbundled, with separate bills submitted for diagnosis, X-rays, setting the fracture, removing the cast, and so on. The rationale for unbundling is usually to provide more detailed records of treatments rendered, but often the result is higher total charges for the parts than would be charged for the entire "package" of services. Also, when applied to multiple providers for a single episode of care, global pricing forces involved providers (e.g., physicians and a hospital) to offer the most cost-effective treatment jointly. A coordinated approach to cost containment may be more effective than separate attempts by each provider to minimize its treatment costs because lowering costs in one phase of treatment can increase costs in another.

Incentives Under Capitation Reimbursement

Under fee-for-service, profits are proportional to volume. The key to provider success is to work harder, increase utilization, and increase profits. Capitation reverses the actions that providers must take to ensure financial success, and providers must adjust accordingly.

Under capitation, profitability relies on efficiency and cost-effective treatment plans. The key to profitability is to work smarter and decrease utilization. Thus, only procedures that are medically necessary should be performed, and treatment should take place in the lowest-cost setting that can provide the appropriate quality of care. Furthermore, capitated providers have an incentive to promote health rather than just treat illness and injury because a healthier population consumes fewer healthcare services.

Comparison of Financial Incentives to Providers

The financial incentives of fee-for-service and capitation reimbursement are compared in exhibit 3.1. The exhibit depicts costs and revenues under the two payment systems. Under both, total costs (TC)—fixed costs (FC) plus variable costs (VC)—are tied directly to volume, meaning greater service volumes result in higher total costs. The revenue lines, which determine how profits and losses are realized, differ between the two systems. Under fee-for-service, the revenue line (Rev) starts at the origin and slopes upward. At zero volume, the provider receives zero revenue. At any positive volume, greater volume results in higher revenue. Under capitation, the revenue line is horizontal, assuming a fixed number of enrollees—meaning revenues are constant across different levels of volume. In each graph, breakeven (BE) occurs when revenues equal total costs.

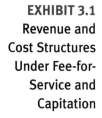

EXHIBIT 3.1 Revenue and Cost Structures Under Fee-for-Service and Capitation

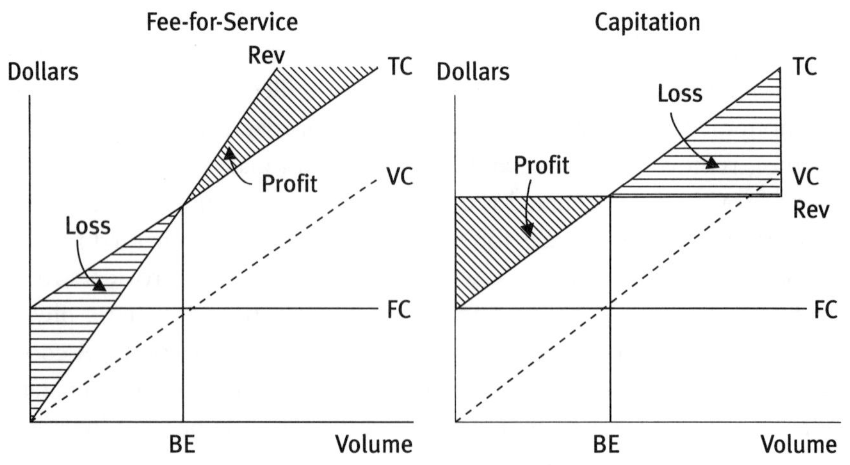

However, as shown in exhibit 3.1, a profound difference exists in how the profits and losses occur. For fee-for-service, all volumes to the left of breakeven produce a loss for the provider, while all volumes to the right of breakeven produce a profit. Thus, the incentive for providers is to raise utilization—increased volume leads to greater profits. The graph of capitation costs and revenues shows that all volume levels to the left of breakeven produce a profit, whereas all volumes to the right of breakeven result in a loss. Under capitation, providers have an incentive to decrease utilization because lower volume leads to higher profits. The only way to increase revenues is to increase the number of covered lives (enrollees).

SELF-TEST QUESTIONS

1. What financial incentives to providers are created by each of the following reimbursement methods:
   a. Cost based
   b. Charge based and discounted charges
   c. Per procedure
   d. Per diagnosis
   e. Per diem
   f. Bundled (global)
   g. Capitation
2. What is the major difference between the financial incentives to providers of fee-for-service and capitation?

Financial Risks to Providers

A key issue facing providers is the impact of the different reimbursement methods on financial risk. For now, think of financial risk in terms of the effect that the reimbursement methods have on profit uncertainty—the greater the chances of losing money, the higher the risk.

Risks Under Fee-for-Service Reimbursement

Cost- and charge-based reimbursements are the least risky for providers because payers more or less ensure that costs will be covered and hence profits will be earned. In cost-based systems, costs are automatically covered, and a profit component typically is added. In charge-based systems, providers typically can set charges high enough to ensure that costs are covered, although discounts introduce uncertainty into the reimbursement process.

In all reimbursement methods except cost based, providers bear the cost-of-service risk (in that costs can exceed revenues). However, a primary difference among the reimbursement types is the provider's ability to influence the revenue–cost relationship. If providers set charge rates for each type of service provided, they can most easily ensure that revenues exceed costs. Furthermore, if providers have the power to set rates above those that would exist in a truly competitive market, charge-based reimbursement could result in higher profits than might cost-based reimbursement.

Prospective payment adds a second dimension of risk to reimbursement contracts because the bundle of services needed to treat a particular patient may be more extensive than that assumed in the payment. However, when the prospective payment is made on a per procedure basis, risk is minimal because each procedure will produce its own revenue. When prospective payment is made on a per diagnosis basis, provider risk increases. If, on average, patients require more intensive treatments, or inpatients a more extended length of stay (LOS), than assumed in the prospective payment amount, the provider must bear the added costs.

When prospective payment is made on a per diem basis, even when stratified, one daily rate usually covers a large number of diagnoses. Because the nature of the services provided could vary widely—because of both varying diagnoses and intensity differences within a single diagnosis—the provider bears the risk that costs associated with the services provided on any day may exceed the per diem rate. Patients with complex diagnoses and greater intensity tend to remain hospitalized longer, and per diem reimbursement does differentiate among different LOSs, but the additional days of stay may be insufficient to make up for the increased resources consumed. In addition, providers bear the risk that the payer, through its utilization review process, will constrain LOS and hence increase intensity during the days that a patient is hospitalized. Under per diem, compression of services and shortened LOS can put significant pressure on providers' profitability.

Under bundled pricing, a more inclusive set of procedures, or providers, are included in one fixed payment. Clearly, the more services that must be rendered for a single payment—or the more providers that have to share a single payment—the more providers are at risk for intensity of services.

Risks Under Capitation Reimbursement

Under capitation, providers assume utilization risk along with the risks assumed under the other reimbursement methods. The assumption of utilization risk has traditionally been an insurance function rather than a provider function. In the traditional fee-for-service system, the financial risk of providing healthcare is shared between purchasers and insurers. Hospitals, physicians, and other providers bear negligible risk because they are paid on the basis of services provided. Insurers bear short-term risk in that payments to providers in any year can exceed the amount of premiums collected. However, poor profitability by insurers in one year usually can be offset by premium increases to purchasers the next year, so the long-term risk of financing the healthcare system is borne by purchasers. Capitation, however, places the burden of short-term utilization risk on providers.

Comparison of Financial Risks to Providers

When provider risk under different reimbursement methods is discussed in this descriptive fashion, it is easy to conclude that capitation is by far the riskiest to providers, while cost- and charge-based reimbursement are by far the least risky. Although this conclusion is not a bad starting point for analysis, financial risk is a complex subject, and we have just scratched the surface. One of the key issues through the remainder of this text is financial risk, so readers will see this topic over and over. For now, keep in mind that different payers use different reimbursement methods. Thus, providers can face conflicting incentives and differing risk, depending on the predominant method of reimbursement.

All prospective payment methods involve a transfer of risk from insurers to providers; that risk increases as the payment unit moves from per procedure to capitation. The added risk does not mean that providers should avoid such reimbursement methods; indeed, refusing to accept contracts with prospective payment provisions would be tantamount to organizational suicide. However, providers must understand the risks involved in prospective payment arrangements, especially their effect on profitability, and make every effort to negotiate a level of payment that is consistent with the risks incurred.

In closing, note that most providers face risk of nonpayment, regardless of reimbursement method. If a user of healthcare services does not have insurance, the patient or patient's family is responsible for payment of total billed charges (or some lesser agreed-upon amount). Because people without health insurance tend to be poor, many of them find it difficult, if not impossible, to pay for healthcare services, which can quickly amount to tens of thousands of dollars. There are two categories of nonpaying patients: (1) patients who have the capacity but are unwilling to pay (the lost revenue attributable to this class of nonpayer is called a *bad debt loss*), and (2) patients who do not have the capacity (are unable) to pay (the lost revenue attributable to these patients is called a *charity*, or *indigent, care loss*).

These classifications are important for two reasons. First, the two types of nonpayment are handled differently on the income statement. Second, it is important that not-for-profit providers be able to document their contributions to society, and one of the most important contributions is willingness to treat indigent patients.

SELF-TEST QUESTIONS

1. What financial risks to providers are created by each of the following reimbursement methods?
   a. Cost based
   b. Charge based and discounted charges
   c. Per procedure
   d. Per diagnosis
   e. Per diem
   f. Bundled (global)
   g. Capitation
2. What is the major difference between the financial risks to providers of fee-for-service and capitation payment systems?

Reimbursement Methods Used by Medicare[1]

Hospital Acute Inpatient Services

The *inpatient prospective payment system (IPPS)* pays per discharge rates, which include two national base payment rates (operating and capital expenses) adjusted to account for two factors that affect the costs of providing care: (1) the patient's condition and treatment and (2) market conditions in the facility's geographic location. Discharges are assigned to one of 754 *Medicare severity diagnosis-related groups (MS–DRGs)*, which are groups of patients with similar clinical problems who are expected to consume similar amounts of hospital resources.

Each MS–DRG has a relative weight that reflects the expected relative cost of inpatients in that group. The payment rates for MS–DRGs in each local market are determined by adjusting the base payment rates to reflect the local input-price level and then multiplying them by the relative weight for each MS–DRG. The operating and capital payment rates are increased for facilities that operate an approved resident training program or that treat a disproportionate share of low-income patients. Rates are reduced for various transfer cases, and *outlier payments* are added for cases that are extraordinarily costly. Both operating and capital payment rates are updated annually (see exhibit 3.2.).

The IPPS payment rates are intended to cover the costs that reasonably efficient providers would incur in providing high-quality care. If the hospital

EXHIBIT 3.2
Medicare Hospital Acute Inpatient Services Payment System

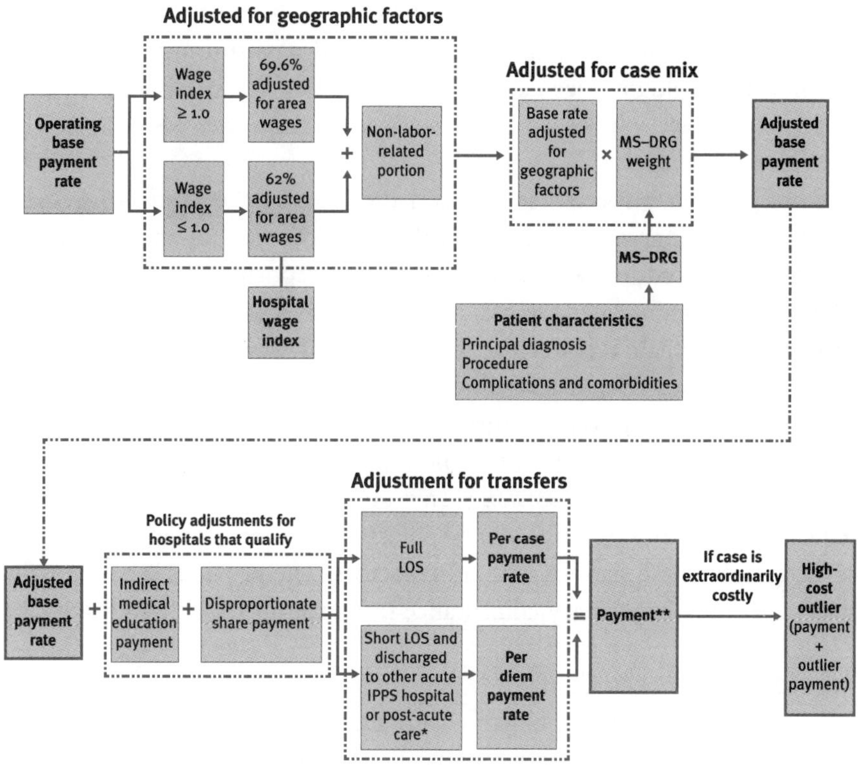

Note: MS–DRG = Medicare severity diagnosis-related group, LOS = length of stay, IPPS = inpatient prospective payment system. Capital payments are determined by a similar system.

* Transfer policy for cases discharged to post-acute care settings applies for cases in 275 selected MS–DRGs.

** Additional payment made for certain rural hospitals.

Source: Reprinted from MedPAC (2018a).

is able to provide the services for less than the fixed reimbursement amount, it can keep the difference. Conversely, if a Medicare patient's treatment costs are more than the reimbursement amount, the hospital must bear the loss.

Outpatient Hospital Services

The *outpatient prospective payment system (OPPS)* is essentially a fee schedule. The unit of payment under the OPPS is the individual service as identified by *HCPCS* (discussed earlier), which contains codes for more than 6,000 distinct services. CMS groups services into *ambulatory payment classifications (APCs)* on the basis of clinical and cost similarity. Each APC has a relative weight that measures the resource requirements of the service and is based on the median cost of services in that APC. CMS sets payments for individual APCs using a conversion factor that translates the relative weights into dollar payment rates and adjustments for geographic differences in input prices. Hospitals also can receive additional payments in the form of outlier adjustments for extraordinarily high-cost services and pass-through payments for some new technologies (see exhibit 3.3.).

Physician Services

Medicare pays for physician services on the basis of the *physician fee schedule.* The unit of payment is the individual service, such as an office visit or a diagnostic procedure, which is classified and reported to CMS according to HCPCS. Payment rates are based on relative weights called *relative value units (RVUs)*, which account for the amount of work required to provide a service, expenses related to maintaining a practice, and liability insurance costs. The values given to these three types of resources are adjusted to reflect variations in local input prices, and the total is multiplied by a standard dollar amount—called the *conversion factor*—to arrive at the payment amount. Medicare's payment rates may also be adjusted to reflect provider characteristics, geographic designations, and other factors. The provider is paid the final amount, less any beneficiary coinsurance (see exhibit 3.4.).

Ambulatory Surgery Centers

In January 2008, Medicare began paying for surgery-related facility services provided in ambulatory surgery centers. The unit of payment is the individual

EXHIBIT 3.3
Medicare Outpatient Hospital Services Payment System

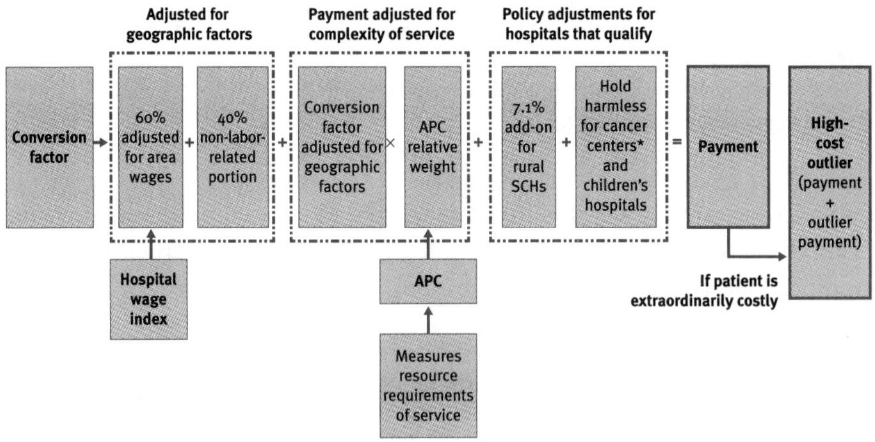

Note: APC = ambulatory payment classification, SCH = sole community hospital. The APC is the service classification system for the outpatient prospective payment system.

*Medicare adjusts outpatient prospective payment system payment rates for 11 cancer hospitals so that the payment-to-cost ratio (PCR) for each cancer hospital is equal to the average PCR for all hospitals minus one percentage point.

Source: MedPAC (2018b).

EXHIBIT 3.4
Medicare Physician Services Payment System

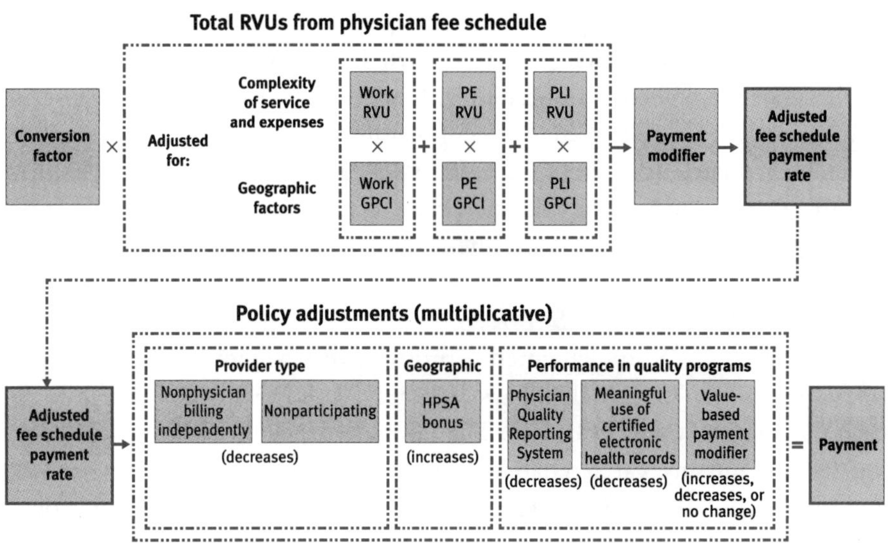

Note: RVU = relative value unit, GPCI = geographic practice cost index, PE = practice expense, PLI = professional liability insurance, HPSA = health professional shortage area. This exhibit depicts Medicare payments only. The fee schedule lists separate PE RVUs for facility and nonfacility settings. Fee schedule payments are often reduced when specified nonphysician practitioners bill Medicare separately, but not when services are provided "incident to" a physician's service.

Source: Reprinted from MedPAC (2018c).

surgical procedure. Each of the nearly 3,600 approved procedures is assigned an APC. These APCs are the same payment groups used in OPPS. The relative weights for most procedures in the ambulatory surgery center payment system are the same as the relative weights in OPPS. Like OPPS, the ambulatory surgical center payment system sets payments for individual services using a conversion factor and adjustments for geographic differences in input prices.

Inpatient Rehabilitation Facilities

In January 2002, CMS implemented the inpatient rehabilitation facility prospective payment system. Inpatient rehabilitation facilities are paid predetermined, per discharge rates based primarily on the patient's condition (diagnoses, functional and cognitive statuses, age) and market area wages. Discharges are assigned to one of 92 intensive rehabilitation categories called *case-mix groups (CMGs)*, which are groups of patients with similar clinical problems. In each of these CMGs, patients are further categorized into one of four tiers on the basis of any comorbidities they have; each tier receives a specific payment that reflects the costliness of patients in that tier relative to others in the CMG.

Psychiatric Hospital Services

In January 2005, CMS implemented the inpatient psychiatric facility prospective payment system, which pays psychiatric hospitals the per diem, routine, ancillary, and capital costs associated with providing covered inpatient psychiatric services. A base per diem payment is adjusted to account for cost-of-care differences related to patient characteristics (age, diagnosis, comorbidities, length of stay) and facility characteristics (local wages, geographic location, teaching status, emergency department status).

Skilled Nursing Facility Services

In July 1998, CMS implemented a prospective payment system for *skilled nursing facilities (SNFs)* that pays facilities a predetermined daily rate for each day of care, up to 100 days. The rates are expected to cover all operating (skilled nursing care, rehabilitation services, other goods and services) and capital costs that efficient facilities would be expected to incur in providing most SNF services. Various high-cost, low-probability ancillary services are covered separately. Patients are assigned to one of 66 categories called *resource utilization groups (RUGs)* on the basis of patient characteristics and service use that are expected to require similar resources. Nursing and therapy weights are applied to the base payment rates of each RUG. Daily base payment rates are also adjusted to account for geographic differences in labor costs.

Home Health Care Services

In October 2000, CMS implemented a prospective payment system that pays home health agencies a predetermined rate for each 60-day episode of home health care. If fewer than five visits are delivered during a 60-day episode, the home health agency is paid per visit by visit type. Patients who receive five or more visits are assigned to one of 153 *home health resource groups*, which are based on clinical and functional status and service use as measured by the Outcome and Assessment Information Set. The payment rates are adjusted to reflect local market input prices and special circumstances, such as high-cost outliers.

Critical-Access Hospitals

The Balanced Budget Act of 1997 created a new category of hospitals: CAHs. Each of 1,348 CAHs is limited to 25 beds, and patients are limited to a four-day length of stay. CAHs primarily operate in rural areas. Unlike most other acute care hospitals (which are paid through prospective payment systems), CAHs are paid by Medicare on the basis of each hospital's reported costs. Each CAH receives 101 percent of the costs it incurs in providing outpatient, inpatient, laboratory and therapy services, and post-acute care in the hospital's swing beds (hospital beds that are used to provide both acute and long-term care). The cost of treating Medicare patients is estimated using cost accounting data from Medicare cost reports.

Hospice Services

Medicare pays hospice providers a daily rate for each day a beneficiary is enrolled in the hospice benefit. Medicare makes a daily payment, regardless of the amount of services provided and on days when no services are provided. The daily payment rates are intended to cover costs of providing services included in patients' care plans. Payments are made according to a fee schedule for four different categories of care: routine home care, continuous home care, inpatient respite care, and general inpatient care. The four categories of care differ by the location and intensity of the services provided, and the base payments for each category reflect variation in expected input cost differences.

Ambulance Services

Medicare pays for ambulance services using a dedicated fee schedule, which has payment rates for nine categories of ground and air ambulance transport. CMS considers historical costs as a basis for establishing relative values for each payment category. These relative values are multiplied by a dollar amount that is standard across all nine categories and then adjusted for geographic differences. This amount is added to a mileage payment to arrive at the total ambulance payment amount. Medicare payments for ambulance services may also be adjusted by one of several add-on payments based on additional geographic characteristics of the transport.

SELF-TEST QUESTIONS

1. What is the IPPS, and how does it work?
2. What is the OPPS, and how does it work?
3. How are physicians reimbursed for providing services to Medicare patients?

Value-Based Purchasing

Value-based purchasing, *value-based payment*, or *Pay for Performance (P4P)* are general terms that refer to any reimbursement scheme that makes meeting performance standards a prerequisite for some or all of a provider's payment. Thus, risk pools are a type of value-based system. Value-based purchasing uses financial incentives to encourage behaviors and influence outcomes that the payer considers desirable. It can be implemented by insurers or purchasers to improve quality and increase productivity among their contract providers. There are examples of value-based purchasing in both public and private insurance reimbursement of physician practices, hospitals, long-term care providers, and home health agencies. Providers may also use value-based purchasing to determine reimbursement of staff in their own organizations. Organizations vary in the ways they pay for performance in two main respects: (1) how they define performance and (2) how they allocate rewards.

Defining Performance

Value-based purchasing requires selection of performance measures and specification of levels of performance. Public and private insurers usually define performance as achieving a specific level of quality. Depending on the program's aims and the data available, some combination of four quality dimensions is usually measured: outcome, process, patient satisfaction, and structure.

Outcome measures reveal whether a provider attained a certain level of healthcare results over a defined period. An example of an outcome measure is the percentage of healthy babies born at a hospital. Numerous factors influence health outcomes beyond provider care. Unadjusted outcome measures are potentially biased to favor providers with healthier patients, so value-based payment measures are frequently adjusted according to risk factors in a patient population. At a minimum, risk adjustment includes age and gender, while more complex adjustment may include health status and other demographic characteristics of the patient population.

Processes of care linked to desired health outcomes are measured through *process measures*. Most process measures circumvent the need to adjust for risk because providers have more control over whether they follow a particular process than they have over the outcome of that process. Process measures typically report the ratio of processes actually performed to the total times the process should have been performed—for example, the percentage of emergency patients with chest pain who receive aspirin.

Patients' satisfaction can also be an indicator of quality. *Patient satisfaction measures* focus on patients' evaluation of the care they experience versus providers' views on the same. Patient satisfaction measures, such as the courtesy afforded to patients by staff, may reflect on more aspects of the care delivered than specific outcome and process measures; however, these types of data are more subjective and may be harder to interpret than outcome and process measures. The Consumer Assessment of Healthcare Providers and Systems is the most common set of surveys used by providers, hospitals, and health plans to assess patient experience in a variety of healthcare settings.

Finally, *structure measures* may be used as indirect measures of quality. For example, a payer may decide that implementation of an EHR will improve the quality of care. As part of a value-based program, it may provide financial incentives for investment in information technology (IT).

Providers that use value-based care to determine staff compensation in their own organizations often include productivity and financial measures in their definition of performance. *Productivity measures*, such as the average number of patient visits per day, provide incentives to treat more patients by working faster or longer hours. *Financial measures*, such as revenue per physician, provide incentives to increase the total revenue of the organization.

Allocating Rewards

Value-based purchasing programs vary with regard to reward criteria and the amount that they reward. In general, value-based rewards may be earned for three types of performance: relative, benchmark, and improvement. *Relative* performance measures how a provider performed in comparison to other providers; for example, a provider that scored better than 75 percent of its peers on a particular measure receives a reward. *Benchmark* performance is based on whether a provider attained a pre-identified score or level of performance. *Improvement* performance measures how much a provider's performance has improved over its performance in a previous period; for example, a provider that increased its score on a particular measure by more than 10 percent receives a reward.

For examples of the three types of performance on which value-based awards may be based, consider cardiac care. When patients go to an emergency department with chest pain, most are supposed to (but do not always) receive aspirin. A value-based purchasing program might specify that, over a certain period, a provider will receive a reward if it: (1) administers aspirin to appropriate patients more often than 90 percent of its peers do (relative performance), (2) administers aspirin to more than 95 percent of appropriate patients (benchmark performance), or (3) increases the percentage of patients who receive aspirin appropriately from 80 percent to 90 percent (improvement performance).

The reward amount can also be determined in several ways. Payment may be a specified bonus for attainment of performance (or deduction for nonattainment). The reward can be calculated as a percentage increase (or decrease) of the normal reimbursement amount. Alternatively, a set amount might be distributed on a per patient basis, in which case the total reward would depend on eligible patient volume. The magnitude of the value-based reward should be enough to provide a meaningful incentive for the desired behavior but not so much that it encourages neglect of other unmeasured performance. Many insurers believe that the rewards should amount to at least 10 percent of providers' earnings, but current award levels are typically set between 3 percent and 10 percent.

Rewards are not always financial, particularly among some public insurance value-based reimbursement initiatives. Nonfinancial incentives include public recognition through distinguished provider ratings, auto-assignment for increased Medicaid market share, and reduced administrative requirements. Nonfinancial disincentives include practice sanctions, such as nonreferral of patients.

Information Requirements of Value-Based Purchasing

A value-based payment system depends on the collection and reporting of accurate data. For many providers, a substantial capital investment in IT may be needed for these tasks. Different payers usually have somewhat different information and technological requirements for data collection and reporting, although universal standards will eventually apply. These requirements often involve specification of timeliness and standard data definitions to allow meaningful comparisons across providers. Many value-based payment systems that use process measures include incentives for the expansion of provider IT capacity. For example, a value-based program in a large physician practice in California includes a two-part measure to calculate performance scores. Points are awarded for clinical patient data integrated at the group level in the first part and for clinical decision support at the point of care in the second part. Clinical decision support tools include telemedicine applications and wireless point-of-care e-prescribing.

Beyond the collection and reporting of data, IT can also facilitate the performance improvement that is the focus of a value-based program. For example, some EHR software can select individuals from a patient list who are due for a mammogram or who have high blood pressure. Automatic physician notification of these patients can increase the likelihood that they will receive the recommended care. IT also can help providers standardize clinical care and thereby attain better quality scores.

The Future of Value-Based Purchasing

As more and more healthcare organizations experiment with different value-based payment designs, the evidence base for their effect on providers and their quality of care will grow. Some important questions have yet to be answered: What level of financial incentive is needed to change provider behavior? Which combinations of incentive designs and performance measures yield the greatest improvements in a population's health status? What are the long-term financial implications of financing value-based programs?

One lesson that resonates across most value-based payment experiences is that provider input and buy-in are crucial elements of any attempt to improve performance through financial incentives. Providers have a vital role to play in the discussion and implementation, and the more effectively they work with insurers, purchasers, and policymakers, the bigger the impact value-based payment will have.

A Value-Based Purchasing Example

Perhaps the best way to learn about value-based purchasing is by example. In the following sections, we discuss the implementation of value-based payment across two dimensions (quality and productivity) at one primary care practice.

Fordham Primary Care (FPC) is a medical group practice that employs three primary care physicians who are each paid an annual salary of $200,000. FPC is located in a state that recently announced a new value-based payment program designed to increase preventive healthcare provided to Medicaid patients. Medicaid patients are a substantial proportion of FPC's patients, so it decides to participate in the Medicaid Value-Based Payment program.

Pay for Quality

The Medicaid value-based payment program defines quality performance on the basis of process measures and allocates rewards on the basis of a benchmark. The process measures are (1) screening mammography for premenopausal women older than 40 who have not been screened within the year, (2) one of five recommended colorectal cancer screening options for men older than 50 who are due for screening, and (3) annual influenza vaccinations for all adults older than 50. Rewards are allocated only to physicians who exceed a benchmark of 95 percent on each of the process measures over a six-month period. For example, a physician will receive a reward only if at least 95 percent of her premenopausal patients older than 40 who have not been screened within the year actually undergo screening mammography. If the benchmark is not achieved, no reward is provided. For physicians who achieve benchmark performance, Medicaid will pay a bonus of $45 times the actual number of eligible Medicaid patients.

FPC collects the data required for participation in the Medicaid value-based payment program. The annual results are shown in exhibit 3.5.

Exhibit 3.5 shows that FPC physicians vary with regard to total number of patients and the percentage of patients who are on Medicaid. Furthermore, not all Medicaid patients are premenopausal women older than 40, men older than 50, or adults older than 50. Thus, only a subset of Medicaid patients count toward value-based rewards; these numbers are shown in the middle section of exhibit 3.5. The Medicaid quality scores for this subset at the bottom of exhibit 3.5 show that Dr. A met the benchmark of 95 percent on all three Medicaid process measures. Dr. B met the benchmark for breast

EXHIBIT 3.5
Quality Data for FPC

	Dr. A	Dr. B	Dr. C
Total number of patients	1,000	1,100	1,200
Percentage who are Medicaid patients	40%	30%	20%
Number of Medicaid patients	400	330	240
Possible number of Medicaid patients eligible for value-based rewards			
Breast cancer screening	160	132	96
Colorectal cancer screening	120	99	72
Influenza vaccination	80	66	48
Medicaid process measures			
Breast cancer screening	99%	95%	95%
Colorectal cancer screening	99%	94%	93%
Influenza vaccination	98%	95%	94%

cancer screening and influenza vaccination only, and Dr. C met the benchmark for breast cancer screening only.

The next step is to calculate the value-based rewards on the basis of each physician's quality performance. The results are shown in exhibit 3.6.

Dr. A met the benchmark for all three Medicaid process measures. Therefore, Dr. A's pay-for-quality reward is 160 × $45 = $7,200 for breast cancer screening, 120 × $45 = $5,400 for colorectal cancer screening, and 80 × $45 = $3,600 for influenza vaccination. Dr. B did not meet the benchmark for colorectal cancer screening, so he receives a pay-for-quality reward for breast cancer screening and influenza vaccination only. Dr. C receives a pay for quality reward for breast cancer screening only.

The exhibit shows that the financial effects of the pay-for-quality program on an individual physician depend on the total number of patients she has, the percentage of these patients who are on Medicaid, the number of these Medicaid patients who count toward the value-based payment program, and whether she meets the benchmark for each Medicaid process measure. Although Dr. A had the least number of patients, she had the highest percentage of Medicaid patients and was the only physician to meet the benchmark for all three process measures. Consequently, Dr. A receives a total value-based reward of $16,200, the highest among the FPC physicians. Dr. B. had more patients than Dr. A had, but he had a lower percentage of Medicaid patients and met the benchmark for breast cancer screening and influenza vaccination only. Dr. B receives a total value-based reward of $8,910, substantially less than Dr. A's reward. Dr. C. had more patients than Drs. A and B, but he had a lower percentage of Medicaid patients and met

EXHIBIT 3.6
FPC Physician Pay for Quality

	Dr. A	Dr. B	Dr. C
Bonus per eligible patient	$ 45	$ 45	$ 45
Number of Medicaid patients who count toward value-based rewards			
Breast cancer screening	160	132	96
Colorectal cancer screening	120	0	0
Influenza vaccination	80	66	0
Pay for quality			
Breast cancer screening	$ 7,200	$5,940	$4,320
Colorectal cancer screening	5,400	0	0
Influenza vaccination	3,600	2,970	0
Total	$16,200	$8,910	$4,320

the benchmark for breast cancer screening only. Dr. C receives a total value-based reward of $4,320.

Pay for Productivity

FPC physicians were enthusiastic about implementing a pay-for-quality program but also concerned that the increased attention to quality may diminish physician productivity. To achieve an appropriate balance of incentives, FPC decided to concurrently implement a pay-for-productivity program. Five percent of total salaries (3 physicians × $200,000 per physician × 5% = $30,000) was set aside for productivity pay, to be allocated at the end of the year in proportion to the volume of patient visits.

The data required for the productivity value-based payment program and the annual results are shown in exhibit 3.7.

Exhibit 3.7 shows that FPC physicians vary with regard to the total number of patients and the average number of visits per patient. Dr. A has the lowest number of patients but the highest average visits per patient. Dr. A may have a higher proportion of elderly or chronically ill patients who require more visits than do other patients. In contrast, Dr. C has the highest number of patients but the lowest average visits per patient, which may indicate a higher proportion of younger, healthier patients. Dr. B is in between Drs. A and C in both total number of patients and average visits per patient.

The next step is to calculate the value-based rewards on the basis of each physician's productivity performance. The results are shown in exhibit 3.8.

Dr. A accounted for 34.3 percent (3,000 out of 8,740) of FPC's total number of patient visits. Therefore, Dr. A's pay-for-productivity reward is

EXHIBIT 3.7
Productivity Data for FPC

	Dr. A	Dr. B	Dr. C	Total
Total number of patients	1,000	1,100	1,200	3,300
Average visits per patient	3.0	2.6	2.4	
Total number of patient visits	3,000	2,860	2,880	8,740

EXHIBIT 3.8
FPC Physician Pay for Productivity

	Dr. A	Dr. B	Dr. C	Total
Percentage of patient visits	34.3%	32.7%	33.0%	100.0%
Pay for productivity	$10,297	$9,817	$9,886	$30,000

34.3% × $30,000 = $10,297. In comparison to Dr. A., Drs. B and C each accounted for a lower percentage of the total number of patient visits and consequently receive a lower pay-for-productivity reward.

Comparison of the Two P4P Programs

Exhibit 3.9 shows the combined effect of the pay-for-quality and pay-for-productivity programs on the compensation of each FPC physician.

Dr. A has the highest compensation after participation in the value-based payment program, primarily because of a substantial pay-for-quality reward. In contrast, Dr. C has the lowest compensation after participation in value-based payment because of a low pay-for-quality reward. There is little difference between the physicians' pay-for-productivity rewards. The physicians may all be similarly busy, or perhaps the number of patient visits is not the best measure of productivity.

Both value-based payment programs demonstrate the challenges of structuring a value-based program that is fair and provides the desired incentives. In the pay-for-quality example, the physicians have an opportunity to earn income in addition to their base compensation of $200,000 by increasing the number of patients who count toward the Medicaid value-based payment program and by meeting the benchmark for each Medicaid process measure. In the pay-for-productivity example, each physician's base compensation is essentially reduced by 5% × $200,000 = $10,000, which each can earn back through productivity. If one physician is more productive than her colleagues, she can earn back more than $10,000; if she is less productive, she will earn back less than $10,000.

EXHIBIT 3.9
FPC Physician Compensation Before and After Participation in Value-based Payment (VBP)

	Dr. A	*Dr. B*	*Dr. C*	*Total*
Compensation before VBP	$190,000	$190,000	$190,000	$570,000
Pay for quality	$ 16,200	$ 8,910	$ 4,320	$ 29,430
Pay for productivity	$ 10,297	$ 9,817	$ 9,886	$ 30,000
Compensation after VBP	$216,497	$208,727	$204,206	$629,430

The source of funds of each value-based payment program is a key difference. The funds for the Medicaid pay-for-quality program come from a source external to the group practice, which increases the practice's total earnings. The funds for the pay-for-productivity program come from the internal earnings of the group practice. Physicians do not compete for pay-for-quality rewards; if one physician performs particularly well, his reward does not affect the compensation of another physician. However, physicians do essentially compete for pay-for-productivity rewards. If one physician is not as productive as his colleagues, his compensation will be relatively lower. The different incentives increase the likelihood that physicians will pay more attention to the "rules of the game" of the productivity value-based payment program.

SELF-TEST QUESTIONS

1. What is the aim of a value-based purchasing program designed by an insurer?
2. What are four dimensions of quality that can define performance in a value-based purchasing scheme?
3. What are three ways of allocating value-based purchasing rewards?
4. What is the role of IT in a value-based purchasing program?
5. On what kinds of performance standards are the largest value-based purchasing initiatives basing their awards?

Health Reform and Payments to Providers

In addition to improving healthcare delivery through focusing on access and quality, health reform has significantly changed the way providers are reimbursed. The key reforms include a move from a fee-for-service model to a prospective payment model, which may include bundled payments or capitation. These new payment methods aim to move reimbursement from a system based on volume to one based on value and better outcomes. These payment methods propose to do the following:

- Encourage providers to deliver care in a high-quality, efficient manner
- Support coordination of care among multiple providers
- Adopt evidence-based care standards and protocols that result in the best outcomes for patients
- Provide accountability and transparency
- Discourage overtreatment or medically unnecessary procedures
- Eliminate or reduce the occurrence of adverse events
- Discourage cost shifting

The implications of health reform for financial management and health insurance are addressed in chapters 1 and 2, respectively. The implications for payments to providers are discussed here.

Centers for Medicaid & Medicare Services Value-Based Programs

CMS states that value-based programs reward healthcare providers with incentive payments for the quality of care they give to people with Medicare. These programs are part of CMS's larger quality strategy to reform how healthcare is delivered and paid for. Value-based programs also support CMS's three-part aim: better care for individuals, better health for populations, and lower cost. Value-based programs are important because they are helping CMS move toward paying providers based on the quality, rather than the quantity, of care they give patients.

There are five original value-based programs; their goal is to link provider quality measures to provider payment:

1. End-Stage Renal Disease (ESRD) Quality Incentive Program (www.cms.gov/Medicare/Quality-Initiatives-Patient-Assessment-Instruments/ESRDQIP/index.html)
2. Hospital Value-Based Purchasing (HVBP) Program (www.cms.gov/Medicare/Quality-Initiatives-Patient-Assessment-Instruments/Value-Based-Programs/HVBP/Hospital-Value-Based-Purchasing.html)
3. Hospital Readmissions Reduction (HRR) Program (www.cms.gov/Medicare/Quality-Initiatives-Patient-Assessment-Instruments/Value-Based-Programs/HRRP/Hospital-Readmission-Reduction-Program.html)

4. Value Modifier (VM) Program (www.cms.gov/Medicare/Quality-Initiatives-Patient-Assessment-Instruments/Value-Based-Programs/VMP/Value-Modifier-VM-or-PVBM.html)
5. Hospital-Acquired Conditions (HAC) Reduction Program (www.cms.gov/Medicare/Quality-Initiatives-Patient-Assessment-Instruments/Value-Based-Programs/HAC/Hospital-Acquired-Conditions.html)

CMS has also created two other value-based programs: the Skilled Nursing Facility Value-Based Purchasing (SNF VBP) Program (www.cms.gov/Medicare/Quality-Initiatives-Patient-Assessment-Instruments/Value-Based-Programs/Other-VBPs/SNF-VBP.html) and the Home Health Value-Based Purchasing (HHVBP) Program (www.cms.gov/Medicare/Quality-Initiatives-Patient-Assessment-Instruments/Value-Based-Programs/Other-VBPs/HHVBP.html).

Centers for Medicaid & Medicare Services Quality Payment Program

The ACA requires Medicare to factor quality into payments for physicians and most clinicians. Quality-based compensation is part of Medicare's effort to shift medicine away from focus on volume. Clinicians can earn additional compensation based on the quality and cost-effectiveness of the care they provide to their patients. Bonuses and penalties are calculated on the basis of performance on quality measures, which vary among specialties.

The Medicare Access and CHIP Reauthorization Act of 2015 (MACRA) ended the sustainable growth rate formula and, by law, required CMS to implement the Quality Payment Program. The Quality Payment Program gives clinicians new tools and resources to help give patients the best possible care. There are two ways for clinicians to participate based on practice size, specialty, location, or patient population: advanced alternative payment models (APMs) (see https://qpp.cms.gov/apms/overview) and the Merit-based Incentive Payment System (MIPS) (see https://qpp.cms.gov/mips/overview).

Centers for Medicaid & Medicare Services Shared Savings Program

Shared savings is an approach to reducing healthcare costs and is a major mechanism used by ACOs. Under shared savings, if a healthcare organization or provider reduces total healthcare spending for its patients below the level that the payer expected, the provider is then rewarded with a portion of the savings. The benefits are twofold: (1) the payer spends less than it would otherwise, and (2) the provider gets more revenue than it expected. The savings can arise from more efficient, cost-effective use of hospital or outpatient services that enhance quality, reduce costs over time, and improve outcomes. It can be applied to hospital episodes of care, including physician services, or to physician office care (see www.cms.gov/Medicare/Medicare-Fee-for-Service-Payment/sharedsavingsprogram/index.html).

Bundled Payment

Bundled payment models are a form of capitation and an alternative payment method to the fee-for-service model. The objective of bundled payments is to promote more efficient use of resources and reward providers for improving the coordination, quality, and efficiency of care. If the cost of services is less than the bundled payment, the physicians and other providers retain the difference. But if the costs exceed the bundled payment, physicians and other providers are not compensated for the difference.

In terms of payment, in some circumstances one entity—an ACO—may receive the bundled payment and subsequently divide the payment among participating physicians and providers. In another situation, the payer may pay the participating physicians and providers independently, but it may adjust each payment according to negotiated predefined rules to ensure that the total payments to all the providers do not exceed the total bundled payment amount. This type of payment method is called ***virtual bundling***. Challenges of bundled payments include the portioning of the payment between the various providers and determining who owns the episode of care.

On January 9, 2018, CMS's Center for Medicare and Medicaid Innovation announced the launch of a new voluntary bundled payment model called Bundled Payments for Care Improvement Advanced (BPCI Advanced). Under BPCI Advanced, participants can earn additional payment if all expenditures for a beneficiary's episode of care are under a spending target that factors in quality (CMS 2018).

SELF-TEST QUESTION

1. Briefly describe the impact of the health reform on payments to providers.

Chapter Key Concepts

Reimbursement methods, risk sharing, and pay-for-performance have a profound influence on the risk and behavior of providers. In this chapter, some of the more important aspects of these topics are discussed. Here are its key concepts:

- When payers pay *billed charges*, they pay according to the schedule of charge rates established by the provider.
- *Negotiated charges*, which are *discounted* from billed charges, are often used by insurers in conjunction with managed care plans such as health maintenance organizations (HMOs) and preferred provider organizations (PPOs).
- Under a *retrospective cost* system, the payer agrees to pay the provider certain allowable costs expected to be incurred in providing services to the payer's enrollees.
- In a *prospective payment system*, the rates paid by payers are determined in advance and are not tied directly to reimbursable costs or billed charges. Typically, prospective payments are made on the basis of the following service definitions: (1) *per procedure*, (2) *per diagnosis*, (3) *per diem* (per day), or (4) *bundled* (global) *pricing*.
- *Capitation* is a flat periodic payment to a physician or other healthcare provider; it is the sole reimbursement for providing services to a defined population. Capitation payments are generally expressed as some dollar amount *per member per month (PMPM)*. In this term, the word *member* typically means an enrollee in some managed care plan—usually an HMO.
- Under fee-for-service, all volumes less than breakeven produce a loss for the provider, while all volumes greater than breakeven produce a profit. Under capitation, all volumes less than breakeven produce a profit, whereas all volumes greater than breakeven produce a loss. Thus, provider incentives under capitation are opposite those under conventional reimbursement.
- In 1983, the federal government adopted the *inpatient prospective payment system (IPPS)* for Medicare hospital inpatient reimbursement. Under IPPS, the amount of the payment is fixed by the patient's *Medicare severity diagnosis-related group (MS-DRG)*.

(continued)

(continued from previous page)

- To provide some cushion for the high costs associated with severely ill patients within each diagnosis, IPPS includes a provision for *outlier payments*.
- In 2000, Medicare reimbursement for hospital-based outpatient care was changed from a cost-based system to the *outpatient prospective payment system (OPPS)*. The payment calculation is similar to that for inpatient care. Also, Medicare recently created prospective payment systems for nursing home and home health care services that are much less generous than the previous cost-based systems.
- Physicians are reimbursed by Medicare through the *resource-based relative value system (RBRVS)*. Under RBRVS, reimbursement is based on three resource components: (1) *physician work*, (2) *practice expenses*, and (3) *malpractice insurance*. Each of these components is given a weight for each of approximately 7,500 procedures. The weights are summed and multiplied by a dollar conversion factor to determine the payment amount.
- *Value-based payment* (VBP) plans use provider payments to incentivize certain behaviors. They usually encourage quality improvement but can be used to motivate physicians to increase productivity or financial contribution to a group practice. Value-based payment programs used in practice vary widely in intent and design.
- *Outcome, process, patient satisfaction,* and *structure* are four dimensions of quality measured by value-based payment programs.
- Financial rewards are given to providers who meet predefined *relative, benchmark*, or *improvement* standards, depending on how the value-based payment program is designed. Dollar amounts provided by value-based payment plans also vary.
- Health reform has significantly changed the way providers are reimbursed. The *new payment methods emphasize value and better patient outcomes* over volume.

This concludes our discussion of reimbursement methods, risk sharing, and value-based payment.

Chapter Models, Problems, and Minicases

The following ancillary resources in spreadsheet format are available for this chapter:

- Problems that test your ability to perform the calculations
- A minicase that is more complicated than the problems and that tests your ability to perform the calculations in preparation for a case. These resources can be accessed online at ache.org/HAP/PinkSong8e.

Selected Case

One case in *Cases in Healthcare Finance*, sixth edition, is applicable to this chapter: "Case 2: Orlando Family Physicians," which focuses on the implementation of a pay-for-performance program by a medical group practice.

References

Centers for Medicare & Medicaid Services (CMS). 2018. "CMS Announces New Payment Model to Improve Quality, Coordination, and Cost-Effectiveness for Both Inpatient and Outpatient Care." Published January 9. www.cms.gov/newsroom/press-releases/cms-announces-new-payment-model-improve-quality-coordination-and-cost-effectiveness-both-inpatient.

MedPAC. 2018a. *Hospital Acute Inpatient Services Payment System.* Revised October. http://medpac.gov/docs/default-source/payment-basics/medpac_payment_basics_18_hospital_final_v2_sec.pdf.

———. 2018b. *Outpatient Hospital Services Payment System.* Revised October. www.medpac.gov/docs/default-source/payment-basics/medpac_payment_basics_18_opd_final_sec.pdf.

———. 2018c. *Physician and Other Health Professionals Payment System.* Revised October. http://medpac.gov/docs/default-source/payment-basics/medpac_payment_basics_18_physician_final_v2_sec.pdf.

Selected Bibliography

Castellucci, M. 2018. "CMS Amps Up Value-Based Payments in 2018 as Other Quality Issues Fall by the Wayside." *Modern Healthcare.* Published December 26. www.modernhealthcare.com/article/20181226/NEWS/181229979.

Daly, R. 2018. "Latest ACO Trends Identified." *hfm*. Published April 20. www.hfma.org/Content.aspx?id=60396.

Harris, J., M. Johnson, and A. Brown. 2018. "Bundled Payments for Care Improvement Advanced: 5 Critical Issues." *hfm*. Published June 1. www.hfma.org/Content.aspx?id=60858.

Marino, D. 2018. "A Blueprint for Building a 'Risk Ready' Healthcare Organization." *hfm*. Published October 1. www.hfma.org/Content.aspx?id=61959.

Optum. 2018. "Navigating Value-Based Reimbursement." *hfm* 72 (6): S1–S4.

Selected Websites

The following websites pertain to the content of this chapter:

- For more information on California's physician value-based initiative, visit the Integrated Healthcare Association website at www.iha.org.
- Bridges to Excellence has an informative website that provides further details on its value-based programs; see www.bridgestoexcellence.org.
- To read more about hospital value-based programs, see the web pages devoted to the topic on the CMS site at www.cms.gov/Medicare/Quality-Initiatives-Patient-Assessment-Instruments/Value-Based-Programs/Value-Based-Programs.html.
- To read more about payment reform, see the website of the Center for Healthcare Quality and Payment Reform at www.chqpr.org.

Note

1. Our purpose here is not to make you an expert in Medicare's payment methods. Most healthcare organizations, other than the smallest, have one or more specialists on the financial staff whose sole responsibility is to keep track of changes in Medicare reimbursement practices. However, Medicare payment systems are used by many payers for many types of providers, so all healthcare managers should have some knowledge of these systems. For excellent summaries of the payment systems used by CMS, see "Payment Basics," published by MedPAC (www.medpac. gov/-documents-/payment-basics).

PART

II

BASIC FINANCIAL MANAGEMENT CONCEPTS

Before we discuss the details of the financial management of healthcare organizations, we must first explain two fundamental topics that are important for you to learn.

Most financial management decisions involve future dollar amounts. For example, when a physician group practice uses debt financing, it is obligated to make a series of future (principal and interest) payments to the lender. Or, when a hospital builds an outpatient surgery center, it expects the investment to provide a series of future cash flows when the center is up and running. To estimate the financial impact of these transactions, the organization must value future dollar amounts. This valuation is called *time value analysis.* Chapter 4 provides the concepts necessary to perform this analysis.

Chapter 5 discusses financial risk and required return. Virtually all financial decisions involve risk. For example, a physician group practice that obtains debt financing may not be able to make the required payments. Or, a hospital that builds a new outpatient surgery center is at risk that the center will take in less cash flow than forecasted when the center was built. Such situations involve financial risk, and to make good financial decisions, managers must be able to define and measure this risk. Furthermore, risk must be translated into required rates of return. For example, to be financially attractive, the new outpatient surgery center must provide an expected rate of return that is sufficient to compensate the hospital for the riskiness of its investment. Chapter 5 provides the tools required to perform this task.

CHAPTER

4

TIME VALUE ANALYSIS

Learning Objectives

After studying this chapter, readers should be able to

- explain why time value analysis is important to healthcare financial management;
- find the present and future values for lump sums, annuities, and uneven cash flow streams;
- apply the opportunity cost principle;
- measure the return on an investment;
- create an amortization table; and
- apply stated, periodic, and effective annual interest rates.

Introduction

The financial value of any asset—whether a *financial asset* (such as a stock or a bond) or a *real asset* (such as a piece of diagnostic equipment or an ambulatory surgery center)—is based on future cash flows. However, a dollar to be received in the future is worth less than a current dollar because a dollar in hand today can be invested, earn interest, and hence be worth more than one dollar in the future. If no investment opportunities existed, a dollar in hand would still be worth more than a dollar to be received in the future because a dollar today can be used for immediate consumption, whereas a future dollar cannot. Because current dollars are worth more than future dollars, valuation analyses must account for cash flow timing differences.

The process of assigning appropriate values to cash flows that occur at different points in time is called *time value analysis*. However, the application of time value analysis to valuation situations is often called *discounted cash flow analysis* because, as you will see later in this chapter, finding present values is called *discounting*. Time value analysis is an important part of many healthcare financial management decisions because many financial analyses involve the valuation of future cash flows. Of all the financial analysis techniques discussed in this text, none is more important than time value analysis. The concepts presented in this chapter are the cornerstones of financial analysis, so a thorough understanding of these concepts is essential to good financial decision-making.

Time Lines

One important tool used in time value analysis is the *time line*. Time lines make it easier to visualize when the cash flows in a particular analysis occur. For an illustration of the time line concept, consider the following five-period time line:

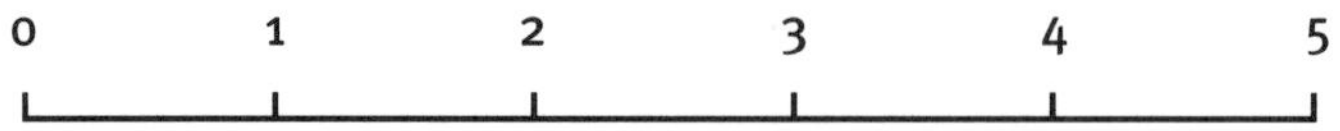

Time 0 is any starting point; time 1 is one period from the starting point, or the end of period 1; time 2 is two periods from the starting point, or the end of period 2; and so on. Thus, the numbers above the tick marks represent ends of periods. Often, the periods are years, but other time intervals—such as quarters, months, or days—are also used when needed to fit the timing of the cash flows being evaluated. If the periods are years, the interval from 0 to 1 would be year 1, and the tick mark labeled 1 would represent both the end of year 1 and the beginning of year 2. In many time value analyses, time 0 (the starting point) is considered to be "today," although the term **today** usually does not literally mean today's date. Rather, time 0 typically identifies the start of the analysis, which begins when the first cash flow occurs.

Cash flows are shown on a time line directly below the tick marks, at the point they are expected to occur. The interest rate relevant to the analysis is sometimes shown directly above the time line in the first period. (In rare cases, it may be appropriate to apply more than one interest rate in a time value analysis. In this situation, interest rates may be shown in multiple periods.) In addition, unknown cash flows—the ones to be determined in the analysis—are sometimes indicated by question marks. Here is an example of a completed time line:

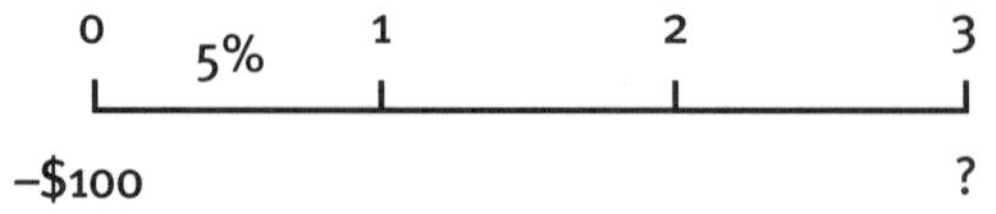

Here, the interest rate for each of the three periods is 5 percent, a *lump-sum* (single amount) investment of $100 is made at time 0, and the time 3 value is to be determined. The $100 is an *outflow* because it is shown as a negative cash flow. (Outflows are often designated by parentheses rather than by minus signs.) In simple analyses, it is not necessary to designate cash flows as inflows and outflows because the analyst is well aware of the economics of the situation. However, more complicated analyses require the correct cash flow designation. Thus, to ensure you are familiar with sign conventions, we use them in most of our illustrations.

Time lines are essential when learning time value concepts, but even experienced analysts use time lines when dealing with complex problems. The time line may be an actual line, as used in this chapter, or it may be a series of columns, or rows, on a spreadsheet. Time lines will be used extensively in the remainder of this text, so get into the habit of creating time lines when conducting time value analyses.

SELF-TEST QUESTION

1. Draw a three-year time line that illustrates the following situation: an investment of $10,000 at time 0; inflows of $5,000 at the end of years 1, 2, and 3; and an interest rate of 10 percent during the entire three-year period.

Future Value of a Lump Sum (Compounding)

On the web at: *ache.org/HAP/PinkSong8e*

The process of going from today's values, or ***present values (Pvs)***, to future values is called ***compounding***. Although compounding is not used extensively in healthcare financial management, it is the best point from which to start learning time value concepts. For an example of ***lump-sum*** compounding, which deals with a single starting dollar amount, suppose that the manager of Meridian Clinic deposits $100 of the clinic's excess cash in a bank account that pays 5 percent interest per year. How much would be in the account at the end of one year?

Before you begin, you need to understand the terms used in the solution:

- Pv = $100 = present value, or beginning amount, of the account.
- I = 5% = interest rate the bank pays on the account per year. The interest amount, which is paid at the end of each year, is based on the balance at the beginning of the year. Expressed as a decimal, I = 0.05.
- INT = dollars of interest earned each year, which equals the beginning amount multiplied by the interest rate. Thus, for Year 1, INT = Pv × I.
- Fv_N = future value, or ending amount, of the account at the end of N years. Whereas Pv is the value now, and Fv_N is the value N years into the future (after the interest earned has been added to the account).

- N = number of years (or periods) involved in the analysis.

If N = 1, Fv_N is calculated as follows:

$$Fv_N = Fv_1 = Pv + INT = Pv + (Pv \times I) = Pv \times (1 + I).$$

The future value at the end of one year, Fv1, equals the present value multiplied by (1 plus the interest rate). This future value relationship can be used to find how much $100 will be worth at the end of one year if it is invested in an account that pays 5 percent interest:

$$Fv_1 = Pv \times (1 + I) = \$100 \times (1 + 0.05) = \$100 \times 1.05 = \$105.$$

Now, what would be the value after five years? Here is a time line that shows the amount at the end of each year:

	0 (5%)	1	2	3	4	5
Beginning amount	−$100					
Interest earned		$ 5	$ 5.25	$ 5.51	$ 5.79	$ 6.08
End-of-year amount		105	110.25	115.76	121.55	127.63

Note the following points:

- The account is opened with a deposit of $100. This deposit is shown as an outflow at year 0. It is an outflow to Meridian because Meridian is depositing the funds with the bank as opposed to receiving the funds from the bank, which would be an inflow.
- Meridian earns $100 × 0.05 = $5 of interest during the first year, so the amount in the account at the end of year 1 is $100 + $5 = $105.
- At the start of the second year, the account balance is $105. Interest of $105 × 0.05 = $5.25 is earned on the now-larger amount, and the account balance at the end of the second year is $105 + $5.25 = $110.25. The year 2 interest, $5.25, is higher than the first year's interest, $5, because $5 × 0.05 = $0.25 in interest was earned on the first year's interest.
- This process continues, and because the beginning balance is higher in each succeeding year, the interest earned increases in each year.

- The total interest earned, \$27.63, is reflected in the balance at the end of year 5, \$127.63.

To better understand the mathematics of compounding, note that the year 2 value—\$110.25—is calculated as follows:

$$\begin{aligned} Fv_2 &= Fv_1 \times (1 + I) \\ &= Pv \times (1 + I) \times (1 + I) \\ &= Pv \times (1 + I)^2 \\ &= \$100 \times (1.05)^2 = \$110.25. \end{aligned}$$

Furthermore, the balance at the end of year 3 is

$$\begin{aligned} Fv_3 &= Fv_2 \times (1 + I) \\ &= Pv \times (1 + I)^3 \\ &= \$100 \times (1.05)^3 = \$115.76. \end{aligned}$$

If we continue the calculation to the end of year 5, we get

$$Fv_5 = \$100 \times (1.05)^5 = \$127.63.$$

A pattern exists in these future value calculations. In general, the future value of a lump sum at the end of N years can be found by applying this equation:

Key Equation 4.1: Future Value of a Lump Sum

$$Fv_N = Pv \times (1 + I)^N.$$

Future values, and most other time values, can be calculated three ways: (1) by using a regular calculator, (2) by using a financial calculator, and (3) by using a spreadsheet.[1] This textbook focuses on the spreadsheet solution technique.

Regular Calculator Solution

A regular (nonfinancial) calculator can be used, either by multiplying the Pv by (1 + I) for N times or by using the exponential function to raise (1 + I) to the Nth power and then multiplying the result by the Pv. The easiest way to find the future value of \$100 after five years when compounded at 5 percent is to enter \$100 and then multiply this amount by 1.05 five times. If the calculator is set to display two decimal places, the answer is \$127.63:

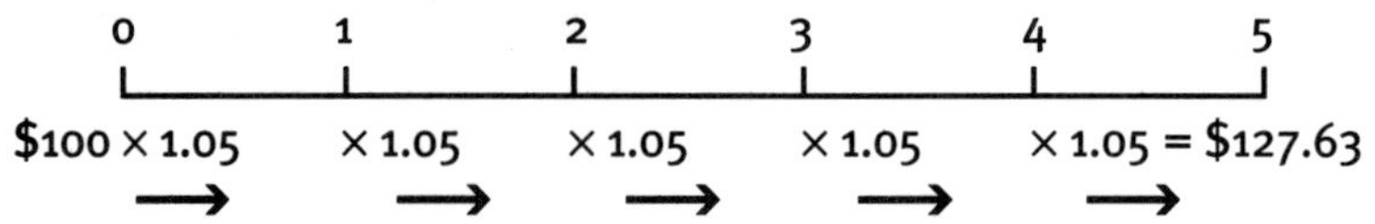

Spreadsheet Solution

The word *compounding* means to add to or increase, so values increase when moving to the right along a time line.

	A	B	C	D
1				
2	5	Nper	Number of periods	
3	$100.00	Pv	Present value	
4	5.0%	Rate	Interest rate	
5				
6	$127.63	= 100*(1.05)^5 (entered into cell A6)		
7				
8	$127.63	=A3*(1+A4)^A2 (entered into cell A8)		
9				
10	$127.63	=Fv(A4,A2,,-A3) (entered into cell A10)		

Spreadsheet programs, such as Excel, are ideally suited for time value analyses. For simple time value calculations, it is easy to enter the appropriate formula directly into the spreadsheet. For example, you could enter the spreadsheet version of the future value equation into cell A6: =100*(1.05)^5. Here, = tells the spreadsheet that a formula is being entered into the cell; * is the spreadsheet multiplication sign; and ^ is the spreadsheet exponential, or power, sign. When this formula is entered into cell A6, the value $127.63 appears in the cell (when formatted with a dollar sign to two decimal places). Note that different spreadsheet programs use slightly different syntax in their time value analyses. The examples presented in this text use Excel syntax.

In most situations, it is more useful to enter a formula that can accommodate changing input values than to embed values in the formula, so it would be better to solve this future value problem with this formula: =A3*(1+A4)^A2, as done in cell A8. Here, the present value ($100) is contained in cell A3, the interest rate (0.05, which is displayed as 5.0%) in cell A4, and the number of periods (5) in cell A2. With this formula, future values can be easily calculated with different starting amounts, interest rates, or number of years by changing the values in the input cells.

Most time value solutions are preprogrammed in the spreadsheet software. The preprogrammed time value formulas are called *functions.* Like any formula, a time value function consists of a number of arithmetic calculations combined into one statement. By using functions, spreadsheet users can save the time and tedium of building formulas from scratch.

Each function begins with a unique name that identifies the calculation to be performed, along with one or more *arguments* (the input values for the calculation) enclosed in parentheses. The best way to access the time value functions is to use the spreadsheet's *function wizard* (also called the *paste* function). For this future value problem, first move the cursor to cell A10 (the cell where you want the answer to appear). Then, click on the function wizard; select "Financial" for the function category and "Fv" (future value) for the function name; and enter A4 for Rate, A2 for Nper (number of periods), and –A3 for Pv. (Note that the Pmt and Type entries are left blank for this problem. Also note that the cell address entered for Pv has a minus sign. This is necessary for the answer to be displayed as a positive number.) Press OK, and the result—\$127.63—appears in cell A10.

Most of the spreadsheet solutions shown in this book follow a similar format. The input values and the output are contained in column A. If a spreadsheet function is used in the solution, the input value (argument) names are shown in column B to the right of the input values. In addition, the formula or function used to calculate the output is shown in column B to the right of the output value. Finally, column C contains the descriptive input names.

The most efficient way to solve most problems involving time value is to use a spreadsheet. However, the basic mathematics behind the calculations must be understood to set up complex problems before solving them. In addition, the underlying logic must be understood to comprehend stock and bond valuation, lease analysis, capital budgeting analysis, and other important healthcare financial management topics.

To help you better understand time value solution techniques, we use a consistent format in the illustrations presented in this chapter:

- We lay out the situation on a time line and show the equation that must be solved.
- We present the mathematical formula, if applicable.
- We present the spreadsheet solution.

Graphic View of the Compounding (Growth) Process

Exhibit 4.1 shows how \$1, or any other lump sum, grows over time at various rates of interest. The data used to plot the curves can be obtained by using any of the solution techniques described in the previous section. Note that the greater the rate of interest, the faster the growth rate. Thus, \$100 on deposit for ten years at a 5 percent interest rate will grow to \$162.89, but the same amount invested at 10 percent interest will grow to \$259.37. The

On the web at: *ache.org/HAP/PinkSong8e*

EXHIBIT 4.1
Relationships Among Future Value, Interest Rates, and Time

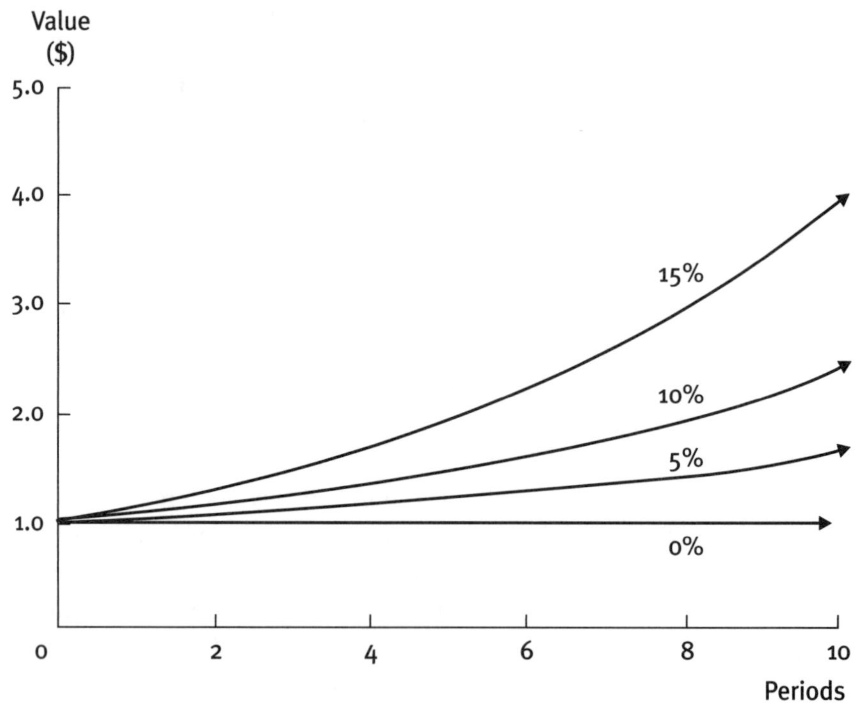

Interest Rate Plot Points

Period	*5%*	*10%*	*15%*
1	1.0500	1.1000	1.1500
2	1.1025	1.2100	1.3225
3	1.1576	1.3310	1.5209
4	1.2155	1.4641	1.7490
5	1.2763	1.6105	2.0114
6	1.3401	1.7716	2.3131
7	1.4071	1.9487	2.6600
8	1.4775	2.1436	3.0590
9	1.5513	2.3579	3.5179
10	1.6289	2.5937	4.0456

interest rate is, in fact, a growth rate: If a lump sum is deposited and earns 5 percent interest, the funds on deposit will grow at a rate of 5 percent per period. Also note that future value concepts are not restricted to bank deposits; they can be applied to any growing, or declining, numerical value such as number of clinic visits or earnings per share.

The Power of Compounding

It is important to understand what is commonly called *the power of compounding*. A relatively small starting value can grow to a large amount over a long period, even when the rate of growth (interest rate) is modest. For example, assume that a new parent places $1,000 in a mutual fund to help pay her child's college expenses, which are expected to begin in 18 years. If the *mutual fund*—a common stock fund holding a large number of securities—earns a return of 10 percent per year, after 18 years the value of the mutual fund account will be $5,560, which is not an inconsequential sum. (Historically, 10 percent has been considered a reasonable estimate for annual returns on a well-diversified portfolio of stocks.

Now, assume that the money is meant to help fund the child's retirement, which, hypothetically, will occur 65 years into the future. The value of the mutual fund account at that time will be $490,371, or nearly a **half-million dollars**, all because of the power of compounding! The moral of this story is clear: When saving for retirement, or for any other purpose, start early.

SELF-TEST QUESTIONS

1. What is compounding? What is interest on interest?
2. What is the basic equation for calculating the future value of a lump sum?
3. What are three solution techniques for solving lump-sum compounding problems? Which technique is the most efficient?
4. What is meant by the power of compounding?

Present Value of a Lump Sum (Discounting)

On the web at: *ache.org/HAP/PinkSong8e*

Suppose that GroupWest Health Plans, which has premium income reserves to invest, has an opportunity to purchase a low-risk security that will pay $127.63 at the end of five years. A local bank is offering 5 percent interest on a five-year certificate of deposit (CD), and GroupWest's managers believe that the security is as safe as the bank CD. The 5 percent interest rate available on the bank CD is GroupWest's *opportunity cost rate*, in that it has the opportunity to earn that return on an investment similar to the security under consideration. (Opportunity costs are discussed in detail in the next section.) How much would GroupWest be willing to pay for this security?

In the previous section, we learned that an initial amount of $100 invested at 5 percent per year would be worth $127.63 at the end of five years. Thus, GroupWest should be indifferent to the choice between $100 today and

$127.63 to be received after five years. Today's $100 is defined as the present value, or Pv, of $127.63 due in five years, when the opportunity cost rate is 5 percent. If the price of the security is less than $100, GroupWest should buy it. If the price is greater than $100, GroupWest should turn the offer down. If the price is exactly $100, GroupWest can buy it or turn it down because $100 is the security's fair value. In general, the present value of a cash flow due N years in the future is the amount that, if it were on hand today, would grow to equal the future amount when compounded at the opportunity cost rate.

Finding present values is called *discounting*, and it is simply the reverse of compounding: If the Pv is known, compound to find the Fv; if the Fv is known, discount to find the Pv. Here are the solution techniques for this discounting problem.

Key Equation 4.2: Present Value of a Lump Sum

$$\text{Compounding: } Fv_N = Pv \times (1 + I)^N.$$

$$\text{Discounting: } Pv = \frac{Fv_N}{(1 + I)^N}.$$

The word ***discount*** means to reduce or to lessen, so values decrease when moving to the left along a time line.

Spreadsheet Solution

One spreadsheet approach would be to enter the applicable formula, as shown to the right of cell A6: =A3/(1+A4)^A2. Here, the future value ($127.63) is contained in cell A3, the interest rate (0.05, which is displayed as 5.0%) in cell A4, and the number of periods (5) in cell A2. With this formula, present values easily can be calculated for different starting future amounts, interest rates, or number of years.

	A	B	C	D
1				
2	5	Nper	Number of periods	
3	$127.63	Fv	Future value	
4	5.0%	Rate	Interest rate	
5				
6	$100.00	=A3/(1+A4)^A2 (entered into cell A6)		
7				
8	$100.00	=Pv(A4,A2,,-A3) (entered into cell A8)		
9				
10				

The function approach is illustrated in cell A8. First, move the cursor to the cell in which you want the answer to appear (here, cell A8). Click on the function wizard; select Financial for the function category and Pv (present value) for the function name; and enter A4 for Rate, A2 for Nper (number of periods), and –A3 for Fv. (The Pmt and Type entries are left blank for this problem. Also, the cell address entered for Fv has a minus sign so that the answer will be displayed as a positive number.) Press OK, and the result—$100.00—appears in cell A8.

Graphic View of the Discounting Process

Exhibit 4.2 shows how the present value of $1, or any other sum, to be received in the future diminishes as the years to receipt increase. Again, the data used to plot the curves can be developed by using any of the solution techniques. The graphs show that (1) the present value decreases and approaches zero as the payment date is extended further into the future; and (2) the greater the rate of decrease, the higher the interest (discount) rate.

Discounting at Work

At relatively high interest rates, funds due in the future are worth little today, and even at moderate discount rates, the present value of a sum due in the distant future is small. For an illustration of discounting at work, consider 100-year bonds. A *bond* is a type of debt security; an investor loans some amount of principal—say, $1,000—to a borrower who promises to pay interest over the life of the bond and return the principal amount at maturity. Typically, the longest maturities for bonds are 30 to 40 years, but in the early 1990s, several firms, including Columbia/HCA Healthcare (now HCA Healthcare; see www.hcahealthcare.com), issued 100-year bonds.

Anyone who would buy a 100-year bond might appear irrational—there is little assurance that the firm will exist in 100 years to repay the amount borrowed. However, consider the present value of $1,000 to be received in 100 years. If the discount rate is 7.5 percent—roughly the interest rate set on the bond when it was issued in 1995—the present value is $0.72. The time value of money erodes the value of the principal repayment to a point where it is worth less than $1 when the bond is purchased. Therefore, the value of the bond stems mostly from the interest stream received in the early years of ownership, and the payments expected during the later years of the bond contribute little to the bond's initial $1,000 value.

EXHIBIT 4.2 Relationships Among Present Value, Interest Rates, and Time

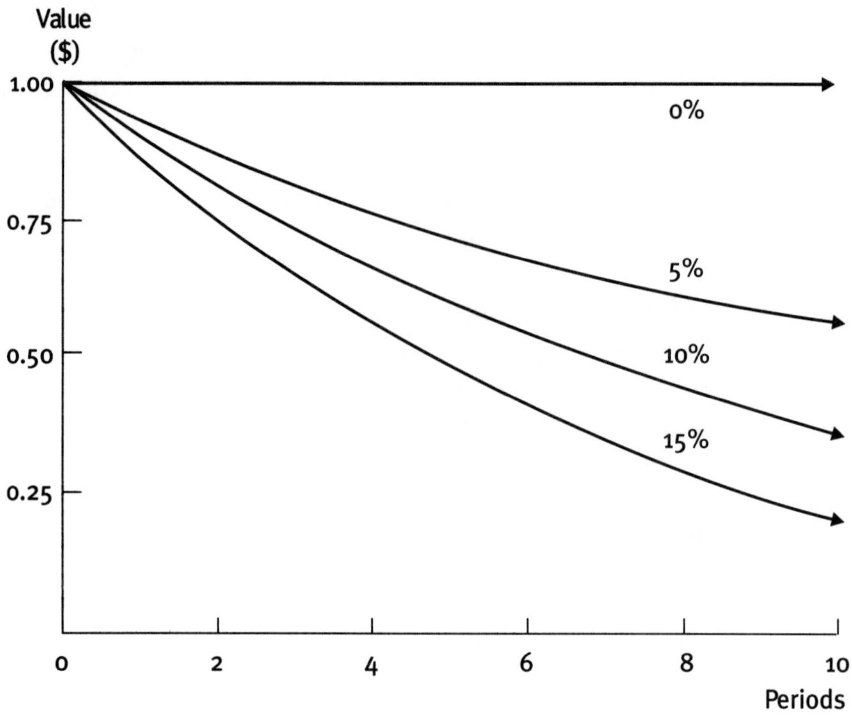

	Interest Rate Plot Points		
Period	*5%*	*10%*	*15%*
1	.9524	.9091	.8696
2	.9070	.8254	.7561
3	.8638	.7513	.6575
4	.8227	.6830	.5718
5	.7835	.6209	.4972
6	.7462	.5634	.4323
7	.7107	.5132	.3759
8	.6768	.4665	.3269
9	.6446	.4241	.2843
10	.6139	.3855	.2472

SELF-TEST QUESTIONS

1. What is discounting? How is it related to compounding?
2. What are the three techniques for solving lump-sum discounting problems?
3. What is the basic equation for calculating the present value of a lump sum?
4. How does the present value of an amount to be received in the future change as the payment date is extended and the interest rate increases?

Opportunity Costs

In the previous section, the opportunity cost concept was used to set the discount rate needed to analyze GroupWest's security investment. This concept plays an important role in time value analysis. For example, suppose an individual had the winning ticket for the Florida lottery and now has $1 million to invest. Should he assign a "cost" to these funds? This money might appear to have zero cost because its acquisition was purely a matter of luck. However, when the lucky individual thinks about what he is going to do with the $1 million, he has to think in terms of the opportunity costs involved. By using the funds to invest in one alternative (e.g., in the stock of Health Management Associates, www.hmacorp.com), the individual forgoes the opportunity to make some other investment (e.g., in US Treasury bonds). Thus, there is an opportunity cost associated with any investment planned for the $1 million, though the lottery winnings were "free."

Because one investment decision automatically negates all other possible investments with the same funds, the cash flows expected to be earned from any investment must be discounted at a rate that reflects the return that can be earned on forgone investment opportunities. The problem is that the number of forgone investment opportunities is virtually infinite, so which one should be chosen to establish the opportunity cost rate? The opportunity cost rate to be applied in time value analysis is the rate that can be earned on alternative investments of **similar risk**. It would not be logical to assign a low opportunity-cost rate to a series of risky cash flows, or vice versa. This concept is one of the cornerstones of financial management, so it is worth repeating. **The opportunity cost rate (i.e., the discount rate) applied to investment cash flows is the rate that can be earned on alternative investments of similar risk.**

If You Win the Powerball, Should You Take the Annuity or the Cash?

Suppose you won the Powerball with a jackpot of $590,500,000. With odds reported at 1 in 175,223,510, you would have been very lucky indeed (Powerball 2019). Winners of the Powerball have two choices for how to receive their winnings. They can take 30 annual payments (in your case, 30 × $19,683,333) or one lump sum (in your case, $370,896,781). Which option should you choose?

The first step is to determine the discount rate that makes the present value of the annuity due equal to the lump sum; in other words, what is the rate of return that makes the present value of 30 annual payments of $19,683,333 equal to the lump sum of $370,896,781? As a starting point, let's try a discount rate of 4 percent. The present value of an annuity due at a discount rate of 4 percent and 30 annual payments of $19,683,333 is

= PV (4%,30, $19683333,,1) = $353,979,444.

This is slightly less than the lump sum, so we know that the discount rate is less than 4 percent. Using Goal Seek, we find that a discount rate of 3.59 percent makes the present value of the annuity due equal to the lump sum. Now what? If you believe that, through careful investing, you can achieve an average annual rate of return greater than 3.59 percent, you should choose the lump sum and invest it accordingly. However, if you believe that it is unlikely you can achieve an average annual rate of return of 3.59 percent, you should choose the annuity. Of course, there are many other financial factors to consider, such as taxes, liquidity, and other assets and liabilities. There are nonfinancial factors as well, such as your family circumstances and age. An 80-year-old Powerball winner likely has a different attitude toward a 30-year annuity than a 20-year-old winner does.

The opportunity cost rate does not depend on the source of the funds to be invested. The primary determinant of this rate is the riskiness of the cash flows being discounted. Thus, the same opportunity cost rate would be applied to a potential investment in Tenet Healthcare Corporation stock, whether the funds needed to make the purchase were won in a lottery, taken out of petty cash, or obtained by selling some landholdings.

Generally, opportunity cost rates are obtained by looking at rates that can be earned or, more precisely, rates that are expected to be earned on securities (such as stocks or bonds). Securities are usually chosen to set opportunity cost rates because their expected returns are more easily estimated than rates of return on real assets such as health maintenance organizations, group practices, hospital beds, magnetic resonance imaging (MRI) machines, and the like. Furthermore, as discussed in chapters 6 and 7, securities generally provide the minimum return appropriate for the amount of risk assumed, so securities returns are a good benchmark for other investments.

To better grasp the opportunity cost concept, assume that Live Oak Community Hospital is considering building a nursing home. The first step in the financial analysis is to forecast the cash flows that the nursing home is expected to produce. These cash flows must be discounted at some opportunity cost rate to determine their present value. Would the hospital's opportunity cost rate be (1) the expected rate of return on Treasury bonds; (2) the expected rate of return on the stock of Enlivant (www.enlivant.com), which operates about 200 assisted living centers; or (3) the expected rate of return on pork belly futures? (Pork belly futures are investments that involve commodity contracts for delivery at some future time.) The answer is the expected rate of return on Enlivant's stock because that rate of return is expected to be earned on alternative investments of similar risk. Treasury securities are very low-risk investments, so they would understate the opportunity cost rate in owning a nursing home. Conversely, pork belly futures are very high-risk investments, so that rate of return is probably too high to apply to Live Oak's nursing home investment.[2]

The source of the funds used for the nursing home investment is **not relevant** to the time value analysis. Live Oak may obtain the needed funds by borrowing or by soliciting contributions, or it may have accumulated excess cash over time. The discount rate applied to the nursing home cash flows depends only on the riskiness of those cash flows and the returns available on alternative investments of similar risk, not on the source of the investment funds.

At this point, you may question the ability of real-world analysts to assess the riskiness of a cash flow stream or to choose an opportunity cost rate with any confidence. Fortunately, the process is not as difficult as it may appear here because businesses have benchmarks that can be used as starting points. (Chapter 9 contains a discussion of how baseline opportunity cost rates are established for capital investments, while chapter 12 presents a detailed discussion on how the riskiness of a cash flow stream can be assessed.)

SELF-TEST QUESTIONS

1. Why does an investment have an opportunity cost rate even when the employed funds have no explicit cost?
2. How are opportunity cost rates established?
3. Does the opportunity cost rate depend on the source of the investment funds?

Solving for Interest Rate and Time

In our examples thus far, four time value analysis variables have been used: Pv, Fv, I, and N. Specifically, the interest rate (I) and the number of years (N), plus either Pv or Fv, have been given. If the values of any three of the variables are known, the value of the fourth can be found.

On the web at: *ache.org/HAP/PinkSong8e*

Solving for Interest Rate (I)

Suppose that FPA, a primary care physician group practice, can buy a bank CD for $78.35 that will return $100 after five years. In this case Pv, Fv, and

N are known, but I—the interest rate that the bank is paying—is not known. Such problems are solved in this way:

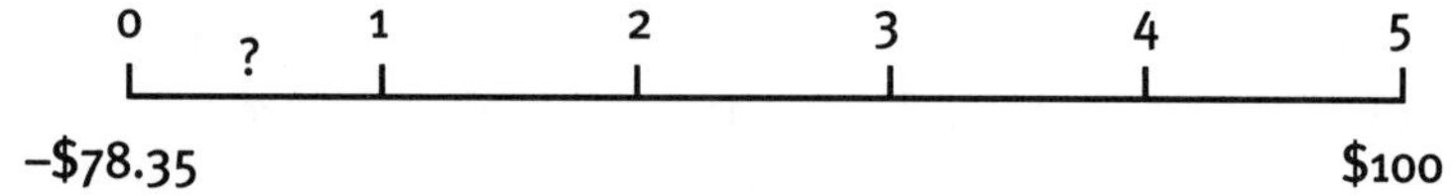

$$Fv_N = Pv \times (1 + I)^N$$
$$\$100 = \$78.35 \times (1 + I)^5$$

Spreadsheet Solution

	A	B	C	D
1				
2	5	Nper	Number of periods	
3	$(78.35)	Pv	Present value	
4	$100.00	Fv	Future value	
5				
6				
7				
8	5.00%	=RATE(A2,,A3,A4) (entered into cell A8)		
9				
10				

Here, the spreadsheet function RATE is used to solve for I, as illustrated to the right of cell A8. First, click on the function wizard; select Financial for the function category and RATE for the function name; and enter A2 for Nper (number of periods), A3 for Pv, and A4 for Fv. (The Pmt and Type entries are left blank for this problem. Also, the Pv was entered as a negative number, as shown on the time line.) Press OK, and the result—5.00%—appears in cell A8. (Some spreadsheet programs display the answer in decimal form unless the cell is formatted to display as a percentage.)

Solving for Time (N)

On the web at: *ache.org/HAP/PinkSong8e*

Suppose that the bank told FPA that a CD pays 5 percent interest each year, that it costs $78.35, and that the group would receive $100 at maturity. How long must the funds be invested in the CD? In this case, Pv, Fv, and I are known, but N—the number of periods—is not known.

Time Line

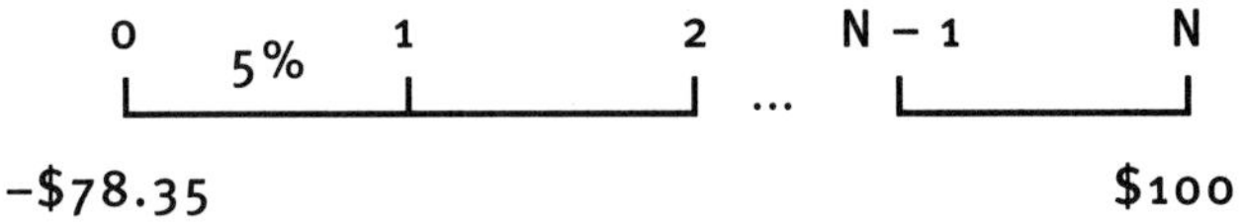

$$Fv_N = Pv \times (1 + I)^N$$
$$\$100 = \$78.35 \times (1.05)^N$$

Spreadsheet Solution

	A	B	C	D
1				
2	5.00%	Rate	Number of periods	
3	$(78.35)	Pv	Present value	
4	$100.00	Fv	Future value	
5				
6				
7				
8	5	=NPER(A2,,A3,A4) (entered into cell A8)		
9				
10				

To solve for time, the spreadsheet function NPER (number of periods) is used. To begin, place the cursor in cell A8 and click on the function wizard. Then select Financial for the function category and NPER for the function name, and enter A2 for Rate, A3 for Pv, and A4 for Fv. (The Pmt and Type entries are left blank for this problem. Also, the Pv was entered as a negative number, as shown on the time line.) Press OK, and the result—5—appears in cell A8.

The Rule of 72

The *Rule of 72* is a simple and quick method for judging the approximate effect of different interest rates on the growth of a lump-sum deposit. It tells us that to find the number of years required to double the value of a lump sum, merely divide the number 72 by the interest rate paid. For example, if the interest rate is 10 percent, it would take 72 ÷ 10 = 7.2 years for the money in an account to double in value. The spreadsheet solution is 7.27 years, so the Rule of 72 is relatively accurate, at least when reasonable interest rates are applied.

In a similar manner, the Rule of 72 can be used to determine the interest rate required to double the money in an account in a given number of years. For example, an interest rate of 72 ÷ 5 = 14.4% is required to double the value of an account in five years. The spreadsheet solution here is 14.9 percent, so the Rule of 72 again gives a reasonable approximation of the correct answer.

SELF-TEST QUESTIONS

1. What are some real-world situations that may require you to solve for interest rate or time?
2. What is the Rule of 72, and how is it used?

Annuities

Whereas lump sums are single dollar amounts, an ***annuity*** is a series of equal amounts paid out at fixed intervals for a specified number of periods. Annuity amounts, which often are called ***payments*** and given the symbol PMT, can occur at the beginning or end of each period. If the payments occur at the end of each period, as they typically do, the annuity is an ***ordinary annuity*** (also called a ***deferred***, or ***regular***, ***annuity***). If payments are made at the beginning of each period, the annuity is an ***annuity due***. Because ordinary annuities are, by far, the most common, the term ***annuity*** without further description usually means an ordinary annuity.

Ordinary Annuities

On the web at: *ache.org/HAP/PinkSong8e*

A series of equal payments at the end of each period constitutes an ordinary annuity. If Meridian Clinic were to deposit $100 at the end of each year for three years in an account that paid 5 percent interest per year, how much would Meridian accumulate at the end of three years? The answer to this question is the ***future value*** of the annuity.

Time Line

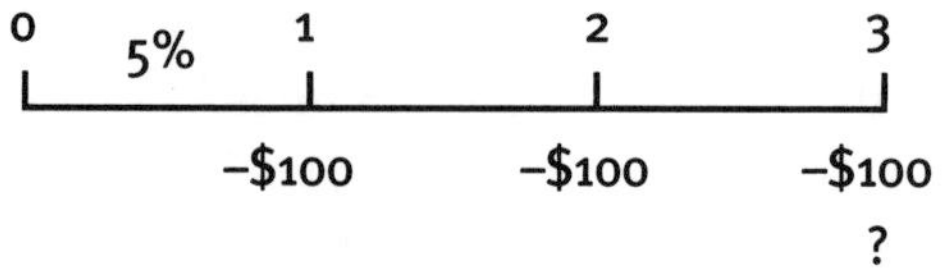

The future value of any annuity occurs at the end of the final period. Thus, for regular annuities, the future value coincides with the last payment.

Spreadsheet Solution

	A	B	C	D
1				
2	3	Nper	Number of periods	
3	$(100.00)	Pmt	Payment	
4	5.0%	Rate	Interest rate	
5				
6				
7				
8	$315.25	=Fv(A4,A2,A3) (entered into cell A8)		
9				
10				

Here, we again use the Fv function, but now we use the payment (Pmt) entry in the function wizard to recognize that the problem involves annuities. Place the cursor in cell A8. Click on the function wizard; select Financial for the function category and Fv for the function name; and enter A4 for Rate, A2 for Nper (number of periods), and A3 for Pmt. (The Pv and Type entries are left blank for this problem.) Press OK, and the result—$315.25—appears in cell A8.

Suppose that Meridian was offered the following alternatives: (1) a three-year annuity with payments of $100 at the end of each year or (2) a lump-sum payment today. Meridian has no need for the money during the next three years. If it chooses the annuity, it would deposit the payments in an account that pays 5 percent interest per year. Similarly, the lump-sum payment would be deposited into the same account. How large must the lump-sum payment be today to make it equivalent to the annuity? In other words, what is the present value of the annuity?

	A	B	C	D
1				
2	3	Nper	Number of periods	
3	$(100.00)	Pmt	Payment	
4	5.0%	Rate	Interest rate	
5				
6				
7				
8	$272.32	=Pv(A4,A2,A3) (entered into cell A8)		
9				
10				

Here, we use the present value function, but again with a payment entry to recognize that the problem involves annuities. Place the cursor in cell A8. Click on the function wizard; select Financial for the function category and Pv for the function name; and enter A4 for Rate, A2 for Nper (number of periods), and A3 for Pmt. (The Fv and Type entries are left blank for this problem.) Press OK and the result—$272.32—appears in cell A8.

One especially important application of the annuity concept relates to loans with constant payments such as mortgages, auto loans, and many business loans. Such loans are examined in more depth in a later section on amortization.

Annuities Due

On the web at: *ache.org/HAP/PinkSong8e*

If the three $100 payments in the previous example had been made at the beginning of each year, the annuity would have been an annuity due. When compared to an ordinary annuity, each payment is shifted to the left one year. Because the payments come in faster, an annuity due is more valuable than an ordinary annuity.

The future value of our example, assuming it is an annuity due, is found as follows:

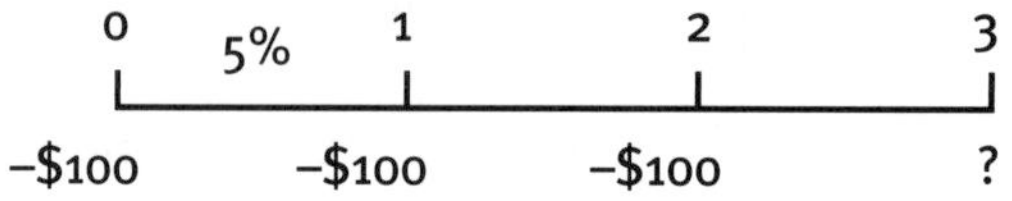

The future value of an annuity due occurs one period after the final payment, while the future value of an ordinary annuity coincides with the final payment. (Remember, by definition, the future value of any annuity occurs at the end of the final period; thus, the future value of a three-year annuity occurs at the end of period 3, whether the annuity is a regular annuity or an annuity due.)

In the case of an annuity due, as compared with an ordinary annuity, all the cash flows are compounded for one additional period; hence, the future value of an annuity due is greater than the future value of a similar ordinary annuity by (1 + I). Thus, the future value of an annuity due also can be found as follows:

$$\begin{aligned} \text{Fv (Annuity due)} &= \text{Fv of a regular annuity} \\ &\quad \times (1 + \text{I}) \\ &= \$315.25 \times 1.05 = \$331.01. \end{aligned}$$

Spreadsheet Solution

	A	B	C	D
1				
2	3	Nper	Number of periods	
3	$(100.00)	Pmt	Payment	
4	5.0%	Rate	Interest rate	
5				
6	$331.01	=Fv(A4,A2,A3,,1) (entered into cell A6)		
7				
8	$331.01	=Fv(A4,A2,A3)*(1+A4) (entered into cell A8)		
9				
10				

One approach (as shown in cell A6) is to use the spreadsheet Fv function, but with a "1" entered for Type (as opposed to a blank). Now, the spreadsheet treats the entries as an annuity due, and $331.01 is displayed as the answer. The solution is the same as for an ordinary annuity, except the result must be multiplied by (1 + Rate), which is (1 + A4) in this example. This solution approach is given in cell A8. The result—$331.01—is the future value of the annuity due.

The present value of an annuity due is found in a similar manner:

Time Line

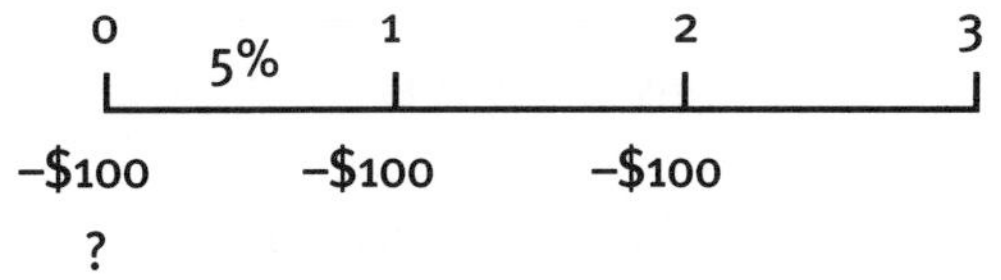

The present value of an annuity due can be thought of as the present value of an ordinary annuity that is compounded for one period, so it also can be found as follows:

$$\text{Pv (Annuity due)} = \text{Pv of a regular annuity} \times (1 + \text{I})$$
$$= \$272.32 \times 1.05 = \$285.94.$$

Spreadsheet Solution

	A	B	C	D
1				
2	3	Nper	Number of periods	
3	$(100.00)	Pmt	Payment	
4	5.0%	Rate	Interest rate	
5				
6	$285.94	=Pv(A4,A2,A3,,1) (entered into cell A6)		
7				
8	$285.94	=Pv(A4,A2,A3)*(1+A4) (entered into cell A8)		
9				
10				

As with future value, one approach (as shown in cell A6) is to use the spreadsheet Pv function, but with a "1" entered for Type (as opposed to a blank). Now, the spreadsheet treats the entries as an annuity due, and $285.94 is displayed as the answer. Note that the solution is the same as for an ordinary annuity, except the function in cell A8 is multiplied by (1 + A4). The result—$285.94—is the present value of the annuity due.

SELF-TEST QUESTIONS

1. What is an annuity?
2. What is the difference between an ordinary annuity and an annuity due?
3. Which annuity has the greater future value: an ordinary annuity or an annuity due? Why?
4. Which annuity has the greater present value: an ordinary annuity or an annuity due? Why?

Perpetuities

On the web at: *ache.org/HAP/PinkSong8e*

Most annuities call for payments to be made over some finite period—for example, $100 per year for three years—but some annuities go on indefinitely, or perpetually. Such annuities are called ***perpetuities***. The present value of a perpetuity is found as follows:

Key Equation 4.3: Present Value of a Perpetuity

$$\text{Pv (Perpetuity)} = \frac{\text{Payment}}{\text{Interest rate}} = \frac{\text{PMT}}{\text{Interest rate}}.$$

For example, some securities issued by General Healthcare, Inc., promise to pay $100 each annually in perpetuity (forever). What would each security be worth if the opportunity cost rate, or discount rate, were 10 percent? The answer is $1,000:

$$\text{Pv (Perpetuity)} = \frac{\$100}{0.10} = \$1{,}000.$$

	A	B	C	D
1				
2				
3	$100.00	Pmt	Payment	
4	10.0%	Rate	Interest rate	
5				
6				
7				
8	$1,000.00	=A3/A4 (entered into cell A8)		
9				
10				

Using a spreadsheet, merely enter the perpetuity formula into a cell, as shown in cell A8.

Suppose interest rates, and hence the opportunity cost rate, rose to 15 percent. What would happen to the security's value? The interest rate increase would lower its value to $666.67:

$$\text{Pv (Perpetuity)} = \frac{\$100}{0.15} = 666.67.$$

Assume that interest rates fell to 5 percent. The rate decrease would increase the perpetuity's value to $2,000:

$$\text{Pv (Perpetuity)} = \frac{\$100}{0.05} = \$2{,}000.$$

As illustrated in the previous equations, the value of a perpetuity changes dramatically when interest (opportunity cost) rates change. All securities' values are affected when such changes occur, but some types—such as perpetuities and long-term government bonds—are more sensitive to interest rate changes than others. Conversely, securities such as short-term government bonds (T-bills) and one-year bank CDs are affected much less when rates change. The risks associated with interest rate changes are discussed in more detail in chapter 6.

SELF-TEST QUESTIONS

1. What is a perpetuity?
2. What happens to the value of a perpetuity when interest rates increase or decrease?

Uneven Cash Flow Streams

The definition of an annuity includes the words *constant amount*, so annuities involve cash amounts that are the same in every period. Although some financial decisions—such as bond valuation—do involve constant cash amounts, most important healthcare financial analyses involve uneven, or nonconstant, amounts. For example, the financial evaluation of a proposed outpatient clinic or MRI facility rarely involves constant cash amounts.

In general, the term *payment (PMT)* is reserved for annuity situations in which the dollar amounts are constant, and the term *cash flow* denotes uneven cash flows (or lump sums).

Present Value

On the web at: *ache.org/HAP/PinkSong8e*

The present value of an uneven cash flow stream is the sum of the present values of the individual cash flows of the stream. For example, suppose Smith Memorial Health System is considering purchasing a new X-ray machine. The hospital's managers forecast that the operation of the new machine would produce the following stream of cash inflows (in thousands of dollars):

0	1	2	3	4	5
	$100	$120	$150	$180	$250

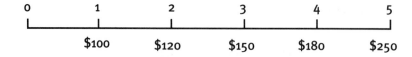

What is the present value of the new X-ray machine investment if the appropriate discount (opportunity cost) rate is 10 percent?

Spreadsheet Solution

	A	B	C	D
1				
2	10.0%	Rate	Interest rate	
3				
4	$100	Value 1	Year 1 CF	
5	$120	Value 1	Year 2 CF	
6	$150	Value 1	Year 3 CF	
7	$180	Value 1	Year 4 CF	
8	$250	Value 1	Year 5 CF	
9				
10	$580.95	=NPV(A2,A4:A8)(entered into cell A10)		

The NPV function calculates the present value of a series, called a spreadsheet *range*, of cash flows. First, enter the cash flow values into consecutive cells in the spreadsheet, as shown in cells A4 through A8. Next, place the discount (opportunity cost) rate in a cell (as in cell A2). Then, place the cursor in cell A10, use the function wizard to select Financial and NPV, and enter A2 as Rate and A4:A8 as Value 1. Press OK, and the value—$580.95—appears in the cell. (The Value 1 entry is the range of cash flows contained in cells A4 through A8. Also, NPV stands for *net present value*, which indicates that the resulting present value is the net of the present values of two or more cash flows.)

The NPV function assumes that cash flows occur at the **end** of each period, so NPV is calculated as of the **beginning** of the period of the first cash flow specified in the range, which is one period before the cash flow occurs. Because the cash flow specified as the first flow in the range is a year 1 value, the calculated NPV occurs at the beginning of year 1, or the end of year 0, which is correct for this illustration. However, if a year 0 cash flow is included in the range, the NPV would be calculated at the beginning of year 0, or the end of year –1, which typically is incorrect. This problem will be addressed in the next major section.

Future Value

The future value of an uneven cash flow stream is found by compounding each payment to the end of the stream and then summing the future values.

On the web at: *ache.org/HAP/PinkSong8e*

Spreadsheet Solution

Most spreadsheet programs do not have a function that computes the future value of an uneven cash flow stream. However, future values can be found by building a formula in a cell.

SELF-TEST QUESTIONS

1. Give two examples of financial decisions that typically involve uneven cash flows.
2. Describe how present values of uneven cash flow streams are calculated using a spreadsheet.
3. What is meant by NPV?

Using Time Value Analysis to Measure Return on Investment

In most investments, an individual or business spends cash today with the expectation of receiving cash in the future. The financial attractiveness of such investments is measured by ***return on investment (ROI)***, or just ***return***. There are two basic ways of expressing ROI: (1) in dollar terms and (2) in percentage terms.

To illustrate the concept, we can reexamine the cash flows expected to be received if Smith Memorial Health System buys its new X-ray machine (shown on the time line in thousands of dollars). In the last section, we determined that the Pv of these flows, when discounted at a 10 percent rate, is $580.95:

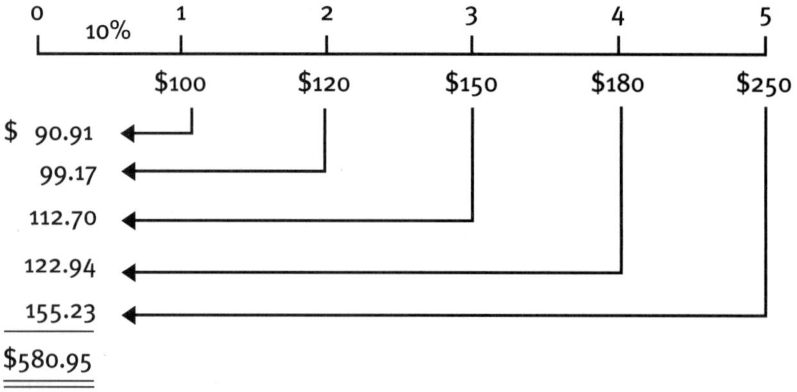

Dollar Return

On the web at: *ache.org/HAP/PinkSong8e*

The $580.95 represents the present value (in financial terms) of the cash flows that the X-ray machine is expected to provide to Smith Memorial Health System. These cash flows are not known with certainty but are the best estimates of the hospital's managers.

To measure the ***dollar return*** on the investment, typically called NPV, the cost of the X-ray machine must be compared to the present value of the expected benefits (the cash inflows). If the machine is expected to cost $500, and the present value of the inflows is $580.95, then the machine's NPV is $580.95 – $500 = $80.95. (Because these amounts are in thousands, the actual NPV is $80,950.) Note that this measure of dollar return incorporates time value through the discounting process. Also, the opportunity cost inherent in the use of the $500,000 is accounted for because the 10 percent discount rate reflects the return that can be earned on alternative investments of similar risk. Thus, the machine is expected to produce an $80,950 return above that required for its riskiness, as accounted for by the 10 percent opportunity cost rate.

The dollar return process can be combined into a single calculation by adding the cost of the machine to the time line:

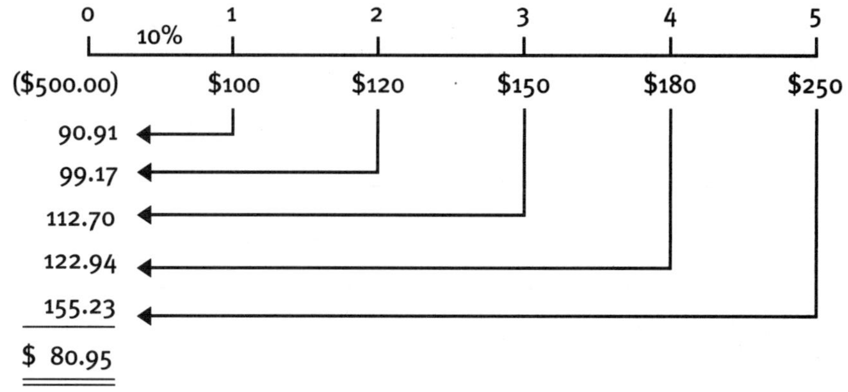

	A	B	C	D
1				
2	10.0%	Rate	Interest rate	
3	$(500)		Year 0 CF	
4	$100	Value 1	Year 1 CF	
5	$120	Value 1	Year 2 CF	
6	$150	Value 1	Year 3 CF	
7	$180	Value 1	Year 4 CF	
8	$250	Value 1	Year 5 CF	
9				
10	$80.95	=NPV(A2,A4:A8) + A3 (entered into cell A10)		

The situation here is the same as in the previous cash flow stream, which did not include the cost of the machine, with the exception of an initial investment outlay of $500 in cell A3. Because the NPV of the cash inflows in cells A4 through A8 represents the value one period before the first (A4) cash flow, we just add the investment outlay to the calculated NPV. This calculation is done in cell A10 by adding A3 to the NPV function. The result—$80.95—appears in that cell.

On the web at: *ache.org/HAP/ PinkSong8e*

Rate of Return

The second way to measure ROI is by ***rate of return***, or ***percentage return***. Rate of return measures the interest rate that must be earned on the investment outlay to generate the expected cash inflows. In other words, this measure provides the expected periodic rate of return on the investment. If the cash flows are annual, as in this example, the rate of return is an annual rate. In effect we are solving for I (the interest rate that equates the present value of the cash inflows to the dollar amount of the cash outlay).

Mathematically, if the Pv of the cash inflows equals the investment outlay, the NPV of the investment is forced to $0. This relationship is shown here:

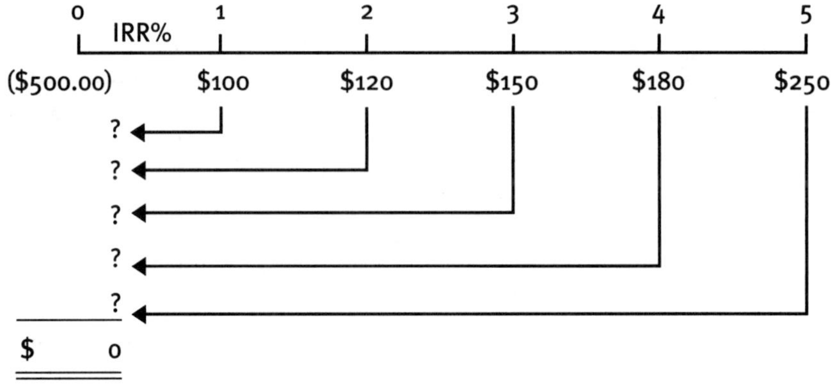

The rate of return on an investment, particularly an investment in plant or equipment, typically is called the ***internal rate of return (IRR)***, a somewhat archaic term that is still used instead of *ROI* or *just rate of return*.

Spreadsheet Solution

	A	B	C	D
1				
2	$(500)	Values	Year 0 CF	
3	$100	Values	Year 1 CF	
4	$120	Values	Year 2 CF	
5	$150	Values	Year 3 CF	
6	$180	Values	Year 4 CF	
7	$250	Values	Year 5 CF	
8				
9	15.3%	=IRR(A2:A7) (entered into cell A9)		

The IRR function is used to calculate rate of return. The entry in the function (A2:A7) specifies the range of cash flows to be used in the spreadsheet calculation. The answer—15.3%—is displayed in cell A9. We have much more to say about investment returns in chapters 6, 7, 11, and 12. For now, an understanding of the basic concept is sufficient.

SELF-TEST QUESTIONS

1. What does ROI mean?
2. Differentiate between dollar return and rate of return.
3. Is the calculation of ROI an application of time value analysis? Explain your answer.

Semiannual and Other Compounding Periods

On the web at: *ache.org/HAP/PinkSong8e*

In all the examples thus far, we assumed that interest is compounded once a year, which is called ***annual compounding***. Suppose, however, that Meridian Clinic puts $100 into a bank account that pays 6 percent annual interest, but it is compounded ***semiannually***, which means interest is paid each six months, so interest is earned more often under semiannual compounding than under annual compounding. How much would the clinic accumulate at the end of one year, two years, or some other period?

For an illustration of semiannual compounding, assume that the $100 is placed into the account for three years. The following situation occurs under annual compounding:

Time Line

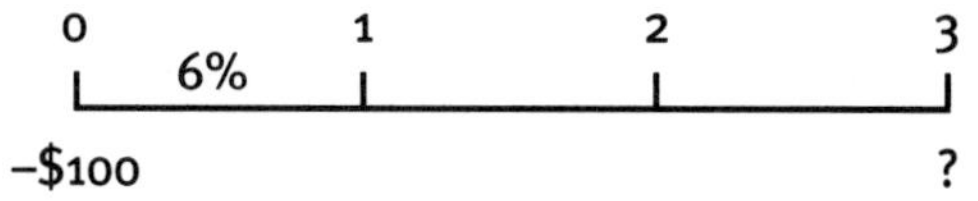

$$Fv_N = Pv \times (1 + I)^N = \$100 \times (1.06)^3$$

Spreadsheet Solution

	A	B	C	D
1				
2	3	Nper	Present Value	
3	$100.00	Pv	Payment	
4	6.0%	Rate	Interest rate	
5				
6	$119.10	=100*(1.06)^3 (entered into cell A6)		
7				
8	$119.10	=A3*(1+A4)^A2 (entered into cell A8)		
9				
10	$119.10	=Fv(A4,A2,,-A3)(entered into cell A10)		

Now, consider what happens under semiannual compounding. Because interest rates usually are stated as annual rates, this situation would be described as 6 percent interest, compounded semiannually. With semiannual compounding, N = 2 × 3 = 6 semiannual periods, and I = 6 ÷ 2 = 3% per semiannual period. Here is the solution:

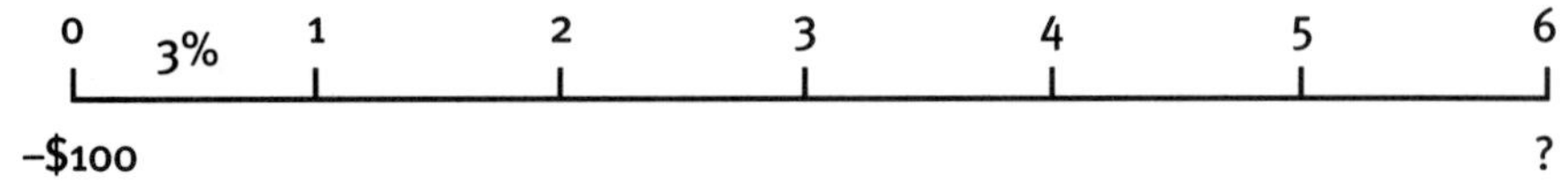

$$Fv_N = Pv \times (1 + I)^N = \$100 \times (1.03)^6$$

Spreadsheet Solution

	A	B	C	D
1				
2	6	Nper	Number of periods	
3	$100.00	Pv	Present value	
4	3.0%	Rate	Interest rate	
5				
6	$119.41	=100*(1.03)^6 (entered into cell A6)		
7				
8	$119.41	=A3*(1+A4)^A2 (entered into cell A8)		
9				
10	$119.41	=Fv(A4,A2,,-A3)(entered into cell A10)		

The $100 deposit grows to $119.41 under semiannual compounding, but only to $119.10 under annual compounding. This result occurs because interest on interest is earned more frequently under semiannual compounding.

Throughout the economy, different compounding periods are used for different types of investments. For example, bank accounts often compound interest monthly or daily, most bonds pay interest semiannually, and stocks generally pay quarterly dividends.[3] Furthermore, the cash flows stemming from capital investments—such as a new hospital wing or new diagnostic equipment—can be analyzed in monthly, quarterly, or annual periods or some other interval. Time value analyses with different compounding periods must be put on a common basis to make meaningful comparisons.

The *stated*, or *nominal, interest rate* in the Meridian Clinic semiannual compounding example is 6 percent. The *effective annual rate (EAR)*, which accounts for intrayear compounding, is the rate that produces the same ending value under annual compounding. In the example, the EAR is the rate that would produce a future value of $119.41 at the end of year 3 under annual compounding. The solution, using Excel's EFFECT function, is 6.09 percent:

	A	B	C	D
1				
2				
3	6.0%	Nominal rate	Nominal interest rate	
4	2	Npery	Number of periods in year	
5				
6				
7	6.09%	=EFFECT(A3,A4) (entered into cell A7)		
8				
9				

Thus, if one bank offered to pay 6 percent interest with semiannual compounding on a savings account, while another offered 6.09 percent with annual compounding, both banks would be paying the same EAR because the ending value is the same under both sets of terms:

Semiannual periods:

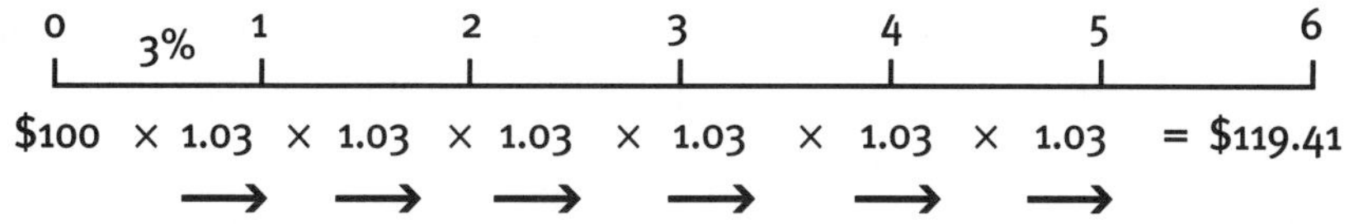

Years:

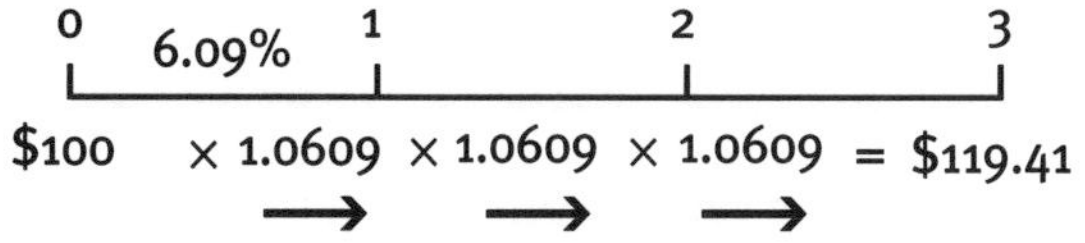

Key Equation 4.4: Effective Annual Rate

The EAR can be determined, if given the stated rate and number of compounding periods per year, by using this equation:

$$\text{Effective annual rate (EAR)} = (1 + I_{\text{Stated}} \div M)^{M} - 1.0.$$

Here, I_{Stated} is the stated (nominal or annual) interest rate and M is the number of compounding periods per year. Note that the term $I_{\text{Stated}} \div M$ is the **periodic** interest rate, so the EAR equation can be restated as follows:

$$\text{Effective annual rate (EAR)} = (1 + \text{Periodic rate})^{M} - 1.0.$$

For an illustration of the use of the EAR equation, consider the situation of a stated rate of 6 percent and semiannual compounding. Here, the EAR is 6.09 percent:

$$\begin{aligned} \text{EAR} &= (1 + 0.06 \div 2)^2 - 1.0 \\ &= (1.03)^2 - 1.0 \\ &= 1.0609 - 1.0 = 0.0609 = 6.09\%. \end{aligned}$$

For another illustration of the EAR concept, consider the interest rate charged on credit cards. Many banks charge 1.0 percent per month and, in their advertising, state that their annual percentage rate (APR) is 12.0 percent.[4] However, the true cost rate to credit card users is the effective annual rate of 12.7 percent:

$$\begin{aligned} \text{EAR} &= (1 + \text{Periodic rate})^{\text{M}} - 1.0 \\ &= (1.01)12 - 1.0 = 0.127 = 12.7\%. \end{aligned}$$

In time value analyses, semiannual compounding—or any compounding that occurs more than once a year—can be handled two ways. First, the input variables can be expressed as periodic variables rather than annual variables. In the Meridian Clinic example, use N = 6 periods rather than N = 3 years, and I = 3% per period rather than I = 6% per year. Second, find the EAR and then use it as an annual rate over the actual number of years. In the example, use I = 6.09% and N = 3 years.

SELF-TEST QUESTIONS

1. What changes must be made in the calculations to determine the future value of an amount being compounded at 8 percent semiannually versus one being compounded at 8 percent annually?
2. From an investor's standpoint, why is semiannual compounding better than annual compounding?
3. How does the EAR differ from the stated (nominal) rate?

Amortized Loans

One important application of time value analysis involves loans that are to be paid off in equal installments over time, such as automobile loans, home mortgage loans, and most business debt other than very short-term loans and long-term bonds. If a loan is to be repaid in equal periodic amounts—monthly, quarterly, or annually—it is called an ***amortized loan.*** The word ***amortize*** comes from the Latin ***mors***, meaning death, so an amortized loan is one that is "killed off" over time.

For example, suppose Santa Fe Healthcare System borrows $1 million from the Bank of New Mexico, to be repaid in three equal installments at the end of each of the next three years. The bank is to receive 6 percent interest on the loan balance that is outstanding at the beginning of each year. The first task in analyzing the loan is to determine the amount Santa Fe must repay each year, or the annual payment. To find this amount, recognize that the loan represents the present value of an annuity of PMT dollars per year for three years, discounted at 6 percent.

	A	B	C	D
1				
2	6.0%	Rate	Interest rate	
3	3	Nper	Number of periods	
4	$1,000,000	Pv	Present value	
5				
6				
7				
8	$374,110	=PMT(A2,A3,-A4) (entered into cell A8)		
9				
10				

Therefore, if Santa Fe pays the bank $374,110 at the end of each of the next three years, the percentage cost to Santa Fe, and the rate of return to the bank, will be 6 percent.

Each payment consists partly of interest and partly of repayment of principal. This breakdown is given in the ***amortization schedule*** shown in exhibit 4.3. The interest component is largest in the first year, and it declines as the outstanding balance of the loan is reduced over time. Coincidentally, the amount of the annual payment that is used to repay the principal amount of the loan increases over time. For tax purposes, a taxable business borrower reports the interest payments in column 3 as a deductible expense each year, while the lender reports these same amounts as taxable income.

The spreadsheet function PMT can be used to construct the amortization table. This function calculates the principal payment for any given input year.

SELF-TEST QUESTIONS

1. When constructing an amortization schedule, how is the periodic payment amount calculated?
2. Does the periodic payment remain constant over time?
3. Do principal and interest remain constant over time? Explain your answer.

A Review of Interest Rate Types

This chapter covers many time value concepts, including three different types of interest rate. In this section, we review these rates.

Stated Rate

The stated (nominal) rate is the rate stated in financial contracts. According to convention, in the stock, bond, mortgage, commercial loan, consumer loan, and other markets, loan terms are expressed in stated rates, which typically are annual rates. However, if compounding is not annual, the stated rate must indicate the number of compounding periods per year. For example, a bank savings account may offer 4 percent interest compounded quarterly, or a money market mutual fund may offer a 3 percent rate with interest paid monthly. The stated rate is not used for calculations (i.e., never use I_{Stated} on a time line or in a spreadsheet formula or function) unless compounding occurs once a year (M = 1). In this case, I_{Stated} = Periodic rate = Effective annual rate.

EXHIBIT 4.3 Loan Amortization Schedule

Year	*Beginning Amount (1)*	*Payment (2)*	*Interest[a] (3)*	*Repayment of Principal[b] (4)*	*Remaining Balance (5)*
1	$1,000,000	$ 374,110	$ 60,000	$ 314, 110	$685,890
2	685,890	374,110	41,153	332,957	352,933
3	352,933	374,110	21,177	352,933	0
		$1,122,330	$122,330	$ 1,000,000	

[a]Interest is calculated by multiplying the loan balance at the beginning of each year by the interest rate. Therefore, interest in year 1 is $1,000,000 × 0.06 = $60,000; in year 2 is $685,890 × 0.06 = $41,153; and in year 3 is $352,933 × 0.06 = $21,177.

[b]Repayment of principal is equal to the payment of $374,110 minus the interest charge for each year.

Periodic Rate

The periodic rate is the rate charged by a lender or paid by a borrower, or any other time value rate, expressed on a per period basis. The rate can be per year, per six months, per quarter, per month, per day, or per any other time interval. For example, a bank may charge 1 percent per month on its credit card loans, or a finance firm may charge 3 percent per quarter on consumer loans.

Periodic rate = $I_{Stated} \div M$, which implies that I_{Stated} = Periodic rate × M, where M is the number of compounding periods per year. For example, consider the finance firm loan at 3 percent per quarter:

$$I_{Stated} = \text{Periodic rate} \times M = 3\% \times 4 = 12\%,$$

and

$$\text{Periodic rate} = I_{Stated} \div M = 12\% \div 4 = 3\% \text{ per quarter.}$$

The periodic rate can be used when cash flows occur more frequently than once a year and the number of cash flows per year corresponds to the number of compounding periods per year. Therefore, for a retirement annuity that provides monthly payments, a semiannual payment bond, a consumer loan with quarterly payments, or a credit card loan with monthly payments, the calculations would use Periodic rate = $I_{Stated} \div M$. The implication in all these examples is that the interest compounding period is the same as the cash flow period. Thus, **the periodic rate can be used directly in calculations only when the cash flow period coincides with the interest rate compounding period (i.e., quarterly payments and quarterly compounding).**

Effective Annual Rate

The EAR is the rate that, under annual compounding (M = 1), would produce the same results as a given stated rate with compounding that occurs more frequently than annually (M > 1). The EAR is found as follows:

$$\begin{aligned} EAR &= (1 + I_{Stated} \div M)^M - 1.0 \\ &= (1 + \text{Periodic rate})^M - 1.0. \end{aligned}$$

For example, suppose that you can use either a 1 percent per month credit card loan or a 3 percent per quarter consumer loan to make a purchase. Which one should you choose? To answer this question, you must express the cost rate of each alternative as an EAR.

$$EAR_{\text{Credit card loan}} = (1 + 0.01)^{12} - 1.0 = (1.01)^{12} - 1.0$$

$$= 1.127 - 1.0 = 0.127 = 12.7\%.$$

$$EAR_{Consumer\ loan} = (1 + 0.03)^4 - 1.0 = (1.03)^4 - 1.0$$
$$= 1.126 - 1.0 = 0.126 = 12.6\%.$$

Thus, the consumer loan is slightly less costly than the credit card loan. This result should have been intuitive because, although both loans have the same 12 percent stated rate, monthly payments would have to be made on the credit card, while under the consumer loan terms, only quarterly payments would have to be made.

The EAR is also used when the interest rate compounding period occurs more often than the period between payments or cash flows. For example, if payments occur semiannually, but interest is compounded quarterly, then the EAR must be used. In this case, the EAR is really an "effective semiannual rate" calculated as $(1 + I_{Stated} \div 4)^2 - 1.0$, which is then applied to the semiannual payment stream.

SELF-TEST QUESTIONS

1. Define the stated rate, the periodic rate, and the effective annual rate.
2. How are these three rates related?
3. Can you think of a situation in which all three of these rates are the same?

Chapter Key Concepts

Financial decisions often involve situations in which future cash flows must be valued. The process of valuing future cash flows is called *time value analysis.* Here are the key concepts behind this type of analysis:

- Analysts use *time lines* to lay out the cash flows involved in a time value analysis.
- *Compounding* is the process of determining the *future value (Fv)* of a lump sum, an annuity, or an uneven cash flow stream.
- *Discounting* is the process of finding the *present value (Pv)* of a lump sum, an annuity, or an uneven cash flow stream.
- An *annuity* is a series of equal, periodic cash flows, which are often called *payments (PMT).*
- If an annuity's payments occur at the end of each period, it is called an *ordinary annuity.*
- If each annuity payment occurs at the beginning of the period rather than at the end, the annuity is an *annuity due.*
- A *perpetuity* is an annuity that lasts forever.
- If an analysis involving more than one cash amount does not meet the definition of an annuity, it is called an *uneven cash flow stream.*
- The financial attractiveness of an investment is measured by its *return on investment (ROI).*
- ROI can be measured in either *dollar* or *percentage* terms.
- Dollar return is measured by *net present value (NPV),* while percentage return is measured by *internal rate of return (IRR).*
- The *stated (nominal) rate* is the annual rate normally quoted in financial contracts.
- The *periodic rate* is the stated rate divided by the number of compounding periods per year.
- If compounding occurs more frequently than once a year, it is often necessary to calculate the *effective annual rate (EAR),* which is the rate that produces the same results under annual compounding as it does under more frequent compounding.
- An *amortized loan* is one that is paid off in equal amounts over a specified number of periods.

(continued)

(continued from previous page)

- An *amortization schedule* shows the amount of each payment that represents interest, the amount used to reduce the principal, and the remaining balance on each payment date.

Time value analysis is one of the cornerstones of healthcare financial management, so you should feel comfortable with this material before moving ahead.

Chapter Models, Problems, and Minicases

The following ancillary resources in spreadsheet format are available for this chapter:

- A chapter model that shows how to perform many of the calculations described in the chapter
- Problems that test your ability to perform the calculations
- A minicase that is more complicated than the problems and tests your ability to perform the calculations in preparation for a case

These resources can be accessed online at ache.org/HAP/PinkSong8e.

Selected Case

One case in *Cases in Healthcare Finance*, sixth edition, can help you learn more about time value analysis: Case 11: Gulf Shores Surgery Centers, which examines the time value analysis techniques discussed in this chapter.

Reference

Powerball. 2019. "Powerball Powerplay." Accessed May 10. www.powerball.com/games/powerball.

Selected Resources

- Aftermarket reference manual for your spreadsheet software
- Help menu for your spreadsheet software

Notes

1. Time value analyses can be performed using mathematical multipliers obtained from tables. At one time, tables were the most efficient way to conduct time value analyses, but new technology (calculators and computers) have made tabular solutions obsolete.
2. Actually, owning a single nursing home is riskier than owning the stock of a firm that has a large number of nursing homes with geographic diversification. Also, an owner of Enlivant's stock can easily sell the stock if things go sour, whereas it would be much more difficult for Live Oak to sell its nursing home. These differences in risk and liquidity suggest that the true opportunity cost rate is probably higher than the return that is expected from owning the stock of a large long-term care company. However, direct ownership of a nursing home implies control, while ownership of the stock of a large firm usually does not. Control rights tend to reduce the opportunity cost rate. The main point here is that, in practice, it may not be possible to obtain a "perfect" opportunity cost rate. Nevertheless, an imprecise one is better than none at all.
3. Some financial institutions pay interest that is compounded *continuously*. Continuous compounding is not relevant to healthcare financial management, so it is not discussed here.
4. The ***annual percentage rate (APR)*** and ***annual percentage yield (APY)*** are terms defined in Truth in Lending and Truth in Savings laws. APR is defined as Periodic rate × Number of compounding periods per year, so it ignores the consequences of compounding. Although the APR on a credit card with interest charges of 1.0 percent per month is 1.0% × 12 = 12.0%, the true effective annual rate as calculated in the text is 12.7 percent.

Integrative Application

The Problem

Achieve Rehabilitation in Kansas City has decided to expand its outpatient department. The building consultants retained by Achieve estimate that, if the building were constructed today, the capital cost would be approximately $15 million. However, the building consultants estimate that construction costs will increase by 2.5 percent per year over the next three years as a result of shortages of some materials and labor.

Achieve is considering two banks for a building fund. First, Lower Plains Bank offers a CD that pays a 5.0 percent interest rate, compounded quarterly. In this account, all funds—whether invested for one, two, or three years—must remain on deposit until the end of the three years. Second, Mid-West Bank offers a money market account that pays 4.95 percent, compounded daily. In this account, all funds may be withdrawn at any time. Achieve projects that it will be able to invest $2.5 million immediately, $5 million in one year, and $7.5 million in two years.

Achieve wants to ensure that it will have the funds it needs to build the new outpatient facility, but it is also concerned about locking up its funds for three years (which the CD would require). Management must decide which bank to use for its building fund.

The Analysis

The first task is to estimate the cost of the new facility three years from now:

Estimated annual rate of increase in building costs	2.5%
Number of years until building is needed	3
Current construction cost of building	$15,000,000
Estimated construction cost in three years	$16,153,359

= FV(rate,nper,,pv)

= FV(2.5%,3,,$15,000,000)

= $16,153,359

The EAR of the investment at each bank is as follows:

	Lower Plains Bank	*Mid-West Bank*
Interest rate	5%	4.95%
Compounding periods per year	4	365
EAR	5.095%	5.074%

=EFFECT(5%,4) = 5.095%

=EFFECT(4.95%,365) = 5.074%

The CD at Lower Plains Bank offers the higher EAR, but management still needs to determine whether either investment will provide the funds it will need in three years.

The ending amount if Achieve decides on the CD offered by Lower Plains Bank is as follows:

Interest rate	5.0%
Number of compounding periods per year	4

		Years on Deposit	*Quarters on Deposit*	*Ending Amount*
1st deposit	$2,500,000	3	12	$ 2,901,886
2nd deposit	$5,000,000	2	8	$ 5,522,431
3rd deposit	$7,500,000	1	4	$7,882,090
Total 3 years from now				$16,306,407

=FV(rate,nper,,pv)

=FV(5% 4,3 × 4,,$2,500,000) = $2,901,886

=FV(5% 4,2 × 4,,$5,000,000) = $5,522,431

=FV(5% 4,1 × 4,,$7,500,000) = $7,882,090.

The ending amount if Achieve decides on the money market account offered by Mid-West Bank is as follows:

Interest rate	4.95%
Number of compounding periods per year	365

		Years on Deposit	Quarters on Deposit	Ending Amount
1st deposit	$2,500,000	3	1,095	$ 2,900,203
2nd deposit	$5,000,000	2	730	$ 5,520,294
3rd deposit	$7,500,000	1	365	$ 7,880,565
Total 3 years from now				$16,301,063

=FV(rate,nper,,pv)

=FV(4.95%/365,3*365,,$2,500,000) = $2,900,203

=FV(4.95%/365,2*365,,$5,000,000) = $5,520,294

=FV(4.95%/365,1*365,,$7,500,000) = $7,880,565.

The difference between the ending amount and the estimated construction cost in three years for each bank is as follows:

	Lower Plains Bank	Mid-West Bank
Ending amount	$16,306,407	$16,301,063
Estimated construction cost	$ 16,153,359	$16,153,359
Difference	$ 153,047	$ 147,703

The Decision

Both investments would provide an ending amount sufficient to pay the estimated construction cost in three years. Although the money market account with Mid-West Bank would result in an ending balance that is less than the CD with Lower Plains Bank, Achieve management decided to invest its funds in the money market account. Management considered that it was worth forgoing ($153,047 – $147,703 =) $5,344 in exchange for the flexibility of being able to withdraw the funds at any time in case of emergencies or changes in construction timing. ■

CHAPTER

5

FINANCIAL RISK AND REQUIRED RETURN

Learning Objectives

After studying this chapter, readers should be able to

- explain the concept of financial risk in general terms,
- define and differentiate between stand-alone risk and portfolio risk,
- define market risk,
- explain the capital asset pricing model (CAPM) relationship between market risk and required return, and
- use the CAPM to determine required returns.

Introduction

Two of the most important concepts in healthcare financial management are financial risk and required return. What is financial risk, how is it measured, and what effect does it have on required return and hence managerial decisions? Because so much financial decision-making involves risk and return, one cannot gain a good understanding of healthcare financial management without having a solid appreciation of risk and return concepts.

If investors—both individuals and businesses—viewed risk as a benign fact of life, it would have little impact on decision-making. However, decision makers are, for the most part, averse to risk and believe it should be avoided. If risks must be taken, there must be a reward for doing so. Thus, investments of higher risk—whether an individual investor's security investment or a radiology group's investment in diagnostic equipment—must offer higher returns to make the investment financially attractive.

This chapter presents basic risk concepts from the perspectives of individual investors and businesses. Healthcare managers must be familiar with both contexts because investors supply the capital that businesses need to function. Unfortunately, merely knowing an investment's risk is not sufficient to make good investment decisions. It is also necessary to translate risk into required rates of return. Thus, the chapter closes with a discussion of the relationship between risk and required return.

The Many Faces of Financial Risk

A full discussion of financial risk would take many chapters, perhaps even an entire book, because financial risk is a complicated subject. First, it depends on whether the investor is an individual or a business. If the investor is an individual, it depends on the *investment horizon*, or the amount of time until the investment proceeds are needed. To make the situation even more complex, it may be difficult to define, measure, or translate financial risk into something usable for decision-making. For example, the risk that individual investors face when saving for retirement is the risk that the amount of funds accumulated will not be sufficient to fund the lifestyle expected during the full term of retirement. Needless to say, incorporating such a definition of risk into investment decisions is not easy. The good news is that our primary interest concerns the financial risk inherent in making decisions in businesses. Thus, our discussion focuses on the fundamental factors that influence the riskiness of real asset investments (e.g., land, buildings, equipment).

Still, two factors complicate our discussion of financial risk. The first complicating factor is that both businesses and investors in businesses are subject to financial risk. There is some risk inherent in the business itself that depends primarily on the type of enterprise. For example, pharmaceutical firms generally face a great deal of risk, while healthcare providers typically have less risk. Investors—stockholders and creditors—bear the riskiness inherent in the business, but the risk is modified by the contractual nature of the securities they hold. For example, the stock of Manor Care is more risky than its debt, although the risk of both securities depends on the inherent risk of a business that operates in the long-term care sector. Not-for-profit firms have the same partitioning of risk, but the inherent riskiness of the business is split between creditors and the **implied** stockholders, who generally are considered to be the community at large.

The second complicating factor is that the riskiness of an investment

To Mortgage or Not to Mortgage

One of the most perplexing financial issues facing well-to-do individuals is the question of whether to take out a mortgage on a house purchase. Alternatively, how big should the mortgage be? For example, assume a couple is retiring and moving to Florida. They are buying a $300,000 house in The Villages ("Florida's Friendliest Retirement Hometown," https://thevillagesflorida.com). Because they sold their house in Boston, which they had lived in for 30 years, for $500,000, they could easily pay cash for their retirement home. However, the real estate agent in Florida encouraged them to obtain a 20-percent-down ($60,000) mortgage and refinance the remaining $240,000. "After all," said the agent, "the interest rate on the mortgage balance is only 5 percent, and you can invest the $240,000 saved in stocks and earn 10 percent. Only a fool would buy a house for cash." What do you think of the agent's advice? On the surface, the agent makes sense, but does risk enter into the decision? Assume that the proposed mortgage has a 15-year maturity and the interest rate on 15-year Treasury securities is 4 percent. Is this information relevant to the decision?

depends on the context in which it is held. For example, a stock held alone is riskier than the same stock held as part of a large portfolio of stocks. Similarly, a magnetic resonance imaging (MRI) system operated independently is riskier than the same system operated as part of a large, geographically diversified business that owns and operates numerous types of diagnostic equipment.

SELF-TEST QUESTION

1. What complications arise when dealing with financial risk in a business setting?

Returns on Investments

The concept of return provides investors with a convenient way to express the financial performance of an investment. To illustrate, suppose you buy ten shares of a stock for $100. The stock pays no dividends, and at the end of one year, you sell the stock for $110. What is the return on your $100 investment?

One way to express an investment's return is in dollar terms:

$$\text{Dollar return} = \text{Amount to be received} - \text{Amount invested}$$
$$= \$110 - \$100 = \$10.$$

If, at the end of the year, you sell the stock for only $90, your dollar return will be –$10.

Although expressing returns in dollars is easy, two problems arise. First, to make a meaningful judgment about the return, you need to know the scale (size) of the investment; a $100 return on a $100 investment is a great return (assuming the investment is held for one year), but a $100 return on a $10,000 investment would be a poor return. Second, you also need to know the timing of the return; a $100 return on a $100 investment is a great return if it occurs after one year, but the same dollar return after 100 years is not very good. The solution to these scale and timing problems is to express investment results as rates of return or percentage returns. For example, when $1,100 is received after one year, the rate of return on the one-year stock investment, is 10 percent:

$$\text{Rate of return} = \text{Dollar return} \div \text{Amount invested}$$
$$= \$100 \div \$1{,}000 = 0.10 = 10\%.$$

The rate of return calculation "standardizes" the dollar return by considering the annual return per unit of investment.

Introduction to Financial Risk

Generically, risk is defined as "a hazard; a peril; exposure to loss or injury." Thus, risk refers to the chance that an unfavorable event will occur. If an individual engages in skydiving, she risks injury or death. If an individual gambles at roulette, he is not risking injury or death but is taking a ***financial risk***. Even when an individual invests in stocks or bonds, she risks losing money in hopes of earning a positive rate of return. Similarly, when a healthcare business invests in new assets—such as diagnostic equipment, new hospital beds, or a new managed care plan—it is taking a financial risk.

For an illustration of basic financial risk, consider two potential personal investments. The first investment consists of a one-year, $1,000 face-value US Treasury bill (T-bill) bought for $950. Treasury bills are short-term federal debt securities that are sold at a ***discount*** (i.e., less than face value) and return ***face***, or ***par***, ***value*** at maturity. The investor expects to receive $1,000 at maturity in one year, so the anticipated rate of return on the T-bill investment is 5.26 percent. To calculate this using a spreadsheet, see the following image.

	A	B	C	D
1				
2	1	Nper	Number of periods	
3	$(950.00)	Pv	Present value	
4	$1,000	Fv	Future value	
5				
6				
7				
8	5.26%	=RATE(A2,,A3,A4) (entered into cell A8)		
9				
10				

The $1,000 payment is fixed by contract (the T-bill promises to pay this amount), and the US government is certain to make the payment unless a national disaster occurs—an unlikely event. Thus, there is virtually a 100 percent probability that the investment will earn the roughly 5.3 percent rate of return expected. In such situations, an investment is defined as ***riskless***, or ***risk free***.[1]

Now, assume that the $950 is invested in a biotechnology partnership that will be terminated in one year. If the partnership develops a new commercially valuable product, its rights will be sold and $2,000 will be received from the partnership, for a rate of return of 110.53 percent.

	A	B	C	D
1				
2	1	Nper	Number of periods	
3	$(950.00)	Pv	Present value	
4	$2,000	Fv	Future value	
5				
6				
7				
8	110.53%	=RATE(A2,,A3,A4) (entered into cell 8)		
9				
10				

On the other hand, if nothing worthwhile is developed, the partnership will be worthless, no money will be received, and the rate of return will be –100 percent.

	A	B	C	D
1				
2	1	Nper	Number of periods	
3	$(950.00)	Pv	Present value	
4	$0.01	Fv	Future value	
5				
6				
7				
8	–100.00%	=RATE(A2,,A3,A4) (entered into cell 8)		
9				
10				

Note that spreadsheets give no solution when the future value is entered as zero, but if a very small number—for example, 0.01—is entered for the future value, the solution for interest rate is –100.00 percent.

Now, assume that there is a 50 percent chance that a valuable product will be developed. In this admittedly unrealistic situation, the expected rate of return—a statistical concept that will be discussed shortly—is the same 5.3 percent as on the T-bill investment: $(0.50 \times 110.53\%) + (0.50 \times [-100\%]) = 5.3\%$. However, the biotechnology partnership is a far cry from being riskless. If things go poorly, the entire $950 investment will be lost, and the realized rate of return will be –100 percent. Because there is a significant chance of earning a return that is far less than expected, the partnership investment is described as being very risky.

Thus, financial risk is related to the probability of earning a return that is less than expected. The greater the chance of low or negative returns, the greater the amount of financial risk.

SELF-TEST QUESTIONS

1. What is the generic definition of risk?
2. Explain the concept of financial risk in general terms.

Risk Aversion

Why are defining and measuring financial risk so important? Because, for the most part, both individual and business investors dislike risk. Suppose you were given a choice between a sure $1 million and the flip of a coin for either $0 or $2 million. You—and just about everyone else—would likely take the $1 million and run. An individual who takes the sure $1 million is ***risk averse***; an individual who is indifferent between the two alternatives, or views them as the same, is ***risk neutral***; and an individual who prefers the gamble to the sure thing is a ***risk seeker***.

Of course, people and businesses do gamble and take chances, so all of us typically exhibit some risk-seeking behavior. However, most individual investors would never put a sizable proportion of their net worth at risk, and most business executives would never "bet the business"—most people are risk averse when it really matters.

What are the implications of risk aversion for financial decision-making? First, given two investments with similar returns but differing risk, investors will favor the lower-risk alternative. Second, investors will require higher returns to invest in higher-risk investments. These typical outcomes of risk averse behavior have a significant impact on many facets of financial decision-making; hence, they will appear repeatedly in later chapters.

SELF-TEST QUESTIONS

1. What is risk aversion?
2. What are the implications of risk aversion for financial decision-making?

Probability Distributions

The chance that an event will occur is called ***probability of occurrence***, or just ***probability***. For example, a weather forecast might predict a 40 percent chance of rain. Or, when rolling a single die, the probability of rolling a two is one out of six, or $1 \div 6 = 0.1667 = 16.67\%$. If all possible outcomes related to a particular event are listed, and a probability is assigned to each outcome, the result is a ***probability distribution***. In the example of the weather forecast, the probability distribution looks like the following text.

Outcome	*Probability*
Rain	0.40 = 40%
No rain	0.60 = 60%
	1.00 = 100%

In the example of the roll of a die, the probability distribution looks like this:

Outcome	*Probability*
1	0.1667 = 16.67%
2	0.1667 = 16.67%
3	0.1667 = 16.67%
4	0.1667 = 16.67%
5	0.1667 = 16.67%
6	0.1667 = 16.67%
	1.0000 = 100.00%

All possible outcomes (i.e., the number of dots showing after the die roll) are listed in the left column, while the probability of each outcome is listed in the right column and expressed as decimals and percentages. If the probability distribution is complete, the probabilities must sum to 1.0, or 100 percent.

Probabilities can also be assigned to possible outcomes—in this case, returns—on personal and business investments. If an individual buys stock, the return will usually come in the form of dividends and capital gains (selling the stock for more than the individual paid for it) or losses (selling the stock for less than the individual paid for it). Because all stock returns are uncertain, there is some chance that the dividends will not be as high as expected, that the stock price will not increase as much as expected, or that the stock price will even decrease. The higher the probability of dividends and stock

The Gambler's Fallacy

On August 18, 1913, at the casino in Monte Carlo, a rare event occurred at the roulette wheel. (A roulette wheel contains black and red spaces, and the ball has roughly a 50/50 chance of landing on either color each time the wheel is spun.) On that day, the ball landed on a black space a record 26 times in a row. As a result, beginning when black had come up a phenomenal 15 times, there was a wild rush to bet on red. As each spin continued to come up black, players doubled and tripled their stakes, and, after 20 spins, many expressed the belief that there was not a chance in a million of another black. By the time the run ended, on the 27th spin, the casino was millions of francs richer.

The players at the roulette wheel that day committed what is known as the *gambler's fallacy*, also called the *Monte Carlo fallacy*. Simply put, the fallacy rests on the assumption that some result must be "due" simply because what has previously happened departs from what was expected to happen. In this example, one spin of

(continued)

(continued from previous page)

the roulette wheel does not affect the next spin. Thus, each time the ball is rolled, there is (ideally) a 50 percent chance of landing on a black and a 50 percent chance of landing on a red. Even after many blacks have occurred in succession, there is still a 50/50 chance of a red because the results of previous spins have no bearing on the outcome of the next spin—the roulette wheel has no memory.

What do you think of the gambler's fallacy? What conditions must hold for the fallacy to apply? Are there situations that might occur that would cause the fallacy to be correct (past results predict future results)? If people are smart enough to recognize the fallacy, why do Las Vegas casino owners make so much money?

prices having subpar performance, the higher the probability that the return will be significantly less than expected and, hence, the greater the risk.

For an illustration of this concept using a business investment, consider a hospital evaluating the purchase of a new MRI system. The cost of the system is an investment, and the net cash inflows from patient utilization of the MRI provide the return. The net cash inflows, in turn, depend on the number of procedures, the charge per procedure, payer discounts, operating costs, and so on. These values typically are not known with certainty but rather are dependent on factors such as patient demographics, physician acceptance, local market conditions, labor costs, and so on. Thus, the hospital faces a probability distribution of returns rather than a single return known with certainty. The greater the probability of returns well below the return anticipated, the greater the risk of the MRI investment.

SELF-TEST QUESTIONS

1. What is a probability distribution?
2. How are probability distributions used in financial decision-making?

Expected and Realized Rates of Return

On the web at: *ache.org/HAP/PinkSong8e*

To be most useful, the concept of financial risk must be defined more precisely than just as "the chances of a return well below that anticipated." Exhibit 5.1 contains the estimated return distributions developed by the financial staff of Suffolk Community Hospital for two proposed investments: (1) an MRI system and (2) a walk-in clinic. Here, each economic state reflects a combination of factors that determine each project's profitability. For example, for the MRI project, the very poor economic state signifies very low physician acceptance and hence very low utilization, very high discounts

EXHIBIT 5.1
Suffolk Community Hospital: Estimated Returns for Two Proposed Investments

Economic State	Probability of Occurrence	Rate of Return if Economic State Occurs (%)	
		MRI	Clinic
Very poor	0.10	−10	−20
Poor	0.20	0	0
Average	0.40	10	15
Good	0.20	20	30
Very good	0.10	30	50
	1.00		

on reimbursements, very high operating costs, and so on. The economic states are defined in a similar fashion for the walk-in clinic.

The *expected rate of return*, defined in the statistical sense, is the weighted average of the return distribution—the weights being the probabilities of occurrence.

Key Equation 5.1: Expected Value of a Return Distribution

$$\begin{aligned} E(R) = {} & (\text{Probability of return 1} \times \text{Return 1}) \\ & + (\text{Probability of return 2} \times \text{Return 2}) \\ & + (\text{Probability of return 3} \times \text{Return 3}) \text{ and so on.} \end{aligned}$$

For example, the expected rate of return on the MRI system, E(RMRI), is 10 percent:

$$\begin{aligned} E(R_{MRI}) &= (0.10 \times [-10\%]) + (0.20 \times 0\%) + (0.40 \times 10\%) \\ &\quad + (0.20 \times 20\%) + (0.10 \times 30\%) \\ &= 10.0\%. \end{aligned}$$

Calculated in a similar manner, the expected rate of return on the walk-in clinic is 15 percent.

Spreadsheet Solution

	A	B	C	D
1				
2	Probability		MRI Rate	
3	of Occurrence		of Return	
4				
5	0.10		−10%	
6	0.20		0%	
7	0.40		10%	
8	0.20		20%	
9	0.10		30%	
10				
11	10.0%	=SUMPRODUCT(A5:A9,C5:C9) (entered into cell A11)		
12				

The expected rate of return is the average return that would result, given the return distribution, if the investment were randomly repeated many times. In this illustration, if 1,000 clinics were built in different areas, each of which faced the return distribution given in exhibit 5.1, the average return on the 1,000 investments would be 15 percent, assuming the returns in each area are independent of one another. However, only one clinic would actually be built, and the realized rate of return could turn out to be less than the expected 15 percent. Therefore, the clinic investment, as well as the MRI investment, is risky.

Expected rate of return expresses expectations for the future. When the managers at Suffolk Community Hospital analyzed the MRI investment, they expected it to earn 10 percent. Now, assume that economic conditions took a turn for the worse and the very poor economic scenario occurred. In this case, the *realized rate of return*, which is the rate of return that the investment produced as measured at termination, would be a −10 percent. It is the potential of realizing a return of −10 percent on an investment that has an expected return of +10 percent that produces risk. Note that in many situations, especially those illustrated in textbooks, the expected rate of return is not achievable. For example, an investment that has a 50 percent chance of a 5 percent return and a 50 percent chance of a 15 percent return has an expected rate of return of 10 percent. Yet, there is zero probability of actually realizing the 10 percent expected rate of return.

SELF-TEST QUESTIONS

1. How is the expected rate of return calculated?
2. What is the economic interpretation of the expected rate of return?
3. What is the difference between the expected rate of return and the realized rate of return?

Stand-Alone Risk

On the web at: *ache.org/HAP/PinkSong8e*

We can look at the two distributions in exhibit 5.1 and intuitively conclude that the investment in the clinic is riskier than the investment in the MRI system because the clinic has a chance of incurring a 20 percent loss, while the worst possible loss on the MRI system is 10 percent. This intuitive risk assessment is based on the *stand-alone risk* of the two investments—that is, we are focusing on the riskiness of each investment under the assumption that it would be the business's only asset (operated in isolation). Portfolio effects are introduced in the next section, but for now we can continue our discussion of stand-alone risk.

Stand-alone risk depends on the "tightness" of an investment's return distribution. If an investment has a tight return distribution (i.e., a distribution with returns falling close to the expected return), it has relatively low stand-alone risk. Conversely, an investment with a return distribution that is "loose" (i.e., a distribution with values well below the expected return) is relatively risky in the stand-alone sense.

It is important to recognize that risk and return are **separate** attributes of an investment. An investment may have a tight distribution of returns and hence low stand-alone risk, but its expected rate of return might be only 2 percent. In this situation, the investment probably would not be financially attractive, despite its low risk. Similarly, a high-risk investment with a sufficiently high expected rate of return would be attractive.[2]

To be useful, any definition of risk must have some measure, or numerical value, so we need some way to specify the "degree of tightness" of an investment's return distribution. One such measure is the variance.

Key Equation 5.2: Variance of an Expected Return Distribution

$$\text{Variance} = (\text{Probability of return 1} \times [\text{Rate of return 1} - E(R)]^2) + (\text{Probability of return 2} \times [\text{Rate of return 2} - E(R)]^2) \text{ and so on.}$$

Variance is a measure of the dispersion of a distribution around its *expected value*, but it is less useful than standard deviation because its measurement unit is percent or dollars squared, which has no economic meaning. *Standard deviation*, which is often indicated by the symbol σ (Greek lowercase sigma), is a common statistical measure of the dispersion of a distribution around its mean—the smaller the standard deviation, the tighter the distribution and hence the lower the riskiness of the investment.

Key Equation 5.3: Standard Deviation of an Expected Return Distribution

Standard deviation = Square root of variance.

For an example calculation of standard deviation, consider the MRI investment's estimated returns listed in exhibit 5.1. Here are the steps:

1. The expected rate of return on the MRI, $E(R_{MRI})$, is 10 percent.
2. The variance of the return distribution is determined as follows:

$$\begin{aligned}\text{Variance} &= (0.10 \times [-10\% - 10\%]^2) + (0.20 \times [0\% - 10\%]^2)\\&\quad + (0.40 \times [10\% - 10\%]^2) + (0.20 \times [20\% - 10\%]^2)\\&\quad + (0.10 \times [30\% - 10\%]^2)\\&= 120.00.\end{aligned}$$

3. The standard deviation is defined as the square root of the variance:

$$\begin{aligned}\text{Standard deviation } (\sigma) &= \sqrt{\text{Variance}}\\&= \sqrt{120.00} = 10.95\%.\end{aligned}$$

Using the same procedure, the clinic investment listed in exhibit 5.1 was found to have a standard deviation of returns of about 18 percent. Because the clinic investment's standard deviation of returns is larger than that of the MRI investment, the clinic investment has more stand-alone risk than the MRI investment. As a general rule, investments with higher expected rates of return have larger standard deviations than investments with smaller expected returns have.[3] This situation occurs in our MRI and clinic example.

In situations where expected rates of return on investments differ substantially, standard deviation may not provide a good picture of one investment's stand-alone risk relative to another. The *coefficient of variation (CV)*, which is defined as the standard deviation of returns divided by the expected return, measures the risk per unit of return and hence standardizes the measurement of stand-alone risk. For example, note that the MRI investment has a CV of 1.10, while the clinic's CV is 1.20:

$$\text{Coefficient of variation} = \text{CV} = \frac{\sigma}{\text{E(R)}}.$$

$$\text{CV}_{\text{MRI}} = 11.0\% \div 10.0\% = 1.10\text{, and}$$

$$\text{CV}_{\text{Clinic}} = 18.0\% \div 15.0\% = 1.20.$$

In this situation, the clinic investment has slightly more risk per unit of return, so it is riskier than the MRI investment, as measured by both standard deviation and coefficient of variation. However, the clinic investment's stand-alone risk, as measured by the coefficient of variation, is not as great relative to the MRI investment as it is when measured by standard deviation. This difference in relative risk occurs because the clinic investment has a higher expected rate of return. Note that coefficient of variation has no units; it is just a raw number.

SELF-TEST QUESTIONS

1. What is stand-alone risk?
2. What are some measures of stand-alone risk?
3. Is one measure better than another?

Standard Deviation of a Historical Return Distribution

On the web at: *ache.org/HAP/PinkSong8e*

Suppose that a sample of returns over some past period is available. The return in period 1 is denoted as r_1, in period 2 as r_2, and in period t as r_t. The average return over the last T periods (r_T) is defined as the following:

Key Equation 5.4: Return of a Historical Return Distribution

$$r_T = \frac{(r_1 + r_2 + \ldots r_t)}{T}.$$

The standard deviation of a sample of returns can then be estimated using this formula:

Key Equation 5.5: Standard Deviation of a Historical Return Distribution

$$S = \sqrt{\frac{(r_1 - r_T)^2 + (r_2 - r_T)^2 + \ldots + (r_t - r_T)^2}{T - 1}}.$$

To illustrate these calculations, consider the following historical returns for a company.

Year	Return
2016	15%
2017	–5%
2018	20%

Using key equation 5.4, the average return is

$$r_T = \frac{15\% - 5\% + 20\%}{3}$$
$$= 10\%.$$

Using key equation 5.5, the standard deviation is

$$S = \sqrt{\frac{(15\% - 10\%)^2 + (-5\% - 10\%)^2 + (20\% - 10\%)^2}{2}}$$
$$= 13.2\%.$$

The average return and standard deviation can also be calculated using Excel's built-in functions, shown here using numerical data rather than cell ranges as inputs:

=AVERAGE(15%,–5%,20%) = 10.0%

=STDEV(15%,–5%,20%) = 13.2%.

The historical standard deviation is often used as an estimate of future variability. Because past variability is often repeated, past variability may be a reasonably good estimate of future risk.

Portfolio Risk and Return

On the web at: *ache.org/HAP/PinkSong8e*

The preceding section developed a risk measure—standard deviation—that applies to investments held in isolation. (We also discussed coefficient of variation, but for now our focus is on standard deviation.) However, most investments are not held in isolation. Instead, they are held as part of a collection, or *portfolio*, of investments. Individual investors typically hold portfolios of **securities** (i.e., stocks and bonds), while businesses generally hold portfolios of **projects** (i.e., product or service lines). When investments are held in portfolios, investors' primary concern is not the realized rate of return on each individual investment but rather the realized rate of return on the entire portfolio. Similarly, the riskiness of each individual investment in the portfolio is not important to the investor; what matters is the aggregate riskiness of the portfolio. Thus, the whole nature of risk, and how it is defined and measured, changes when one recognizes that investments are not held in isolation but rather as parts of portfolios.

Portfolio Returns

Consider the realized returns for the seven investment alternatives listed in exhibit 5.2. The single investment alternatives (investments A, B, C, and D) could be projects undertaken by South West Clinics, Inc., or they could be securities. The remaining three alternatives in exhibit 5.2 are portfolios. Portfolio AB consists of a 50 percent investment in investment A and a 50 percent investment in investment B (e.g., $10,000 invested in A, and $10,000

EXHIBIT 5.2
Realized Returns for Four Individual Investments and Three Portfolios

Year	*Rate of Return*						
	A	B	C	D	AB	AC	AD
1	−10%	30%	−25%	15%	10%	−17.5%	2.5%
2	0	20	−5	10	10	−2.5	5.0
3	10	10	15	0	10	12.	5.0
4	20	0	35	25	10	27.5	22.5
5	30	−10	55	35	10	42.5	32.5
Rate of return	10.0%	10.0%	15.0%	17.0%	10.0%	12.5%	13.5%
Standard deviation	15.8%	15.8%	31.6%	13.5%	0.0%	23.7%	13.3%

invested in B). Portfolio AC is an equal-weighted portfolio of investments A and C. Portfolio AD is an equal-weighted portfolio of investments A and D. As shown at the bottom of the table, investments A and B both have a 10 percent expected rate of return, while the expected rates of return for investments C and D are 15 percent and 17 percent, respectively. Investments A and B have identical stand-alone risk (i.e., standard deviations of 15.8 percent), while investments C and D have greater stand-alone risk than investments A and B have.

The ***rate of return on a portfolio,*** $R_{Portfolio}$, is the weighted average of the returns on the investments that make up the portfolio, the weights being the proportion of the total portfolio invested in each asset:

Key Equation 5.6: Return on a Portfolio

$R_{Portfolio} = (w_1 \times R_1) + (w_2 \times R_2) + (w_3 \times R_3)$ and so on, where w_1 is the proportion of investment 1 in the overall portfolio and R_1 is the rate of return on investment 1, and so on.

Thus, the rate of return on Portfolio AB is 10 percent:

$$R_{AB} = (0.5 \times 10\%) + (0.5 \times 10\%) = 5\% + 5\% = 10\%,$$

while the rate of return on Portfolio AC is 12.5 percent, and on AD, 13.5 percent.

Alternatively, the rate of return on a portfolio can be calculated by looking at the portfolio's return distribution. For example, consider the return distribution for portfolio AC contained in exhibit 5.2. The portfolio return in each year is the weighted average of the returns on investments A and C in that year. For example, the return on portfolio AC in year 1 is $(0.5 \times [-10\%]) + (0.5 \times [-25\%]) = -17.5\%$. Portfolio AC's return in each other year is calculated similarly. Portfolio AC's return distribution now can be used to calculate its rate of return:

$$\begin{aligned} R_{AC} &= (0.20 \times [-17.5\%]) + (0.20 \times [-2.5\%]) + (0.20 \times 12.5\%) \\ &\quad + (0.20 \times 27.5\%) + (0.20 \times 42.5\%) \\ &= 12.5\%. \end{aligned}$$

This value is the same as that calculated from the rates of return of the two portfolio components:

$$R_{AC} = (0.5 \times 10\%) + (0.5 \times 15\%) = 12.5\%.$$

Portfolio Risk: Two Investments

When an investor holds a portfolio of investments, the portfolio is in effect a stand-alone investment, so the riskiness of the portfolio is measured by the standard deviation of portfolio returns, which is the previously discussed measure of stand-alone risk. How does the riskiness of the individual investments in a portfolio combine to create the overall riskiness of the portfolio? Although the rate of return on a portfolio is the weighted average of the returns on the component investments, a portfolio's standard deviation (i.e., riskiness) is generally **not** the weighted average of the standard deviations of the individual components. The portfolio's riskiness may be smaller than the weighted average of each component's riskiness. Indeed, the riskiness of a portfolio may be less than the least risky portfolio component, and, under certain conditions, a portfolio of risky assets may even be riskless.

A simple example can be used to illustrate this concept. Suppose that an individual is given an opportunity to flip a coin once. If it comes up heads, he wins $10,000, but if it comes up tails, he loses $8,000. This bet is reasonable; the expected dollar return is (0.5 × $10,000) + (0.5 × [−$8,000]) = $1,000. However, it is a highly risky proposition; the individual has a 50 percent chance of losing $8,000. Thus, because of risk aversion, most people would refuse to make the bet, especially if the $8,000 potential loss would result in financial hardship.

Alternatively, suppose that individual is given the opportunity to flip the coin 100 times, and he would win $100 for each head but lose $80 for each tail. It is possible, although unlikely, that he would flip all heads and win $10,000. It is also possible but unlikely that he would flip all tails and lose $8,000. The chances are high that he would flip close to 50 heads and 50 tails and net about $1,000. Even if he flipped a few more tails than heads, he would still make money on the gamble.

Although each flip is a risky bet in the stand-alone sense, collectively, the individual has a low-risk proposition. In effect, the multiple flipping has created a portfolio of investments; each flip of the coin can be thought of as one investment, so the individual now has a 100-investment portfolio. Furthermore, the return on each investment is independent of the returns on the other investments; the individual has a 50 percent chance of winning on each flip of the coin regardless of the results of the previous flips. By combining the flips into a single gamble (i.e., into an investment portfolio), the gambler can reduce the risk associated with each bet. In fact, if the gamble consisted of a large number of flips—say, 1,000—almost all risk would be eliminated; the probability of a near-equal number of heads and tails would be high, and the result would be a sure profit. Risk reduction is inherent in the portfolio because the negative consequences of tossing a tail are offset by the positive consequences of tossing a head.

To examine portfolio effects in more depth, consider portfolio AB in exhibit 5.2. Each investment (A and B) is risky when held in isolation; each has a standard deviation of returns of 15.8 percent. However, a portfolio of the two investments has a rate of return of 10 percent in every possible state of the economy; hence, it offers a riskless 10 percent return. This result is verified by the value of zero for portfolio AB's standard deviation of returns. The reason investments A and B can be combined to form a riskless portfolio is that their returns have an inverse relationship. Thus, in economic states when A's returns are relatively low, those of B are relatively high, and vice versa, so the gains on one component in the portfolio exactly offset losses in the other component.

The movement relationship of two variables (i.e., their tendency to move either together or in opposition) is called *correlation*. The *correlation coefficient*, represented by the variable *r*, measures this relationship. Investments A and B can be combined to form a riskless portfolio because the returns on A and B are *perfectly negatively correlated*, which is designated by r = –1.0. For every year during which investment A has a return higher than its average return, investment B has a return lower than its average return, and vice versa.

The opposite of perfect negative correlation is *perfect positive correlation*, which is designated by r = +1.0. Returns on two perfectly positively correlated investments move up and down together over time. When the returns on two investments are perfectly positively correlated, combining the investments into a portfolio will not lower risk; the standard deviation of the portfolio is merely the weighted average of the standard deviations of the two components. To better understand the impact of perfect positive correlation, consider portfolio AC in exhibit 5.2. Its rate of return, R_{AC}, is 12.5 percent and its standard deviation is 23.7%.

Because there is a perfect positive correlation between the returns on A and C, portfolio AC's standard deviation is the weighted average of the component standard deviations:

$$\sigma_{AC} = (0.5 \times 15.8\%) + (0.5 \times 31.6\%)$$
$$= 23.7\%.$$

There is no risk reduction in this situation. The risk of the portfolio is less than the risk of investment C, but it is more than the risk of investment A. Forming a portfolio does not reduce risk when the returns on the two components are perfectly positively correlated; the portfolio merely **averages** the risk of the two investments.

What happens when a portfolio is created with two investments that have positive, but not perfectly positive, correlation? Combining the two investments can eliminate some, but not all, risk. To illustrate the concept, consider portfolio AD in exhibit 5.2. This portfolio has a standard deviation of returns of 13.3 percent, so it is risky. However, portfolio AD's standard deviation is less than the weighted average of its components' standard deviations, (0.5 × 15.8%) + (0.5 × 13.5%) = 14.7%. The correlation coefficient between the return distributions for A and D is 0.64, which indicates that the two investments are positively correlated, but the correlation is less than +1.0. Thus, combining two investments that are positively, but not perfectly, correlated lowers risk but does not eliminate it.[4]

Because returns correlation is the factor that drives risk reduction, a logical question here is, What is the correlation among the returns on "real world" investments? Generalizing about the correlations among real-world investment alternatives is difficult. However, it is safe to say that the return distributions of two randomly selected investments—whether they are real assets in a hospital's portfolio of projects or financial assets in an individual's investment portfolio—are almost never perfectly correlated; hence, correlation coefficients are rarely –1.0 or +1.0. In fact, it is almost impossible to find actual investment opportunities with returns that are negatively correlated with one another or even to find investments with returns that are uncorrelated (r = 0). Because all investment returns are affected to a greater or lesser degree by general economic conditions, investment returns tend to be positively correlated with one another. However, because investment returns are not affected identically by general economic conditions, returns on most real-world investments are not perfectly positively correlated.

The correlation coefficient between the returns of two randomly chosen investments will usually fall in the range of +0.3 to +0.8. Returns on investments that are similar in nature, such as two inpatient projects in a hospital or two stocks in the same industry, typically have return correlations at the upper end of this range. Conversely, returns on dissimilar projects or securities tend to have correlations at the lower end of the range.

For real-world correlations, consider exhibit 5.3, which shows the correlation coefficients between several investment classes. The base for all correlations is the Standard & Poor's Index (S&P 500), which is a diversified portfolio of large-firm stocks. Adding asset classes with negative or low correlation to traditional investments such as the S&P 500 can increase portfolio diversification.

Portfolio Risk: Many Investments

Businesses are not restricted to two projects, and individual investors are not restricted to holding two-security portfolios. Most firms have tens—or even thousands—of individual projects (i.e., product or service lines), and most individual investors hold many different securities or mutual funds that may be composed of a multitude of individual securities. Thus, what is most relevant to financial decision-making is not what happens when two investments

EXHIBIT 5.3
January 2009–December 2018 Correlations Among Selected Asset Classes

Investment 1	*Investment 2*	*Correlation coefficient*
Investment grade bonds	S&P 500	–0.06
Cash	S&P 500	–0.08
Commodities	S&P 500	0.52
Currencies	S&P 500	–0.52
Global indexes	S&P 500	0.97
Hedge funds	S&P 500	0.74
International equity	S&P 500	0.87
Long/short equity funds	S&P 500	0.83
Managed futures funds	S&P 500	0.15
Real estate investment trusts	S&P 500	0.73
S&P 500	S&P 500	1.00

Source: Guggenheim Investments (2019).

EXHIBIT 5.4
Portfolio Size and Risk

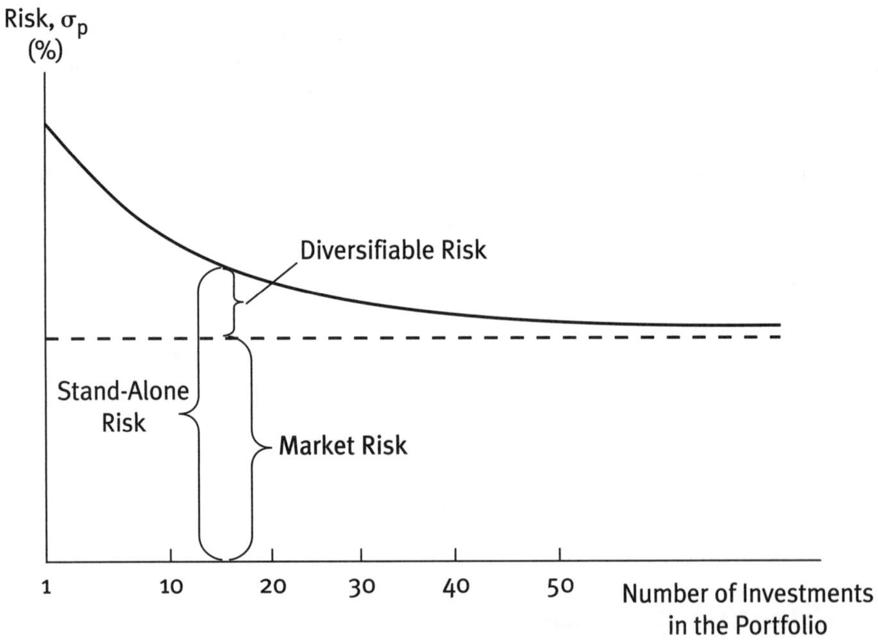

are combined into portfolios but rather what happens when many investments are combined.

To better understand the risk impact of creating large portfolios, consider exhibit 5.4. The graph illustrates the riskiness inherent in randomly selected portfolios of one, two, three, four investments, and so on, considering the correlations that occur among real-world investments. The plot is based on **historical** annual returns on common stocks traded on the New York Stock Exchange (NYSE), but the conclusions are applicable to portfolios made up of any type of investment, including healthcare providers that offer many different types of services.

The riskiness inherent in an average one-investment portfolio is relatively high, as measured by the standard deviation of annual returns. The average two-investment portfolio has a lower standard deviation, so an average two-investment portfolio is less risky than a single investment of average risk. The average three-investment portfolio has an even lower standard deviation of returns, so an average three-investment portfolio is even less risky than an average two-investment portfolio. As more investments are randomly added to create larger portfolios, the average riskiness of the portfolio decreases. However, as more and more investments are added, the incremental risk reduction of adding even more assets decreases. Regardless of how many investments are added, some risk remains in the portfolio.[5]

The rationale for investors' inability to eliminate all risk, even when holding very large portfolios, is worth repeating: All risk cannot be eliminated because the returns on the component investments are positively correlated with one another (although not perfectly so). In other words, all investments, both real and financial, are affected to a greater or lesser extent by overall economic conditions.

Diversifiable Risk Versus Market Risk

Exhibit 5.4 shows what happens as investors create ever larger portfolios. As the size of a randomly created portfolio increases, the riskiness of the portfolio decreases. Thus, a large proportion of the stand-alone risk inherent in an individual investment can be eliminated if it is held as part of a large portfolio. For example, if a stock investor wanted to eliminate as much stand-alone risk as possible, he would have to own more than 6,500 stocks. Fortunately, it is not necessary to purchase all the stocks individually because mutual funds that mimic all of the major stock indexes are available.[6] A portfolio that consists of a large number of stocks is called the *market portfolio* because it consists of the entire stock market, or at least one entire segment of the stock market. Studies have found that the market portfolio has only about one-half the standard deviation of an average stock. However, it is not necessary for individual investors to own the market portfolio to take advantage of the risk-reducing benefits of diversification. As illustrated in exhibit 5.4, most of the benefit can be obtained by holding about 50 randomly selected stocks. Such a collection of investments is called a *well-diversified portfolio*.

The part of the stand-alone riskiness of a single investment that can be eliminated by diversification (i.e., by holding it as part of a well-diversified portfolio) is called *diversifiable risk*. The part of the riskiness of a single investment that cannot be eliminated by diversification is called ***market risk***. Every investment—whether it is the stock of Tenet Healthcare (www.tenet health.com) held by an individual investor or an MRI system operated by a hospital—has some diversifiable risk that can be eliminated and some market risk that cannot be diversified away.

Diversifiable risk, as seen by individuals who invest in stocks, is caused by events that are unique to a single business, such as new product or service introductions, strikes, and lawsuits. Because these events are essentially random and influence only one business, their effects can be eliminated by diversification. When one stock in a portfolio does worse than expected because of a negative event unique to that firm, another stock in the portfolio will do better than expected because of a positive event unique to that firm. On average, bad events in some firms will be offset by good events in others, so lower-than-expected returns will be offset by higher-than-expected returns, leaving the investor with an overall portfolio return closer to that expected than would be the case if only a single stock were held.

The stand-alone risk of an investment can be broken down into two parts:

Key Equation 5.7: Diversifiable Versus Market Risk

Stand-alone risk = Diversifiable risk + Market risk.

Diversifiable risk is that portion of the stand-alone risk of an investment that can be eliminated by placing it in a well-diversified portfolio, while market risk is the risk that remains (cannot be diversified away).

The same logic can be applied to a business with a portfolio of projects. Perhaps hospital returns generated from inpatient surgery are less than expected because of the trend toward outpatient procedures, but these lower returns may be offset by greater-than-expected returns generated from the delivery of state-of-the-art diagnostic services. (If the hospital offered both inpatient and outpatient surgery, it would be ***hedging*** itself against the trend toward more outpatient procedures because reduced demand for inpatient surgery would be offset by increased demand for outpatient surgery.)

The main point here is that the negative impact of random events that are unique to a particular firm, or to a firm's product or service, can be offset by positive events in other firms or in other products or services. Thus, the risk caused by random, unique events can be eliminated by portfolio diversification. Individual investors can diversify by holding many securities, and businesses can diversify by operating many projects.

Note that not all investments benefit to the same degree from portfolio risk-reducing effects. Some have a large amount of diversifiable risk and hence experience a great deal of risk reduction when added to a well-diversified portfolio. Others do not benefit nearly as much from portfolio risk reduction. For example, consider adding the stock of Tenet Healthcare, a hospital management company, to two portfolios. The first portfolio consists of the stocks of 50 healthcare providers. The second portfolio consists of the stocks of 50 randomly selected firms from many different industries. Much less risk reduction will occur when the Tenet stock is added to the healthcare provider portfolio than when it is added to the randomly selected portfolio because Tenet's returns are more highly correlated with healthcare providers than with firms in other industries. In other words, the lower the correlation, the greater the risk reduction.

This logic tells us there is more risk reduction inherent in adding a nursing home to a hospital business than there is in adding it to a long-term care firm that already owns a large number of such investments. Recognize, however, that managing a nursing home is probably more difficult for managers of a hospital business than for managers of a firm that specializes in long-term care.

Unfortunately, not all risk can be diversified away. Market risk—the risk that remains even in well-diversified portfolios—stems from factors (e.g., wars, inflation, recessions, high interest rates) that systematically affect all stocks in a portfolio or all products or services produced by a business. For example, the increasing power of managed care organizations or governmental payers could lower reimbursement levels for all services offered by a hospital. Because the market risk inherent in single investments cannot be eliminated, even well-diversified investors—whether they are individuals with large securities portfolios or diversified healthcare businesses with many different service lines—face a considerable amount of risk.

Implications for Investors

The ability to eliminate a portion of the stand-alone riskiness inherent in individual investments has two significant implications for investors—whether the investor is an individual who holds securities or a business that offers products or services:

1. **Holding a single investment is not rational.** Holding a portfolio can eliminate much of the stand-alone riskiness inherent in individual investments. Investors who are risk averse should seek to eliminate all

diversifiable risk. Individual investors can easily diversify their personal investment portfolios by buying many individual securities or mutual funds that hold diversified portfolios. Businesses cannot diversify their investments as easily as individuals can, but businesses that offer a diverse line of products or services are less risky than businesses that rely on a single product or service.

2. **Because an investment held in a portfolio has less risk than an investment held in isolation, the traditional stand-alone risk measure of standard deviation is not appropriate for individual assets when they are held as parts of portfolios.** Thus, it is necessary to rethink the definition and measurement of financial risk for such assets. (Note, though, that standard deviation remains the correct measure for the riskiness of an investor's portfolio because the portfolio is, in effect, a single asset held in isolation.)

SELF-TEST QUESTIONS

1. What is a portfolio of assets?
2. What is a well-diversified portfolio?
3. What happens to the risk of a single investment when it is held as part of a portfolio of assets?
4. Explain the differences between stand-alone risk, diversifiable risk, and market risk.
5. Why should all investors hold well-diversified portfolios rather than individual assets?
6. Is standard deviation the appropriate risk measure for an individual asset?
7. Is standard deviation the appropriate risk measure for an investor's portfolio of assets? Explain your answer.

The Relevant Risk of a Stock

If investors are risk averse, they will demand a premium for bearing risk; that is, the higher the risk of a security, the higher its expected return must be to induce investors to buy it or to hold it. All risk except that related to broad market movements can easily be diversified away. This implies that investors are primarily concerned with the risk of their portfolios rather than the risk of the individual securities in the portfolio. How, then, should the risk of an individual stock be measured? The *capital asset pricing model (CAPM)* provides one answer to that question. A stock might be quite risky if held by itself, but—because diversification eliminates about half of its risk—the stock's relevant risk is its contribution to a well-diversified portfolio's risk, which is much smaller than the stock's stand-alone risk.

A well-diversified portfolio has only market risk. Therefore, the CAPM defines the relevant risk of an individual stock as the amount of risk that the stock contributes to the market portfolio, which is a portfolio containing all stocks. The relevant measure of risk is called *beta*, and the beta of stock i is calculated as

Key Equation 5.8: Beta

$$b_i = (\sigma_i \div \sigma_m) \times r_{im},$$

where

σ_i = standard deviation of stock i's returns,

σ_m = standard deviation of the market's returns, and

r_{im} = correlation coefficient between stock i's returns and the market's returns.

This equation shows that a stock with a high standard deviation, σ_i, will have a high beta, which means that, other things held constant, the stock contributes a lot of risk to a well-diversified portfolio. This makes sense, because a stock with high stand-alone risk will tend to destabilize a portfolio. Note too that a stock with a high correlation with the market, r_{im}, will also tend to have a large beta and hence be risky. This also makes sense, because a high correlation means that diversification is not helping much—the stock will perform well when the portfolio is also performing well, and the stock will perform poorly when the portfolio is also performing poorly.

The beta of any portfolio of investments is simply the weighted average of the individual investments' betas:

Key Equation 5.9 Portfolio Beta

$$b_{Portfolio} = (w_1 \times b_1) + (w_2 \times b_2) + (w_3 \times b_3) + (w_i \times b_i) \text{ and so on.}$$

Here, $b_{Portfolio}$ is the beta of the portfolio, which measures the volatility of the entire portfolio; w_i is the fraction of the portfolio invested in each particular asset; and b_i is the beta coefficient of that asset. For ease of illustration, assume that an investor has only the four stocks listed in the following table.

Stock	*Beta (b_i)*	*Weight in portfolio (w_i)*
1	0.6	25%
2	1.0	25%
3	1.4	25%
4	1.8	25%

The weighted average of the stock betas is the portfolio beta:

$$b_{Portfolio} = (0.6 \times 0.25) + (1.0 \times 0.25) + (1.4 \times 25\%) + (1.8 \times 25\%)$$
$$= 1.20.$$

There are four key points about beta that you should know.

1. Beta determines how much risk a stock contributes to a well-diversified portfolio. If all the stocks' weights in a portfolio are equal, then a stock with a beta that is twice as big as another stock's beta contributes twice as much risk.
2. The average of all stocks' betas is equal to 1; the beta of the market also is equal to 1. Intuitively, this is because the market return is the average of all the stocks' returns.
3. A stock with a beta greater than 1 contributes more risk to a portfolio than does the average stock, and a stock with a beta less than 1 contributes less risk to a portfolio than does the average stock.
4. Most stocks have betas that are between about 0.4 and 1.6.

Estimating Beta

The CAPM is an *ex ante* model, which means that all of the variables represent before-the-fact, expected values. In particular, the beta coefficient used by investors should reflect the relationship between a stock's expected return and the market's expected return during some future period. However, people generally calculate betas using data from some past period and then assume that the stock's risk will be the same in the future as it was in the past.

Many analysts use four to five years of monthly data, although some use 52 weeks of weekly data. To illustrate, we use the four years (2015–2018) of monthly returns from the file named Ch05 Model.xlsx on the Health Administration Press's website. Calculate the betas of HCA Healthcare (http://hcahealthcare.com), Community Health Systems (www.chs.net), and Tenet Healthcare (www.tenethealth.com) using key equation 5.8:

	Market (S&P 500)	*Community Health Systems*	*Tenet Healthcare*	*HCA Healthcare*
Symbol	GSPC	CYH	THC	HCA
Standard deviation	3.3%	20.7%	14.4%	7.0%
Correlation with the market		0.37	0.36	0.36
$b_i = (\sigma_i / \sigma_m) \times r_{im}$		2.32	1.58	0.77

Source: Yahoo (2019).

Suppose you plot a stock's returns on the *y*-axis (vertical) of a graph and the market portfolio's returns on the *x*-axis (horizontal). The formula for the slope of a regression line is exactly equal to the formula for beta in key equation 5.8. Therefore, to estimate beta for a security, you can estimate a regression with the stock's returns on the *y*-axis and the market's returns on the *x*-axis using the equation

$$r_{it} = a_i + b_i\, r_{Mt} + e_{it},$$

where r_{it} and r_{Mt} are the actual returns for the stock and the market for date t; a_i and b_i are the estimated regression coefficients; and e_{it} is the estimated error at date t. Exhibit 5.5 illustrates this approach for Community Health Systems and HCA. The blue dots represent each of the 48 data points, with the stock's returns on the *y*-axis and the market's returns on the *x*-axis. We used the Trendline feature in Excel to show the regression equation on the charts (these are the dotted line). It is also possible to use Excel's SLOPE function to estimate the slope from a regression: SLOPE(known_y's, known_x's). Exhibit 5.5 shows that Community Health Systems has an estimated beta of 2.32 and HCA has an estimated beta of 0.77, the same values that we calculated earlier using key equation 5.8. The black line is the plot of market versus market (a 45-degree line with a slope of 1.00.)

Notice that the slope of the regression line of Community Health Systems (2.32) is steeper than the slope of the market line (1.00), suggesting that Community Health Systems is riskier than the market. Conversely, the slope of the regression line of HCA (0.77) is flatter than the market, suggesting that HCA is less risky than the market.

It is important to remember that beta cannot be observed; it can only be estimated. Community Health Systems has an estimated beta of 2.32. What does that mean? By definition, the average beta for all stocks is equal to 1, so Community Health Systems contributes 132 percent more risk to a well-diversified portfolio than does a typical stock (assuming they have the

EXHIBIT 5.5
Monthly Stock Returns of Community Health Systems and the S&P 500, 2014–2018

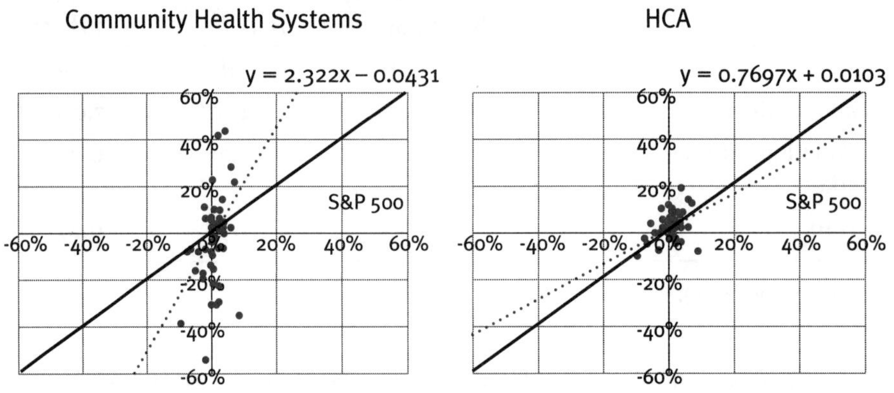

same portfolio weight). HCA has an estimated beta of 0.77, meaning that it contributes 23 percent less risk to a well-diversified portfolio than does a typical stock. When the market is doing well, a high-beta stock such as Community Health Systems tends to do better than an average stock, and when the market does poorly, a high-beta stock also does worse than an average stock. The opposite is true for a low-beta stock: When the market soars, the low-beta stock tends to go up by a smaller amount; when the market falls, the low-beta stock tends to fall less than the market.

The Relationship Between Risk and Return and the Capital Asset Pricing Model

This chapter contains much discussion of the definition and measurement of financial risk. However, the ability to define and measure is of no value in financial decision-making unless risk can be related to return. Planners must consider the question, How much return is required to compensate investors for assuming a given level of risk? In this section, we focus on setting required rates of return on stock investments because the basic theory of risk and return was developed with these in mind. In later chapters, the focus is on setting required rates of return on individual projects in firms.

The relationship between the market risk of a stock, as measured by its market beta, and its required rate of return is given by the CAPM. To begin, some basic definitions are needed:

- $E(R_i)$ = Expected rate of return on stock i—any stock.
- $R(R_i)$ = Required rate of return on stock i.

- RF = Risk-free rate of return. In a CAPM context, RF is generally measured by the return on long-term US Treasury bonds (T-bonds).
- b_i = Market beta coefficient of stock i. The market beta of an average-risk stock is $b_A = 1.0$.
- $R(R_M)$ = Required rate of return on a portfolio that consists of all stocks, which is the market portfolio. $R(R_M)$ is also the required rate of return on an average ($b_A = 1.0$) stock.
- RP_M = Market risk premium = $R(R_M) - RF$. This is the additional return over the risk-free rate required to compensate investors for assuming average ($b_A = 1.0$) risk.
- RP_i = Risk premium on stock $_i$ = $[R(R_M) - RF] \times b_i = RP_M \times b_i$. Stock i's risk premium is less than, equal to, or greater than the premium on an average stock, depending on whether its beta is less than, equal to, or greater than 1.0. If $b_i = b_A = 1.0$, then $RP_i = RP_M$.

Using these definitions, the CAPM relationship between risk and required rate of return is expressed by the following equation, which specifies a line called the *security market line (SML)*:

Key Equation 5.10: Security Market Line (SML)

Required return on stock i = Risk-free rate + Risk premium for stock i

Required return on stock i = Risk-free rate + (Beta of stock i) × (Market risk premium)

$$R(R_i) = RF + (R[R_M] - RF) \times b_i$$
$$= RF + (RP_M \times b_i).$$

The SML equation shows that a stock's required return is determined by the risk-free rate, the market risk premium, and beta.

The Risk-Free Rate

A stock's required return begins with the RF. To induce an investor to take on a risky investment, they will need a return that is at least as big as the risk-free rate. The yield on long-term Treasury bonds is often used to measure the risk-free rate when estimating the required return with the CAPM.

The Market Risk Premium

The market risk premium is the difference between the required rate of return on the market, $R[R_M]$, and the risk-free rate, RF:

$$\text{Market risk premium} = R[R_M] - RF$$
$$\text{Market risk premium} = RP_{M.}$$

The market risk premium (RP_M) is the extra rate of return that investors require to invest in the stock market rather than purchase risk-free securities. The size of the market risk premium depends on the degree of risk aversion that investors have on average. When investors are very risk averse, the market risk premium is high; when investors are less concerned about risk, the market risk premium is low. In this example, T-bonds yield an RF of 6 percent, and an average share of stock has a required rate of return ($R(R_M)$) of 10 percent, so RP_M is 4 percentage points. If the degree of risk aversion is increased, $R(R_M)$ might increase to 12 percent, which would cause RPM to increase to 6 percentage points. Thus, the greater the overall degree of risk aversion, the higher the required rate on the market and hence the higher the required rates of return on all stocks.

The Risk Premium for an Individual Stock

The risk premium for an individual stock (RPi) is equal to the product of the stock's beta and the market risk premium:

$$\text{Risk premium for stock i} = (\text{Beta of stock i}) \times (\text{Market risk premium})$$
$$\text{Risk premium for stock i} = (R[R_M] - RF) \times b_i$$
$$\text{Risk premium for stock i} = (RP_M \times b_i).$$

For an illustration of the use of the SML, assume that the RF is 6 percent and the $R[R_M]$ is 10 percent. For a low-risk stock with $b_{Low} = 0.5$, the risk premium for the stock RP_{Low} is

$$= (R[R_M] - RF) \times b_i$$
$$= (RP_M \times b_i)$$
$$= (10\% - 6\%) \times 0.5$$
$$= (4\%) \times 0.5$$
$$= 2\%.$$

The Required Rate of Return for an Individual Stock

According to the SML, the required rate of return on the low-risk stock is

$$R(R_{Low}) = \text{Risk-free rate} + \text{Risk premium for low-risk stock}$$
$$R(R_{Low}) = RF + RP_{Low}$$
$$R(R_{Low}) = 6\% + 2\%$$

$R(R_{Low}) = 8\%.$

If a high-risk stock has $b_{High} = 2.0$, then its required rate of return is 14 percent, as we see here:

$$R(R_{High}) = 6\% + (10\% - 6\%) \times 2.0$$
$$R(R_{High}) = 6\% + (4\%) \times 2.0$$
$$R(R_{High}) = 6\% + 8\%$$
$$R(R_{High}) = 14\%.$$

An average stock with $b_{Average} = 1.0$ has a required return of 10 percent, the same as the market return, which can be seen if we figure it in the following way:

$$R(R_{Average}) = 6\% + (10\% - 6\%) \times 1.0$$
$$R(R_{Average}) = 6\% + (4\%) \times 1.0$$
$$R(R_{Average}) = 6\% + 4\%$$
$$R(R_{Average}) = 10\% = R(R_M).$$

The SML is often depicted in graphical form, as in exhibit 5.6, which shows the SML when RF = 6 percent and $R(R_M)$ = 10 percent.

Here are the relevant points concerning the graph:

- Required rates of return are shown on the *y*-axis, while risk as measured by market beta is shown on the *x*-axis.
- Riskless securities have $b_i = 0$; therefore, RF is the *y*-axis intercept.

EXHIBIT 5.6
Security Market Line

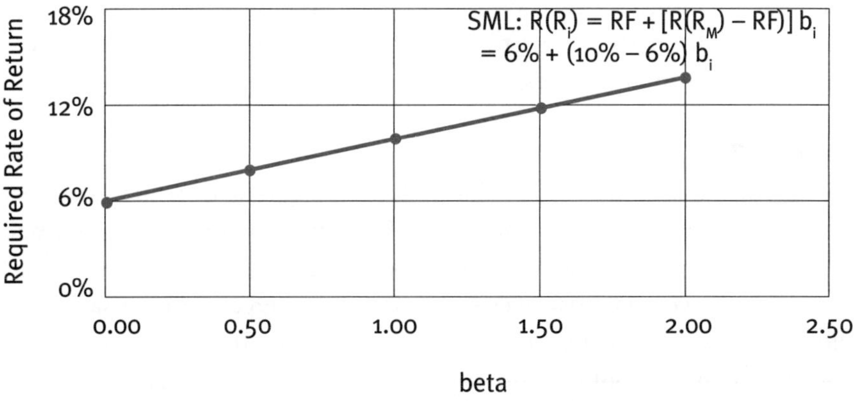

- The slope of the SML reflects the degree of risk aversion in the economy. The greater the average investor's aversion to risk, (1) the steeper the slope of the SML, (2) the greater the risk premium for any stock, and (3) the higher the required rate of return on stocks.
- The *y*-axis intercept reflects the level of expected inflation. The higher inflation expectations are, the greater both RF and $R(R_M)$ are, and thus the higher the SML plots on the graph.
- The values previously calculated for the required rates of return on stocks with $b_i = 0.5$, $b_i = 1.0$, and $b_i = 2.0$ agree with the values shown on the graph.

Both the SML and a firm's position on it change over time because of changes in interest rates, investors' risk aversion, and individual firms' betas. Thus, the SML, as well as a firm's risk, must be evaluated on the basis of current information. The SML, its use, and how its input values are estimated are covered in greater detail in chapter 9.

Required Return and Changes in Expected Inflation or Risk Aversion

Change in Expected Inflation

Exhibit 5.7 shows the impact on the SML of a 2 percent increase in expected inflation. The change causes the risk-free interest rate to increase from 6 percent to 8 percent, but there is no change in the market risk premium (10% – 6% = 12% – 8% = 4%). This happens because, as the risk-free rate changes, so will the required return on the market, and this will, other things held constant, keep the market risk premium stable. Exhibit 5.7 also shows that the increase in expected inflation leads to an identical increase in the required rate of return on all assets, because the same risk-free rate is built into the required rate of return on all assets. For example, the $R[R_M]$ (and the average stock) increases from 10 percent to 12 percent. Other risky securities' returns also rise by 2 percentage points.

Change in Risk Aversion

The slope of the security market line reflects the extent to which investors are averse to risk: The steeper the slope of the line, the greater the average investor's aversion to risk. Suppose all investors were indifferent to risk—that is, suppose they were not risk averse. If RF were 6 percent, then risky assets would also provide an expected return of 6 percent. If there were no risk aversion then there would be no risk premium, and the SML would be a horizontal line. As risk aversion increases, so does the risk premium, and this

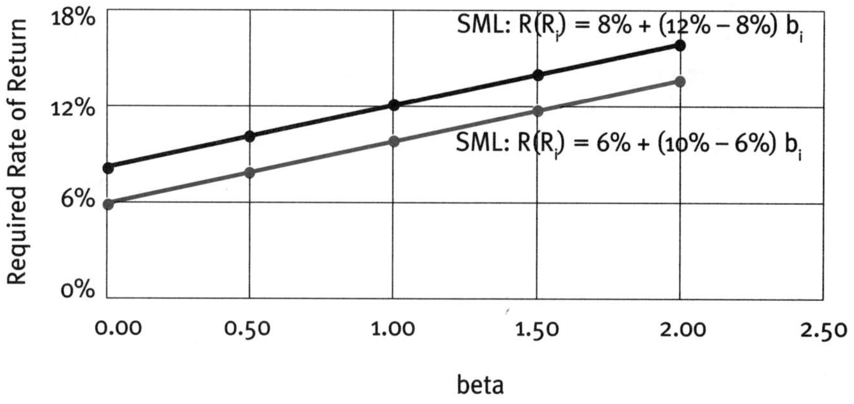

EXHIBIT 5.7
Shift in the SML Caused by an Increase in Expected Inflation

causes the slope of the SML to become steeper. Exhibit 5.8 illustrates the impact of an increase in risk aversion on the SML. The $R[R_M]$ rises from 10 percent to 12.5 percent. The returns on other risky assets also rise, and the effect of this shift in risk aversion is greater for riskier securities. For example, the required return on a stock with b_i = 0.5 increases by only 1.25 percentage points, from 8.5 percent to 9.75 percent; the required return on a stock with b_i = 1.0 increases by 2.5 percentage points, from 10.0 percent to 12.5 percent; and the required return on a stock with b_i = 1.5 increases by 3.75 percentage points, from 12.0 percent to 15.75 percent.

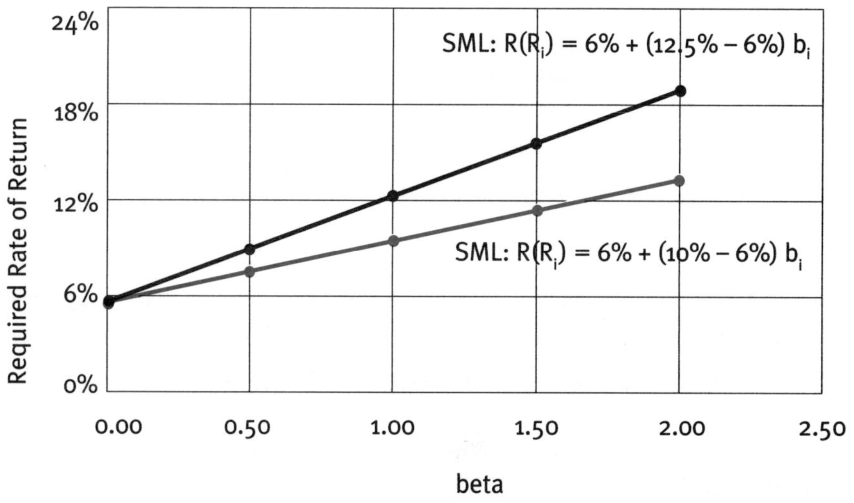

EXHIBIT 5.8
Shift in the SML Caused by an Increase in Investor Risk Aversion

Comparison of Required Return to Expected Return

The CAPM conceptualizes the required return on stock i, $R(R_i)$, as the risk-free rate plus the extra return (i.e., the risk premium) needed to induce an investor to hold the stock. That is, for a given level of risk as measured by beta, what rate of expected return does an investor require to compensate them for bearing that risk? $R(R_i)$ can be considered to be the minimum expected return that is required by an average investor.

How do investors use $R(R_i)$? If the expected rate of return, $E(R_i)$, is less than $R(R_i)$, an investor would not purchase stock i or would sell it if it is owned. If $E(R_i)$ is greater than $R(R_i)$, an investor would purchase stock i, and an individual would be indifferent about the purchase if $E(R_i) = R(R_i)$.

Suppose an investor is considering purchase shares of Regis Healthcare, which has a beta of 1.1 and an expected rate of return, $E(R_{Regis})$, of 15 percent. If the RF is 6 percent and the $R[R_M]$ is 10 percent, then the required rate of return on Regis Healthcare, $R(R_{Regis})$, is

$$R(R_i) = RF + (R[R_M] - RF) \times b_i$$
$$R(R_{Regis}) = 6\% + (10\% - 6\%) \times 1.1$$
$$R(R_{Regis}) = 10.4\%.$$

In this circumstance, the expected rate of return is greater than the required rate of return for Regis Healthcare, so an investor would purchase the stock. In summary,

- if $E(R_i) > R(R_i)$, an investor would purchase stock i;
- if $E(R_i) = R(R_i)$, an investor would be indifferent about purchase of stock i, and
- if $E(R_i) < R(R_i)$, an investor would not purchase stock i.

Some Final Thoughts About Beta and the Capital Asset Pricing Model

The CAPM is more than just an abstract theory described in textbooks. It is widely used by analysts, investors, and corporate managers. However, despite its intuitive appeal, at least serious concerns are prompted by the CAPM:

1. It is built on a restrictive set of assumptions that does not conform well to real-world conditions.
2. It is impossible to prove. Studies that do demonstrate the linear relationship between market risk and required return prove nothing

because the results stem from the mathematical properties of the model, not because it is theoretically correct.

3. Some studies find no relationship between stocks' returns and market betas.
4. The market betas that are actually used in the CAPM measure the historical relative volatility of a stock, but conditions often change. Thus, its future volatility, which is of real concern to investors, might be quite different from its past volatility.

Despite these concerns, the CAPM is extremely appealing because it is simple and logical. It focuses on the impact that a single investment has on a portfolio, which in most situations is the correct way to think about risk. Furthermore, it tells us that the required rate of return on an investment comprises the risk-free rate, which compensates investors for time value, plus a risk premium that is a function of investors' attitudes toward risk in the aggregate and the specific portfolio risk of the investment being evaluated. Because of these points, the CAPM is an important conceptual tool. However, its actual use to set required rates of return must be viewed with some caution. We have more to say about this topic in chapter 9.

SELF-TEST QUESTIONS

1. What is the CAPM?
2. What is the appropriate measure of risk in the CAPM?
3. Write out the equation for the SML, and graph it.
4. How do changes in risk aversion and inflation expectations affect the SML?
5. What are the pros and cons regarding the CAPM?

Chapter Key Concepts

This chapter has covered the important ideas of financial risk and return. Here are its key concepts:

- Risk definition and measurement are important in financial management because, in general, decision makers are *risk averse*, requiring higher returns from investments that have higher risk.
- *Financial risk* is associated with the prospect of returns that are less than anticipated. The higher the probability that the return will be far less than anticipated, the greater the risk.

(continued)

(continued from previous page)

- The riskiness of investments held in isolation, called ***stand-alone risk***, can be measured by the dispersion of the rate of return distribution about its ***expected value***. One commonly used measure of stand-alone risk is the ***standard deviation*** of the return distribution.
- Most investments are not held in isolation but rather as part of ***portfolios***. Individual investors hold portfolios of securities, and businesses hold portfolios of projects (i.e., products and services).
- When investments with returns that are less than perfectly positively correlated are combined in a portfolio, risk is reduced. The risk reduction occurs because less-than-expected returns on some investments are offset by greater-than-expected returns on other investments. However, among real-world investments, it is impossible to eliminate all risk because the returns on all assets are influenced by overall economic conditions.
- The portion of the stand-alone risk of an investment that can be eliminated by holding the investment in a portfolio is called ***diversifiable risk***, while the risk that remains is called ***portfolio risk***.
- The ***beta coefficient of a portfolio of investments*** is the weighted average of the betas of the components of the portfolio—the weights being the proportion of the overall investment in each component. Therefore, the weighted average of corporate betas of all projects in a business must equal 1.0, while the weighted average of all projects' market betas must equal the market beta of the firm's stock.
- The ***capital asset pricing model (CAPM)*** is an equilibrium model that describes the relationship between market risk and required rates of return.
- The ***security market line (SML)*** provides the actual risk and required rate of return relationship. The required rate of return on any stock i is equal to the risk-free rate plus the market-risk premium times the stock's market beta coefficient: $R(R_i) = RF + [R(R_M) - RF] \times b_i = RF + (RP_M \times b_i)$.

This concludes our discussion of basic financial management concepts, which include time value analysis, financial risk, and required rate of return. In the next chapter—titled "Debt Financing"—we begin our coverage of capital acquisition.

Chapter Models, Problems, and Minicases

The following ancillary resources in spreadsheet format are available for this chapter:

- A chapter model that shows how to perform many of the calculations described in the chapter
- Problems that test your ability to perform the calculations
- A minicase that is more complicated than the problems and that tests your ability to perform the calculations in preparation for a case

These resources can be accessed online at ache.org/HAP/PinkSong8e.

Selected Case

One case in *Cases in Healthcare Finance*, sixth edition, is applicable to this chapter: Case 12: Mid-Atlantic Specialty, Inc.

References

Guggenheim Investments. 2019. "Asset Class Correlation Map." Accessed May 22. www.guggenheiminvestments.com/mutual-funds/resources/interactive-tools/asset-class-correlation-map.

Yahoo. 2019. "Quote Lookup." Accessed January 1. https://finance.yahoo.com.

Selected Bibliography

Bannow, T. 2018. "Looking Hard Before They Leap: Getting ACOs to Move to Advanced Risk-Taking Models Hasn't Been Easy." *Modern Healthcare* 48 (41): 16.

Beck, W., C. Kelly-Aduli, and B. B. Sanderson. 2018. "Protecting Revenue at Risk." *Healthcare Financial Management* 72 (4): 62–67.

Brigham, E. F., and P. R. Daves. 2017. "Risk and Return: Part I." In *Intermediate Financial Management*, 13th ed. Mason, OH: South-Western Cengage Learning.

———. 2017. "Risk and Return: Part II." In *Intermediate Financial Management*, 13th ed. Mason, OH: South-Western Cengage Learning.

Friesen, C. A. 2018. "Assessing Risk Calls for Stewardship." *Healthcare Financial Management* 72 (4): 22.

Kotecki, L. 2018. "Reaping the Benefits of an Actuarial Mindset." *Healthcare Financial Management* 72 (4): 50–54.

Luthi, S. 2018. "Azar Hints at 'Bold' Risk-Based Medicare Payment Models." *Modern Healthcare* 48 (37): 2.

Puchley, T., and C. Toppi. 2018. "ERM: Evolving from Risk Assessment to Strategic Risk Management." *Healthcare Financial Management* 72 (4): 44–49.

Ratliff, D., and E. A. Jordahl. 2018. "Finding Reality in a Cloud of Possibility." *Healthcare Financial Management* 72 (3): 68–69.

Tuten, P. 2018. "Building an ERM Framework for Value-Focused Health Care." *Healthcare Financial Management* 72 (4): 34–43.

Selected Websites

The following websites pertain to this chapter:

- For stock market (company) betas, see www.reuters.com/finance. In the search bar, enter the stock symbol of a firm (e.g., THC). On the list of tabs beneath the company name, click Companies. Choose yours from the list, then click Financials. The beta for the company is reported in a table along with other stock market data and financial ratios.
- Try Morningstar for information about the riskiness of mutual funds at www.morningstar.com. Type in a fund symbol—for example, VFINX for the Vanguard 500 Index Fund—into the search bar. Then, click on the Ratings and Risk tab. The next screen will display several risk (volatility) measures, including standard deviation.

Notes

1. If inflation is considered, the T-bill investment is not truly risk free. The *real return*, which recognizes inflation effects, is uncertain because it depends on the amount of inflation realized over the year.
2. In markets that are *efficient*, low-risk investments will have low expected returns, while high-risk investments will have high expected returns. However, not all markets are efficient. See chapter 7 for a complete discussion of market efficiency.
3. See note 2.
4. A portfolio of two investments has lower risk than that of either component only when the correlation coefficient between the returns on the two investments is less than the ratio of the standard deviations,

when this ratio is constructed with the lower standard deviation in the numerator. For example, for portfolio AD to have less risk than both A and D, the correlation coefficient between the returns on A and D must be less than σ_A/σ_D = 11.0% ÷ 12.1% = 0.91. The actual correlation coefficient is 0.53, so the condition is met in this example.

5. Although stocks can be combined with complex investments (derivatives) to form riskless portfolios, our emphasis here is on real-assets investments.
6. The Wilshire 5000 Index, also called the *Total Stock Market Index*, mimics the returns of all publicly traded US stocks.

Integrative Application

The Problem

A patient of Greenacre Hospital recently made a substantial donation in gratitude for the excellent care she received during a recent hospital stay. The money will be added to a board-designated fund that can be used only for cancer research. Gail Simmons is the chair of the investment committee of Greenacre's board, which has been asked to invest the funds. The committee is considering investment in two stocks: New Coast Biotech (NCB) and Valley Nursing Homes (VNH). The returns of the two stocks and the market over the past five years are shown in the following table.

Year	*NCB (%)*	*VNH (%)*	*Market (%)*
1	14	13	12
2	19	7	10
3	–16	–5	–12
4	3	1	1
5	20	11	15

The risk-free rate is 6 percent, and the market risk premium is 5 percent. Gail has reviewed the recommendations of various financial advisors. The average expected return of NCB is 12 percent and of VNH is 10 percent. The committee must decide whether to invest in NCB, VNH, or both stocks.

The Analysis

The =SLOPE function in Excel can be used to determine the betas:

NCB is b = 1.3471, and

VNH is b = 0.6508.

The required rates of return are as follows:

NCB is R(Ri) = 6% + 5% (1.3471) = 12.7355%, and

VNH is R(Ri) = 6% + 5% (0.6508) = 9.2540%.

The expected rates of return are as follows:

NCB is E(Ri) = 12%, and

VNH is E(Ri) = 10%.

The Decision

The committee decided to invest in VNH because its expected rate of return is greater than its required rate of return, whereas the expected rate of return of NCB is less than its required rate of return. ■

PART

III

CAPITAL ACQUISITION

Healthcare organizations need assets to provide services. For example, hospitals need facilities and equipment to provide inpatient and outpatient services, while clinics require similar (but somewhat different) assets to provide their services. To obtain these assets, healthcare organizations need capital (money). A large hospital requires a very large amount of capital (some hospitals have more than $1 billion of capital), while a small home health business requires a relatively small amount of capital. Regardless of size, all healthcare organizations need capital to acquire the facilities, equipment, and other assets needed to run the business.

Many different types of capital are available to healthcare organizations. Debt financing is supplied by lenders, while equity financing is obtained from owners (in the case of for-profit businesses) and from the community at large (in the case of not-for-profit businesses). In addition to using traditional financing (debt and equity), healthcare organizations can obtain the use of facilities and equipment by leasing. Because different types of financing have different characteristics, managers must understand the differences between the types of capital and the impact of these differences on the financial condition of the business. Furthermore, to better understand how capital suppliers decide how much to charge for capital, managers need to know how securities are valued.

The three chapters in this section—chapters 6 through 8—introduce you to the types of capital available to healthcare organizations and the valuation of this capital in the marketplace.

CHAPTER

6

DEBT FINANCING

Learning Objectives

After studying this chapter, readers should be able to

- describe how capital is allocated in the economy;
- discuss the various types of debt—including both long-term and short-term—and their features;
- discuss credit ratings and their importance;
- discuss the yield curve and the components that make up the interest rate on a debt security;
- describe how securities in general are valued; and
- assess the value of debt securities and their yields to maturity.

Introduction

To operate, a business must have assets, and to acquire assets, it must raise *capital.* Capital comes in two basic forms: debt and equity. This chapter focuses on debt financing, while chapter 7 focuses on equity financing. To understand the importance of debt financing to healthcare businesses, consider the fact that providers, on average, finance their assets with roughly 5 percent short-term debt, 30 percent long-term debt, and 65 percent equity. Thus, more than one-third of providers' financing comes from debt. This chapter discusses many facets of debt financing, including important background information on how interest rates are set in the economy.

Unfortunately, the term *debt* can be interpreted in two ways. First, debt can refer to everything on the right side (lower section) of a balance sheet that is not equity, including interest-bearing debt and non-interest-bearing liabilities, such as accruals and trade credit (accounts payable). For some purposes, this all-inclusive definition is appropriate. Second, debt can refer only to interest-bearing debt supplied by *creditors,* such as banks and bondholders. For purposes of this chapter, we will use the second definition and confine our discussion to interest-bearing debt. Other types of liabilities—specifically accruals and trade credit—are discussed in chapter 15.

There are many different types of debt with hundreds of different features. If we were to discuss all of the debt types and their features, this chapter would be too long to be manageable. Thus, the chapter focuses on key issues, while the chapter 6 supplement (found online at ache.org/HAP/PinkSong8e) contains material that is useful and relevant but not essential to understanding the fundamentals of debt financing.

The Cost of Money

Capital in a free economy is allocated through the price system. The ***interest rate*** is the price paid to obtain debt capital, whereas in the case of equity capital in for-profit firms, investors' returns come in the form of ***dividends*** and ***capital gains*** (or ***losses***). The four most fundamental factors that affect the supply of and demand for investment capital, and hence the cost of money, are (1) investment opportunities, (2) time preferences for consumption, (3) risk, and (4) inflation. To see how these factors operate, visualize the situation facing Alicia Ibarra, a nurse-entrepreneur who is planning to start a new home health agency. Alicia does not have sufficient personal funds to finance the business, so she must go to the debt markets to borrow additional capital.

Investment Opportunities

If Alicia estimates that the business will be highly profitable, she will be able to pay creditors a higher interest rate than if it is barely profitable. Thus, her ability to pay for borrowed capital depends on the business's investment opportunities: the higher the profitability of the business, the higher the interest rate that Alicia can afford to pay lenders for use of their savings. In periods of tight credit, high-profitability businesses will be able to afford debt financing, while low-profitability businesses will not be able to pay the prevailing level of interest rates.

Time Preferences for Consumption

The interest rate that lenders will charge depends, in large part, on their time preferences for consumption. For example, one potential lender, Jane Adams, is saving for retirement, so she may be willing to loan funds at a relatively low interest rate because her preference is for future consumption. Another person, Jelani Washington, has a young family to support, so he may be willing to lend funds out of current income, forgoing consumption, but only if the interest rate is very high. Jelani is said to have a high time preference for consumption and Jane a low time preference. If the entire population of an economy were living right at the subsistence level, time preferences for current consumption would necessarily be high, aggregate savings would be low, interest rates would be high, and debt capital would be difficult to obtain.

Risk

The risk inherent in the prospective home health care business, and thus in Alicia's ability to repay the loan, will also affect the return that lenders would require—the higher the perceived risk, the higher the interest rate. Investors are unwilling to lend to high-risk businesses unless the interest rate is higher than the rate on loans to low-risk businesses.

Inflation

Finally, because the value of money in the future is affected by inflation, the higher the expected rate of inflation, the higher the interest rate lenders will demand. To simplify matters, the illustration implied that Jane and Jelani would lend directly to businesses that need capital, but in most cases, the funds would pass through a ***financial intermediary***, such as a bank or mutual fund.

SELF-TEST QUESTIONS

1. What is the "price" of debt capital?
2. What four factors affect the cost of money?

Long-Term Debt

One of the most important ways of categorizing debt is by ***maturity***, or the length of the loan. In general, debt is categorized as long-term or short-term. Although the definitions of "long" and "short" depend on the type of debt under discussion, in most situations ***short-term debt*** is defined as having a maturity of one year or less, while ***long-term debt*** has a maturity of more than one year. Even when the focus is solely on long-term debt, there are still hundreds of different types, if not more. In the following sections, we briefly discuss the types of debt most commonly used by healthcare businesses.

SELF-TEST QUESTION

1. What is the difference between short-term debt and long-term debt?

Term Loans

A *term loan* (the abbreviated version of the term *long-term loan*) is a contract under which a borrower agrees to make a series of payments, on specified dates, to the lender. These payments consist of *principal* (which is the amount borrowed) and *interest* (which is the return the lender receives from the borrower for use of the capital). In general, term loans are negotiated directly between the borrowing business and a financial institution—generally, a bank, a mutual fund, an insurance company, or a pension fund. Thus, term loans are *private placements* as opposed to *public offerings*, which are typically used on bonds—the other major type of long-term debt.

Most term loans have maturities in the range of two to ten years, with an average of about four years. Term loans usually are amortized in equal installments over the life of the loan, so part of the principal of the loan is retired with each payment. For example, Sacramento Cardiology Group has a $100,000 five-year term loan with Bank of America to fund the purchase of new diagnostic equipment. The interest rate on the fixed-rate loan is 10 percent, which obligates the group to five end-of-year payments of $26,379.75. Thus, loan payments total $131,898.75, of which $31,898.75 is interest and $100,000 is repayment of principal.

Term loans have three major advantages over bonds (debt sold to the general public): (1) speed, (2) flexibility, and (3) low issuance costs. Because term loans are negotiated directly between the lender and the borrower, formal documentation is minimized. The key provisions of the loan can be worked out much more quickly and with more flexibility than can those for a public issue, and it is not necessary for a term loan to go through a complicated registration process. A further advantage of term loans over publicly held debt is future flexibility. If many different investors hold a debt issue, it is virtually impossible to alter the terms of the agreement, even if new economic conditions may make such changes desirable. With a term loan, the borrower can generally negotiate with the lender to work out modifications in the contract.

The interest rate on a term loan can be fixed for the life of the loan or variable. If fixed, the rate will be close to the rate on bonds of equivalent maturity for firms of comparable risk. If variable, the rate usually will be set at a certain number of percentage points over an *index rate*, such as the prime rate.[1] Then, when the index rate goes up or down, so does the rate on the outstanding balance of the term loan.

Although term loans have many advantages, there are two potential disadvantages. First, there is a limit to the size of a term loan. Although they can be large—such as when multiple banks combine to make a loan of $100 million or more—most term loans are relatively small, with an average of less than $1 million. Also, lenders typically will not extend term loans to the maturity that businesses can attain in a bond financing, which makes term loans inappropriate for use in financing assets with long lives, such as land and buildings.

SELF-TEST QUESTION

1. Describe the key features of a term loan.

Bonds

Like a term loan, a *bond* is a long-term contract under which a borrower agrees to make payments of interest and principal to the holder of the bond (the lender) on specific dates. Although bonds are similar in many ways to term loans, a bond issue generally is registered with the Securities and Exchange Commission (SEC); advertised; offered to the public in relatively small increments—say, $1,000 or $5,000—through investment bankers; and sold to many different investors (lenders). Indeed, thousands of individual and institutional investors may participate when a firm, such as Tenet Healthcare (www.tenethealth.com), sells a bond issue, while there is generally only one lender in the case of a term loan.

Bonds are categorized as either government (Treasury), corporate, or municipal. *Government*, or *Treasury*, *bonds* are issued by the US Treasury and are used by the federal government to raise money.[2] Corporate and municipal bonds are discussed in detail in the following sections.

Corporate Bonds

Corporate bonds are issued by large investor-owned businesses (corporations), while *municipal bonds* are issued by governments and governmental agencies other than federal. In this section, the primary focus is on corporate bonds, but much of the discussion also is relevant to municipal bonds. The unique features of municipal bonds will be discussed in the next major section.

Although bonds generally have maturities in the range of 20 to 30 years, shorter maturities, as well as longer maturities, are occasionally used. In 1995, HCA Healthcare (see hcahealth.com) issued $200 million of 100-year bonds, following the issuance of 100-year bonds by Disney and Coca-Cola in 1993. Ultra-long-term bonds had not been issued by any firm since the 1920s and have not been issued since. Unlike term loans, bonds usually pay only interest over the life of the bond, and the entire amount of principal is returned to bondholders at maturity.

Most bonds have a **fixed** interest rate, which locks in the current rate for the entire maturity of the bond and hence minimizes interest payment uncertainty. However, some bonds have a **floating**, or **variable, rate** that is tied to some interest rate index, so the interest payment fluctuates as the general level of interest rates rises and falls. Floating-rate bonds are more prevalent when rates are high, when the yield curve (which is discussed later in the chapter) has a steep upward slope, or when both of these conditions are present. Floating-rate bonds are riskier to the issuer because interest rates can rise in the future, but virtually all such debt has call provisions (discussed later) that permit issuers to replace the floating-rate debt with fixed-rate debt if conditions so dictate. Conversely, floating-rate bonds are less risky to buyers, so they carry an initial interest rate that is lower than that set on similar fixed-rate issues.

Some bonds do not pay periodic interest but are sold at a substantial discount from face (principal) value. Such bonds, called *zero-coupon bonds*, provide the investor (lender) with capital appreciation rather than interest income. For example, a zero-coupon bond with a $1,000 face value and ten-year maturity might sell for $385.54 when issued. An investor who buys the bond would realize a 10 percent annual rate of return if they held the bond to maturity, even though they would receive no interest payments along the way. (Note, however, that for tax purposes, the return to zero-coupon bond investors is treated as interest income rather than capital gains income.) Other bonds, instead of paying interest in cash, pay coupons that grant the lender additional bonds (or a proportion of an additional bond). These bonds are called *payment-in-kind (PIK)* bonds. PIK bonds usually are issued by companies in poor financial condition and hence tend to be highly risky.

In rare cases, bonds have *step-up provisions*, meaning the interest rate paid on the bond is increased if the bond's rating is downgraded. (A bond's rating is downgraded when the issuing company's financial condition has deteriorated. Bond ratings are discussed in a later section.) A step-up provision is risky for the issuing company because they must pay a higher interest rate at the worst possible time—when their financial condition weakens. Conversely, such a provision reduces the risk to buyers (lenders).

The bottom line here is that bonds in general, and corporate bonds in particular, come in many different flavors. In a healthcare financial management text, we can only scratch the surface.

Municipal Bonds

Whereas corporate bonds are issued by investor-owned businesses, *municipal bonds*, or *munis*, are issued by states and their political subdivisions, including counties and cities. Although most municipal bonds are backed by the taxing power of the issuing entity, *revenue bonds* are backed by the revenues derived from facilities—such as toll roads and airports—deemed to be beneficial to the community. Of importance to healthcare managers, not-for-profit healthcare providers are entitled to issue such securities through government-sponsored healthcare financing authorities.

Because the interest on municipal debt is exempt from federal income taxes, as well as state income taxes in the state of issue, investors are willing to accept lower interest rates on such debt than on comparable-risk taxable debt. For example, assume that the interest rate on a highly rated, long-term corporate bond was 6.2 percent, while the rate on a similar-risk healthcare muni was 5.0 percent. To an individual investor in the 32 percent federal tax bracket, the muni bond's equivalent taxable yield is 5.0% ÷ (1 − 0.32) = 5.0% ÷ 0.68 = 7.35%, or about 1.2 percentage points above the corporate bond. It is easy to see why investors in high tax brackets are so enthusiastic about municipal bonds. On the surface, it might appear that the ability to obtain debt financing at relatively low rates (5.0 percent versus 6.2 percent in our example) creates a cost-of-financing advantage for not-for-profit providers. However, as we discuss in chapter 10, this advantage is offset by the ability of taxable providers to deduct interest expense from taxable income.

The issuance of municipal bonds by healthcare providers is big business. In 2018, not-for-profit healthcare companies issued more than $15 billion of municipal bonds, and the total amount of debt outstanding is almost $200 billion. Most municipal bonds are sold in *serial* form—that is, a portion of the issue matures (comes due) periodically, anywhere from 6 months to 30 years or more after issue. Whereas most federal government (Treasury) and corporate bonds are held by institutions, about half of all healthcare municipal bonds outstanding are held by individual investors.

In contrast to corporate bonds, municipal bonds are not required to be registered with the SEC. However, prior to bringing municipal debt to market, issuers are required to prepare an *official statement* that contains relevant financial information about the issuer and the nature of the bond issue. In addition, issuers are required to (1) provide annual financial statements that update the information contained in the official statement and (2) release information on material events that can affect bond values as such events occur. This information is not sent directly to investors but rather goes to data banks that can be easily accessed by investment bankers, mutual fund managers, and institutional investors. In theory, by making the information available to investment bankers who handle public trades, any individual who wants to buy or sell a municipal bond will also have access to information that affects the bond's value.

For an illustration of the use of municipal bonds by a healthcare provider, consider the $56 million in municipal bonds issued in March 2018 by the Bay Area Health Facilities Authority. The authority is a public body created under Florida's Health Facilities Authorities Law for the sole purpose of issuing health facilities municipal revenue bonds for qualifying healthcare providers. For this particular bond issue, the provider is Cape Coral Medical Center, a not-for-profit hospital, and the primary purpose of the issue is to raise funds to build and equip a new children's wing. The bonds are secured solely by the revenues of Cape Coral, so the municipal conduit agency—the Bay Area Health Facilities Authority—has no responsibility whatsoever regarding the interest or principal payments on the issue. Exhibit 6.1 shows the maturities and interest rates associated with the issue.

Note the following points:

- The issue is a *serial issue*—that is, the $56 million in bonds is composed of 13 series, or individual issues, with maturities ranging from 1 year to 30 years.
- Because the yield curve on municipal bonds was normal, or upward sloping, at time of issue, the interest rates increase across the series as the maturities increase. (The yield curve is discussed in the chapter supplement.)
- The bonds that mature in 2028, 2038, and 2048 have sinking fund provisions (which we discuss in a later section) that require the hospital

EXHIBIT 6.1
Cape Coral Medical Center Municipal Bond Issue: Maturities, Amounts, and Interest Rates

*Approximate Maturity**	*Amount*	*Interest Rate (%)*
2019	$ 705,000	2.8
2020	740,000	3.2
2021	785,000	3.5
2022	825,000	3.6
2023	880,000	3.8
2024	925,000	3.9
2025	985,000	4.0
2026	1,050,000	4.1
2027	1,115,000	4.2
2028	1,190,000	4.3
2033	5,590,000	4.6
2038	9,435,000	4.9
2048	31,775,000	5.0
	$56,000,000	

*All serial issues mature on March 1 of the listed year.

to place a specified dollar amount with a trustee each year to ensure that funds are available to retire the issues as they become due.

- Although it is not shown in the exhibit, the hospital's annual ***debt service requirements***—the amount of principal and interest that it has to pay on the issue—are relatively constant over time.

The purpose of structuring the series so that the debt service requirements are spread evenly over time is to match the maturity of the issue to the maturity of the asset being financed. Think about it this way: The children's wing has an operational life of about 30 years, and during this time, it will be generating revenues more or less evenly and its value will decline more or less evenly. Thus, the hospital has structured the debt series so that the debt service requirements can be met by the revenues expected to be generated by the children's wing. At the end of 30 years, the debt will be paid off, and Cape Coral Medical Center will probably be planning for a major renovation or a replacement facility that will be funded, at least in part, by a new debt issue.

SELF-TEST QUESTIONS

1. Describe the primary features of long-term debt securities.
2. What is the primary motivation for investors to purchase municipal bonds?
3. Describe the major differences between corporate and municipal bonds.
4. What is a serial issue, and why is it used?

Short-Term Debt

Thus far, we have focused on long-term debt. However, as pointed out in the introduction to this chapter, healthcare providers use about 5 percent short-term debt in their total financing mix. This section provides some of the details associated with short-term debt financing, generally loans with a maturity of one year or less.

Short-term credit has two primary advantages over long-term debt. First, a short-term loan can be obtained much faster than can long-term credit. Lenders will insist on a more thorough credit assessment (financial examination) before extending long-term credit, and the loan agreement will have to be spelled out in considerable detail because much more can happen during the life of a 30-year bond than during the life of a 6-month loan. Thus, businesses that require funds in a hurry look to the short-term markets.

Second, if the need for funds is temporary (seasonal or cyclical), a firm may not want to commit to long-term debt for the following four reasons:

1. Issuance costs are generally higher on long-term debt than on short-term debt. (Issuance costs—sometimes called *flotation costs*—are the administrative costs associated with obtaining financing. For debt financing, these costs include legal and accounting fees, printing costs, loan application fees, and credit assessment fees, among others.)
2. Although long-term debt can be repaid early, provided the loan agreement includes a prepayment provision, prepayment penalties can be expensive. Accordingly, if a firm thinks its need for funds may diminish in the near future, it should choose short-term debt for the flexibility it provides.
3. Long-term loan agreements typically contain restrictive covenants that constrain the firm's future actions. Short-term credit agreements are generally much less onerous in this regard.
4. The interest rate on short-term debt generally is lower than the rate on long-term debt. Thus, when coupled with lower issuance costs, short-term debt can have a significant total cost advantage over long-term debt.

Despite these advantages, short-term credit has one serious disadvantage: It subjects the firm to more risk than does long-term financing. First, if a firm borrows on a long-term basis, its interest costs will be relatively stable over time, but if it uses short-term credit, its interest expense can fluctuate widely. For example, the short-term rate (the prime rate) that banks charge large corporations more than tripled over a two-year period in the early 1980s, rising from 6.25 percent to 21 percent. Many businesses that had borrowed heavily on a short-term basis could not meet their rising interest costs; as a result, business bankruptcies hit record levels during that period. Exposure to increasing interest rates is called *rollover risk*.

Second, the principal amount on short-term debt comes due on a regular basis. If the financial condition of a business deteriorates, the business may be unable to repay this debt when it matures. Furthermore, the business may be in such a weak financial position that the lender will not extend the loan. For the borrower, such a scenario can cause severe problems, which (like unexpectedly high interest rates) can force the business into bankruptcy. The risk that a business will not be able to roll over, or renew, its short-term debt is called *renewal risk*.

Because of the added risk associated with short-term debt, most businesses use such debt solely to meet short-term financing needs (such as to pay for a temporary buildup of medical supplies to meet seasonal demand). To meet more permanent debt financing needs (such as to pay for construction of a new outpatient surgery center), businesses typically use long-term debt.

SELF-TEST QUESTIONS

1. What are the advantages and disadvantages of short-term debt versus long-term debt?
2. Explain the difference between rollover risk and renewal risk.

Credit Ratings

Since the early 1900s, corporate and municipal bonds, as well as other types of debt, have been assigned credit ratings that reflect their probability of going into default. In addition to individual debt issues, a business's overall financial capacity (or *creditworthiness*) can be rated. The three major credit rating agencies are Fitch Ratings (Fitch), Moody's Investors Service (Moody's), and Standard & Poor's Corporation (S&P). On large issues, more than one agency rates the debt, while on smaller deals, one agency is sufficient.

In general, the ratings of these agencies are consistent with one another, although occasionally the agencies will give different ratings to the same firm or issue. Although there are minor variations in the rating grades among the three agencies, the S&P issue ratings, given in exhibit 6.2, are representative. Furthermore, in the discussion to follow, reference to the S&P code implies similar ratings by the other agencies.

Note that debt with a BBB rating or higher is called *investment grade*, which is the lowest-rated debt that many institutional investors are permitted by law to hold. BB and lower debt, called *junk debt*, is more speculative in nature because it has a much higher probability of going into default than does higher-rated debt.

Rating Criteria

Although the rating assignments are subjective, they are based on both qualitative characteristics and quantitative factors. Clearly, quantitative analyses that assess financial condition are an important consideration in the rating process. In addition, the quality and effectiveness of management, organizational structure, competitiveness of the service area, risks associated with medical staff and third-party payer relationships, and local demographic and economic considerations all influence credit ratings.

Analysts at the rating agencies have consistently stated that no precise formula is used to set a credit rating; many factors are taken into account, but not in a mathematically precise manner. Statistical studies have supported this

EXHIBIT 6.2
S&P Issue Credit Ratings

Rating	*Description*
AAA	AAA is the highest rating assigned. The issuer's capacity to meet the debt obligation is extremely strong.
AA	This rating differs from AAA by only a small degree. The issuer's capacity to meet the debt obligation is very strong.
A	The obligation is somewhat more susceptible to adverse changes in circumstances and economic conditions than those with higher ratings. However, the issuer's capacity to meet its financial commitment is still strong.
BBB	The obligation has adequate protection. However, adverse economic conditions or changing circumstances are more likely to weaken the issuer's capacity to meet its obligation. Debt rated lower than BBB is regarded as having significant speculative characteristics.
BB	This rating is less vulnerable to nonpayment than other speculative issues. However, ongoing uncertainties or exposure to adverse conditions can lead to inadequate capacity to meet the financial commitment.
B	The issuer currently has the capacity to meet the obligation, but adverse conditions will likely lead to inadequate capacity.
CCC	This issue is currently vulnerable to nonpayment. The issuer's ability to meet its obligation depends on favorable conditions. Unfavorable conditions are likely to lead to nonpayment.
CC	This obligation is highly vulnerable to nonpayment.
C	This rating is typically used on an obligation when a bankruptcy petition has been filed but payments are still being made.
D	The obligation is in default.

Note: The credit rating agencies use "modifiers" for ratings below AAA. For example, S&P uses a plus and minus system. Thus, in the A rating category, A+ designates the strongest, and A– the weakest.

contention. Researchers who have tried to predict debt ratings on the basis of quantitative data alone have had only limited success, which indicates that the agencies do use a good deal of subjective judgment in the rating process.

Importance of Credit Ratings

Credit ratings are important to both businesses and investors. First, a credit rating is an indicator of the default risk of the debt, or of the business as a whole, so the rating has a direct, measurable influence on the interest rate required by investors and hence on the firm's cost of debt capital. Second, most corporate bonds are purchased by institutional investors rather than by individuals. Many of these institutions are restricted by law or charter to investment-grade securities. Also, most individual investors who buy municipal bonds are unwilling to purchase high-risk bonds. Thus, if an issue has a rating below BBB, the issuer will have a harder time selling the debt because the number of potential purchasers will be reduced. Because of its higher risk and more restricted market, low-grade debt typically carries much higher interest rates than does high-grade debt. (We will illustrate the impact of credit rating on interest rates in the next major section.)

Rating Changes

A change of credit rating will have a significant effect on the business's ability to obtain debt capital and on the cost of that capital. Rating agencies continually review current information about issuers and debt that has been rated. If a major change occurs in an issuer's near-term or long-term credit outlook, the issuer's ratings are placed under review for possible change. For example, S&P will announce that a firm, or issue, has been placed on *CreditWatch* with either a positive or a negative implication. Such an announcement warns investors that a firm, or one or more of its issues, is under review and a rating change could occur. If circumstances dictate such a change, the rating agency will later announce an upgrade or a downgrade.

In addition to the routine review of credit ratings, an announcement that a firm plans to sell a new debt issue, or to merge with another firm and pay for the acquisition by issuing new debt, will trigger agency reviews and possibly lead to a rating change. Thus, if a business's situation has deteriorated somewhat, but its debt has not been reviewed and downgraded, it may choose to use a term loan or short-term debt to raise capital rather than to finance through a public bond issue that would require re-grading. This strategy is used to postpone a rating agency review until the situation has had time to improve.

SELF-TEST QUESTIONS

1. What are the major rating agencies?
2. What are some criteria that the rating agencies use when assigning ratings?
3. What impact do debt ratings have on the cost of debt to the issuing firm?

Interest Rate Components

Although interest rates are set by the interaction of supply and demand for debt capital, the suppliers of debt capital (creditors) base their decisions for each debt security on a minimum required rate of return (interest rate), which depends on several components. By understanding these components, one can gain insights into why interest rates change over time, differ among borrowers, and even differ on separate issues by the same borrower.

The base on which all interest rates are built is the *real risk-free rate (RRF)*. The RRF is the rate that investors would demand on a debt security that is totally **riskless** when there is **no inflation**. Although difficult to measure, the RRF is thought to fall somewhere in the range of 2 percent to 4 percent under normal conditions. However, actions by the Federal Reserve can cause the RRF to fall outside of this range for some periods, especially when applied to short-term interest rates. Note that in the real world, inflation is rarely zero, and most debt securities have some risk. Thus, the actual interest rate on a given debt security will typically be higher than the RRF.

Criticisms of Credit Rating Agencies

Large rating agencies (RAs), such as S&P, have come under increasing criticism in recent years for a multitude of reasons. Here are just a few.

First, the RAs are too cozy with the companies they rate. The close relationships with management, which include frequent meetings along with advice on actions companies should take to maintain current ratings, foster a familial atmosphere that interferes with independent, unbiased rating judgments. Furthermore, because the RAs are paid by the companies they rate, rather than the investors they are meant to protect, a clear conflict of interest exists.

Second, because the rating business is reputation based (why pay attention to a rating that is not recognized by others?), barriers to market entry are high, and the RAs are oligopolists. (An *oligopoly* is a market that is dominated by just a few sellers.) This means that the RAs are somewhat immune to forces that apply to competitive markets and, to an extent, can set their own rules.

Finally, in many instances, the debt markets (through lower bond prices) have indicated a company's deteriorating credit quality many months before a rating downgrade occurred.

These facts have led many observers to suggest that, rather than relying on ratings, investors and regulators should use credit spreads to make judgments about credit risk. (Credit spreads reflect the difference in yields between interest rates on "safe" debt, such as Treasury securities, and rates on risky debt, such as B-rated bonds.)

Inflation Premium

Inflation has a major impact on interest rates because it erodes the purchasing power of the dollar and lowers the value of investment returns. Creditors, which are the suppliers of debt capital, are well aware of the impact of inflation. Thus, they build an *inflation premium (IP)* into required interest rates that is equal to the expected inflation rate over the life of the security.

For example, suppose that the RRF is 2 percent and that inflation is expected to be 2 percent during the next year. Hence, the IP is equal to 2 percent. The rate of interest on a one-year riskless debt security would be 2% + 2% = 4%. The combination of the RRF and IP is called the *risk-free rate (RF)*. Thus, the risk-free rate incorporates inflation expectations but does not incorporate risk factors. In this example, the RF is 4 percent.

The rate of inflation built into interest rates is the rate of inflation **expected in the future**, not the rate experienced in the past. Thus, the latest reported inflation data may show an annual inflation rate of 1 percent, but that rate is for a past period. If investors expect a 2 percent inflation rate in the future, 2 percent would be built into the current rate of interest. Also, the inflation rate built into the inflation premium is the average rate of inflation expected **over the life of the security.** Thus, the inflation rate built into a one-year debt security is the expected inflation rate for the next year, but the inflation rate built into a 30-year security is the average rate of inflation expected over the next 30 years.

Default Risk Premium

The risk that a borrower will default (not make the payments promised) has a significant impact on the interest rate set on a debt security. This risk, along with the possible consequences of default, is captured by a *default risk premium (DRP).* Treasury securities have no default risk; thus, they carry the lowest interest rates on taxable securities in the United States. For corporate and municipal bonds, the higher the bond's rating, the lower its default risk. All else the same, the lower the default risk, the lower the DRP and hence the interest rate.

Exhibit 6.3 lists the interest rates on some representative long-term bonds with different ratings in March 2018. The difference between the interest rate on a T-bond and that on a corporate bond with similar maturity, liquidity, and other features is the DRP. Therefore, if the bonds listed were otherwise similar, the DRP would be 3.4% – 3.0% = 0.4 of a percentage point (40 basis points) for AAA corporate bonds, 3.5% – 3.0% = 0.5 of a percentage point (50 basis points) for AA corporate bonds, 3.6% – 3.0% = 0.6 percentage point (60 basis points) for A corporate bonds, and so on. Bonds rated below BB are called *junk bonds*, and such bonds tend to have large DRPs. For example, the DRP for CCC-rated corporate bonds is a whopping 8.0 percentage points. The DRPs for tax-exempt healthcare bonds are calculated by using the rate on AAA-rated bonds as the basis because there are no tax-exempt T-bonds. Thus, tax-exempt DRPs are not "pure" DRPs—as in the case of corporate bonds, which can be compared to default-free Treasury securities.

In addition to the probability of default, the DRP incorporates a second risk factor called *recovery risk.* For example, consider an issuer that has both mortgage bonds and subordinated debentures outstanding (a debenture is a type of debt instrument that has no collateral backing and relies on the creditworthiness and reputation of the issuer), each carrying the same default rating. Yet, if default occurred, the mortgage bondholders would have a much better chance of recovering the full amount due to them than would the debenture holders (because the debenture holders have no collateral). Thus, the DRP would be higher on the debenture than on the mortgage bond, though both bonds have the same credit rating.

EXHIBIT 6.3 Representative Long-Term Interest Rates in March 2018

	Interest Rate	
Rating	*Taxable (%)*	*Tax-Exempt (%)*
US Treasury	3.0	—
AAA	3.7	2.7
AA	3.5	2.8
A	3.6	3.1
BBB	3.9	4.1
BB	5.1	4.8
B	6.0	5.3
CCC	11.0	7.5

Default risk premiums change over time as the degree of investors' risk aversion changes. For example, if investors believe that businesses will face a tougher operating environment in the future than they did in the immediate past, DRPs will increase. Conversely, if the future is expected to bring an improved operating environment, DRPs will decrease.

Liquidity Premium

A liquid asset is one that can be sold quickly at a predictable fair market price and thus can be converted to a known amount of cash on short notice. Active markets, which provide liquidity, exist for Treasury securities and for the stocks and bonds of large corporations. Securities issued by small businesses, including healthcare providers that issue municipal bonds, are somewhat *illiquid*—they can be sold to raise cash, but they do not sell quickly or at a predictable price. Furthermore, illiquid assets require more effort to sell and hence have relatively high *transactions costs.* Transactions costs include commissions, fees, spreads between asking and selling prices, and other expenses associated with selling an investment. Securities issued by very small businesses, which typically have only a local presence, are very illiquid.

If a security is illiquid, debt suppliers will add a *liquidity premium (LP)* when they set their required interest rate. It is difficult to measure LPs with precision, but a differential of at least 2 percentage points is thought to exist between the least liquid and the most liquid financial assets of similar default risk and maturity.

Price Risk Premium

As we demonstrate in a later section, the market value (price) of a long-term debt security declines sharply when interest rates rise. Because interest rates can and do rise, all long-term debt securities, including Treasury bonds, have an element of risk called *price risk*. For example, if an individual bought a 20-year Treasury bond for $1,000 in November 2017, when the long-term interest rate on such securities was about 2.6 percent, and held it until November 2018, when T-bond rates were roughly 3.4 percent, the value of the bond would have declined to about $889. This decline would represent a loss of about 11.1 percent, which demonstrates that long-term bonds—even US Treasury bonds—are not riskless.

As a general rule, the price risk of the debt of any organization—from the US government to HCA to Cape Coral Medical Center—increases as the maturity of the debt lengthens. Therefore, a *price risk premium (PRP)*, which increases as the term to maturity lengthens, must be included in the interest rate. The effect of PRPs is to raise interest rates on long-term debt relative to those on short-term debt. This premium, like the others, is extremely difficult to measure, but it seems to vary over time; it rises when interest rates are more volatile and uncertain, and it falls when they are more stable. In recent years, the PRP on 30-year T-bonds has been in the range of 0.5–2 percentage points.

Call Risk Premium

Bonds that are callable can be redeemed by the issuer prior to maturity, and hence buyers have uncertain holding periods. This uncertainty makes callable bonds riskier for investors than those that are noncallable. To compensate for bearing call risk, investors charge a *call risk premium (CRP)* on callable bonds. The amount of the premium depends on such factors as the interest rate on the bond, current interest rate levels, and time to first call. Historically, CRPs have been in the range of 30 to 50 basis points.

Combining the Components

When all the interest rate components listed earlier are taken into account, the interest rate on any debt security is expressed as follows:

$$\text{Interest rate} = \text{RRF} + \text{IP} + \text{DRP} + \text{LP} + \text{PRP} + \text{CRP}.$$

For example, assume that RRF is 2 percent and inflation is expected to average 3 percent in the coming year. Because T-bills have no default, liquidity, or call risk and almost no price risk, the interest rate on a one-year T-bill would be 5 percent:

$$\begin{aligned}\text{Interest rate}_{\text{T-bill}} &= \text{RRF} + \text{IP} + \text{DRP} + \text{LP} + \text{PRP} + \text{CRP}\\ &= 2\% + 3\% + 0 + 0 + 0 + 0 = 5\%.\end{aligned}$$

As discussed previously, the combination of RRF and IP is the risk-free rate, so the RF is 5 percent. In general, the rate of interest on short-term Treasury securities (T-bills) is used as a proxy for the short-term RF.

Consider the callable 30-year, A-rated bonds issued by HCA. Assume that these bonds have an inflation premium of 4 percent; default risk, liquidity, and price risk premiums of 1 percent each; and a CRP of 40 basis points. Under these assumptions, the HCA bonds would have an interest rate of 9.4 percent:

$$\text{Interest rate}_{\text{30-year bonds}} = \text{RRF} + \text{IP} + \text{DRP} + \text{LP} + \text{PRP} + \text{CRP}$$
$$= 2\% + 4\% + 1\% + 1\% + 1\% + 0.4\% = 9.4\%.$$

When interest rates are viewed as the sum of a base rate plus premiums for inflation and risk, it is easy to visualize the underlying economic forces that cause interest rates to vary among different issues and over time.

SELF-TEST QUESTIONS

1. Write out the equation for the required interest rate on a debt security.
2. What is the difference between the RRF and the RF?
3. Do the interest rates on Treasury securities include a DRP? An LP? A PRP? Explain your answer.
4. Does the DRP incorporate only the probability of default? Explain your answer.
5. What is price risk? What types of debt securities have the largest price risk premium?

Term Structure of Interest Rates

Usually, short-term interest rates are lower than long-term interest rates. The relationship between long- and short-term rates—which is called the *term structure of interest rates*—is important to healthcare managers (who must decide whether to borrow by issuing long- or short-term debt) and to investors (who must decide whether to buy long- or short-term debt). Thus, it is important to understand how interest rates on long- and short-term debt are related to one another and what causes their relative positions to shift.

To examine the current term structure, look up the interest rates on debt of various maturities by a single issuer (e.g., the US Treasury) in a source such as the *Wall Street Journal* or the *Federal Reserve Bulletin*. For example, the tabular section of exhibit 6.4 lists interest rates for Treasury securities of different maturities on three dates. The set of data for a given date, when plotted on a graph, is called a *yield curve*. As shown in the exhibit, the yield curve changes both position and shape over time. (Current interest rates are readily available online; for example, see www.marketwatch.com/tools/pftools.)

Exhibit 6.4 shows yield curves for US Treasury securities, but the curves could have been constructed for similarly rated corporate or municipal (tax-exempt) bonds. In each case, the yield curve would be approximately the same shape but would differ in vertical position. For example, had the yield curve been constructed for Brookdale Senior Living (www.brookdale.com/en.html), a for-profit nursing home operator with more than 600 locations, it would fall above the Treasury curve because interest rates on corporate debt include default risk premiums, while Treasury rates do not. Conversely, the curve for Cape Coral Medical Center, a not-for-profit hospital, typically would fall below the Treasury curve because the tax-exemption benefit, which lowers the interest rate on tax-exempt securities, generally outweighs

EXHIBIT 6.4
US Treasury Bond Interest Rates on Three Dates

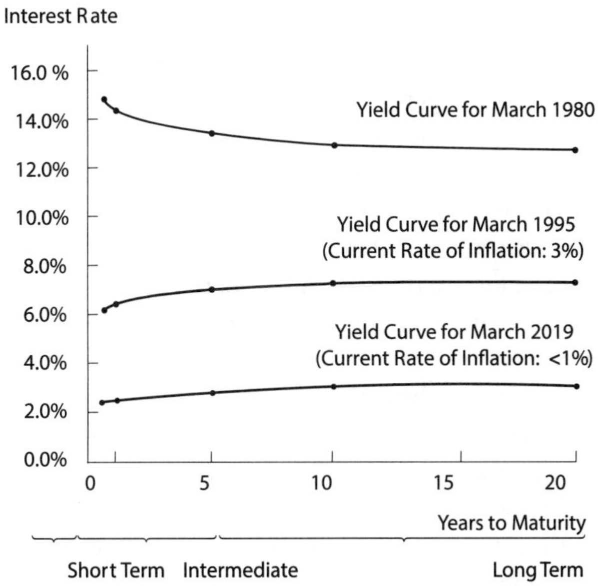

	Interest Rate		
Term to Maturity	*March 1, 1980*	*March 1, 1995*	*March 1, 2019*
6 months	15.0%	6.2%	2.5%
1 year	14.0	6.4	2.6
5 years	13.5	7.1	2.6
10 years	12.8	7.2	2.8
20 years	12.5	7.6	3.0

the default risk premium. In every case, however, the riskier the issuer (i.e., the lower the bonds are rated), the higher the yield curve plots on the graph.

Because long-term rates have historically been higher than short-term rates, at most times the yield curve is upward sloping. An ***upward-sloping curve*** would be expected if the inflation premium is relatively constant across all maturities because the price risk premium applied to long-term issues will push long-term rates above short-term rates. Because an upward-sloping yield curve is most prevalent, this shape is also called a ***normal yield curve***, as illustrated by the curves for March 1995 and March 2019. Conversely, a yield curve that slopes downward is called an ***inverted***, or ***abnormal***, ***yield curve***. Thus, in exhibit 6.4, the yield curve for March 1980 is inverted. In addition, yield curves can be "kinked" or can take other shapes, such as flat, but the yield curve is normal (upward sloping) most of the time.

Healthcare managers use yield curve information to make decisions regarding debt maturities. For example, assume that it is March 2018 and that the yield curve for that month in exhibit 6.4 applies to Cape Coral Medical Center. Also assume that the hospital plans to issue $10 million of debt to finance a new outpatient clinic with a 20-year life. If it borrowed in 2019 on a short-term basis—say, for one year—Cape Coral's interest cost for that year would be 2.6 percent, or $260,000. If it used long-term (20-year) financing, its cost would be 3.0 percent, or $300,000. Therefore, at first glance, it would seem that Cape Coral should use short-term debt.

However, if the hospital uses short-term debt, it will have to renew the loan every year at the then-current short-term rate. Although unlikely, interest rates could return to their March 1980 levels. If they do, at some time in the future, the hospital could be paying 14 percent, or $1.4 million per year. Conversely, if Cape Coral used long-term financing in 2019, its interest costs would remain constant at $300,000 per year, so an increase in interest rates in the economy would not hurt the hospital.

Does this example suggest that businesses should always avoid short-term debt? Not necessarily. If Cape Coral had borrowed on a long-term basis for 3.0 percent in March 2019, it would be at a major disadvantage if interest rates remained low. Its interest expense would be locked in at $300,000 per year, while any competitors that used short-term debt that cost 1.9 percent would be able to renew the debt continually at the lower rate, or even less. Conversely, inflation expectations could push interest rates up to record levels. If that situation occurred, all borrowers would wish that they had borrowed on a long-term basis in 2019.

Financing decisions would be easy if managers could forecast future interest rates with any confidence. Unfortunately, predicting future interest rates with consistent accuracy is somewhere between difficult and impossible—people who make a living by selling interest rate forecasts say it is difficult, but many others say it is impossible. Sound financial policy, therefore, calls for using a mix of long- and short-term debt, as well as equity, in such a manner that the business can survive in all but the most severe and hence unlikely interest rate environments. Furthermore, the optimal financing policy depends on the maturities of the firm's assets: In general, to reduce risk, managers try to match the maturities of the financing with the maturities of the assets being financed. The issue of optimal debt maturities is addressed in more detail in chapter 10.

SELF-TEST QUESTIONS

1. What is a yield curve, and what information is needed to create this curve?
2. What is the difference between a normal yield curve and an inverted one?
3. If short-term rates are lower than long-term rates, why may a business still choose to finance with long-term debt?
4. Explain the following statement: "A firm's financing policy depends in large part on the nature of its assets."

Advantages and Disadvantages of Debt Financing

From the viewpoint of the issuer, there are several advantages to using debt financing as opposed to equity financing (discussed in chapter 7):

- The cost of debt is independent of a business's earnings, so creditors do not participate if profits soar. All of the "excess" value created by good business decisions accrues to the owner(s) of for-profit businesses. For not-for-profit businesses, the value created can be used to further the mission of the organization.
- Because of the tax deductibility of interest for investor-owned businesses and the ability of not-for-profit firms to issue tax-advantaged (municipal) debt, the risk-adjusted component cost of debt is lower than that of common stock.
- The owners of a for-profit business do not have to share control with creditors.
- The use of debt financing enables not-for-profit businesses to offer more services than they could using only equity financing.

The major disadvantages are as follows:

- Because debt service (interest plus principal repayment) costs are fixed, a decline in operating income can result in default and possibly bankruptcy.
- As we discuss in chapter 10, the use of debt financing increases the riskiness of the business and hence increases both debt and equity costs.
- Debt has a fixed maturity date—therefore, it must be repaid when due. If the business's financial capacity at the time of a large principal repayment is limited, financial problems can result.
- Debt contracts, especially those for long-term debt, often contain covenants that restrict managerial actions.
- The amount of debt that can be raised at "reasonable" interest rates is limited.

SELF-TEST QUESTION

1. What are the primary advantages and disadvantages of debt financing compared to equity financing?

Securities Valuation

Now that you understand the basic features of debt securities, the next step is to learn how investors value them. Your reaction at this point might be, "Why should I have to worry about securities valuation when what I really want to learn about is healthcare financial management?" Securities valuation concepts are important to healthcare managers for many reasons. Here are just a few:

- The lifeblood of any business is capital. The most common reason for small business failures is insufficient capital. Therefore, it is vital that healthcare managers understand how investors make investment allocation decisions.
- For investor-owned businesses, stock price maximization is an important, if not primary, goal, so healthcare managers of for-profit businesses must know how investors value the firm's securities to understand how managerial actions affect stock price.
- To make financially sound investment decisions regarding real assets (facilities and equipment), healthcare managers need to estimate the

business's cost of capital, and a knowledge of securities valuation is essential to this process.

- All healthcare managers must grapple with the decision of how much debt financing, as opposed to equity, the business should use. An understanding of securities valuation is critical to this decision.
- Real assets, such as hospital beds and diagnostic equipment, are valued in the same general way as securities. Thus, securities valuation provides healthcare managers with an excellent foundation for learning real asset valuation, which is the heart of capital investment decision-making in businesses.

In essence, we use the basic concepts presented here, with modifications, in chapters 7, 9, 10, 11, and 12.

SELF-TEST QUESTION

1. Why are securities valuation concepts important to healthcare financial management?

The General Valuation Model

Because the financial values of investment opportunities (both real assets and securities) stem from streams of expected cash flows, most investments are valued by the same four-step process:

1. **Estimate the expected cash flow stream**. Estimating the cash flow stream involves estimating both the expected cash flows and the times that they are expected to occur. For some types of investments, such as bonds, the estimation process is easy—the interest and principal repayment stream are fixed by contract. For other types of investments, such as a new service line, the estimation process can be difficult.
2. **Assess the riskiness of the cash flow stream**. For some investments, such as Treasury securities, it is fairly easy to assess the riskiness of the estimated cash flow stream. For other investments, it may be very difficult.
3. **Set the required rate of return**. Once the riskiness is assessed, the opportunity cost principle is applied to set the required rate of return. By making one investment, the funds are no longer available to make alternative investments. Thus, the required rate of return on the cash flow stream is established on the basis of the risk assessment and the returns available on alternative investments of similar risk.

4. **Discount the expected cash flows and sum the present values.** Each cash flow is discounted at the asset's required rate of return (opportunity cost rate), and the present values are summed to find the value of the asset.

The following time line formalizes the general valuation process:

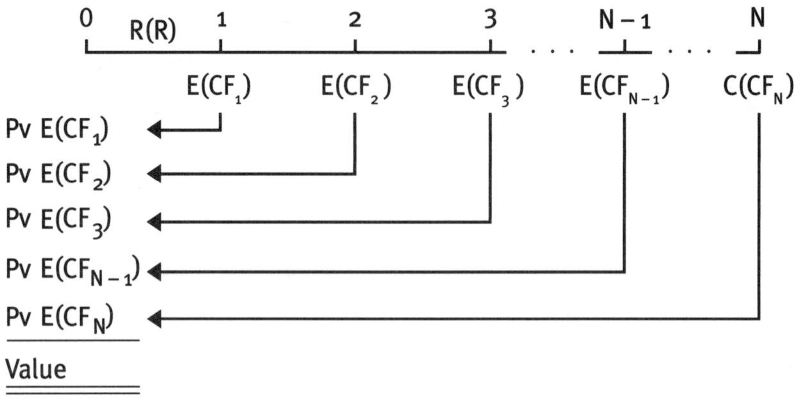

Here, $E(CF_t)$ is the expected cash flow in each period *t*; R(R) is the periodic required rate of return (the opportunity cost rate) on the investment; and N is the number of periods for which cash flows are expected. The periods can be months, quarters, semiannual periods, or years, depending on the frequency of the cash flows expected from the investment.

The general valuation model can be applied to both financial assets (securities), such as stocks and bonds, and real (physical) assets, such as buildings, equipment, and even whole businesses. However, the model can be used only when the cash flows expected from the investment can be estimated with some confidence. Each asset type requires a somewhat different application of the general valuation model, but the basic approach remains the same. In this chapter, the general valuation model is applied to debt securities. In later chapters, the model is applied to common stocks, real assets such as diagnostic equipment, and to entire businesses.

SELF-TEST QUESTIONS

1. What is the general valuation model?
2. Under what conditions can it be used?

Debt Valuation

Unless they have unusual features, debt securities are valued by applying the general valuation model without much modification. We will use a 15-year bond to illustrate debt valuation, but the techniques discussed here are applicable to most types of debt.

To begin our discussion, let's review some basic bond terminology:

- **Par value**. The *par*, or *face, value* is the stated value of the bond. It is often set at $1,000 or $5,000. The par value generally represents the amount of money the business borrows (per bond) and promises to repay at some future date.
- **Maturity date**. Bonds generally have a specified *maturity date* on which the par value will be repaid. For example, Big Sky Healthcare, a for-profit hospital system, issued $50 million worth of $1,000 par value bonds on January 1, 2018. The bonds will mature on December 31, 2033, so they had a 15-year *maturity* at the time of issue. The effective maturity of a bond declines each year after it was issued. Thus, at the beginning of 2019, Big Sky's bonds will have a 14-year maturity, and so on.
- **Coupon rate**. A bond requires the issuer to pay a specific amount of interest each year or, more typically, each six months. The rate of interest is called the *coupon interest rate* or just *coupon rate.* The rate may be variable, in which case it is tied to some index—for example, 2 percentage points above the prime rate. More commonly, the rate will be fixed over the life (maturity) of the bond. For example, Big Sky's bonds have a 10 percent coupon rate, so each $1,000 par value bond pays 0.10 × $1,000 = $100 in interest each year. The dollar amount of annual interest, in this case $100, is called the *coupon payment.*

Origins of the Term *Coupon Payment*

The term *coupon payment* dates back to the time when all bonds were *bearer bonds* and physical possession of the bond certificate provided proof of ownership. Coupons, one for each scheduled interest payment over the life of the bond, were printed on the certificate. Here is an example of a coupon from the 1922 Mecca Temple (New York) construction bonds:

To collect an interest payment, bondholders would remove, or "clip," the appropriate coupon and send it to the issuer or take it to a bank, where it would be exchanged for the dollar payment. Today, all bonds are registered bonds, and the issuer (through an agent) automatically sends interest payments to the registered owner.

- **New issues versus outstanding bonds**. A bond's value is determined by its coupon payment—the higher the coupon payment, other things held constant, the higher its value. At the time a bond is issued, its coupon rate is generally set at a level that will cause the bond to sell at its par value. In other words, the coupon rate is set to match investors' required rate of return on the bond (called the *going rate*). A bond that has just been issued is called a *new issue*. After the bond has been on the market for about a month, it is classified as an *outstanding bond* or a *seasoned issue*. New issues sell close to par, but because a bond's coupon payment is generally fixed, changing economic conditions—and hence the overall level of interest rates—will cause a seasoned bond to sell for more or less than its par value.
- **Debt service requirements**. Firms that issue bonds are concerned with their total debt service requirements, which include interest expense and repayment of principal. For Big Sky, the debt service requirement is 0.10 × \$50 million = \$5 million per year until maturity. In 2033, the firm's debt service requirement will be \$5 million in interest plus \$50 million in principal repayment, for a total of \$55 million. In Big Sky's case, only interest is paid until maturity, so the entire principal amount must be repaid at that time. As we discussed earlier, many municipal bonds are serial issues structured so that the debt service requirements are relatively constant over time. In this situation, the issuer pays back a portion of the principal each year.

The Basic Bond Valuation Model

On the web at: *ache.org/HAP/PinkSong8e*

Bonds generally call for the payment of a specific amount of interest for a specific number of years and for the repayment of par on the bond's maturity date. Thus, a bond represents an annuity plus a lump sum, and its value is found as the present value of this cash flow stream:

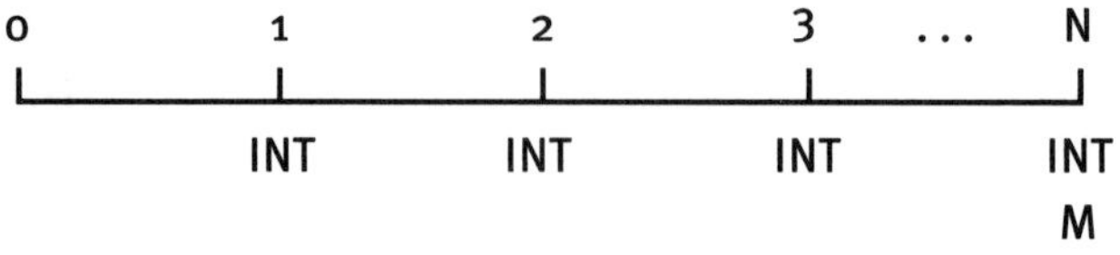

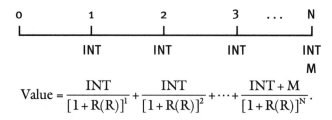

$$\text{Value} = \frac{\text{INT}}{[1+\text{R(R)}]^1} + \frac{\text{INT}}{[1+\text{R(R)}]^2} + \cdots + \frac{\text{INT}+\text{M}}{[1+\text{R(R)}]^N}.$$

Here,

INT = dollars of interest paid each year = Coupon rate × Par value.

M = par, or maturity, value.

R(R) = required rate of return on the bond, which, in general, depends on the returns available on alternative investments of similar risk. For bonds, these returns depend on the real risk-free rate, inflation expectations, and the riskiness of the security.

N = number of years until maturity. N declines each year after the bond is issued.

Here are the cash flows from Big Sky's bonds on a time line:

0	1	2	...	13	14	15
	$100	$100		$100	$100	$ 100
						1,000

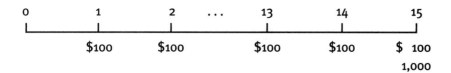

If the bonds had just been issued, and the coupon rate was set at the going interest rate for bonds of this risk, then R(R) = 10 percent. Because the value of the bond is merely the present value of its cash flows, discounted to time 0 at a 10 percent discount rate, the value of the bond at issue was $1,000:

Present value of a 15-year, $100 payment annuity at 10 percent	= $ 760.61
Present value of a $1,000 lump sum discounted 15 years	= 239.39
Value of bond	= $1,000.00

The value of the bond can be found using a spreadsheet.

	A	B	C	D
1				
2	10.0%	Rate	Interest rate	
3				
4	$100	Value 1	Year 1 coupon	
5	$100	Value 1	Year 2 coupon	
6	$100	Value 1	Year 3 coupon	
7	$100	Value 1	Year 4 coupon	
8	$100	Value 1	Year 5 coupon	
9	$100	Value 1	Year 6 coupon	
10	$100	Value 1	Year 7 coupon	
11	$100	Value 1	Year 8 coupon	
12	$100	Value 1	Year 9 coupon	
13	$100	Value 1	Year 10 coupon	
14	$100	Value 1	Year 11 coupon	
15	$100	Value 1	Year 12 coupon	
16	$100	Value 1	Year 13 coupon	
17	$100	Value 1	Year 14 coupon	
18	$1,100	Value 1	Year 15 coupon + Principal	
19				
20	$1,000.00	=NPV(A2,A4:A18) (entered into cell A20)		

Note that we used the NPV function to value the bond. Also note that cell A18 contains 1,100 as the entry, which reflects the $100 interest payment in Year 15 plus the $1,000 return of principal.

If R(R) remained constant at 10 percent over time, what would be the value of the bond one year after it was issued? Now, the term to maturity is only 14 years—that is, N = 14. As shown in the following spreadsheet, the bond's value remains at $1,000:

	A	B	C	D
1				
2	10.0%	Rate	Interest rate	
3				
4	$100			
5	$100	Value 1	Year 1 coupon	
6	$100	Value 1	Year 2 coupon	
7	$100	Value 1	Year 3 coupon	
8	$100	Value 1	Year 4 coupon	
9	$100	Value 1	Year 5 coupon	
10	$100	Value 1	Year 6 coupon	
11	$100	Value 1	Year 7 coupon	
12	$100	Value 1	Year 8 coupon	
13	$100	Value 1	Year 9 coupon	
14	$100	Value 1	Year 10 coupon	
15	$100	Value 1	Year 11 coupon	
16	$100	Value 1	Year 12 coupon	
17	$100	Value 1	Year 13 coupon	
18	$1,100	Value 1	Year 14 coupon + Principal	
19				
20	$1,000.00	=NPV(A2,A5:A18) (entered into cell A20)		

Note that the spreadsheet has the same inputs as when the bond had 15 years to maturity; however, the range listed in the NPV function was changed from A4:A18 to A5:A18 to reflect only 14 years to maturity.

Suppose that interest rates in the economy fell after the Big Sky bonds were issued and, as a result, R(R) decreased from 10 percent to 5 percent. The coupon rate and par value are fixed by contract, so they remain unaffected by changes in interest rates, but now the discount rate is 5 percent rather than 10 percent. At the end of the first year, with 14 years remaining, the value of the bond would be $1,494.93:

	A	B	C	D
1				
2	5.0%	Rate	Interest rate	
3				
4	$100			
5	$100	Value 1	Year 1 coupon	
6	$100	Value 1	Year 2 coupon	
7	$100	Value 1	Year 3 coupon	
8	$100	Value 1	Year 4 coupon	
9	$100	Value 1	Year 5 coupon	
10	$100	Value 1	Year 6 coupon	
11	$100	Value 1	Year 7 coupon	
12	$100	Value 1	Year 8 coupon	
13	$100	Value 1	Year 9 coupon	
14	$100	Value 1	Year 10 coupon	
15	$100	Value 1	Year 11 coupon	
16	$100	Value 1	Year 12 coupon	
17	$100	Value 1	Year 13 coupon	
18	$1,100	Value 1	Year 14 coupon + Principal	
19				
20	$1,494.93	=NPV(A2,A5:A18) (entered into cell A20)		

Here, we changed only the required rate of return in cell A2. The arithmetic of the bond value increase should be clear: Lower discount rates lead to higher present values. But what is the logic behind it? The fact that R(R) has fallen to 5 percent means that if an individual had $1,000 to invest, she could buy new bonds such as Big Sky's—on average, 10 to 20 businesses sell new bonds daily—except that these new bonds would pay only $50 in interest each year. Naturally, she would favor $100 over $50 and would be willing to pay more than $1,000 for Big Sky's bonds. All bond buyers would recognize this rationale; as a result, the Big Sky bonds would be bid up in price to $1,494.93, at which point they would provide the same rate of return as that provided by new bonds of similar risk: 5 percent.

If interest rates stay constant at 5 percent over the next 14 years, what would happen to the value of a Big Sky bond? It would fall gradually from $1,494.93 at present to $1,000 at maturity, when the firm will redeem each bond for $1,000. This point can be illustrated by calculating the value of the bond one year later, when it has only 13 years remaining to maturity:

	A	B	C	D
1				
2	5.0%	Rate	Interest rate	
3				
4	$100			
5	$100			
6	$100	Value 1	Year 1 coupon	
7	$100	Value 1	Year 2 coupon	
8	$100	Value 1	Year 3 coupon	
9	$100	Value 1	Year 4 coupon	
10	$100	Value 1	Year 5 coupon	
11	$100	Value 1	Year 6 coupon	
12	$100	Value 1	Year 7 coupon	
13	$100	Value 1	Year 8 coupon	
14	$100	Value 1	Year 9 coupon	
15	$100	Value 1	Year 10 coupon	
16	$100	Value 1	Year 11 coupon	
17	$100	Value 1	Year 12 coupon	
18	$1,100	Value 1	Year 13 coupon + Principal	
19				
20	$1,469.68	=NPV(A2,A6:A18) (entered into cell A20)		

This time, we changed the range to A6:A18 to reflect 13 years to maturity. The resulting value of the bond is $1,469.68.

If an individual purchased the bond at a price of $1,494.93 and then sold it one year later with interest rates still at 5 percent, she would realize a capital loss of $1,494.93 – $1,469.68 = $25.25. The rate of return on the bond over the year consists of an *interest*, or *current*, *yield* plus a *capital gains yield*:

Key Equation 6.1: Current Yield on a Bond

Current yield = Annual coupon payment ÷ Beginning price
= $100 ÷ $1,494.93 = 0.0669 = 6.69%.

Key Equation 6.2: Capital Gains Yield on a Bond

Capital gains yield = Annual capital gain (or loss) ÷ Beginning price
= –$25.25 ÷ $1,494.93 = –0.0169 = –1.69%.

Key Equation 6.3: Rate of Return (Total Yield) on a Bond

$$\text{Rate of return (Total yield)} = \text{Total dollar return} \div \text{Beginning price}$$
$$= (\$100 - \$25.25) \div \$1{,}494.93$$
$$= \$74.75 \div \$1{,}494.93 = 0.0500 = 5.00\%.$$

Or,

$$\text{Total yield} = \text{Current yield} + \text{Capital gains yield}$$
$$= 6.69\% + (-1.69\%) = 5.00\%.$$

Had interest rates risen from 10 percent to 15 percent during the first year after issue rather than fallen, the value of Big Sky's bonds would have declined to \$713.78 at the end of the first year. If interest rates held constant at 15 percent, the bond would have a value of \$720.84 at the end of the second year, so the total yield to investors during year 2 would be

Current yield	= \$100 ÷ \$713.78	= 0.1401	= 14.01%.
Capital gains yield	= \$7.06 ÷ \$713.78	= 0.0099	= 0.99%.
Rate of return, or total yield	= \$107.06 ÷ \$713.78	= 0.1500	= 15.00%.

Exhibit 6.5 graphs the values of the Big Sky bond over time, assuming that interest rates will remain constant at 10 percent, fall to 5 percent and remain at that level, and rise to 15 percent and remain constant at that level. The exhibit illustrates the following important points:

- Whenever the required rate of return on a bond equals its coupon rate, the bond will sell at its par value.
- When interest rates—and hence required rates of return—fall after a bond is issued, the bond's value rises above its par value and the bond sells at a *premium*.
- When interest rates—and hence required rates of return—rise after a bond is issued, the bond's value falls below its par value and the bond sells at a *discount*.
- Bond prices on outstanding issues and interest rates are inversely related. Increasing rates lead to falling prices, and decreasing rates lead to increasing prices.
- The price of a bond will always approach its par value as its maturity date approaches, provided the issuer does not default on the bond.

EXHIBIT 6.5 Time Path of the Value of a 15-Year, 10 Percent Coupon, $1,000 Par Value Bond When Interest Rates Are 5 Percent, 10 Percent, and 15 Percent

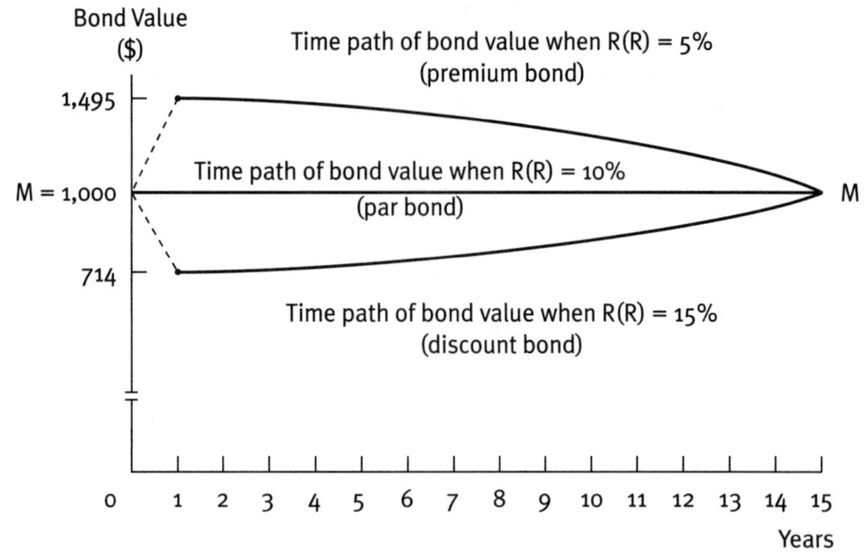

Year	Bond Value at R(R) = 5%	R(R) = 10%	R(R) = 15%
0	—	$1,000.00	—
1	$1,494.93	1,000.00	$ 713.78
2	1,469.68	1,000.00	720.84
3	1,443.16	1,000.00	728.97
.	.	.	.
.	.	.	.
.	.	.	.
13	1,092.97	1,000.00	918.71
14	1,047.62	1,000.00	956.52
15	1,000.00	1,000.00	1,000.00

Note, however, that interest rates do **not** remain constant over time, so in reality, a bond's price fluctuates as interest rates in the economy fluctuate and as the bond's term to maturity decreases. Still, regardless of interest rate movements, a bond's value will approach its par value as the maturity date gets closer and closer.

Zero-Coupon Bonds

Zero-coupon bonds pay no interest at all during the life of the bond, so an investor's cash flows consist solely of the return of par value at maturity. Because there are no interest payments, when the bond is issued, its value is much less than par value, so the bond originally sells at a discount. Thus, zero-coupon bonds also are called ***original issue discount bonds.***

Zero-coupon bonds are valued in the same way as regular (coupon) bonds, only there are no coupon payments to contribute to the bond's value. For example, assume that Big Sky's 15-year bond issue discussed in the previous section was a zero-coupon bond. Assuming a 10 percent required rate of return, the bond's value would be $239.39:

	A	B	C	D
1				
2	10.0%	Rate	Interest rate	
3				
4	$ –	Value 1	Year 1 coupon	
5	$ –	Value 1	Year 2 coupon	
6	$ –	Value 1	Year 3 coupon	
7	$ –	Value 1	Year 4 coupon	
8	$ –	Value 1	Year 5 coupon	
9	$ –	Value 1	Year 6 coupon	
10	$ –	Value 1	Year 7 coupon	
11	$ –	Value 1	Year 8 coupon	
12	$ –	Value 1	Year 9 coupon	
13	$ –	Value 1	Year 10 coupon	
14	$ –	Value 1	Year 11 coupon	
15	$ –	Value 1	Year 12 coupon	
16	$ –	Value 1	Year 13 coupon	
17	$ –	Value 1	Year 14 coupon	
18	$1,000	Value 1	Year 15 coupon + Principal	
19				
20	$239.39	=NPV(A2,A4:A18) (entered into cell A20)		

Note that we zeroed out all cash flows except the principal payment at maturity. (Because cells A4 through A18 were formatted as accounting values, zeroes are displayed as dashes.)

Zero-coupon bonds have some advantages as well as disadvantages when compared to coupon bonds. The primary advantage to issuers is that no payments have to be made to bondholders until the maturity date. As we will explain in a later section, the primary advantage to buyers is that there are no coupon payments to reinvest.

Yield to Maturity

On the web at: *ache.org/HAP/PinkSong8e*

Up to this point, a bond's required rate of return and cash flows have been used to determine its value. However, investors' required rates of return on securities generally are not listed in either the print or online media. But current prices can be easily found—at least on bonds that are actively traded—by looking in many newspapers, including the *Wall Street Journal*, or online. Suppose that the Big Sky bond had 14 years remaining to maturity and the bond was selling at a price of $1,494.93. What percentage (rate of) return, or *yield to maturity* (*YTM*), would be earned if the bond was bought at this price and held to maturity assuming no default occurs? To find the answer, 5 percent, use a spreadsheet as follows:

	A	B	C	D
1				
2	($1,494.93)	Values	Bond price	
3	$100	Values	Year 1 coupon	
4	$100	Values	Year 2 coupon	
5	$100	Values	Year 3 coupon	
6	$100	Values	Year 4 coupon	
7	$100	Values	Year 5 coupon	
8	$100	Values	Year 6 coupon	
9	$100	Values	Year 7 coupon	
10	$100	Values	Year 8 coupon	
11	$100	Values	Year 9 coupon	
12	$100	Values	Year 10 coupon	
13	$100	Values	Year 11 coupon	
14	$100	Values	Year 12 coupon	
15	$100	Values	Year 13 coupon	
16	$1,100	Values	Year 14 coupon + Principal	
17				
18	5.0%	=IRR(A2:A16) (entered into cell A18)		

Note that the IRR function is used to calculate YTM. The YTM can be thought of as the expected rate of return on the bond.[3] It is similar to the total rate of return calculated in the previous section. For a bond that sells at par, the YTM consists entirely of an interest yield, but if the bond sells at a discount or premium, the YTM consists of the current yield plus a positive or negative capital gains yield.

Yield to Call

On the web at: *ache.org/HAP/PinkSong8e*

A callable bond is one that can be *called* (redeemed) by the issuer prior to maturity. Because the maturity of the bond is shortened if it is called, callable bonds have both a YTM and a *yield to call (YTC)*. The YTC is similar to the YTM, except that it carries an assumption that the bond will be called. Thus, the YTC is calculated like the YTM, except that *N* reflects the number of years until the bond will be called, as opposed to years to maturity, and *M* reflects the call price rather than the maturity value.

For example, suppose the Big Sky bond had ten years of call protection when it was issued. There are now nine years to the date of first call, and the bond is selling at a price of $1,494.93. Furthermore, there is a $100 call premium that must be paid by the borrower if the issue is called at the earliest possible date. What YTC would be earned if the bond were bought at this price and held to first call, at which time it was redeemed for $1,000 + $100 = $1,100? The answer is 4.2 percent:

	A	B	C	D
1				
2	($1,494.93)	Values	Bond price	
3	$100	Values	Year 1 coupon	
4	$100	Values	Year 2 coupon	
5	$100	Values	Year 3 coupon	
6	$100	Values	Year 4 coupon	
7	$100	Values	Year 5 coupon	
8	$100	Values	Year 6 coupon	
9	$100	Values	Year 7 coupon	
10	$100	Values	Year 8 coupon	
11	$1,200	Values	Year 9 coupon + Principal + Call premium	
12				
13	4.20%	=IRR(A2:A11) (entered into cell A13)		

Note that cell A11 contains $1,200: the par value of the bond ($1,000) plus the $100 call premium plus the $100 coupon payment for year 9.

A question now faces potential investors in this bond: Should they expect to earn its 5.0 percent YTM or its 4.2 percent YTC? Of course, the answer depends on whether the bond will be called. There is no way of knowing with certainty today when, or even if, the bond will be called. We do know that the bond is selling at a large premium now, and if interest rates do not change much over the next nine years, the bond will likely be selling for more than $1,100 when first callable. If that is the situation, it is likely that the bond will be called, and hence the YTC is probably a better estimate of the expected rate of return than is the YTM. On the other hand, if the bond is currently selling at a discount, and interest rates are expected to be relatively constant over the next nine years, it is likely that the bond will not be called and thus the YTM would be the appropriate measure of the return on the bond. Unfortunately, no one knows today what interest rates will be nine years in the future.

Bond Values with Semiannual Coupons

Virtually all bonds issued in the United States pay interest semiannually, or every six months. To apply the preceding valuation concepts to semiannual bonds, we must modify the bond valuation procedures as follows:

On the web at: *ache.org/HAP/PinkSong8e*

- The annual interest payment, INT, must be divided by two to determine the dollar amount paid **each six months**.
- The number of years to maturity, N, must be multiplied by two to determine the number of **semiannual interest periods**.

- The annual required rate of return, R(R), must be divided by two to determine the **semiannual required rate of return**.

For an illustration of the use of the semiannual bond valuation model, assume that the Big Sky bonds pay $50 every six months rather than $100 annually. Thus, each interest payment is only half as large, but there are twice as many of them. When the going rate of interest is 5 percent annually, which translates to 2.5 percent semiannually, the value of Big Sky's bonds with 14 years (28 semiannual periods) left to maturity is $1,499.12:

	A	B	C	D
1				
2	28	Nper	Number of periods	
3	$50.00	Pmt	Payment (coupon amount)	
4	$1,000.00	Fv	Future value (principal)	
5	2.5%	Rate	Interest rate	
6				
7				
8	$1,499.12	= –PV(A5,A2,A3,A4) (entered into cell A8)		
9				
10				

Note several points regarding this spreadsheet calculation. First, we could have used the NPV function, as we did in the previous bond valuation examples. However, to do so we would require a range with 28 cell entries for coupon payments, so we elected to use the Pv function to avoid all these entries. Second, when we use the Pv function for bond valuation, function wizard entries include both Pmt and Fv because bonds have both coupon payments and a maturity (principal) payment. Finally, we placed a minus sign in front of the function name (Pv) so that the value would be displayed as a positive number.

Similarly, if the bond were selling for $1,400 with 14 years to maturity, its YTM would be 5.80 percent:

	A	B	C	D
1				
2	28	Nper	Number of periods	
3	$(1,400.00)	Pv	Present value (bond price)	
4	$50.00	Pmt	Payment (coupon amount)	
5	$1,000.00	Fv	Future value (principal)	
6				
7				
8	2.90%	=RATE(A2,A4,A3,A5) (entered into cell A8)		
9				
10				

Here, we used the RATE function to calculate the YTM. The value shown in cell A8, 2.90 percent, is the **periodic (semiannual) YTM**, so we must multiply it by two to get the annual YTM. The effective annual YTM on the bond is somewhat greater than the 5.80 percent that was calculated.[4] However, it is convention in the bond markets to quote all rates on a stated (annual) basis, so the procedures outlined in this section are correct when bonds—all of which have semiannual coupons—are being compared. However, when the returns on securities that have different periodic payments are being compared, all rates of return should be expressed as effective annual rates.

Interest Rate Risk

Interest rates change over time, which causes two types of investment risk generally classified as *interest rate risk.* First, an increase in interest rates causes the values of outstanding bonds to decline. Because interest rates can rise, bondholders face the risk of losses on their holdings. This risk is called *price risk.* Second, many bondholders buy bonds to build funds for future use. These bondholders reinvest the interest and principal cash flows as they receive them. If interest rates fall, bondholders will earn a lower rate on the reinvested cash flows, which will have a negative impact on the future value of their holdings. This risk is called *reinvestment rate risk.*

Price Risk

For an illustration of price risk, suppose you bought some of Big Sky's 10 percent bonds when they were issued at a price of $1,000. As illustrated earlier, if interest rates rise, the value of the bonds will fall. An investor's exposure to price risk depends on the maturity of the bonds. Exhibit 6.6, which shows the values of 1-year and 14-year bonds at several different market interest rates, illustrates price risk. Notice how much more sensitive the value of the 14-year bond is to changes in interest rates. For bonds with similar coupons, the longer the maturity of the bond, the greater its price change in response to a given change in interest rates. Thus, investors in bonds with longer maturities are exposed to more price risk.[5]

Reinvestment Rate Risk

Although a 1-year bond exposes the buyer to less price risk than a 14-year bond does, the 1-year bond carries more reinvestment rate risk. Here's why: If the holding period is more than one year, investing in a 1-year bond means that the principal and interest will have to be reinvested at the end of the first year. If interest rates fall, the return earned during the second year will be less than the return earned during the first year. Reinvestment rate risk is the second dimension of interest rate risk.

EXHIBIT 6.6
Value of Long- and Short-Term 10 Percent Annual Coupon Rate Bonds at Different Market Interest Rates

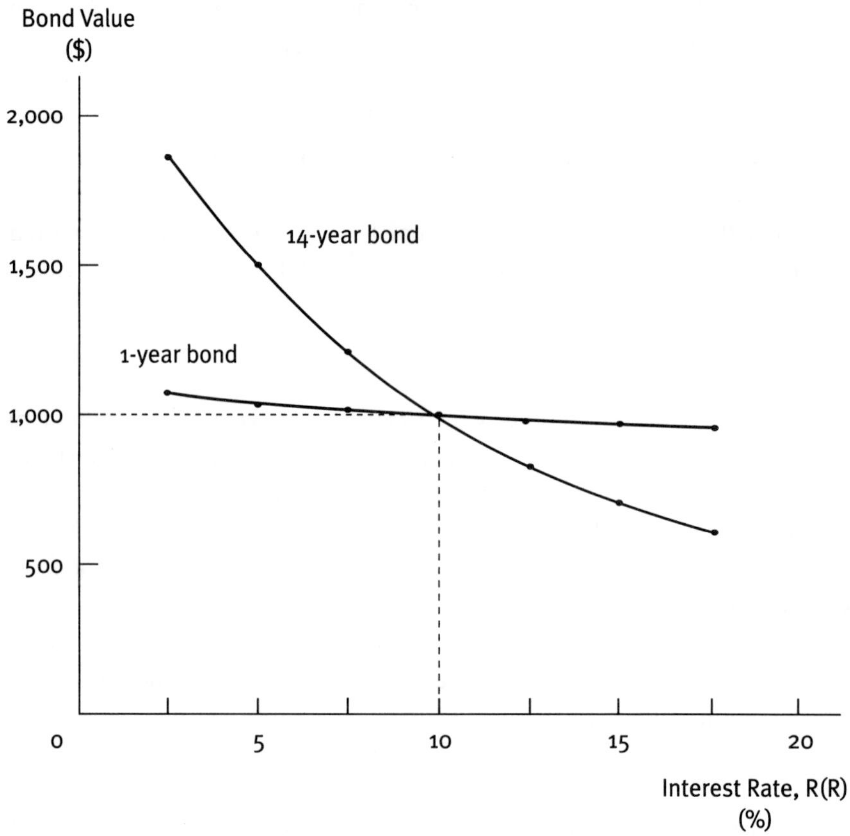

Current Market Interest Rate, R(R)	*Bond Value*	
	1-Year Bond	*14-Year Bond*
2.5%	$1,073.17	$1,876.82
5.0	1,047.62	1,494.93
7.5	1,023.26	1,212.23
10.0	1,000.00	1,000.00
12.5	977.78	838.45
15.0	956.52	713.78
17.5	936.17	616.25

Minimizing Interest Rate Risk

Clearly, bond investors face both price risk and reinvestment rate risk as a result of interest rate fluctuations over time. Which risk is most meaningful to a particular investor depends on the circumstances, but in general, interest rate risk is reduced by matching the maturity of the bond with the anticipated *investment horizon*. For example, suppose Hilldale Community Hospital received a $5 million contribution and plans to use it in five years to build a new neonatal care center. By investing the contribution in five-year bonds, the hospital would minimize its interest rate risk because it would be matching its investment horizon. Price risk would be minimized because the bond will mature in five years; Hilldale will receive par value regardless of the level of interest rates at that time. Reinvestment rate risk is also minimized because only the interest on the bond would have to be reinvested, which is a less risky situation than if both principal and interest had to be reinvested. Note that if Hilldale invested in a zero-coupon bond, reinvestment rate risk would be eliminated. Price risk, however, can never be completely eliminated, in the sense that a forced sale of a bond prior to maturity in a higher interest rate environment would result in a loss of principal. Interest rate risk is but one of many financial risks facing healthcare businesses. Fortunately, various techniques can be used to mitigate such risks. We discuss financial risk management in some detail in chapter 18 (Financial Risk Management), which is available exclusively online at ache.org/HAP/PinkSong8e.

How Safe Are Treasury Bonds?

In the popular press, Treasury bonds (T-bonds) are commonly referred to as being ultrasafe. The party line goes something like this: "The US Treasury issues various securities of differing maturities. Like any widely traded security, you can buy them when they are issued and hold them to maturity or buy and sell them in the market at any time. Because Treasury securities are backed by the US government, they are the ultimate safe investment."

But are T-bonds, which have the longest maturities of all Treasury securities, really the ultimate safe investment? It all depends on how you define the word *safe*. Sure, they are safe from default risk, but they carry a great deal of price risk. To illustrate, in the summer of 2018, the interest rate on 30-year T-bonds was roughly 3 percent. If you bought a 30-year bond then at its $1,000 par value and interest rates rose to 6 percent in 2019, your bond, with 29 years left to maturity, would be worth only $590.03. If interest rates continued to rise, to 8 percent in 2020, the bond, with 28 years left to maturity, would be worth only $445.50. (In 1981, the rate on 30-year T-bonds was more than 13 percent, so the numbers in this illustration are in the realm of possibility.) Sure, T-bonds are safe from default risk, but they carry a high level of price risk.

SELF-TEST QUESTIONS

1. How are bonds valued?
2. What is a zero-coupon bond?
3. What is meant by a bond's YTM? By its YTC?
4. Differentiate price risk from reinvestment rate risk.

Chapter Key Concepts

This chapter provides an overview of debt financing, including discussion on the determination of interest rates and the characteristics of the major types of debt securities. Here are its key concepts:

- Any business must have assets to operate; to acquire assets, the business must raise *capital*. Capital comes in two basic forms: (1) *debt* and (2) *equity* (or *fund*) capital.
- Capital is allocated through the price system; a price is charged to "rent" money. Lenders charge *interest* on funds they lend, while equity investors receive *dividends* and *capital gains* in return for letting the firm use their money.
- *Term loans* and *bonds* are long-term debt contracts under which a borrower agrees to make a series of interest and principal payments on specific dates to the lender. A term loan is generally sold to one, or a few, lenders, while a bond is typically offered to the public and sold to many different investors.
- Many different types of bonds exist, including *Treasury*, *corporate*, and *municipal bonds*. Prevailing interest rates, the bond's riskiness, and tax consequences determine the return required on each type of bond.
- *Revenue bonds* are municipal bonds that pledge the revenues derived from projects, such as roads or bridges, airports, water and sewage systems, and not-for-profit healthcare facilities, as security for the bonds.
- Bonds are assigned *ratings* that reflect their probability of going into default. The higher a bond's rating, and the greater the

(continued)

(continued from previous page)

probability of recovering bondholder capital if default should occur, the lower its interest rate.

- The *interest rate* on a debt security is composed of the real risk-free rate (RRF) plus premiums that reflect inflation (IP), default risk (DRP), liquidity (LP), price risk (PRP), and call risk (CRP): Interest rate = RRF + IP + DRP + LP + PRP + CRP.
- The relationship between the yields on securities and the securities' maturities is known as the *term structure of interest rates*. The *yield curve* is a graph of this relationship.
- Debt financing has several advantages and disadvantages when compared to equity financing. The primary advantages are fixed payments, lower costs, and no control rights, whereas the primary disadvantage is the additional risk that debt financing brings to the business.
- Bonds call for the payment of a specific amount of *interest* for a specific number of years, and for the *repayment of par* on the bond's maturity date. Like the value of most assets, a bond's value is simply the present value of the expected cash flow stream.
- The annual rate of return on a bond consists of an *interest*, or *current*, *yield* plus a *capital gains yield*. If we assume that interest rates are constant, a bond selling at a *discount* yields positive capital gains, whereas a bond selling at a *premium* yields negative capital gains.
- A bond's *yield to maturity (YTM)* is the rate of return earned on a bond if it is held to maturity and no default occurs. The YTM for a bond that sells at par consists entirely of an interest yield, but if the bond sells at a discount or premium, the YTM consists of the current yield plus a positive or negative capital gains yield.
- Bondholders face *price risk* because bond values change when interest rates change. In general, the longer the maturity of the bonds, the greater the price risk.
- Bondholders face *reinvestment rate risk* when the investment horizon exceeds the maturity of the bond issue.

Debt is a major source of capital for health services organizations, so healthcare managers must be familiar with debt concepts. In chapter 7, we discuss equity financing, the second major type of capital.

Chapter Models, Problems, and Minicases

The following ancillary resources in spreadsheet format are available for this chapter:

- A chapter model that shows how to perform many of the calculations described in the chapter
- Problems that test your ability to perform the calculations
- A minicase that is more complicated than the problems and tests your ability to perform the calculations in preparation for a case

These resources can be accessed online at ache.org/HAP/PinkSong8e.

Selected Cases

There are no cases that focus on the institutional details of debt financing. However, the following case in *Cases in Healthcare Finance*, sixth edition, can help you understand bond valuation: Case 13: Pacific Healthcare (A), which focuses on the valuation of corporate bonds as opposed to the managerial decisions inherent in floating a bond issue. Another case that focuses on related material is Case 14: Senior Care Enterprises, which focuses on the bond refunding decision. (Note that bond refunding is covered in the chapter 6 supplement.)

Selected Bibliography

Arduino, K. 2018. "Healthcare Capital Markets Outlook: Short-Term Opportunities Versus Long-Term Uncertainty." *Healthcare Financial Management* 72 (5): 36–43.

———. 2017. "Amid Change, Focus on Nimbleness and Affordability." *Healthcare Financial Management* 71 (2): 58–59.

———. 2017. "Time to Revisit Private Placement Debt." *Healthcare Financial Management* 71 (10): 92–93.

Bruton, P. W. 2018. "The Rise, Fall, and Possible Return of Variable-Rate Demand Bonds." *Healthcare Financial Management* 72 (5): 50–54.

Healthcare Financial Management Association. 2018. "Optimizing Capital Structure Decisions Under the New Tax Law." *Healthcare Financial Management* 72 (8): A1–A4.

Jordahl, E. A. 2017. "Contemplating the Case for Terminating Swaps." Healthcare Financial Management Association. Published December 1. www.hfma.org/Content.aspx?id=57108.

Lalangas, E., D. Kroll, and A. Carlson. 2018. "The Tax Cuts and Jobs Act Takeaways for Healthcare Finance Leaders." *Healthcare Financial Management* 72 (4): 28–31.

Sahrbeck, J. B. 2015. "Timing Tax-Exempt Bond Refunds." *Healthcare Financial Management* 69 (9): 112, 114.

Selected Websites

The following websites pertain to the content of this chapter:

- For term structure data in the form of a table and a graph of the yield curves for Treasury and municipal securities, see www.bloomberg.com/markets/rates-bonds.
- For current (updated daily) interest rate information, see the Federal Reserve site at www.federalreserve.gov/releases/h15/. This site includes data on commercial paper, corporate bonds, and other rates in addition to the rates on Treasury securities.
- The S&P website provides a great deal of information on bond ratings. See www.standardandpoors.com.

Notes

1. The *prime rate* is the base rate that banks charge on loans to businesses. Theoretically, the prime rate is set separately by each bank, but in practice all banks follow the lead of the major New York City banks, so there is usually a single prime rate in the United States. The prime rate changes—sometimes rapidly—as economic conditions (primarily inflation expectations) change. In mid-2018, the prime rate was 5.25 percent.
2. Treasury bonds, or T-bonds, have original maturities at issue of more than ten years. The Treasury also issues notes, called *T-notes*, which have maturities of more than one year (up to ten years), and bills, called *T-bills*, which have maturities of one year or less. Note that the names of Treasury securities are fixed at issue even though their maturities shorten over time. Thus, a 30-year T-bond that was issued

25 years ago now has only five years remaining to maturity, but it is still classified as a bond, not a note.

3. If the probability of default on the bond is anything other than zero, the expected rate of return on the bond is less than the YTM. Also, the calculation of YTM assumes that the coupon payments are reinvested at the YTM rate. Thus, if interest rates over the life of the bond are above the YTM, the realized rate of return will be higher than the YTM. Similarly, if interest rates over time are less than the YTM, the realized return will be less than the YTM.
4. The effective annual YTM is $(1.029)^2 - 1.0 = 1.0588 - 1.0 = 0.0588 =$ 5.88%, as compared to the stated rate of 5.80%.
5. In reality, price risk is more related to a debt security's duration than to its maturity. Duration, which can be thought of as the average maturity of a debt issue—including both interest and principal payments—is discussed in online chapter 18.

Integrative Application

The Problem

QuickCare, a not-for-profit system that owns and operates 34 walk-in clinics in central Florida, is planning to build and operate 10 more clinics over the next few years. They estimate that land, construction, and start-up costs for the clinics will be $100 million, and they plan to raise the necessary funds by issuing tax-exempt (municipal) bonds. Furthermore, their investment bankers believe that two maturities are most attractive at this time: 5-year bonds that would require a fixed interest rate of 3.5 percent and 20-year bonds with a fixed rate of 5 percent. You have been asked by the CEO to make a recommendation as to which maturity to use. Also, he is interested in investing personally in the bonds and wants to know what would happen to the value of each bond if interest rates rise by 1 percentage point during the first year of issue and the bonds had remaining maturities of 4 years and 19 years. (Experts predict that it is more likely that interest rates will increase in the future rather than decrease.) Finally, he would like to know what total return he would earn during the first year if the interest rate increase took place. Perform the analysis on a per bond basis assuming a par value of $1,000. Also, for convenience, assume the bonds have annual coupons.

The Analysis

First, calculate the value of each bond after one year if interest rates increase to 4.5 percent on the 5-year bond and 6.0 percent on the 20-year bond.

5-Year Bond

	A	B	C	D
1				
2	4	Nper	Number of payments	
3	$35.00	Pmt	Payment (coupon amount)	
4	$1,000.00	Fv	Future value (principal)	
5	4.5%	Rate	Interest rate	
6				
7				
8	$964.12	= –PV(A5,A2,A3,A4) (entered into cell A8)		
9				
10				

20-Year Bond

	A	B	C	D
1				
2	19	Nper	Number of payments	
3	$50.00	Pmt	Payment (coupon amount)	
4	$1,000.00	Fv	Future value (principal)	
5	6.0%	Rate	Interest rate	
6				
7				
8	$888.42	= –PV(A5,A2,A3,A4) (entered into cell A8)		
9				

These values ($964.12 for the 5-year bond and $888.42 for the 20-year bond) illustrate price risk—when interest rates rise in the economy, the values of existing bonds decline. Now, consider the total returns.

5-Year Bond

Current yield = Annual coupon payment ÷ Beginning price

= $35 ÷ $1,000.00 = 0.0350 = 3.50%.

Capital gains yield = Annual capital gain (or loss) ÷ Beginning price

= –$35.88 ÷ $1,000.00 = –0.0359 = –3.59%.

Rate of return (Total yield) = Total dollar return ÷ Beginning price

= ($35.00 – $35.88) ÷ $1,000.00

= –$0.88 ÷ $1,000.00 = –0.0009 = –0.09%.

Or,

Total yield = Current yield + Capital gains yield

= 3.50% + (–3.59%) = –0.09%.

20-Year Bond

Current yield = Annual coupon payment ÷ Beginning price

= $50 ÷ $1,000.00 = 0.0500 = 5.00%.

Capital gains yield = Annual capital gain (or loss) ÷ Beginning price

= –$111.58 ÷ $1,000.00 = –0.1116 = –11.16%.

Total yield = Current yield + Capital gains yield

= 5.00% + (–11.16%) = –6.16%.

The Decision

First, consider the maturity decision for QuickCare. The business would minimize its financing risk by using the longer-term (20-year) bond because it better matches the maturity (useful life) of the assets being financed. Also, with interest rates expected to increase, a longer-term issue would lock in the current low rates. Thus, the board agreed to use the 20-year bonds to finance the new clinics.

Now, what about the CEO's personal investment decision? If interest rates increase, the 5-year bond would have a total loss of 0.09 percent during the first year, while the loss on the 20-year bond would be 6.16 percent. Furthermore, if interest rates continued to increase, the 20-year bond would be subjected to larger future losses. The shorter-term (five-year) bond, on the other hand, would mature in five years, and the principal could be reinvested at a higher interest rate. Thus, the CEO probably would be better off investing in short-term bonds. Of course, this advice assumes that the expert predictions are correct, but they are often wrong. ■

CHAPTER

7

EQUITY FINANCING

Learning Objectives

After studying this chapter, readers should be able to

- explain the rights and privileges associated with common stock ownership,
- discuss the different methods by which new common stock is sold,
- describe the market for common stock,
- explain how not-for-profit businesses obtain "equity" financing,
- value stocks and calculate their expected rates of return, and
- explain the concept of market efficiency and its implications for investors and managers.

Introduction

Debt financing concepts were discussed in chapter 6, including how interest rates are set in the economy, types of debt, and how various debt features affect the interest rate on any particular issue. The second major source of capital for healthcare businesses is *equity financing*. Proprietorships and partnerships raise equity capital through owner contributions, while for-profit corporations obtain equity financing through the sale of stock. For-profit businesses also obtain equity capital by retaining earnings. Not-for-profit corporations raise equivalent financing—sometimes called *fund capital*—through contributions and grants and by retaining earnings. From a financial perspective, common stock and fund financing serve the same basic purpose, so the generic term *equity* is used to refer to all nondebt capital, regardless of a business's ownership.

In this chapter, we discuss the same general issues that were presented in chapter 6 but focus on equity financing. Like debt financing, there are many different types of equity with many different features. If we were to discuss all of these features, along with the methods for selling stock to investors, this chapter would be too long to be manageable. Thus, it focuses on key issues, while the chapter 7 online supplement contains material that is useful and relevant but not essential to understanding the fundamentals of equity financing.

Rights and Privileges of Common Stockholders

Common stockholders are the owners of for-profit corporations and as such have certain rights and privileges. The most important of these rights and privileges are discussed in this section.

Claim on Residual Earnings

The reason most people buy common stocks is to gain the right to a proportionate share of a corporation's residual earnings. A corporation's net income, which is the residual earnings after all expenses have been paid, belongs to the common stockholders. For many corporations—particularly mature ones—some portion of net income will be paid out to common stockholders as ***dividends***. Although the predominant timing of dividend payments is quarterly, some corporations are now changing to annual dividends to reduce the administrative costs associated with such payments. The portion of net income that is retained in the business will be invested in new assets, which presumably will increase the business's earnings over time and hence contribute to even greater dividends in the future.

An increasing dividend stream means that the stock will be more valuable in the future than it is today because dividends will be higher—say, in five years—than they are today. Thus, common stockholders typically expect to be able to sell the stock they purchased at some time in the future at a price higher than they paid for it and hence realize a ***capital gain***. For an illustration of the payment of dividends, consider exhibit 7.1, which lists the annual per share dividend payment and earnings, as well as the average annual stock price, for Big Sky Healthcare from 2008 through 2018. Over the ten growth periods, Big Sky's dividend grew by 275 percent, or at an average annual growth rate of 14.1 percent. At the same time, the firm's stock price grew by 247 percent, which equates to an average annual growth rate of 13.2 percent.

Note that Big Sky's dividend growth was not a constant 14.1 percent each year. Many corporations hold the dividend constant for several years to allow earnings to climb to a point where they can support a higher dividend payment. For example, Big Sky kept its dividend at $0.23 a share from 2009 through 2011, while earnings per share were flat at about $0.55.

In general, managers are reluctant to reduce dividends because investors interpret lower dividends as a signal that management forecasts poor times ahead. Thus, when Big Sky saw its earnings per share tumble from $1.25 in 2014 to $0.45 in 2015, it maintained its $0.58 per share dividend.

EXHIBIT 7.1
Big Sky Healthcare: Dividends, Earnings, and Stock Price, 2008–2018

Year	*Annual per Share Dividend ($)*	*Annual per Share Earnings ($)*	*Average Annual Stock Price ($)*
2008	0.20	0.48	7.70
2009	0.23	0.55	10.95
2010	0.23	0.52	11.00
2011	0.23	0.58	10.40
2012	0.48	0.85	15.30
2013	0.52	1.10	18.70
2014	0.58	1.25	20.60
2015	0.58	0.45	19.50
2016	0.65	1.35	23.20
2017	0.70	1.50	24.40
2018	0.75	1.55	26.70

Big Sky was able to pay a cash dividend that exceeded earnings in 2015 because the firm's cash flow, which is roughly equal to net income plus depreciation, easily supported the dividend. When earnings picked up again in 2016, Big Sky increased its dividend to $0.65.

Over the entire period, Big Sky proved to be an excellent investment for stockholders. For example, assume that you bought the stock for $7.70 in 2008, received a $0.20 dividend payment, and then sold the stock one year later for $10.95. For simplicity, assume that the dividend payment was paid at the end of the one-year holding period rather than quarterly. Thus, you paid $7.70, and one year later you received $10.95 + $0.20 = $11.15. The total return earned was Total profit ÷ Amount of investment = ($11.15 − $7.70) ÷ $7.70 = 0.448 = 44.8%. Note, however, that investors who bought Big Sky's stock in 2010 or 2014 and then sold it one year later would have had a capital loss—rather than a capital gain—on the sale. Of course, they would have received quarterly dividends over the one-year holding period. We will have much more to say about stock valuation later in the chapter. Also, for more information about corporate dividend policy as well as other distributions, see chapter 17 (Distributions to Owners: Bonuses, Dividends, and Repurchases), which is available exclusively online at ache.org/HAP/PinkSong8e.

Control of the Firm

Common stockholders have the right to elect the board of directors, who in turn elect the officers who will manage the corporation. In small, privately owned corporations, the major stockholders typically assume all of the management leadership positions. In large, publicly owned firms, managers typically have some stock, but their personal holdings are insufficient to allow them to exercise voting control. Thus, the management of most publicly owned corporations can be removed by the stockholders if they decide a management team is not effective.

Various state and federal laws stipulate how stockholder control is to be exercised. First, corporations must hold an election of directors periodically—usually once per year, at an annual meeting. In many corporations, one-third of the directors are elected each year for a three-year term. Each share of stock has one vote; thus, the owner of 1,000 shares has 1,000 votes.[1] Stockholders can appear at the annual meeting and vote in person, but typically they transfer their right to vote to a second party by means of a *proxy*. Management always solicits stockholders' proxies and usually gets them. However, if the common stockholders are dissatisfied with current management, an outside group may solicit the proxies in an effort to overthrow management and take control of the business. This is known as a *proxy fight*. In addition, one corporation can take over another by purchasing a majority of the outstanding stock. A *hostile takeover* occurs when such a control change takes place without approval by the board of directors of the business being bought.

Obviously, managers who do not have majority control are concerned about proxy fights and hostile takeovers. One of the most common tactics to thwart hostile takeovers is to place a *poison pill* provision in the corporate charter. A poison pill typically permits stockholders of the corporation that is taken over to buy shares of the resulting business entity at a greatly reduced price. Obviously, shareholders at the acquiring business do not want an outside group to get bargain-priced stock, so such provisions effectively stop hostile takeovers. Although poison pill provisions of this type might appear to be illegal, they have withstood many court challenges. The ultimate effect of poison pills is to force acquiring firms to get the approval of the board of directors of the *target* firm prior to the takeover. Although the stated reason for poison pills is to protect shareholders against a hostile takeover at a price that is too low, many people believe that they protect entrenched managements as least as much as stockholders.

The Preemptive Right

Common stockholders often have the right—called the *preemptive right*—to purchase any new shares sold by the corporation. In some states, the preemptive right is mandatory; in others, it can be specified in the corporate charter.

The purpose of the preemptive right is twofold. First, it protects current stockholders' position of control. Without this safeguard, the management of a corporation under criticism from stockholders could secure its position by issuing and then purchasing a large number of additional shares.

Management would thereby gain a controlling position in the corporation and frustrate the outside stockholders.

Second, and more important, it protects stockholders against dilution of value. For example, suppose HealthOne HMO has 1,000 shares outstanding at a price of $100 per share, so the total market value of the firm is $100,000. If an additional 1,000 shares were sold at $50 a share, bringing in an additional $50,000, the total market value of HealthOne's stock would theoretically increase to $150,000. When the new total market value is divided by the new number of shares outstanding, the value per share drops to $75. HealthOne's original stockholders would lose $25 per share, and the new stockholders would realize an instant profit of $25 per share. Thus, selling common stock at a price below the current market price dilutes its value and, at the same time, transfers wealth from the current stockholders to those who purchase the new shares. The preemptive right prevents such wealth transfers.

SELF-TEST QUESTIONS

1. In what forms do common stock investors receive returns?
2. How do common stockholders exercise their right of control?
3. What is the preemptive right, and what is its purpose?

Selling New Common Stock

New stock usually is sold to raise equity capital—however, new stock sometimes is issued without raising new capital. For example, new stock may be distributed to current shareholders when a portion of the company, usually a subsidiary, is divested (given) to shareholders in a *spin-off*. When stock is issued to raise new equity capital, the new shares may be sold in one of six ways:

1. On a pro rata basis to existing stockholders through a rights offering
2. Through investment bankers to the general public in a public offering
3. To a single buyer, or a very small number of buyers, in a private placement
4. To employees through an employee stock purchase plan
5. Through a dividend reinvestment plan
6. Through a direct purchase plan

The following sections provide more information on these methods.

Rights Offering

As discussed earlier, common stockholders often have the preemptive right to purchase any additional shares sold by the firm. If the preemptive right is contained in the firm's charter, the firm **must** offer any newly issued common stock to existing stockholders. If the charter does not prescribe a preemptive right, the firm can choose to sell to its existing stockholders or to the public at large. If it sells to the existing stockholders, the stock sale is called a *rights offering*. Each stockholder is issued an option to buy a certain number of new shares at a price below the existing market price, and the terms of the option are listed on a certificate called a *stock purchase right*, or simply a *right*. If a stockholder does not wish to purchase additional shares in the firm, he can sell the rights to some other person who does want to buy the stock.

Public Offering

If the preemptive right exists in a firm's charter, it must sell new stock through a rights offering. If the preemptive right does not exist, the firm may choose to offer the new shares to the general public through a *public offering*. We discuss procedures for public offerings in detail in the chapter 7 supplement.

Private Placement

In a *private placement*, also called a *direct placement*, securities are sold to one or just a few investors—generally institutional investors. Private placements are most common with bonds, but they also occur with stocks. The primary advantages of private placements are lower *issuance costs* and greater speed because the shares do not have to go through the Securities and Exchange Commission (SEC) registration process.

The primary disadvantage of a private placement is that, because they have not been registered with the SEC, the securities must be sold initially to an "accredited" investor—usually a bank, insurance company, mutual fund, or pension fund. Furthermore, in the event that the original purchaser wants to sell the securities, they must be sold to other accredited investors, including individuals with a net worth of $1,000,000 or income exceeding $200,000. Because there are thousands of institutions and millions of individuals that are considered by the SEC to be accredited investors, private placements now play an important role in capital acquisition, especially when smaller amounts, say, less than $50 million of capital, are being raised.

To illustrate a private placement, consider the 2018 equity sale by Immune-Onc Therapeutics, a company that is trying to develop new immunotherapeutic treatments for cancer (www.immune-onc.com). Immune-Onc raised more than $33 million in equity from the sale. In total, the company has raised more than $40 million through private unregistered securities offering.

Employee Purchase and Employee Stock Ownership Plans

Many firms have plans that allow employees to purchase stock on favorable terms. First, under executive incentive *stock option plans*, key managers are given options to purchase stock. These managers generally have a direct, material influence on the firm's fortunes, so if they perform well, the stock price will go up and the options will become valuable. Second, there are plans for lower-level employees. For example, Texas HealthPlans, Inc., a regional investor-owned HMO, permits employees who are not participants in its stock option plan to allocate up to 10 percent of their salaries to its *stock purchase plan*, and the funds are then used to buy newly issued shares at 85 percent of the market price on the purchase date. Often the firm's contribution—in this case, the 15 percent discount—is not vested in an employee until five years after the purchase date. Thus, the employee cannot realize the benefit of the firm's contribution without working an additional five years. This type of plan is designed both to improve employee performance and to reduce turnover.

Third, under an *employee stock ownership plan (ESOP)*, the stock is purchased for employees out of a share of the firm's profits. In an ESOP, firms can claim a tax credit equal to a percentage of wages, provided that the funds are used to buy newly issued stock for the benefit of employees. Because ESOPs enjoy favorable tax treatment, and because they are thought to create a more loyal and productive workforce, many firms have created such plans in recent years. Now, around 10,800 firms have ESOPs that cover 14.4 million employees.

Dividend Reinvestment Plan

During the 1970s, many large corporations instituted *dividend reinvestment plans (DRIPs)*, whereby stockholders can automatically reinvest their dividends in the stock of the paying corporation. There are two types of DRIPs: (1) plans that involve only "old" stock that is already outstanding, and (2) plans that involve newly issued stock. In either case, the stockholder must pay income taxes on the amount of the dividends even though stock, rather than cash, is received.

Under both types of DRIPs, stockholders must choose between continuing to receive cash dividends and using the cash dividends to buy more stock in the corporation. Under the "old" stock type of plan, a bank, which acts as a trustee, takes the total funds available for reinvestment from each quarterly dividend, purchases the corporation's stock on the open market, and allocates the shares purchased to the participating stockholders on a pro rata basis. The brokerage costs of buying the shares are low because of volume purchases, so these plans benefit small stockholders who do not need cash for current consumption.

The "new" stock type of DRIP provides for dividends to be invested in newly issued stock; hence, these plans raise new capital for the firm. No fees are charged to participating stockholders, and some firms offer the new stock at a discount of 3 to 5 percent below the prevailing market price. The firms absorb these costs as a trade-off against the issuance costs that would be incurred if the stock were sold through investment bankers rather than through the DRIP.

Direct Purchase Plan

In recent years, many corporations have established ***direct purchase plans***, which allow individual investors to purchase stock directly from the firm. Many of these plans grew out of DRIPs, which were expanded to allow participants to purchase shares in addition to those purchased through the DRIPs. In direct purchase plans, investors usually pay nominal or no brokerage fees, and many plans offer convenient features such as fractional share purchases, automatic purchases by bank debit, and quarterly statements.

Although employee purchase plans, DRIPs, and direct purchase plans are an excellent way for employees and individual investors to purchase stock, they typically do not raise large sums of new capital for the business. Other methods must be used when equity needs are great.

SELF-TEST QUESTIONS

1. What is a rights offering?
2. What is a private placement, and what are its primary advantages over a public offering?
3. Briefly, what is an employee stock purchase plan?
4. What is a dividend reinvestment plan?
5. What is a direct purchase plan?

The Market for Common Stock

Some corporations are so small that their common stock is not actively traded; rather, they are owned by only a few people who usually are the managers. Such firms are said to be ***privately held***, or ***closely held***, and the stock is said to be a ***closely held stock***.

The stocks of most small, publicly owned corporations are not listed on an exchange and hence are called ***unlisted***. Such stocks trade in the *over-the-counter (OTC)* market, which consists of a network of dealers connected by computer. The roughly 10,000 companies that are traded in the OTC market usually are highly risky and typically do not meet the standards required to be accepted on an exchange.

Most large, publicly owned corporations are *listed* on one of the stock exchanges—either the NASDAQ (which formerly stood for the National Association of Securities Dealers Automated Quotations) or the "Big Board" (the New York Stock Exchange [NYSE]). For example, AgeX Therapeutics, Inc. (www.agexinc.com), which develops therapeutics for age-related degenerative disease, was listed on the NYSE in 2014. More than 3,300 stocks are listed on the NASDAQ exchange, while roughly 2,800 are listed on the NYSE, but because of the larger size of its listed firms, the NYSE historically has dominated the NASDAQ in terms of the market value of stocks listed.

To have its stock listed on an exchange, a corporation must meet the exchange's minimum requirements regarding size, number of shareholders, and number of shares held by outsider investors, which is called *float*. Float is important to an exchange because shares held by insiders trade much less frequently than do shares held by outsiders. If the float is small, there will be limited trading, and the exchange, as well as investors, will gain little from the listing.

Many people believe that listing is beneficial to both the firm and its stockholders. Listed firms receive a certain amount of free advertising and publicity, and their listed status may enhance their prestige and reputation. These factors, as well as the safeguards against illegal trading practices, may have a positive impact on sales and stock price. However, improvements in telecommunications and digital processing of trades have lowered transaction costs to the point at which differences between trading on an exchange and on the OTC market are inconsequential. Furthermore, listing on an exchange does not add much cachet to large firms with well-recognized names.

Institutional investors—such as pension funds, insurance firms, and mutual funds—own about 60 percent of all common stocks. However, the institutions buy and sell relatively actively, so they account for about 75 percent of all transactions. Thus, the institutions have the greatest influence on the prices of individual stocks.

Stock market transactions can be classified into three categories:

1. **The new issue market**. A small firm typically is owned by its management and a handful of private investors. At some point, if the firm is to grow further, its stock must be sold to the general public, which is referred to as *going public*. The market for stock that is in the process of going public is often called the *new issue market*, and the issue is called an *initial public offering (IPO)*. For example, in

November 2018, Vapotherm, Inc. (https://vapotherm.com)—a medical technology company that develops, manufactures, and markets noninvasive ventillary support devices—raised close to $56 million in an IPO by selling 4 million shares at $14 per share.

2. **The primary market**. Also in November 2018, Acadia Pharmaceuticals, Inc.—a biopharmaceutical company focused on discovering and developing innovative medicines that address unmet needs (www.acadia-pharm.com)—sold more than 10.8 million shares of new common stock at a price of $18.51 per share for an aggregate offering of almost $200 million, before underwriting discounts, commissions, and estimated expenses. Because the shares sold were newly created, the issue was defined as a *primary market* offering, but because the business was already publicly held, the offering was not an IPO. Corporations prefer to obtain equity by retaining earnings because of the issuance costs and market pressure associated with the sale of new common stock. Still, if a firm requires more equity funds than can be generated from retained earnings, a stock sale may be necessary.
3. **The secondary market**. If the owner of 100 shares of Tenet Healthcare (www.tenethealth.com) sells her stock, the trade is said to have occurred in the *secondary market*. Thus, the market for *outstanding*, or used, shares is defined as the secondary market. More than 1.5 million shares of Tenet were bought and sold daily on the NYSE in 2018, but the firm did not receive a dime from these transactions.

SELF-TEST QUESTIONS

1. What is an IPO?
2. What is the difference between selling Tenet shares in the primary market and selling the firm's shares in the secondary market?
3. What is the difference between a listed stock and an unlisted stock?

The Decision to Go Public

Most businesses start as proprietorships or partnerships, and then if they are successful and grow, they find it useful to convert to a corporation. Initially, the stock of most corporations is owned by the business's founders, key employees, and often a few investors—usually *venture capitalists*—who may or may not be actively involved in management.[2] However, if growth continues, at some point most firms go public. The advantages and disadvantages of public stock ownership are discussed next.

Advantages of Going Public

- **Permits stock diversification for founders**. As a business grows and becomes more valuable, its founders often have most of their wealth tied up in their ownership position. By selling some of their stock during the IPO or sometime thereafter, the founders can better diversify their holdings, thereby reducing the riskiness of their personal portfolios.
- **Increases liquidity**. The stock of a closely held firm is very illiquid: It has no ready market. If one of the owners wants to sell some shares to raise cash, it will be difficult to find a buyer, and even if one can be found, there is no established price on which to base the sale. Going public creates liquidity and solves these problems.
- **Facilitates raising new corporate cash**. If a privately held firm needs to raise new equity, it must either get it from the current owners, who may not want to put additional capital into the business, or seek outside investors. However, often the firm finds it difficult to get outsiders to contribute equity capital to a closely held business because they are at the mercy of the founders, who have a controlling interest. For example, the founders, who typically are the managers, can vote themselves excessive compensation packages, have private self-serving dealings with the business, and even withhold the business's financial information from outside investors. There are few positions as vulnerable as being an outside stockholder in a closely held firm. Going public—which requires both public disclosure and regulation by the SEC—greatly reduces these problems and hence makes it much easier for the business to raise equity capital.
- **Establishes a value for the business**. There are several reasons why it is useful for the marketplace to establish the equity value of a business. When the owner of a closely held business dies, tax appraisers must set a value on the ownership position. If the value is too high, the estate is treated unfairly, but if the value is too low, the taxpayers lose. A firm that is publicly held has an established value. Similarly, if a firm gives incentive stock options to key employees, they cannot estimate a value for those options unless the stock is publicly traded.
- **Allows private equity investors to cash out**. During the 1990s and early 2000s, private equity investors purchased the stocks of many publicly owned companies, thereby converting those companies to private ownership. A prime example was the 2006 purchase of HCA (https://hcahealthcare.com) by three private equity firms. At the time

of the purchase, the new owners of HCA planned to "cash out" by taking the company public again at some future date after they had taken steps to increase the value of the enterprise. That cash out took place in March 2011, when HCA sold 126.2 million shares for $30 each, raising about $3.79 billion. This transaction marked the largest private-equity backed IPO in US history.

Disadvantages of Going Public

- **Cost of reporting**. A publicly owned firm must file quarterly and annual reports with the SEC and various state agencies. Such reports are costly to produce, especially for smaller firms that do not have the internal resources to prepare them. For example, the annual cost of complying only with the Sarbanes-Oxley Act of 2002—which specifies corporate financial reporting duties and responsibilities—can easily top $10 million (Protiviti 2016).
- **Disclosure**. In most situations, the managers of large firms would prefer to keep operating and financial data private rather than have them available to the firm's competitors. Similarly, the owners of smaller firms may not want to disclose their net worth, and because a publicly owned firm must disclose the number of shares owned by its officers, directors, and major stockholders, it is easy for anyone to estimate the net worth of the insiders—or at least the portion due to the owners of the business. For example, Select Medical Corporation (www.selectmedical.com), which operates more than 1,000 specialty hospitals and clinics, chose to *go private* in 2004. The shares held by the public were purchased by management and private investors, and the company became (again) privately held. The reason given for this action was that it is "easier to operate" as a private company.
- **Self-dealings**. The owners/managers of closely held firms have many opportunities for various types of questionable but legal self-dealings, including the payment of above-market salaries; nepotism; personal transactions with the business, such as lease arrangements; overgranting of stock options and warrants; and other fringe benefits that go far beyond what the marketplace sets as reasonable. Such self-dealings become harder to sustain when a firm becomes public because doing so ultimately creates a board of directors that exercises true oversight.
- **Inactive market and low price**. If a corporation is very small, its shares will not be frequently traded, its stock will not really be liquid, and its market price will often be a poor measure of the stock's value. In addition, security analysts will not follow the stock. If this situation persists, the corporation will not realize much of the benefit associated with going public.

- **Control**. In many businesses, the most dramatic increase in shareholder wealth occurs when a proxy fight or hostile takeover takes place. In addition, these acts motivate managers to pursue stockholder wealth maximization with some zeal. Conversely, such acts often result in removal of the managers at the acquired firm. If the managers maintain a controlling interest, their jobs are secure. In most cases, going public ultimately leads to loss of control by the founding owners or managers.

Conclusions on Going Public

There are no hard and fast rules regarding when, or even if, a closely held firm should go public. This decision is different for each business and should be made on the basis of the unique circumstances surrounding the business and its stockholders. If a firm does decide to go public, either by selling new common stock to raise capital or by selling stock held by insiders, the key issue is setting the price at which the shares will be offered. The current owners want the price to be as high as possible because the higher the price, the smaller the proportion of the firm that they will have to relinquish to obtain a specified dollar amount of equity financing. On the other hand, potential buyers want the price set as low as possible. We will discuss the process of setting the price on an IPO in a later section.

SELF-TEST QUESTIONS

1. What are the primary advantages of going public?
2. What are the disadvantages of going public?

Advantages and Disadvantages of Common Stock Financing

In this section, we briefly discuss the advantages and disadvantages of financing with common stock, with emphasis on its features as compared to debt financing.

Advantages of Financing with Common Stock

- **Has no fixed charges**. Common stock does not obligate the business to fixed charges. If the business does not generate sufficient earnings, it does not have to pay dividends on its common stock. Conversely, if the business uses debt financing, it must make the promised interest and principal payments regardless of the earnings it generates. If it uses preferred stock financing, dividend payments, for all practical purposes, are mandatory and the par value typically must be repaid according to a set schedule. (Preferred stock financing is discussed in the chapter 7 supplement.)

- **Has no maturity date**. Common stock has no maturity date; it is permanent capital that does not have to be "paid back."
- **Creates additional debt capacity**. Because equity financing strengthens the position of creditors, common stock financing increases access to the debt markets and lowers the cost of debt financing.
- **May be easier to sell**. Common stock can, at times, be sold more easily than debt, especially when the firm is small and growing rapidly, which almost by definition makes it risky. It appeals to some investors because (1) it offers a higher expected rate of return than does preferred stock or debt, (2) it provides a better hedge against inflation than do fixed return securities, and (3) it has tax advantages over debt investments.[3]

Disadvantages of Financing with Common Stock

- **Dilutes control**. The sale of common stock normally gives voting rights to new investors, which dilutes the control of current owners. For this reason, equity financing often is not used unless absolutely necessary by small firms whose owners or managers are unwilling to share control with outsiders. However, as we discussed in a previous section, a special class of common stock can be used that does not confer voting rights.
- **Dilutes value**. Debt financing has a fixed cost, so creditors do not share in the success of a business beyond what is promised in the debt agreement. New common stock, however, "dilutes the equity" in the sense that there are more claims on the residual earnings of the business.
- **Issuance costs**. As discussed in the supplement to this chapter, the issuance (legal, accounting, and sales) costs associated with a new stock issue are higher than the costs associated with a similar-sized preferred stock or debt issue.
- **Negative signaling**. Investors may perceive the sale of new common stock as a negative signal, which would put downward pressure on the stock price. The reason for such an interpretation is the assumption that managers know more about future prospects for the firm than do outside shareholders. Furthermore, it typically is in the business's best interest to issue new common stock only when it is overvalued in the marketplace. Thus, a new stock issue—especially one by mature firms with limited growth potential—can be interpreted as a signal that managers believe the stock to be overvalued.

SELF-TEST QUESTION

1. What are the advantages and disadvantages associated with common stock financing?

Equity in Not-for-Profit Corporations

Although technically not-for-profit corporations do not use equity financing, they have equivalent financing which, on the balance sheet, is called either *net assets* or *fund capital*. Because this capital performs the same function as equity in for-profit businesses, we will refer to it here as "equity."

Investor-owned corporations have two sources of equity financing: (1) retained earnings and (2) new stock sales. Not-for-profit corporations can, and do, retain earnings, but they do not have access to the equity markets—that is, they cannot sell stock to raise equity capital. Not-for-profit corporations can, however, raise equity capital through *government grants* and *charitable contributions*. Federal, state, and local governments are concerned about the provision of healthcare services to the general population. Therefore, these entities often make grants to not-for-profit providers to offset the costs of services rendered to patients who cannot pay for those services. Sometimes these grants are nonspecific, but often providers are required to offer specific services, such as neonatal intensive care to infants from low-income families.

As for charitable contributions, individuals, as well as businesses, are motivated to contribute to health services organizations for a variety of reasons, including concern for the well-being of others, the recognition that often accompanies large contributions, and tax deductibility. Because only contributions to not-for-profit corporations qualify as tax deductible, this source of funding is, for all practical purposes, not available to investor-owned entities. Although charitable contributions are not a substitute for profit retentions, charitable contributions can be a significant source of fund capital. For example, the Association for Healthcare Philanthropy reported that total gifts to not-for-profit hospitals in recent years have averaged about $8 billion annually.

Most not-for-profit hospitals received their initial start-up equity capital from religious, educational, or governmental entities, and today some hospitals continue to receive funding from these sources. However, since the 1970s, these sources have provided a much smaller proportion of hospital funding, forcing not-for-profit hospitals to rely more on retained earnings and charitable contributions. Furthermore, federal programs such as the Hill-Burton Act (which provided large amounts of funds for hospital expansion following World War II) have been discontinued, and state and local governments (which are also facing significant financial pressures) are finding it more and more difficult to fund grants to healthcare providers.

Finally, as we discussed in chapter 1, there is a growing trend among legislative bodies and tax authorities to force not-for-profit hospitals to "earn" their favorable tax treatment by providing a certain amount of charity care to indigent patients. Even more severe, some cities have pressured not-for-profit hospitals to make "voluntary" payments to the city to make up for the lost property-tax revenue. All of these trends tend to reduce the ability of not-for-profit health services organizations to raise equity capital by grants and contributions. The result is increased reliance on making money the "old-fashioned way"—by earning it.

On the surface, investor-owned corporations appear to have a significant advantage in raising equity capital. In theory, new common stock can be issued at any time and in any amount. Conversely, charitable contributions are much less certain. The planning, solicitation, and collection periods can take years, and pledges are not always collected, so funds that were counted on may not materialize. Also, the proceeds of new stock sales may be used for any purpose, but charitable contributions often are *restricted*, in which case they can be used only for the designated purpose.

However, managers of investor-owned corporations do not have complete freedom to raise capital in the equity markets. If market conditions are poor and the stock is selling at a low price, a new stock issue can be harmful to the firm's current stockholders. In addition, a new stock issue can be viewed by investors as a signal by management that the firm's stock is overvalued, so new stock issues tend to have a negative impact on the firm's stock price. The bottom line here is that investor-owned businesses—especially those in fast-growing industries—do have

The Green Bay Packers

What do the Green Bay Packers have in common with the Mayo Clinic? It turns out that they are both not-for-profit organizations, but there is a surprising difference: The Packers have stockholders. The Green Bay Packers, Inc., became a publicly owned, not-for-profit corporation in 1923, when the original articles of incorporation were filed with Wisconsin's secretary of state. The corporation is governed by a board of directors and a seven-member executive committee. Today, 5,011,558 shares are owned by 360,760 stockholders, but these shares are not like most stock. They pay no dividends and cannot be sold on the open market; they can only be sold back to the corporation at the same price at which they were purchased. Furthermore, any profits earned by the corporation must be donated to charity.

One of the more remarkable business stories in American sports, the team has been kept financially viable over the years by its shareholders. Fans have come to the team's financial rescue on several occasions, including the sale of $24 million in stock in 1998 for stadium improvements. To protect against someone taking control of the team, the articles of incorporation prohibit any person from owning more than 200,000 shares.

Even some not-for-profit healthcare corporations issue stock, although it is rarely done. Typically, this form of not-for-profit corporation is used initially to finance not-for-profit clinics, whereby the physicians who will practice in the clinic contribute the start-up capital. When a physician leaves the clinic, her initial capital investment is returned.

a financing advantage over not-for-profit businesses. However, the advantage is not so great as to create market dominance. If the advantage were significant, we would likely find many fewer not-for-profit businesses in the healthcare sector than currently exist.

SELF-TEST QUESTIONS

1. What sources of equity (fund capital) do not-for-profit businesses have?
2. Do investor-owned businesses have a significant financing advantage over not-for-profit businesses?

Common Stock Valuation

For many reasons, the valuation of the common stocks of for-profit businesses is a difficult and perplexing process. Furthermore, the model used depends on the characteristics of the issuing business. For stock valuation purposes, there are three types of corporations:

1. **Start-up**. Start-up businesses generally pay no dividends because all earnings must be reinvested in the business to finance growth. To make matters worse, start-up firms often take years to make a profit, so there is no track record of positive earnings to use as a basis for a cash flow forecast. Under such conditions, traditional cash flow valuation models cannot be applied because the value of such firms stems more from potential opportunities than from existing product or service lines. Even if most of the opportunities do not materialize, one or two can turn into blockbusters and hence create a highly successful firm. Option pricing techniques, can—at least in theory—be used to value the stock of such firms. In reality, such valuations are not much better than shots in the dark, so stock prices are based more on qualitative factors, including emotions, than on anything else. As a result, the stock prices of start-up businesses typically are volatile.
2. **Earnings but no dividends**. As a firm passes through its initial start-up phase, it often reaches a point where it has more or less predictable positive earnings but still requires reinvestment of these earnings, so no dividends are paid. In such cases, it is possible to first value the entire business, and then from this value derive the value of the firm's stock. In such a valuation, the expected earnings stream is discounted, or *capitalized*, to find the current value of the corporation.

Then the value of the debt is stripped off to estimate the value of the common stock.

3. **Dividend payment**. More mature corporations generally pay a relatively predictable dividend, so the future dividend stream can be forecast with reasonable confidence. In such cases, the common stock can be valued on the basis of the present value of the expected dividend stream. We illustrate this approach in the following sections.

Definitions

Common stocks with a predictable dividend stream can be valued using the general valuation model discussed in chapter 6 applied to the expected dividends. Before we present the model, here are some definitions:

- $E(D_t)$ = Dividend the stockholder **expects** to receive at the end of year t. D_0 is the most recent dividend, which has already been paid and is known with certainty; $E(D_1)$ is the first dividend expected and for valuation purposes is assumed to be paid at the end of one year; $E(D_2)$ is the dividend expected at the end of two years; and so forth. $E(D_1)$ represents the first cash flow a new purchaser of the stock will receive. D_0, the dividend that has just been paid, is known with certainty, but all future dividends are expected values, so the estimate of any $E(D_t)$ may differ among investors. (Note that stocks generally pay dividends quarterly, so, theoretically, we should evaluate them on a quarterly basis. However, in stock valuation, most analysts work on an annual basis because the data generally are not precise enough to warrant the refinement of a quarterly model. In recent years, a few companies have started paying annual—as opposed to quarterly—dividends. The rationale for doing so is that the administrative expenses associated with dividend payments are reduced significantly.)
- P_0 = Actual *market price* of the stock today.
- $E(P_t)$ = Expected price of the stock at the end of each year t. $E(P_0)$ is the *value* of the stock today, which is based on a particular investor's estimate of the stock's expected dividend stream and riskiness; $E(P_1)$ is the price expected at the end of one year; and so on. Thus, whereas P_0 is fixed and identical for all investors, $E(P_0)$ will differ among investors depending on each investor's assessment of the stock's riskiness and dividend stream. $E(P_0)$, each investor's estimate of the stock's value today, can be above or below P_0, the current stock price, but an investor would buy the stock only if her estimate of $E(P_0)$ were equal to or greater than P_0.
- $E(g_t)$ = Expected growth rate in dividends in each future year t. Different investors may use different $E(g_t)$s to evaluate a firm's stock.

In reality, $E(g_t)$ is normally different for each year t. However, the valuation process can be simplified by assuming that E(gt) is constant across time.

- $R(R_s)$ = Required rate of return on the stock, considering both its riskiness and the returns available on other investments.
- $E(R_s)$ = Expected rate of return on the stock. $E(R_s)$ can be greater than, less than, or equal to $R(R_s)$, but an investor would buy the stock only if his $E(R_s)$ were equal to or greater than $R(R_s)$. Note that $E(R_s)$ is an **expectation**. For example, a return of 15 percent may be expected if Tenet Healthcare Corporation stock were purchased today. If market conditions or Tenet's prospects take a turn for the worse, however, the realized return may end up being much lower than that expected, perhaps even negative.
- $E(D_1) \div P_0$ = Expected *dividend yield* on a stock during the first year. If a stock is expected to pay a dividend of \$1 during the next 12 months, and if its current price is \$10, its expected dividend yield is \$1 ÷ \$10 = 0.10 = 10%.
- $[E(P_1) - P0] \div P0$ = Expected *capital gains yield* on the stock during the first year. If the stock sells for \$10 today and is expected to rise to \$10.50 at the end of the year, the expected capital gain is $E(P_1) - P_0$ = \$10.50 – \$10.00 = \$0.50, and the expected capital gains yield is $[E(P_1) - P0]/P0$ = \$0.50 ÷ \$10 = 0.050 = 5%.

Expected Dividends as the Basis for Stock Values

In the chapter 6 discussion of debt valuation, the value of a bond was found by adding the present value of the interest payments over the life of the bond to the present value of the bond's maturity, or par, value. In essence, a bond's value is the present value of the cash flows expected from the bond. The value of a stock according to the dividend valuation model is similarly found as the present value of a stream of cash flows. What are the cash flows that dividend-paying stocks provide to their holders? First, consider an investor who buys a stock with the intention of holding it in his family forever. In this situation, all the investor and his heirs will receive is a stream of dividends, and the value of the stock today is calculated as the present value of an infinite stream of dividends.

Consider the more typical case in which an investor expects to hold the stock for a finite period and then sell it. What would be the value of the stock in this case? The value of the stock is again the present value of the expected dividend stream. To understand this concept, recognize that, for any individual investor, expected cash flows consist of expected dividends plus the expected price of the stock when it is sold. However, the sale price received by the current investor will depend on the dividends some future investor expects to receive. Therefore, for all present and future investors in total, expected cash flows must be based on expected future dividends. In other words, unless a business is liquidated or sold to another concern, the cash flows it provides to its stockholders consist only of a stream of dividends; therefore, the value of a share of its stock must be the present value of that expected dividend stream.

The validity of this concept can also be confirmed by asking the following: Suppose that an investor buys a stock and expects to hold it for one year. She will receive dividends during the year plus the value E(P1) when selling out at the end of the year, but what will determine the value of E(P1)? It will be determined as the present value of the dividends during year 2 plus the stock price at the end of that year, which in turn will be determined as the present value of another set of future dividends and an even more distant stock price. This valuation can be continued infinitely, and the ultimate result is that the value of a stock is the present value of its expected dividend stream, regardless of the holding period of the investor who performs the analysis. On occasion, stock shares could have additional value, such as the value of a controlling interest when an investor buys 51 percent of a firm's outstanding stock or the added value brought about by a takeover bid. However, in this model, the sole value inherent in stock ownership stems from the dividends expected to be paid by the corporation to its shareholders.

Investors periodically lose sight of the long-run nature of stocks as investments and forget that to sell a stock at a profit, they must find a buyer who will pay the higher price. Suppose that a stock's value is analyzed on the basis of expected future dividends and the conclusion is that the stock's market price exceeded a reasonable value. If an investor buys the stock anyway, he would be following the "bigger fool" theory of investment: The investor may be a fool to buy the stock at its excessive price, but he believes that, when ready to sell, an even bigger fool can be found.

The concept that the value of a stock is the present value of the expected dividend stream holds, regardless of the pattern of growth. It is not even necessary to project the stream for more than, say, 50 years. Because of the time value of money, dividends beyond that point contribute an insignificant amount to a stock's value today. It is generally not possible to have much confidence in dividend values projected over a 50-year period, so stock valuation using the dividend valuation model must be viewed as an approximation.

Constant Growth Stock Valuation

Sometimes, the projected stream of dividends follows a pattern, making it possible to develop a simplified (i.e., easier to evaluate) version of the dividend valuation model. This section discusses the most common simplifying assumption: *constant growth*.

Although the dividends of only a few firms grow at a constant rate, the assumption of constant growth is often made because doing so renders the forecasting of individual dividends over a long period unnecessary. Furthermore, many mature businesses come close to meeting constant growth assumptions. For a constant growth firm, the expected dividend growth rate is constant for all years, so $E(g_1) = E(g_2) = E(g_3)$ and so on, which implies that $E(g^t)$ becomes merely E(g). Under this assumption, the dividend in any future year t may be forecast as $E(D_t) = D_0 \times [1 + E(g)]_t$, where D_0 is the last dividend paid, and hence known with certainty, and E(g) is the constant expected rate of dividend growth. Alternatively, each year's dividend is E(g) percent greater than the previous dividend, so $E(D_t) = E(D_t - 1) \times [1 + E(g)]$.

Consider the following example. If Minnesota Health Systems (MHS), Inc., just paid a dividend of \$1.82 (i.e., D_0 = \$1.82), and if investors expect a 10 percent constant dividend growth rate, the dividend expected in one year is $E(D_1)$ = \$1.82 × (1 + 0.10) = \$2.00; $E(D_2)$ is \$1.82 × $(1 + 0.10)^2$ = \$2.20; and the dividend expected in five years is $E(D_5)$ = \$1.82 × $(1 + 0.10)^5$ = \$2.93. This method of estimating future dividends can be used to estimate MHS's expected future cash flow stream (i.e., the dividends) for some time into the future—say, 50 years. Then, the present values of this stream can be summed to find the value of MHS's stock.

The Value of a Constant Growth Stock

When E(g) is assumed to be constant, a stock can be valued using a simplified model called the *constant growth model*, seen in the following equation.

On the web at: *ache.org/HAP/PinkSong8e*

Key Equation 7.1: Constant Growth Model (Valuation)

$$E(P_0) = \frac{D_0 \times [1 + E(g)]}{R(R_S) - E(g)} = \frac{E(D_1)}{R(R_S) - E(g)}$$

where $R(R_s)$ is the required rate of return on the stock. If D_0 = \$1.82, E(g) = 10%, and $R(R_s)$ = 16% for MHS, the value of its stock would be \$33.33:

$$E(P_{MHS}) = \frac{1.82 \times 1.10}{0.16 - 0.10} = \frac{\$2.00}{0.06} = \$33.33.$$

	A	B	C	D
1				
2	$1.82	D_0	Last dividend payment	
3	10.0%	E(g)	Expected growth rate	
4	16.0%	$R(R_s)$	Required rate of return	
5				
6				
7				
8	$33.37	=A2*(1+A3)/(A4 – A3) (entered into cell A8)		
9				
10				

Note a small rounding difference between the hand-calculated answer (where the first expected dividend was rounded to $2.00) and the spreadsheet solution.

For the constant growth model to be valid, the required rate of return on the stock must be greater than the constant dividend growth rate—that is, $R(R_s)$ must be greater than E(g). If the constant growth model is used when $R(R_s)$ is not greater than E(g), the results will be meaningless. However, for a stock to qualify as a constant growth stock, its dividends must be expected to grow at the constant growth rate forever, or at least for a very long time. Stocks can have an E(g) that is greater than $R(R_s)$ for short periods, but E(g) cannot exceed $R(R_s)$ over the long run because a company's growth rates are limited by general economic growth. Although the constant growth model is applied here to stock valuation, it can be used in any situation in which cash flows are growing at a constant rate.

How does an investor determine her required rate of return on a particular stock, $R(R_s)$? One way is to use the security market line (SML) of the capital asset pricing model, which we discussed in chapter 5. Assume that MHS's market beta, as reported by a financial advisory service, is 1.6. Also assume that the risk-free interest rate (the rate on long-term Treasury bonds) is 5 percent and the required rate of return on the market is 12 percent. According to the SML, the required rate of return on MHS's stock is 16.0 percent:

Key Equation 7.2: Security Market Line (SML)

$$\begin{aligned} R(R_{MHS}) &= RF + [R(R_M) - RF] \times b_{MHS} \\ &= 5\% + (12\% - 5\%) \times 1.6 \\ &= 5\% + (7\% \times 1.6) \\ &= 5\% + 11.2\% = 16.2\% \approx 16\%. \end{aligned}$$

Remember, in the SML, RF is the risk-free rate; $R(R_M)$ is the required rate of return on the market or the required rate of return on a b = 1.0 stock; and b_{MHS} is MHS's market beta.

	A	B	C	D
1				
2	1.6	b	Beta coefficient	
3	5.0%	RF	Risk-free rate	
4	12.0%	$R(R_M)$	Required return on market	
5				
6				
7				
8	16.2%	=A3+(A4 – A3)* A2 (entered into cell A8)		
9				
10				

Growth in dividends occurs primarily as a result of growth in earnings per share (EPS). Earnings growth, in turn, results from a number of factors, including the inflation rate in the economy and the amount of earnings the firm retains and reinvests. Regarding inflation, if output in units is stable and if both sales prices and input costs increase at the inflation rate, EPS also will grow at the inflation rate. EPS will grow as a result of the reinvestment, or plowback, of earnings as well. If the firm's earnings are not all paid out as dividends (i.e., if a fraction of earnings is retained), the dollars of investment behind each share will rise over time, which should lead to growth in productive assets and hence growth in earnings and dividends.

In the constant growth model, the most critical input is E(g)—the expected constant growth rate in dividends. Investors can make their own E(g) estimates on the basis of historical dividend growth, but E(g) estimates are also available from brokerage and investment advisory firms.

Expected Rate of Return on a Constant Growth Stock

The constant growth model can be rearranged to solve for $E(R_s)$, the *expected rate of return*. In the model's normal form, $R(R_s)$ is the required rate of return, but when the model is transformed, the expected rate of return, $E(R_s)$, is found. This transformation requires that the required rate of return equal the expected rate of return, or $R(R_s) = E(R_s)$. This equality holds if the stock is in equilibrium, a condition we will discuss later in the chapter. After solving the constant growth model for $E(R_s)$, this expression is obtained:

On the web at: *ache.org/HAP/PinkSong8e*

Key Equation 7.3: Constant Growth Model (Rate of Return)

$$E(R_s) = \frac{D_0 \times [1 + E(g)]}{P_0} + E(g) = \frac{E(D_1)}{P_0} + E(g).$$

If an investor buys MHS's stock today for \$33.33 (P_0), expects the stock to pay a dividend of \$2.00 one year from now [$E(D_1)$], and expects dividends to grow at a constant rate of 10 percent in the future [E(g)], the expected rate of return on that stock is 16 percent:

$$E(R_{MHS}) = \frac{\$2.00}{\$33.33} + 10\% = 6\% + 10\% = 16\%.$$

In this form, $E(R_s)$—the expected total return on the stock—consists of an expected dividend yield [$E(D1)/P_0$] of 6% and an expected growth rate or capital gains yield [E(g)] of 10 percent.

	A	B	C	D
1				
2	\$33.33	P_0	Stock price	
3	\$2.00	$E(D_{1)}$	Next expected dividend	
4	10.0%	E(g)	Expected growth rate	
5				
6				
7				
8	16.0%	=A3/A2+A4 (entered into cell A8)		
9				
10				

Suppose this analysis had been conducted on January 1, 2019, so P_0 = \$33.33 is MHS's January 1, 2019, stock price, and $E(D_1)$ = \$2.00 is the dividend expected at the end of 2019. What is the value of $E(P_1)$, the firm's expected stock price at the end of 2019 (the beginning of 2020)? The constant growth model would again be applied, but this time the 2016 dividend, $E(D_2) = E(D_1) \times [1 + E(g)] = \$2.00 \times 1.10 = \$2.20$, would be used:

$$E(P_1) = \frac{E(D_2)}{R(R_{MHS}) - E(g)} = \frac{\$2.20}{0.06} = \$36.67.$$

Notice that $E(P_1)$ = \$36.67 is 10 percent greater than P_0 = \$33.33: \$33.33 × 1.10 = \$36.67. Thus, a capital gain of \$36.67 – \$33.33 = \$3.34 would be expected during 2019, which produces a capital gains yield of 10 percent:

$$\text{Capital gains yield} = \frac{\text{Capital gain}}{\text{Beginning price}} = \frac{\$3.34}{\$33.33} = 0.100 = 10\%.$$

If the analysis were extended, in each future year the expected capital gains yield would always equal E(g) because the stock price would grow at the 10 percent constant dividend growth rate. The expected dividend yield in 2020 (year 2) can be found as follows:

$$\text{Dividend yield} = \frac{E(D_2)}{E(P_1)} = \frac{\$2.20}{\$36.67} = 0.060 = 6\%.$$

The dividend yield for 2021 (year 3) can also be calculated; again, it would be 6 percent. Thus, for a constant growth stock, the following valuation conditions must hold:

- The dividend is expected to grow forever, or at least for a long time, at a constant rate, E(g).
- The stock price is expected to grow at this same rate.
- The expected dividend yield is a constant.
- The expected capital gains yield is also a constant and is equal to E(g).
- The expected rate of return in any year t—which is equal to the expected dividend yield plus the expected capital gains yield (growth rate)—is expressed by this equation: $E(Rt) = [E(D_{t+1}) \div E(P_t)] + E(g)$.

The term *expected* should be clarified—it means expected in a statistical sense. Thus, if MHS's dividend growth rate is expected to remain constant at 10 percent, this means that the growth rate in each year can be represented by a probability distribution with an expected value of 10 percent, not that the growth rate is expected to be exactly 10 percent in each future year. In this sense, the constant growth assumption is reasonable for many large, mature businesses.

Nonconstant Growth Stock Valuation

Some firms exhibit constant dividend growth, or at least growth close enough to apply the constant growth model. However, many businesses do not. For example, some businesses that have not yet fully matured but have a solid dividend record may be growing much faster today than they will over the long term. At some point in time, as the business matures, the growth will fall to a steady rate. Also, some dividend-paying firms may temporarily suspend the dividends because of a temporary downturn, but they may have every intention of picking up the dividends when conditions improve. If a

On the web at: *ache.org/HAP/PinkSong8e*

business is not expected to exhibit more or less constant growth in dividends in the future, the constant growth model cannot be used.

To find the value of a nonconstant growth stock, assuming that the growth rate will eventually stabilize to some steady rate, we proceed as follows:

- Estimate the stock's dividend stream on a year-by-year basis, stopping at the first dividend in the constant growth phase.
- Find the present value of the dividends during the period of nonconstant growth.
- Find the expected price of the stock at the end of the nonconstant growth period, at which point it has become a constant growth stock, and discount this price back to the present.
- Add the dividend and price components to find the value of the stock.

For an illustration of the process for valuing nonconstant growth stocks, suppose the following facts exist:

$R(R_s)$ = Stockholders' required rate of return = 16%.

N = Years of nonconstant growth = 3.

$E(g_n)$ = Rate of growth in dividends during the nonconstant growth period = 30%. (Note that the growth rate during the nonconstant growth period could vary from year to year.)

$E(g_c)$ = Steady (constant) growth rate after the nonconstant period = 10%.

D_0 = last dividend paid = \$1.82.

The valuation process, which is tedious but not difficult, is explained in the steps below:

1. Find the expected dividends during the nonconstant growth phase (years 1, 2, and 3 in this case) plus the first dividend of the constant growth phase (year 4) by multiplying each dividend by one plus the growth rate expected in the coming year:

$$D_0 = \$1.82.$$

$$D_1 = D_0 \times 1.30 = \$1.82 \times 1.30 = \$2.366.$$

$$D_2 = D_1 \times 1.30 = \$2.366 \times 1.30 = \$3.076.$$

$$D_3 = D_2 \times 1.30 = \$3.076 \times 1.30 = \$3.999.$$

$$D_4 = D_3 \times 1.10 = \$3.999 \times 1.10 = \$4.399.$$

2. Find the present values of the dividends that occur during the nonconstant growth phase, remembering that D_0 just occurred and thus does not contribute to the stock's value:

$$PV\ D_1 = \$2.366 \div (1.16)^1 = \$2.040.$$
$$PV\ D_2 = \$3.076 \div (1.16)^2 = \$2.286.$$
$$PV\ D_3 = \$3.999 \div (1.16)^3 = \$2.562.$$

3. The stock price expected at the end of year 3 (the beginning of year 4) can be found using the constant growth model because dividends are expected to grow at a constant rate of 10 percent in year 4 and beyond. This price captures the value of all dividends beyond year 3. Calculate the stock price at the end of year 3 and then discount this value to year 0:

$$E(P) = \frac{D_4}{R(R_s) - E(g)} = \frac{\$4.399}{0.16 - 0.10} = \$73.317.$$
$$PV\ E(_3) = \$73.32 \div (1.16)^3 = \$46.971.$$

4. Add the present values to find the value of the stock today:

$$E(P_0) = \$2.040 + \$2.286 + \$2.562 + \$46.971$$
$$= \$53.859 \approx \$53.86.$$

	A	B	C	D
1				
2	30.0%	$E(g_n)$	Nonconstant growth rate	
3	10.0%	$E(g_c)$	Constant growth rate	
4	16.0%	$R(R_s)$	Required rate of return	
5	$1.82	D_0	Last dividend payment	
6				
7	$2.366	=A5*(1+A2) (entered into cell A7)		
8	$3.076	=A7*(1+A2) (entered into cell A8)		
9	$3.999	=A8*(1+A2) (entered into cell A9)		
10	$4.398	=A9*(1+A3) (entered into cell A10)		
11	$73.307	=A10/(A4–A3) (entered into cell A11)		
12				
13	$53.85	=NPV(A4,A7:A9)+PV(A4,3,,–A11) (entered into cell A13)		

Here, we calculated the future dividend stream in cells A7 through A9 and the future stock price in cells A10 and A11. (The dividend in cell A10 is needed only to calculate the future stock price in cell A11.) Then, in cell

A13, we calculated the present values of the three-year dividend stream and future stock price and added them together. (Note a small rounding difference between the calculator and spreadsheet solutions.)

Although this illustration shows *supernormal growth*—in which the dividends are currently growing at a higher rate than the steady rate—the procedures illustrated here can be used with any pattern of nonconstant growth. This model can be used only in cases where the dividend stream returns to constant growth at some not-too-distant point in time.

Stock Valuation by the Free Cash Flow Method

Earlier, we described three potential business situations that dictate the nature of the stock valuation process: start-up, earnings but no dividends, and dividend paying. In this section, we briefly describe the valuation process when earnings are more or less predictable but the corporation pays no dividends. This method is called the *free cash flow method*, because it focuses on cash flows **available** for distribution to investors rather than dividends paid to stockholders.

Free cash flow is defined as Net income + Interest expense – Funds reinvested in the business. Thus, free cash flow represents the amount of money available to a business to pay its investors, including both equity investors (stockholders) and debt investors (debtholders). To conduct the valuation, future free cash flows are estimated and either the constant or nonconstant growth model is used to find their present value, which represents the total value of business. Note that the discount rate used to find the present value is the corporate cost of capital rather than the cost of equity, because the cash flows being discounted represent the aggregate risk to investors, including both stockholders and debtholders.

To briefly illustrate the free cash flow method, assume that for-profit Tampa Physician's Hospital (TPH) has a present value of free cash flows of $50 million. Because this value must be shared by stockholders and debtholders, to focus on stock value it is necessary to first subtract the value that belongs to debtholders. Assuming that the market value of TPH's debt is $10 million, $50 million – $10 million = $40 million is left as the total value of the corporation's common stock. Finally, if there are 5 million shares of common stock outstanding, the value of each share would be $40 million ÷ $5 million = $8 million.

Valuation using free cash flow as the basis is used extensively when valuing businesses that do not have an established dividend track record. Thus, we revisit this approach in chapter 16 (Business Combinations and Valuation).

SELF-TEST QUESTIONS

1. What are three methods for valuing common stocks, and when does each apply?
2. Write out and explain the dividend valuation model for a constant growth stock in both the valuation and expected rate of return forms.
3. What are the assumptions of the constant growth model?
4. What are the key features of constant growth regarding dividend yield and capital gains yield?
5. What are the key features of the nonconstant growth model?
6. Explain how to estimate stock value using the free cash flow method.

Security Market Equilibrium

Investors will want to buy a security if its expected rate of return exceeds its required rate of return or, put another way, when its value exceeds its current price. Conversely, investors will want to sell a security when its required rate of return exceeds its expected rate of return (i.e., when its current price exceeds its value). When more investors want to buy a security than sell it, its price is bid up. When more investors want to sell a security than buy it, its price falls. In *equilibrium*, these two conditions must hold:

1. **The expected rate of return on a security must equal its required rate of return to the marginal investor**. This means that no investor who owns the stock believes that its expected rate of return is less than its required rate of return, and no investor who does not own the stock believes that its expected rate of return is greater than its required rate of return. (The *marginal investor* is the investor who is most likely to be the buyer or the seller on the next trade and hence has the greatest influence on stock prices.)
2. **The market price of a security must equal its value to the marginal investor**. If these conditions do not hold, trading will occur until they do. Of course, security prices are not constant. A security's price can swing wildly when new information becomes available that changes investors' expectations concerning the security's cash flow stream or risk, or when the general level of returns (i.e., interest rates) changes. However, evidence suggests that securities prices—especially

of securities that are actively traded, such as those issued by the US Treasury or by large firms—adjust rapidly to disequilibrium situations. Thus, most people believe that the bonds of the US Treasury and the bonds and stocks of major corporations are generally in equilibrium. The key to the rapid movement of security prices toward equilibrium is informational efficiency, which is discussed in the next section.

SELF-TEST QUESTIONS

1. What is meant by security market equilibrium?
2. What securities are most likely to be in equilibrium?
3. What is meant by the term *marginal investor*?

Informational Efficiency

A securities market—say, the market for long-term US Treasury bonds—is *informationally efficient* if (1) all information relevant to the values of the securities traded can be obtained easily and at a low cost and (2) the market contains many buyers and sellers who act rationally in response to this information. If these conditions hold, current market prices will have embedded in them all information of possible relevance; hence, future price movements will be based solely on new information as it becomes known. The *efficient markets hypothesis (EMH)*, which has three forms, formalizes the theory of informational efficiency:

1. The *weak form* of the EMH holds that all information contained in **past price movements** is fully reflected in current market prices. Therefore, information about recent trends in a security's price, or a bond's yield, is of no value in choosing which securities will "outperform" other securities.
2. The *semistrong form* of the EMH holds that current market prices reflect all **publicly available information**. Therefore, it makes no sense to spend hours and hours analyzing economic data and financial reports because whatever information you might find—good or bad—has already been absorbed by the market and embedded in current prices.
3. The *strong form* of the EMH holds that current market prices reflect **all relevant information**, whether publicly available or privately held. If this form holds, then even investors with "inside information," such as corporate officers, would find it impossible to earn abnormal

returns—returns in excess of that justified by the riskiness of the investment.

The EMH, in any of its three forms, is a hypothesis rather than a proven law, so it is not necessarily true. However, hundreds of empirical tests have been conducted to try to prove, or disprove, the EMH, and the results are relatively consistent. Most tests support the weak and semistrong forms of the EMH for well-developed markets, such as the US markets for large firms' stocks and bond issues and for Treasury securities. Supporters of these forms of the EMH note that there are 100,000 or so full-time, highly trained, professional analysts and traders operating in these markets. Furthermore, many of these analysts and traders work for businesses such as Citibank, Fidelity Investments, Merrill Lynch, Prudential, and the like that have billions of dollars available to take advantage of undervalued securities. Finally, as a result of disclosure requirements and electronic information networks, new information about these heavily followed securities is almost instantaneously available. Therefore, security prices in these markets adjust almost immediately as new developments occur, and hence prices reflect all publicly available information.

Virtually no one, however, believes that the strong form of the EMH holds. Studies of legal purchases and sales by people with inside information indicate that insiders can make abnormal profits by trading on that information. It is even more apparent that insiders can make abnormal profits if they trade illegally on specific information that has not been disclosed to the public, such as a takeover bid, a research and development breakthrough, and the like.

The EMH has important implications both for individual investment decisions and for business financing decisions. Because security prices appear to generally reflect all public information, most actively followed and traded securities are in equilibrium and fairly valued. Being in equilibrium, however, does not mean that new information cannot cause a security's price to soar or to plummet, but it does mean that most securities are neither undervalued nor overvalued. Therefore, over the long run, an investor with no inside information can expect to earn only a return on a security that compensates her for the amount of risk assumed. In the short run—for example, a year—an investor can expect to earn only a return that is the same as the average for securities of equal risk. In other words, investors should not expect to "beat the market" after adjusting for risk. Also, because the EMH applies to the major bond markets, bond prices and hence interest rates reflect all current public information. Future interest rates are impossible to forecast consistently because interest rates change in response to new information.

For managers, the EMH indicates that managerial decisions generally should not be based on perceptions about the market's ability to properly price the firm's securities or on perceptions about which way interest rates will move. In other words, managers generally should not try to time new stock issues to catch high prices or new bond issues to catch low interest rates. However, in some situations, managers may have information about their own firms that is unknown to the public. This condition is called *asymmetric information*, which can affect managerial decisions. For example, suppose a drug manufacturer has made a breakthrough in Alzheimer research but wants to maintain as much secrecy as possible about the new drug. During final development and testing, the firm might want to delay any new securities offerings because securities can probably be sold under more favorable terms once the announcement is made. Managers can, and should, act on inside information for the benefit of their firms, but inside information cannot legally be used for personal profit.

Are markets really efficient? If markets were not efficient, the better managers of stock and bond mutual funds and pension plans would be able to consistently outperform the broad averages over long periods. In fact, few managers can consistently better the broad averages. In any year, some mutual fund managers will outperform the market and others will underperform the market. This fact is known with certainty, but for an investor to beat the market by investing in mutual funds, she must identify the successful managers beforehand, which seems difficult, if not impossible, to do.

Despite evidence to the contrary, many theorists, and even more Wall Street experts, believe that pockets of inefficiency do exist. In some cases, entire markets may be inefficient. For example, the markets for the securities issued by small firms may be inefficient because there is either an insufficient number of analysts ferreting out information on these companies

Behavioral Finance

Behavioral finance is a field of study that proposes psychology-based theories to explain stock market anomalies. Proponents argue that investors are not nearly as rational as traditional finance theory makes them out to be. Of course, the idea that psychology drives stock market movements flies in the face of the EMH. In fact, behaviorists (as they are called) contend that, rather than being unusual, irrational behavior is commonplace. Here is one of the experiments they cite to support that view.

Suppose you are given a choice of a sure $50 or coin flip in which you could win either $100 or nothing. Most people would pocket the sure $50. Now, suppose you are confronted with this choice: a sure loss of $50 or a coin flip in which you could lose either $100 or nothing. Now, most people would choose the coin toss, although the value inherent in flipping the coin is equivalent in both scenarios. The idea here is that people tend to view the possibility of recouping a loss as more important than the possibility of greater gain.

The priority of avoiding losses also affects investor behavior. It is common for investors to watch a particular stock plummet in value but refuse to sell because it would "lock in" the loss coupled with the belief that the price will eventually bounce back to the value it had once achieved. Although behavioral finance offers no investment miracles, perhaps it can help investors train themselves to watch their own behavior and, in turn, avoid mistakes that would be detrimental to their personal wealth.

or an insufficient number of investors trading these securities. Many people also believe that individual securities traded in efficient markets are occasionally priced inefficiently, or that investor emotions can drive prices too high during raging bull markets (such as the one seen in the 1990s) or too low during whimpering bear markets (such as the one between 2007 and 2009). Indeed, if investors are driven more by greed and emotion than by rational assessments of security values, markets may not really be as efficient as claimed by supporters of the EMH.

Benjamin Graham (2016), a well-respected stock market pundit, described the EMH as a theory that "could have great practical importance if it coincided with reality." Graham proposed that the price of every stock consists of two components: investment value and a speculative element. Investment value measures the worth of all the cash flows a company will generate in the future, while the speculative element is driven by sentiment and emotions, such as hope, greed, fear, and regret. The market is highly efficient at identifying investment value. However, the speculative element is prone to large and rapid swings that can, at times, swamp investment value.

Whether the market is truly efficient, partially efficient, or totally inefficient seems to have little bearing on how easy it is to beat. We know this because the so-called investment experts would have much better results than they do, as evidenced by the fact that only 3 percent of actively managed mutual funds deliver results that exceed those merely the result of chance.

In closing our discussion of market efficiency, we can discuss what it means to "beat the market." First, consider the short run—say, one year. You may hold a portfolio of stocks that realizes a 20 percent return in a given year. Is that a good return? Yes. Over the past 80 or so years, a diversified investment in stocks averaged an annual return of roughly 10 percent. However, the 20 percent return in any given year does not mean that you beat the market in that year. To actually beat the market, you must realize a return that is higher than the average return on similar portfolios of stocks (portfolios that have the same risk as yours). If the average return (benchmark) on a similar-risk portfolio for that year was 25 percent, some portfolios did better than average and others did worse, including yours. If market efficiency holds, however, those that did better in one year will not be able to consistently beat the relevant benchmark year after year.

What about the long run? Over the long run—say, ten or more years—beating the market means a return in excess of that commensurate with the riskiness undertaken. For stocks, this means an average annual return of roughly 10 percent (based on historical performance).

We really do not know whether it is possible to beat the market by skill or whether it is just a matter of luck. Nevertheless, it is wise for both investors and managers to consider the implications of market efficiency when making investment and financing decisions. Investors who believe that they can beat the market should at least recognize that there is a lot of evidence that tells us that most people who try to do so will ultimately fail.

SELF-TEST QUESTIONS

1. What two conditions must hold for markets to be efficient?
2. Briefly, what is the EMH?
3. What are the implications of the EMH for investors and managers?
4. What is meant by the phrase "beat the market"?

The Risk/Return Trade-Off

Most financial decisions involve alternative courses of action. For example, should a hospital invest its excess funds in Treasury bonds that yield 4 percent or in Tenet bonds that yield 6 percent? Should a group practice buy a replacement piece of equipment now or wait until next year? Should a joint venture outpatient diagnostic center purchase a small, limited-use MRI (magnetic resonance imaging) system or a large, and more expensive, multipurpose system?

Generally, alternative courses of action have different expected rates of return, and one may be tempted to accept automatically the alternative with the higher expected return. However, this approach to financial decision-making would be incorrect. In efficient markets, alternatives that offer higher returns also entail higher risk. The correct question to ask when making financial decisions is not which alternative has the higher expected rate of return but which alternative has the higher return **after adjusting for risk**. In other words, which alternative has the higher return over and above the return commensurate with that alternative's riskiness?

For an illustration of the *risk/return trade-off*, suppose Tenet stock has an expected rate of return of 12 percent, while its bonds yield (and have an expected rate of return of) 6 percent. Does this mean that investors should flock to buy the firm's stock and ignore the bonds? No. The higher expected rate of return on the stock merely reflects that the stock is riskier than the bonds. Investors who are not willing to assume much risk will buy Tenet's bonds, while those that are less risk averse will buy the stock. From the perspective of Tenet's managers, financing with stock is less risky than financing with debt, so the firm is willing to pay the higher cost of equity to limit the firm's risk exposure.

Despite the hypothesized efficiency of major securities markets, the markets for products and services (i.e., the markets for real assets, such as MRI systems, and services, such as inpatient healthcare) are usually not efficient; hence, returns are not necessarily related to risk. Thus, hospitals, group practices, and other healthcare businesses can make real-asset investments and achieve returns in excess of those required to compensate for the riskiness of the investment. Furthermore, the market for *innovation* (i.e., the market for ideas) is not efficient. Thus, it is possible for people such as Mark Zuckerberg, one of the founders of Facebook, to become multibillionaires at a relatively young age. However, when excess returns are found in the product, service, or idea markets, new entrants quickly join the innovators, and competition over time usually forces rates of return down to efficient market levels. The result is that later entrants can expect only returns that are commensurate with the risks involved.

SELF-TEST QUESTIONS

1. Explain the meaning of the term *risk/return trade-off.*
2. In what markets does this trade-off hold?

Chapter Key Concepts

This chapter contains a wealth of material on equity financing and how securities are brought to market. Here are its key concepts:

- The most important *common stockholder* rights are a claim on the firm's residual earnings, control, and the preemptive right.
- New common stock may be sold by for-profit corporations in six ways: (1) on a pro rata basis to existing stockholders through a *rights offering*; (2) through investment bankers to the general public in a *public offering*; (3) to a single buyer, or a small number of buyers, in a *private placement*; (4) to employees through an *employee stock purchase plan*; (5) to shareholders through a *dividend reinvestment plan*; and (6) to individual investors by *direct purchase*.
- A *closely held corporation* is one that is owned by a few individuals who typically are the firm's managers.
- A *publicly owned corporation* is one that is owned by a relatively large number of individuals who are not actively involved in its management.
- Not-for-profit firms do not have access to the equity markets. However, *charitable contributions*, which are tax deductible to the donor, and *governmental grants* constitute unique equity sources for not-for-profit firms.

(continued)

(continued from previous page)

- Under the dividend valuation model, the *value* of a share of stock is found by *discounting* the stream of *expected dividends* by the stock's required rate of return.
- The value of a stock whose dividends are expected to grow at a constant rate for many years is found by applying the *constant growth model*:

$$E(P_0) = \frac{D_0 \times [1 + E(g)]}{R(R_S) - E(g)} = \frac{E(D_1)}{R(R_S) - E(g)}.$$

- The *expected rate of return* on a stock consists of an *expected dividend yield* plus an *expected capital gains yield*. For a constant growth stock, both the expected dividend yield and the expected capital gains yield are constant over time, and the expected rate of return can be found using this equation:

$$E(R_s) = \frac{D_0 \times [1 + E(g)]}{P_0} + E(g) = \frac{E(D_1)}{P_0} + E(g).$$

- The *efficient markets hypothesis (EMH)* holds that (1) stocks are always in equilibrium and fairly valued, (2) it is impossible for an investor to beat the market consistently, and (3) managers should not try to forecast future interest rates or time security issues.
- In efficient markets, alternatives that offer higher returns must also have higher risk; this condition is called the *risk/return trade-off*. The implication is that investments must be evaluated on the basis of both risk and return.

This concludes our discussion of the features and valuation of equity financing. In chapter 8, we discuss lease financing, which is an alternative to debt and equity financing.

Chapter Models, Problems, and Minicases

The following ancillary resources in spreadsheet format are available for this chapter:

- A chapter model that shows how to perform many of the calculations described in the chapter

- Problems that test your ability to perform the calculations
- A minicase that is more complicated than the problems and tests your ability to perform the calculations in preparation for a case

These resources can be accessed online at ache.org/HAP/PinkSong8e.

Selected Case

The following case in *Cases in Healthcare Finance*, sixth edition, focuses on the mechanics of equity valuation: Case 15: Pacific Healthcare (B).

References

Graham, B. 2006. *The Intelligent Investor: The Definitive Book on Value Investing*. New York: Collins Business Essentials.

Protiviti. 2016. *Understanding the Costs and Benefits of SOC Compliance*. Accessed May 24, 2019. www.protiviti.com/sites/default/files/united_states/insights/2016-sox-survey-protiviti.pdf.

Selected Bibliography

Anderson, D. G., M. Potter, and D. E. Morris. 2018. "Improving Performance and Enhancing Innovation with Venture Investing." *Healthcare Financial Management* 72: 44–53.

Arduino, K. 2018. "Healthcare Capital Markets Outlook: Short-Term Opportunities Versus Long-Term Uncertainty." *Healthcare Financial Management* 72 (5): 36–43.

Bannow, T. 2018. "High Prices Test Private Equity's Ability to Close Healthcare Deals." *Modern Healthcare* 48 (29): 8.

Dillingham, W. J. 2018. "Recent Trends in Healthcare Philanthropy and Foundations." *Healthcare Financial Management* 72 (3): 54–59.

Fama, E. F., and K. R. French. 2009. "Luck Versus Skill in the Cross Section of Mutual Fund Returns." Working paper, Tuck School of Business at Dartmouth. http://papers.ssrn.com/sol3/papers.cfm?abstract_id=1356021.

Healthcare Financial Management Association. 2018. "Optimizing Capital Structure Decisions Under the New Tax Law." *Healthcare Financial Management* 72 (8): A1–A4.

Jarvis, W. F. 2011. "Endowment Income for the Post-Reform Era." *Healthcare Financial Management* 65 (5): 132.

Lalangas, E., D. Kroll, and A. Carlson. 2018. "The Tax Cuts and Jobs Act Takeaways for Healthcare Finance Leaders." *Healthcare Financial Management* 72 (4): 28–31.

Livingston, S. 2018. "Surge in Private Equity Deals Causes Some Alarm." *Modern Healthcare* 48 (25): 8.

Selected Websites

The following websites pertain to this chapter:

- To learn more about stock exchanges, see the NYSE site at www.nyse.com. You can research listing requirements as well as learn how the NYSE works. Also, see the NASDAQ site at www.nasdaq.com.
- To learn about ESOPs, see the website of the Employee Stock Ownership Association at www.esopassociation.org.
- To learn more about DRIPs, see the DRIP investor site at www.dripinvestor.com.

Notes

1. In the typical voting procedure, a stockholder who owns 1,000 shares can cast 1,000 votes for each director whose seat is contested. An alternative voting procedure, called *cumulative voting*, is used at some corporations. Here, the 1,000-share stockholder would get 3,000 votes if three seats were being contested, and he can cast all of them for one director. Cumulative voting helps small groups of shareholders gain a voice on the board.
2. Venture capitalists are individuals and firms that supply capital to small start-up businesses that do not have the track record necessary to obtain capital from banks or public markets. This type of financing is referred to as *first-round financing*. The capital may be in the form of debt or equity, but debt investments usually are accompanied by stock options or some other "equity kicker" that gives the venture capitalist an ownership position in the business. Although many venture capital investments never pan out, those that do typically create huge returns when the venture capitalists "cash out" after the successful firm has gone public.
3. If a stock is held for more than one year, any profit is classified as a long-term capital gain and hence taxed at a lower rate than is ordinary income. Furthermore, taxes are not paid until the stock is sold, so there is a time value of money benefit.

Integrative Application

The Problem

Sally Randolph is a surgical nurse at Wellford Surgery Centers (WSC), a small for-profit ambulatory surgery center owner and operator whose stock is thinly traded in the OTC market. A few nights ago, Sally received a call from her mother asking for some advice regarding a stock recommendation. Her mother said that her broker had recommended adding 1,000 shares of WSC stock to the family's retirement portfolio. Because Sally worked at WSC, her mother thought that Sally might have some special insights. Also, Sally's mother just read a short article in an investment magazine regarding market efficiency and behavioral finance, and she asked what impact these ideas have on the broker's recommendation.

Sally was finishing up her healthcare master's in business administration at a local university, so she thought this would be a good opportunity to apply some of the stock valuation concepts she had learned. To begin, she looked up some basic data:

WSC beta coefficient = 1.2.

Yield on treasury bonds = 7.0%.

Market risk premium = 5.0 percentage points.

Last dividend paid = \$2.00.

Expected growth rate = a constant 6.0%, or alternatively
= 10.0% for 3 years and 5.0% constant growth thereafter.

Current stock price = \$33.00.

Now, she must use this information to make some judgments about whether her mother should follow the broker's advice.

The Analysis

First, use the security market line (SML) of the capital asset pricing model to estimate the required rate of return on the stock:

$$R(R_{WSC}) = RF + (R[R_M] - RF) \times b_{WSC} = RF + (RP_M \times b_{WSC})$$

$$= 7.0\% + (5.0\% \times 1.2) = 13.0\%.$$

Next, estimate the current value of the stock using the constant growth valuation model:

$$E(P_{WSC}) = D_0 \times [1 + E(g)] \div [R(R_s) - E(g)]$$
$$= \$2.00 \times 1.06 \div [0.13 - 0.06] = \$2.12 \div 0.07 = \$30.29.$$

Alternatively, use the expected rate of return version of the model:

$$E(R_{WSC}) = [D_0 \times [1 + E(g)]] \div P_0 + E(g) = E(D_1) \div P_0 + E(g)$$
$$= \$2.12 \div \$33.00 + 6.0\% = 6.4\% + 6.0\% = 12.4\%.$$

Finally, use the nonconstant growth model to estimate WSC's current value:

$$D_0 = \$2.00.$$
$$D_1 = D_0 \times 1.10 = \$2.000 \times 1.10 = \$2.200.$$
$$D_2 = D_1 \times 1.10 = \$2.200 \times 1.10 = \$2.420.$$
$$D_3 = D_2 \times 1.10 = \$2.420 \times 1.10 = \$2.662.$$
$$D_4 = D_3 \times 1.05 = \$2.662 \times 1.05 = \$2.795.$$
$$E(P_3) = D4 \div [R(Rs) - E(g)] = \$2.795 \div [0.13 - 0.05] = \$2.795 \div 0.08 = \$34.938.$$
$$PV\ D_1 = \$2.200 \div (1.13)1 = \$1.947.$$
$$PV\ D_2 = \$2.420 \div (1.13)2 = \$1.895.$$
$$PV\ D_3 = \$2.662 \div (1.13)3 = \$1.845.$$
$$PV\ E(P_3) = \$34.938 \div (1.13)3 = \$24.214.$$
$$E(P_0) = \$1.947 + \$1.895 + \$1.845 + \$24.214 = \$29.901 \sim \$29.90.$$

The Decision

Sally estimated the current value of WSC's stock to be $30.29 using the constant growth dividend model and $29.90 using the nonconstant growth model. Considering all the uncertainties involved in the valuation processes, $30 seems a reasonable final estimate. However, the current stock price is $33, so it appears that the stock is overvalued by the market and hence should not be bought. (Alternatively, the constant growth expected rate of return on the stock is 12.4 percent, while Sally's required rate of return is 13.0 percent. Because the expected return is less than that required, the stock should not be purchased.)

However, these judgments require that (1) the valuation estimates are correct and (2) the market for WSC's stock is efficient. If the market is not efficient (perhaps because the stock is infrequently traded), the current price may not reflect all public information and new information may cause the price to soar as opposed to fall to Sally's value estimate. Sally, wisely, declined to offer an opinion regarding the stock recommendation. However, she did suggest that her mother think about buying a low-cost, well-diversified mutual fund for her retirement portfolio rather than invest in individual stocks. ■

CHAPTER

8

LEASE FINANCING

Learning Objectives

After studying this chapter, readers should be able to

- describe the different types of leases,
- explain how lease financing affects financial statements and taxes,
- analyze basic lease transactions from the perspectives of both the lessee and the lessor, and
- discuss the factors that create value in lease transactions.

Introduction

Businesses generally own fixed (capital) assets, but it is the use of the buildings and equipment that is important to the business, not their ownership. One way to obtain the use of such assets is to raise debt or equity capital and then use this capital to buy the assets. An alternative way to obtain the use of fixed assets is to lease them. Prior to the 1950s, leasing was generally associated with real estate—land and buildings. Today, almost any kind of fixed asset can be leased.

Leasing is used extensively in the health services field. For example, it is estimated that 35 percent to 40 percent of all medical equipment used in the United States is leased. In 2018 alone, healthcare providers leased more than $10 billion worth of equipment. Diagnostic imaging devices account for about half of all provider leasing, with a typical lease term of about five years. In addition to diagnostic equipment, there has been increasing use of leasing to acquire information technology, which is consuming a larger and larger proportion of healthcare businesses' capital expenditures.

Lease Parties and Types

There are two parties to any lease transaction. The user of a leased asset is called the *lessee*, while the owner of the property—usually the manufacturer or a leasing company—is called the *lessor*. ("Lessee" is pronounced "less-EE" [not "lease-ee"], and "lessor" is pronounced "LESS-or.")

Historically, leases have been classified in one of three categories: (1) operating leases, (2) finance leases, and (3) combination leases. In this section, we discuss these informal classifications. In later sections, we will discuss more formal classifications used by accountants and by the Internal Revenue Service (IRS).

Operating Leases

Operating leases generally provide for both financing and maintenance in addition to use of the asset. IBM was one of the pioneers of operating lease contracts. Computers and office copiers—together with automobiles, trucks, and medical diagnostic equipment—are the primary types of assets involved in operating leases. Ordinarily, operating leases require the lessor to maintain and service the leased equipment, and the cost of the maintenance is built into the lease payments.

Another important characteristic of operating leases is partial amortization. The lease contract is usually written for a period considerably shorter than the expected economic life of the leased asset; thus, the payments required under the lease contract are not sufficient for the lessor to recover the full cost of the equipment. However, the lessor can expect to recover all costs eventually by lease renewal payments, by releasing the equipment to other lessees, or through sale of the equipment.

Finally, operating leases often contain a *cancellation clause*, which gives the lessee the right to cancel the lease and return the equipment before the expiration of the basic lease agreement. This feature is important to the lessee because it means that the equipment can be returned if it is rendered obsolete by technological advances or if it is no longer needed because of a decline in the lessee's business.

Finance Leases

Finance leases, which are also called *capital leases*, are differentiated from operating leases in that they (1) typically do not provide for maintenance service, (2) typically are not cancelable, (3) generally are executed for a period that approximates the useful life of the asset, and hence (4) are fully amortized—that is, the lessor receives rental payments equal to the full cost of the leased asset plus a return on the funds employed.

A lease is classified as a finance lease if one or more of the following conditions exist:

- Under the terms of the lease, ownership of the property is effectively transferred from the lessor to the lessee.

- The lessee can purchase the property at less than its true market value when the lease expires.
- The lease runs for a period equal to or greater than 75 percent of the asset's life. Thus, if an asset has a ten-year life and the lease is written for eight years, the lease must be capitalized.
- The present value of the lease payments is equal to or greater than 90 percent of the initial value of the asset. The discount rate used to calculate the present value of the lease payments must be the lower of (1) the rate used by the lessor to establish the lease payments, which is discussed later in the chapter; and (2) the rate of interest that the lessee would have to pay for new debt with a maturity equal to that of the lease. Note that any maintenance payments embedded in the lease payment must be stripped out prior to checking this condition (FASB 2016).

In a typical finance lease, the lessee selects the item it requires and negotiates the price and delivery terms with the manufacturer. The lessee then arranges to have a leasing firm (lessor) buy the equipment from the manufacturer, and the lessee simultaneously executes a lease agreement with the lessor. The lessee is generally given an option to renew the lease at a reduced rate on expiration of the initial lease agreement. However, under a "pure" finance lease, the initial lease cannot be canceled. Also, the lessee generally pays the insurance premiums and any property taxes due on the leased property.

The terms of the lease call for full amortization of the lessor's investment plus a rate of return on the unamortized balance, which is close to the percentage rate the lessee would have paid on a secured term loan. For example, if a radiology group practice would have to pay 10 percent for a term loan to buy an X-ray machine, the lessor would build a rate of about 10 percent into the lease contract. The parallel to borrowing is obvious in a finance lease. Under a secured loan arrangement, the lender would normally receive a series of equal payments just sufficient to amortize (pay off) the loan and to provide a specified rate of return on the outstanding loan balance. Under a finance lease, the lease payments are set up exactly the same way—the payments are just sufficient to return the full purchase price to the lessor, plus a stated return on the lessor's investment.

A *sale and leaseback* is a special type of finance lease, often used with real estate, that can be arranged by a user that currently owns some asset. Here, the user sells the asset to another party and simultaneously executes an agreement to lease the property back for a stated period under specific terms. In a sale and leaseback, the lessee receives an immediate cash payment in exchange for a future series of lease payments that must be made to rent the asset sold.

Combination Leases

Although the distinction between operating and finance leases has historical significance, today many lessors offer leases under a wide variety of terms. Therefore, in practice, leases often do not fit exactly into the operating lease or finance lease category but rather combine some features of each. For example, many of today's finance leases contain cancellation clauses, which historically have been associated only with operating leases. However, when used in finance leases, these clauses generally include prepayment provisions whereby the lessee must make penalty payments sufficient to enable the lessor to recover some or all of the remaining lease payments.

SELF-TEST QUESTIONS

1. What is the difference between an operating lease and a finance lease?
2. What is a sale and leaseback?
3. Explain the features of a combination lease.

Per Procedure Versus Fixed Payment Leases

Lease (rental) payments on operating leases can be structured in two different ways. Under *fixed payment* terms, an agreed-on fixed amount is made to the lessor periodically—usually monthly. With this type of payment, the cost to the lessee is known with certainty. Under *per procedure (per use)* terms, a fixed amount is paid each time the equipment is used. In essence, a per procedure lease converts a lessee's fixed cost for the equipment (which is independent of volume) into a variable cost (which is directly related to volume). We will have more to say about per procedure leases later in the chapter.

SELF-TEST QUESTION

1. How do per procedure and fixed payment operating lease terms differ?

Tax Effects

For both investor-owned and not-for-profit healthcare businesses, tax effects can play an important role in the lease-versus-buy decision.

For investor-owned businesses, the full amount of lease payments is a tax deductible expense for the lessee **provided that the IRS agrees that a particular contract is a genuine lease and not simply a loan that is called a lease**. Thus, it is important that a lease contract be written with terms that are acceptable to the IRS. A lease that complies with all of the IRS requirements for taxable businesses is called a *guideline*, or *tax-oriented, lease.* In a guideline lease, ownership tax benefits (primarily depreciation) accrue to the lessor and the lessee's lease payments are fully tax deductible. A lease that does not meet the tax guidelines is called a *nonguideline*, or *non-tax-oriented, lease.* For this type of lease, the lessee can deduct only the implied interest portion of each lease payment. However, the lessee is effectively the owner of the leased equipment; thus, the lessee, rather than the lessor, receives the tax depreciation benefit.

The main provisions of the tax guidelines are as follows:

- The lease term, including any extensions or renewals at a fixed rental rate, must not exceed 80 percent of the estimated useful life of the equipment at the commencement of the lease transaction. Thus, at the projected end of the lease, the property must have an estimated remaining life equal to at least 20 percent of its original life. Furthermore, the remaining useful life must not be less than one year. This requirement limits the maximum term of a guideline lease to 80 percent of

LASIK and Per Use Leases

LASIK—commonly referred to as laser eye surgery or laser vision correction—is a type of refractive surgery for the correction of myopia, hypermetropia, and astigmatism. The surgery is performed by an ophthalmologist who uses a laser to reshape the cornea to improve visual acuity. For most patients, LASIK provides a permanent alternative to eyeglasses or contact lenses. As of 2018, more than 19 million such procedures have been performed in the United States.

LASIK surgery was first approved by the Food and Drug Administration for use in the United States in the early 1990s, after its successful application in other countries. At the time, the equipment itself cost about $100,000. Initially, there was significant uncertainty regarding the effectiveness and patient acceptance of the procedure, and hence the volume of surgeries was highly speculative. The end result was that most ophthalmologists were unwilling to risk the $100,000 purchase price.

To encourage widespread use, the manufacturer, along with other lessors, offered to lease the equipment to physicians on a per procedure (per use) basis. The lease required no upfront payment and the lessor handled equipment maintenance and any required repairs. In addition, the lessor provided delivery and installation along with all required technical training for a per use charge of roughly $800. The end result was a fixed contribution of about $1,200 for each procedure performed, which first covers all other operating costs and then flows to profit. Under a traditional fixed payment lease, the risk of low volume is borne by the practice, but under a per use lease, this risk is assumed by the lessor. At anticipated volumes, the per use lease cost more than a fixed payment lease, but the per use lease provided protection (insurance) for the lessee against low volumes.

Because of the attractiveness of the per use lease financing option to ophthalmologists, LASIK surgery took off like gangbusters and today remains one of their leading revenue sources.

the asset's useful life. Note that an asset's useful life is normally much longer than its tax depreciation class life.
- The equipment's estimated value (in constant dollars without adjustment for inflation) at the projected expiration of the lease must equal at least 20 percent of its value at the start of the lease. Note that the estimated value of the asset at the end of the lease is called the *residual value.* This requirement also has the effect of limiting the maximum lease term.
- Neither the lessee nor any related party can have the right to purchase the property from the lessor at a price substantially less than its fair market value.
- Neither the lessee nor any related party can pay or guarantee payment of any part of the price of the leased equipment. Simply put, the lessee cannot make any investment in the equipment, other than through the lease payments.
- The leased equipment must not be "limited use" property, which is equipment that can be used only by the lessee or a related party at the end of the lease.

If the contract is classified as a tax-oriented lease, then the lessor is entitled to the tax benefits of ownership, including depreciation and any investment tax credits. The lessor also bears the responsibilities of ownership, such as maintenance expenses. The reverse is true for a non-tax-oriented lease: The lessee retains the tax benefits and pays for the maintenance. The IRS guidelines mean that almost all operating leases are tax-oriented leases and almost all finance leases are non-tax-oriented leases.

The reason for the IRS's concern about lease terms is that, without restrictions, a business can set up a "lease" transaction that calls for rapid lease payments, which would be deductible from taxable income. The effect would be to depreciate the equipment over a much shorter period than the IRS allows in its depreciation guidelines. For example, suppose that New England Laboratories, Inc., an investor-owned corporation that owns clinical laboratories in New Hampshire, Maine, Massachusetts, and Vermont, planned to acquire a $2 million computer that has a three-year life for tax purposes. According to current tax laws (Modified Accelerated Cost Recovery System [MACRS]), the annual depreciation allowances would be $660,000 in year 1; $900,000 in year 2; $300,000 in year 3; and $140,000 in year 4. If New England Laboratories were in the 30 percent federal-plus-state tax bracket, the depreciation would provide a tax savings of 0.30 × $660,000 = $198,000 in year 1; $270,000 in year 2; $90,000 in year 3; and $42,000 in year 4, for a total savings of $600,000. At a 6 percent discount rate, the present value of these tax savings would be $568,081.

Now, suppose the firm could acquire the computer through a one-year lease arrangement with First Bank of Boston for a payment of $2 million, with a one-dollar purchase option. If the $2 million payment were treated as a lease payment, it would be fully deductible, so it would provide tax savings of 0.30 × $2,000,000 = $600,000 versus a present value of only $568,081 for the depreciation shelters associated with ownership. Thus, the lease payment and the depreciation would both provide the same total amount of tax savings—30 percent of $2 million, or $600,000—but the savings would come in faster, and hence have a higher present value, with the one-year lease. This acceleration would benefit businesses, but it would be costly to the government and hence to individual taxpayers. For this reason, the IRS has established the rules just described for defining a lease for tax purposes.

Even though leasing can be used only within limits to speed up the effective depreciation schedule, there are still times when substantial tax benefits can be derived from a leasing arrangement. For example, if an investor-owned hospital has a large construction program that has generated so much depreciation that it has no current tax liabilities, then depreciation shelters are not very useful. In this case, a leasing company set up by a profitable business, such as General Electric, can buy the equipment, receive the depreciation shelters, and then share these benefits with the hospital by charging lower lease payments.[1] This issue will be discussed in detail later in the chapter, but the point to be made now is that if businesses are to obtain tax benefits from leasing, the lease contract must be written in a manner that will qualify it as a true lease under IRS guidelines. Any questions about the tax status of a lease contract must be resolved by the potential lessee prior to signing the contract.

Not-for-profit businesses also benefit from tax laws, but in a different way. Because not-for-profit corporations do not obtain tax benefits from depreciation, the ownership of assets has no tax-related value. However, lessors, which are all taxable businesses, do benefit from ownership. This benefit, in turn, can be shared with the lessee in the form of lower rental payments. Note, however, that the cost of tax-exempt debt to not-for-profit firms can be lower than the after-tax cost of debt to taxable firms, so leasing is not automatically less costly to not-for-profit businesses than borrowing in the tax-exempt markets and buying.

A special type of financial transaction—called a *tax-exempt lease*—has been created for not-for-profit businesses. Legally, this transaction is not really a lease, but it has all of the general characteristics of one. The major difference between a tax-exempt lease and a conventional lease is that the implied interest portion of the lease payment is not classified as taxable income to the lessor. Thus, a portion of the lease payment received by the lessor is exempt from federal income taxes. The rationale for this tax treatment is that the interest paid on most debt financing used by not-for-profit organizations is tax exempt to the lender, and a lessor is, in actuality, a lender. Tax-exempt leases provide a greater after-tax return to lessors than do conventional leases, so some of this "extra" return can be passed back to the lessee in the form of lower lease payments. Thus, a not-for-profit lessee's payments on tax-exempt leases can be lower than the payments on conventional leases.

SELF-TEST QUESTIONS

1. What is the difference between a guideline and a nonguideline lease?
2. What are some provisions that would make a lease nonguideline?
3. Why should the IRS care about lease provisions?
4. What is a tax-exempt lease?

Reporting Leases on Financial Statements

Previously, neither the leased asset nor the liabilities under an operating lease contract appeared on the lessee's balance sheet. This type of financing is often called *off-balance-sheet financing*, which makes it difficult for investors to identify an organization's true financial obligations. The Financial Accounting Standards Board (FASB) recently issued new financial reporting standards for operating leases that effectively eliminate off-balance-sheet financing for leases. Under the new Accounting Standards Update (ASU 2016-02), any lease lasting more than a year must be capitalized by reporting it on the balance sheet as a liability and an asset. In short, operating leases now appear on the balance sheet under their own accounts. Consistent with the new accounting standards, the leased asset will appear as both the asset (described as a "right-of-use" asset) and a lease liability.

Regardless of current accounting rules, from an economic (financial) perspective, a lease has the same economic consequences for a business as a loan in which the asset is pledged as collateral. If a firm signs a lease contract, its obligation

Financial Accounting Standards Board Changes to Lease Accounting Guidelines

FASB Statement 13, "Accounting for Leases," which has been in effect since 1977, spells out in detail the conditions under which a lease must be capitalized and the procedures for capitalizing it. FASB is the primary organization promulgating the rules that form the basis of generally accepted accounting principles (GAAP), which, in turn, guide the preparation of financial statements. FASB recently established a significant new Accounting Standards Update (ASU 2016-02) for leasing that goes into effect in 2019 for most organizations.

Although a complete discussion of the changes is beyond the scope of this text, the most important change is that any operating

(continued)

to make lease payments is just as binding as if it had signed a loan agreement; failure to make lease payments has the potential to bankrupt a firm, just as failure to make principal and interest payments on a loan can result in bankruptcy. Thus, leases are considered the same as debt for capital structure purposes, and they have roughly the same effects as debt on the financial condition of the firm.

However, there are some legal differences between loans and leases, mostly involving the rights of lessors versus lenders when a business in financial distress reorganizes or liquidates. In most financial distress situations, lessors fare better than lenders do, so lessors may be more willing than would lenders to deal with firms in poor financial condition. At a minimum, lessors may be willing to accept lower rates of return than lenders would when dealing with financially distressed firms because their risks are lower.

(continued from previous page)

lease greater than or equal to 12 months in length appears on the balance sheet, whereas previously operating leases only appeared on the income statement as an expense. This change has the ability to affect a firm's debt balance; however, there is room for the language of the lease to ensure that it is not considered a portion of a firm's debt. Rather, all fixed payment leases would be accounted for in the same way on the balance sheet—all leased property would be listed by lessees on the asset side as "right-to-use assets" and on the liability side as "lease liabilities."

Over the term of the lease, leased assets would be depreciated by the straight-line method and lease liabilities would be decreased by the rental payments made. For all practical purposes, the leased assets and liabilities will balance one another, so the primary effect will be to increase both sides of the balance sheet by a like amount. The ultimate purpose of the proposed rule is to eliminate operating leases as a source of off-balance-sheet financing and hence report all leases directly on the balance sheet.

SELF-TEST QUESTIONS

1. Why were some leases referred to as off-balance-sheet financing prior to 2019?
2. How are leases accounted for in a lessee's financial statements?

Evaluation by the Lessee

Leases are evaluated by both the lessee and the lessor. The lessee must determine whether leasing an asset is less costly than obtaining equivalent alternative financing and buying the asset, and the lessor must decide what the lease payments must be to produce a rate of return consistent with the riskiness of the investment. This section focuses on the lessee's analysis.

A degree of uncertainty exists regarding the theoretically correct way to evaluate lease-versus-purchase decisions, and complex decision models have been developed to aid in the analysis. However, the simple analysis given here, coupled with judgment, is sufficient to prevent a lessee from entering into a lease agreement that is clearly not in its best interests. In the typical case, the events leading to a lease arrangement follow this sequence:

- The business decides to acquire a particular building or piece of equipment; this decision is based on the standard capital budgeting procedures discussed in chapters 11 and 12. The decision to acquire the asset is **not an issue** in the typical lease analysis; this decision was made previously as part of the capital budgeting process. In lease analysis, we are concerned simply with whether to obtain the use of the property by lease or by purchase (how to finance the acquisition).
- Once the business has decided to acquire the asset, the next question is how to finance its acquisition. A well-run business does not have excess cash lying around, and even if it does, there are opportunity costs associated with its use.
- Funds to purchase the asset can be obtained by borrowing; by retaining earnings; or, if the business is investor owned, by selling new equity. If the firm is not-for-profit, perhaps the funds can be raised by soliciting contributions for the project. Some combination of these sources can also be used. Alternatively, the asset can be leased.

Because a lease is roughly comparable to a loan in the sense that both have a similar impact on a business's financial condition, the appropriate comparison when making lease decisions is the cost of lease financing versus the cost of debt financing. The comparison of lease financing to debt financing is valid regardless of how the asset actually would be financed if it were not leased. The asset may be purchased with available cash if not leased or financed by a new equity sale or a cash contribution. However, because leasing is a substitute for debt financing and hence uses up a business's debt capacity, the appropriate comparison would still be to debt financing.

Simplified Example

To better understand the basic elements of lease analysis, consider this simplified example. Nashville Radiology Group (the Group) needs to use a $100 piece of diagnostic equipment for two years, and the Group must choose between leasing and buying the machine. (The actual cost is $100,000, but let's keep the numbers simple.) If the Group purchases the machine, the bank will lend the Group the needed $100 at a rate of 10 percent on a two-year, simple interest loan. Thus, the Group would have to pay the bank $10 in interest at the end of each year, plus return the $100 in principal at the end of year 2. For simplicity, assume that, if the Group purchases the machine, it can depreciate the entire cost over two years for tax purposes by the straight-line method, resulting in tax depreciation of $50 in each year. Furthermore, the Group's tax rate is 30 percent. Thus, the depreciation expense produces a tax savings, or *tax shield*, of \$50 × 0.30 = \$15 each year. Also for simplicity, assume that the machine's value at the end of two years (its residual value) is estimated to be \$0.

Alternatively, the Group can lease the asset under a guideline lease for two years for a payment of \$55 at the end of each year. The analysis for the lease-versus-buy decision consists of (1) estimating the cash flows associated with borrowing and buying the asset—that is, the flows associated with debt financing; (2) estimating the cash flows associated with leasing the asset; and (3) comparing the two financing methods to determine which has the lower cost. Here are the borrow-and-buy flows:

Cash Flows if the Group Buys	*Year 0*	*Year 1*	*Year 2*
Equipment cost	(\$100)		
Loan amount	100		
Interest expense		(\$10)	(\$ 10)
Tax savings from interest		3	3
Principal repayment			(100)
Tax savings from depreciation	0	15	15
Net cash flow	\$ 0	\$ 8	(\$ 92)

The net cash flow is zero in year 0, positive in year 1, and negative in year 2. Because the operating cash flows (the revenues and operating costs) will be the same regardless of whether the machine is leased or purchased, they can be ignored. Cash flows that are not affected by the decision at hand are said to be ***nonincremental*** to the decision. Here are the cash flows associated with the lease:

Cash Flows if the Group Leases	*Year 0*	*Year 1*	*Year 2*
Lease payment		(\$ 55)	(\$55)
Tax savings from payment		16.5	16.5
Net cash flow	\$ 0	(\$38.5)	(\$38.5)

Note that the two sets of cash flows reflect the tax savings associated with interest expense, depreciation, and lease payments, as appropriate. If the lease had not met IRS guidelines, ownership would have resided with the lessee, and the Group would have depreciated the asset for tax purposes whether it had been "leased" or purchased. Furthermore, only the implied interest portion of the lease payment would be tax deductible. Thus, the analysis for a nonguideline lease would consist of simply comparing the after-tax financing flows on the loan with the after-tax lease payment stream.

To compare the cost streams of buying and leasing, we must put them on a present value basis. As we will explain later, the correct discount rate is the lessee's after-tax cost of debt, which for the Group is 10% × (1 – T) = 10% × (1 – 0.3) = 7%. Applying this rate, we find the present value cost of buying to be $72.88 and the present value cost of leasing to be $69.61. Because leasing has the lower present value of costs, it is the less costly financing alternative, so the Group should lease the asset.

This simplified example shows the general approach used in lease analysis, and it also illustrates a concept that can simplify the cash flow estimation process. Look back at the loan-related cash flows if the Group buys the machine, which consist of the interest expense, tax savings from interest, and principal repayment. The after-tax loan-related flows are –$7 in year 1 and –$107 in year 2. When these flows are discounted to year 0 at the 7 percent after-tax cost of debt, their present value is –$100, which is the negative of the loan amount shown in year 0. This equality results because we first used the cost of debt to estimate the future financing flows, and we then used this same rate to discount the flows back to Year 0, all on an after-tax basis. In effect, the loan amount positive cash flow and the loan cost negative cash flows cancel one another out. Here is the cash flow stream associated with buying the asset after the Year 0 loan amount and the related Year 1 and Year 2 flows have been removed:

Cash Flows if the Group Buys	*Year 0*	*Year 1*	*Year 2*
Cost of asset	($100)		
Tax savings from depreciation		$15	$15
Net cash flow	($100)	$15	$15

The present value cost of buying here is $72.88, which is the same number we found earlier. The two approaches will always produce consistent estimates regardless of the specific terms of the debt financing—as long as the discount rate is the after-tax cost of debt, the cash flows associated with the loan can be ignored.

More Realistic Example

To examine a more realistic example of lease analysis, consider the following lease-versus-buy decision facing the Nashville Radiology Group:

- The Group plans to acquire a new computer system that will automate the Group's clinical records, as well as its accounting, billing, and collection processes. The computer has an economic life of eight years and costs $200,000 (delivered and installed). However, the Group plans to lease the equipment for only four years because it believes that computer technology is changing rapidly and wants the opportunity to reevaluate the situation at that time.

- The Group can borrow the required $200,000 from its bank at a before-tax cost of 10 percent.
- The computer's estimated scrap value is $5,000 after eight years of use, but its estimated residual value when the lease expires after four years of use is $20,000. Thus, if the Group buys the equipment, it would expect to receive $20,000 before taxes when the equipment is sold in four years.
- The Group can lease the equipment for four years at a rental charge of $57,000, payable at the beginning of each year, but the lessor will own the equipment on expiration of the lease. (The lease payment schedule is established by the potential lessor, as described in a later section, and the Group can accept, reject, or negotiate it.)
- The lease contract stipulates that the lessor will maintain the computer at no additional charge to the Group. However, if the Group borrows money to buy the computer, it will have to bear the cost of maintenance, which would be performed by the equipment manufacturer at a fixed contract rate of $2,500 per year, payable at the beginning of each year.
- The computer falls in the MACRS five-year class life, the group's marginal tax rate is 30 percent, and the lease qualifies as a guideline lease under a special IRS ruling. (Refer to chapter 1 to review tax depreciation, if necessary.)

Dollar Cost Approach

On the web at: *ache.org/HAP/PinkSong8e*

Exhibit 8.1 shows the steps involved in a complete *dollar cost analysis.* As in the simplified example, our approach here is to compare the dollar cost of owning (borrowing and buying) to the dollar cost of leasing. All else the same, the lower-cost alternative is preferable. Part I of the exhibit is devoted to the costs of borrowing and buying. Here, line 1 shows the equipment's cost, and line 2 shows the maintenance expense; both are cash costs or outflows. Note that whenever an analyst is setting up cash flows on a time line, one of the first decisions to be made is what time interval will be used—that is, months, quarters, years, or some other period. As a starting point, we generally assume that all cash flows occur at the end of each year. If, at some point later in the analysis, we conclude that another interval is better, we will change it. Longer intervals—such as years—simplify the analysis but introduce some inaccuracies because all cash flows do not occur at the end of the year. For example, tax benefits occur quarterly because businesses pay taxes on a quarterly basis. On the other hand, shorter intervals—such as months—often are used for lease analyses because lease payments typically occur monthly. For ease of illustration, we are using annual flows in this example.

Line 3 shows the maintenance tax savings, and because maintenance expense is tax deductible, the Group saves 0.30 × \$2,500 = \$750 in taxes by virtue of paying the maintenance fee. Line 4 shows the depreciation tax savings, which is the depreciation expense multiplied by the tax rate. For example, the MACRS allowance for the first year is 20 percent, so the depreciation expense is 0.20 × \$200,000 = \$40,000, and the depreciation tax savings is 0.30 × \$40,000 = \$12,000.

Lines 5 and 6 show the residual value cash flows. The residual value is estimated to be \$20,000, but the tax book value after four years of depreciation is \$34,000. Thus, the Group is losing \$14,000 for tax purposes, which produces the 0.3 × \$14,000 = \$4,200 tax savings shown as an inflow in line

EXHIBIT 8.1
Lessee's Dollar Cost Analysis

	Year 0	Year 1	Year 2	Year 3	Year 4
I. Cost of Owning (Borrowing and Buying)					
1. Net purchase price	(\$200,000)				
2. Maintenance cost	(2,500)	(\$2,500)	(\$ 2,500)	(\$ 2,500)	
3. Maintenance tax savings	750	750	750	750	
4. Depreciation tax savings		12,000	19,200	11,400	\$ 7,200
5. Residual value					20,000
6. Residual value tax					4,200
7. Net cash flow	(\$201,750)	\$10,250	\$17,450	\$ 9,650	\$31,400
8. PV cost of owning =	(\$145,097)				
II. Cost of Leasing					
9. Lease payment	(\$ 55,000)	(\$55,000)	(\$55,000)	(\$55,000)	
10. Tax savings	16,500	16,500	16,500	16,500	
11. Net cash flow	(\$ 38,500)	(\$38,500)	(\$38,500)	(\$38,500)	
12. PV cost of leasing =	(\$139,536)				

III. Cost Comparison

13. Net advantage to leasing (NAL) = PV cost of leasing − PV cost of owning
= −\$139,536 − (−\$145,097) = \$5,561.

Note: The MACRS depreciation allowances are 0.20, 0.32, 0.19, and 0.12 in years 1 through 4, respectively. In practice, a lease analysis such as this one would be done on a monthly basis using a spreadsheet program.

6. Line 7, which sums the component cash flows, shows the net cash flows associated with borrowing and buying.

Part II of exhibit 8.1 contains an analysis of the cost of leasing. The lease payments, shown in line 9, are $55,000 per year; this rate, which includes maintenance, was established by the prospective lessor and offered to the Group. If the Group accepts the lease, the full amount will be a deductible expense, so the tax savings, shown in line 10, is 0.30 × Lease payment = 0.30 × $55,000 = $16,500. The net cash flows associated with leasing are shown in line 11.

The final step is to compare the net cost of owning with the net cost of leasing. First, we must put the annual cash flows associated with owning and leasing on a common basis by converting them to present values, which brings up the question of the proper rate at which to discount the net cash flows. We know that the riskier the cash flows, the higher the discount rate used to find the present value will be. This same principle was observed in our discussion of security valuation, and it applies to all discounted cash flow analyses, including lease analysis. Just how risky are the cash flows under consideration here? Most of them are relatively certain, at least when compared with the types of cash flow estimates associated with stock investments or with the Group's operating cash flows. For example, the loan payment schedule is set by contract, as is the lease payment schedule. The depreciation expenses are also established by law and not subject to change, and the annual maintenance fee is fixed by contract as well. The tax savings are somewhat uncertain, but they will be as projected as long as the Group's marginal tax rate remains at 30 percent. The residual value is the least certain of the cash flows, but even here, the Group's management is fairly confident because there are a great deal of historical data available to help make the estimate.

Because the cash flows under the lease and under the borrow-and-purchase alternatives are both relatively certain, they should be discounted at a relatively low rate. What market-determined rate is readily available that reflects relatively low risk? Most analysts recommend that the firm's cost of debt financing be used, and this rate seems reasonable in our example. However, the Group's cost of debt—10 percent—must be adjusted to reflect the tax deductibility of interest payments because this benefit of borrowing and buying is not accounted for in the cash flows. Thus, the Group's effective cost of debt becomes Before-tax cost × (1 − Tax rate) = 10% × 0.7 = 7%. Accordingly, the cash flows in lines 7 and 11 are discounted at a 7 percent rate. The resulting present values are $145,097 for the cost of owning and $139,536 for the cost of leasing, as shown in lines 8 and 12. Leasing is the lower-cost financing alternative, so the Group should lease, rather than buy, the computer.

The cost comparison can be formalized by defining the *net advantage to leasing (NAL)* as follows:

Key Equation 8.1: Net Advantage to Leasing (NAL)

$$\text{NAL} = \text{PV cost of leasing} - \text{PV cost of owning}$$
$$= -\$139{,}536 - (-\$145{,}097) = \$5{,}561.$$

The positive NAL indicates that leasing creates more value than buying, so the Group should lease the equipment. Indeed, the value of the Group is increased by $5,561 if it leases, rather than buys, the computer.

Percentage Cost Approach

On the web at: ache.org/HAP/PinkSong8e

The Group's lease-versus-buy decision can also be analyzed using *percentage cost analysis*, which involves comparing the effective cost rate on the lease to the effective cost rate on the loan. Signing a lease is similar to signing a loan contract—the firm has the use of the equipment but must make a series of payments under either type of contract. We know the effective cost rate built into the loan: It is the 7 percent after-tax interest rate. If the after-tax cost rate in the lease is less than 7 percent, there is an advantage to leasing.

Exhibit 8.2 sets forth the cash flows needed to determine the percentage cost of the lease. Here is an explanation of the exhibit:

- The first step is to calculate the leasing-versus-owning cash flows. We do so by subtracting the owning cash flows shown in line 7 from the leasing cash flows shown in line 11 (see exhibit 8.2). The differences are the incremental cash flows that relate to the Group if it leases, rather than buys, the computer.

EXHIBIT 8.2 Lessee's Percentage Cost

	Year 0	*Year 1*	*Year 2*	*Year 3*	*Year 4*
1. Leasing cash flow	($38,500)	($38,500)	($38,500)	($38,500)	$0
2. Less: Owning cash flow	(201,750)	10,250	17,450	9,650	31,400
3. Leasing-versus-owning cash flow	$163,250	($48,750)	($55,950)	($48,150)	($31,400)

NAL = $5,561.
IRR = 5.4%.

- Note that exhibit 8.2 consolidates the analysis shown in exhibit 8.1 into a single set of net cash flows. At this point, we can discount the net (consolidated) cash flows shown in line 3 of exhibit 8.2 by 6 percent to obtain the NAL, \$5,561. In exhibit 8.1, we discounted the owning and leasing cash flows separately and then subtracted their present values to obtain the NAL. In exhibit 8.2, we subtracted the cash flows first to obtain a single set of flows and then found their present value. The end result is the same.
- The consolidated cash flows provide good insight into the economics of leasing. If the Group leases the computer, it avoids having to lay out the cash required to buy the equipment in year 0, but it is then obligated to make a series of cash outflows for four years. In marketing materials, leasing companies are quick to point out that leasing does not require a large, upfront cash outlay (\$163,250 in this example). However, they are not so quick to mention that the "cost" to save this outlay is an obligation to make payments over the next four years. Leasing makes sense financially (disregarding other factors) only if the savings are worth the cost.
- By inputting the leasing-versus-owning cash flows listed in exhibit 8.2 into a spreadsheet and using the internal rate of return (IRR) function, we can find the cost rate inherent in the cash flow stream: 5.6 percent. This rate is the equivalent after-tax cost rate implied in the lease contract. Because this cost rate is lower than the 7 percent after-tax cost rate on a regular loan, leasing is less expensive than borrowing and buying. Thus, the percentage cost analysis confirms the NAL analysis.

Some Additional Points

So far, we have discussed the main features of a lessee's analysis, including both dollar cost and percentage cost approaches. Before we move on to the lessor's analysis, note the following points:

- The dollar cost and percentage cost approaches will always lead to the same decision. Thus, one method is as good as the other from a decision standpoint.
- If the net residual value cash flow (residual value and tax effect) is considered riskier than the other cash flows in the analysis, it is possible to account for this differential risk by applying a higher discount rate to this flow, which results in a lower present value. Because the net residual value flow is an inflow in the cost-of-owning analysis, a lower present value leads to a higher present value cost of owning. Thus, increasing residual value risk decreases the attractiveness of owning an asset. For example, assume that the Group's managers

believe that the computer's residual value is much riskier than the other flows in exhibit 8.1. Furthermore, they believe that 10 percent, rather than 7 percent, is the appropriate discount rate to apply to the residual value flows. When the exhibit 8.1 analysis is modified to reflect this risk, the present value cost of owning increases to \$149,314, while the NAL increases to \$15,070. The riskier the residual value, **all else the same**, the more favorable leasing becomes, because residual value risk is borne by the lessor. However, all else will generally not be the same. Increasing residual value risk would cause the lessor to increase the lease payment, thereby making the lease less attractive to the lessee.

- As we discuss in chapter 11, net present value (NPV) is the dollar value of a project, assuming that it is financed using debt and equity financing. In lease analysis, the NAL is the additional dollar value of a project attributable to leasing, as opposed to conventional (debt) financing. Thus, to approximate the value of a leased asset to the firm, we increase the project's NPV by the amount of the NAL:

Key Equation 8.2: Adjusted NPV

$$\text{Adjusted NPV} = \text{NPV} + \text{NAL}.$$

The value added through leasing, in some cases, can turn unprofitable (negative NPV) projects into profitable (positive adjusted NPV) projects. Thus, projects (assets) that are marginally unprofitable when evaluated on the basis of conventional financing should be reevaluated on the basis of lease financing (if available) to see whether alternative financing will make the project financially acceptable.

SELF-TEST QUESTIONS

1. Explain how the cash flows are structured in conducting a dollar-based NAL analysis.
2. What discount rate should be used when lessees perform lease analyses?
3. What is the economic interpretation of the NAL?
4. What is the economic interpretation of a lease's IRR?

Evaluation by the Lessor

On the web at: *ache.org/HAP/PinkSong8e*

Thus far, we have considered lease analysis from the lessee's viewpoint. It is also useful to analyze the transaction as the lessor sees it: Is the lease a good investment for the party that *writes* the lease (i.e., the party that buys the asset)? The lessor will generally be a specialized leasing firm; a bank or bank affiliate; or a manufacturer, such as Siemens Healthcare, that uses leasing by an affiliated entity as a marketing tool.

Any potential lessor needs to know the rate of return on the capital invested in the lease. This information is also useful to the prospective lessee because lease terms on large leases are generally negotiated; so, the lessor and the lessee should know one another's position. The lessor's analysis involves (1) determining the net cash outlay, which is usually the invoice price of the leased equipment less any lease payments made in advance; (2) determining the periodic cash inflows, which consist of the lease payments minus income taxes and any maintenance expenses the lessor must bear; (3) estimating the after-tax residual value of the property when the lease expires; and (4) determining whether the rate of return on the lease is adequate for the riskiness of the investment.

To illustrate the lessor's analysis, we assume the same facts for the Nashville Radiology Group lease and this situation. The potential lessor is Medicomp, Inc. (https://medicompinc.com), a commercial leasing company that specializes in leasing computers to healthcare providers. Medicomp's marginal federal-plus-state tax rate is 30 percent. To provide maintenance to the Group, Medicomp must contract with the computer manufacturer under the same terms available to the Group—that is, $2,500 at the beginning of each year. Medicomp views computer lease arrangements as relatively low-risk investments. There is, however, some small chance of default on the lease, so Medicomp typically assumes that a lease investment is about as risky as buying AA-rated corporate bonds. Because four-year, AA-rated bonds are yielding 7.5 percent at the time of the analysis, Medicomp can earn an after-tax yield of $7.0\% \times (1 - T) = 7.0\% \times 0.7 = 4.9\%$ on such investments. Thus, 4.9 percent is the after-tax return that Medicomp can obtain on alternative investments of similar risk (the opportunity cost rate).

The lease analysis from the lessor's standpoint is developed in exhibit 8.3. Here, we see that the cash flows to the lessor are similar to those for the lessee shown in exhibit 8.1. Line 1 shows the purchase price of the computer—$ 200,000. Line 2 shows the maintenance costs, while line 3 lists the tax savings attributable to these costs. Line 4 shows the depreciation tax savings, or tax shields, that accrue to the owner of the computer. In line 5, we

EXHIBIT 8.3 Lessor's Analysis

	Year 0	Year 1	Year 2	Year 3	Year 4
1. Net purchase price	($200,000)				
2. Maintenance cost	(2,500)	($ 2,500)	($ 2,500)	($ 2,500)	
3. Maintenance tax savings	750	750	750	750	
4. Depreciation tax savings		12,000	19,200	11,400	$ 7,200
5. Lease payment	55,000	55,000	55,000	55,000	
6. Tax on lease payment	(16,500)	(16,500)	(16,500)	(16,500)	
7. Residual value					20,000
8. Tax on residual value					4,200
9. Net cash flow	($ 163,250)	$48,750	$ 55,950	$ 48,150	$31,400

NPV = $1,712
IRR = 5.4%.

show the annual lease rental payment as an inflow, while the taxes that must be paid on the rental payments are shown in line 6. Lines 7 and 8 show the residual value and resulting taxes (tax savings in this case). Finally, the cash flows are summed in line 9.

The value (NPV) of the lease to Medicomp is found by discounting the line 9 cash flows at the firm's after-tax opportunity cost of capital—4.9 percent—and then summing the resultant present values. (When using a spreadsheet for the analysis, use the NPV function.) For Medicomp, the NPV of the lease investment is $1,712, which means that the firm is somewhat better off, on a present value basis, if it writes the lease rather than investing in comparable-risk AA-rated bonds. If the NPV of the lease were negative, Medicomp would be better off investing in the bonds. Because we saw earlier that the lease is also advantageous to the Group, the transaction is beneficial to both the lessee and the lessor.

We can also calculate Medicomp's expected percentage rate of return on the lease by finding the IRR of the net cash flows shown in line 9 of exhibit 8.3. Simply use a spreadsheet's IRR function to find the answer: 5.4 percent. Thus, the lease provides a 5.4 percent after-tax return to Medicomp, which exceeds the 4.9 percent after-tax return available on alternative investments of similar risk: AA-rated, four-year bonds. So, using either the dollar-rate-of-return (NPV) method or the percentage-rate-of-return (IRR) method, we obtain the same result: The lease appears to be a satisfactory investment for Medicomp.

Note, however, that the lease investment is actually slightly more risky than the alternative bond investment because the residual value cash flow is less certain than a principal repayment. Thus, Medicomp would probably require a rate of return somewhat above the 4.9 percent promised on the bond investment, and the higher the risk of the residual value, the higher the required return. Also, note that the lessor's NPV analysis can be extended by using a higher discount rate on the residual value cash flows than that used on the other flows. Doing so lowers the NPV and hence makes the lease investment look less attractive than the bond investment.

SELF-TEST QUESTIONS

1. What discount rate is used in a lessor's NPV analysis?
2. What is the economic interpretation of the lessor's NPV? The lessor's IRR?

Lease Analysis Symmetry

Let's stop for a moment and compare the cash flows in exhibits 8.2 and 8.3. Upon examination, we find that the cash flows to the lessee and lessor are symmetrical. They differ in sign, but their values are the same. This symmetry occurs because there are only two parties to a lease transaction, and our example assumed that the parties would pay the same amount for the computer, pay taxes at the same rate, forecast the same residual value, and so on. Thus, a cash inflow to one party becomes a cash outflow to the other. Taken one step further, if the cost of debt to the lessee in our example had equaled the opportunity cost to the lessor, the NPV to the lessor would be equal, but opposite in sign, to the lessee's NAL. Therefore, if all of the input values had been the same to both lessee and lessor, Medicomp's NPV would have been a **negative** $5,561.

From this simple observation, we conclude that when there is symmetry between the lessor and the lessee—same tax rates, costs, and so on—leasing is a *zero-sum game*.[2] If the lease is attractive to the lessee, the lease is unattractive to the lessor, and vice versa. However, conditions often are such that leasing can be of benefit to both parties. This situation arises because of differences in tax rates, estimated residual values, or the ability to bear residual value risk. We will explore this issue in detail in a later section.

SELF-TEST QUESTIONS

1. What is lease analysis symmetry?
2. What impact does this symmetry have on the economic viability of leasing?

Setting the Lease Payment

On the web at: *ache.org/HAP/PinkSong8e*

In the preceding sections, we evaluated the lease assuming that the lease payments had already been specified. However, as a general rule (especially in large leases), the parties will work out the terms of the lease, including the size of the lease payments. In situations where the lease terms are not negotiable (which is often the case for small leases), the lessor must still go through the same type of analysis, setting terms that provide a target rate of return and then offering these terms to the potential lessee on a take-it-or-leave-it basis.

Competition in the leasing industry will force lessors to build market-related returns into their lease payment schedules. For an illustration, suppose Medicomp—after examining other alternative investment opportunities—decides that the 5.4 percent return on the Nashville Radiology Group lease is too low and that the lease should provide an after-tax return of 6.3 percent. What lease payment schedule would provide this return?

To answer this question, note again that exhibit 8.3 contains the lessor's cash flow analysis. If the basic analysis is done on a spreadsheet, it is easy to change the lease payment until the lease's NPV = $0 at a 6.3 percent discount rate or, equivalently, until its IRR = 6.3 percent. We did this with our spreadsheet lease evaluation model, and we found that the lessor must set the lease payment at $56,248 to obtain an expected after-tax rate of return of 6.3 percent. However, if this lease payment is not consistent with market rates, the Group may be able to strike a better deal with another lessor.

SELF-TEST QUESTION

1. How do lessors set the lease payment amount?

Leveraged Leases

On the web at: *ache.org/HAP/PinkSong8e*

In the early days of lease transactions, only two parties were involved: (1) the lessor, who put up the front money, and (2) the lessee, who used the asset. In recent years, however, a new type of lease—the *leveraged lease*—has come into widespread use. (In financial parlance, the term *leverage* means the use of debt financing.) Under a leveraged lease, the lessor arranges to borrow part of the required funds, generally giving the lender a lien on the property being leased, or a first mortgage if the lease is for real estate. (To meet IRS guidelines for leveraged leases, the lessor must have a minimum 20 percent equity interest in the lease, so the maximum amount of leverage that can be used is 80 percent of the purchase price.)

In a leveraged lease, the lessor still receives the tax benefits associated with depreciation. However, the lessor now has a riskier position because of its use of debt financing. Incidentally, whether a lease is leveraged is not important to the lessee; from the lessee's standpoint, the method of analyzing a proposed lease is unaffected by whether or not the lessor borrows part of the required capital.

The analysis in exhibit 8.3 can be easily modified if the lessor borrows part of the required $200,000, making the transaction a leveraged lease. First, we would add a set of lines to exhibit 8.3 to show the financing cash flows. The interest component would represent another tax deduction, while the loan repayment would constitute an additional cash outlay. The "initial cost" would be reduced by the amount of the loan. With these changes made, a new NPV and IRR can be calculated and used to evaluate whether the lease would be a good investment.

For an illustration of this concept, assume that Medicomp can borrow $100,000 of the $200,000 purchase price at a rate of 7 percent on a four-year, simple interest loan. Exhibit 8.4 contains the lessor's leveraged lease analysis. Line 1 shows the unleveraged lease cash flows from exhibit 8.3, while the leveraging cash flows are shown in lines 2 through 5. The net cash flows to Medicomp are shown in line 6. The NPV of the leveraged lease is $1,712, which is also the NPV of the unleveraged lease. In this situation, leveraging had no impact on the lessor's per lease NPV. This result occurred because the cost of the loan to the lessor—4.9 percent after taxes—equals the discount rate, so the leveraging cash flows are netted out on a present value basis.

Note, though, that the lessor has a net investment of only $63,250 in the leveraged lease compared to a net investment of $163,250 in the unleveraged lease. Therefore, the lessor has the opportunity to invest in a total of

EXHIBIT 8.4
Leveraged Lease Analysis

	Year 0	*Year 1*	*Year 2*	*Year 3*	*Year 4*
1. Unleveraged cash flow	($163,250)	$48,750	$55,950	$48,150	$31,400
2. Loan amount	100,000				
3. Interest		(7,000)	(7,000)	(7,000)	(7,000)
4. Interest tax savings		2,100	2,100	2,100	2,100
5. Principal repayment					(100,000)
6. Net cash flow	($ 63,250)	$43,850	$51,050	$43,250	($73,500)

NPV = $1,712.
IRR = 14.6%.

$163,250 ÷ $63,250 = 2.6 identical leveraged leases for the same $163,250 investment required to finance a single unleveraged lease, producing a total net present value of 2.6 × $1,712 = $4,451. The effect of leverage on the lessor's return is also reflected in the leveraged lease's IRR. The IRR of the leveraged lease is 14.6 percent, which is substantially higher than the 5.4 percent after-tax return on the unleveraged lease.

Leveraged leases can provide lessors with higher expected rates of return (IRRs) and higher NPVs per dollar of invested capital than unleveraged leases. However, such leases are also riskier for the same reason that any leveraged investment is riskier. Sophisticated lessors use simulations similar to those described in chapter 12 to assess the riskiness associated with leveraged leases. Then, given the apparent riskiness of the lease investment, the lessor can decide whether the returns built into the contract are sufficient to compensate for the risks involved.

SELF-TEST QUESTIONS

1. What is a leveraged lease?
2. How does leveraging affect the lessee's analysis?
3. What is the usual impact of lease leveraging on the lessor's expected rate of return and risk?

Motivations for Leasing

We noted earlier that leasing is a zero-sum game unless there are lease analysis differentials between the lessee and the lessor. In this section, we discuss some of the differentials that motivate lease agreements.

Tax Differentials

Many leases are driven by tax differentials. Historically, the typical tax asymmetry arose between highly taxed lessors and lessees with low tax rates. These low tax rates may be the result of low profitability or tax shields (primarily depreciation) that are sufficient to reduce taxable income to a small amount, even to zero. In such situations, the lessor can take the leased asset's depreciation tax benefits and then share this value with the lessee. Many other possible tax motivations exist, including tax differentials between not-for-profit providers and investor-owned lessors, as well as the alternative minimum tax.

The *alternative minimum tax (AMT)*, which roughly amounts to 20 percent of profits as **reported to shareholders**, is designed to force profitable firms to pay at least some taxes. The AMT was instituted because the use of accelerated depreciation for tax purposes, along with other tax shelters, allowed many businesses that report significant income to stockholders to pay little or no federal income taxes.

Firms exposed to heavy tax liabilities under the AMT naturally seek ways to reduce reported income. Leasing can be beneficial because firms can use a relatively short period for the lease and consequently have a high annual payment, resulting in lower reported profits and a lower AMT liability. Note that the lease payments do not have to qualify as a deductible expense for regular tax purposes; all they need to do is reduce reported income shown on a firm's income statement.

Lessors have designed spreadsheet models to deal with AMT considerations, and they are generating a substantial amount of leasing business as a direct result of the AMT. Thus, one of the important motivations for leasing is tax differential.

Ability to Bear Obsolescence (Residual Value) Risk

Leasing is an attractive financing alternative for many high-tech items that are subject to rapid and unpredictable technological obsolescence. For example, assume that a small, rural hospital wants to acquire an MRI (magnetic resonance imaging) device. If it buys the MRI equipment, it is exposed to the risk of technological obsolescence. In a relatively short time, some new technology might be developed that makes the current system almost worthless, and this large economic depreciation can create a severe financial burden on the hospital. Because it does not use much equipment of this nature, the hospital would bear a great deal of risk if it buys the MRI device.

Conversely, a lessor that specializes in state-of-the-art medical equipment might be exposed to significantly less risk. By purchasing and then leasing many different high-tech items, the lessor benefits from portfolio diversification; over time, some items will lose more value than the lessor expected, but these losses will be offset by other items that retain more value than expected. Also, lessors are especially familiar with the markets for used medical equipment, so they can both estimate residual values better and negotiate better prices when the asset is resold than can a hospital. Because the lessor is better able to bear residual value risk than the hospital, the lessor can charge a premium for bearing this risk that is less than the premium inherent in ownership.

Some lessors also offer programs that guarantee that the leased asset will be modified as necessary to keep it abreast of technological advancements. For an increased rental fee, lessors will provide upgrades to keep the leased equipment current regardless of the cost. To the extent that lessors are better able to forecast such upgrades; negotiate better terms from manufacturers; and, by greater diversification, control the risks involved with such upgrades, it may be cheaper for businesses to obtain state-of-the-art equipment by leasing than by buying.

Ability to Bear Utilization Risk

As we discussed earlier in the chapter, per procedure (per use) leases are gaining popularity among healthcare providers. In this type of lease, instead of a fixed annual or monthly payment, the lessor charges the lessee a fixed amount for each procedure performed (each use of the asset). For example, the lessor may charge the hospital $300 for every scan performed using a leased MRI device, or it may charge $400 per scan for the first 50 scans in each month and $200 for each scan above 50. Because the hospital's MRI revenues depend on the amount of utilization, and because the per procedure lease changes the hospital's costs for the MRI from a fixed payment to a variable payment, the hospital's risk is reduced.

However, the conversion of the payment to the lessor from a fixed amount to an uncertain stream increases the lessor's risk. In essence, the lessor is now bearing the utilization (operating) risk of the MRI. Although the passing of risk often produces no net benefit, a per procedure lease can be beneficial to both parties **if the lessor is better able than the lessee to bear the utilization risk**. As we discussed earlier, if the lessor has written a large number of per procedure leases, some of the leases will be more profitable than expected and some will be less profitable than expected, but if the lessor's expectations are unbiased, the aggregate return on all the leases will be close to that expected.

Ability to Bear Project Life Risk

Leasing can also be attractive when a business is uncertain about how long an asset will be needed. Consider the following example. Hospitals sometimes offer services that are dependent on a single staff member—for example, a physician who does liver transplants. To support the physician's practice, the hospital might have to invest millions of dollars in equipment that can be used only for this procedure. The hospital will charge for the use of the equipment, and if things go as expected, the investment will be profitable. However, if the physician dies or leaves the hospital staff, and if no other qualified physician can be recruited to fill the void, the project must be terminated and the equipment becomes useless to the hospital. A lease with a cancellation clause would permit the hospital to simply return the equipment to the lessor. The lessor would charge a premium for the cancellation clause because such clauses increase the riskiness of the lease to the lessor. The increased lease cost would lower the expected profitability of the project, but it would provide the hospital with an option to abandon the equipment, and such an option can have a value that exceeds the incremental cost of the cancellation clause. The leasing company would be willing to write this option because it is in a better position to remarket the equipment—either by writing another lease or by selling it outright.

Maintenance Services

Some businesses find leasing attractive because the lessor is able to provide better or less expensive maintenance services (or both). For example, MEDTRANSPORT, Inc., a for-profit ambulance and medical transfer service, leased 25 ambulances and transfer vans. The lease agreement, with a lessor that specializes in purchasing, maintaining, and then reselling automobiles and trucks, permitted the replacement of an aging fleet that MEDTRANSPORT had built up over several years. "We are pretty good at providing emergency services and moving sick people from one facility to another, but we aren't very good at maintaining an automotive fleet," said MEDTRANSPORT's CEO.

Lower Information Costs

Leasing may be financially attractive for smaller businesses that have limited access to debt markets. For example, a small, recently formed physician group practice may need to finance one or more diagnostic devices, such as an electrocardiogram (EKG) machine. The group has no credit history, so it would be relatively difficult, and hence costly, for a bank to assess the group's credit risk. Some banks might think the loan is not even worth the effort. Others might be willing to make the loan, but only after building the high cost of credit assessment into the cost of the loan. On the other hand, some lessors specialize in leasing to group practices, so their analysts have assessed the financial worthiness of hundreds, or even thousands, of group practices. Thus, it would be relatively easy for them to make the credit judgment, and hence they might be more willing than conventional lenders to provide the financing and charge lower rates.

Lower Risk in Bankruptcy

Finally, for firms that are poor credit risks, leasing may be less expensive than buying. As discussed earlier, in the event of financial distress leading to reorganization or liquidation, lessors generally have more secure claims than do lenders. Thus, lessors may be willing to write leases to firms with poor financial characteristics that are less costly than loans offered by lenders, if such loans are even available.

Liquidity Preservation

Most of the promotional material prepared by lessors states that the biggest advantage of leasing is that it preserves liquidity—that is, by leasing, a business avoids using cash resources to make the initial outlay required to purchase the asset. Although the statement is true, it ignores the fact that the lessee becomes contractually obligated to make a series of payments to the lessor. The alternative to leasing—borrowing and buying—also enables a business to avoid using current cash to buy the asset because the loan amount is used to make the purchase; hence, it also preserves liquidity. Under the borrow-and-buy scenario, the potential lessee again is obligated to make a series of payments, but this time to the lender. When one carefully considers the situation, it is obvious that leasing is advantageous only when it costs less than borrowing and buying.

There are other reasons that might motivate firms to lease an asset rather than buy it. Often, these reasons are difficult to quantify, so they cannot be easily incorporated into a numerical analysis. Nevertheless, a sound lease analysis must begin with a quantitative analysis, and then qualitative factors can be considered before making the final lease-or-buy decision.

SELF-TEST QUESTIONS

1. What are some economic factors that motivate leasing—that is, what asymmetries might exist that make leasing beneficial to both lessors and lessees?
2. Would it ever make sense to lease an asset that has a negative NAL when evaluated by a conventional lease analysis? Explain your answer.
3. Does leasing lead to increased credit availability?
4. What is your reaction to this statement: "Leasing is preferable to buying because it preserves the business's liquidity"?

Chapter Key Concepts

In this chapter, we discuss leasing decisions from the standpoints of the lessee and lessor. Here are its key concepts:

- Lease agreements often are categorized as *operating leases* or *finance leases*.
- The IRS has specific guidelines that apply to lease arrangements. A lease that meets these guidelines is called a *guideline*, or

(continued)

(continued from previous page)

tax-oriented, lease because the IRS permits the lessee to deduct the lease payments. A lease that does not meet IRS guidelines is called a *nonguideline*, or *non-tax-oriented, lease*. In such leases, ownership resides with the lessee rather than with the lessor.

- Going forward, both operating and finance leases are shown as an asset and liability on the balance sheet in accordance with the new accounting standards.
- The lessee's analysis consists of a comparison of the costs and benefits associated with leasing the asset and the costs and benefits associated with owning the asset. Two analytical techniques can be used: (1) the *dollar-cost (NAL) method* and (2) the *percentage-cost (IRR) method.*
- One of the key issues in the lessee's analysis is the appropriate discount rate. Because the cash flows in a lease analysis are known with relative certainty, the appropriate discount rate is the *lessee's after-tax cost of debt.* A higher discount rate may be used on the *residual value* if it is substantially riskier than the other flows.
- In a *lessor's analysis*, the return on a lease investment is compared with the return available on alternative investments of similar risk.
- In a *leveraged lease*, the lessor borrows part of the funds required to buy the asset. Generally, the asset is pledged as collateral for the loan.
- Leasing is motivated by differentials between lessees and lessors. Some of the more common reasons for leasing are (1) *tax rate differentials*, (2) *alternative minimum taxes*, (3) *residual risk bearing*, and (4) *lack of access* to conventional debt markets.

This chapter concludes our discussion of lease financing. Furthermore, it wraps up the coverage of part III (capital acquisition). In chapter 9, we begin our coverage of cost of capital and capital structure decisions.

Chapter Models, Problems, and Minicases

The following ancillary resources in spreadsheet format are available for this chapter:

- A chapter model that shows how to perform many of the calculations described in the chapter

- Problems that test your ability to perform the calculations
- A minicase that is more complicated than the problems and tests your ability to perform the calculations in preparation for a case

These resources can be accessed online at ache.org/HAP/PinkSong8e.

Selected Case

One case in *Cases in Healthcare Finance*, sixth edition, is applicable to this chapter: Case 17: Seattle Cancer Center, which focuses on leasing decisions from the perspectives of both the lessee and lessor.

Reference

Financial Accounting Standards Board (FASB). 2016. "FASB Issues New Guidance on Lease Accounting." Published February 25. www.fasb.org/jsp/FASB/FASBContent_C/NewsPage&cid=1176167901466.

Selected Bibliography

Berman, M. 2016. "New Lease Accounting and Health Care." *Healthcare Financial Management* 70 (5): 78–83.

Conner, B. 2016. "Can Cloud Computing Impact Your EBITDA?" *Healthcare Financial Management* 70 (9): 36–38.

Healthcare Financial Management Association. 2016. "Using Equipment Financing to Increase Cash Flow." *Healthcare Financial Management* 70 (9): A1–A4.

Jordahl, E. A., M. Robbins, and M. Sedlmeier. 2016. "Meeting New Equipment Needs and Reducing Capital Costs." *Healthcare Financial Management* 70 (7): 60–62.

Parrott, B. 2018. "Why Age Is Not Enough: A Better Approach to Equipment Replacement." *Healthcare Financial Management* 72 (5): 44–49.

Selected Websites

The following websites pertain to the content of this chapter:

- To obtain information about leasing from the Equipment Leasing and Finance Association (an association of equipment lessors), see www.elfaonline.org.

- For one example of a leasing company that has a large medical equipment component, see www.acgcapital.com.
- The following webpage contains a glossary of leasing terminology: www.equipmentfinanceadvantage.org/efl01/glossary.cfm.
- Although not directly related to healthcare equipment leasing, the following website contains a wealth of information on automobile leases: www.leasesource.com.

Notes

1. In fact, General Electric has a subsidiary, GE Capital Corporation, which is one of the largest lessors in the world. The subsidiary was originally set up to finance consumers' purchases of GE's durable goods, such as refrigerators and washing machines, but it has become a major player in the commercial loan and leasing markets.
2. The zero-sum-game feature of leasing can be useful in debugging lease analysis models. Whenever we build a new spreadsheet model that contains both the lessee's and the lessor's analyses, we test it by trying symmetrical input values for the lessee and lessor. If the lessee's NAL and lessor's NPV are not equal, but opposite in sign, there is something wrong with the model.

Integrative Application

The Problem

Brooklyn Family Medicine, a for-profit group practice, has decided to acquire a new top-of-the-line EKG machine. One alternative would be to purchase the equipment outright for $40,000. If purchased, the practice could borrow the amount needed from a local bank at a 10 percent annual interest rate. Also, if purchased, the practice would have to sign a maintenance contract with a vendor that would cost $1,000 annually, *payable at year end*. Alternatively, the practice could lease the machine on a four-year guideline lease with a payment of $10,000, *payable at the beginning of each year*. The lease includes maintenance. The EKG machine falls into the MACRS three-year class (allowances are 33, 45, 15, and 7 percent in years 1 through 4, respectively), the machine's estimated residual value is $10,000, and the practice's federal-plus-state tax rate is 30 percent. In addition, the CEO of Brooklyn Family Medicine believes that the recent election of a new state governor could result in a reduction of the practice's tax rate from 30 percent to 25 percent, but she does not know how this will affect the analysis. The decision at hand is whether to buy or to lease the equipment.

The Analysis

	Year 0	*Year 1*	*Year 2*	*Year 3*	*Year 4*
I. Cost of Owning (Borrowing and Buying)					
1. Net purchase price	($40,000)				
2. Maintenance cost		($ 1,000)	($ 1,000)	($ 1,000)	($ 1,000)
3. Maintenance tax savings		300	300	300	300
4. Depreciation tax savings		3,960	5,400	1,800	840
5. Residual value					10,000
6. Residual value tax					(3,000)
7. Net cash flow	($ 40,000)	$ 3,260	$ 4,700	$ 1,100	$ 7,140
8. PV cost of owning @ 7% =	($26,503)				
II. Cost of Leasing					
9. Lease payment	($10,000)	($10,000)	($10,000)	($10,000)	
10. Tax savings	3,000	3,000	3,000	3,000	
11. Net cash flow	($ 7,000)	($ 7,000)	($ 7,000)	($ 7,000)	0

	Year 0	Year 1	Year 2	Year 3	Year 4
12. PV cost of leasing					
@ 7% =	($25,370)				

III. Cost Comparison

13. Net advantage to leasing (NAL) = PV cost of leasing – PV cost of owning
= −25,370 – (– 26,503)) = $1,133.

If the tax rate falls to 25 percent, then the PV of the cost of leasing increases to $27,004, the PV of the cost of owning increases to $28,201, and the NAL increases to $1,197. Both the cost of leasing and the cost of owning increase because the tax shield is smaller when the tax rate falls. However, the reduction in the tax shield for leasing is less than the reduction for owning, so the NAL increases.

The Decision

With a positive NAL, leasing is the lower cost-financing alternative. Furthermore, if the tax rate falls as the CEO predicts, this makes leasing even more attractive. Therefore, the CEO of Brooklyn Family Medicine decided to lease the EKG machine. ■

PART

IV

COST OF CAPITAL AND CAPITAL STRUCTURE

In part III, you learn that businesses use two primary forms of capital (financing): debt and equity. You also learn that these two types of capital have different characteristics—that is, they present businesses with financing choices that bring different risks and potential rewards.

In part IV, we discuss two important topics related to the financing choices made by businesses. The first, cost of capital (covered in chapter 9), involves measuring the costs associated with a business's financing. Providers of business capital expect to earn a return on the funds they provide; this expectation means that businesses incur costs to use capital. With an estimate of these costs, managers can make better decisions regarding capital allocation (i.e., which assets should be acquired).

The second topic, capital structure, is covered in chapter 10. Businesses have a choice regarding how much debt versus equity capital should be used to finance the business's assets. This choice affects the riskiness of the business, the cost of its financing, and hence its potential profitability. Chapter 10 discusses the factors that affect this decision.

CHAPTER

9

COST OF CAPITAL

Learning Objectives

After studying this chapter, readers should be able to

- describe the general process for estimating a business's corporate (overall) cost of capital;
- estimate the component costs of debt and equity as well as the corporate cost of capital for any healthcare business, including not-for-profit and small businesses;
- describe the uncertainties inherent in the cost-of-capital estimation process; and
- explain the economic meaning of the corporate cost of capital and how it is used in capital investment decisions.

Introduction

The cost of capital is an extremely important concept in healthcare financial management. All businesses—whether large, small, investor-owned, or not-for-profit—have to raise funds to buy the assets required to meet their strategic objectives. Hospitals, nursing homes, clinics, group practices, and so on need buildings, equipment, and inventories to provide services. The funds to acquire these assets come in many shapes and forms, including contributions; profit retention; equity sales to stockholders; and debt capital supplied by creditors, such as banks, bondholders, lessors, and suppliers. Most of the capital raised by organizations has a cost that is either explicit (such as the interest payments on debt) or implicit (such as the opportunity cost associated with equity capital). Because many business decisions require the cost of capital as an input, managers must understand the cost-of-capital concept and know how to both estimate the costs of capital for their firms and properly apply the estimate when making capital investment decisions.

Overview of the Cost-of-Capital Estimation Process

The ultimate goal of the cost-of-capital estimation process is to estimate the business's *corporate cost of capital (CCC)*, which represents the blended, or average, cost of a business's financing mix. This cost, in turn, is used as the required rate of return on the business's capital investment opportunities. For example, assume Bayside Memorial Hospital, a not-for-profit integrated delivery system, has a CCC of 10.2 percent. If a new MRI (magnetic resonance imaging) investment is expected to return at least 10.2 percent, it is financially attractive to the business. If the MRI is expected to return less than 10.2 percent, the investment will have an adverse effect on the business's financial soundness. Here, we assume that the project under consideration has average risk—that is, the same risk as the overall business. As we discuss later in this chapter and in chapter 12, the CCC must be adjusted to reflect project risk when it differs from the overall risk of the business.

The CCC is a weighted average of the *component* (i.e., debt and equity) *costs*, adjusted for tax effects. After the component costs have been estimated, they are combined to form the CCC. Thus, the first step in the cost-of-capital estimation process is to estimate both the cost of debt and the cost of equity. However, before the mechanics of cost estimation are discussed, some other issues regarding the estimation process must be addressed.

What Capital Components Should Be Included?

The first task in estimating a business's CCC is to determine which sources of capital, shown on the right side of the business's balance sheet, should be included in the estimate. In general, the CCC focuses on the cost of *permanent capital* (long-term capital) because these sources are used to finance capital asset acquisitions. Thus, for most firms, the capital components included in the corporate-cost-of-capital estimate are equity and long-term debt. Typically, short-term debt is used only as temporary financing to support seasonal or cyclical fluctuations in volume, and hence assets, so it is not included in the cost-of-capital estimate. However, if a firm does use short-term debt as part of its permanent financing mix, it should be included in the cost-of-capital estimate. (We discuss why short-term debt is not well suited for financing permanent assets in chapter 10.)

Do Taxes Need to Be Considered?

In developing component costs, investor-owned businesses face the issue of tax effects. Should the component costs be estimated on a before- or after-tax basis? As we discuss in chapter 10, the use of debt financing creates a tax benefit because interest expense is tax deductible, while the use of equity financing has no impact on taxes. This tax benefit can be handled in several ways when working with capital costs, but the most common way is to include it in the cost-of-capital estimate. Thus, the tax benefit associated with debt financing will be recognized in the component-cost-of-debt estimate, resulting in an after-tax cost of debt.

Should the Focus Be on Historical or Marginal Costs?

Two different sets of capital costs can be measured: (1) ***historical***, or ***embedded***, ***costs***, which reflect the cost of funds raised in the past, and (2) ***new***, or ***marginal***, ***costs***, which measure the cost of funds to be raised in the future. Historical costs are important for many purposes. For example, payers that reimburse on a cost basis are concerned with embedded costs, as are taxing authorities. However, the primary purpose in developing a business's CCC is to use it in making capital investment decisions, which involve future asset acquisitions and future financing. For these purposes, the relevant costs are the marginal costs of new funds to be raised during some future planning period—say, the coming year—and not the cost of funds raised in the past.

SELF-TEST QUESTIONS

1. What is the basic concept of the CCC?
2. What financing sources are typically included in a firm's cost-of-capital estimate?
3. Should the component costs be estimated on a before-tax basis or an after-tax basis?
4. Should the component-cost estimates reflect historical costs or marginal costs?

Estimating the Cost of Debt

On the web at: *ache.org/HAP/PinkSong8e*

Although the cost-of-capital estimation process is the same, some of the details of component-cost estimation differ depending on the type of business. We begin our discussion by focusing on large businesses—primarily publicly traded for-profit businesses. Along the way, we point out some of the differences in cost estimation between investor-owned and not-for-profit businesses. Then, later in the chapter, we will discuss some unique features of cost-of-capital estimation in small businesses.

It is unlikely that a business's managers will know at the start of a planning period the exact types and amounts of debt the firm will issue in the future; the type of debt used will depend on the specific assets to be financed and on market conditions as they develop over time. However, they do know what types of debt the business usually issues. For example, Bayside typically uses bank debt to raise short-term funds to finance seasonal or cyclical working capital needs, and it uses 30-year tax-exempt (municipal) bonds to raise long-term debt capital. Because Bayside does not use short-term debt to finance permanent assets, its managers include only long-term debt in their corporate-cost-of-capital estimate, and they assume that this debt will consist solely of 30-year tax-exempt bonds.

Suppose that Bayside's managers are developing the system's corporate-cost-of-capital estimate for the coming year. How should they estimate the ***cost of debt***? Most managers of large businesses would begin by discussing current and prospective interest rates with their firms' investment bankers, which are institutions that help businesses obtain financing. Assume that the municipal bond underwriter at Suncoast Securities, Inc., Bayside's investment banker, stated that a new 30-year tax-exempt healthcare issue would require semiannual interest payments of \$30.50 (\$61 annually) for each \$1,000 par value bond issued. Thus, municipal bond investors currently require a \$61 ÷ \$1,000 = 0.061 = 6.1% return on Bayside's 30-year bonds. This rate of return required by investors (the interest rate) establishes the cost of debt to Bayside.

How the Choice of Issuing Authority Affects Hospital Debt Financing Costs

Hospitals need to know how their choice of bond-issuing authority affects debt financing costs. States vary in the vehicles that not for-profit organizations can use to issue tax-exempt debt: (1) a single statewide authority, (2) local authorities, or (3) local and statewide authorities. In a 2013 study, Caryl Carpenter and Patrick Bernet found that, all other things being equal, bonds issued by statewide authorities have lower yields than bonds issued by local authorities. Investors recognize that statewide authorities have greater oversight of not-for-profit hospitals and are less likely to issue bonds for highly risky institutions. In addition, investors are more familiar with the policies and procedures of large, statewide authorities, and that transparency may lead to a lower cost of capital. Although lower yields may be offset by higher issuance costs for statewide authorities, the services provided in exchange for the higher issuance costs—including enhanced information and protection for bondholders—may benefit both the investors and the issuing hospitals.

Source: Carpenter and Bernet (2013).

The true cost of debt to Bayside would be somewhat higher than 6.1 percent because the system must incur ***issuance***, or ***flotation***, ***costs*** (such as legal, accounting, and marketing expenses) to sell the bonds. However, flotation costs are often small, especially on debt financing, so their impact on the cost of debt estimate is inconsequential, especially when the uncertainty inherent in the cost of capital estimation process is considered. Therefore, as we will discuss later in the chapter, it is common practice to ignore flotation costs when estimating a business's cost of capital. Bayside follows this practice, so its managers would estimate the component cost of debt as 6.1 percent:

$$\text{Tax-exempt component cost of debt} = \text{R(R}_\text{d}) = 6.1\%.$$

If Bayside's current outstanding debt were actively traded, the current *yield to maturity (YTM)* on this debt could be used to estimate the cost of new debt. For example, assume that Bayside has an actively traded outstanding issue that has a 7 percent coupon rate with semiannual payments, currently sells for $1,114.69, and has 25 years remaining to maturity. Using a spreadsheet, we determine that the semiannual YTM on this bond is 3.05 percent:

	A	B	C	D
1				
2	50	Nper	Number of periods	
3	$(1,114.69)	Pv	Present value (bond price)	
4	$35.00	Pmt	Payment (coupon amount)	
5	$1,000.00	Fv	Future value (principal)	
6				
7				
8	3.05%	=RATE(A2,A4,A3,A5) (entered into cell A8)		
9				
10				

Because this rate is semiannual, the resulting solution, 3.05 percent, must be multiplied by two to get the annual YTM, resulting in a cost of debt estimate of 6.1 percent.[1]

Using the YTM on an outstanding issue to estimate the cost of new debt works reasonably well when the remaining life of the old issue approximates the anticipated maturity of the new issue. If this is not the case, yield curve differentials may cause the estimate to be biased. For example, if the yield curve were upward sloping in the 25- to 30-year range, the YTM on a 25-year outstanding issue would understate the actual cost of a new 30-year issue. If the understatement is material, an adjustment can be made on the basis of the current yield curve on Treasury securities. For example, suppose the yield on 25-year T-bonds is 5.5 percent and the yield on 30-year T-bonds is 5.7 percent, a difference of 0.2 percentage points. The 6.1 percent estimate for Bayside's cost of debt based on outstanding 25-year bonds could be increased to 6.3 percent to account for yield curve differentials.

A taxable healthcare provider would use one or more of the techniques described here to estimate its before-tax cost of debt. However, the tax benefits of interest payments must then be incorporated into the estimate. For a for-profit business, the after-tax component cost of debt is calculated as follows:

Key Equation 9.1: After-Tax Cost of Debt

$$\text{After-tax cost of debt} = R(R_d) \times (1 - T).$$

Here, $R(R_d)$ is the before-tax cost of debt (required interest rate) and T is the tax rate.

For example, consider Ann Arbor Health Care, Inc., a publicly traded for-profit business. The firm's investment bankers indicate that a new 30-year corporate bond issue that has Ann Arbor's BBB rating would require an interest rate of 10 percent. Because the firm's federal-plus-state tax rate is 40 percent, its after-tax cost of debt estimate is lowered to 6 percent:

$$\text{After-tax cost of debt} = R(R_d) \times (1 - T)$$
$$= 10\% \times (1 - 0.30) = 10\% \times 0.60 = 6\%.$$

By reducing Ann Arbor's component cost of debt from 10 percent to 6 percent, the cost-of-debt estimate has incorporated the benefit associated with interest payment tax deductibility.

In general, the **effective** cost of debt is roughly comparable between investor-owned and not-for-profit firms of similar risk. Investor-owned firms have the benefit of tax deductibility of interest payments, while not-for-profit firms have the benefit of being able to issue lower-cost tax-exempt debt. Under normal economic conditions, these two benefits are roughly the same, resulting in a similar cost of debt. In our illustrations, the effective cost of debt is 7.0 percent for Ann Arbor, an investor-owned firm, and 6.1 percent for Bayside, a similar not-for-profit business.

SELF-TEST QUESTIONS

1. What are some methods used to estimate a business's cost of debt?
2. For investor-owned firms, how is the before-tax cost of debt converted to an after-tax cost?
3. Does the effective cost of debt differ materially between businesses that are similar in all respects except ownership?

Estimating the Cost of Equity to Large Investor-Owned Businesses

Large investor-owned businesses (corporations) raise equity capital by selling new common stock and by retaining earnings for use by the firm rather than paying them out as dividends to shareholders.[2] Not-for-profit businesses raise equity capital through contributions and grants and by generating an excess of revenues over expenses, none of which can be paid out as dividends.

This section describes how to estimate the cost of equity capital for large investor-owned businesses. The next major section focuses on large not-for-profit businesses, while the cost-of-equity estimation for small businesses is discussed later in the chapter.

The cost of debt is based on the return (interest rate) that investors require on debt securities, and the *cost of equity* to investor-owned businesses can be defined similarly: It is the rate of return that investors require on the firm's common stock. At first glance, equity raised through **retained earnings** may appear to be a costless source of capital to investor-owned businesses. After all, dividend payments must be paid at some point in time on any new shares of stock that are issued, but no such payments are required on funds obtained by retaining earnings. The reason that a cost of capital must be assigned to all forms of equity financing involves the *opportunity cost principle.* An investor-owned firm's net income literally belongs to its common stockholders. Employees are compensated by wages, suppliers are compensated by cash payments for supplies, bondholders are compensated by interest payments, governments are compensated by tax payments, and so on. The residual earnings of a firm—its net income—belong to the stockholders and "pay the rent" on stockholder-supplied capital.

The firm can either pay out earnings in the form of dividends or retain earnings for reinvestment in the business. If it retains part of the earnings, it incurs an opportunity cost; stockholders could have received those earnings as dividends and then invested this money in stocks, bonds, real estate, commodity futures, or any other investment. Thus, the firm should earn on its retained earnings at least as much as its stockholders can earn on alternative investments of similar risk. If the firm cannot earn as much as stockholders can in similar risk investments, the firm's net income should be paid out as dividends rather than retained for reinvestment in the business. What rate of return can stockholders expect to earn on other investments of equivalent risk? The answer is $R(R_e)$, the required rate of return on equity (ROE). Investors can earn this return either by buying more shares of the firm in question or by buying the stock of similar businesses.

Whereas debt is a contractual obligation with an easily estimated cost, the cost of equity is not nearly as easy to estimate. Large, investor-owned businesses use three primary methods in the estimation process: (1) the capital asset pricing model (CAPM), (2) the discounted cash flow (DCF) model, and (3) the debt-cost-plus-risk-premium method. These methods should not be regarded as mutually exclusive, for no single approach dominates the estimation process. In practice, all approaches should be used to estimate the cost of equity, and then the final value should be chosen on the basis of the managers' confidence in the data at hand.

Capital Asset Pricing Model Approach

The CAPM, which was first discussed in chapter 5, is a widely accepted finance model that specifies the equilibrium risk–return relationship on common stocks. Basically, the model assumes that investors consider only one risk factor when setting required rates of return: the volatility of returns on the stock relative to the volatility of returns on a well-diversified portfolio called the *market portfolio*, or just the *market*. The measure of risk in the CAPM is the stock's *market beta*. The market, which is a large collection of stocks often proxied by the Standard & Poor's Index (S&P 500), has a beta of 1.0. A stock with a beta of 2.0 has twice the volatility of returns as the market, while a stock with a beta of 0.5 has half the volatility of returns as the market. Because relative volatility measures market risk, a low-beta stock (which has a beta less than 1.0) is less risky than the market, while a high-beta stock (which has a beta greater than 1.0) is more risky than the market.

Under the CAPM, the equation that relates risk to return is called the *security market line (SML)*:

Key Equation 9.2: Security Market Line of the Capital Asset Pricing Model

$$R(R_e) = RF + [R(R_M) - RF] \times b_i$$
$$= RF + (RP_M \times b_i).$$

In this equation,

- $R(R_e)$ = required rate of return on equity;
- RF = risk-free rate;
- $R(R_M)$ = required rate of return on the market;
- b_i = beta coefficient of the stock in question;
- $[R(R_M) - RF)] = RP_M$ = market risk premium, the premium above the risk-free rate that investors require to buy a stock with average risk; and
- $(RP_M) \times b_i$ = stock risk premium, the premium above the risk-free rate that investors require to buy the stock in question.

Managers can calculate the required rate of return on a firm's stock given estimates of the risk-free rate, RF; the beta of the firm's stock, bi; and the required rate of return on the market, R(RM). This result, in turn, can be used as one estimate of the firm's cost of equity.

Estimating the Risk-Free Rate

The starting point for the CAPM cost-of-equity estimate is RF, the risk-free rate. Unfortunately, there is no unambiguous proxy for this rate. Treasury securities are essentially free of default risk, but long-term T-bonds will suffer capital losses if interest rates rise, and a portfolio invested in short-term T-bills will provide a volatile earnings stream because the rate paid on T-bills varies over time.

Because we cannot, in practice, find a truly riskless rate on which to base the CAPM, what rate should we use? Most analysts use a rate on long-term Treasury bonds (versus a T-bill rate). There are many reasons for favoring a T-bond rate, including the fact that T-bill rates are volatile because they are directly affected by actions taken by the Federal Reserve Board. Perhaps the most persuasive argument is that common stocks have traditionally been viewed as long-term investments, so stock returns should embody the long-term inflation expectations embodied in bonds, rather than the short-term inflation expectations embodied in bills. On this account, the cost of equity should be more highly correlated with T-bond rates than with T-bill rates.

The rates on Treasury bonds vary with the maturity of the bond. In recent years, the US Treasury has emphasized the use of shorter maturity debt. The Treasury even suspended the issue of 30-year bonds from 2001 to 2006. This action caused the *Wall Street Journal* to change its "benchmark" long-term interest rate from 30-year Treasuries to 10-year Treasuries. As a result, many analysts use the 10-year or 20-year Treasury bond rate as the basis for the CAPM risk-free rate.

Estimating the Market Risk Premium

The market risk premium, $RP_M = [R(R_M) - RF]$, can be estimated on the basis of historical returns or expected returns. The most complete, accurate, and up-to-date historical returns study is published annually by Morningstar. It examines market data over long periods (from 1926 to the present) to determine the average annual rates of return and standard deviations of various classes of securities.[3] By examining the spread between the historical rates of return on stocks and Treasury bonds, it is possible to obtain the historical average risk premium of stocks over T-bonds. The data suggest that this risk premium is about 6 to 7 percentage points when arithmetic average returns are used and about 4 to 5 percentage points when geometric average returns are used.

However, the basic returns data have large standard deviations, so one must use historical averages with caution. Also, in years such as 2000–2002 and 2008, bonds had higher returns than stocks, which would indicate a negative risk premium. In addition, when stock returns are abnormally high, the average risk premium increases, while the opposite occurs when stock returns are abnormally low. This impact on the historical average is the opposite of what it should be, as low stock returns indicate an increasing risk premium, and vice versa.

Finally, the choice of the beginning and ending periods can have a major impact on the calculated risk premiums. All of these considerations suggest that the historical average risk premium should be used with caution, although in some situations it may be the only measure available. As one businessman muttered after listening to a professor give a lecture on the CAPM: "Beware of academics bearing gifts!"

The historical approach to risk premiums assumes that investors expect future results, on average, to equal past results. However, as we noted, the historical risk premium varies greatly depending on the period selected, and, in any event, investors today probably expect results in the future to be different from those achieved many years ago, all of which are included and given equal weight in the historical returns data. The questionable assumption that future expectations are equal to past realizations—together with the sometimes nonsensical results obtained when calculating historical risk premiums—has led to the search for expected (forward-looking) risk premiums.

The most common approach to estimating expected market risk premiums uses the DCF model to estimate the expected market rate of return, E(RM). Then, assuming market equilibrium, the expected rate of return is used as the proxy for the required rate of return, R(RM). Finally, RF is subtracted to obtain the estimate for the expected market risk premium. Many financial services firms publish forecasts of the expected rate of return on the market, and these values can be used as inputs into the CAPM.

Clearly, there is no good answer to the question of how to estimate the CAPM market risk premium. Still, it has to be done to use the CAPM method to estimate a firm's cost of equity. It is our view that the risk premium is driven primarily by equity investors' attitudes toward risk, and there are good reasons to believe that investors are less risk averse today than they were 50 years ago. The advent of pension plans, Social Security, health and disability insurance, and dual-income families means that investors can take on more risk with their stock investments, which lowers the market risk premium.

The bottom line is that we favor a market risk premium of about 5 percentage points, but we would have a hard time arguing against someone using a premium anywhere in the range of 4 to 6 percentage points. We believe that investor risk aversion is relatively stable but not absolutely constant from year to year. When stock prices are relatively high, investors are less risk averse, so we use a smaller risk premium. Conversely, we use a larger premium (but still in the range) when stock prices are relatively low. There is no way to prove that a particular risk premium value is right or wrong, although we would be suspicious of an estimated premium that is much less than 4 percentage points or much greater than 6 percentage points.

Estimating Beta

The last parameter needed for a CAPM cost-of-equity estimate is the beta coefficient. Recall from chapter 5 that a stock's beta is a measure of its volatility relative to that of an average stock and that betas are generally estimated from the stock's characteristic line, which is estimated by running a linear regression between past returns on the stock in question and past returns on some chosen market index.

Unfortunately, historical betas show how risky a stock was *in the past*, whereas investors are interested in *future* risk. A given firm might have appeared safe in the past, but things may have changed and its future risk may be judged to be higher than its past risk, or vice versa. The hospital sector presents a good example. Prior to 1983, when the sector operated on a cost-plus basis, investor-owned hospitals were among the bluest of the blue chips. However, when prospective payment began, the sector became riskier. The increasing market power of managed care plans has further added to hospitals' risk.

When we use a historical beta in a CAPM framework to measure the firm's cost of equity, we are implicitly assuming that future risk is the same as past risk. This assumption would be troublesome for a hospital in 1983, but what about most firms in most years? As a general rule, is future risk sufficiently similar to past risk to warrant the use of historical betas in a CAPM framework? For individual firms, historical betas are often unstable, so past risk is often **not** a good predictor of future risk. Nevertheless, most managers use beta estimates published on various financial websites but—with the knowledge that, like any other estimate, the betas may be imprecise.

Exhibit 9.1 contains the betas of some representative investor-owned healthcare businesses. According to this limited selection, healthcare business lines, like all businesses, appear to exhibit large differences in market risk for stockholders.

Illustration of the CAPM Approach

For an illustration of the CAPM approach, consider Ann Arbor Health Care, which has a beta coefficient, *b*, of 1.50. Furthermore, assume that the current yield on T-bonds, RF, is 6.0 percent and that the best estimate for the

On the web at: *ache.org/HAP/PinkSong8e*

EXHIBIT 9.1
Beta Coefficients for Selected Healthcare Businesses

Company	*Symbol*	*Primary Line of Business*	*Beta*
AmerisourceBergen Corporation	ABC	Pharmaceuticals	1.43
Amgen Inc.	AMGN	Biotechnology	0.90
Community Health Systems, Inc.	CYH	Acute care hospitals	4.11
DaVita Inc.	DVA	Dialysis services	1.65
HCA Healthcare, Inc.	HCA	Acute care facilities	1.27
Humana, Inc.	HUM	Managed care	1.02
Laboratory Corporation of America Holdings	LH	Clinical laboratory	1.23
McKesson Corporation	MCK	Medical supplies	1.54
Medtronic plc	MDT	Medical equipment	0.66
Merck & Co., Inc.	MRK	Pharmaceuticals	0.31
Pfizer Inc.	PFE	Pharmaceuticals	0.54
Quest Diagnostics Incorporated	DGX	Diagnostic testing	0.98
Tenet Healthcare Corporation	THC	Acute care hospitals	2.18
UnitedHealth Group Incorporated	UNH	Managed care	0.89
Universal Health Services, Inc.	UHS	Acute care facilities	1.21

Source: Data obtained from Yahoo Finance on May 23, 2019. Beta is calculated from three-year, monthly data.

current market risk premium, RP_M, is 5 percentage points. In other words, the current required rate of return on the market, $R(R_M)$, is 11.0 percent. All required input parameters have been estimated. The SML equation can be completed as follows:

$$\begin{aligned} R(R_e) &= RF + [R(R_M) - RF] \times b_{AAHS} \\ &= 6.0\% + (11.0\% - 6.0\%) \times 1.50 \\ &= 6.0\% + (5.0\% \times 1.50) \\ &= 6.0\% + 7.5\% = 13.5\%. \end{aligned}$$

Thus, according to the CAPM, Ann Arbor's required rate of ROE is 13.5 percent.

What does the 13.5 percent estimate for $R(R_e)$ imply? In essence, equity investors believe that Ann Arbor's stock, with a beta of 1.50, is more risky than an average stock with a beta of 1.00. With a risk-free rate of 6.0 percent and a market risk premium of 5 percentage points, an average firm, with b = 1.0, has a required rate of ROE of 6.0% + (5.0% × 1.00) = 6.0% + 5.0% = 11.0%. Thus, according to the CAPM, equity investors require 250 basis points (2.50 percentage points) more return for investing in Ann Arbor, with b = 1.50, than in an average stock, with b = 1.00.

There is a great deal of uncertainty in the CAPM estimate of the cost of equity. Some of this uncertainty stems from the fact that there is no assurance that the CAPM is correct (i.e., the CAPM accurately describes the risk/return preference of stock investors). In addition, a great deal of uncertainty exists in the input parameter estimates, especially the beta coefficient. Because of these uncertainties, it is highly unlikely that Ann Arbor's true, but unobservable, cost of equity is 13.5 percent. Thus, instead of picking single values for each parameter, it may be better to develop high and low estimates and then combine all of the high and low estimates to develop a range, rather than a point estimate, for the CAPM cost of equity.

Discounted Cash Flow Approach

The second procedure for estimating the cost of equity is the *DCF method*. As we discussed in chapter 7, the value of a stock with a predictable dividend stream can be found as the present value of that expected dividend stream. Furthermore, if the dividend is expected to grow each year at a constant rate, E(g), the *constant growth model* can be used to estimate the expected rate of ROE, $E(R_e)$:

$$E(R_e) = \frac{D_0 \times [1 + E(g)]}{P_0} + E(g) = \frac{E(D_1)}{P_0} + E(g) = R(R_e).$$

Because stock prices typically are in equilibrium, the expected rate of return, $E(R_e)$, is also the required rate of return, $R(R_e)$.

Estimating the Current Stock Price

As in the CAPM approach, there are three input parameters in the DCF model. Current stock price is readily available for actively traded firms from many financial websites. Currently, Ann Arbor's stock price is \$40, so P_0 = \$40.

Estimating the Next Dividend Payment

Next year's dividend payment is also relatively easy to estimate. If you are one of Ann Arbor's managers, you can look in the firm's five-year financial plan for the dividend estimate. If you are an outsider, dividend data on larger publicly traded firms are available from many financial websites. Current dividend information can also be used as a basis for estimating next year's dividend. Ann Arbor is followed by several analysts at major brokerage houses, and their consensus estimate for next year's dividend payment is \$2.50, so for purposes of this analysis, $E(D_1)$ = \$2.50.

Estimating the Expected Growth Rate

The expected growth rate, E(g), is the most difficult of the DCF model parameters to estimate. Here, we discuss several methods for estimating E(g).

Using Historical Growth Rates to Forecast Future Growth

If growth rates in earnings and dividends have been relatively stable in the past and if investors expect these trends to continue, the past realized growth rate may be used as an estimate of the expected future growth rate. For an illustration of this concept, consider exhibit 9.2, which lists earnings per share (EPS) and dividends per share (DPS) data from 2010 to 2019 for Ann Arbor. Ten years (nine growth periods) of data are shown in the exhibit, but we could have used 15 years, 5 years, or some other historical period. There is no rule about the appropriate number of years to analyze when calculating historical growth rates. However, the period chosen should reflect, to the extent possible, the longest period **that replicates conditions expected in the future**.

The easiest historical growth rate to calculate is the compound rate between two dates, called the *point-to-point rate*. For example, EPS grew at an annual rate of 6.8 percent from 2010 to 2019, and DPS grew at a 7.2 percent rate during this same period. Note that the point-to-point growth rate can change radically if we use two other points. For example, if we calculate the five-year EPS growth rate from 2014 to 2019, we would obtain only 2.8 percent. This radical change occurs because the point-to-point rate is extremely sensitive to the beginning and ending years chosen.

To alleviate the problem of beginning and ending year sensitivity, some analysts use the *average-to-average method*, which reduces the sensitivity of the growth rate to beginning and ending year values. The 2010–2012

EXHIBIT 9.2
Ann Arbor Health Care: Historical EPS and DPS Data

Year	*EPS ($)*	*DPS ($)*
2010	2.95	1.24
2011	3.07	1.32
2012	3.22	1.32
2013	3.40	1.52
2014	4.65	1.72
2015	5.12	1.92
2016	5.25	2.00
2017	5.20	2.20
2018	5.12	2.20
2019	5.35	2.32

average EPS is ($2.95 + $3.07 + $3.22) ÷ 3 = $3.08, the average 2017–2019 EPS is ($5.20 + $5.12 + $5.35) ÷ 3 = $5.22, and the number of years of growth between the two averages is 2011 to 2018 = 7. The average-to-average DPS growth rate is 8.2 percent, and the average-to-average EPS growth rate is 7.8 percent. Note that we are calculating compound annual growth rates, which are much easier to interpret than a single growth rate over the entire period.

A third way, and in our view the best, to estimate historical growth rates is by *log-linear least squares regression*.[4] The regression method considers all data points in the series; thus, this method is the least likely to be biased by a randomly high or low beginning or ending year. The only practical way to estimate a least squares growth rate is to use a computer or a financial calculator. Using a spreadsheet's data regression capability, we find the growth rate in earnings to be 7.9 percent, while the growth rate in dividends is 7.7 percent.

When earnings and dividends are growing at approximately the same rate, we can have more confidence in the resultant growth rate forecast. However, if EPS and DPS historically have grown at different rates, something will have to change in the future because these two series cannot grow at different rates indefinitely. There is no rule for handling differences in historical earnings and dividend growth rates; differences simply demonstrate in yet another way the problems of using historical growth as a proxy for expected future growth. Like many aspects of healthcare finance, judgment is required when estimating growth rates.

Exhibit 9.3 summarizes the historical growth rates just discussed. It is obvious that one can take a given set of historical data and, depending on the years and the calculation method used, obtain a large number of different growth rates. If past growth rates have been stable, investors might base future expectations on past trends. While this approach is reasonable, it is seldom feasible; one rarely finds much historical stability. Therefore, the use of historical growth rates in a DCF analysis must be applied with judgment and also used, if at all, in conjunction with the estimation methods discussed next.

EXHIBIT 9.3
Ann Arbor Health Care: Historical Growth Rates, 2010–2019

Method	*EPS (%)*	*DPS (%)*	*Average (%)*
Point to point	6.84%	7.21%	7.02%
Average to average	7.84%	8.16%	8.00%
Log-linear regression	7.72%	7.70%	7.71%

Retention Growth Model

The *retention growth method* is another method for estimating the expected growth rate in dividends:

$$E(g) = \text{Retention ratio} \times \text{Expected ROE}.$$

This model produces a constant growth rate, and when we use it, we are, by implication, making four important assumptions: (1) We expect the payout ratio, and thus the retention ratio, to remain constant; (2) we expect the ROE on new investments to equal the firm's current ROE, which implies that we expect the ROE to remain constant; (3) the firm is not expected to issue new common stock, or if it does we expect this new stock to be sold at a price equal to its book value; and (4) future projects are expected to have the same degree of risk as the firm's existing assets.

Ann Arbor has had an average ROE of about 14 percent over the past ten years. The ROE has been relatively steady, but even so, it has ranged from a low of 8.9 percent to a high of 17.6 percent during this period. In addition, the firm's dividend payout ratio has averaged 0.45 over the past ten years, so its retention ratio has averaged 1.0 – 0.45 = 0.55. Using these data, the retention growth method gives a divided growth estimate of 7.7 percent:

$$E(g_{AAHS}) = 0.55 \times 14\% = 7.7\%.$$

This figure, together with the historical EPS and DPS growth rates summarized in exhibit 9.3, might lead us to conclude that Ann Arbor's expected dividend growth rate is in the range of 7.0 percent to 8.0 percent.

Analysts' Forecasts

A third growth-rate estimation technique uses security analysts' forecasts. Analysts forecast and then publish growth rate estimates for most of the larger publicly owned businesses. For example, Value Line provides such forecasts on about 1,700 stocks, and all of the larger brokerage houses provide similar forecasts. Also, many online sites provide dividend forecast data. Finally, several data collection firms compile analysts' forecasts on a regular basis and provide summary information—such as the median and range of forecasts—on widely followed businesses. These growth-rate summaries—such as the ones compiled by the organization Lynch, Jones & Ryan, Inc., in its *Institutional Brokers Estimate System (I/B/E/S*, and currently owned by Thomson Reuters) and by Zacks Investment Research—can be ordered for a fee and obtained either as a hard copy or through download. In addition, some data are available for free on the web.

The problem for our purposes is that most analysts' forecasts correctly assume nonconstant growth. For example, some analysts that follow Ann Arbor are forecasting a 12.0 percent annual growth rate in earnings and dividends over the next five years, followed by a steady-state (constant) growth rate of 6.5 percent. A simple way to handle this situation is to use the nonconstant growth forecast to develop a proxy constant growth rate. Computer simulations indicate that dividends beyond year 50 contribute little to the value of any stock—the present value of dividends beyond year 50 is virtually zero, so for practical purposes, anything beyond that point can be ignored. If we consider only a 50-year horizon, we can develop a weighted-average growth rate and use it as a constant growth rate for cost-of-capital purposes. For Ann Arbor, we assumed a growth rate of 12.0 percent for five years followed by a growth rate of 6.5 percent for 45 years, which produced an arithmetic average annual growth rate of $(0.10 \times 12.0\%) + (0.90 \times 6.5\%) = 7.0\%$.[5]

Illustration of the DCF Approach

For an illustration of the DCF approach, consider the data developed thus far for Ann Arbor. The firm's current stock price, P_0, is \$40, and its next expected annual dividend, $E(D_1)$, is \$2.50. Thus, the firm's DCF estimate of $E(R_e) = R(R_e)$, according to the DCF model, is

On the web at: *ache.org/HAP/PinkSong8e*

$$E(R_e) = \frac{E(D_1)}{P_0} + E(g)$$

$$= \frac{\$2.50}{\$40} + E(g) = 6.25\% + E(g).$$

With an E(g) estimate range of 7 percent to 8 percent, the midpoint—7.5 percent—will be used as the final estimate. Thus, the DCF point estimate for Ann Arbor's cost of equity is $6.25\% + 7.5\% = 13.75\% \approx 13.8\%$. Note, however, that it might be best to think of this estimate as a range of values—say, from 13.3 percent to 14.3 percent—because of the uncertainty in the growth rate estimate.

If a company's dividends are expected to grow at a constant rate forever, a simple model can be used to value its stock:

Key Equation 9.3: Constant Growth Dividend Valuation Model

$$E(R_e) = \frac{D_0 \times [1 + E(g)]}{P_0} + E(g) = \frac{E(D_1)}{P_0} + E(g).$$

Here, $E(R_e)$ is the expected rate of return on equity, which in equilibrium equals $R(R_e)$, the required rate of return on equity. D_0 is the last dividend paid; E(g) is the expected constant dividend growth rate; P_0 is the current stock price; and $E(D_1)$ is the next expected dividend.

Debt-Cost-Plus-Risk-Premium Approach

On the web at: *ache.org/HAP/PinkSong8e*

The *debt-cost-plus-risk-premium approach* relies on the assumption that stock investments are riskier than debt investments; hence, the cost of equity for any business can be thought of as the before-tax cost of debt to **that business** plus a risk premium:

$$R(R_e) = R(R_d) + \text{Risk premium.}$$

The cost of debt is relatively easy to estimate, so the key input to this model is the risk premium. Note that the risk premium used here is **not** the same as the market risk premium used in the CAPM. The market risk premium is the amount that investors require above the **risk-free rate** to invest in average-risk common stocks. Here, we need the risk premium above the **before-tax cost of debt**. How might this new risk premium be estimated? Using previous data, we know that the cost of equity for an average risk (b = 1.0) stock is 11.0 percent. Furthermore, the cost of debt for an average firm, which has roughly an A rating, is 7.0 percent. Thus, for an average firm, the risk premium of the cost of equity over the cost of debt is 11.0% – 7.0% = 4.0 percentage points.

Empirical work suggests that, in recent years, the risk premium used in the debt-cost-plus-risk-premium model has ranged from 3 to 5 percentage points. When interest rates are high in the economy, this risk premium tends to be at the lower end of the range, while lower interest rates often lead to higher-risk premiums. Perhaps the biggest weakness of this approach is that there is no assurance that the risk premium for the average firm is the same as the risk premium for the firm in question, which in this case is Ann Arbor. Thus, the risk premium method does not have the theoretical precision that the other models do. On the other hand, the input values required by the debt-cost-plus-risk-premium model are fewer and easier to estimate than in the other models.

A business's cost of equity can be estimated by adding a risk premium to the business's before-tax cost of debt:

Key Equation 9.4: Debt Cost Plus Risk Premium Model

$$R(R_e) = R(R_d) + \text{Risk premium.}$$

Here, $R(R_e)$ is the cost of equity, $R(R_d)$ is the before-tax cost of debt, and the risk premium is the amount of return required above the cost of debt to induce investors to buy the business's stock.

With a cost of debt estimate of 10.0 percent and a current risk premium estimate of 4.0 percentage points, the debt-cost-plus-risk-premium estimate for Ann Arbor's cost of equity is 14.0 percent:

$$R(R_e) = R(R_d) + \text{Risk premium}$$
$$= 10.0\% + 4.0\% = 14.0\%.$$

Comparison of the Capital Asset Pricing Model, Discounted Cash Flow, and Debt-Cost-Plus-Risk-Premium Methods

We have discussed three methods for estimating the cost of equity. The CAPM estimate for Ann Arbor is 13.5 percent, the DCF estimate is 13.8 percent, and the debt-cost-plus-risk-premium estimate is 14.0 percent. At this point, most analysts would conclude that there is sufficient consistency in the results to warrant the use of 13.8 percent, or thereabout, as the final estimate of the cost of equity for Ann Arbor. If the three methods had produced widely different estimates, Ann Arbor's managers would have had to use their judgment regarding the relative merits of each estimate and then chosen the estimate, or some average of the estimates, that seemed most reasonable under the circumstances. If one of the estimates is clearly out of the ballpark, it would be best to discard that estimate rather than average it in with the others. In general, the choice of which methods and weights to use in making the final estimate would be based on the managers' confidence in the input parameters and the relative values of each approach.

SELF-TEST QUESTIONS

1. Describe the CAPM approach to estimating a business's cost of equity.
2. What is the best proxy for the risk-free rate in the CAPM? Why?
3. What are the three types of beta that can be used in the CAPM?
4. Describe the DCF approach to estimating a business's cost of equity.
5. What are three common methods for estimating the future dividend growth rate for use in the DCF model?
6. Describe the debt-cost-plus-risk-premium approach to estimating a business's cost of equity.
7. Is there a difference between the risk premium used in the CAPM and the one used in the debt-cost-plus-risk-premium model?
8. How would you choose among widely different estimates of $R(R_e)$?

Estimating the Cost of Equity to Not-for-Profit Businesses

Not-for-profit businesses raise equity (i.e., fund) capital in two basic ways: (1) by receiving contributions and grants and (2) by earning an excess of revenues over expenses (retained earnings). In this section, we discuss some views regarding the cost of fund capital and then illustrate how this cost might be estimated.

Our primary purpose in this chapter is to develop a CCC estimate that can be used in capital budgeting decisions. Thus, the estimated "costs" represent the cost of using capital to purchase fixed assets, rather than for alternative uses. What is the cost of using equity capital for real-asset investments in not-for-profit businesses? At least five positions can be taken on this question:

1. **Fund capital has a zero cost**. The rationale here is that (1) contributors do not expect a monetary return on their contributions and that (2) the firm's stakeholders, especially the patients who pay more for services than warranted by the firm's tangible costs, do not require an explicit return on the capital retained by the firm. Because no explicit monetary return is required by the suppliers of fund capital, its cost is zero.
2. **Fund capital has a cost equal to the return forgone on marketable securities investments**. When a not-for-profit firm receives contributions or retains earnings, it can always invest these funds in marketable securities (highly liquid, safe securities) rather than immediately use these funds to purchase real assets (property and equipment). Thus, fund capital has an opportunity cost that should be acknowledged; this cost is roughly equal to the return available on a portfolio of short-term, low-risk securities such as T-bills. Because such securities provide relatively low returns, the cost of fund capital is relatively small.
3. **Fund capital has a cost equal to the expected growth rate of the business's assets**. To better understand the logic here, assume that a hospital in a growing city must increase its services to meet growing demand and, because it does not have excess capacity, its total assets must increase by 8 percent per year to keep pace with the increasing patient load. Because the left side of the balance sheet (total assets) must increase by 8 percent, the right side (total capital) also must increase by the same amount to keep the balance sheet balanced. To increase its capital without increasing the proportion of debt used to finance its assets, the hospital must grow its fund capital at an 8 percent rate. In this way, it can finance asset growth by growing

both debt and equity at the same 8 percent rate as assets and hence hold the relative amount of debt constant. If the hospital earned zero return on its fund capital, its equity base would remain constant over time, and the only way it could add new assets would be to take on additional debt without matching equity (and hence drive up its debt ratio) or rely solely on contributions to provide the needed equity. In general, reliance on contribution capital is highly risky, and, at some point, lenders will be unwilling to provide additional debt financing, so it would be difficult to support the desired growth without a return on the equity invested.

Even if no volume growth is expected, a not-for-profit business must earn a return on its fund capital just to replace its existing asset base as assets wear out or become obsolete. This ROE is required because new assets will cost more than the old ones being replaced as a result of technological advances and inflation, so depreciation cash flow in itself will not be sufficient to replace older assets as needed. The bottom line here is that not-for-profit firms must earn an ROE merely to support dollar growth in assets, and the greater the growth rate—including that caused by inflation—the greater the cost of fund capital.

4. **Fund capital has a cost equal to that required to maintain the business's creditworthiness.** One of the factors that rating agencies consider when assigning credit ratings is the profitability of the business; all else the same, the higher the profitability, the higher the credit rating. In general, managers of not-for-profit healthcare businesses have some target credit rating that they wish to maintain. Failure to maintain a sound credit rating increases both the cost of debt (interest rate) and the difficulties involved in obtaining future debt financing. Rating agencies periodically publish financial measures that they believe to be appropriate for each credit rating. In addition, numerous providers of hospital financial data publish financial measure averages by bond rating. For example, if the average A-rated hospital has an ROE of 7 percent, and a not-for-profit hospital wants to maintain an A rating, its target ROE (and hence cost of fund capital) should be about 7 percent.
5. **Fund capital has a cost equal to the cost of equity to similar for-profit businesses.** The rationale here rests on the opportunity cost concept as discussed in the second argument, but the opportunity cost is now defined as the return available from investing fund capital in alternative investments of **similar risk rather than from investing in low-risk marketable securities.**

For an illustration of this position, suppose Bayside, a not-for-profit corporation, receives $500,000 in contributions in 2019 and also retains $4.5 million in earnings, so it has $5 million of new fund capital available for investment. The $5 million can be (1) used to purchase assets related to its core business, such as an outpatient clinic or diagnostic equipment; (2) temporarily invested in securities, with the intent of purchasing healthcare assets sometime in the future; (3) used to retire debt; (4) used to pay management bonuses; (5) placed in a non-interest-bearing account at a bank; and so on. By using this capital to invest in real assets (property and equipment), Bayside is deprived of the opportunity to use this capital for other purposes, so an opportunity cost must be assigned that reflects the riskiness associated with an equity investment in hospital assets. What return is available on securities with similar risk to an equity investment in hospital assets? The answer is the return expected from investing in the stock of an investor-owned hospital business, such as Ann Arbor Health Care. Instead of using fund capital to purchase real healthcare assets, Bayside can always use the funds to buy the stock of a hospital business, such as Ann Arbor, and delay the purchase of a real asset until sometime in the future.

Of these five positions, which should prevail in practice? Unfortunately, the answer is not clear-cut. However, at a minimum, a not-for-profit business should require a return on its equity investment in real assets that is at least as large as its projected asset growth rate. In that way, the business is setting the minimum rate of return that will, if it is actually achieved, ensure that the forecasted growth rate can be achieved. Thus, the expected growth rate sets the minimum required rate of return, and hence the minimum cost of equity, for not-for-profit businesses. On the other hand, if the rating agency's target ROE is greater than the growth rate, it would be prudent to use this value as the cost of equity to ensure the business maintains its creditworthiness.

However, to recover **all opportunity costs** fully, including the opportunity cost of employing equity capital in real assets, the real-asset investments must

Choosing a Cost of Equity When Estimates Vary Widely

Suppose you are estimating the cost of capital for a large, publicly traded for-profit hospital chain. First, you estimated the cost of debt to be 7.2 percent. Then, you applied all three methods for estimating the hospital's cost of equity, with the following results:

CAPM: 13.6%
DCF: 6.8%
Debt cost plus risk premium: 11.2%

Your next task is to choose a single value for the cost of equity.

How do you estimate a single value from these widely different estimates? Should you merely average the three estimates or should other factors be considered? Does the fact that the DCF estimate is less than the cost of debt influence your decision? What is your best single (point) estimate for the hospital's cost of equity?

offer an expected return equal to the return expected on similar-risk securities investments. Thus, the "true" economic cost of equity to a not-for-profit healthcare provider is the rate that can be earned on stock investments in similar investor-owned firms. By using this cost of equity, a not-for-profit business is requiring that all costs, including full opportunity costs, be considered in the cost-of-capital estimate.

Although we believe the full opportunity cost approach to be most correct theoretically, many would argue that the unique mission of not-for-profit businesses precludes securities investments as realistic alternatives to healthcare property-and-equipment investments because securities investments do not contribute directly to the mission of providing healthcare services. If that is the case, the cost of fund capital should be the greater of the expected growth rate or the rate required to maintain creditworthiness. On the other hand, full opportunity costs do not have to be recovered on every new capital investment. Not-for-profit firms do invest in negative profit projects that benefit their stakeholders, but we believe that managers should be aware of the financial opportunity costs inherent in such investments. We have more to say about this issue in chapter 11.

SELF-TEST QUESTIONS

1. Is there a cost of equity for not-for-profit businesses?
2. How can this cost be estimated?

Estimating the Corporate Cost of Capital

On the web at: *ache.org/HAP/PinkSong8e*

The final step in the cost-of-capital estimation process is to combine the debt and equity cost estimates to form the CCC. As we discuss in chapter 10, each business has a target capital structure in mind, which is defined as the particular mix of debt and equity that causes its overall cost of capital to be minimized. Furthermore, when a business raises new capital, it generally tries to finance in a way that will keep the actual capital structure reasonably close to its target over time. The CCC for any business, regardless of ownership, is calculated using the following equation:

Key Equation 9.5: Corporate Cost of Capital

$$CCC = [w_{ed} \times R(R_d) \times (1 - T)] + [w_e \times R(R_e)].$$

Here, CCC is the corporate cost of capital, w_{ed} is the weight of debt financing in the optimal (target) capital structure, $R(R_d)$ is the cost of debt, T is the tax rate, w_e is the weight of equity, and $R(R_e)$ is the cost of equity.

Here, w_{ed} and w_e are the target weights for debt and equity, respectively. The cost of the debt component, $R(R_d)$, will be an average if the firm uses several types of debt for its permanent financing. Alternatively, the equation can be expanded to include multiple debt terms. Investor-owned businesses would use their marginal tax rate for T, while T would be zero for not-for-profit firms.

The CCC represents the cost of each **new** dollar of capital raised at the margin. It is **not** the average cost of all the dollars that the firm has raised in the past. Our primary interest is in obtaining a cost of capital for use in capital investment analysis; for such purposes, a marginal cost is required. The CCC formula implies that each new dollar of capital will consist of both debt and equity that is raised, at least conceptually, in proportion to the firm's target capital structure.

Investor-Owned Businesses

For an illustration of the CCC calculation for investor-owned businesses, consider Ann Arbor, which has a target capital structure of 60 percent debt and 40 percent equity. As previously estimated, the firm's before-tax cost of debt, $R(R_d)$, is 10.0 percent; its tax rate, T, is 30 percent; and its cost of equity, $R(R_e)$, is 13.8 percent. Using these data, we estimate Ann Arbor's CCC to be 9.7 percent:

$$\begin{aligned} CCC_{AAHS} &= [w_d \times R(R_d) \times (1 - T)] + [w_e \times R(R_e)] \\ &= [0.60 \times 10.0\% \times (1 - 0.30)] + [0.40 \times 13.8\%] \\ &= 9.7\%. \end{aligned}$$

Conceptually, every dollar of new capital that Ann Arbor obtains consists of 60 cents of debt (with an after-tax cost of 7.0 percent) and 40 cents of equity (with a cost of 13.8 percent). The average cost of each new dollar is 9.7 percent. In any one year, Ann Arbor may raise all of its required new capital by issuing debt, by retaining earnings, or by selling new common stock. Over the long run, Ann Arbor plans to use 60 percent debt financing and 40 percent equity financing, so these weights are appropriate for the cost-of-capital calculation.

Not-for-Profit Businesses

The CCC for not-for-profit businesses is developed in the same way as for investor-owned businesses. For an illustration, consider the following example. If we assume a target capital structure of 50 percent debt and 50 percent equity and use the estimates of the component costs developed earlier, the CCC for Bayside is 10.0 percent:

$$\begin{aligned} CCC_{BMH} &= [w_d \times R(R_d) \times (1 - T)] + [w_e \times R(R_e)] \\ &= [0.50 \times 6.1\% \times (1 - 0)] + [0.50 \times 13.8\%] \\ &= 10.0\%. \end{aligned}$$

The primary reason that Bayside's corporate-cost-of-capital estimate is greater than Ann Arbor's is that Ann Arbor uses more debt financing in its target mix and hence uses more of the lower-cost financing component. Perhaps Ann Arbor, as a hospital system, has lower business risk and hence can carry more debt in its optimal financing structure. (This issue is pursued in chapter 10.)

Businesses, regardless of ownership, cannot raise unlimited amounts of new capital in any given year at a constant cost. Eventually, as more new capital is raised, investors will require higher returns on debt and equity capital, even if the capital is raised in accordance with the firm's target structure. Thus, the CCCs estimated here for Ann Arbor and Bayside are valid only when the amount required for capital investment falls within each business's normal range. If capital is required in amounts that far exceed those normally raised, the CCC must be subjectively adjusted upward to reflect the higher costs involved.

SELF-TEST QUESTIONS

1. What is the general formula for finding the CCC?
2. What weights should be used in the formula? Why?
3. What is the primary difference between the CCCs for investor-owned and not-for-profit firms?
4. Is the CCC constant regardless of the amount of new capital required? Explain your answer.

An Economic Interpretation of the Corporate Cost of Capital

Thus far, the focus of the cost of capital discussion has been on the mechanics of the estimation process. Now, it is worthwhile to step back from the mathematics of the process and examine the economic interpretation of the CCC.

The component-cost estimates (the costs of debt and equity) that make up a business's CCC are based on the returns that investors require to supply capital to the firm. In turn, investors' required rates of return are based on the opportunity costs borne by investing in the debt and equity of the business in question, rather than in alternative investments of similar risk. These opportunity costs to investors, when combined to estimate the CCC, establish the **opportunity cost** to the business—that is, the CCC is the return that the business can earn by investing in alternative security investments that have the same risk its own real assets have. From a pure financial perspective, if a business cannot earn its CCC on new capital investments, no new investments should be made and no new capital should be raised. If existing investments are not earning the CCC, they should be terminated, the assets liquidated, and the proceeds returned to investors for reinvestment elsewhere.

Note that the CCC sets the minimum return required on real-asset investments **regardless of the actual financing anticipated during the planning period**—that is, even if Ann Arbor planned to finance all new capital investments with debt financing, which has an estimated after-tax cost of 7.0 percent, the appropriate cost of capital to the firm is 9.7 percent. The rationale is that the debt financing cannot be obtained at the current cost rate without Ann Arbor's equity base, so from an economic perspective, the new capital investments are actually being financed using both equity and debt—that is, being financed at the firm's target capital structure.

However, the CCC is not the appropriate minimum rate of return for all new real-asset investments. The required rates of return set by investors on the business's debt and equity are based on perceptions regarding the riskiness of their investments, which, in turn, are based on two factors: (1) the inherent riskiness of the business and (2) the amount of debt financing used. Thus, the firm's inherent business risk and capital structure are embedded in its CCC estimate.

Because different firms have different business risk and use different proportions of debt financing, different firms have different CCCs. Different capital costs are most pronounced for firms in different industries; stocks of high-tech businesses, for example, often have higher beta values than healthcare stocks do. Still, even firms in the same industry can have different business risk, and capital structure differences among such firms can compound CCC differences.

The primary purpose of estimating a business's CCC is to help make capital budgeting decisions—that is, the cost of capital will be used as the benchmark capital budgeting *hurdle rate*, which is the minimum return necessary for a project to be attractive financially. The firm can always earn its cost of capital by investing in securities that in the aggregate have the same risk as the firm's assets, so it should not invest in real assets unless it can earn at least as much. However, remember that the CCC reflects opportunity costs based on the aggregate risk of the firm (i.e., the riskiness of the firm's average project). Thus, the CCC can be applied without modification only to projects under consideration that have average risk, where average is defined as that applicable to the firm's currently held assets in the aggregate. If a project under consideration has risk that differs significantly from that of the firm's average asset, the CCC must be adjusted to account for the differential risk when the project is being evaluated.[6]

For example, Ann Arbor's CCC—9.7 percent—is probably appropriate for use in evaluating a new outpatient clinic that has risk similar to the hospital's average project, which involves the provision of both inpatient and outpatient services. Clearly, it would not be appropriate to apply Ann Arbor's 9.7 percent CCC without adjustment to a new project that involves establishing a managed care subsidiary; this project does not have the same risk as the hospital's average asset.

As discussed in chapter 5, investors require higher returns for riskier investments. Thus, a high-risk project must have a higher *project cost of capital* than a low-risk project does. Exhibit 9.4 illustrates the relationships among project risk, the CCC, and project cost of capital. The exhibit illustrates that Ann Arbor's 9.7 percent CCC is the appropriate hurdle rate **only** for an **average risk** project such as project A, which has the same risk as the

EXHIBIT 9.4
Ann Arbor Health Care: Corporate and Project Costs of Capital

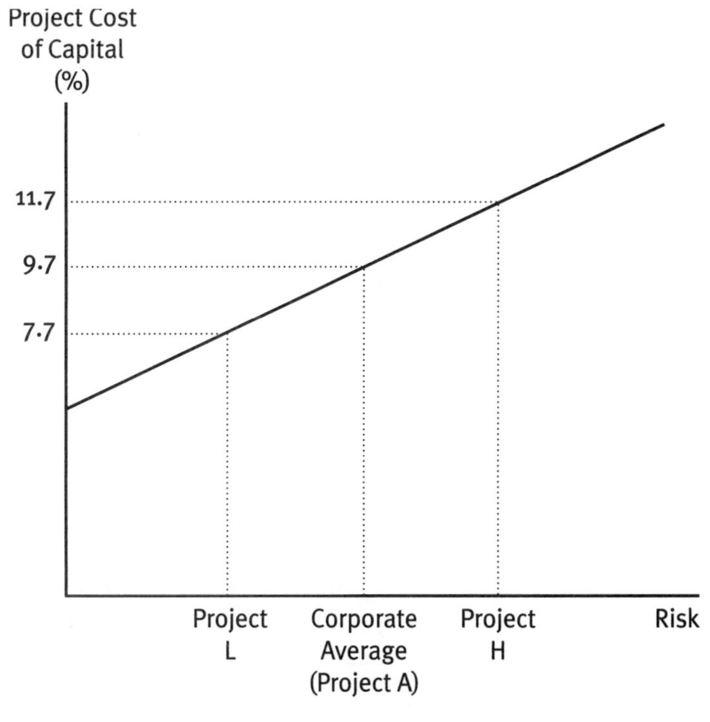

aggregate business. Project L, which has less risk than Ann Arbor's average project, has a project cost of capital of 7.7 percent, which is less than the CCC. Conversely, Project H, which has more risk than the average project, has a higher project cost of capital of 11.7 percent.

The key point here is that the CCC is merely a **benchmark** that will be used as the basis for estimating project costs of capital. It is not a one-size-fits-all rate that can be used with abandon whenever an opportunity cost is needed in a financial analysis. This point is revisited in chapter 12, when capital investment risk considerations are addressed.

SELF-TEST QUESTIONS

1. Explain the economic interpretation of the CCC.
2. Is the CCC affected by short-term financing plans? Explain your answer.
3. Is the CCC the appropriate opportunity cost for all projects that a business evaluates?
4. Draw a graph similar to the one shown in exhibit 9.4 and explain its implications.

Flotation Costs

In our discussion of the CCC, we have ignored flotation (issuance) costs, which are the administrative costs and fees required to bring new securities to market. Under some circumstances, such costs can be large, especially for equity issues. One way of handling flotation costs is to incorporate them into the CCC estimate, which has the effect of increasing the CCC. Here are some points to consider regarding flotation costs:

- Mature for-profit businesses rarely issue new common stock. Rather, it is cheaper to obtain equity capital by earnings retention, which eliminates flotation costs. Furthermore, flotation costs on public debt issues are relatively small, while such costs on private placements are near zero. Thus, only businesses that must go to the equity markets frequently bear substantial flotation costs.
- There is considerable uncertainty inherent in the cost-of-capital estimation process. Thus, attempting to fine-tune the resulting estimate by incorporating flotation costs may be an exercise in futility.
- When flotation costs are significant, they can be incorporated into the decision-making process by adding them to the cost of the capital

investments under consideration. Thus, if new capital to fund a business's new investments requires $2 million in flotation costs, this dollar cost can be assigned directly to the projects under consideration.

For these reasons, we have chosen not to incorporate flotation costs into the estimation process.[7]

SELF-TEST QUESTION

1. Are flotation costs relevant to the CCC estimate? Explain your answer.

Divisional Costs of Capital

The CCC reflects the riskiness of the overall business in the aggregate. If a firm has only one line of business, the CCC can be used—with appropriate risk adjustments—on most projects under consideration. However, the CCC may not be the appropriate benchmark (starting point) for projects that are in a line of business that differs from the overall firm.

When a firm has multiple divisions that operate in different business lines, it may be best to estimate a *divisional cost of capital* for each division and use these estimates as the benchmarks for all capital project evaluations. The assumption here is that capital budgeting analyses will be conducted at the divisional level, so the best benchmark for such analyses is the one that reflects the riskiness of each division's business line.

For an illustration of this concept, consider the following example. A for-profit healthcare system might, along with its provider network, have one subsidiary that invests primarily in real estate for medical uses and another subsidiary that runs an HMO (health maintenance organization). Clearly, each of these subsidiaries has its own unique business risk and optimal capital structure. The low-risk, high-debt-capacity real estate subsidiary might have a divisional cost of capital of 8 percent, while the high-risk, low-debt-capacity HMO subsidiary might have a cost of capital of 12 percent. The health system, which consists of these two divisions plus provider assets, would likely have a cost of capital that falls between 8 and 12 percent—say, 10 percent.

If all capital budgeting decisions in the system were made on the basis of the system's 10 percent CCC, the process would be biased in favor of the higher-risk HMO subsidiary. The cost of capital would be too low for the HMO subsidiary and too high for the real-estate subsidiary. Over time, this cost-of-capital bias would result in acceptance of too many HMO projects and too few real-estate projects, which would skew the business-line mix toward HMO assets and hence increase the overall riskiness of the system. Of course, the answer to this problem is to use subsidiary costs of capital rather than the CCC in the capital budgeting decision process.

Unlike individual project costs of capital, subsidiary costs of capital often can be estimated with some confidence because it is usually possible to identify publicly traded firms that are predominantly in the same line of business as the subsidiary. For example, the cost of capital for the HMO subsidiary can be estimated by looking at the debt and equity costs of the major for-profit managed care companies, such as Humana and UnitedHealth Group. This approach, in which a publicly traded firm in the same line of business is used as a proxy for a nonpublicly traded business, is called the ***pure play*** approach. If market data are at hand for pure play firms, it is relatively easy to develop subsidiary costs of capital.

As a final check in the process of estimating divisional costs of capital, note that the CCC must equal the weighted average—say, by proportion of assets—of all of the subsidiary costs of capital. If it does not, there are problems in the estimation process that must be resolved.

SELF-TEST QUESTION

1. Explain the concept of divisional costs of capital.

Warning! Warning! Warning!

We have spent a great deal of time describing how the corporate (or divisional) cost of capital is estimated for any business. In addition, we have discussed the interpretation and use of the corporate (or divisional) cost of capital as a hurdle rate in evaluating new capital investment proposals. Once the effort has been expended to estimate the cost of capital, there is a strong tendency (especially among students) to treat the estimate as a one-size-fits-all number—that is, "we have a project to consider—no sweat, use the cost-of-capital estimate as the hurdle rate." Unfortunately, the corporate (or divisional) cost of capital cannot be applied willy-nilly. As we discussed earlier, if the project being evaluated does not have average risk, a risk adjustment—as illustrated in exhibit 9.4—must be applied.

Equally important, if the project under consideration is in a line of business that is **unrelated to the core business**, the corporate (or divisional) cost of capital **cannot** be used. For example, assume that a hospital is considering acquiring a medical group practice. Is it appropriate to use the hospital's CCC as the base hurdle rate in the analysis? The answer is no! Because the project being evaluated (a medical practice) is in a different line of business than the hospital, the CCC is not relevant to the analysis. The appropriate cost of capital is one developed using the pure play method (discussed in the next section) with practice management businesses as the proxy.

SELF-TEST QUESTION

1. When is it appropriate to apply the CCC when evaluating a new project proposal? When is it inappropriate?

Cost-of-Capital Estimation for Small Businesses

The guidance given thus far in the chapter focuses on the cost-of-capital estimation process for large healthcare businesses. What if the business is small, such as a solo practice; a small group practice; or a small, freestanding hospital? The estimation process is the same as described, but the manner in which the component costs are estimated must be handled differently.

Estimating the Cost of Debt

Small businesses typically obtain the bulk of their debt financing from commercial banks, so a business's commercial loan officer will be able to provide some insights on the cost of future debt financing. Alternatively, managers of small businesses can look to marketplace activity for guidance—that is, the interest rate currently being set on the debt issues of similar-risk firms can be used as an estimate of the cost of debt. Here, similar risk can be judged by subjective analysis (same industry, similar size, similar use of debt, and so on). In many cases, the prime rate gives small businesses a benchmark for bank loan rates. If the business has borrowed from commercial banks in the past, its managers will know the historical premium charged above the prime rate for the business's bank debt. An awareness of the current interest rate environment generally permits managers to make a reasonable estimate for their own business's cost of debt, even when the business is small.

Estimating the Cost of Equity

Although estimating the cost of debt for a small business is relatively easy, the cost-of-equity estimate is more problematic because such businesses do not have publicly traded stock.

Debt-Cost-Plus-Risk-Premium Approach

Perhaps the easiest way to estimate the cost of equity of a small business is to use the debt-cost-plus-risk-premium method. Because the cost of debt is relatively easy to estimate, it is equally easy to add some risk premium—say,

4 percentage points—to the business's before-tax cost of debt to obtain its cost-of-equity estimate. However, this estimate can be considered only a ballpark estimate because the risk premiums applicable to small businesses may not be the same as those estimated for large firms.

Pure Play Approach

As an alternative, a proxy publicly traded firm in the same line of business can be identified and its beta used to estimate the equity risk of the small business. This approach is the pure play method first mentioned in the last major section. For example, suppose the beta for a publicly traded practice management firm is 0.88. **If the riskiness inherent in practice management is the same as the risk involved in the ownership of a small group practice**, a beta of 0.88 can be used to proxy such ownership risk. Then, the CAPM approach can be used to estimate the small business's cost of equity.

To use the pure play approach for a small business, we must assume that the risk to the owners of the publicly traded proxy firm is the same as the risk to the owners of the small business. However, there are several important differences between the ownership of stock in a large corporation and the ownership of, say, a small group practice. First, the geographic and business-line diversification of a large business typically makes ownership less risky than a similar position in a small, localized single-line business. In effect, the portfolios of business projects of large firms are better diversified than the portfolios of small firms. Second, most stockholders of large businesses hold that stock as part of a well-diversified investment. In a small group practice, employment earnings are highly correlated with investment returns on the practice. Third, stock owned in an investment portfolio is highly liquid—the owner can sell it quickly at a fair market price with a single phone call. Conversely, an ownership position in a group practice is difficult to sell.

All of these factors suggest that the cost of equity to a small, owner-managed business is higher, perhaps much higher, than that calculated using the CAPM and a proxy company. Unfortunately, finance theory cannot tell us how much higher.

Build-Up Method

An approach called the *build-up method* is commonly used to estimate the cost of equity for small businesses. Here, the cost of equity of a similar large business is used as the base, or starting point. Then, various adjustments, or premiums, are added to account for the differences between large and small businesses.

- **Size premium**. Although returns data on businesses as small as a group practice are not readily available, studies using historical returns data indicate that the cost of equity for the smallest stocks (those in the bottom decile of market value) listed on the New York Stock Exchange is about 4 percentage points higher than the cost of equity for large businesses (those in the S&P 500). This premium—added to compensate for the additional risk inherent in the ownership of small, as opposed to large, businesses—is called the ***size premium***. It can be argued that the size premium is even larger than 4 percentage points for firms so small that their equity is not publicly traded. The bottom line here is that when the cost of equity of a small business is estimated on the basis of equity costs to similar large businesses, an additional premium must be added to account for the size differential.

- **Liquidity premium**. Because an ownership position in a small business is less liquid than the stock of a large corporation, a liquidity premium is commonly added when estimating the cost of equity for a small business. This premium is generally thought to be about 2 percentage points. Note, however, that if an investor has a control position (more than 50 percent ownership), some of the risk associated with small business ownership is reduced.
- **Unique risk premium**. Some small businesses have unique risk. For example, the success of a start-up business might depend on new, unproven technology, or the success of a small business might depend on the intellectual capital or managerial prowess of one person. In such situations, an equity investment is **very** risky, and it is not uncommon to add a premium of 5 or more percentage points to account for such unique risk.

For an illustration of the use of the build-up method, consider a small medical practice. The cost of equity to a large practice management company is found as follows:

$$\begin{aligned} R(R_e) &= RF + [R(R_M) - RF] \times b \\ &= 6.0\% + (11.0\% - 6.0\%) \times 0.88 \\ &= 6.0\% + (5.0\% \times 0.88) = 10.4\%. \end{aligned}$$

Here, we used a pure play beta of 0.88, along with the market data used in previous examples, to obtain a base cost of equity of 10.4 percent.

Now, using the build-up method, and assuming a size premium of 4 percentage points and a liquidity premium of 2 percentage points, we obtain a cost of equity estimate of

$$\text{Cost of equity} = 10.4\% + 4.0\% + 2.0\% = 16.4\%.$$

If any unique risk is identified for this practice, the cost-of-equity estimate could be even higher.

Although the estimation process clearly is more difficult, it may be even more important for small businesses to recognize their CCCs than it is for large businesses. The reason is that in small businesses, owners often have their livelihoods, as well as their equity investment, tied to the business. Using the techniques described in this section, even a small business owner can attempt to estimate her business's CCC.

SELF-TEST QUESTIONS

1. What problems do small businesses face when estimating the CCC?
2. What is the size premium? Liquidity premium? Unique risk premium?
3. Describe the build-up method for estimating a small business's cost of equity.

Factors That Influence a Business's Cost of Capital

The CCC estimate for any business is influenced by several factors. Some are external to the business, but some can be influenced by managerial actions.

Factors That Cannot Be Influenced

- **The level of interest rates**. The factor that perhaps has the greatest impact on a business's cost of capital is the general level of interest rates, which typically is a function of inflation expectations. In the early 1980s, interest rates were very high; hence, CCCs were very high. In such circumstances, only projects that will yield a very high return are acceptable; as a result, capital investment is low. Conversely, in recent years, interest rates in the United States have been low, so the costs of capital have been relatively low.
- **Tax rates**. High corporate tax rates lead to a lower cost of capital because the cost of debt for investor-owned businesses is reduced by one minus the tax rate. At the same time, differential personal taxes encourage the use of one form of capital over another. For example, a capital gains tax rate that is lower than the ordinary tax rate lowers the cost of equity to taxable businesses relative to the cost of debt and hence encourages the use of equity financing. High personal tax rates also affect the cost of debt to not-for-profit businesses because high tax rates make tax-exempt debt more attractive to investors and hence lower the cost of tax-exempt (municipal) debt capital.

Factors That Can Be Influenced

- **Capital structure policy**. As we discuss in the next chapter, the optimal capital structure is the structure that produces the lowest cost of capital to the business. Thus, businesses that are not using the optimal proportion of debt financing have a CCC that is higher than necessary.
- **Capital investment policy**. A business's capital investment policy defines its line of business, which establishes the basic risk of the business. If a business adds more and more risky assets to its fixed asset portfolio, its CCC will increase. Likewise, the addition of low-risk assets will lower the cost of capital. Do not forget, however, that the CCC is merely a benchmark, and new projects that have differential risk as compared with the business as a whole must use a cost of capital that differs from the CCC.

SELF-TEST QUESTION

1. What are the factors that affect the CCC estimate?

Chapter Key Concepts

This chapter discusses the CCC, which is important to the financial well-being of healthcare businesses. Here are its key concepts:

- The cost of capital to be used in capital budgeting decisions is the *weighted average* of the various types of permanent capital the firm uses, typically debt and common equity.
- The *component cost of debt* is the *after-tax* cost of new debt. For taxable businesses, it is found by multiplying the before-tax cost of new debt by (1 – T), where T is the firm's marginal tax rate, so the component cost of debt is $R(R_d) \times (1 - T)$. For not-for-profit businesses, the debt is often tax-exempt, but no other tax effects apply, so the component cost of debt is merely the tax-exempt $R(R_d)$.
- The *cost of equity* for an investor-owned business is the rate of return investors require on the firm's common stock. For large businesses, it is usually estimated by three methods: (1) the capital asset pricing model (CAPM) approach, (2) the discounted

(continued)

(continued from previous page)

cash flow (DCF) approach, and (3) the debt-cost-plus-risk-premium approach.

- In the *CAPM* approach, the firm's beta coefficient is multiplied by the market risk premium to determine the firm's risk premium, and this risk premium is added to the risk-free rate to obtain the firm's cost-of-equity estimate.
- The best proxy for the *risk-free rate* is the yield on long-term T-bonds.
- The market risk premium can be estimated either *historically* or *prospectively*.
- The *DCF* approach uses the dividend valuation model, which requires the current stock price, last dividend paid, and dividend growth rate to estimate the cost of equity.
- The growth rate can be estimated from historical dividend data (by using the *retention growth model*) or from securities analysts' forecasts.
- The *debt-cost-plus-risk-premium* approach adds a risk premium to the firm's cost-of-debt estimate to obtain the cost-of-equity estimate.
- For not-for-profit businesses, the *cost of equity (fund capital)* can be approximated by the cost of equity of similar investor-owned firms. This approach considers the opportunity costs associated with the use of equity capital.
- Alternatively, the cost of equity to not-for-profit businesses can be set as the greater of the expected asset growth rate and the rate required to maintain creditworthiness. This approach does not consider opportunity costs, but it does recognize that a ROE is required if the business is to maintain a sound financial posture.
- Each firm has a *target capital structure*, and the target weights are used to estimate the firm's *corporate cost of capital (CCC)*:

$$CCC = [w_d \times R(R_d) \times (1 - T)] + [w_e \times R(R_e)].$$

- When making *capital investment decisions*, the firm will use the CCC as the *hurdle rate* for **average-risk** projects. Note, however, that the CCC is irrelevant if the project being analyzed is in a different line of business than the core business.

(continued)

(continued from previous page)

- If a business has multiple divisions that operate in different business lines, it is best to estimate a *divisional cost of capital* for each division.
- The CCC for small businesses is estimated by using the same techniques as applied for large businesses. However, the estimation of the component costs—particularly the cost of equity—is more difficult.
- The *build-up method* is used to estimate the cost of equity for a small business. This method uses the cost of equity of a similar large business as the starting point and then adds (1) a *size premium*, (2) a *liquidity premium*, and (3) a *unique risk premium*.
- Several factors influence the cost-of-capital estimate for any business, including (1) the *current level of interest rates*, (2) *tax rates*, (3) *capital structure policy*, and (4) *capital investment policy*.

The concepts developed in this chapter are used extensively throughout the text, especially in capital structure decisions (chapter 10) and in capital budgeting decisions (chapters 11, 12).

Chapter Models, Problems, and Minicases

The following ancillary resources in spreadsheet format are available for this chapter:

- A chapter model that shows how to perform many of the calculations described in the chapter
- Problems that test your ability to perform the calculations
- A minicase that is more complicated than the problems and tests your ability to perform the calculations in preparation for a case.

These resources can be accessed online at ache.org/HAP/PinkSong8e8.

Selected Case

One case in *Cases in Healthcare Finance*, sixth edition, is applicable to this chapter: Case 17: Southeastern Homecare, which focuses on the cost of capital estimation process for both investor-owned and not-for-profit businesses.

References

Carpenter, C. E., and P. M. Bernet. 2013. "How the Choice of Issuing Authority Affects Hospital Debt Financing Costs." *Healthcare Financial Management* 67 (5): 80–84.

Yahoo. 2019. "Quote Lookup." Accessed May 23. https://finance.yahoo.com.

Selected Bibliography

Arduino, K. 2018. "Healthcare Capital Markets Outlook: Short-Term Opportunities Versus Long-Term Uncertainty." *Healthcare Financial Management* 72 (5): 36–43.

Brigham, E. F., and M. C. Ehrhardt. 2013. "Chapter 9." In *Financial Management: Theory and Practice,* 14th ed. Mason, OH: South-Western Cengage Learning.

Cleverley, W. O. 1982. "Return on Equity in the Hospital Industry: Requirement or Windfall?", *Inquiry* (Summer): 150–59.

Conrad, D. A. 1984. "Returns on Equity to Not-for-Profit Hospitals: Theory and Implementation." *Health Services Research* (April): 41–63.

Healthcare Financial Management Association. 2018. "Capital Planning and Finance: Charting the Reallocation of Scarce Resources." Published May 1. www.hfma .org/Content.aspx?id=60612.

———. 2018. "Optimizing Capital Structure Decisions Under the New Tax Law." *Healthcare Financial Management* 72 (8): A1–A4.

Jordahl, E. A. 2017. "Contemplating the Case for Terminating Swaps." Healthcare Financial Management Association. Published December 1. www.hfma.org/ Content.aspx?id=57108.

Jordahl, E. A., R. Freel, and D. Ratliff. 2016. "Four Current Market Concepts for Advance Refunding." *Healthcare Financial Management* 70 (12): 70–71.

Jordahl, E. A., M. Robbins, and M. Sedlmeier. 2016. "Meeting New Equipment Needs and Reducing Capital Costs." *Healthcare Financial Management* 70 (7): 60–62.

TD Bank. "Optimizing Capital Structure Decisions Under the New Tax Law." *Healthcare Financial Management* 72 (8): A1–A4.

Selected Websites

The selected websites listed at the end of chapters 6 and 7 are applicable to cost-of-capital estimation.

- For some interesting information related to cost-of-capital estimation, see the Duff & Phelps website at http://duffandphelps.com/.
- For an illustration of a real-world cost-of-capital calculation, see the Expectations Investing website at http://expectationsinvesting.com. Click on Online Tutorials, followed by How Do You Calculate a Company's Cost of Capital?
- The TeachMeFinance website features several tutorial-type discussions that cover various aspects of financial management. For a cost-of-capital tutorial, go to www.teachmefinance.com and click on Cost of Capital in the list along the left side of the page.

Notes

1. A question arises here as to whether the stated rate or the effective annual rate should be used in the cost-of-debt estimate. In general, the difference will be inconsequential, so most analysts opt for the easier approach, which is simply to use the stated rate. (The effective annual rate in this example is $[1.0305]^2 - 1.0 = 6.19\%$ versus a 6.1 percent stated rate.) More important, most capital budgeting analyses use end-of-year cash flows to approximate cash flows that occur throughout the year—in effect creating stated, as opposed to effective, cash flows. For consistency, we prefer to use a cost of capital that does not recognize intrayear compounding—the cash flows will be understated, but so will the cost of capital.
2. Only a few firms in the health services sector use preferred stock financing, so we will not include preferred stock in our cost-of-capital examples. If preferred stock is used as a source of permanent financing, it should be included in the cost-of-capital estimate, and its cost would be estimated using procedures similar to those discussed for the cost of debt.
3. See the *Ibbotson SBBI 2013 Classic Yearbook: Market Results for Stocks, Bonds, Bills, and Inflation 1926–2012* (Morningstar Inc., 2013) for a complete discussion of historical risk premiums, including a discussion of arithmetic and geometric averages.
4. Log-linear regression is a standard time-series linear regression in which the data points are plotted as natural logarithms. The advantage of a log-linear regression is that the slope of the regression line is the average annual growth rate, assuming continuous compounding. In a

standard time-series linear regression of EPS or DPS, the slope of the regression line is the average annual dollar change.

5. The calculation given in the text produces an *arithmetic average* growth rate. A better measure of average growth is the *geometric average* growth rate, which is calculated as follows to be 7 percent:

$$(1.12)5 \times (1.065)45 = (1 + x)^{50}$$
$$1.76234 \times 17.01110 = (1 + x)^{50}$$
$$29.97934 = (1 + x)50$$
$$1 + x = (29.97934)1/50$$
$$1 + x = 1.070$$
$$x = 0.070 = 7.0\%.$$

The equation is asking: What annual growth rate in dividends over the entire 50-year period is equivalent to growth at 12 percent for 5 years, followed by growth at 6.5 percent for 45 years? The answer is an annual growth rate of 7 percent.

6. In theory, the cost of capital should also be adjusted when projects under evaluation have optimal capital structures that differ from the business's target mix. Thus, if a project under evaluation by Ann Arbor had a *debt capacity* of 80 percent, versus 60 percent debt for the average project, this differential should be considered when evaluating the project. However, in reality, debt capacities for individual projects typically are impossible to estimate, so the adjustments made to the CCC usually are confined to risk differentials.

Integrative Application

The Problem

The director of capital budgeting for See-Saw Inc., manufacturer of orthopedic surgery tools, is considering a plan to expand production facilities to meet an increase in demand. She estimates that this expansion will produce a rate of return of 11 percent. The firm's target capital structure calls for a debt/equity ratio of 0.8. See-Saw currently has a bond issue outstanding that will mature in 25 years and has a 7 percent annual coupon rate. The bonds have a par value of $1,000 and are currently selling for $804. The firm has maintained a constant growth rate, E(g), of 6 percent. See-Saw's next expected dividend, E(D1), is $2 and its current stock price, P_0, is $40. Its tax rate is 30 percent. See-Saw is considering funding its expansion with debt only, and any new debt will have a 25-year maturity. The director has to determine whether See-Saw should undertake the expansion.

The Analysis

The CCC sets the minimum return required on real-asset investments regardless of the actual financing anticipated during the planning period. That is, even if See-Saw planned to finance all new capital investments with debt financing, the appropriate cost of capital is the CCC. The rationale is that the debt financing cannot be obtained at the current cost rate without See-Saw's equity bases, so from a financial perspective, the new capital investments are actually being financed using both equity and debt—that is, being financed at the firm's target capital structure.

The cost of common equity can be estimated by the DCF:

$$E(R_e) = E(D1) / P_0 + E(g)$$

$$E(R_e) = \$2 / \$40 + .06 = 11\%$$

The cost of debt can be estimated by the yield to maturity on the current debt:

=RATE(nper,pmt,pv,fv)

=RATE(25,$70,–$804,$1000) = 8.99%

In determining the capital structure weights, note that the debt/equity = 0.8, or 4/5 for example:

Debt	4
Equity	5
Debt + equity	9

Therefore, the capital structure weights are

Debt ÷ (Debt + equity)	4 / 9 = 0.44
Equity / (Debt + equity)	5 / 9 = 0.56

The corporate cost of capital is

$$CCC = [w_d \times R(R_d) \times (1 - T)] + [w_e \times R(R_e)]$$

$$CCC = [0.44 \times 8.99\% \times (1 - 0.3)] + [0.56 \times 11\%]$$

$$CCC = 8.9\%$$

The Decision

Because the expected rate of return is (11.0 – 8.9 =) 2.1 percentage points higher than the CCC, the director decided to undertake the expansion. Of course, the analysis assumed that the planned expansion of production facilities has the same risk as the average See-Saw project. If the project were of higher (lower) risk, the CCC would have had to be adjusted upward (downward). ■

CHAPTER

10

CAPITAL STRUCTURE

Learning Objectives

After studying this chapter, readers should be able to

- explain the effects of debt financing on a business's risk and return,
- briefly describe the primary capital structure theories and their implications for managers, and
- discuss the factors that influence the choice between debt and equity financing.

Introduction

In chapter 9, when we discussed a business's corporate cost of capital, we noted that the weights used in the calculation represent the optimal, or target, mix of debt and equity financing. These weights are defined by the *capital structure* decision. We explain in chapter 10 that managers analyze a number of quantitative and qualitative factors and then establish the *optimal*, or *target*, *capital structure* for the business. Often, because of uncertainties in the estimation process, the target is expressed as a range rather than as a point value. The target will undoubtedly change over time as conditions internal and external to the business change, but at any given moment, managers have a specific capital structure in mind.

The target structure plays a major role in a business's financing decisions. If less than the optimal amount of debt is on hand, new financings will be biased toward the use of debt. Conversely, if too much debt is on the books, equity will be the first choice for new capital. The key here is that one of the most important factors that influences financing decisions is the target capital structure. Managers prefer to finance in a way that keeps the business's capital structure on target.

Once the optimal capital structure—and hence the optimal amount of debt—is identified, managers must consider the optimal maturity structure of the debt component. Should the business's debt be all long-term, all short-term, or some combination of the two? This chapter addresses the optimal capital structure and optimal maturity structure decisions in detail.

Impact of Debt Financing on Risk and Return

One of the most important concepts in capital structure decisions is the impact of debt financing on a business's risk and return.[1] The best way to present this concept is by illustration. Assume that a new business, Super Dental, Inc., is being formed. The business requires $200,000 in assets to begin operation, and only two financing alternatives are available to it: (1) all equity or (2) 50 percent debt and 50 percent equity.

Exhibit 10.1 contains the business's projected starting balance sheet and first year's income statement under the two financing alternatives. To begin, consider the balance sheets shown in the top portion of the table. The business will require $100,000 in current assets and $100,000 in fixed assets to begin operations. Because asset requirements depend on the nature and size of the business rather than on how the business will be financed, the asset side of the balance sheet is unaffected by the financing mix. However, the capital, or claims, side of the balance sheet is influenced by the choice of financing. Under the all-equity alternative, the owners must put up the entire $200,000 needed to purchase the assets. If 50 percent debt financing is used, the owners will contribute only $100,000, and the remaining $100,000 will be obtained from creditors—say, a bank loan with a 10 percent interest rate.

EXHIBIT 10.1 Super Dental, Inc.: Projected Financial Statements Under Two Financing Alternatives

Balance Sheets		
	All Equity	*Debt/Equity*
Current assets	$100,000	$ 100,000
Fixed assets	100,000	100,000
Total assets	$200,000	$ 200,000
Bank loan (10% cost)	$ 0	$ 100,000
Total equity	200,000	100,000
Total claims	$ 200,000	$ 200,000
Income Statements		
Revenues	$ 150,000	$ 150,000
Operating costs	100,000	100,000
Operating income (EBIT)	$ 50,000	$ 50,000
Interest expense	0	10,000
Taxable income	$ 50,000	$ 40,000
Taxes (30%)	15,000	12,000
Net income	$ 35,000	$ 28,000
Return on equity	17.5%	28%
Total dollar return to investors	$ 35,000	$ 38,000

Now, consider the impact of the two financing alternatives on Super Dental's projected income statement. First-year revenues are projected to be \$150,000 and operating costs are forecast at \$100,000, so the business's operating income—earnings before interest and taxes (EBIT)—is expected to be \$50,000. Because the method of financing does not affect revenues and operating costs, the operating income projection is the same under both financing alternatives. However, interest expense must be paid if debt financing is used, so the debt/equity alternative results in a 0.10 × \$100,000 = \$10,000 annual interest charge, while no interest expense occurs if the business is entirely financed with equity. The result is taxable income of \$50,000 under the all-equity alternative and lower taxable income of \$40,000 under the 50 percent debt alternative. Because the business anticipates being taxed at a 30 percent federal-plus-state rate, the expected tax liability is 0.30 × \$50,000 = \$15,000 under the all-equity alternative and 0.30 × \$40,000 = \$12,000 for the debt/equity alternative. Finally, when taxes are deducted from the income stream, Super Dental projects a net income of \$35,000 if it chooses all-equity financing and \$28,000 if 50 percent debt financing is used.

At first glance, all-equity financing appears to be the best strategy. If the business uses 50 percent debt financing, its projected net income will fall by \$35,000 – \$28,000 = \$7,000. But the conclusion that debt financing is bad requires closer examination. Business owners are less concerned with net income than with the return they expect on their equity investment. Perhaps the most meaningful measure of return to a business's owners is the rate of return on equity, or just return on equity (ROE), which is defined as Net income ÷ Total equity. Under all-equity financing, the projected ROE is \$35,000 ÷ \$200,000 = 0.175 = 17.5%. But with 50 percent debt financing, projected ROE increases to \$28,000 ÷ \$100,000 = 28%. The key here is that although net income decreases with debt financing, so does the amount of owner-supplied capital, and the equity requirement decreases proportionally more than does net income.

The end result is that the use of debt financing increases the expected ROE. Why does this positive result

Debt Use in the Healthcare Sector

Capital structure theory has identified several factors as being important to the capital structure decision. Two of the most important are the amount of business risk and the asset structure of the organization. Firms with greater business risk tend to use less debt financing, and firms with a large quantity of brick-and-mortar assets, which can be used as loan collateral, tend to use more debt financing.

Now, consider three important healthcare fields: hospitals, medical equipment manufacturers, and biotechnology companies. On average, which of these fields do you believe uses the most debt financing and which uses the least? Which field sits in the middle? How did you reach your conclusions? Does it make any difference if the hospitals are for-profit or not-for-profit? After you have your answers, you can go to https://finance.yahoo.com/sector/healthcare to see if you were right. Choose some key firms and go to their statistics page to check their debt/equity ratios.

happen? There is no magic here. The key is in the tax code: Interest expense is tax deductible for investor-owned businesses, while dividend distributions are not. To understand the impact of the tax deductibility of interest, take another look at the income statements in exhibit 10.1. The total dollar return to all investors, including owners and creditors, is $35,000 in net income if all-equity financing is used, but it is $28,000 in net income plus $10,000 of interest, for a total of $38,000, when 50 percent debt financing is used. Where did the "extra" $3,000 come from? The answer is, "from the tax man." Taxes are $15,000 if Super Dental is all-equity financed but only $12,000 when 50 percent debt financing is used, and $3,000 less in taxes means $3,000 more for investors. Because debt financing reduces taxes, more of a business's operating income (EBIT) is available for distribution to investors, including owners and creditors.

Super Dental's financing decision appears to be clear. Given only the two alternatives, Super Dental should use the 50 percent debt alternative because it provides the owners with the higher return on investment. Unfortunately, like the proverbial no free lunch, there is a catch. The use of debt financing not only increases owners' return but also increases their risk.

To understand the risk-increasing characteristics of debt financing, consider exhibit 10.2. Here, we recognize that Super Dental, like all businesses, is risky. The owners do not know precisely what the first year's revenues and operating costs will be. Assume, for illustrative purposes, that Revenues – Operating costs = Operating income can be as low as $0 or as high as $100,000 in the business's first year of operations. Furthermore, assume that there is a 25 percent chance that the worst case will occur, a 25

EXHIBIT 10.2 Super Dental, Inc.: Partial Income Statements in an Uncertain World

	All Equity			*Debt/Equity*		
Probability	0.25	0.50	0.25	0.25	0.50	0.25
Operating income (EBIT)	$0	$50,000	$100,000	$0	$50,000	$100,000
Interest expense	0	0	0	10,000	10,000	10,000
Taxable income	$0	$ 50,000	$ 100,000	($10,000)	$40,000	90,000
Taxes (30%)	0	15,000	30,000	(3,000)	12,000	27,000
Net income	$0	$ 35,000	70,000	($ 7,000)	$28,000	63,000
ROE	0%	17.5%	35%	−7%	28%	63%
Expected ROE		17.5%			28%	
Standard deviation of ROE		12.4%			24.7%	

percent chance that the best case will occur, and a 50 percent chance that the exhibit 10.1 forecast, with an operating income of $50,000, will be realized.

The assumptions regarding uncertainty about the future profitability of the business lead to three different ROEs for each financing alternative. The expected ROEs are the same as when we ignored uncertainty—that is, 17.5 percent if Super Dental is all-equity financed and 28 percent when 50 percent debt financing is used. However, the uncertainty in operating income produces uncertainty, and hence risk, in owners' returns. If we measure owners' risk by the standard deviation of ROE, we see that the return is more risky when 50 percent debt financing is used. More precisely, owners' risk is twice as much in the 50 percent debt financing alternative: 24.7 percent standard deviation of ROE versus 12.4 percent standard deviation in the zero-debt alternative.

Intuitively, this risk increase occurs because the use of debt financing imposes a fixed cost—the $10,000 interest expense—on an uncertain income stream. In other words, the fixed interest payment must be made regardless of the level of operating income. The insertion of the fixed interest expense magnifies the variability of all values below the insertion point. Note that the increased risk is apparent without performing any standard deviation calculations. Under all-equity financing, the worst result is an ROE of zero. However, with 50 percent debt financing, the owners can realize an ROE of –7 percent. (Here, an assumption is made that the business's $10,000 loss could be used to offset the owners' personal income, resulting in a $3,000 tax savings. If this were not the case, the loss would be even worse.) In fact, with no operating income to pay the $10,000 interest due if the worst-case scenario occurs, the owners would have to either put up additional personal funds or declare the business bankrupt. Clearly, the use of 50 percent debt financing has increased the riskiness of the equity investment in the business.

This simple example illustrates two key points about the use of debt financing:

1. The use of debt financing increases the percentage return (ROE) to a business's owners. Note, however, that for the use of debt financing to increase owners' returns, the basic (inherent) return on the business must be greater than the interest rate on the debt. The basic return on the business in the Super Dental illustration is 25 percent ($50 in operating income divided by $200 in assets), and debt financing costs only 10 percent, so the use of debt financing increases ROE.
2. While the use of debt financing increases owners' return, it also increases owners' risk. In the Super Dental example, we saw that 50 percent debt financing doubled the risk to owners (as measured by standard deviation of ROE).

Super Dental's ultimate decision regarding financial structure is not clear-cut. One alternative—no debt—has a lower expected ROE but also lower risk. The second alternative—50 percent debt—offers a higher expected ROE but only at the price of higher risk. To complicate matters even more, there are an almost unlimited number of debt-level choices available to the business, not just the 50/50 mix used in the illustration. Later sections will try to resolve the dilemma facing Super Dental, but first we need to introduce two other concepts.

SELF-TEST QUESTIONS

1. What is the impact of debt financing on a business's risk and return?
2. Why does the use of debt financing leverage up (increase) owners' return?

Business and Financial Risk

In chapter 5, we discussed several different dimensions of risk, including stand-alone risk and portfolio (corporate and market) risk. Now, we introduce two new dimensions: (1) business risk and (2) financial risk. Here, the term *financial risk* has a specific connotation—as opposed to its use in chapter 5, where, in the generic sense, it means the risk arising from business transactions as opposed to other types of risk, such as risk to life and limb. Note that the concepts of business and financial risk apply just as much to not-for-profit businesses as they do to for-profit businesses, but in not-for-profits the risk concepts apply to the business's noncreditor stakeholders, including the community at large, rather than to the business's owners.

Business Risk

Business risk is the inherent riskiness of a business as seen by its owners. It is measured by the uncertainty inherent in the business's ROE, **assuming that no debt financing is used**. In other words, business risk is the riskiness of a business's assets, assuming they are all-equity financed. For an illustration of business risk, consider Santa Fe Hospitals, Inc., a **debt-free**, investor-owned hospital chain that operates in the southwestern United States. Exhibit 10.3 provides some insights into the firm's business risk.

The top graph gives both security analysts and Santa Fe's management an idea of the historical variability of ROE and, consequently, how the firm's ROE might vary in the future. This graph also shows that Santa Fe's ROE is growing slowly, so the relevant variability of ROE is the dispersion about the

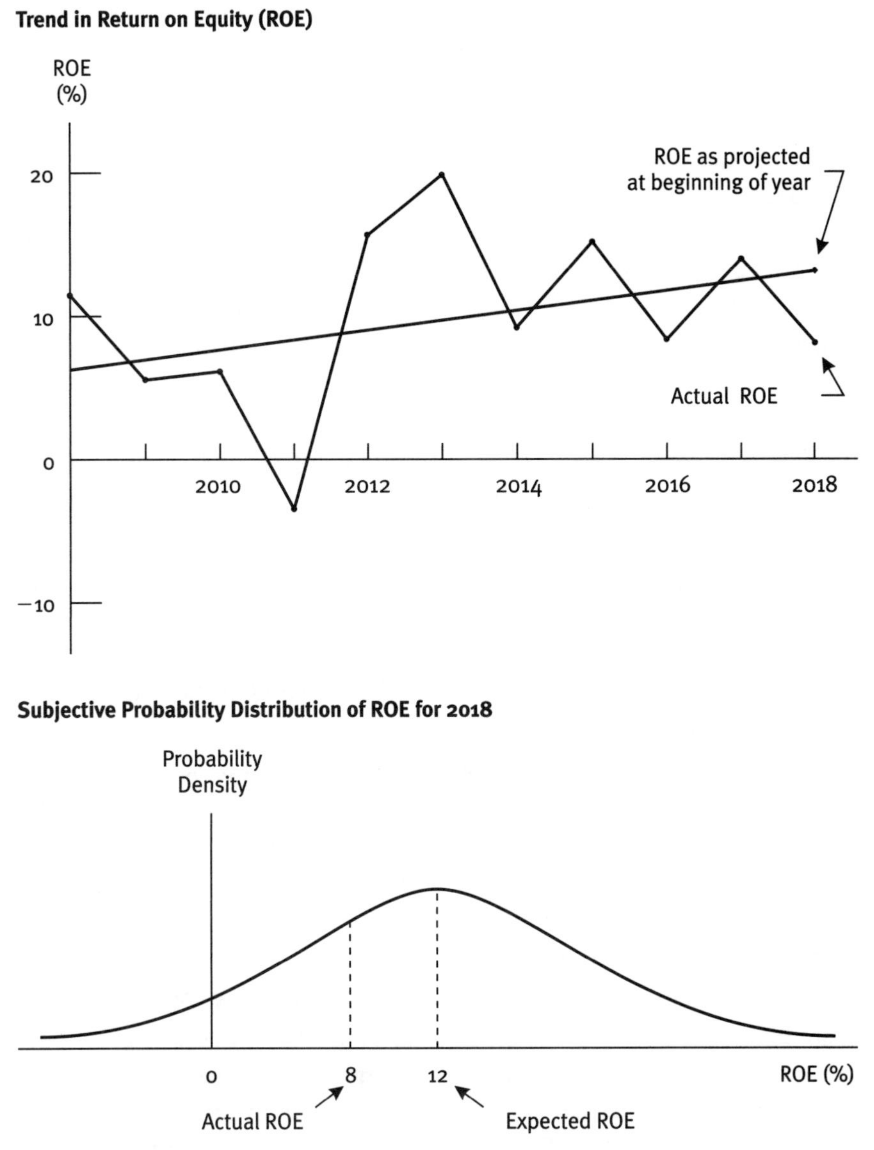

EXHIBIT 10.3
Santa Fe Hospitals: Trend in ROE, 2008–2018, and Subjective ROE Distribution, 2018

trend line rather than the overall standard deviation of historical ROE. The bottom graph shows the beginning-of-year subjectively estimated probability distribution of Santa Fe's ROE for 2018, based on the trend line in the top graph of exhibit 10.3. As both graphs indicate, Santa Fe's actual ROE in 2018 was only 8 percent, well below the expected value of 12 percent.

Santa Fe's past fluctuations in ROE were caused by many factors—changes in the economy, actions by competing hospitals, revisions to payer mix, changes in payment policies of third-party payers, variation labor costs, and so on. Similar events will undoubtedly occur in the future, and because they do, Santa Fe's realized ROE will almost always be higher or lower than the projected level. Furthermore, there is always the possibility that some event that permanently depresses the company's earning power might occur. For example, the federal government could move to a single-payer system with dramatically reduced hospital reimbursement rates.

Because Santa Fe uses no debt financing, the uncertainty regarding its future ROE defines the firm's business risk. The key point here is that we are trying to measure the riskiness of the business before it is influenced by the use of debt financing. Business risk varies not only from industry to industry but also among firms in a given industry. Furthermore, business risk can change over time. As mentioned in the previous chapter, hospitals were regarded for years as having little business risk, but events in the 1980s and 1990s—primarily the move of governmental payers to prospective payment and the increasing bargaining power of managed care plans—greatly increased the sector's business risk.

Business risk depends on a number of factors, including the following:

- **Demand (volume) variability**. The more stable the demand for a business's products or services, other things held constant, the lower its business risk.
- **Sales price variability**. Businesses whose products or services are sold in markets with highly volatile prices are exposed to more business risk than are firms whose sales prices are more stable.
- **Input cost variability**. Businesses whose input costs—labor, materials, and capital—are highly uncertain are exposed to more business risk than are firms with more certain input costs.
- **Ability to respond to changing market conditions**. Some businesses are better able than others to respond to changing market conditions. For example, some hospitals are in a better position to raise their own prices when input costs rise. Other hospitals are more adept at cutting costs if the need arises. The greater the ability to respond to changing market conditions, the lower the degree of business risk, other things held constant.
- **Liability exposure uncertainty**. The greater the uncertainty in liability losses, the greater the business risk. For example, hospitals that perform a large number of high-risk surgeries face more liability risk than do hospitals with a limited surgery program.
- **Operating leverage**. *Operating leverage* measures the proportion of fixed costs, as opposed to variable costs, in a business's cost structure. If a business has a high percentage of fixed costs, which by definition

do not decline when demand falls off, it is exposed to a relatively high degree of business risk.

Each of the factors that influence business risk is determined partly by industry characteristics, but each of them also can be influenced to some extent by managerial decisions. For example, consider operating leverage. Higher fixed costs generally are associated with highly technical, capital-intensive businesses and industries. Thus, hospitals have higher fixed costs, relative to total costs, than do home health care agencies. Also, healthcare providers that employ highly skilled workers who must be retained and paid even during periods of low utilization have a relatively high proportion of fixed costs.

To what extent can businesses control their operating leverage? To a large extent, operating leverage is determined by industry characteristics. Firms such as drug manufacturers, hospitals, and ambulatory care clinics simply must make heavy investments in fixed assets and labor, which results in a high proportion of fixed costs and hence high operating leverage. On the other hand, firms such as home health agencies generally have significantly lower fixed-cost proportions and hence lower operating leverage. Still, although industry factors do exert a major influence, all businesses have some control over their operating leverage. For example, a hospital can expand its diagnostic imaging capability either by buying a new imaging device or by leasing it on a per procedure basis.[2] If the hospital purchased the device, the hospital would incur fixed costs, but the device's per procedure operating costs would be relatively low. If the hospital leased the device, the hospital would have lower fixed costs, but the variable—per procedure—costs for the device would be higher. Thus, by its financing decisions, and also by its capital investment decisions, a business can influence its operating leverage and hence its basic business risk.

Financial Risk

Financial risk is the additional risk placed on owners as a result of the decision to use debt financing. Conceptually, a business has a certain amount of risk inherent in its operations—this is its business risk. However, the use of debt financing, or *financial leverage*, concentrates (increases) the risk seen by the business's owners. Because the return to debt suppliers is fixed by contract and is independent of fluctuations in the business's revenues and costs, creditors bear none of the firm's business risk. For an illustration of this concept, consider the Super Dental example. The business can be financed by either \$200,000 of equity or \$100,000 of equity and \$100,000 of debt. The use of debt financing concentrates the business risk of the enterprise, which is fixed, on a smaller equity base and hence increases owners' risk.

Business and financial risk can be easily measured. Refer again to exhibit 10.2. The standard deviation of ROE to Super Dental if it uses no debt financing—σ_{ROE} (U), where U stands for unleveraged (no debt)—measures its business risk. The standard deviation of ROE at any positive debt level—σ_{ROE} (L), where L stands for leveraged (some debt)—measures the risk borne by owners. Because the use of debt financing concentrates the risk to owners, σ_{ROE} (L) is always greater than σ_{ROE} (U). Financial risk is the difference between the actual risk seen by owners and the inherent business risk of the enterprise, or σ_{ROE} (L) – σ_{ROE} (U). Applying these measures to Super Dental, we see that its business risk is σ_{ROE} (U) = 12.4% and its risk under 50 percent debt financing is σ_{ROE} (L) = 24.7%, so the financial risk at that level of debt is σ_{ROE} (L) – σ_{ROE} (U) = 24.7% – 12.4% = 12.3%. Operating leverage and financial leverage normally work in the same way; they both increase expected ROE, but they also increase the risk borne by owners. Operating leverage affects the business risk of the enterprise, while financial leverage affects its financial risk.

SELF-TEST QUESTIONS

1. What is business risk? How can it be measured?
2. What are some determinants of business risk?
3. What is operating leverage?
4. What is financial risk? How can it be measured?
5. What are the similarities between operating leverage and financial leverage?

Capital Structure Theory

The preceding discussion points out that the use of debt financing increases the expected ROE, but from the perspective of the business's owners, it also increases the risk of the business. The obvious question now is whether the benefit of debt financing (increased expected return) exceeds the cost of debt financing (increased risk). *Capital structure theory* attempts to determine the relationship between the amount of debt financing and the value of a business; thus, its goal is to determine, after risk is considered, whether the use of financial leverage is beneficial. The theory is directly applicable to investor-owned businesses, but it also provides some guidance for not-for-profit businesses. Although capital structure theory does not provide a complete answer to the optimal capital structure question, it does provide many insights into the value of debt financing versus equity (or fund) financing. Thus, an understanding of capital structure theory will aid managers in making capital structure decisions.

The Modigliani–Miller Models

Until 1958, capital structure theories were little more than loose assertions about investor behavior rather than carefully constructed models that could be tested by formal statistical studies. In what has been called the most influential set of financial papers ever published, ***Franco Modigliani and Merton Miller (MM)*** addressed the capital structure issue in a rigorous, scientific fashion and set off a chain of research that continues to this day.[3]

To begin, MM made the following assumptions, some of which were later relaxed:

- The business risk of an enterprise can be measured by the standard deviation of earnings before interest and taxes (σ_{EBIT}). Firms with the same degree of business risk are said to be in a ***homogeneous risk class.***
- All present and prospective investors have identical estimates of each firm's future EBIT—that is, investors have ***homogeneous expectations*** about expected future corporate earnings and the riskiness of those earnings.
- Stocks and bonds are traded in ***perfect capital markets.*** This assumption implies, among other things, that there are no brokerage costs and that investors—both individual and institutions—can borrow at the same rate as corporations.
- The debt of businesses and individuals is ***riskless,*** so the interest rate on debt is the risk-free rate. Furthermore, this situation holds regardless of how much debt a business, or an individual, uses.
- All cash flows are perpetuities—that is, businesses are assumed to have ***zero growth*** with an "expectationally constant" EBIT, and its bonds are perpetuities. Expectationally constant means that investors expect EBIT to be constant, but the realized value, or the value after the fact, can be different from the expected level.

MM Without Taxes

MM first performed their analysis under the assumption that there are no corporate or personal income taxes. On the basis of the preceding assumptions, and in the absence of taxes, they proposed and then algebraically proved two propositions:[4]

Proposition I

The value of any business, V, is established by discounting its expected net operating income (EBIT when T = 0) at a constant rate that is appropriate for its risk class, regardless of the amount of debt financing used:

Key Equation 10.1: Value of a Firm Assuming No Taxes

$$V_L = V_U = \frac{\text{EBIT}}{\text{CCC}} = \frac{\text{EBIT}}{R(R_{eU})}.$$

Here, the subscripts L and U designate levered (with debt financing) and unlevered (without debt financing) businesses in a given risk class, CCC is the corporate cost of capital, and $R(R_{eU})$ is the required rate of return on equity for an unlevered (zero debt) business. The key point is that the discount rate used to determine the value of the business is a constant—CCC = $R(R_{eU})$—regardless of the amount of debt financing used, and because EBIT is unaffected by debt financing, the value of the business also is a constant. Because V, as established by Proposition I, is a constant regardless of the level of debt financing, **under the MM model with no taxes, the value of a business is independent of its leverage**. This statement also implies that (1) the CCC to any business is completely independent of its capital structure and (2) the CCC for all businesses with the same business risk (in the same risk class) is equal to the cost of equity to an unlevered firm in that risk class, regardless of the amount of debt financing used.

Proposition II

The cost of equity to a levered firm, $R(R_{eL})$, is equal to (1) the cost of equity to an unlevered firm in the same risk class, $R(R_{eU})$, plus (2) a risk premium that depends on both the differential between the costs of equity and debt to an unlevered firm and the amount of leverage used:

Key Equation 10.2: Cost of Equity to a Levered Firm Assuming No Taxes

$$R(R_{eL}) = R(R_{eU}) + \text{Risk premium} =$$
$$R(R_{eU}) + \{[R(R_{eU}) - R(R_d)] \times (D \div E)\}.$$

Here, D = the market value of the business's debt, E = the market value of the business's equity, and $R(R_d)$ = the constant cost of debt. Proposition II states that **as a business's use of debt increases, its cost of equity also increases, in a mathematically precise manner**.

Taken together, the two MM propositions imply that the inclusion of debt in a business's capital structure will not increase its value because the benefits of the less costly debt financing (as compared to equity financing) will be exactly offset by an increase in the riskiness, and hence in the cost, of the business's equity. Thus, MM theory implies that **in a world without taxes, both the value of a firm and its CCC are unaffected by its capital structure**.

MM used an *arbitrage proof* to support their propositions.[5] They showed that, under their assumptions, if two firms differed only (1) in the way they are financed and (2) in their total market values, investors would sell shares of the higher-valued firm, buy those of the lower-valued firm, and continue this process until the firms had exactly the same market value. Thus, the actions of investors would ensure that the two firms had identical market values. Once the values are proved to be equal, the two MM propositions are the logical result.

Note that each of the assumptions listed in the beginning of this section is necessary for the arbitrage proof to work. For example, if the firms are not identical in business risk, the arbitrage process cannot be invoked. We will discuss further implications of the assumptions later in the chapter.

MM with Corporate Taxes

MM's original work, published in 1958, assumed zero taxes. In 1963, MM published a second article that **included corporate tax effects**. With corporate income taxes, the authors concluded that the use of financial leverage will increase a business's value. When businesses are subject to income taxes, the MM propositions are as follows.

Proposition I

The value of a levered firm is equal to (1) the value of an unlevered firm in the same risk class plus (2) the gain from leverage, which is the present value of the tax savings and which equals the corporate tax rate, T, multiplied by the amount of debt the firm uses, D:[6]

Key Equation 10.3: Value of a Levered Firm with Corporate Taxes

$$V_L = V_U + (T \times D).$$

The important point here is that, when corporate taxes are introduced, the value of a levered business exceeds that of a similar unlevered business by the amount T × D. Note also that the differential increases as the use of debt increases, so a business's value is maximized at virtually 100 percent debt financing.

To find the MM value for V_U for any business, recognize that all businesses are assumed to have zero growth and a constant EBIT, and all earnings are paid out as dividends. Thus, the total market value of a business's equity, E, can be found using perpetuity valuation techniques as follows:

$$E = \frac{\text{Dividends}}{R(R_e)} = \frac{\text{Net income}}{R(R_e)} = \frac{\{\text{EBIT} - [R(R_d) \times D]\} \times (1 - T)}{R(R_e)}.$$

With zero debt, D = \$0 and the total value of the firm is its equity value, so

Key Equation 10.4: Value of Unlevered Firm with Corporate Taxes

$$E = V_U = \frac{\text{EBIT} \times (1 - T)}{R(R_{eU})}.$$

Proposition II

The cost of equity to a levered firm is equal to (1) the cost of equity to an unlevered firm in the same risk class (equal business risk) plus (2) a risk premium that depends on the differential between the costs of equity and debt to an unlevered firm, the amount of financial leverage used, **and the corporate tax rate**:

Key Equation 10.5: Cost of Equity to a Levered Firm with Corporate Taxes

$$R(R_{eL}) = R(R_{eU}) + \text{Risk premium}$$
$$= R(R_{eU}) + \{[R(R_{eU}) - R(R_d)] \times (1 - T) \times (D \div E)\}.$$

Notice that proposition II here is identical to the corresponding without-tax equation, except for the term (1 − T). Because (1 − T) is less than 1.0 for any positive tax rate, the imposition of corporate taxes causes the cost of equity to rise at a slower rate when debt is used than it did in the absence of taxes. It is this characteristic, along with the fact that the effective cost of debt is reduced because of the tax deductibility of interest, that produces the proposition I result—namely the increase in firm value as leverage increases.

Illustration of the MM Models

For an illustration of the MM models, assume that the following data and conditions hold for New England Clinical Laboratories, Inc., an old, established firm that operates in several no-growth areas in rural Maine, New Hampshire, and Vermont:

- New England currently has no debt; it is an all-equity firm.
- Expected EBIT = \$2.4 million. EBIT is not expected to increase over time, so New England is in a no-growth situation.
- New England pays out all of its income as dividends because no retained earnings are required to finance growth. (Worn-out assets are replaced using depreciation cash flow.)
- If New England begins to use debt, it can borrow at a rate $R(R_d) = 8\%$. This borrowing rate is constant, and it is independent of the amount of debt used. Any money raised by selling debt would be used to retire common stock, so New England's assets and EBIT would remain constant.
- The risk of New England's assets, and thus its EBIT, is such that its shareholders require a rate of return, $R(R_{eU})$, of 12 percent if no debt is used.

With Zero Taxes

To begin, assume that there are no taxes, so T = 0%. At any level of debt, proposition I can be used to find New England's value, \$20 million:

$$V_L = V_U = \frac{\text{EBIT}}{R(R_{eU})} = \frac{\$2.4 \text{ million}}{0.12} = \$20.0 \text{ million.}$$

With zero debt, the \$20 million represents all-equity value. Now, assume that New England decides to use \$10 million of debt financing. According to proposition I, its total value will not change, so the business's equity value must fall to \$10 million:

$$E = V - D = \$20 \text{ million} - \$10 \text{ million} = \$10 \text{ million.}$$

This decrease occurs because the \$10 million of new debt financing is used to repurchase \$10 million of existing equity.

We can also find New England's cost of equity, $R(R_{eL})$, and its CCC at a debt level of \$10 million. First, we use proposition II to find $R(R_{eL})$, New England's levered cost of equity:

$$\begin{aligned} R(R_{eL}) &= R(R_{eU}) + \{[R(R_{eU}) - R(R_d)] \times (D \div E)\} \\ &= 12\% + \{[12\% - 8\%] \times (\$10 \text{ million} \div \$10 \text{ million})\} \\ &= 12\% + 4.0\% = 16.0\%. \end{aligned}$$

Now, we can find the firm's CCC:

$$\begin{aligned} CCC &= [w_d \times R(R_d) \times (1 - T)] + [w_e \times R(R_{eL})] \\ &= [(\$10 / \$20) \times 8\% \times 1.0] + [(\$10 / \$20) \times 16.0\%] = 12.0\%. \end{aligned}$$

We can easily expand the illustration to show New England's value and CCC at various debt levels. We would see that in an MM world without taxes, financial leverage does not matter: The value of the firm and its overall cost of capital are independent of the amount of debt financing used. The key to this result is that the additional risk imposed by the use of debt financing increases the cost of equity just enough to counteract any benefit that results from the fact that debt costs are lower than equity costs. In essence, each of these security classes is priced—has a required rate of return—such that the business is indifferent to the choice. Debt costs less than equity, but to the business it is a riskier form of financing than equity. Thus, each type of capital is priced correctly on the basis of the risk it brings to a business, so the financing mix does not affect the value of the firm.

With Corporate Taxes

For an illustration of the MM model with corporate taxes, assume that all of the previous assumptions hold except these two:

1. Expected EBIT = \$4 million.
2. New England has a 30 percent federal-plus-state tax rate, so T = 30%.

Note that we increased New England's EBIT from \$2.4 million to \$4 million to make the numerical comparison between the two models easier. If we had not, the **introduction of corporate taxes have lowered New England's value by Expected EBIT × (1 – T) = \$2.4 million × 0.7 = \$1.68 million.**

When New England has zero debt but pays taxes, and its expected EBIT is increased to \$4 million, its value with zero debt financing is \$20 million:

$$V_U = \frac{EBIT \times (1 - T)}{R(R_{eU})} = \frac{\$4 \text{ million} \times 0.7}{0.12} = \$23.3 \text{ million.}$$

With \$10 million of debt in a world with taxes, proposition I indicates that New England's total market value rises to \$26.3 million.

$$V_L = V_U + (T \times D) = \$23.3 \text{ million} + (0.3 \times \$10 \text{ million}) = \$26.3 \text{ million.}$$

Therefore, the value of New England's equity must be \$16.3 million:

$$E = V_L - D = \$26.3 \text{ million} - \$10 \text{ million} = \$16.3 \text{ million.}$$

To find New England's cost of equity and its CCC at a debt level of \$10 million, we first use proposition II to find the levered cost of equity:

$$\begin{aligned} R(R_{eL}) &= R(R_{eU}) + \{[R(R_{eU}) - R(R_d)] \times (1 - T) \times (D / E)\} \\ &= 12\% + [(12\% - 8\%) \times 0.7 \times (\$10 \text{ million} / \$16.3 \text{ million})] \\ &= 12\% + 1.71\% = 13.71\%. \end{aligned}$$

Then, we can find the firm's weighted average cost of capital:

$$\begin{aligned} CCC &= [w_d \times R(R_d) \times (1 - T)] + [w_e \times R(R_{eL})] \\ &= [(\$10 / \$26.3) \times 8\% \times 0.7] + [(\$16.3 / \$26.3) \times 13.71\%] \\ &= 10.6\%. \end{aligned}$$

Again, we can easily expand the illustration to include additional debt levels. We see that in an MM world with corporate taxes, financial leverage does matter: The value of the firm is maximized and its overall cost of capital is minimized if it uses virtually 100 percent debt financing. Furthermore, we know that the increase in value solely results from the tax deductibility of interest payments, which causes both the cost of debt and the increase in the cost of equity with leverage to be reduced by (1 – T). With the tax deductibility of interest payments, the cost of debt is now less than that warranted by the risk it brings to a business; hence, businesses prefer debt to equity, which remains fairly priced in relationship to the risk it brings to a business.

SELF-TEST QUESTIONS

1. What is the single most important conclusion of the MM zero-tax model?
2. What is the single most important conclusion of the MM model with corporate taxes?
3. What is the underlying cause of the "gain from leverage" in the MM model with corporate taxes?

The Miller Model

On the web at: *ache.org/HAP/PinkSong8e*

Although MM included **corporate** taxes in the second version of their model, they did not extend the model to analyze the effects of **personal** taxes. However, Merton Miller later introduced a model designed to show how leverage affects firms' values when both personal and corporate taxes are taken into account.[7] To explain Miller's model, let us begin by defining T_c as the corporate tax rate, T_e as the personal tax rate on equity returns, and T_d as the personal tax rate on debt returns. Note that equity returns typically come partly as dividends and partly as capital gains, so T_e is a weighted average of the effective tax rates on dividends and capital gains, while essentially all debt income comes from interest, which is taxed at investors' top rates.

With personal taxes included, and **under the remaining assumptions used in the earlier MM models**, the value of an unlevered firm is found by the following equation:

Key Equation 10.6: Value of Unlevered Firm with Corporate and Personal Taxes

$$V_U = \frac{EBIT \times (1 - T_C) \times (1 - T_e)}{R(R_{eU})(1 - T_e)}.$$

Note that equation 10.6 is identical to equation 10.4, except for the addition of the $(1 - T_e)$ term, which adjusts for personal taxes. Now, the numerator shows how much of a business's operating cash flow is available to investors after the unlevered firm itself pays corporate income taxes and the equityholders subsequently pay personal taxes on the equity income. In effect, the numerator is the perpetual after-all-taxes cash flow stream to equity investors. Because the denominator is the after-tax return on equity, the $(1 - T_e)$ term cancels out and we are left with equation 10.4. Therefore, personal taxes do not change the value of the unlevered firm, other things held constant.

The Miller model, which can be derived using an arbitrage proof similar to the one used to prove the MM models, is as follows:

Key Equation 10.7: Value of a Levered Firm with Corporate and Personal Taxes

$$V_L = V_U + \left\{\left[1 - \frac{(1 - T_c) \times (1 - T_e)}{1 - T_d}\right] \times D\right\}.$$

Here are some relevant points about the Miller model:

- The term bracketed by [ ], when multiplied by D, is the new gain from leverage. It replaces $T = T_c$ in the earlier MM model with corporate taxes.

- If we ignore all taxes (i.e., if $T_c = T_e = T_d = 0$), the bracketed term reduces to zero, so, in that case, the Miller model is the same as the original MM model without taxes.
- If we ignore personal taxes (i.e., if $T_e = T_d = 0$), the bracketed term reduces to T_c, so the Miller model reduces to the MM model with corporate taxes.
- If the effective personal tax rates on stock and bond incomes were equal (i.e., if $T_e = T_d$), the bracketed term would again reduce to T_c.
- If $(1 - T_c) \times (1 - T_e) = 1 - T_d$, the bracketed term would go to zero and the value of using leverage would also be zero. This result implies that the tax advantage of debt to the firm would be exactly offset by the personal tax advantage of equity. Under this condition, capital structure would have no effect on a firm's value or its cost of capital, so we would be back to MM's original zero-tax theory.

Because the tax rate on dividends and capital gains is less than the tax rate on ordinary income (generally 20 percent versus 24, 32, or 35 percent), and because taxes on capital gains are deferred, the effective tax rate on equity income is less than the effective tax rate on debt income.[8] This being the case, what would the Miller model predict as the gain from leverage? To answer this question, assume that the tax rate on corporate income is T_c = 30%, the effective rate on bond income is T_d = 35%, and the effective rate on stock income is T_e = 20%. Using these values in the Miller model, we find that a levered firm's value increases over that of an unlevered firm by 14 percent of the market value of corporate debt:

$$
\begin{aligned}
\text{Gain from leverage} &= \left[1 - \frac{(1 - T_c) \times (1 - T_e)}{1 - T_d}\right] \times D \\
&= \left[1 - \frac{(1 - 0.30) \times (1 - 0.20)}{1 - 0.35}\right] \times D \\
&= [1 - 0.86] \times D = [0.14] \times D.
\end{aligned}
$$

Note that, with these data, the MM model with corporate taxes would indicate a gain from leverage of $T_c \times D = 0.30 \times D$, or 30 percent of the amount of corporate debt. Thus, with these assumed tax rates, the addition of personal taxes to the model significantly lowers the benefit derived from corporate debt financing. In general, whenever the effective tax rate on equity income is lower than the effective rate on debt income, the Miller model produces a lower gain from leverage than that produced by the MM with corporate taxes model. The fact that personal tax rates favor equity investments means that interest rates must be higher (than in the absence of personal taxes) on corporate debt financing to attract debt capital. These higher interest rates reduce the value of debt financing to businesses and hence lower the gain from leverage.

In his paper, Miller argued that firms in the aggregate would issue a mix of debt and equity securities such that the before-tax yields on corporate securities and the personal tax rates of the investors who bought these securities would adjust until equilibrium was reached. At equilibrium, $(1 - T_d)$ would equal $(1 - T_c) \times (1 - T_e)$, so, as we noted earlier, the tax advantage of debt to the firm would be exactly offset by personal taxation and capital structure would have no effect on a firm's value or its cost of capital. Thus, according to Miller, the conclusions derived from the original MM zero-tax model are correct!

Others have extended and tested Miller's analysis. Generally, these extensions disagree with Miller's conclusion that there is no advantage to the use of corporate debt. In the United States, the effective tax rate on equity income is lower than the effective tax rate on debt income, so it appears that there is an advantage to the corporate use of debt financing. However, Miller's work does show that personal taxes offset some of the benefits of corporate debt, so the tax advantages of corporate debt probably are fewer than those implied by the earlier MM model that considered only corporate taxes.

SELF-TEST QUESTIONS

1. How does the Miller model differ from the MM model with corporate taxes?
2. What are the implications of the Miller model under various tax assumptions?
3. What is the primary implication of the Miller model given the current tax situation in the United States?

Criticisms of the MM and Miller Models

The conclusions of each of the three models follow logically from their initial assumptions: If the assumptions are correct, the resulting conclusions must be reached. However, academics and managers have voiced concern over the validity of these models, and virtually no businesses follow the recommendations of any of the models. Use of the MM zero-tax model leads to the conclusion that capital structure does not matter, but we observe some regularities in structure within industries. Furthermore, when used with "reasonable" tax rates, use of both the MM model with corporate taxes and the Miller model lead to the conclusion that firms should use 100 percent debt financing. That situation is not observed in practice except by firms whose equity has been eroded by operating losses. Those who disagree with the MM and Miller models and their suggestions for financial policy generally attack the models on the grounds that their assumptions do not reflect real-world conditions. Some of the main objections include the following:

- MM and, later, Miller assume that personal and corporate leverage are perfect substitutes. However, an individual investing in a levered firm has less loss exposure, and hence more limited liability, than if he used "homemade" leverage by taking on personal debt. This increased personal risk exposure would tend to restrain investors from engaging in the type of arbitrage required to derive the models, and impeded arbitrage can cause the models to be incorrect.
- Brokerage costs were assumed away in the MM and Miller models. However, brokerage and other transaction costs do exist, and they too impede the arbitrage process.
- MM initially assumed that both businesses and individual investors can borrow at the risk-free rate. Although risky debt has been introduced into the analysis by others with no significant change in results, it is still necessary to assume that both corporations and investors can borrow at the same rate to reach the MM and Miller conclusions. Although major institutional investors probably can borrow at the corporate rate, many institutions are not allowed to borrow to buy securities. Furthermore, most individual investors must borrow at higher rates than those paid by large corporations.
- The MM and Miller models assume that there are no costs associated with financial distress. These costs are discussed in the next section.

SELF-TEST QUESTIONS

1. Should we accept one of the models presented thus far as being correct? Why or why not?
2. In your view, which of the assumptions used in the models is most likely to invalidate them?

Financial Distress Costs

Some of the assumptions inherent in the MM and Miller models can be relaxed, and when this is done, their basic conclusions remain unchanged. However, as we discuss next, when financial distress costs are added, the MM and Miller results are altered significantly.

A number of firms experience *financial distress* each year, and some are forced into bankruptcy. Financial distress includes, but is not restricted to, bankruptcy, and when it occurs, several things can happen, including the following:

- Arguments between claimants often delay the liquidation of assets. Bankruptcy cases can take many years to settle, and during this time equipment loses value, buildings are vandalized, inventories become obsolete, and so on.
- Lawyer's fees, court costs, and administrative expenses can absorb a large part of a business's value. Together, the costs of physical deterioration plus legal fees and administrative expenses are called the *direct costs of bankruptcy*.
- Managers generally lose their jobs when a firm fails. Knowing this, the managers of a business in financial distress often take actions that keep it alive for the short run but dilute its long-run value. For example, a hospital in financial distress may fail to modernize or may sell off valuable nonessential assets at bargain prices to raise cash or cut costs so much that it impairs the quality of its services and erodes its long-run market position.
- Stakeholders of organizations experiencing financial difficulties are aware of the problems and often take actions that further damage troubled firms. For example, patients may go elsewhere, suppliers may be reluctant to sell on credit, and medical staff may be difficult to recruit and retain. Suboptimal managerial actions associated with financial distress, as well as the costs imposed by stakeholders, are called the *indirect costs of financial distress*. Of course, a business in financial distress may incur these costs even if it does not go into bankruptcy; bankruptcy is just one point in the continuum of financial distress.

All things considered, the direct and indirect costs associated with financial distress are high, but financial distress typically occurs only if a firm uses debt financing because debt-free businesses rarely experience financial distress. Therefore, the greater the use of debt financing, and the larger the fixed interest charges, the greater the probability that a decline in earnings will lead to financial distress and, hence, the higher the probability that costs of financial distress will be incurred.

An increase in the probability of incurring financial distress raises a firm's cost of equity capital and hence lowers the current value of the firm's equity. Furthermore, the probability of incurring financial distress increases with leverage, causing the expected present value cost of financial distress to rise as more and more debt financing is used. A firm's creditors also feel the effects of financial distress. Businesses that experience financial distress have a higher probability of defaulting on debt payments, so the expectation of financial distress influences creditors' required rates of return: the higher the probability of incurring financial distress, the higher the required return on debt. Thus, as a firm uses more and more debt financing and hence increases the probability of incurring financial distress, its cost of debt also increases.

SELF-TEST QUESTIONS

1. Describe some financial distress costs.
2. How are financial distress costs related to the use of financial leverage?

Trade-Off Models

Both the MM with corporate taxes and Miller models as modified to reflect financial distress costs are described as ***trade-off models***—that is, the optimal capital structure is found, at least conceptually, by balancing the tax shield benefits of leverage against the financial distress costs of leverage, so the costs and benefits are "traded off" against one another.

Model Structure

If the MM model with corporate taxes were correct, a firm's value would rise continuously as it moved from zero debt toward 100 percent debt: The equation $V_L = V_U + (T \times D)$ shows that $T \times D$ (hence V_L) is maximized if D is at a maximum. Recall that the rising component of value, $T \times D$, results directly from the tax shelter provided by interest on the debt. However, the present value of the costs associated with potential future financial distress would cause V_L to decline as the level of debt increases. Therefore, in the MM with corporate taxes model, the relationship between a firm's value and its use of leverage takes this form when financial distress costs are added:

Key Equation 10.8: Value of a Levered Firm with Financial Distress

$$V_L = V_U + (T \times D) - \text{PV of expected financial distress costs.}$$

The relationship expressed in this equation is graphed in exhibit 10.4. The tax shelter effect dominates until the amount of debt reaches point A. After point A, financial distress costs become increasingly important, offsetting some of the tax advantages. At point B, the marginal tax shelter benefits of additional debt are exactly offset by the marginal disadvantages of debt, and beyond point B, the marginal disadvantages outweigh the marginal benefits.

The Miller model can also be modified to reflect financial distress costs. The equation would be identical to that developed for the MM with corporate taxes model, except that the gain-from-leverage term, T × D, would be adjusted to reflect the addition of personal taxes. In either the MM or Miller models, the gain from leverage can at least be roughly estimated, but the value reduction resulting from potential financial distress costs is almost entirely subjective. We know that these costs must increase as the use of debt financing rises, but we simply do not know the specific functional relationship.

Model Implications

The trade-off models are not capable of specifying precise optimal capital structures, but they do enable us to make three statements about debt usage:

EXHIBIT 10.4
Net Effect of Financial Leverage on the Value of the Firm

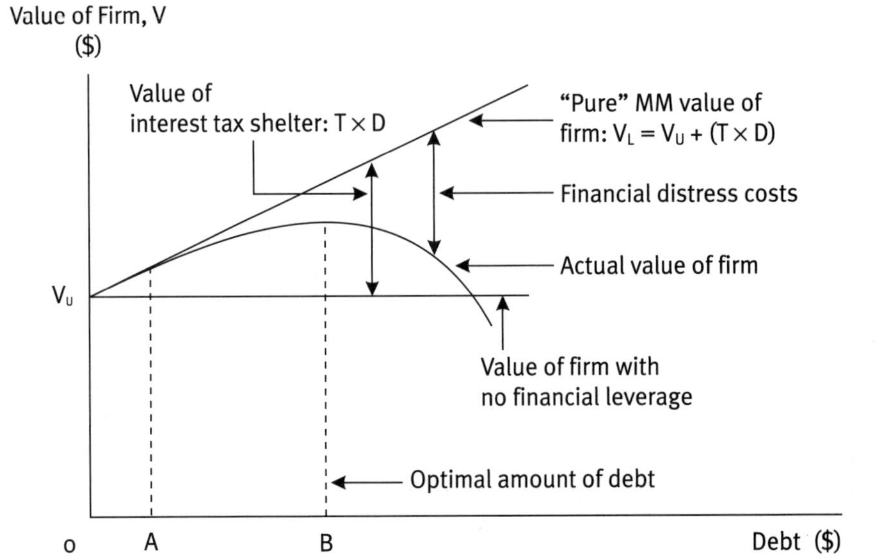

1. Higher-risk businesses, as measured by the variability of returns on the business's assets, ought to borrow less than lower-risk firms, with other things being equal. The greater this variability, the greater the probability of financial distress at any level of debt and, hence, the greater the expected costs of distress. Thus, firms with lower business risk can borrow more before the expected costs of distress offset the tax advantages of borrowing.
2. Businesses that employ tangible assets, such as real estate and standardized equipment, should borrow more than firms whose value is derived either from intangible assets, such as intellectual capital and goodwill, or from growth opportunities. The costs of financial distress depend not only on the probability of incurring distress but also on what happens if distress occurs. Specialized assets, intangible assets, and growth opportunities are more likely than standardized, tangible assets to lose value if financial distress occurs.
3. Businesses that are currently paying taxes at the highest rate, and that are likely to continue to do so in the future, should carry more debt than should firms with current or prospectively lower tax rates. High corporate tax rates lead to greater benefits from debt financing; hence, high-tax-rate firms can carry more debt, other factors held constant, before the tax shield is offset by financial distress costs.

According to the trade-off models, each business should set its target capital structure such that its costs and benefits of leverage are balanced at the margin because such a structure will maximize its value. We would expect to find actual target structures that are consistent with the three points just noted. Furthermore, we would generally expect to find that firms in an industry have similar capital structures because such firms have roughly the same types of assets, business risk, and profitability.

The Empirical Evidence

The trade-off models have intuitive appeal because they lead to the conclusion that both no debt and all debt are bad, while a "moderate" debt level is good. However, we must ask ourselves whether these models explain actual behavior. If they do not, we must search for other explanations or assume that managers, and hence investors, are acting irrationally, which is an assumption that we are unwilling to make.

The trade-off models do have some empirical support. For example, businesses that have primarily tangible assets tend to borrow more heavily than do firms whose value stems from intangibles and growth opportunities. However, other empirical evidence refutes the trade-off models. First, several studies have examined models of financing behavior to see whether firms' financing decisions reflect adjustment toward a target capital structure. These studies provide some evidence that they do, but the explanatory power of the models is low, suggesting that trade-off models capture only a part of actual behavior. Second, no study has clearly demonstrated that a firm's tax rate has a predictable, material effect on its capital structure. In fact, firms used debt financing long before corporate income taxes even existed. Finally, actual debt ratios tend to vary widely across apparently similar firms, whereas the trade-off models suggest that the use of debt should be relatively consistent within industries.

All in all, empirical support for the trade-off models is not strong, which suggests that other factors not incorporated into these models are also at work. In other words, the trade-off models do not tell the full story.

SELF-TEST QUESTIONS

1. What is a trade-off model of capital structure?
2. What are the implications of the trade-off models for capital structure decisions?
3. Does empirical evidence support the trade-off models?

Asymmetric Information Model of Capital Structure

The asymmetric information model of capital structure traces back to the work done in the 1960s by Gordon Donaldson. Donaldson conducted an extensive survey of investor-owned corporations to find out how managers make financing decisions and reached the following conclusions:

- Businesses prefer to finance with internally generated funds—that is, with retained earnings and depreciation cash flow.
- Businesses set target dividend payout ratios on the basis of their expected future investment opportunities and their expected future cash flows. The target payout ratio is set at a level such that expected retentions plus depreciation cash flow will meet expected capital expenditure requirements.
- Dividends are "sticky" in the short run because firms are reluctant to make major changes in the dollar dividend, and they are especially reluctant to cut the dividend. Thus, in any given year, depending on realized cash flows and actual investment opportunities, a business may or may not have sufficient internally generated funds to cover its capital expenditures.

- If a business has more internal cash flow than is needed for capital investment, it will invest the excess in marketable securities or use the funds to retire debt.
- If a business has insufficient internal cash flow to finance its capital investments, it will first draw down its marketable securities portfolio, then issue debt, then issue convertible bonds—bonds that can be exchanged in the future for common stock—and then only as a last resort will it sell new equity.

Thus, Donaldson observed a "pecking order" of financing, not the balanced approach that is called for by the trade-off models. Indeed, the pecking order causes firms to move away from, rather than toward, a well-defined capital structure because equity funds are raised in two forms: (1) retained earnings at the top of the pecking order and (2) new common stock sales at the bottom.

For many years, no theoretical model was available to explain this behavior, so academics did not give Donaldson's survey results much credence. Then, Stewart C. Myers proposed the ***asymmetric information model*** of capital structure.[9] The model is based on two assumptions: (1) Managers know more about their firm's future prospects than do investors, and (2) managers are motivated to maximize the wealth of their firm's current shareholders.

If managers think that their firm's equity is undervalued, they will be motivated to use debt financing because selling stock at a "bargain" price is detrimental to the firm's existing shareholders. However, if managers think that their firm's equity is overvalued, they will be motivated to issue new common stock. By issuing stock for more than it is actually worth, managers transfer value from the buyers of the new stock to existing shareholders. Thus, managers are motivated to issue new stock only when they believe that the stock is overvalued. Because equity investors are rational, they treat new common stock issues as "signals" that management considers the stock to be overvalued. Thus, investors revise their expectations for the firm downward and the stock price falls.[10]

Because new equity issues have an adverse effect on stock price, managers are reluctant to issue new stock. Although large amounts of new stock are issued each year, the vast majority are issued by small, rapidly growing firms that have large capital needs and hence little choice. Equity issues by mature firms are relatively rare. If external financing is required, debt is the first choice and new common stock will be used only in unusual circumstances. Thus, the asymmetric information model leads managers to act in accordance with Donaldson's pecking order.

Because managers want to avoid issuing new stock, especially when it might be least advantageous, it becomes prudent for firms to maintain a ***reserve borrowing capacity*** that can be used whenever capital investments require an unusually large amount of external capital. By maintaining a reserve borrowing capacity and then tapping it when necessary, managers can avoid issuing new common stock under unfavorable conditions.

Note that the degree of information asymmetry and its impact on investors' perceptions differ substantially across firms. For example, the degree of asymmetry is typically much greater in the pharmaceutical industry than in the hospital field because success in the drug industry depends on secretive proprietary research and development. Thus, managers in the drug industry hold significantly more information about their firm's prospects than do outside analysts and investors. Also, start-up businesses with limited capital and good growth opportunities are recognized for having to use external financing, so investors do not view new stock offerings by such firms with as much concern as they view new offerings by mature firms with limited growth opportunities. Thus, although the asymmetric information theory is applicable to all investor-owned firms, its influence on managerial decisions varies from firm to firm and over time.

SELF-TEST QUESTIONS

1. Briefly explain the asymmetric information model of capital structure.
2. What does the model suggest about capital structure decisions?

Summary of the Capital Structure Models

The great contribution of the trade-off models of MM, Miller, and their followers is their ability to identify the specific benefits and costs of using debt—the tax effects, financial distress costs, and so on. Before these models were developed, no capital structure theory existed, and we had no systematic way of analyzing the effects of debt financing. The trade-off model is summarized in exhibit 10.5. The top graph shows the relationships between the debt ratio and the cost of debt, cost of equity, and the CCC. Both the cost of equity and the effective (after-tax) cost of debt rise steadily with increases in leverage, but the rate of increase accelerates at higher debt levels, reflecting the increased probability of incurring financial distress and its attendant costs. The CCC first declines, then hits a minimum, and then begins to rise. Note that a business's CCC is minimized and its value is maximized **at the same capital structure**. Also note that the general shapes of the curves apply once

EXHIBIT 10.5 Summary of the Trade-Off Models

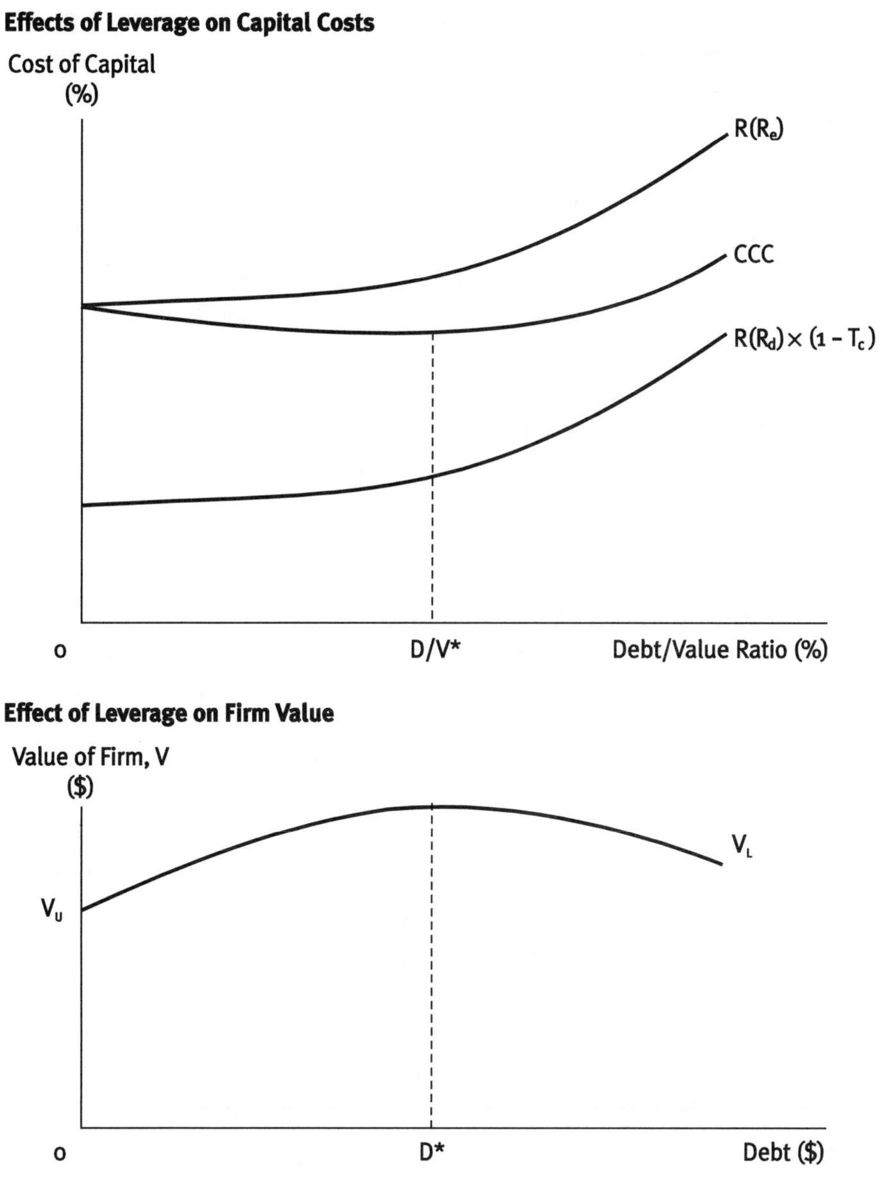

we consider the effects of financial distress costs, regardless of whether we are using the MM with corporate taxes model or the Miller model.

The fact that the same capital structure both minimizes the cost of capital and maximizes value should be no surprise. The value of any business is nothing more than the present value of its expected after-tax operating income stream. What discount rate is used to find the present value? The answer is the CCC. Therefore, by minimizing its CCC, a business is automatically creating the greatest value.

Unfortunately, it is extremely difficult for financial managers to quantify the costs and benefits of debt financing to their firms, so it is virtually impossible to pinpoint the capital structure that truly maximizes a business's value. Most experts believe that such a structure exists for every taxable business but that it changes substantially over time as the nature of the business and the capital markets changes. Most experts also believe that, as shown in the lower graph of exhibit 10.5, the relationship between firm value and leverage is relatively flat; thus, relatively large deviations from the optimal structure can occur without materially affecting a business's value.

Now, consider the asymmetric information model. Because of asymmetric information, investors know less about a firm's prospects than its managers do. Furthermore, managers try to maximize value for current stockholders, not new ones, so if the firm has excellent prospects, management will not want to issue new shares; however, if things look bleak, a new stock offering may be sold. Therefore, investors take a stock offering to be a signal of bad news, so stock prices tend to decline when new issues are announced. As a result, new equity financing can be expensive, and this factor must be incorporated into the capital structure decision. Its effect is to motivate firms to maintain a reserve borrowing capacity, which permits future investment opportunities to be financed by debt when internal funds are insufficient.

By combining the two theories, we obtain this possible explanation for the capital structure decisions of taxable firms:

- Debt financing provides benefits because of the tax deductibility of interest. Hence, firms should have some debt in their capital structures.
- However, financial distress costs place limits on debt usage—beyond some point, these costs offset the tax advantage of debt.
- Finally, because of asymmetric information, businesses maintain a reserve borrowing capacity to take advantage of good investment opportunities and, at the same time, avoid having to issue stock at distressed prices.

SELF-TEST QUESTIONS

1. Do the capital structure models provide managers with quantifiable guidance regarding optimal capital structures?
2. Summarize the information that capital structure models provide to decision makers.

Application of Capital Structure Theory to Not-for-Profit Firms

So far, the discussion of capital structure theory has focused on investor-owned businesses. Do the models presented in this chapter apply to not-for-profit firms? No rigorous research has been conducted into the optimal capital structures of not-for-profit firms, but some loose analogies can be drawn. Although not-for-profit businesses do not receive a direct tax subsidy when debt financing is used, they do have access to the tax-exempt debt market, which provides an indirect tax subsidy. (If not-for-profits had to issue taxable debt, their costs of debt would be higher.) Thus, not-for-profit firms receive about the same tax advantages from the use of debt financing as do investor-owned firms.

What about the costs associated with equity (fund) financing? As discussed in chapter 9, from a pure opportunity cost perspective, a not-for-profit firm's fund capital has a cost that is roughly equivalent to the cost of equity of a similar investor-owned firm. Thus, we would expect the opportunity cost of fund capital to rise as more and more debt financing is used, just as for an investor-owned firm. After all, the use of debt financing increases the risk to the stakeholders of the organization. Furthermore, not-for-profit firms are subject to the same types of financial distress costs that are borne by investor-owned firms, so these costs are equally applicable. Even if the cost of equity is measured by the return required to support growth or maintain creditworthiness, increased risk means that a higher required rate of return is appropriate; hence, higher risk leads to a higher cost of fund capital.

Thus, we would expect the trade-off models to be roughly applicable to not-for-profit businesses and for such firms to have optimal capital structures defined, at least in theory, as a trade-off between the costs and benefits of debt financing. Note, however, that the asymmetric information model is not applicable to not-for-profit firms because such firms do not sell common stock.

Although the trade-off models may be generally applicable to not-for-profit businesses, a problem arises in practice because for-profit firms have more or less unlimited access to equity capital. Thus, if they have more capital investment opportunities than they can finance with retained earnings and debt financing, investor-owned firms can always raise the needed funds by a new stock issue. (According to the asymmetric information theory, managers may not want to issue new stock, but the opportunity still exists.) In addition, it is easy for investor-owned firms to alter their capital structures. If they are financially underleveraged—using too little debt—they can simply issue more debt and use the proceeds to repurchase stock. On the other hand, if they are financially overleveraged—using too much debt—they can issue additional shares and use the proceeds to refund debt.

Not-for-profit businesses do not have access to the equity markets; their sole source of "equity" capital is through governmental grants, private contributions, and excess revenues (retained earnings). Thus, managers of not-for-profit organizations do not have the same degree of flexibility in either capital investment or capital structure decisions as do their proprietary counterparts.

The reduced access to equity capital means that it is often necessary for not-for-profit firms to (1) delay new projects, even profitable ones, because of funding insufficiencies and (2) use more than the theoretically optimal amount of debt because that is the only way that needed services can be financed. Although these actions may be required in certain situations, not-for-profit managers must recognize that such strategies increase costs. Project delays mean that needed services are not being provided on a timely basis. Using more debt than optimal pushes the firm beyond the point of the greatest net benefit of debt financing and hence drives capital costs up. If a not-for-profit firm is forced into a situation where it is using more than the optimal amount of debt financing, its managers should plan to reduce the firm's level of debt as soon as the situation permits.

The ability of a not-for-profit business to garner governmental grants, attract private contributions, and generate excess revenues plays an important role in establishing its competitive position. A firm that has an adequate amount of fund capital can operate at its optimal capital structure and thus minimize capital costs. If insufficient fund capital is available, too much financial leverage is then used and the result is higher capital costs. Consider two not-for-profit hospitals that are similar in all respects, except that one has more fund capital and can operate at its optimal structure while the other has insufficient fund capital and thus must use more debt financing than optimal. The hospital with insufficient fund capital must operate at an inefficient capital structure. The former has a significant competitive advantage because it can offer either more services at the same cost by using additional (suboptimal) debt financing or matching services at lower costs. Thus, sufficient fund capital provides the flexibility to offer all of the necessary services and still operate at the lowest capital cost structure. Just like firms that have low operating cost structures, firms that are at their optimal capital structures—and hence have a low capital cost structure—have an advantage over their competitors that have higher capital cost structures.

SELF-TEST QUESTIONS

1. Do the capital structure models apply to not-for-profit firms?
2. Why is capital structure important to not-for-profit firms?

Making the Capital Structure Decision

Although the trade-off and asymmetric information theories of capital structure provide many insights into the capital structure decision, theories alone cannot provide managers with a numerical answer. Thus, managers must apply judgment along with quantitative analysis.

Quantitative Analysis

Businesses typically have a financial planning model that forecasts their financial statements five years into the future. This model creates pro forma income statements and balance sheets on the basis of a large number of inputs, including financing decisions. By varying the future debt-equity mix, managers can get a feel for the impact of capital structure on future financial performance; hence, this model can provide information that is valuable to the capital structure decision.

Qualitative Analysis

The judgmental analysis involves several different factors, and in one situation a particular factor might have great importance, while the same factor might be relatively unimportant in another situation. This section discusses some of the more important judgmental issues that should be taken into account.

Long-Run Viability

Managers of businesses that provide vital healthcare services have a responsibility to the community to provide those services for generations. Thus, they must refrain from using financial leverage to the point where the firm's long-run viability is endangered.

Managerial Conservatism

Well-diversified investors have eliminated most, if not all, of the diversifiable risk from their portfolios. Therefore, the typical investor can tolerate some chance of financial distress because a loss on one stock will probably be offset by random gains on other stocks in the investor's portfolio. However, managers of investor-owned firms often view financial distress with more concern because they typically are not well diversified in their careers, so the present value of their expected earnings can be seriously affected by the onset of financial distress. For this reason, managers might be more "conservative" in their use of leverage than the average stockholder would desire. If so, they would set somewhat lower target capital structures than those that maximize firm value.

For not-for-profit firms, one can argue that managerial conservatism is appropriate. Not-for-profit firms have no shareholders, and many of the stakeholders are typically not well diversified in their relationships with the firm. Thus, these stakeholders have much more to lose if the firm fails than do well-diversified shareholders of investor-owned firms.

Lender and Rating Agency Attitudes

Regardless of a manager's own analysis of the proper leverage for her firm, there is no question that lenders' and rating agencies' attitudes are frequently important determinants of financial structures. In the majority of cases, corporate managers discuss the firm's financial structure with lenders and rating agencies and give much weight to their advice. Also, if a particular firm's management is so confident of the future that it seeks to use leverage beyond the norms for its industry, its lenders may be unwilling to accept such debt increases, or they may do so only at a high price.

Rating agencies publish data that give managers the rough relationship between the use of debt financing and debt rating. For example, exhibit 10.6 lists the relationship between financial leverage and debt rating for not-for-profit hospitals as reported by Standard & Poor's. In general, the greater the use of debt, the lower the debt rating. Furthermore, managers typically want

EXHIBIT 10.6
Relationship Between Financial Leverage and Debt Rating for Not-for-Profit Hospitals

Debt Rating	*Long-Term Debt/Capital Ratio (%)*
AA+	21.9
AA	24.7
AA–	30.1
A+	35.0
A	41.1
A–	48.1
BBB+	45.8
BBB/BBB-	60.3
Speculative	69.5

Notes: Data are updated annually. *Capital* is defined as long-term debt plus equity.
Source: Data from S&P Global (2017).

to maintain some target debt rating—say, A. If a hospital wants to target an A rating, according to the data in exhibit 10.6, it should set an optimal capital structure of about 35 percent. Note, however, that factors other than financial leverage affect debt ratings, so the ratios provided by the rating agencies should be considered only rough guidance.

Reserve Borrowing Capacity

Under the asymmetric information model, businesses should maintain a reserve borrowing capacity that preserves the ability to issue debt at favorable terms if unanticipated needs arise. For example, suppose Merck (www.Merck.com) had just successfully completed a research and development program on a new drug and its internal projections forecast much higher earnings in the future. However, the new earnings are not yet anticipated by investors and hence are not reflected in the price of its stock. Merck's managers would not want to issue stock; they would prefer to finance with debt until the higher earnings materialize and are reflected in the stock price, at which time the firm can sell an issue of common stock, retire the debt, and return to its target capital structure. To maintain a reserve borrowing capacity, firms generally use less debt under "normal" conditions and hence present a stronger financial picture than they otherwise would. The use of less debt is not suboptimal from a long-run standpoint, although it might appear so if viewed strictly on a short-run basis.

Industry Averages

Presumably, managers act rationally, so the capital structures of other firms in the industry, particularly the industry leaders, should provide insights into the optimal structure. In general, there is no reason to believe that the managers of one firm are better than the managers of any other firm. Thus, if one firm has a capital structure that is significantly different from other firms in its industry, the managers of that firm should identify the unique circumstances that contribute to the anomaly. If unique circumstances cannot be identified, it is doubtful that the firm has identified the correct target structure.

Control of Investor-Owned Corporations

The effect that a firm's choice of securities has on a management's position of control may also influence its capital structure decision. If a firm's management barely has majority control—just over 50 percent of the stock—but is not in a position to buy any more stock, debt may be the choice for new financing. On the other hand, a management group that is not concerned about voting control may decide to use equity rather than debt if the firm's financial situation is so weak that the use of debt might subject the firm to serious risk of default.

Asset Structure

Firms whose assets are suitable as security for loans tend to use debt rather heavily because the use of collateral provides access to lower-cost debt financing. Thus, hospitals tend to be highly leveraged, but firms involved in technological research employ relatively little debt. Also, if the firm's assets carry high business risk, it will be less able to use financial leverage than a firm with low business risk will be. Accordingly, factors such as sales stability and operating leverage, which influence business risk, also influence firms' optimal capital structure. Thus, the greater the amount of "hard" assets and the lower the business risk, the greater the amount of debt financing used.

Growth Rate

Other factors being the same, faster-growing firms must rely more heavily on external capital—slow growth can be financed with retained earnings, but rapid growth generally requires the use of external funds. As postulated in the information asymmetry theory, businesses first use debt financing to meet external funding needs. Furthermore, the flotation costs involved in selling common stock exceed those incurred when selling debt. Thus, rapidly growing firms tend to use more debt than do slower-growth firms.

Profitability

Highly profitable firms do not need to use much debt financing because their high rates of return enable them to rely primarily on retained earnings. This behavior is consistent with the asymmetric information theory.

Taxes

Interest is a deductible expense, while dividends are not deductible, so the higher a firm's corporate tax rate, the greater the advantage of using corporate debt.

Clearly, some of the considerations that go into the capital structure decision are quantitative and some are qualitative. Thus, in practice, the decision requires a great deal of judgment. As mentioned earlier, businesses often use forecasting models to assess the impact of alternative capital structures on financial health, but the final decision always involves some judgment.

SELF-TEST QUESTIONS

1. Is the capital structure decision mostly objective or subjective?
2. What are some of the factors that managers must consider when setting a business's optimal capital structure?

Capital Structure Decisions for Small Investor-Owned Businesses

Capital structure theory, and its prescriptions for business behavior, is based on large corporations, in which owners and managers are separate groups and the securities issued are publicly traded. Thus, like its application to not-for-profit businesses, the application of capital structure theory to small investor-owned businesses results in more questions than answers.

In small businesses—say, a medical practice of one or a few physicians—the situation changes dramatically. Now, it is common to distribute returns to the owner–managers through salary bonuses as opposed to dividends. What makes this situation different? The key to the value of debt financing is that interest on debt financing is tax deductible to a business, while dividends on equity financing are not. In other words, interest is paid from pretax income, while dividends are paid from after-tax income. This asymmetric tax deductibility of interest creates the value inherent in the use of debt. As proved by MM, if there were no differential tax effects (the zero-tax case), the increase in riskiness to owners would exactly offset the benefits associated with a cost of debt that is lower than the cost of equity. The tax impact makes the effective cost of debt lower than that appropriate for the risk that it brings to the business, and this "externality" drives the value of debt financing.

When dividends to equityholders are paid in the form of bonuses, they, too, are tax deductible to the business. Thus, we are in a situation in which there are tax advantages inherent in both debt and equity financing. Debt financing still leverages up owners' return, but the increase in risk that debt financing brings to owners either partially or fully offsets the increase in ROE. Thus, there is no clear value-increasing benefit to debt financing.

Should such small businesses still use debt financing? The answer is probably yes because owner–managers often cannot provide the amount of equity capital needed by the business. If owners do not have the capital needed by the business, and control considerations preclude bringing in outside equity, debt financing is the only choice. In addition, the use of debt financing means that less of the owners' wealth is tied up in the business, so owners are better diversified in their personal investments.

Interestingly, the debt used by small businesses can be obtained either by the business or by the owners as personal debt, which would then be contributed to the business as equity. This situation amounts to the "homemade" leverage argument made by MM in their proofs. In general, if the business can borrow at a lower interest rate than the individual owners can, business debt makes sense, and vice versa. However, the issue becomes cloudy because, under many forms of organization, personal debt has different liability characteristics than business debt has. Adding to the complexity, the owners of small businesses typically have to sign personal guarantees on business debt, which further blurs the line between business and personal debt.

The bottom line here is that each small business situation is unique, and no guidance for capital structure decision-making is applicable to all small businesses.

SELF-TEST QUESTION

1. Do the general prescriptions for capital structure decisions apply to small businesses? Explain your answer.

Chapter Key Concepts

This chapter presents a variety of topics related to capital structure decisions. Here are its key concepts:

- The use of debt financing increases the *rate of return* to owners, but it also increases their *risk*.
- *Business risk* is the inherent riskiness in a firm's operations if it uses no debt financing. *Financial risk* is the additional risk that is concentrated on the business's owners when debt financing is used.
- In 1958, Franco Modigliani and Merton Miller (MM) startled the academic community by proving, under a restrictive set of assumptions including *zero taxes*, that capital structure is irrelevant because a business's value is not affected by its financing mix.
- MM later added *corporate taxes* to their model, leading to the conclusion that capital structure does matter and that businesses should use almost 100 percent debt financing to maximize value.

(continued)

(continued from previous page)

- The MM model with corporate taxes illustrates that the benefits of debt financing stem solely from the *tax deductibility of interest payments.*
- Much later, Miller extended the model to include *personal taxes.* The introduction of personal taxes reduces, but does not eliminate, the benefits of debt financing. Thus, the *Miller model* also prescribes 100 percent debt financing.
- The addition of *financial distress costs* to either the MM corporate tax model or the Miller model results in a *trade-off model.* Here, the marginal costs and benefits of debt financing are balanced against one another, and the result is an optimal capital structure that falls somewhere between 0 percent and 100 percent debt.
- *Not-for-profit firms* face a set of benefits and costs associated with debt financing similar to those faced by investor-owned firms, so the trade-off model is at least partially applicable to them. However, the inability to sell equity may keep a not-for-profit firm's capital structure above the optimal point, at least temporarily.
- The *asymmetric information model*, which is based on the assumption that managers have better information than investors do, postulates that there is a preferred order to financing: retained earnings (and depreciation); then debt; and, as a last resort, new common stock.
- The asymmetric information model prescribes that businesses maintain a *reserve borrowing capacity* so that they can always issue debt on reasonable terms rather than be forced into a new equity issue at the wrong time.
- Unfortunately, capital structure theory does not provide neat, clean answers to the optimal capital structure question. Thus, many factors must be considered when actually choosing a firm's target capital structure, and the final decision will be based on both analysis and judgment.
- In very small investor-owned businesses, such as a solo or small group medical practice, the situation is complicated by the fact that the owners and managers are the same people.

This chapter concludes our discussion of the cost of capital and capital structure. In chapters 11 and 12, we discuss capital budgeting decisions.

Chapter Models, Problems, and Minicases

The following ancillary resources in spreadsheet format are available for this chapter:

- A chapter model that shows how to perform many of the calculations described in the chapter
- Problems that test your ability to perform the calculations
- A minicase that is more complicated than the problems and tests your ability to perform the calculations in preparation for a case

These resources can be accessed online at ache.org/HAP/PinkSong8e.

Selected Case

One case in *Cases in Healthcare Finance*, sixth edition, is applicable to this chapter: Case 18: RN Temp, Inc., which focuses on the choice between debt and equity financing for a for-profit business.

Reference

S&P Global. 2017. *U.S. Not-For-Profit Health Care System Median Financial Ratios—2016 vs. 2015.* Standard & Poor's. Published August 24. www.spratings.com//documents/20184/908554/US_PF_Event_Webcast_hc91417_art7.pdf/ec5e0239-2fb3-4341-826c-3ff7dfe38124.

Selected Bibliography

Arduino, K. 2018. "Healthcare Capital Markets Outlook: Short-Term Opportunities Versus Long-Term Uncertainty." *Healthcare Financial Management* 72 (5): 36–43.

Brigham, E. F., and M. C. Ehrhardt. 2016. "Chapter 21." In *Financial Management: Theory and Practice,* 15th ed. Mason, OH: South-Western Cengage Learning.

Donaldson, G. 1961. *Corporate Debt Capacity: A Study of Corporate Debt Policy and the Determination of Corporate Debt Capacity.* Cambridge, MA: Harvard Graduate School of Business Administration.

Healthcare Financial Management Association. "Optimizing Capital Structure Decisions Under the New Tax Law." *Healthcare Financial Management* 72 (8): A1–A4.

Jordahl, E. A. 2017. "Contemplating the Case for Terminating Swaps." Healthcare Financial Management Association. Published December 1. www.hfma.org/Content.aspx?id=57108.

Jordahl, E. A., R. Freel, and D. Ratliff. 2016. "Four Current Market Concepts for Advance Refunding." *Healthcare Financial Management* 70 (12): 70–71.

Marsh, P. 1982. "The Choice Between Equity and Debt: An Empirical Study." *Journal of Finance* 37 (1): 121–44.

Modigliani, F., and M. H. Miller. 1965. "The Cost of Capital, Corporation Finance and the Theory of Investment: Reply." *American Economic Review* 55 (3): 524–27.

———. 1963. "Corporate Income Taxes and the Cost of Capital: A Correction." *American Economic Review* 53 (3): 433–43.

———. 1958. "The Cost of Capital, Corporation Finance and the Theory of Investment." *American Economic Review* 48 (3): 261–97.

Ratliff, D., and E. A. Jordahl. 2018. "Finding Reality in a Cloud of Possibility." *Healthcare Financial Management* 72 (3): 68–69.

Taggart, R. 1977. "A Model of Corporate Financing Decisions." *Journal of Finance* 32 (5): 1467–84.

Selected Websites

The following websites pertain to the content of this chapter:

- Ohio State University maintains a website with video clips by various finance professionals briefly discussing topics of relevance to this course. (Unfortunately, the clips do not include healthcare executives.) To access the clips, go to https://fisher.osu.edu/academic-departments/department-finance, click Resources and then Video Series. This will lead you to the available videos.
- If you are interested in learning more about the consequences of Miller and Modigliani's work as it pertains to stock repurchases, you may find Dr. Robert Shiller's lecture, available through Open Yale Courses, to be of interest. That video can be accessed at http://oyc.yale.edu/economics/econ-252-08/lecture-11#transcript.
- Finally, you may take the opportunity to explore the work of Merton H. Miller by reading his Nobel Peace Prize lecture, which can be

found at www.nobelprize.org/prizes/economic-sciences/1990/miller/biographical. Click on Read the Lecture toward the bottom of the page.

Notes

1. The use of preferred stock has roughly the same effect on a business's risk and return, and hence capital structure decision, as does debt financing. However, most businesses in the health services sector do not use preferred stock.
2. Per procedure leases are discussed in chapter 8.
3. In a 1979 survey of Financial Management Association members, the original MM article was judged to have had the greatest impact on the field of finance of any work ever published. See Cooley, P. L., and J. L. Heck. 1981. "Significant Contributions to Finance Literature." *Financial Management* (Tenth Anniversary Issue): 23–33.
4. MM actually developed three propositions, but the third one is not material to our discussion.
5. *Arbitrage* is the simultaneous buying and selling of essentially identical assets at different prices. The buying increases the price of the undervalued asset, and the selling decreases the price of the overvalued asset. Arbitrage operations will continue until prices have been adjusted to the point where the arbitrageur can no longer earn a profit. At this point, the prices are in equilibrium.
6. The annual interest expense associated with D dollars of debt financing is R(Rd) × D, and the resulting tax savings is $T \times R(R_d) \times D$. Because MM assumed that all cash flows are perpetuities, the present value of the tax savings stream is $[T \times R(R_d) \times D] \div R(R_d) = T \times D$.
7. See Miller, M. H. 1977. "Debt and Taxes." *Journal of Finance* (May): 261–75. The paper was first presented as the presidential address at the 1976 meeting of the American Finance Association.
8. Over the past 25 years, the tax rate on equity income has changed several times, resulting in a dividend tax rate that has been less than the tax rate on debt (interest) income during some periods and equal to the rate on debt income during other periods. However, the fact that capital gains taxes are deferred into the future while taxes on debt income must be paid when the interest is received makes the effective tax rate on equity income lower than the effective rate on debt income, even when the statutory rates are the same.

9. See Myers, S. C. 1984. "The Capital Structure Puzzle." *Journal of Finance* (July): 575–92. It is interesting to note that, like the Miller model, Myers's paper was presented as a presidential address to the American Finance Association.
10. Many studies support the contention that the announcement of a new stock issue prompts a decrease in stock price. For example, one study found that stock prices decline about 3 percent following the announcement of a new stock issue. See P. Asquith and D. W. Mullins, Jr., 1986, "Equity Issues and Offering Dilution," *Journal of Financial Economics* (June): 61–89.

Integrative Application

The Problem

STU Rehabilitation currently has no debt. An in-house research group has just been assigned the job of determining whether the firm should change its capital structure. Because of the importance of the decision, management has also hired the investment banking firm of Morgan & Company to conduct a parallel analysis of the situation. Both analyses will use the MM with taxes framework (incorporating the probability of financial distress). Mr. Harris, the in-house analyst who has a good knowledge of the firm and is confident of his ability to predict the firm's probability of financial distress at various levels of debt, has decided to estimate the optimal capital structure as the one that maximizes the value of the levered firm. Ms. Martinez, the Morgan & Company consultant who has a good knowledge of capital market conditions and is confident of her ability to predict the firm's debt and equity costs at various levels of debt, has decided to estimate the optimal capital structure as the one that minimizes the firm's corporate cost of capital.

The following data are relevant to both analyses:

EBIT per year, in perpetuity: $4 million
Tax rate: 30%
Required rate of return on equity (unlevered): 12%
PV of financial distress costs: $8 million

The cost-of-capital schedule predicted by Ms. Martinez and the probabilities of financial distress predicted by Mr. Harris are as follows (where FD is financial distress):

	Debt Level (in millions of dollars)							
	$0	*$2*	*$4*	*$6*	*$8*	*$10*	*$12*	*$14*
$R(R_d)$	—	8.0%	8.3%	9.0%	10.0%	11.0%	13.0%	16.0%
$R(R_e)$	12.00%	12.25%	12.75%	13.00%	13.15%	13.40%	14.65%	17.00%
Prob (FD)	0%	0%	5%	7%	10%	17%	47%	90%

The problem is to determine the level of debt that Mr. Harris would recommend and the level of debt that Ms. Martinez would recommend.

The Analysis

Mr. Harris's analysis is summarized in the following exhibit

	Debt Level (in millions of dollars)							
	\$0	*\$2*	*\$4*	*\$6*	*\$8*	*\$10*	*\$12*	*\$14*
V_U	\$23.33	\$23.33	\$23.33	\$23.33	\$23.33	\$23.33	\$23.33	\$23.33
$T \times D$	\$ 0.00	\$ 0.60	\$ 1.20	\$ 1.80	\$ 2.40	\$ 3.00	\$ 3.60	\$ 4.20
PV of FD	\$ 0.00	\$ 0.00	\$ 0.40	\$ 0.56	\$ 0.80	\$ 1.36	\$ 3.76	\$ 7.20
V_L	\$23.33	\$23.93	\$24.13	\$24.57	\$24.93	\$24.97	\$23.17	\$20.33

The table shows that the optimal capital structure occurs at a debt level of \$10 million: At this amount of debt, the value of the levered firm (V_L) is maximized at \$24.97 million. This value is obtained as follows:

$$VU = \frac{\text{EBIT} \times (1 - T)}{R(R\ R_{eU})} = \frac{\$4 \text{ million} \times 0.7}{0.12} = \$23.33 \text{ million}$$

$$T \times D = 0.3 \times \$10 \text{ million} = \$3.00 \text{ million}$$

$$\text{PV of FD} = 17\% \times \$8 \text{ million} = \$1.36 \text{ million}$$

$$V_L = \$23.33 \text{ million} + \$3.00 \text{ million} - \$1.36 \text{ million} = \$24.97 \text{ million}$$

Ms. Martinez's analysis is summarized as follows:

	Debt Level (in millions of dollars)							
	\$0	*\$2*	*\$4*	*\$6*	*\$8*	*\$10*	*\$12*	*\$14*
$E = V_L - D$	\$23.33	\$21.93	\$20.13	\$18.57	\$16.93	\$14.97	\$11.17	\$6.33
$w_d = D / V_L$	0%	8%	17%	24%	32%	40%	52%	69%
$w_e = E / V_L$	100%	92%	83%	76%	68%	60%	48%	31%
CCC	12.00%	11.69%	11.61%	11.36%	11.18%	11.12%	11.78%	13.01%

The table shows that the optimal capital structure occurs at a debt level of \$10 million. At this amount of debt, the CCC is minimized at 10.4 percent. This value is obtained as follows:

$$E = V_L - D = \$24.97 \text{ million} - \$10.00 \text{ million} = \$14.97 \text{ million}$$

$$w_d = D / V_L = \$10.00 \text{ million} / \$24.97 \text{ million} = 40\%$$

$$w_e = E / V_L = \$14.97 \text{ million} / \$24.97 \text{ million} = 60\%$$

$$CCC = [w_d \times R(R_d) \times (1 - T)] + [w_e \times R(R_{eL})]$$
$$= [40\% \times 11.0\% \times 0.7] + [60\% \times 13.4\%] = 11.12\%.$$

The Decision

STU Rehabilitation decided to issue $10 million of debt. At this level of debt, the value of the firm is maximized and the CCC is minimized. ■

PART

V

CAPITAL ALLOCATION

In parts III and IV, we focused on capital acquisition (long-term financing), including capital structure decisions and cost-of-capital estimation—in other words, how businesses raise the funds used to buy needed land, buildings, and equipment and the cost of those funds. Now, we turn our attention to the capital allocation decision—or how those funds can be deployed (spent) in the most financially efficient manner. The overall process of choosing the projects to be undertaken by a business is called *capital budgeting*.

Our discussion of capital allocation spans two chapters. Perhaps the most critical part of capital budgeting involves cash flow estimation, because the financial attractiveness of proposed projects stems solely from the cash flows they are expected to produce. Chapter 11 covers the basic concepts of capital budgeting, including how to estimate a project's cash flows and how to measure its expected financial impact.

In addition to cash flow estimation, an important consideration in capital budgeting is project risk. Chapter 12 explains how to assess the riskiness of a project and incorporate that assessment into the capital budgeting decision process.

CHAPTER

11

CAPITAL BUDGETING

Learning Objectives

After studying this chapter, readers will be able to

- explain how managers use project classifications and postaudits in the capital budgeting process;
- discuss the role of financial analysis in health services capital budgeting decisions;
- discuss the key elements of cash flow estimation, breakeven analysis, and profitability analysis; and
- conduct basic capital budgeting analyses.

Introduction

Chapters 9 and 10 described how healthcare managers estimate their business's corporate cost of capital and make capital structure decisions. Now, we change our focus to fixed-asset acquisition decisions, which entail the acquisition of new facilities or equipment. Because such decisions require the use, or expenditure, of capital, they are called ***capital investment***, or ***capital budgeting***, ***decisions***. The term ***capital budgeting*** is used because the listing of projects to be undertaken in some future planning period, along with their total dollar cost, is called the ***capital budget***. Capital budgeting decisions are of fundamental importance to the success or failure of any business because a firm's capital budgeting decisions, more than anything else, shape its future.

The discussion of capital budgeting is divided into two chapters. Chapter 11 provides an overview of the capital budgeting process, a discussion of the key elements of project cash flow estimation, and an explanation of the basic techniques used to assess a project's breakeven characteristics and profitability. Chapter 12 considers capital budgeting risk analysis and the optimal capital budget.

Capital budgeting decisions are among the most critical decisions that healthcare managers must make. First, and most important, the results of capital budgeting decisions generally affect the business for an extended period. If a business invests too heavily in facilities and equipment (fixed assets), it will have too much capacity and its costs will necessarily be too high. On the other hand, a business that invests too little in fixed assets may face two problems: (1) technological obsolescence and (2) inadequate capacity. A healthcare provider without the latest technology will lose patients to its more up-to-date competitors and will deprive its patients of the best healthcare diagnostics and treatments available. A provider with inadequate capacity may lose a portion of its market share to competitors, which would then require it to increase its marketing costs or aggressively reduce prices to regain the lost share.

Effective capital budgeting procedures provide several benefits to businesses. A business that forecasts its needs for capital assets well in advance can plan the purchases carefully and thus negotiate the highest-quality assets at the best prices. In addition, asset expansion typically involves substantial expenditures, and because large amounts of funds are not usually on hand, they must be raised externally. Good capital budgeting practices enable a business to identify its financing needs and sources well in advance, which ensures the lowest possible capital procurement costs and availability of funds as they are needed.

SELF-TEST QUESTIONS

1. Why are capital budgeting decisions so crucial to the success of a business?
2. What are the benefits of effective capital budgeting procedures?

Project Classifications

Although benefits can be gained from the careful analysis of capital investment proposals, such efforts can be costly. For certain types of projects, a relatively detailed analysis may be warranted; for others, cost–benefit studies suggest that simpler procedures should be used. Accordingly, healthcare businesses generally classify projects into categories and then analyze those in each category differently. For example, Ridgeland Community Hospital, a not-for-profit hospital, uses the following classifications:

- **Category 1: Mandatory replacement**. This category consists of expenditures required to replace worn-out or damaged equipment necessary to the operations of the hospital. In general, these expenditures are mandatory, so they are usually made without going through an elaborate decision process.

- **Category 2: Discretionary replacement**. This category includes expenditures made to replace serviceable but obsolete equipment. The purpose of these projects generally is to lower costs or to provide more clinically effective services. Because category 2 projects are not mandatory, a more detailed analysis is generally required to support the expenditure than that needed for category 1 projects.
- **Category 3: Expansion of existing products, services, or markets**. This category includes expenditures made to increase capacity or to expand in markets currently served. These decisions are more complex, so still more detailed analysis is required, and the final decision is made at a higher level in the organization.
- **Category 4: Expansion into new products, services, or markets**. This category consists of projects necessary to provide new products or services or to expand into geographic areas not currently served. Such projects involve strategic decisions that can change the fundamental nature of the hospital, and they normally require the expenditure of large sums of money over long periods. Invariably, a particularly detailed analysis is required, and the board of trustees generally makes the final decision as part of the hospital's strategic planning process.
- **Category 5: Safety or environmental projects**. This category consists of expenditures necessary to comply with government orders, labor agreements, accreditation requirements, and so on. Unless the expenditures are large, category 5 expenditures are treated like category 1 expenditures.
- **Category 6: Other**. This category is a catchall for projects that do not fit neatly into any of the previous categories. The primary determinant of how category 6 projects are evaluated is the amount of funds required. In general, relatively simple analysis and only a few supporting documents are required for replacement decisions and safety or environmental projects, especially those that are mandatory. A more detailed analysis is required for expansion and other projects.

Note that, in each category, projects are classified by size. Larger projects require increasingly detailed analysis and approval at a higher level in the hospital. For example, department heads can authorize spending up to $25,000 on discretionary replacement projects, while the full board of directors must approve expansion projects that cost more than $5 million.

SELF-TEST QUESTIONS

1. What is the primary advantage of classifying capital projects?
2. What are some typical classifications?
3. What role does project size (cost) play in the classifications?

The Role of Financial Analysis in Health Services Capital Budgeting

For investor-owned businesses, for which shareholder wealth maximization is an important goal, the role of financial analysis in investment decisions is clear. Projects that will contribute to shareholder wealth should be undertaken, while those that will not should be ignored. However, what about not-for-profit businesses that do not have shareholder wealth maximization as a goal? In such businesses, the appropriate goal is providing quality, cost-effective service to the communities served. (A strong argument can be made that investor-owned firms in the health services sector should also have this goal.) In this situation, capital budgeting decisions must consider many factors besides a project's financial implications. For example, the needs of the medical staff and the good of the community must be taken into account. In some instances, these noneconomic factors will outweigh financial considerations.

Nevertheless, good decision-making, and hence the future viability of health services organizations, requires that the financial impact of capital investments be fully recognized. If a business takes on a series of highly unprofitable projects that meet nonfinancial goals, and such projects are not offset by other profitable projects, the business's financial condition will deteriorate. If this situation persists over time, the business will eventually lose its financial viability and may even be forced into bankruptcy and closure.

Because bankrupt businesses obviously cannot meet a community's needs, even managers of not-for-profit businesses must consider a project's potential impact on the firm's financial condition. Managers may make a conscious decision to accept a project with a poor financial prognosis because of its nonfinancial virtues, but it is important that managers know the financial impact up front, rather than be surprised when the project drains the firm's financial resources. Financial analysis provides managers with relevant information about a project's financial impact and hence helps managers make better decisions, including decisions based primarily on nonfinancial considerations.

SELF-TEST QUESTIONS

1. What is the role of financial analysis in capital budgeting decision-making in for-profit firms?
2. Why is the financial analysis of projects important in not-for-profit businesses?

Overview of Capital Budgeting Financial Analysis

The financial analysis of capital investment proposals typically involves the following four steps:

1. Estimate the project's expected cash flows, which consist of
   a. the capital outlay, or cost;
   b. the operating cash flows; and
   c. the terminal (ending) cash flow. (Cash flow estimation is discussed in the next section.)
2. Assess the riskiness of the estimated cash flows. (Risk assessment is discussed in chapter 12.)
3. Given the riskiness of the project, estimate the project's cost of capital (opportunity cost, or discount, rate). As discussed in chapter 9, a business's corporate cost of capital reflects the aggregate risk of the business's assets—that is, the riskiness inherent in the average project. If the project being evaluated does not have average risk, the corporate cost of capital must be adjusted.
4. Assess the financial impact of the project, including profitability. Several measures can be used for this purpose; we will discuss five in this chapter.

SELF-TEST QUESTION

1. Describe the four steps in capital budgeting financial analysis.

Cash Flow Estimation

The most important—but also the most difficult—step in evaluating capital investment proposals is cash flow estimation: the investment outlays, the annual net operating flows expected when the project goes into operation, and the cash flows associated with project termination. Many variables are involved in cash flow forecasting, and many individuals and departments participate in the process. It is difficult to make accurate projections of the revenues and costs associated with a large, complex project, so forecast errors can be large. Thus, it is essential that risk analyses be performed on prospective projects. One manager with a good sense of humor developed the following five principles of capital-budgeting cash flow estimation:

1. It is difficult to forecast cash flows, especially those that occur in the future.
2. Those who live by the crystal ball soon learn how to eat ground glass.
3. The moment you forecast cash flows, you know that you are wrong; you just do not know by how much and in what direction.
4. If you are right, never let your bosses forget.
5. An expert is someone who has been right at least once.

It is hard to overstate the difficulty and importance of correctly forecasting a project's cash flows. However, if the principles discussed in the next sections are observed, errors that often arise in the process can be minimized. Also, because cash flow estimation is so difficult, chapter 12 presents several techniques managers use to measure and account for cash flow uncertainty.

Identifying the Relevant Cash Flows

In the evaluation of a new capital investment, the relevant cash flows are the project's *incremental cash flows*, which are defined as the difference between the firm's cash flows in each period if the project is undertaken and the firm's cash flows if the project is not undertaken:

$$\text{Incremental CF}_t = \text{CF}_{t(\text{Firm with project})} - \text{CF}_{t(\text{Firm without project})}.$$

Here, the subscript t specifies a period—normally years—so CF_0 is the cash flow during year 0, which is generally assumed to be the beginning of the project; CF_1 is the cash flow during the year 1, CF_2 is the cash flow during year 2, and so on. In practice, the early cash flows, particularly those in year 0, are usually cash outflows—the costs associated with getting the project "up and running." As the project begins to generate operating revenues, the cash flows normally turn positive.

Cash Flow Versus Accounting Income

Accounting income statements prepared in accordance with generally accepted accounting principles are in some respects a mix of apples and oranges. For example, accountants deduct labor costs (which are cash outflows) from revenues (which may not be entirely cash). (For healthcare providers, most of the collections are from third-party payers, and payment may not be received until several months after the service is provided.) At the same time, the income statement does not recognize capital outlays (which are cash flows), but it does deduct depreciation expense (which is not a cash flow). In capital investment decisions, it is critical that the decision be based on the actual dollars that flow into and out of the business because a business's true profitability—and hence its ability to provide healthcare services—depends on its cash flows and not on income as reported in accordance with generally accepted accounting principles. Note, however, that accounting items can influence cash flows because items such as depreciation can affect tax or reimbursement cash flows.

Cash Flow Timing

Financial analysts must be careful to account for the timing of cash flows. Accounting income statements are for periods, such as years or quarters, so they do not reflect exactly when revenues and expenses occur during the period. In theory, capital budgeting cash flows should be analyzed exactly as they occur. Of course, there must be a compromise between accuracy and simplicity. A time line with daily cash flows would, in theory, provide the most accuracy, but daily cash flow estimates are difficult to perform, unwieldy to use, and probably no more accurate than annual cash flow estimates. Thus, in most cases, analysts assume all cash flows occur at year-end. However, for some projects, it may be useful to assume cash flows occur every six months or even to forecast quarterly or monthly cash flows.

Project Life

One of the first decisions that must be made in forecasting a project's cash flows is the life of the project: Do we need to forecast cash flows for 20 years, or is a period of 5 years sufficient? Many projects, such as a new hospital wing or an ambulatory care clinic, potentially have very long lives—perhaps as long as 50 years. In theory, a cash flow forecast should extend for the full life of a project, yet most managers would have little confidence in any cash flow forecasts beyond the near term. Thus, most organizations set an arbitrary limit on the project life assumed in capital budgeting analyses—often five or ten years. If the forecasted life is less than the arbitrary limit, the forecasted life is used to develop the cash flows. If the forecasted life exceeds the limit, project life is truncated and the operating cash flows beyond the limit are ignored in the analysis.

Although cash flow truncation is a practical solution to one problem, it creates another problem—the value inherent in the cash flows beyond the truncation point is lost to the project. This problem can be addressed either objectively or subjectively. The standard procedure at some organizations is to estimate the project's *terminal value*, which is a proxy for the value of the cash flows beyond the truncation point. Often, the terminal value is estimated as the liquidation value of the project at that point in time. If the terminal value is too difficult to estimate, the fact that some portion of the project's cash flow stream is being ignored should, at a minimum, be subjectively recognized by decision-makers. The saving grace is that cash flows well into the future typically contribute a relatively small amount to a project's profitability. For example, a $100,000 terminal value projected ten years into the future contributes only about $38,500 to the project's initial value when the cost of capital (discount rate) is 10 percent.

Sunk Costs

A *sunk cost* refers to an outlay that has already occurred or has been irrevocably committed, so it is an outlay that is unaffected by the current decision to accept or reject the project. For example, suppose that in 2019, Ridgeland Community Hospital is evaluating the purchase of a lithotripter system. For help with the decision, the hospital hired and paid $10,000 to a consultant in 2018 to conduct a marketing study. Is this 2018 cash flow relevant to the 2019 capital investment decision? The answer is **no**. The $10,000 is a sunk cost; Ridgeland cannot recover it whether the lithotripter is purchased or not. Costs, such as sunk costs, as well as other cash flows that are not relevant to an analysis, are called *nonincremental cash flows*. Sometimes a project appears to be unprofitable when all of the associated costs, including sunk costs, are considered. However, on an **incremental** basis, the project may be profitable and should be undertaken. Thus, the correct treatment of sunk costs may be critical to the decision.

Assume for a moment that Ridgeland goes ahead with the lithotripter project. Then, in 2020, when conducting a periodic analysis of the historical profitability of the project, the $10,000 cost of the consultant's report might be included because it was part of the total cash flows attributable to the project. Still, when making the 2019 decision regarding whether to go ahead with the project, the $10,000 is nonincremental and hence not relevant to the decision.

Opportunity Costs

All relevant *opportunity costs* must be included in a capital investment analysis. Note that one opportunity cost involves the use of the capital. When Ridgeland uses its capital to invest in a lithotripter system, it cannot use the same capital to invest in, say, a new surgical suite. The opportunity cost associated with capital use is accounted for in the project's cost of capital, which is used to discount the project's expected cash flows and represents the return that the business can earn by investing in alternative investments of similar risk. Thus, the opportunity cost associated with capital is automatically considered in a project analysis by the mathematics of the discounting process.

There are other types of opportunity costs, and all such costs should be built into a project's cash flows. For example, assume that Ridgeland's lithotripter would be installed in a freestanding facility and that the hospital currently owns the land on which the facility would be constructed. The hospital purchased the land ten years ago at a cost of $50,000, but the current market value of the property is $130,000, net of taxes (if applicable) and fees. When evaluating the lithotripter, should we disregard the value of the land because no cash outlay is necessary? The answer is "no," because there is an opportunity cost inherent in the use of the property. Using the property for the lithotripter facility deprives Ridgeland of its use for anything else. The hospital might use the property for a walk-in clinic, an ambulatory surgery center, or a parking garage rather than sell it, but the best measure of the property's value to Ridgeland—and hence the opportunity cost inherent in its use—is the cash flow that can be realized by selling it. By considering the property's current market value, the hospital is letting market forces assign a value to the land's best alternative use. Thus, the lithotripter project should have a $130,000 opportunity cost charged against it. Note that the opportunity cost is the property's $130,000 net market value, regardless of whether the property was acquired for $50,000 or $200,000.

Effect on the Business's Other Projects

Capital budgeting analyses must consider the effect of the project under consideration on the business's other projects. When the effect is negative, it is often called *cannibalization* because the project is expected to "eat away" at other revenues. For example, assume that some of the patients who are expected to use Ridgeland's new lithotripter would have been treated surgically at the hospital, so these surgical revenues will be lost if the lithotripter facility goes into operation. Thus, the incremental revenues to Ridgeland are the revenues attributable to the lithotripter less the revenues lost from forgone surgery services. Of course, the costs saved by losing these surgery patients would be a benefit to the lithotripter project and hence should also be considered in the analysis. Note, however, that if the surgical patients would be lost to competitors that are buying lithotripters, the loss of these patients does not affect the lithotripter project analysis because these losses would occur whether the lithotripter project is accepted or not.

Thus far, we have focused on the negative impact of a new project on other services. The impact can be positive. For example, new patients who use the lithotripter may at the same time use other services provided by the hospital, such as imaging services. In this situation, the incremental cash flows generated by the lithotripter patients' utilization of other services should be credited to the lithotripter project. In theory, if the lithotripter brings new patients to the hospital who otherwise would go elsewhere, all of the profits from these patients should be attributed to the lithotripter project. Of course, such cash flows would be difficult to estimate. If possible, both positive and negative effects on other projects should be quantified; at a minimum, they should be noted so that the final decision-maker is aware of their existence.

Shipping and Installation Costs

When a firm acquires new equipment, it often incurs substantial costs for shipping and installation. These charges are added to the invoice price of the equipment to determine the overall cost of the project. Also, the full cost of the equipment, including shipping and installation charges, is used as the basis for calculating depreciation expense. Thus, if Ridgeland purchases intensive care monitoring equipment that costs $200,000 but another $50,000 is required for shipping and installation, the full cost of the equipment would be $250,000, and this amount would be the starting point (cost basis) for both tax calculations (when applicable) and all depreciation calculations.

Changes in Net Working Capital

Normally, expansion projects require additional inventories, and added patient services also lead to additional accounts receivable. The increase in these current asset accounts must be financed, just as an increase in fixed assets must be financed. (To keep the balance sheet balanced, we must offset any increases on the left side with increases on the right side.) However, accounts payable and accruals will probably also increase as a result of the expansion, and these current liability additions will reduce the cash needed to finance the increase in inventories and receivables. The difference between the increase in current assets and the increase in current liabilities that **directly result** from a new project is called a *change in net working capital.*

If the change in net working capital is positive—that is, if the increase in current assets exceeds the increase in current liabilities—this amount is as much a cost to the project as is the cost of the asset itself. Thus, the project must be charged an amount additional to the cost of the new asset to reflect the net financing needed for the current asset accounts. Similarly, if the change in net working capital is negative, the project is generating a working capital cash inflow because the increase in liabilities exceeds the project's current asset requirements, and this cash flow partially offsets the cost of the asset being acquired.

As the project approaches termination, inventories will be sold off and not replaced, receivables will be converted to cash, and no new receivables will be created. In effect, the business will recover its investment in net working capital when the project is terminated. This recovery will produce a cash flow that is equal, but opposite in sign, to the change in net working capital cash flow that arises at the beginning of a project.

For healthcare providers, the change in net working capital often is small and can be ignored without materially affecting the analysis. In addition, because the initial change in net working capital is exactly offset at project termination, its impact is reduced. However, when a large project has a significant change in net working capital, failure to consider the net investment in current assets will result in an overstatement of the project's profitability, which can lead to a faulty analysis.

Inflation Effects

Inflation effects can have a considerable influence on a project's profitability, so inflation must be considered in any sound capital budgeting analysis. As discussed in chapter 9, a business's corporate cost of capital is based on its costs of debt and equity, which in turn are estimated on the basis of investors' required rates of return. Because investors must protect themselves against the loss of purchasing power as a result of inflation, they incorporate an inflation premium into their required returns. For example, a debt investor might require a 5 percent return on a 10-year bond in the absence of inflation. However, if inflation is expected to average 4 percent over the coming ten years, the investor would require a 9 percent return.

Because inflation effects are already embedded in the corporate cost of capital, and because this rate is the benchmark used to discount the cash flows in our profitability measures, it is necessary to ensure that inflation effects are also built into the project's estimated cash flows. If cash flow estimates do not include inflation effects (**real** cash flows), and a discount rate that does include inflation effects is used (**nominal** discount rate), the profitability of the project will be biased downward (understated).

The most effective way to deal with inflation is to build inflation effects into each cash flow component using the best available information about how each component will be affected. For example, per procedure reimbursement rates may be expected to increase at a 4 percent rate, labor costs may be expected to increase at an 8 percent rate, supply costs may be expected to increase at a 2 percent rate, and so on. Because it is impossible to estimate future inflation rates with much precision, inflation sometimes is assumed to be **neutral**—that is, inflation is assumed to affect all revenues and costs, except depreciation, equally. However, such an assumption rarely reflects the actual situation facing healthcare businesses. So, in general, different inflation rates should be applied to each cash flow component. Inflation adds to the uncertainty, or riskiness, of capital budgeting, as well as to its complexity. Fortunately, spreadsheet programs are available to help with inflation analysis, so the mechanics of inflation adjustments are not difficult.

Cash Flow Estimation Bias

As stated previously, cash flow estimation is the most critical, and the most difficult, part of the capital budgeting process. Cash flow components, such as volume and reimbursement rates, often must be forecast many years into the future, and estimation errors are bound to occur, some of which can be large. However, large businesses evaluate and accept many projects every year, and as long as cash flow estimates are unbiased and the errors are random, the estimation errors will tend to offset one another—that is, some cash flow estimates will be too high and some will be too low. However, in the aggregate for all projects, the realized cash flows will be close to the estimates, so realized total profitability will be close to that expected.

Unfortunately, there are strong indications that capital budgeting cash flow forecasts are not unbiased; rather, managers tend to be overly optimistic in their forecasts. As a result, revenues tend to be overstated and costs tend to be understated. The result is an upward bias in estimated profitability. This bias may occur because managers often are rewarded on the basis of the size of their divisions or departments, so they have an incentive to maximize the number of projects accepted rather than the profitability of the projects. Managers also may be emotionally attached to their projects and become unable to objectively assess a project's potential.

Top management can use two procedures to identify cash flow estimation bias. First, if a project is judged to be highly profitable as compared to the business's average project, this question should be asked: What is the underlying cause of this project's high profitability? If the business has some underlying advantage—such as a monopoly position in a managed care market or a superior reputation in providing a specific service, such as organ transplants—there may be a logical rationale supporting the high profitability. If no such factor can be identified, senior management should be concerned about the possibility of estimation bias. Even when these factors exist, the project's profitability will likely be eroded at some point in the future by competitive pressure from other businesses seeking to capture the high profitability inherent in the project.

Second, the postaudit process, which we discuss later in this chapter, will help to identify divisions and departments that habitually overstate or understate project profitability. (It is difficult to identify projects whose cash flows are understated because many of those projects will be rejected, and hence no cash flow comparisons can be made. When competing firms undertake projects of the type that are being rejected, we should be especially suspicious that underestimation bias is present.) Many firms now identify managers and divisions that typically submit biased cash flow estimates and compensate for this bias in the decision process by reducing cash inflows that are thought to be too rosy or by increasing the cost of capital to such projects.

Strategic Value

In the previous section, we discussed the problem of cash flow estimation bias, which can cause a project's profitability to be overstated. Another problem that can occur in cash flow estimation is underestimation of a project's true profitability. Underestimation results when a project's *strategic value*—the value of future investment opportunities that can be undertaken only if the project currently under consideration is accepted—is not recognized.

For example, consider a hospital management company analyzing a management contract for a hospital in Hungary, which would be its first move into Eastern Europe. On a stand-alone basis, this project might be unprofitable, but the project might provide entry into the Eastern European market, which would likely unlock the door to a whole range of highly profitable new projects. For another example, consider Ridgeland's decision to start a kidney transplant program. The financial analysis of this project showed the program to be unprofitable, but Ridgeland's managers considered kidney transplants to be the first step in an aggressive transplant program that would not only be profitable in itself but also enhance the hospital's reputation for technological and clinical excellence and thus contribute to the hospital's overall profitability.

In theory, the best approach to dealing with strategic value is to forecast the cash flows from follow-on projects, estimate their probabilities of occurrence, and then add the expected cash flows from the follow-on projects to the cash flows of the project under consideration. In practice, this is usually impossible to do—either the follow-on cash flows are too nebulous to forecast or the potential follow-on projects are too numerous to quantify. In most situations, the strategic value of a project stems from the **options** inherent in it. Thus, at a minimum, decision-makers must recognize that some projects have strategic value, and this value should be qualitatively considered when making capital budgeting decisions.

Strategic value is but one type of added value that arises when projects have embedded in them options that may or may not be exercised (taken advantage of) in the future. Options that are inherent in projects, as opposed to options on securities, are called *real*, or *managerial*, *options*. In the next chapter, we further discuss real options and their implications for a project's risk and value.

SELF-TEST QUESTION

1. Briefly discuss the following concepts associated with cash flow estimation:
   a. Incremental cash flow
   b. Cash flow versus accounting income
   c. Cash flow timing
   d. Project life
   e. Sunk costs
   f. Opportunity costs
   g. Effects on other projects
   h. Shipping and installation costs
   i. Changes in net working capital
   j. Inflation effects
   k. Cash flow estimation bias
   l. Strategic value

Cash Flow Estimation Example

On the web at: *ache.org/HAP/PinkSong8e*

Up to this point, we have discussed a number of key concepts related to cash flow estimation. In this section, we present an example that illustrates some of the concepts already covered and introduces several others that are important to good cash flow estimation.

The Basic Data

Consider the situation facing Ridgeland in its evaluation of a new MRI (magnetic resonance imaging) system. The system costs \$1.5 million, and the hospital would have to spend another \$1 million on shipping, site preparation, and installation. Because the system would be installed in the hospital, the space to be used has a very low, or zero, market value to outsiders, so no opportunity cost has been assigned to account for the value of the space.

The MRI site is estimated to generate weekly usage (volume) of 40 scans, and each scan would, on average, cost the hospital \$15 in supplies. The site is expected to operate 50 weeks per year, with the remaining two weeks devoted to maintenance. The estimated average charge per scan is \$500, but

25 percent of this amount, on average, is expected to be lost to indigent patients, contractual allowances, and bad-debt losses. Thus, the average net revenue expected from each scan is $375. Ridgeland's managers developed the project's forecasted revenues by conducting the revenue analysis contained in exhibit 11.1.

The MRI site would require two technicians, prompting an incremental increase in annual labor costs of $50,000, including fringe benefits. **Cash** overhead costs would increase by $10,000 annually if the MRI site is activated. The equipment would require maintenance, which would be furnished by the manufacturer for an annual fee of $150,000, payable at the end of each year of operation. For book (financial statement) purposes, the MRI site would be depreciated by the straight-line method over a five-year life.

The MRI site is expected to operate for five years, at which time the hospital's master plan calls for a brand-new imaging facility. The hospital plans to sell the MRI system at that time for an estimated $750,000 salvage value, net of removal costs. The inflation rate is estimated to average 5 percent over the period, and this rate is expected to apply to all revenues and costs except depreciation. Ridgeland's managers initially assume that projects under evaluation have average risk; thus, the hospital's 10 percent corporate cost of capital is the appropriate project cost of capital. In chapter 12, we demonstrate that a risk assessment of the project may indicate that a different cost of capital is appropriate.

EXHIBIT 11.1 Ridgeland Community Hospital: MRI Site Revenue Analysis

Payer	*Number of Scans per Week*	*Charge per Scan*	*Total Charges*	*Basis of Payment*	*Net Payment per Scan*	*Total Payments*
Medicare	10	$500	$ 5,000	Fixed fee	$370*	$ 3,700
Medicaid	5	500	2,500	Fixed fee	350*	1,750
Private insurance	9	500	4,500	Full charge	500	4,500
Blue Cross	5	500	2,500	% of charge	420*	2,100
Managed care	7	500	3,500	% of charge	390*	2,730
Self-pay	4	500	2,000	Full charge	55**	220
Total	40		$20,000			$15,000
Average			$ 500			$ 375

*Net of contractual allowances

**Net of bad-debt losses

Although the MRI project is expected to draw some patients from the hospital's other imaging systems, new MRI patients are expected to generate revenues for some of the hospital's other departments. On net, the two effects are expected to balance out—that is, the cash flow gain from other services used by the new MRI patients is expected to offset the cash flow loss from other imaging systems.

Cash Flow Analysis

The first step in the financial analysis is to estimate the MRI site's net cash flows. This analysis is presented in exhibit 11.2. Here are the key points of the analysis by line number:

- **Line 1**. Line 1 contains the estimated cost of the MRI system. In general, capital budgeting analyses assume that the first cash flow, normally an outflow, occurs at the end of year 0. Note that expenses, or cash outflows, are shown in parentheses.
- **Line 2**. The related shipping, site preparation, and installation expense—$1 million—is also assumed to occur at year 0.
- **Line 3**. Gross revenues = Weekly volume × Weeks of operation × Charge per scan = 40 × 50 × $500 = $1,000,000 in the first year. The 5 percent inflation rate is applied to all charges and costs that would likely be affected by inflation, so the gross revenue amount shown in line 3 increases by 5 percent over time. Although most of the operating revenues and costs would occur more or less evenly over the year, it is difficult to forecast exactly when most of the flows would occur. Furthermore, there is significant potential for large errors in cash flow estimation. For these reasons, operating cash flows are often assumed to occur at the end of each year.

  Also, we assume that the MRI system could be put into operation quickly. If this were not the case, the first year's operating flows would be reduced because it would be a partial year of operations. In some situations, it might take several years from the first cash outflow to the point where the project is operational and begins to generate operating cash inflows.
- **Line 4**. Deductions from charges are estimated to average 25 percent of gross revenues, so in Year 1, 0.25 × $1,000,000 = $250,000 of gross revenues would be uncollected. This amount increases each year by the 5 percent inflation rate.
- **Line 5**. Line 5 contains the net revenues in each year, line 3–line 4. An alternative format for the cash flow analysis would be to replace lines 3, 4, and 5 with a single line that shows Net revenues = Weekly volume × Weeks of operation × Net charge per scan, which for the first year would be 40 × 50 × $375 = $750,000.

EXHIBIT 11.2

Ridgeland Community Hospital: MRI Site Cash Flow Analysis

	Annual Cash Flows					
	0	*1*	*2*	*3*	*4*	*5*
1. System	($1,500,000)					
2. Related expenses	(1,000,000)					
3. Gross revenues		$1,000,000	$1,050,000	$1,102,500	$1,157, 625	$1,215,506
4. Deductions		250,000	262,500	275,625	289,406	303,877
5. Net revenues		$ 750,000	$ 787,500	$ 826,875	$ 868,219	$ 911,630
6. Labor costs		50,000	52,500	55,125	57,881	60,775
7. Maintenance costs		150,000	157,500	165,375	173,644	182,326
8. Supplies		30,000	31,500	33,075	34,729	36,465
9. Incremental overhead		10,000	10,500	11,025	11,576	12,155
10. Depreciation		350,000	350,000	350,000	350,000	350,000
11. Operating cash flow		$ 160,000	$ 185,500	$ 212,275	$ 240,389	$ 269,908
12. Taxes	0	0	0	0	0	0
13. Net operating cash flow		$ 160,000	$ 185,500	$ 212,275	$ 240,389	$ 269,908
14. Depreciation		350,000	350,000	350,000	350,000	350,000
15. Net salvage value						750,000
16. Net cash flow	($2,500,000)	$ 510,000	$ 535,500	$ 562,275	$ 590,389	$1,369,908

Note: Calculations are rounded.

- **Line 6**. Labor costs are forecasted to be $50,000 during the first year but will increase over time at the 5 percent inflation rate.
- **Line 7**. Maintenance fees must be paid to the manufacturer at the end of each year of operation. These fees are assumed to increase at the 5 percent inflation rate.
- **Line 8**. Each scan uses $15 of supplies, so supply costs in the first year total 40 × 50 × $15 = $30,000, which are expected to increase each year by the inflation rate.
- **Line 9**. If the project is accepted, overhead cash costs will increase by $10,000 in the first year. Note that the $10,000 in cash costs is related directly to the acceptance of the MRI project. Existing overhead costs that are arbitrarily allocated to the MRI site are not incremental cash flows and thus should not be included in the analysis. Overhead costs are also assumed to increase over time at the inflation rate.
- **Line 10**. For book purposes, depreciation in each year is calculated by the straight-line method, assuming a five-year depreciable life. The depreciable basis is equal to the capitalized cost of the project, which includes the cost of the asset and related expenses, less the estimated salvage value. Thus, the depreciable basis is ($1,500,000 + $1,000,000) – $750,000 = $1,750,000. Then, the straight-line depreciation in each year of the project's five-year depreciable life is (1 ÷ 5) × $1,750,000 = $350,000. Note that depreciation is based solely on acquisition costs, so it is unaffected by inflation. Also, note that the cash flows in exhibit 11.2 are presented in a generic format that can be used by both investor-owned and not-for-profit hospitals.

  Depreciation expense is not a cash flow but an accounting convention that prorates the cost of a long-term asset over its productive life. Because Ridgeland is tax exempt, depreciation will not affect taxes, and because depreciation is added back to the cash flows in line 14, depreciation can be totally omitted from the cash flow analysis.
- **Line 11**. Line 11 shows the project's operating cash flow in each year, which is merely net revenue less all operating expenses.
- **Line 12**. Line 12 contains zeros because Ridgeland is a not-for-profit hospital and hence does not pay taxes.
- **Line 13**. Ridgeland pays no taxes, so the project's net operating cash flow equals its operating cash flow.
- **Line 14**. Because depreciation—a noncash expense—was deducted in line 10, it must be added back to the project's net operating cash flow in each year to obtain each year's net cash flow.
- **Line 15**. Finally, the project is expected to be terminated after five years, at which time the MRI system will be sold for an estimated

$750,000. This salvage value cash flow is shown in line 15 as an inflow at the end of year 5.

- **Line 16**. The project's net cash flows are shown in line 16. The project requires a $2.5 million investment at year 0 but then generates cash inflows over its five-year operating life.

Note that the exhibit 11.2 cash flows do not include any allowance for interest expense. On average, Ridgeland will finance new projects in accordance with its target capital structure, which consists of 50 percent debt financing and 50 percent equity (fund) financing. The costs associated with this financing mix, including interest costs, are incorporated into Ridgeland's corporate cost of capital of 10 percent. Because the cost of debt financing is included in the discount rate that will be applied to the cash flows, we would be counting interest expense twice if we also incorporated it into the cash flow estimates.

The cash flow analysis in exhibit 11.2 can be easily modified to reflect tax implications if the analyzing firm is taxable. For example, assume that the MRI project is being evaluated by Ann Arbor Health Care Inc., an investor-owned hospital chain. Furthermore, assume that all of the project data presented earlier apply to Ann Arbor, except that (1) the MRI falls into the Modified Accelerated Cost Recovery System (MACRS) five-year class for tax depreciation and (2) the firm has a 30 percent tax rate. Exhibit 11.3 contains Ann Arbor's cash flow analysis. Note the following differences:

- **Line 10**. First, depreciation expense must be modified to reflect tax depreciation rather than book depreciation. As discussed in chapter 1, tax depreciation is calculated using the MACRS. To determine the MACRS depreciation allowance in any year, multiply the asset's depreciable basis (without considering its estimated salvage value) by the appropriate depreciation factor. In the MRI illustration, the depreciable basis is $2.5 million, and the MACRS factors for the five-year class are 0.20, 0.32, 0.19, 0.12, 0.11, and 0.06 in years 1 to 6, respectively. Thus, the tax depreciation in year 1 is 0.20 × $2,500,000 = $500,000; in year 2 the depreciation is 0.32 × $2,500,000 = $800,000; and so on.
- **Line 12**. Taxable businesses must reduce the operating cash flow in line 11 by the amount of taxes. Taxes, which appear in line 12, are computed by multiplying the pretax operating cash flow in line 11 by the business's marginal tax rate. For example, the project's taxes for year 1 are 0.30 × $10,000 = $3,000. Note that the taxes shown for year 2 are a negative $79,350. In this year, the project is expected to lose $264,500, so Ann Arbor's taxable income, assuming

its existing projects are profitable, will be reduced by this amount if the project is undertaken. This reduction in taxable income would lower the firm's tax bill by T × Taxable income reduction = 0.30 × \$264,500 = \$79,350.[1]

- **Line 14**. The MACRS depreciation amount, because it is a noncash expense, is added back on line 14.
- **Line 15**. Investor-owned firms normally incur a tax liability on the sale of a capital asset at the end of the project's life. According to the Internal Revenue System (IRS), the value of the MRI system at the end of year 5 is the *tax book value*, which is the depreciation that remains on the tax books. In the illustration, five years' worth of depreciation would be taken, so only one year of depreciation remains. The MACRS factor for year 6 is 0.06, so by the end of Year 5, Ann Arbor has expensed 0.94 of the MRI's depreciable basis and the remaining tax book value is 0.06 × \$2,500,000 = \$150,000. Thus, according to the IRS, the value of the MRI system is \$150,000. When Ann Arbor sells the system for its estimated salvage value of \$750,000, it realizes a "profit" of \$750,000 – \$150,000 = \$600,000 and must repay the IRS an amount equal to 0.3 × \$600,000 = \$180,000. The \$180,000 tax bill recognizes that Ann Arbor took too much depreciation on the MRI system, so it is a *recapture* of the excess tax benefit taken over the five-year life of the system. The \$180,000 in taxes reduces the cash received from the sale of the MRI equipment, so the salvage value net of taxes is \$750,000 – \$180,000 = \$570,000.

As can be seen by comparing line 16 in exhibits 11.2 and 11.3, all else the same, the taxes paid by investor-owned firms tend to reduce a project's net operating cash flows and net salvage value and hence reduce the project's profitability.

Replacement Analysis

We used Ridgeland's MRI project to illustrate how the cash flows from an *expansion project* are analyzed. All businesses, including Ridgeland, also make *replacement decisions*, which consider acquiring a new asset to replace an existing asset that could, if not replaced, continue in operation. The cash flow analysis for a replacement decision is somewhat more complex than that for an expansion decision because the cash flows from the existing asset must be considered.

Again, the key to cash flow estimation is to focus on the incremental cash flows. If the new asset is acquired, the existing asset can be sold, so the current market value of the existing asset is a cash inflow at time 0 in the analysis. The incremental flows are the cash flows expected from the replacement asset less the flows that the existing asset produces. By applying the

EXHIBIT 11.3

Ann Arbor Health Care: MRI Site Cash Flow Analysis

	Annual Cash Flows					
	0	*1*	*2*	*3*	*4*	*5*
1. System	($1,500,000)					
2. Related expenses	(1,000,000)					
3. Gross revenues		$1,000,000	$1,050,000	$1,102,500	$1,157, 625	$1,215,506
4. Deductions		250,000	262,500	275,625	289,406	303,877
5. Net revenues		$ 750,000	$ 787,500	$ 826,875	$ 868,219	$ 911,630
6. Labor costs		50,000	52,500	55,125	57,881	60,775
7. Maintenance costs		150,000	157,500	165,375	173,644	182,326
8. Supplies		30,000	31,500	33,075	34,729	36,465
9. Incremental overhead		10,000	10,500	11,025	11,576	12,155
10. Depreciation		500,000	800,000	475,000	300,000	275,000
11. Operating cash flow		$ 10,000	($ 264,500)	$ 87,275	$ 290,389	$ 344,908
12. Taxes		3,000	(79,350)	26,183	87,117	103,472
13. Net operating cash flow		$ 7,000	$ 185,150	$ 61,093	$ 203,272	$ 241,436
14. Depreciation		500,000	800,000	475,000	300,000	275,000
15. Net salvage value						570,000
16. Net cash flow	($2,500,000)	$ 507,000	$ 614,850	$ 536,093	$ 503,272	$1,086,436

incremental cash flow concept, we can estimate the correct cash flows for replacement decisions.

SELF-TEST QUESTIONS

1. Briefly describe how a project cash flow analysis is constructed.
2. Is it necessary to include depreciation expense in a cash flow analysis for a not-for-profit provider? Explain your answer.
3. What are the key differences between cash flow analyses performed by investor-owned and not-for-profit organizations?
4. How do expansion and replacement project analyses differ?

Breakeven Analysis

Breakeven analysis is used to gain insights into the potential profitability and risk of a project. Furthermore, breakeven analysis often is useful in evaluating operational decisions that do not require an initial capital investment, such as expanding the hours of a clinic. Although breakeven analysis can be applied in many different ways, we focus here on two types of breakeven: (1) utilization (volume) breakeven and (2) time breakeven (payback).

Utilization (Volume) Breakeven

For an illustration of utilization breakeven, first consider how it can be applied to operating cash flows. Specifically, we can examine operating breakeven in year 1. From exhibit 11.2, we know that 40 scans per week would produce a net cash flow in year 1 of $510,000. How many scans per week would be necessary to reach operating breakeven in year 1? In other words, how many scans per week are required to generate a positive net cash flow in year 1? Exhibit 11.4 contains the year 1 net cash flow at different utilization levels. As indicated by the data, the project breaks even in year 1 if the hospital performs 12 scans per week. Of course, the actual analysis typically would be performed using a spreadsheet model.

Utilization breakeven can also be applied to the entire project. Here, we want to know the answer to this question: What weekly utilization would allow the hospital to break even economically—that is, to recover all of the costs associated with the project, including capital costs? When the analysis is modeled on a spreadsheet, answers to these types of questions are easy to obtain. As we discuss in a later section, economic breakeven occurs when a project's net present value equals zero or just turns positive. In Ridgeland's MRI project, economic breakeven occurs at a weekly volume of 39 scans, so the project in its entirety just breaks even when the hospital averages 39 scans

EXHIBIT 11.4
Ridgeland Community Hospital: MRI Site Year 1 Breakeven Analysis

Number of Scans per Week	*Year 1 Net Cash Flow*
0	($210,000)
5	(120,000)
10	(30,000)
11	(12,000)
12	6,000
13	24,000
14	42,000
15	60,000
20	150,000
30	330,000
40	510,000

per week over the five-year forecasted life of the project. Such information is clearly useful to Ridgeland's managers. If they feel strongly that utilization will exceed 39 scans per week, it is highly likely that the project will be economically profitable. Conversely, if they believe that utilization will be less than the breakeven level, the project will probably be unprofitable. Also, if, as in this situation, the projected volume is just above breakeven, a small forecasting error can make a project appear profitable on paper when, in reality, it would be unprofitable if undertaken.

This type of breakeven analysis can be applied to cash flow inputs other than volume. For example, it would be useful for Ridgeland's managers to know the project's breakeven salvage value. Using a spreadsheet, we can easily use trial and error (or even more easily use Excel's Goal Seek capability) to find the economic breakeven point for salvage value: about $617,000. Thus, even if the MRI is worth only $617,000 at the end of five years as opposed to the actual estimate of $750,000, the project remains financially worthwhile (or at least neutral).

Time Breakeven (Payback)

The ***payback***, or ***payback period***, measures time breakeven. Payback is defined as the expected number of years required to recover the investment in the project. For an illustration, consider the net cash flows for the MRI project contained in exhibit 11.2. The best way to determine the project's payback is to construct the project's cumulative cash flows as shown in exhibit 11.5. Here, the cumulative cash flow in each year is the sum of the annual cash flows up to and including that year. For example, the cumulative cash flow in year 2 is –$2,500,000 + $510,000 + $535,500 = –$1,454,500.

EXHIBIT 11.5
Ridgeland Community Hospital: MRI Site Cumulative Cash Flows

Year	*Annual Cash Flow*	*Cumulative Cash Flow*
0	($2,500,000)	($2,500,000)
1	510,000	(1,990,000)
2	535,500	(1,454,500)
3	562,275	(892,225)
4	590,389	(301,836)
5	1,369,908	1,068,072

Payback = 4 + $301,836 ÷ $1,369,908 = 4.22 years.

Because the cumulative cash flows turn positive in year 5, the $2.5 million investment in the MRI site would be recovered some time during year 5. If the project's cash flows are assumed to come in evenly during the year, breakeven would occur $301,836 ÷ $1,369,908 = 0.22 of the way through year 5, so the payback is 4.22 years.

Many years ago, managers used payback as the primary financial evaluation tool in project analyses. For example, a business might accept all projects with paybacks of less than five years. However, payback has two serious deficiencies when it is used as a project selection criterion. First, payback ignores all cash flows that occur after the payback period. For example, assume that Ridgeland is evaluating a competing project that has the same cash flows as the MRI project in years 0 through 5. However, the alternative project has a cash inflow of $2 million in year 6. Both projects would have the same payback, 4.22 years, and hence be ranked the same, even though the alternative project clearly is better from a financial perspective. Second, payback ignores the opportunity costs associated with the capital employed. For these reasons, payback generally is no longer used as the primary evaluation tool.

However, payback is useful in capital investment analysis. The shorter the payback, the more quickly the funds invested in a project become available for redeployment in the organization, and hence the more liquid the project. Also, cash flows expected in the distant future are generally more difficult to forecast than near-term cash flows, so projects with shorter paybacks generally are less risky than those with longer paybacks. Therefore, payback is often used as a rough measure of a project's *liquidity* and *risk*.

Another measure, the ***discounted payback***, is similar to the "regular" payback, except that the cash flows in each year are discounted by the project's cost of capital before the payback is calculated. Thus, discounted payback solves the regular payback's problem of not considering the project's cost of capital in the payback calculation. For an illustration of discounted payback, consider exhibit 11.6. Here, we have created a new column labeled

EXHIBIT 11.6
Ridgeland Community Hospital: MRI Site Cumulative Discounted Cash Flows

Year	*Annual Cash Flow*	*Discounted Cash Flow*	*Cumulative Discounted Cash Flow*
0	($2,500,000)	($2,500,000)	($2,500,000)
1	510,000	463,636	(2,036,364)
2	535,500	442,562	(1,593,802)
3	562,275	422,446	(1,171,356)
4	590,389	403,244	(768,112)
5	1,369,908	850,605	82,493

Discounted payback = 4 + 768,112 ÷ 850,605 = 4.90 years.

Discounted Cash Flow. Each entry in this column is the matching annual cash flow discounted at the 10 percent cost of capital for the number of years it occurs into the future. For example, the discounted year 2 cash flow is $\$535,500 \div (1.10)^2 = \$442,562$. The discounted payback is 4 + (768,112 ÷ 850,605) = 4.90 years. Because time value is recognized in the discounted payback, it is longer than the regular payback of 4.22 years.

SELF-TEST QUESTIONS

1. Why is breakeven information valuable to decision-makers?
2. Describe several types of breakeven analysis.
3. What is the difference between regular payback and discounted payback?

Return on Investment Analysis

Up to this point, the chapter has focused on cash flow estimation and breakeven analysis. Perhaps the most important element in a project's financial analysis is expected profitability, which generally is assessed by ***return on investment (ROI)*** measured either in dollars or in percentage rate of return. In the next sections, we present one dollar measure (net present value) and two rate-of-return measures (internal rate of return, modified internal rate of return).

Net Present Value

Net present value (NPV) is a profitability measure that uses the discounted cash flow (DCF) techniques discussed in chapter 4, so it is often referred to as a *DCF measure.* To apply the NPV method, we proceed as follows:

- Find the present (time 0) value of each net cash flow, including inflows and outflows, discounted at the project cost of capital.
- Sum the present values. This sum is the project's NPV.
- If the NPV is positive, the project is profitable, and the higher the NPV, the more profitable the project. If the NPV is zero, the project breaks even in terms of profit. If the NPV is negative, the project is unprofitable.

Assuming a project cost of capital of 10 percent, the NPV of Ridgeland's MRI project is calculated as follows:

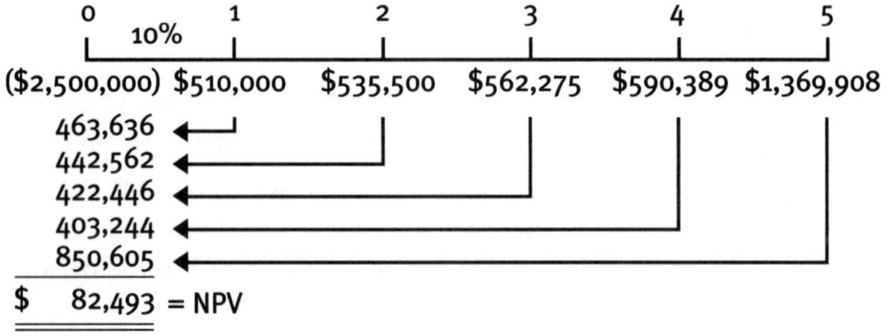

Spreadsheets have NPV functions that easily perform the mathematics given the cash flows and cost of capital.[2] Here is one example of a spreadsheet calculation for the project:

	A	B	C	D
1				
2	10.0%		Project cost of capital	
3	$(2,500,000)		Cash flow 0	
4	510,000		Cash flow 1	
5	535,500		Cash flow 2	
6	562,275		Cash flow 3	
7	590,389		Cash flow 4	
8	1,369,908		Cash flow 5	
9				
10	$82,493	=NPV(A2,A4:A8)+A3 (entered into cell A10)		

Note that we have merely entered the net cash flows into the spreadsheet. In a typical project analysis, the spreadsheet would be used for the entire cash flow analysis, with the last line of the cash flows being the net cash flows. The project's NPV is calculated in cell A10 using the NPV function. The first entry in the function (A2) is the discount rate (project cost of capital), while the second entry (A4:A8) designates the range of cash flows from years 1 through 5. Because the NPV function calculates NPV one period before the first cash flow entered in the range, it is necessary to start the range with year 1 rather than year 0. Finally, to complete the calculation in cell A10, A3 (the initial outlay) is added to the NPV function. The end result—$82,493—is displayed in cell A10.

The rationale behind the NPV method is straightforward. An NPV of zero signifies that the project's cash inflows are just sufficient to (1) return the capital invested in the project and (2) provide the required rate of return on that invested capital. In other words, the project just breaks even in an economic sense, which considers **all costs** associated with the employment of capital. If a project has a positive NPV, it is generating excess cash flows, and these excess cash flows are available to management to reinvest in the firm and, for investor-owned firms, to pay bonuses or dividends. In investor-owned businesses, NPV is a direct measure of the project's contribution to owners' wealth. If a project has a negative NPV, its cash inflows are insufficient to compensate the business for the capital invested or perhaps will not ever recover the invested capital, so the project is unprofitable and acceptance would cause the financial condition of the business to deteriorate.

The NPV of the MRI project is $82,493, so on a present value basis the project is projected to generate a cash flow excess of more than $80,000. Thus, the project is economically profitable, and its acceptance would have a positive impact on Ridgeland's financial condition.

Internal Rate of Return

Whereas NPV measures a project's dollar profitability, ***internal rate of return (IRR)***—which is another DCF profitability measure—measures a project's percentage profitability or expected rate of return. Mathematically, the IRR is defined as the discount rate that equates the present value of the project's expected cash inflows to the present value of the project's expected cash outflows, so the IRR is simply the discount rate that forces the NPV of the project to equal zero.

For Ridgeland's MRI project, the IRR is the discount rate that causes the sum of the present values of the cash inflows to equal the $2.5 million cost of the project:

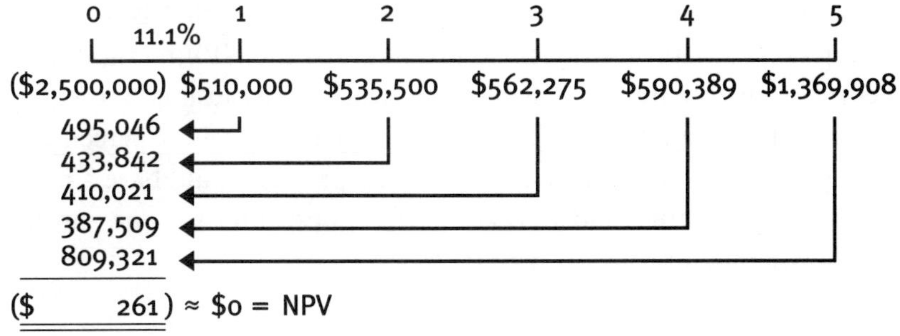

When all of the MRI project's cash flows are discounted at 11.1 percent, the NPV of the project is approximately zero. Thus, the MRI project's IRR is 11.1 percent. Put another way, the project is expected to generate an 11.1 percent rate of return on its $2.5 million investment.

Spreadsheets have IRR functions that calculate IRRs rapidly. Simply input the project's cash flows into the spreadsheet and compute the IRR:

	A	B	C	D
1				
2	$(2,500,000)		Cash flow 0	
3	510,000		Cash flow 1	
4	535,500		Cash flow 2	
5	562,275		Cash flow 3	
6	590,389		Cash flow 4	
7	1,369,908		Cash flow 5	
8				
9	11.1%	=IRR(A2:A7) (entered into cell A9)		

The entry in the IRR function (A2:A7) specifies the range of cash flows to be used in the spreadsheet calculation. The answer—11.1 percent—is displayed in cell A9.

If the IRR exceeds the project cost of capital, a surplus remains after recovering the invested capital and paying for its use, and this surplus accrues to the firm's stockholders (in Ridgeland's case, to its stakeholders). On the other hand, if the IRR is less than the project cost of capital, taking on the project imposes a cost on the firm's stockholders or stakeholders. The MRI project's 11.1 percent IRR exceeds the project's 10 percent cost of capital. Thus, as measured by the IRR, the MRI project is profitable and its acceptance would enhance Ridgeland's financial condition.

Comparison of the NPV and IRR Methods

Consider a project with a zero NPV. In this situation, the project's IRR must equal its cost of capital. The project has zero profitability, and acceptance would neither enhance nor diminish the firm's financial condition. To have a positive NPV, the project must have an IRR that is greater than its cost of capital; a negative NPV signifies a project with an IRR that is less than its cost of capital. Thus, projects deemed profitable by the NPV method will also be deemed profitable by the IRR method. In the MRI example, the project would have a positive NPV for all costs of capital less than 11.1 percent. If the cost of capital is greater than 11.1 percent, the project would have a negative NPV. In effect, the NPV and IRR are perfect substitutes for one another in estimating whether a project is profitable.

Modified Internal Rate of Return

In general, academics prefer the NPV profitability measure. This preference stems from two factors: (1) NPV measures profitability in dollars, which is a direct measure of the project's contribution to the value of the business, and (2) both the NPV and IRR methods—because they are discounted cash flow techniques—require an assumption about the rate at which project cash flows can be reinvested, and the NPV method has the better assumption.

To better understand the second point, consider the MRI project's year 2 net cash flow of $535,500, as shown in exhibit 11.2. The discounting process inherent in the NPV and IRR methods automatically assigns a reinvestment rate to this cash flow—that is, both the NPV and IRR methods assume that Ridgeland has an opportunity to reinvest the $535,500 year 2 cash flow in other projects, and each method automatically assigns a reinvestment rate to this flow for years 3, 4, and 5. The NPV method assumes reinvestment at the project cost of capital (10 percent), while the IRR method assumes reinvestment at the IRR rate (11.1 percent). Which is the better assumption—reinvestment at the cost of capital or reinvestment at the IRR rate? Typically, a business will take on all projects that exceed its cost of capital. Thus, at the margin, the returns from capital reinvested in the firm are more likely to be at, or close to, the cost of capital than at the project's IRR, especially for projects with exceptionally high or low IRRs. Furthermore, a business can obtain outside capital at a cost roughly equal to the cost of capital, so cash flows generated by a project could be replaced by capital having this cost. Thus, in general, reinvestment at the cost of capital is a better assumption than reinvestment at the IRR rate, so NPV is theoretically a better measure of profitability than IRR.[3]

Though academics strongly favor the NPV method, practicing managers

> ### Accounting Rate of Return
>
> The *accounting rate of return (ARR)* uses accounting information to measure the profitability of an investment. Although there are alternative ways of performing the calculation, the generic formula is as follows:
>
> Accounting rate of return =
> Average net profit ÷ Average investment.
>
> Here, both profit and investment are measured in accounting terms and averaged over the life of the project. For example, a five-year project that cost $100,000 and has a zero salvage value would have an average investment of $100,000 ÷ 5 = $20,000. If the aggregate profit over the five years was forecast to be $25,000, the average annual net profit would be $5,000. Thus, the project's ARR would be $5,000 ÷ $20,000 = 25%.
>
> Proponents of the ARR cite the following advantages:
>
> 1. It is simple to use and understand.
> 2. It can be readily calculated from accounting data, unlike NPV and IRR.
> 3. It incorporates the entire stream of income as opposed to looking at only a single year.
>
> What is your opinion of the ARR? Does it have any weaknesses compared to NPV and IRR? Should healthcare organizations use ARR to make capital budgeting decisions?

prefer the IRR method because it is more intuitive for most people to analyze investments in terms of percentage rates of return than dollars of NPV. Thus, an alternative rate of return measure has been developed that eliminates the primary problem with the IRR method. This measure is the ***modified internal rate of return (MIRR)***, and it is calculated as follows:

- Discount all the project's net cash outflows back to year 0 at the project cost of capital. This value is called the ***present value of costs.***
- Compound all the project's net cash inflows forward to the last (terminal) year of the project, at the project cost of capital. This value is called the ***inflow terminal value.***
- The discount rate that forces the present value of the inflow terminal value to equal the present value of costs is defined as the MIRR.

Applying these steps to Ridgeland's MRI project produces a MIRR of about 10.7 percent:

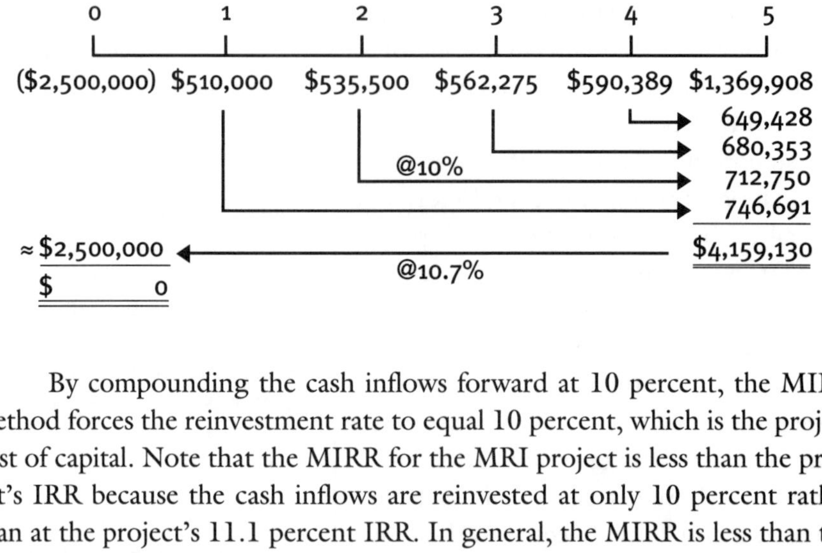

By compounding the cash inflows forward at 10 percent, the MIRR method forces the reinvestment rate to equal 10 percent, which is the project cost of capital. Note that the MIRR for the MRI project is less than the project's IRR because the cash inflows are reinvested at only 10 percent rather than at the project's 11.1 percent IRR. In general, the MIRR is less than the IRR when the IRR is greater than the cost of capital, but it is greater than the IRR when the IRR is less than the cost of capital. In effect, the IRR overstates the profitability of profitable projects and understates the profitability of unprofitable projects. By forcing the correct reinvestment rate, the MIRR method provides decision-makers with a theoretically better measure of a project's expected rate of return than does the IRR.

Here is the spreadsheet solution for MIRR:

	A	B	C	D
1				
2	10.0%		Project cost of capital	
3	$(2,500,000)		Cash flow 0	
4	510,000		Cash flow 1	
5	535,500		Cash flow 2	
6	562,275		Cash flow 3	
7	590,389		Cash flow 4	
8	1,369,908		Cash flow 5	
9				
10	10.7%	=MIRR(A3:A8,A2,A2) (entered into cell 10)		

The MIRR function was placed in cell A10. The first entry in the function (A3:A8) is the range of cash flows, while the next two entries (A2,A2) are the project cost of capital. (The MIRR function allows the reinvestment rate to differ from the project cost of capital: The first of the two entries is the project cost of capital, and the second is the reinvestment rate. For our purposes, the two rates are the same.) The resulting MIRR—10.7 percent—is displayed in cell A10.

In closing our discussion, note that use of the MIRR method has another advantage over the IRR method besides calculating the proper reinvestment rate. Primarily, it is not subject to the problems that might occur when a project has **nonnormal** cash flows. A project with normal cash flows has one or more outflows followed by one or more inflows, while one with nonnormal cash flows has outflows occurring after one or more inflows have occurred. In the nonnormal situation, it is possible for a project to have two IRRs or even to have no IRR. These unusual results occur because of the mathematics of the IRR calculation. Because the MIRR calculation is not subject to these problems, it is the only rate-of-return measure available for some projects.

SELF-TEST QUESTIONS

1. Briefly describe how to calculate NPV, IRR, and MIRR.
2. Explain the rationale behind each method.
3. Why is MIRR a better rate-of-return measure than IRR?
4. Do the three methods lead to the same conclusions regarding project profitability? Explain your answer.

Some Final Thoughts on Breakeven and Profitability Analysis

We have presented several approaches to breakeven analysis and three profitability measures. In the course of our discussion, we purposely compared the methods against one another to highlight their relative strengths and weaknesses, but in the process we may have created the impression that businesses would use only one method in the decision process. Today, virtually all capital budgeting decisions of financial consequence are analyzed by computer; hence, it is easy to calculate and list numerous breakeven measures along with NPV, IRR, and MIRR. Because each measure contributes slightly different information about the financial consequences of a project, it would be foolish for decision makers to focus on a single financial measure. Thus, we believe that a thorough financial analysis of a new project should include numerous financial measures and that capital budgeting decisions are enhanced if all the information inherent in all of the measures is considered.

However, just as it would be foolish to ignore any of the quantitative measures, it would also be foolish to base capital budgeting decisions solely on these measures. The uncertainties in the cash flow estimates for many projects are such that the resulting quantitative measures can be viewed only as rough estimates. Furthermore, organizational missions and strategic factors are important elements in capital budgeting decision-making. Thus, qualitative factors should play an important role in the decision process. (We discuss one approach, project scoring, in a later section.)

Finally, as mentioned, managers should be cautious of potential projects that have high expected profitability. In a highly competitive environ ment, there would be no highly profitable projects available because the marketplace would have already identified these opportunities and taken advantage of them. Thus, high-profitability projects must have some underlying rationale, such as market dominance or innovation, that justifies the profitability. Even then, under most circumstances, the project's high profitability will be eroded over time by competition.

SELF-TEST QUESTIONS

1. Should capital budgeting analyses look at only one breakeven or profitability measure? Explain.
2. Why should qualitative factors also play a role in capital budgeting decisions?
3. Why should projects that have high expected profitability be viewed with some skepticism?

Evaluating Projects with Unequal Lives

On the web at: *ache.org/HAP/PinkSong8e*

On occasion, businesses must choose between two ***mutually exclusive projects*** that have unequal lives. (Two projects are mutually exclusive when acceptance of one implies rejection of the other.) When this situation arises, if the project with the shorter life will be replicated in the future, an adjustment to the normal capital budgeting process is necessary. We now discuss two procedures—(1) the replacement chain method and (2) the equivalent annual annuity method—to illustrate the problem and show how to deal with it.

Suppose American Dental Equipment Corporation is planning to modernize its production facilities and, as part of the process, is considering either installing a conveyor system (project C) or using forklift trucks (project F) to move materials from the parts department to the main assembly line. Exhibit 11.7 shows the expected net cash flows and the NPVs for these two mutually exclusive alternatives. We see that project C, when discounted at the firm's 11.5 percent corporate cost of capital, has the higher NPV and thus appears to be the more profitable project.

Replacement Chain (Common Life) Method

Although the analysis in exhibit 11.7 suggests that project C is the more profitable project, the analysis is incomplete and this conclusion is actually incorrect. If the firm chooses project F, it will have an opportunity to make a similar investment in three years, and if cost and revenue conditions continue at the exhibit 11.7 levels, this second, or replication, investment will also be profitable. However, if the firm chooses project C, it will not have this second investment opportunity. Therefore, to make a proper comparison between the three-year and six-year projects, we can apply the ***replacement chain (common life)*** method—that is, find the extended NPV of project F over a

EXHIBIT 11.7 Expected Net Cash Flows for Projects C and F

Year	*Project C*	*Project F*
0	($40,000)	($20,000)
1	8,000	7,000
2	14,000	13,000
3	13,000	12,000
4	12,000	—
5	11,000	—
6	10,000	—
NPV @ 11.5%	$ 7,165	$ 5,391

six-year period by assuming the project will be replicated, and then compare this extended NPV with the NPV of project C over the same period.

The NPV for project C, as calculated in exhibit 11.7, is already over the six-year common life. For project F, however, we must take three additional steps: (1) determine the NPV of the replication project three years hence, (2) discount this NPV back to the present, and (3) sum the two components to obtain the project's extended NPV. If we assume that the replication project will have the same cash flows as the original project, then project F's extended NPV is $9,280:

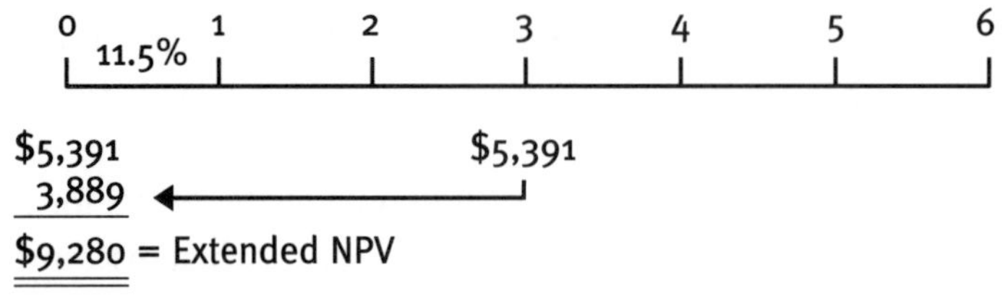

Because project F's six-year (extended) NPV is greater than project C's six-year NPV, project F is more profitable when the opportunity to replicate the project is considered. Note that this time line analysis uses NPVs to summarize project F's estimated cash flows. An alternative approach to the analysis is to place the annual cash flows on the time line:

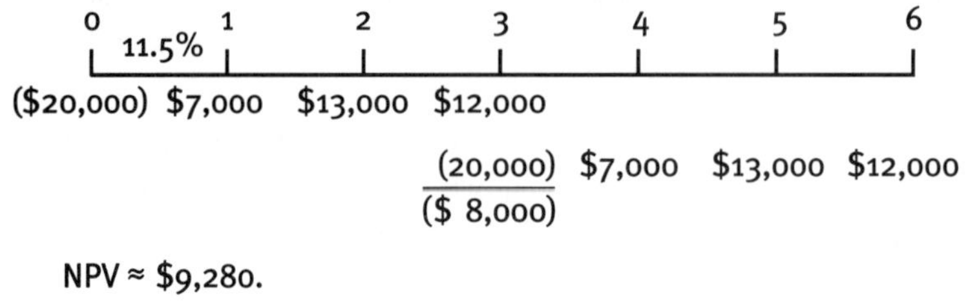

Clearly, the former method is simpler. However, if the cash flows for the replicated project are not the same as the cash flows for the initial project, the more complex individual cash flow method must be used. By showing each cash flow, the analysis can accommodate changes in project cash flows that are expected to occur when the project is replicated.

Equivalent Annual Annuity Method

Although the preceding example illustrates why an extended approach is necessary if two mutually exclusive projects with different lives are being analyzed, the analysis is generally more complex in practice. For example, one project might have a six-year life and the other a ten-year life. This comparison would require a replacement chain analysis over 30 years, which is the lowest common multiple of the two lives. In such a situation, it is simpler to use the *equivalent annual annuity (EAA)* approach.

The EAA method involves three steps:

1. Find each project's NPV over its original life. In exhibit 11.7, we see that NPV_C = \$7,165 and NPV_F = \$5,391.
2. For each project, find the annuity (constant value) cash flow over the project's original life that has the same present value as the project's NPV. This cash flow is the EAA. Here is the concept shown on a time line for project F:

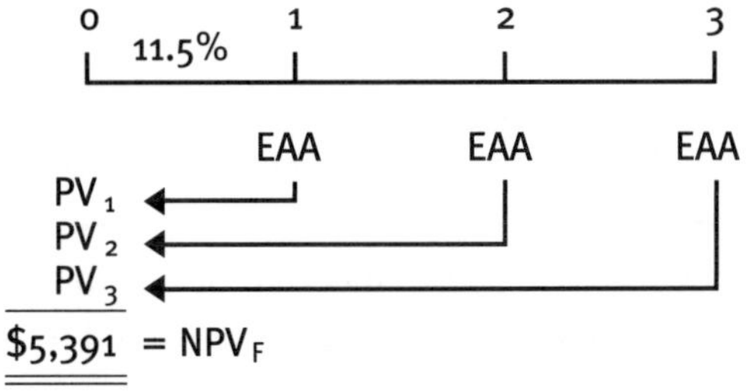

   To find the value of EAA_F on a financial calculator, enter 5,391 (or −5,391) as the PV, I = 11.5, and N = 3. Then, solve for payment (PMT), which turns out to be 2,225. Thus, the EAA for project F is \$2,225. When discounted at the project cost of capital (11.5 percent), this annuity stream over the original life of the project (three years) has a present value equal to project F's NPV (\$5,391). The EAA for project C—\$1,718—is calculated in a similar manner. Thus, project C has an NPV that is equivalent to an annuity of \$1,718 per year for six years, while project F's NPV is equivalent to an annuity of \$2,225 for three years.
3. Now, when projects are replicated—assuming that the cash flows remain the same—they earn the same NPV over and over, which is equivalent to replicating the project's EAA over time. Thus, over any common life, whether 6 years or 30 years, the project with the higher EAA will have the higher NPV because its equivalent cash flow will be higher in every year. Because project F has the higher EAA, under the assumption of constant cash flow replication it is more profitable than project C.

The EAA method is generally easier to apply, but the replacement chain method is often easier to explain to decision-makers. Still, the two methods always lead to the same results if consistent assumptions are used.

When should managers worry about unequal life analysis? As a general rule, the unequal life issue does not arise for independent projects; it is an issue only when mutually exclusive projects are being analyzed. However, even for mutually exclusive projects, it is not always appropriate to extend the analysis to a common life. Extension should be done only if there is a high probability that the projects will be replicated beyond their original lives.

Several weaknesses are inherent in the types of analyses just described. First, if inflation is expected, replacement cost will probably be higher than the initial cost and both revenues and operating costs will probably rise, so the static conditions built into the example would not be appropriate. Second, future replacements may use different technologies, which might also change the project's replication cash flows. Third, it is difficult enough to estimate the lives of most projects, so estimations of the lives of a future series of projects are often just speculation.

In view of these problems, no experienced manager would be too concerned about comparing mutually exclusive projects with lives of, say, eight years and ten years. Given all of the uncertainties in the estimation process, such projects can, for all practical purposes, be assumed to have the same life. Still, it is important to recognize that a problem does exist if mutually exclusive projects that will be replicated have substantially different lives. When the managers of Ann Arbor encounter such problems, they build expected inflation, possible efficiency gains, or both directly into the cash flow estimates and then use the replacement chain approach to estimate the projects' extended NPVs. The cash flow estimation is more complicated than in our example, but the concepts involved are the same.

SELF-TEST QUESTIONS

1. Is it always necessary to adjust project cash flows to account for unequal lives?
2. Briefly describe the two methods for adjusting for unequal lives.

Economic Life Versus Physical Life (Abandonment Value)

Customarily, projects are analyzed as though the business will operate the project over its full *physical life*. However, full-life operation may not be the best course of action financially; it may be best to terminate a project before the end of its potential life because doing so can materially affect a project's estimated profitability. Termination of a project before the end of its physical life is called *abandonment*, and the key to making this decision is a project's *abandonment value*. For example, consider Ridgeland's proposal to establish a taxable medical transportation division that would offer specialized medical transportation services to Ridgeland's patients and others in the community. The project's cash flows are contained in exhibit 11.8. For simplicity, we have shortened the physical life of the project to three years. The project's investment and operating cash flows are shown in the second column, while the third column contains the project's abandonment values. Abandonment values are equivalent to net salvage values, except they have been estimated for each year of the project's physical life.

Using a 10 percent cost of capital, the NPV over the project's three-year physical life, with zero abandonment value, is –\$11,743. Thus, the project is unprofitable when the single alternative of a three-year life with a zero salvage value is considered. However, what would its NPV be if the project were abandoned after two years? In this situation, Ridgeland would receive operating cash flows for two years, plus the \$190,000 abandonment value at the end of year 2, and the project's NPV would be \$13,802. Thus, the project is profitable if Ridgeland operates it for only two years and then sells it. To complete the abandonment analysis, note that if the project were abandoned after one year, its NPV would be –\$25,455.

The *economic life* of the project, which is the life that produces the highest economic value (NPV), is two years. As a general rule, if profitability were the sole criterion in capital budgeting decisions, a project should be abandoned when the net abandonment value is greater than the present value of all cash flows beyond the abandonment point (discounted to the abandonment point). For example, if Ridgeland were to operate the division for one year, the abandonment value at that point would be \$300,000, but the present value at year 1 of the cash flows beyond year 1 would be \$187,500 $\div (1.10)^1$ + \$190,000 $\div (1.10)^1$ = \$343,182, assuming abandonment at the end of year 2. The year 1 abandonment value is less than the year 1 present value of continuing the project, so the project should not be abandoned at this point. However, a similar analysis at the end of year 2 shows that the

EXHIBIT 11.8
Medical Transportation Division's Projected Cash Flows

Year	*Initial Investment and Operating Cash Flows*	*End of Year Net Abandonment Value*	*NPV if Abandoned at the End of the Year Listed*
0	(\$480,000)	\$480,000	\$ 0
1	200,000	300,000	(25,455)
2	187,500	190,000	13,802
3	175,000	0	(11,743)

Note: The project cost of capital is 10 percent.

abandonment value would be greater than the discounted value of future cash flows, so abandonment at year 2 would produce the greater profitability. This conclusion is the same that we reached when calculating the NPVs of each possible project life. In essence, the abandonment decision involves comparing the abandonment cash flows to the cash flows associated with continuing the project to determine the most profitable course of action.

In this illustration, we examined the concept of abandonment by looking at a project in its initial evaluation stage. However, project performance should be examined on a regular basis, and those that are not meeting financial goals should, if feasible, be abandoned. (Project performance is reviewed in the postaudit process, which we discuss in a later section.) Once a project is up and running, two different types of abandonment can occur: (1) sale by a business of a still-valuable product or service line because some other party can operate the line more efficiently and (2) abandonment of a product or service line because it is losing money.

The first type can be illustrated by Ridgeland's sale of its two walk-in clinics to a physician group. Although the clinics were profitable to Ridgeland, the physician group could presumably operate them more efficiently and hence was willing to pay the hospital a premium over the value the clinics would have if they remained under hospital control.

The second type of abandonment can be illustrated by Northeast Medical Health Plan's decision to discontinue its HMO (health maintenance organization) operation in Boston. Although Northeast's GoodHealth plan had proved profitable in several areas, competition in the Boston market proved destructive, so the firm decided to cut its losses.

SELF-TEST QUESTIONS

1. Define economic life, as opposed to physical life.
2. Should projects be viewed as having one fixed life, or should they be considered as having alternative lives?

Capital Budgeting in Not-for-Profit Businesses

Although the capital budgeting techniques discussed up to this point are appropriate for use by both investor-owned and not-for-profit businesses, a not-for-profit business has the additional consideration of meeting its charitable mission. In this section, we discuss two models that extend the capital budgeting decision to not-for-profit firms.

Except for the discussion of strategic value, the financial analysis techniques discussed so far have focused exclusively on the cash flow implications of a proposed project. Some healthcare businesses, particularly not-for-profit providers, have the goal of producing social services along with commercial services. For such firms, the proper analysis of proposed projects must systematically consider the *social value* of a project along with its pure financial, or cash flow, value.

When social value is considered, the *total net present value (TNPV)* of a project can be expressed as follows:

Key Equation 11.1: Net Present Social Value Model

$$TNPV = NPV + NPSV.$$

Here, NPV represents the conventional NPV of the project's cash flow stream and NPSV is the *net present social value* of the project. The NPSV term, which represents managers' assessment of the social value of the project in dollar terms, clearly differentiates capital budgeting in not-for-profit firms from that in investor-owned firms (Wheeler and Clement 1990).

In evaluating each project, a project is acceptable if its TNPV is greater than or equal to zero. In other words, the sum of the project's financial and social values is at least zero, so when both facets of value are considered, the project has positive (or at least nonnegative) worth. Not all projects will have social value, but if a project does, it is considered formally in this decision model. However, no project should be accepted if its NPSV is negative, even if its TNPV is positive. Furthermore, to ensure the financial viability of the business, the sum of the NPVs of all projects initiated in a planning period must equal or exceed zero. If this restriction were not imposed, social value could displace financial value over time, and a firm cannot continue to provide social value without maintaining financial integrity.

NPSV is the sum of the present (year 0) values of each year's social value. In essence, the suppliers of fund capital to a not-for-profit firm never receive a cash return on their investment. Instead, they receive a return on their investment in the form of social dividends. These dividends take the form of services with social value to the community, such as charity care, medical research and education, and myriad other services that (for one reason or another) do not pay their own way. A service provided to a patient at a price equal to or greater than its cost does not create social value. Similarly, if governmental entities purchase care directly for beneficiaries of a program or support research, the resulting social value is created by the payer and not by the provider of the services.

In estimating a project's NPSV, first it is necessary to estimate the social value of the services provided by the project in each year and to determine the discount rate to apply to those services. When a project provides services to individuals who are willing and able to pay for those services, the value of those services is captured by the amount they actually pay. Thus, the value of the services provided to those who cannot pay—or to those who cannot pay the full amount—can be estimated by the average net price paid by the individuals who are able to pay. This approach to valuing social services has intuitive appeal, but certain points merit further discussion:

- Price is a fair measure of value only if the payer has the capacity to judge the true value of the service provided. Many observers of the health services field would argue that information asymmetries between the provider and the purchaser inhibit the purchaser's ability to judge true value.
- Because most payments for healthcare services are made by third-party payers, price distortions may result. For example, insurers may be willing to pay more for services than an individual would pay in the absence of insurance, or the existence of monopsony power by Medicare may result in a net price that is less than individuals would be willing to pay.
- A great deal of controversy exists over the true value of treatment in many situations. Suppose that some people are entitled to whatever healthcare is available, regardless of cost, and are not required to pay for the care personally. Even though society as a whole must cover the bill, people may demand a level of care that is of questionable value. For example, should $500,000 be spent to keep a comatose 92-year-old patient alive for a few more days? If the true value of such expenditure is zero, assigning a $500,000 value just because that is its cost makes little sense.

Despite these potential problems, it still seems reasonable to assign a social value to many—but not all—healthcare services on the basis of the price that others are willing to pay for those services.

The second requirement to estimating the NPSV of a project is to apply the discount rate to the annual social value stream. Like the required rate of return on equity for not-for-profit firms, there has been considerable controversy over the proper discount rate to apply to future social values. However, contributors of fund capital clearly can capture social value two ways. First, as is commonly done, contributions can be made directly to not-for-profit organizations. Second, contributors can always invest the funds in a portfolio of securities and then use the proceeds to purchase the healthcare services directly. In the second situation, there would be no tax consequences on the portfolio's return because the contributed proceeds would qualify for tax exemption, but the contributor would lose the tax exemption on the full amount of the funds placed in the portfolio. Because the second alternative exists, providers should require a return on their social value stream that approximates the return available on the equity investment in for-profit firms that offer the same services.

The NPSV model formalizes the capital budgeting decision process applicable to not-for-profit healthcare businesses. Although few organizations actually attempt to quantify NPSV, not-for-profit providers should, at a minimum, subjectively consider the social value inherent in projects under consideration.

Managers of not-for-profit businesses, as well as most managers of investor-owned businesses, recognize that nonfinancial factors should be considered in any capital budgeting analysis. The NPSV model examines only one other factor, and it is difficult to implement in practice. Thus, many firms use a quasi-subjective project-scoring approach to capital budgeting decisions that attempts to capture both financial and nonfinancial factors. Exhibit 11.9 illustrates one such approach, the *project scoring matrix*, used by Ridgeland.

Ridgeland ranks projects on three dimensions: (1) stakeholder factors, (2) operational factors, and (3) financial factors. In each dimension, multiple factors are examined and assigned scores that range from two points for very favorable impact to negative one point for negative impact. The scores in each dimension are added to obtain scores for stakeholder, operational, and financial factors, and then the dimension scores are aggregated to obtain a total score for the project. The total score gives Ridgeland's managers a feel for the relative values of projects under consideration when all factors, including financial, are taken into account.

The Three-Step Budgeting Process

In today's economic climate, hospitals are more strapped for cash than ever. Increasingly facing problems accessing the capital needed to finance new projects, hospitals' capital budgeting decisions are becoming increasingly constrained. With limited capital, limited projects can be undertaken—meaning those that are put into play need to be carefully chosen, with an emphasis on an objective, analytic decision-making process.

Unfortunately, rather than using a more rigorous analysis, many organizations navigate the capital planning process by using a simple three-step budgeting process, which can be described as follows: (1) the total available capital is determined; (2) department managers are asked to prioritize projects by A, B, and C levels; and (3) projects are approved in priority order until the funds are exhausted.

Based on what you have learned about capital budgeting, can you think of some drawbacks to this approach? Further, can you think of why the methods described in this chapter might be superior to this process? Finally, understanding that the real-world practice of healthcare financial management is often far removed from the theory behind it, can you think of some reasons some managers choose to use this process instead of a more sophisticated analysis?

Source: Information from Casolari and Womack (2010).

EXHIBIT 11.9
Project Scoring Matrix

	Relative Score			
Criteria	*2*	*1*	*0*	*−1*
Stakeholder				
Physicians	Strongly support	Support	Neutral	Opposed
Employees	Helps morale a lot	Helps morale a little	No effect	Hurts morale
Visitors	Greatly enhances visit	Enhances visit	No effect	Hurts image
Social value	High	Moderate	None	Negative
Operational				
Outcomes	Greatly improves	Improves	No effect	Hurts outcomes
Length of stay	Documented decrease	Anecdotal decrease	No effect	Increases
Technology	Breakthrough	Improves current	Adds to current	Lowers
Productivity	Large decrease in FTEs	Decrease in FTEs	No change in FTEs	Adds FTEs
Financial				
Life cycle	Innovation	Growth	Stabilization	Decline
Payback	Less than 2 years	2–4 years	4–6 years	Over 6 years
IRR	Over 20%	15–20%	10–15%	Less than 10%
Correlation	Negative	Uncorrelated	Somewhat positive	Highly positive
Stakeholder factors score	________			
Operational factors score	________			
Financial factors score	________			
Total score	________			

Ridgeland's managers recognize that the scoring system is completely arbitrary, so a project with a score of 16, for example, may be more or less than twice as good as a project with a score of 8. Nevertheless, use of the project scoring matrix forces managers to address multiple issues when making capital budgeting decisions. Although Ridgeland's approach should not be used at other organizations without modification for firm- and industry-unique circumstances, it does provide insight into how a matrix might be developed that is unique to a firm.

SELF-TEST QUESTIONS

1. Describe the NPSV model of capital budgeting.
2. Describe the construction and use of a project scoring matrix.

The Postaudit

Capital budgeting is not a static process. If there is a long lag between a project's acceptance and its implementation, any new information concerning capital costs or the project's cash flows should be analyzed before the actual start-up occurs. Furthermore, the performance of each project should be monitored throughout the project's life. The process of formally monitoring project performance over time is called the *postaudit*. It involves comparing actual results with those projected by the project's sponsors; explaining why differences occur; and analyzing potential changes to the project's operations, including replacement or termination.

The postaudit has several purposes:

- **Improve forecasts**. When managers systematically compare their projections to actual outcomes, estimates tend to improve. Conscious or unconscious biases can be identified and, one hopes, eliminated; new forecasting methods are sought as the need for them becomes apparent; and managers tend to do everything better, including forecasting, if they know that their actions are being monitored.
- **Develop historical risk data**. Postaudits permit managers to develop historical data on new project analyses regarding risk and expected rates of return. As we discuss in chapter 12, these data can be used to make judgments about the relative risk of future projects.
- **Improve operations**. Businesses are run by managers, and they can perform at higher or lower levels of efficiency. When a forecast is made by the surgery department, for example, the department director and

medical staff are, in a sense, putting their reputations on the line. If costs are above predicted levels and utilization is below expectations, the people involved will strive, within ethical bounds, to improve the situation and bring results into line with forecasts. As one hospital CEO put it, "You academics worry only about making good decisions. In the health services sector, we also have to worry about making decisions good."

- **Reduce losses**. Postaudits monitor the performance of projects over time, so the first indication that termination or replacement should be considered often arises when the postaudit indicates that a project is performing poorly.

SELF-TEST QUESTIONS

1. What is a postaudit?
2. Why are postaudits important to the efficiency of a business?

Using Capital Budgeting Techniques in Other Contexts

The techniques developed in this chapter can help healthcare managers make a number of different types of decisions in addition to project selection. One example is the use of NPV and IRR to evaluate corporate merger opportunities. Healthcare businesses often acquire other firms to increase capacity, to expand into other service areas, or for other reasons. A key element of any merger analysis is the valuation of the target firm. Although the cash flows in such an analysis typically are structured differently from those in project analysis, the same evaluation tools are applied. We demonstrate the use of these techniques in the business valuation section of chapter 16.

Managers also use capital budgeting techniques when deciding whether to divest assets or reduce staffing. Like capital budgeting, these actions require an analysis of the impact of the decision on the business's cash flows. When cutting personnel, businesses typically spend money up front in severance payments but then receive benefits in the form of lower labor costs in the future. When assets are sold, the pattern of cash flows is reversed—that is, cash inflows occur when the asset is sold, but any future cash inflows associated with the asset are sacrificed. (If future cash flows are negative, the decision—at least from a financial perspective—should be easy.) In both situations, the techniques discussed here, perhaps with modification, can be applied to assess the financial consequences of the action.

SELF-TEST QUESTION

1. Can capital budgeting tools be used in different settings? Explain your answer.

Chapter Key Concepts

This chapter discusses the basic capital budgeting process. Here are its key concepts:

- *Capital budgeting* is the process of analyzing potential expenditures on fixed assets and deciding whether the firm should undertake those investments.
- The *capital budgeting* process requires the firm to (1) estimate the project's expected cash flows, (2) assess the riskiness of those flows, (3) determine the appropriate cost of capital at which to discount those flows, and (4) determine the project's profitability and breakeven characteristics.
- The most important, but also the most difficult, step in analyzing a project is estimating the *incremental cash flows* that the project will generate.
- In determining incremental cash flows, *opportunity costs* (the cash flows forgone by using an asset) must be considered, but *sunk costs* (cash outlays that cannot be recouped) are not included. Further, any impact of the project on the firm's *other cash flows* must be included in the analysis.
- *Tax laws* generally affect investor-owned firms in three ways: (1) taxes reduce a project's operating cash flows, (2) tax laws prescribe the depreciation expense that can be taken in any year, and (3) taxes affect a project's salvage value cash flow.
- Capital projects often require an investment in *net working capital* in addition to the investment in fixed assets. Such increases represent a cash outlay that, if material, must be included in the analysis. This investment is recovered when the project is terminated.
- *Cash flow estimation bias* can result if managers are overly optimistic in their forecasts. Estimation bias should be identified and dealt with in the decision process.

(continued)

(continued from previous page)

- A project may have some *strategic value* that is not accounted for in the estimated cash flows. At a minimum, strategic value should be noted and considered qualitatively in the analysis.
- The *effects of inflation* must be considered in project analyses. The best procedure is to build inflation effects directly into the component cash flow estimates.
- *Breakeven analysis* provides decision-makers with insights concerning a project's profitability, liquidity, and risk. Time breakeven is measured by the *payback period.*
- *Net present value (NPV)*, which is simply the sum of the present values of all the project's net cash flows when discounted at the project cost of capital, measures a project's dollar profitability. An NPV greater than $0 indicates that the project is profitable after all costs—including the opportunity cost of capital—have been considered. Further, a higher NPV indicates a more profitable project.
- *Internal rate of return (IRR)*, which is the discount rate that forces a project's NPV to equal zero, measures a project's percentage rate-of-return profitability. If a project's IRR is greater than its cost of capital, the project is profitable, and the higher the IRR, the more profitable the project.
- The NPV and IRR profitability measures provide identical indications of profitability—that is, a project that is judged to be profitable by its NPV will also be profitable by its IRR. However, when mutually exclusive projects are being evaluated, NPV might rank a different project higher than IRR. This difference can occur because the two measures have different *reinvestment rate assumptions*—IRR assumes that cash flows can be reinvested at the project's IRR, while NPV assumes that cash flows can be reinvested at the project's cost of capital.
- The *modified internal rate of return (MIRR)*, which forces a project's cash flows to be reinvested at the project's cost of capital, is a better measure of a project's percentage rate of return than the IRR is.
- If mutually exclusive projects have *unequal lives*, the analysis may need to be adjusted to place the projects on an equal life basis. This adjustment can be made using either the *replacement chain* method or the *equivalent annual annuity (EAA)* method.

(continued)

(continued from previous page)

- A project's profitability may be enhanced if it can be *abandoned* before the end of its physical life.
- The *net present social value (NPSV)* model formalizes the capital budgeting decision process for not-for-profit firms.
- Firms often use *project scoring* subjectively to incorporate a large number of factors, including financial and nonfinancial factors, into the capital budgeting decision process.
- The *postaudit* is a key element in capital budgeting. By comparing actual results to predicted results, decision-makers can improve both their operations and their cash flow estimation process.
- Capital budgeting techniques are used in a wide variety of settings in addition to project evaluation.

This concludes our discussion of the basics of capital budgeting. In the next chapter, we discuss risk assessment and incorporation—key issues in capital budgeting analysis.

Chapter Models, Problems, and Minicases

The following ancillary resources in spreadsheet format are available for this chapter:

- A chapter model that shows how to perform many of the calculations described in the chapter
- Problems that test your ability to perform the calculations
- A minicase that is more complicated than the problems and tests your ability to perform the calculations in preparation for a case

These resources can be accessed online at ache.org/HAP/PinkSong8e.

Selected Case

Because chapters 11 and 12 contain related material, most of the applicable cases require material from both chapters and hence are listed at the end of the next chapter. However, one case in *Cases in Healthcare Finance*, sixth edition, is applicable solely to this chapter: Case 4: Tulsa Memorial Hospital, which focuses on estimating the breakeven volume of a walk-in clinic.

References

Casolari, C., and S. Womack. 2010. "Prioritizing Capital Projects When Cash Is Scarce." *Healthcare Financial Management* 64 (3): 114, 116.

Wheeler, J. R. C., and J. P. Clement. 1990. "Capital Expenditure Decisions and the Role of the Not-for-Profit Hospital: An Application of the Social Goods Model." *Medical Care Review* (Winter): 467–86.

Selected Bibliography

Arduino, K. 2018. "The Increasing Importance of Strategic Capital Planning." *Healthcare Financial Management* 72 (2): 76–77.

Brigham, E. F., and M. C. Ehrhardt. 2013. "Chapter 11." In *Financial Management: Theory and Practice*, 14th ed. Mason, OH: South-Western Cengage Learning.

Guimond, J. P. 2016. "Have You Looked at Your Capital Process Lately?" *Healthcare Financial Management* 70 (5): 64–69.

Hegwer, L. R. 2016. "Capital Planning for a New Era." *Healthcare Financial Management* 70 (5): 60–63.

Jasuta, L. 2016. "Rolling Capital/Managing Investments in a Value-Based Care World." *Healthcare Financial Management* 70 (6): 82–89.

Parrott, B. 2018. "Why Age Is Not Enough: A Better Approach to Equipment Replacement." *Healthcare Financial Management* 72 (5): 44–49.

Pohlman, R. A., E. S. Santiago, and F. L. Markel. 1988. "Cash Flow Estimation Practices of Large Firms." *Financial Management* (Summer): 71–79.

Pruitt, S. W., and L. J. Gitman. 1987. "Capital Budgeting Forecast Biases: Evidence from the *Fortune* 500." *Financial Management* (Spring): 46–51.

Selected Website

The TeachMeFinance website has several tutorial-type discussions that cover various aspects of financial management. For a capital budgeting tutorial, go to www.teachmefinance.com/capitalbudgeting.html.

Notes

1. If Ann Arbor did not have taxable income to offset in year 2 and had no taxable income to offset in previous years, the loss would have to be carried forward and hence the tax benefit would not be immediately realized. In this situation, the tax shield value of the loss

would be reduced because it would be pushed into the future rather than recognized immediately. Note that IRS regulations pertaining to the carryback of losses change often to reflect changing economic conditions. At this time (2018), businesses can elect to carry back losses three, four, or five years.

2. The NPV is the same as the cumulative discounted cash flow shown for year 5 in exhibit 11.6. In essence, NPV can be thought of as the total cumulative discounted cash flow of the project.
3. One can argue that not-for-profit businesses do not have unlimited access to capital, and thus such firms cannot replace project cash flows with external capital. Furthermore, not-for-profit businesses usually do not have sufficient capital to accept all projects that have positive NPVs, so the return on a not-for-profit firm's marginal project may not equal the firm's cost of capital. Nevertheless, for not-for-profit businesses, the average aggregate return on projects will usually be close to the firm's cost of capital, so the cost of capital is still a better reinvestment rate than the project's IRR, especially when projects with exceptionally high or low IRRs are being evaluated.

Integrative Application

The Problem

The Scampini Clinic recently purchased a new ultrasound machine. The machine cost $22,500, and it is expected to generate net after-tax operating cash flows (including depreciation) of $6,250 per year, starting in year 1. The machine has a five-year expected life, and the clinic's cost of capital is 10 percent. The expected salvage values of the machine at the end of each year are given in the following table:

Year	*Salvage Value*
0	$22,500
1	$ 17,500
2	$ 14,000
3	$ 11,000
4	$ 5,000
5	$ 0

The clinic must decide whether to operate the machine until the end of its five-year physical life or earlier.

The Analysis

The operating cash flows and salvage value for each year of the expected life of the ultrasound machine are as follows:

Year	*Operating Cash Flow*	*Salvage Value*
0	($22,500)	$22,500
1	$ 6,250	$ 17,500
2	$ 6,250	$ 14,000
3	$ 6,250	$ 11,000
4	$ 6,250	$ 5,000
5	$ 6,250	$ 0

If the clinic operates the machine for one year only, the NPV of the investment at a cost of capital of 10 percent would be as follows:

$$\text{NPV} = -\$22{,}500 + \frac{(\$6{,}250 + \$17{,}500)}{1.10} = -\$909$$

$$= -\$22{,}500 + \text{NPV}\ (10\%, \$6{,}250 + \$17{,}500) = -\$909.$$

If the clinic operates the machine for two to five years, the NPV of the investment at a cost of capital of 10 percent would be as follows:

At 2 years: = –\$22,500 + NPV (10%, \$6,250, \$6,250 + \$14,000) = –\$83

At 3 years: = –\$22,500 + NPV (10%, \$6,250, \$6,250, \$6,250 + \$11,000) = \$1,307

At 4 years: = –\$22,500 + NPV (10%, \$6,250, \$6,250, \$6,250, \$6,250 + \$5,000) = \$727

At 5 years: = –\$22,500 + NPV (10%, \$6,250, \$6,250, \$6,250, \$6,250, \$6,250 + \$0) = \$1,192

The Decision

The clinic decided to operate the ultrasound machine for three years, which is when the NPV is maximized at \$1,307. Positive salvage values can only raise the expected NPV and IRR of a project. However, negative salvage values (e.g., removal and disposal costs) could lower NPV and IRR. ■

CHAPTER

12

PROJECT RISK ANALYSIS

Learning Objectives

After studying this chapter, readers should be able to

- describe the three types of risk relevant to capital budgeting decisions,
- discuss the techniques used in project risk assessment,
- conduct a project risk assessment,
- discuss several types of real options and their impact on a project's value, and
- explain how risk is incorporated into the capital budgeting process.

Introduction

Chapter 11 covered the basics of capital budgeting, including cash flow estimation, breakeven analysis, and profitability measures. This chapter extends the discussion of capital budgeting to include risk analysis, which is composed of three elements: (1) defining the type of risk relevant to the project, (2) measuring the project's risk, and (3) incorporating that risk assessment into the capital budgeting decision process. Although risk analysis is a key element in all financial decisions, the importance of capital investment decisions to a healthcare organization's success makes risk analysis vital.

The higher the risk associated with an investment, the higher its required rate of return. This principle is just as valid for healthcare businesses that make capital expenditure decisions as it is for individuals who make personal investment decisions. Thus, the ultimate goal in project risk analysis is to ensure that the cost of capital used as the discount rate in a project's profitability analysis properly reflects the riskiness of that project. The corporate cost of capital, which is covered in detail in chapter 9, reflects the cost of capital to the organization on the basis of its aggregate risk—that is, the riskiness of the business's average project.

In project risk analysis, a project's risk is assessed relative to the firm's average project: Does the project have average risk, below-average risk, or above-average risk? The corporate cost of capital is then adjusted to reflect any differential risk, resulting in a project cost of capital. In general, high-risk projects are assigned a project cost of capital that is higher than the corporate cost of capital, average risk projects are evaluated at the corporate cost of capital, and low-risk projects are assigned a discount rate that is less than the corporate cost of capital. (Note that when capital budgeting is conducted at the divisional level, the adjustment process is handled in a similar manner but the starting value is the divisional cost of capital.)

Types of Project Risk

Three types of project risk can be defined and, at least in theory, measured:

1. **Stand-alone risk**, which views the risk of a project as if it were held in isolation and hence ignores portfolio effects in the firm and among equity investors
2. **Corporate risk**, which views the risk of a project in the context of the business's portfolio of projects
3. **Market risk**, which views a project's risk from the perspective of the business's owners, who are assumed to hold a well-diversified portfolio of stocks[1]

The type of risk that is most relevant to a particular capital budgeting decision depends on the business's ownership and the number of projects the business operates.

Stand-Alone Risk

Stand-alone risk is present in a project whenever there is a chance of a return that is less than the expected return. A project is risky whenever its cash flows are not known with certainty because uncertain cash flows mean uncertain profitability. Furthermore, the greater the probability of a return far below the expected return, the greater the risk. Stand-alone risk can be measured by the *standard deviation* of the project's profitability (return on investment [ROI]), as measured typically by net present value (NPV) or internal rate of return (IRR). Because standard deviation measures the dispersion of a distribution about its expected value, the larger the standard deviation, the greater the probability that the project's profitability (NPV or IRR) will be far below that expected.

An alternative measure of stand-alone risk is the project's *coefficient of variation*, which is the standard deviation divided by the project's expected NPV. Conceptually, stand-alone risk is relevant in only one situation: when a not-for-profit firm is evaluating its first project. In this situation, the project will be operated in isolation, so no portfolio diversification is present; that is, the business does not have a collection of different projects, nor does it have stockholders who hold diversified portfolios of stocks.

Corporate Risk

In reality, businesses usually offer many different products or services and thus can be thought of as having a large number (perhaps even hundreds) of individual projects. For example, MinuteMan Healthcare, a New England HMO (health maintenance organization), offers healthcare services to a large number of diverse employee groups in numerous service areas, and each different group can be considered a separate project. In this situation, the stand-alone risk of a project (service line) under consideration by MinuteMan is not relevant because the project will not be held in isolation. The relevant risk of a new project to MinuteMan is its contribution to the HMO's overall risk—the impact of the project on the variability of the overall profitability of the business. This type of risk, which is relevant when the project is part of a not-for-profit business's portfolio of projects, is called *corporate risk.*

A project's corporate risk depends on the context (i.e., the firm's other projects), so a project may have high corporate risk to one business but low corporate risk to another, particularly when the two businesses operate in widely different industries.

Market Risk

Market risk is generally viewed as the relevant risk for projects being evaluated by investor-owned businesses. The goal of shareholder (owner) wealth maximization implies that a project's returns as well as its risk should be defined and measured from the owners' perspective. The riskiness of an individual project to a well-diversified owner is not the risk the project would have if it were owned and operated in isolation (i.e., stand-alone risk), nor is it the contribution of the project to the riskiness of the business (i.e., corporate risk). Most business owners hold a large diversified portfolio of stocks of many firms, which can be thought of as a large diversified portfolio of individual projects. Thus, the risk of any single project to a for-profit business's owners is its contribution to the riskiness of their well-diversified stock portfolios.

SELF-TEST QUESTIONS

1. What are the three types of project risk?
2. How is each type of project risk measured, both in absolute and relative terms?

Relationships Among Stand-Alone, Corporate, and Market Risks

After discussing the three types of project risk and the situations in which each is relevant, it is tempting to say that stand-alone risk is almost never important because not-for-profit businesses should focus on a project's corporate risk and investor-owned businesses should focus on a project's market risk. Unfortunately, the situation is not that simple. First, it is almost impossible in practice to quantify a project's corporate or market risk because it is extremely difficult—some practitioners would say impossible—to estimate the prospective return distributions for given economic states for either the project, the firm as a whole, or the market. If these return distributions cannot be estimated, the appropriate beta cannot be estimated, and hence a project's corporate or market risk cannot be quantified.

Fortunately, as demonstrated in the next section, it is possible to get a rough idea of the relative stand-alone risk of a project. Thus, managers can make statements such as "project A has above-average risk, project B has below-average risk, and project C has average risk," all in the stand-alone sense. After a project's stand-alone risk has been assessed, the primary factor in converting stand-alone risk to corporate or market risk is correlation. If a project's returns are expected to be highly positively correlated with the firm's returns, high stand-alone risk translates to high corporate risk. Similarly, if the firm's returns are expected to be highly correlated with the stock market's returns, high corporate risk translates to high market risk. The same relationships hold when the project is judged to have average or low stand-alone risk.

Most projects will be in a firm's primary line of business and hence will be in the same line of business as the firm's average project. Because all projects in the same line of business are generally affected by the same economic factors, such projects' returns are usually highly correlated. When this situation exists, a project's stand-alone risk is a good proxy for its corporate risk. Furthermore, most projects' returns are also positively correlated with the returns on other assets in the economy; that is, most assets have high returns when the economy is strong and low returns when the economy is weak. When this situation holds, a project's stand-alone risk is a good proxy for its market risk.

Thus, for most projects, the stand-alone risk assessment also provides good insights into a project's corporate and market risk. The only exception is a situation in which a project's returns are expected to be independent of, or negatively correlated to, the business as a whole. In these situations, considerable judgment is required because the stand-alone risk assessment will over-state the project's corporate risk. Similarly, if a project's returns are expected to be independent of or negatively correlated to the market's returns, the project's stand-alone risk will overstate its market risk.

An additional problem arises with investor-owned healthcare businesses. Finance theory specifies that investor-owned businesses should focus on market risk when making capital budgeting decisions. However, most healthcare businesses (even proprietary ones) have corporate goals that focus on the provision of quality healthcare services in addition to owner (shareholder) wealth maximization. Furthermore, a proprietary healthcare business's stability and financial condition, which primarily depend on corporate risk, are important to all the firm's other stakeholders: its managers, physicians, patients, community, and so on. Some financial theorists even argue that stockholders, including those that are well diversified, consider factors other than market risk when setting required returns. This point is especially meaningful for small businesses because their owners and managers are not well diversified in their relationship to the business. Considering all the factors, it may be reasonable for managers of investor-owned healthcare businesses, particularly small ones, to be just as concerned about corporate risk as are managers of not-for-profit businesses. Fortunately, in most real-world situations, a project's risk in the corporate sense will be the same as its risk in the market sense.[2]

SELF-TEST QUESTIONS

1. Name and define the three types of risk relevant to capital budgeting.
2. How are these risks related?
3. Should managers of investor-owned providers focus exclusively on a project's market risk?

Risk Analysis Illustration

On the web at: *ache.org/HAP/PinkSong8e*

To illustrate project risk analysis, consider Ridgeland Community Hospital's evaluation of a new MRI (magnetic resonance imaging) system presented in chapter 11. Exhibit 12.1 contains the project's cash flow analysis. If all of the project's component cash flows were known with certainty, the project's projected profitability would be known with certainty and hence the project would have no risk. However, in most project analyses, future cash flows—and hence profitability—are uncertain and, in many cases, highly uncertain, so risk is present.

The component cash flow distributions and their correlations with one another determine the project's profitability distribution and hence the

EXHIBIT 12.1
Ridgeland Community Hospital: MRI Site Cash Flow Analysis

	Annual Cash Flows					
	0	*1*	*2*	*3*	*4*	*5*
1. System cost	($1,500,000)					
2. Related expenses)	(1,000,000)					
3. Gross revenues		$1,000,000	$1,050,000	$1,102,500	$1,157,625	$1,215,506
4. Deductions		250,000	262,500	275,625	289,406	303,876
5. Net revenues		$ 750,000	$ 787,500	$ 826,875	$ 868,219	$ 911,630
6. Labor costs		50,5000	52,500	55,125	57,881	60,775
7. Maintenance costs		150,000	157,500	165,375	173,644	182,326
8. Supplies		30,000	31,500	33,075	34,729	36,465
9. Incremental overhead		10,000	10,500	11,025	11,576	12,155
10. Depreciation		350,000	350,000	350,000	350,000	350,000
11. Operating cash flow		$ 160,000	$ 185,500	$ 212,275	$ 240,389	$ 269,908
12. Taxes		0	0	0	0	0
13. Net operating cash flow		$ 160,000	$ 185,500	$ 212,275	$ 240,389	$ 269,908
14. Depreciation		350,000	350,000	350,000	350,000	350,000
15. Net salvage value						750,000
16. Net cash flow	($2,500,000)	$ 510,000	$ 535,500	$ 562,275	$ 590,389	$1,369,908

Profitability measures:
Net present value (NPV) = $82,493.
Internal rate of return (IRR) = 11.1%.

project's risk. In the following sections, three quantitative techniques for assessing a project's risk are discussed: (1) sensitivity analysis, (2) scenario analysis, and (3) Monte Carlo simulation. In a later section, we present a qualitative approach to risk assessment.

SELF-TEST QUESTIONS

1. What condition creates project risk?
2. What makes one project riskier than another?
3. What type of risk is initially assessed?

Sensitivity Analysis

On the web at: *ache.org/HAP/PinkSong8e*

Historically, ***sensitivity analysis*** has been classified as a risk assessment tool. In reality, it is not very useful in assessing a project's risk. However, it does have significant value in project analysis, so we discuss it in some detail here.

Many of the variables that determine a project's cash flows are subject to some type of probability distribution, not known with certainty. If the realized value of such a variable is different from its expected value, the project's profitability will differ from its expected value. Sensitivity analysis indicates exactly how much a project's profitability—NPV, IRR, or modified internal rate of return (MIRR)—will change in response to a given change in a single input variable, with all other input variables held constant.

Sensitivity analysis begins with the *base case* developed using expected values (in the statistical sense) for all uncertain variables. For example, assume that Ridgeland's managers believe that all of the MRI project's component cash flows—except for weekly volume and salvage value—are known with relative certainty. The expected values for these variables (volume = 40, salvage value = $750,000) were used in exhibit 12.1 to obtain the base case NPV of $82,493. Sensitivity analysis is designed to provide managers with the answers to such questions as, What if volume turns out to be more or less than the expected level? What if salvage value turns out to be more or less than expected? (Typically, more than two variables would be examined in a sensitivity analysis. We use only two to keep the illustration manageable.)

In a sensitivity analysis, each uncertain input variable typically is changed by a fixed percentage amount above and below its expected value, while all other variables are held constant at their expected values. Thus, all input variables except one are held at their base case values. The resulting NPVs (or IRRs or MIRRs) are recorded and plotted. Exhibit 12.2 contains the NPV sensitivity analysis for the MRI project, assuming that there are two uncertain variables: (1) volume and (2) salvage value.

EXHIBIT 12.2
MRI Project Sensitivity Analysis

	Net Present Value	
Change from Base Case Level (%)	*Volume*	*Salvage Value*
−30	($814,053)	($ 57,215)
−20	(515,193)	(10,646)
−10	(216,350)	35,923
0	82,493	82,493
+10	381,335	129,062
+20	680,178	175,631
+30	979,020	222,200

Note that the NPV is a constant $82,493 when there is no change in either of the uncertain variables because a 0 percent change recreates the base case. The values in exhibit 12.2 give managers a feel for which input variable will have the greatest impact on the MRI project's profitability—the larger the NPV change for a given percentage input change, the greater the impact. Considering only these two variables, we see that the MRI project's NPV is affected by changes in volume to a much greater degree than it is by changes in salvage value.

Often, the results of sensitivity analyses are shown in graphical form. For example, the exhibit 12.2 sensitivity analysis is graphed in exhibit 12.3. Here, the slopes of the lines show how sensitive the MRI project's NPV is to changes in each of the uncertain input variables—the steeper the slope, the more sensitive the NPV is to a change in the variable. Note that the sensitivity lines intersect at the base case values—0 percent change from base case level and $82,493. Also, spreadsheet models are ideally suited for performing sensitivity analyses because such models automatically recalculate NPV when an input value is changed and facilitate graphing.[3]

Exhibit 12.3 illustrates that the MRI project's NPV is very sensitive to volume and only mildly sensitive to changes in salvage value. A sensitivity plot that has a negative slope indicates that **increases** in the value of that variable **decrease** the project's NPV. If two projects were being compared, the one with the steeper sensitivity lines would be regarded as riskier because a relatively small error in estimating a variable—for example, volume—would produce a large difference in the project's realized NPV. Thus, a realized volume that turns out to be smaller than that expected means that the project's actual NPV will be far less than that expected. If information were available on the sensitivity of NPV to input changes to Ridgeland's average project, similar judgments regarding the riskiness of the MRI project could be made, but they would be relative to the firm's average project.

EXHIBIT 12.3
Sensitivity Analysis Graph

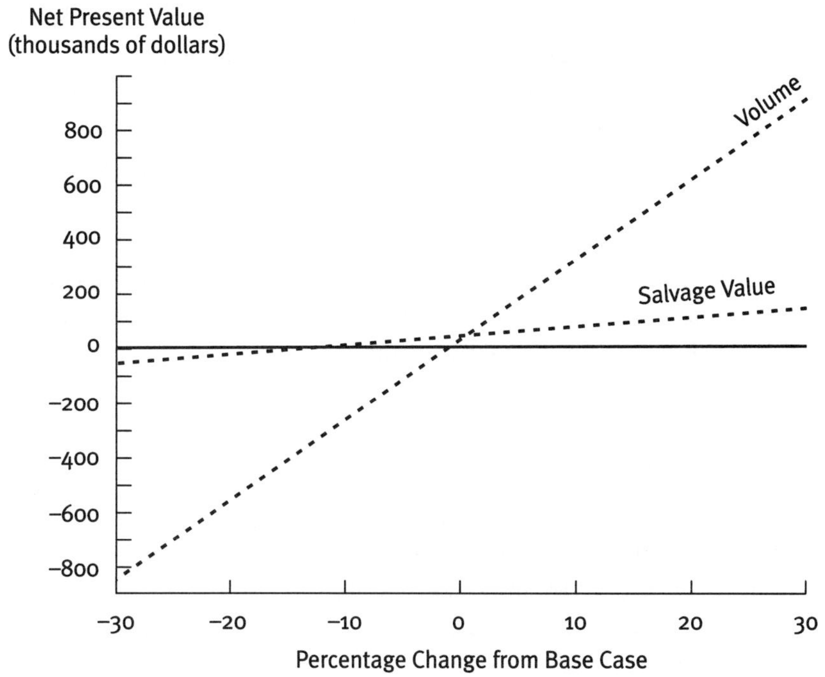

Although sensitivity analysis historically has been thought of as a risk assessment tool, it has severe limitations in this role. For example, suppose that Ridgeland had a contract with an HMO that guaranteed a minimum MRI volume at a fixed reimbursement rate. In that situation, volume would not contribute to project risk at all, despite the sensitivity analysis showing NPV to be highly sensitive to changes in volume. In general, a project's stand-alone risk depends on the sensitivity of its profitability to changes in key input variables and the ranges of likely values of these variables. Because sensitivity analysis considers only the first factor, its results can be misleading. Furthermore, sensitivity analysis does not consider interactions among the uncertain input variables; it considers each variable independently.

Despite its shortcomings in risk assessment, sensitivity analysis does provide managers with valuable information. First, it provides some breakeven information about the project's uncertain variables. For example, exhibits 12.2 and 12.3 show that just a small decrease in expected volume makes the project unprofitable, whereas the project remains profitable even if salvage value falls by more than 10 percent. Although somewhat rough, this breakeven information is clearly valuable to Ridgeland's managers. (The breakeven points can be easily refined by using Excel's Goal Seek capability.)

Second, and perhaps more important, sensitivity analysis helps managers identify which input variables are most critical to the project's profitability and hence to the project's financial success. In this MRI example, volume is clearly the key input variable of the two that were examined, so Ridgeland's managers should ensure that the volume estimate is the best possible. The concept here is that Ridgeland's managers have a limited amount of time to spend on analyzing the MRI project, and sensitivity analysis enables them to focus on what's most important.

The ability to identify the critical input variables is also useful post-audit. If the project is performing poorly and changes must be made, such changes will have the greatest positive impact if they are made to one of the critical variables. In our illustration, if the MRI project is initiated but its profitability is not meeting forecasts, it clearly is better to focus on increasing volume than on increasing the salvage value.

SELF-TEST QUESTIONS

1. Briefly describe sensitivity analysis.
2. What type of risk does it attempt to measure?
3. Is sensitivity analysis a good risk assessment tool? If not, what is its value in the capital budgeting process?

Scenario Analysis

On the web at: *ache.org/HAP/PinkSong8e*

Scenario analysis is a stand-alone risk-analysis technique that considers (1) the sensitivity of NPV or another profitability measure to changes in key variables, (2) the likely range of variable values, and (3) the interactions among the variables. To conduct a scenario analysis, managers pick a "bad" set of circumstances (e.g., low volume, low salvage value), an average or "most likely" set, and a "good" set (e.g., high volume, high salvage value). The resulting input values are then used to create a probability distribution of NPV.

For an illustration of scenario analysis, assume that Ridgeland's managers regard a drop in weekly volume below 30 scans as very unlikely; they also feel that a volume above 50 is also improbable. On the other hand, salvage value can be as low as $500,000 or as high as $1 million. The **most likely** values are 40 scans per week for volume and $750,000 for salvage value. Thus, a volume of 30 and a $500,000 salvage value define the lower bound (or **worst-case** scenario), while a volume of 50 and a salvage value of $1 million define the upper bound (or **best-case** scenario).

Ridgeland can now use the worst-, most likely, and best-case values for the input variables to obtain the NPV corresponding to each scenario. Ridgeland's managers used a spreadsheet model to conduct the analysis, and exhibit 12.4 summarizes the results. The most likely case results in a positive

NPV, the worst case produces a large negative NPV, and the best case results in an even larger positive NPV. These results, along with each scenario's probability of occurrence, can now be used to determine the expected NPV and standard deviation of NPV. Suppose that Ridgeland's managers estimate that there is a 20 percent chance that the worst case will occur, a 60 percent chance that the most likely case will occur, and a 20 percent change that the best case will occur. Of course, it is difficult to estimate scenario probabilities with any confidence, and, in most situations, the probabilities used will not be symmetric. For example, in an environment of increasing managed care penetration and increasing competition among providers, the probability may be higher for the worst-case scenario than for the best-case scenario.

Exhibit 12.4 contains a discrete distribution of returns, so the expected NPV can be found as follows:

$$\begin{aligned}\text{Expected NPV} &= (0.20 \times [-\$819{,}844]) + (0.60 \times \$82{,}493)\\ &\quad + (0.20 \times \$984{,}829)\\ &= \$82{,}493.\end{aligned}$$

The expected NPV in the scenario analysis is the same as the base case NPV—$82,493. The results are consistent because, when coupled with the scenario probabilities, the values of the uncertain variables used in the scenario analysis—30, 40, and 50 scans for volume and $500,000, $750,000, and $1 million for salvage value—produce the same expected values that were used in the exhibit 12.1 base case analysis. If inconsistencies exist between the base case NPV and the expected NPV in the scenario analysis, the two analyses have inconsistent input assumptions. In general, such inconsistencies should be identified and removed to ensure that common assumptions are used throughout the project risk analysis. However, remember that our purpose here is to conduct a risk assessment, not to measure profitability. Ultimately,

EXHIBIT 12.4 MRI Project Scenario Analysis

Scenario	*Probability of Outcome*	*Volume*	*Salvage Value*	*NPV*
Worst case	0.20	30	$ 500,000	($ 819,844)
Most likely case	0.60	40	750,000	82,493
Best case	0.20	50	1,000,000	984,829
Expected value		40	$ 750,000	$ 82,493
Standard deviation				$ 570,688

we will use the base case (expected value) cash flows to reassess the project's profitability when we have completed the risk assessment.

The standard deviation of NPV, as shown here, is $570,688:

$$\sigma_{NPV} = [0.20 \times (-\$819{,}844 - \$82{,}493)^2 + 0.60 \times (\$82{,}493 - \$82{,}493)^2 + 0.20 \times (\$984{,}829 - \$82{,}493)2]^{1/2} = \$570{,}688,$$

while the coefficient of variation (CV) of NPV is 6.9:

$$CV = \frac{\sigma_{NPV}}{\text{Expected NPV}} = \frac{\$570{,}688}{\$82{,}493} = 6.9.$$

The MRI project's standard deviation and coefficient of variation measure its stand-alone risk. Suppose that when a similar scenario analysis is applied to Ridgeland's aggregate cash flows (average project), the result is a coefficient of variation of NPV in the range of 2.5 to 5.0. Then, on the basis of its stand-alone risk measured by coefficient of variation, along with subjective judgments, Ridgeland's managers might conclude that the MRI project is riskier than the firm's average project, so it would be classified as a high-risk project.

Scenario analysis can also be interpreted in a less mathematical way. The worst-case NPV—a loss of about $800,000—is an estimate of the worst possible financial consequences of the MRI project. If Ridgeland can absorb such a loss in value without much impact on its financial condition, the project does not pose significant financial danger to the hospital. Conversely, if such a loss would mean financial ruin for the hospital, its managers might be unwilling to undertake the project, regardless of its profitability under the most likely and best-case scenarios. Note that the risk of the project is not changing in these two situations. The difference is in the organization's ability to bear the risk inherent in the project.

While scenario analysis provides useful information about a project's stand-alone risk, it is limited in two ways. First, it considers only a few discrete states of the economy and hence provides information on only a few potential profitability outcomes for the project. In reality, an almost infinite number of possibilities exist. Although the illustrative scenario analysis contained only three scenarios, it can be expanded to include more states of the economy—say, five or seven. However, there is a practical limit on how many scenarios can be included in a scenario analysis.

Second, scenario analysis—at least as normally conducted—implies a definite relationship among the uncertain variables involved. For example, our analysis assumed that the worst value for volume (30 scans per week) would occur at the same time as the worst value for salvage value ($500,000) because the worst-case scenario is defined by combining the worst possible value of each uncertain variable. Although this relationship (all worst values occurring together) may hold in some situations, it may not hold in others. If volume is low, for example, maybe the MRI will withstand less wear and tear and hence be worth more after five years of use. The worst value for volume, then, should be coupled with the best salvage value. Conversely, poor volume may be symptomatic of poor medical effectiveness of the MRI and hence lead to limited demand for used equipment and a low salvage value. Scenario analysis tends to create extreme profitability values for the worst and best cases because it automatically combines all worst and best input values, even if these values have only a remote chance of occurring together. This problem can be mitigated, but not eliminated, by assigning relatively low probabilities to the best and worst cases. The next section describes a method of assessing a project's stand-alone risk that deals with these two problems.

SELF-TEST QUESTIONS

1. Briefly describe scenario analysis.
2. What type of risk does it attempt to measure?
3. What are its strengths and weaknesses?

Monte Carlo Simulation

Monte Carlo simulation, so named because it developed out of work on the mathematics of casino gambling, describes uncertainty in terms of **continuous** probability distributions, which have an infinite number of outcomes rather than just a few **discrete** values. Thus, Monte Carlo simulation provides a more realistic view of a project's risk than does scenario analysis and can be installed on personal computers as an add-on to a spreadsheet program. Because most financial analysis today is done with spreadsheets, Monte Carlo simulation is now accessible to virtually all health services organizations, both large and small.

The first step in a Monte Carlo simulation is to create a model that calculates the project's net cash flows and profitability measures, just as was done for Ridgeland's MRI project. The relatively certain variables are estimated as single, or point, values in the model, while continuous probability distributions are used to specify the uncertain cash flow variables. After the model has been created, the simulation software automatically executes the following steps:

1. The Monte Carlo program chooses a single random value for each uncertain variable on the basis of its specified probability distribution.
2. The values selected for each uncertain variable, along with the point values for the relatively certain variables, are combined in the model to estimate the net cash flow for each year.
3. Using the net cash flow data, the model calculates the project's profitability—for example, as measured by NPV. A single completion of these three steps constitutes one iteration, or *run*, in the Monte Carlo simulation.
4. The Monte Carlo software repeats these steps many times (e.g., 5,000). Because each run is based on different input values, each run produces a different NPV.

The ultimate result of the simulation is an NPV probability distribution based on a large number of individual scenarios, which encompasses almost all of the likely financial outcomes. Monte Carlo software usually displays the results of the simulation in both tabular and graphical forms and automatically calculates summary statistical data such as expected value, standard deviation, and skewness.[4]

For an illustration of Monte Carlo simulation, again consider Ridgeland's MRI project. As in the scenario analysis, the illustration has been simplified by specifying the distributions for only two key variables: (1) weekly volume and (2) salvage value. Weekly volume is not expected to vary by more than ±10 scans from its expected value of 40 scans. Because this situation is symmetrical, the normal (bell-shaped) distribution can be used to represent the uncertainty inherent in volume. In a normal distribution, the expected value ±3 standard deviations will encompass almost the entire distribution. Thus, a normal distribution with an expected value of 40 scans and a standard deviation of 10 ÷ 3 = 3.33 scans is a reasonable description of the uncertainty inherent in weekly volume.

A triangular distribution was chosen for salvage value because it specifically fixes the upper and lower bounds, whereas the tails of a normal distribution are, in theory, limitless. The triangular distribution is also used extensively when the input distribution is nonsymmetrical because it can easily accommodate skewness. Salvage value uncertainty was specified by a triangular distribution with a lower limit of \$500,000, a most likely value of \$750,000, and an upper limit of \$1 million.

The basic MRI model containing these two continuous distributions was used, plus a Monte Carlo add-on to the spreadsheet program, to conduct a simulation with 5,000 iterations. The output is summarized in exhibit 12.5, and the resulting probability distribution of NPV is plotted in exhibit

12.6. The mean, or expected, NPV ($82,498) is about the same as the base case NPV and expected NPV indicated in the scenario analysis ($82,493). In theory, all three results should be the same because the expected values for all input variables are the same in the three analyses. However, some randomness exists in the Monte Carlo simulation that leads to an expected NPV that is slightly different from the others. The more iterations that are run, the more likely the Monte Carlo NPV will be the same as the base case NPV, assuming that the assumptions are consistent.

The standard deviation of NPV is lower in the simulation analysis because the NPV distribution in the simulation contains values within the

EXHIBIT 12.5 Simulation Results Summary

Expected NPV	$ 82,498
Minimum NPV	($ 951,760)
Maximum NPV	$ 970,191
Probability of a positive NPV	62.8%
Standard deviation	$256,212
Skewness	0.002

EXHIBIT 12.6 NPV Probability Distribution

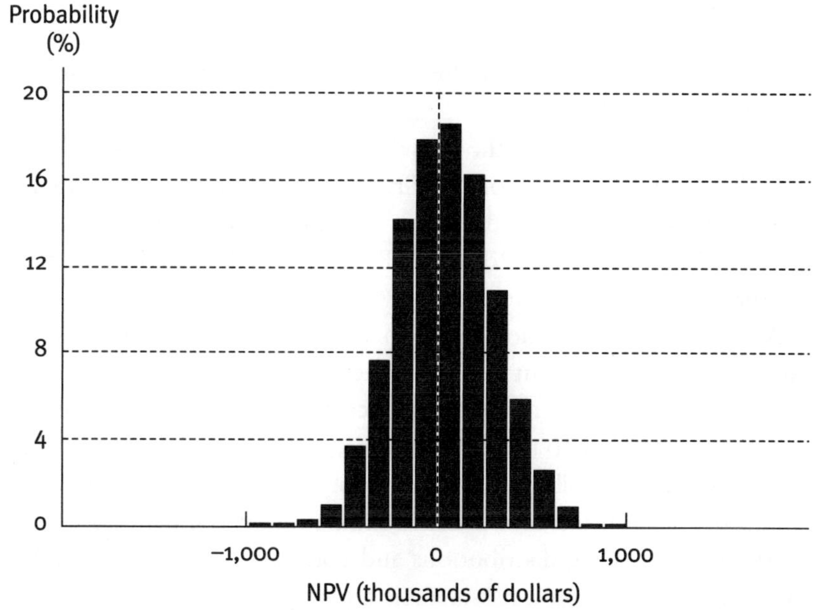

entire range of possible outcomes, while the NPV distribution in the scenario analysis contains only the most likely value and the best-case and worst-case extremes. In this illustration, one value for volume uncertainty was specified for all five years; that is, the value chosen by the Monte Carlo software for volume in year 1—for example, 40 scans—was used as the volume input for the remaining four years in that iteration of the simulation analysis. As an alternative, the normal distribution for year 1 can be applied to each year separately, which would allow the volume forecasts to vary from year to year. Then, the Monte Carlo software might choose 35 as the value for year 1, 43 as the year 2 input, 32 for year 3, and so on. This approach, however, probably does not do a good job of describing real-world behavior; high usage in the first year presumably means strong acceptance of the MRI system and hence high usage in the remaining years. Similarly, low usage in the first year probably portends low usage in future years.

The volume and salvage value variables were treated as independent in the simulation; that is, the value chosen by the Monte Carlo software from the salvage value distribution was not related to the value chosen from the volume distribution. Thus, in any run, a low volume can be coupled with a high salvage value and vice versa. If Ridgeland's managers believe that high utilization at the hospital indicates a strong national demand for MRI systems, they can specify a positive correlation between these variables. A positive correlation would tend to increase the riskiness of the project because a low-volume pick in one iteration cannot be offset by a high–salvage value pick. Conversely, if the salvage value is more a function of the technological advances that occur over the next five years than local utilization, it may be best to specify the variables as independent, as was done.

As in scenario analysis, the project's simulation results must be compared with a similar analysis of the firm's average project. If Ridgeland's average project were considered to have less stand-alone risk when a Monte Carlo simulation was conducted, the MRI project would be judged to have above-average (high) stand-alone risk.

Monte Carlo simulation has two primary advantages over scenario analysis: (1) All possible input variable values are considered, and (2) correlations among the uncertain inputs can be incorporated into the analysis. However, there is a downside to these two advantages: Although it is mechanically easy to input the probability distributions for the uncertain variables as well as their correlations into a Monte Carlo simulation, it is much more difficult to determine what those distributions and correlations are. The problem is that the more information a risk-analysis technique requires, the harder it is to develop the data with any confidence; hence, managers are left with an elegant result of questionable value.

SELF-TEST QUESTIONS

1. Briefly, what is Monte Carlo simulation?
2. What type of risk does it attempt to measure?
3. What are its strengths and weaknesses?

Qualitative Risk Assessment

In some situations, it may be difficult to conduct a quantitative risk assessment because the input variable estimates are nebulous. In other situations, a quantitative assessment may be possible, but a verification of results provides managers with additional confidence. More and more healthcare organizations are using qualitative risk assessment techniques to confirm quantitative assessment results or as the sole basis for the risk assessment.

Qualitative risk assessment is based on the answers to a set of questions. For example, one large healthcare clinic uses these questions:

- Does the project require additional market share or represent a new service initiative?
- Is the project outside the scope of current management expertise?
- Does the project require difficult-to-recruit physicians, nurses, or technical specialists?
- Will the project pit the organization against a strong competitor?
- Does the project involve new, unproven technology?

Each "yes" answer is assigned one point (while each "no" answer receives zero points). If the total point count for the project is zero, it is judged to have low risk; one or two points indicate moderate risk, and three or more points indicate high risk. Although such a subjective approach appears to have little theoretical basis, a closer examination reveals that each question in the list seen earlier is tied to cash flow uncertainty. The greater the number of "yes" answers, the greater the cash flow uncertainty and hence the greater the stand-alone risk of the project.

The value of using the qualitative risk assessment approach in conjunction with a quantitative risk assessment is that it forces managers to think about project risk in alternative frameworks. If the quantitative and qualitative assessments do not agree, the project's risk assessment requires more consideration.

After some discussion, Ridgeland's managers concluded that the MRI project's qualitative risk assessment score was 3. Thus, the quantitative and qualitative assessments reached the same conclusion: The project has high risk.

SELF-TEST QUESTIONS

1. Describe qualitative risk assessment.
2. Why does a qualitative risk assessment work?
3. Assume a quantitative risk assessment has been conducted on a project. Is a qualitative risk assessment necessary?

Incorporating Risk into the Decision Process

Thus far, the MRI illustration has demonstrated that a project's riskiness is difficult to quantify. It may be possible to reach a general conclusion that one project is more or less risky than another or to compare the riskiness of a project with the business as a whole, but it is difficult to develop a good measure of project risk. This lack of precision in measuring project risk adds to the difficulties involved in incorporating differential risk into the capital budgeting decision.

There are two methods for incorporating project risk into the capital budgeting decision process: (1) the certainty equivalent method, which adjusts a project's expected cash flows to reflect project risk, and (2) the risk-adjusted discount rate method, which deals with differential risk by changing the cost of capital. Although most businesses use the risk-adjusted discount rate method, there are some theoretical advantages to using the certainty equivalent method. Furthermore, it raises some interesting issues related to the risk-adjustment process.

How Many Scenarios in a Scenario Analysis?

In the scenario analysis of Ridgeland's MRI project, we used three scenarios. However, three is no magic number, given that the more scenarios used, the more information is obtained from the analysis. Furthermore, more scenarios lessen the problem associated with extreme values because the best- and worst-case scenarios can be assigned low probabilities (which are probably realistic) without causing the risk inherent in the project to be understated.

Although more scenarios add additional realism and provide more information for decision makers, a greater number of scenarios increases forecasting difficulty and makes the analysis more time-consuming. Furthermore, the greater the number of scenarios, the more difficult it is to interpret the results. Thus, the entire process is easier if three scenarios are used rather than, say, nine.

What do you think? Are three scenarios sufficient or should more be used? How many scenarios are too many? Is it better to have an odd number than an even number of scenarios? Is there an optimal number of scenarios?

Certainty Equivalent Method

The *certainty equivalent (CE) method* directly follows the economic concept of *utility*.[5] Under the CE approach, managers must first evaluate a cash flow's risk and then specify how much money, with certainty, would be required for an individual to be indifferent between the riskless (certain) sum and the risky cash flow's expected value. For example, suppose that a rich eccentric offered someone the following choices:

- Flip a coin. If it is a head, the individual receives \$1 million; if it is a tail, the individual receives nothing. The expected value of the gamble is (0.5 × \$1,000,000) + (0.5 × \$0) = \$500,000, but the actual outcome will be either zero or \$1 million, so the gamble is highly risky.
- Do not flip the coin. Simply pocket \$400,000 in cash.

If the individual is indifferent to the two alternatives, \$400,000 is defined to be her CE amount for this particular risky expected \$500,000 cash flow. The riskless \$400,000 provides that individual with the same satisfaction (utility) as the risky \$500,000 expected return.

In general, investors are risk averse, so the CE amount for this gamble will be something less than the \$500,000 expected value. Each individual would have his own CE value—the greater the individual's degree of risk aversion, the lower the CE amount.

The CE concept can be applied to capital budgeting decisions, at least in theory, in this way:

- Convert each net cash flow of a project to its CE value. Here, the riskiness of each cash flow is assessed, and a CE cash flow is chosen on the basis of that risk. The greater the risk, the greater the difference between the expected value and its lower CE value. (If a cash outflow is being adjusted, the CE value is higher than the expected value. The unique risk adjustments required on cash outflows will be discussed in a later section.)
- Once each cash flow is expressed as a CE, discount the project's CE cash flow stream by the risk-free rate to obtain the project's ***differential risk adjusted NPV.***[6] Here, the term "differential risk-adjusted" implies that the unique riskiness of the project, as compared to the overall riskiness of the business, has been incorporated into the decision process. The risk-free rate is used as the discount rate because CE cash flows are analogous to risk-free cash flows.
- A positive differential risk-adjusted NPV indicates that the project is profitable even after adjusting for differential (project-specific) risk.

The CE method is simple and neat. Furthermore, it can easily handle differential risk among the individual cash flows. For example, the final year's CE cash flow might be adjusted downward an additional amount to account for salvage value risk if that risk is considered to be greater than the risk inherent in the operating cash flows.

Unfortunately, there is no practical way to estimate a risky cash flow's CE value. No benchmarks are available to inform the estimate, so each individual would have her own estimate, and they can vary significantly. Also, the risk assessment techniques—for example, scenario analysis—focus on profitability and hence measure the stand-alone risk of a project in its entirety. This process provides no information about the riskiness of individual cash flows, so there is no basis for adjusting each cash flow to reflect its own unique risk.

Risk-Adjusted Discount Rate Method

In the *risk-adjusted discount rate (RADR) method*, expected cash flows are used in the valuation process, and the risk adjustment is made to the discount rate (the opportunity cost of capital). All average-risk projects are discounted at the business's corporate cost of capital, which represents the opportunity cost of capital for average-risk projects; high-risk projects are assigned a higher cost of capital; and low-risk projects are discounted at a lower cost of capital.

One advantage to using the RADR method is that it has a starting benchmark: the business's corporate cost of capital. This discount rate reflects the riskiness of the business in the aggregate, or the riskiness of the firm's average project. Another advantage is that project risk-assessment techniques identify a project's aggregate risk—the combined risk of all of the cash flows—and the RADR applies a single adjustment to the cost of capital rather than attempts to adjust individual cash flows. However, the disadvantage is that, typically, there is no theoretical basis for setting the size of the RADR adjustment, so the amount of adjustment remains a matter of judgment.

There is one additional disadvantage to using the RADR method. RADR combines the factors that account for time value (the risk-free rate) and the adjustment for risk (the risk premium): Project cost of capital = Differential risk-adjusted discount rate = Risk-free rate + Risk premium. The CE approach, on the other hand, keeps risk adjustment and time value separate—time value in the discount rate and risk adjustment in the cash flows. By lumping together risk and time value, the RADR method compounds the risk premium over time, just as interest compounds over time. This compounding of the risk premium means that the RADR method automatically assigns more risk to cash flows that occur in the distant future, and the farther into the future, the greater the implied risk. Because the CE method assigns risk to each cash flow individually, it does not impose assumptions regarding the relationship between risk and time.

The RADR model is one method used to incorporate risk in the capital budgeting decision process. It is based on the following concept:

Key Equation 12.1: Risk-Adjusted Discount Rate (RADR) Theoretical Model

Project cost of capital = Risk-free rate + Risk premium.

The idea here is that the risk-free rate accounts for the time value of money, while the risk premium accounts for the unique (below average, average, or above average) risk of the project. The RADR method as it is normally used—with a constant discount rate applied to all cash flows of a project—implies that risk increases with time. This implication imposes a greater burden on long-term projects, so short-term projects tend to look better financially than do long-term projects. For most projects, the assumption that risk increases over time is probably reasonable because cash flows are more difficult to forecast the farther one moves into the future. However, managers should be aware that the RADR approach automatically penalizes distant cash flows, and an additional explicit penalty based solely on cash flow timing is not warranted unless some specific additional risk can be identified.

SELF-TEST QUESTIONS

1. What are the differences between the CE and RADR methods for risk incorporation?
2. What assumptions about time and risk are inherent in the RADR method?
3. How do most businesses incorporate differential risk into the capital-budgeting decision process?

Final Risk Assessment and Incorporation for the MRI Project

In most project risk analyses, it is impossible to assess the project's corporate or market risk quantitatively, and managers are left with only an assessment of the project's stand-alone risk. However, like the MRI project, most projects being evaluated are in the same line of business as the firm's other projects, and the profitability of most firms is highly correlated with the overall economy. Thus, stand-alone, corporate, and market risk are usually highly correlated, which suggests that managers can get a feel for the relative risk of most projects on the basis of the quantitative and qualitative analyses conducted to assess the project's stand-alone risk. In Ridgeland's case, its managers concluded that the MRI project, with its above-average stand-alone risk, also had above-average corporate risk, which is the risk most relevant to not-for-profit organizations; hence, the project was categorized as a high-risk project.

The business's corporate cost of capital provides a basis for estimating a project's differential RADR—average-risk projects are discounted at the corporate cost of capital, high-risk projects are discounted at a higher cost of capital, and low-risk projects are discounted at a rate below the corporate cost of capital. Unfortunately, there is no good way of specifying exactly how much higher or lower these discounts rates should be; given the present state of the art, risk adjustments are necessarily judgmental and somewhat arbitrary.

Ridgeland's standard procedure is to add 4 percentage points to its 10 percent corporate cost of capital when evaluating high-risk projects and to subtract 2 percentage points when evaluating low-risk projects. Thus, to estimate the high-risk MRI project's differential risk-adjusted NPV, the project's expected (base case) cash flows shown in exhibit 12.1 are discounted at 10% + 4% = 14%. This rate is called the *project cost of capital*, as opposed to the corporate cost of capital, because it reflects the risk characteristics of a specific project rather than the aggregate risk characteristics of the business. The resultant NPV is –$200,017, so the project becomes unprofitable when the analysis is adjusted to reflect its high risk. Ridgeland's managers may still decide to go ahead with the MRI project, but at least they know that its expected profitability is not sufficient to make up for its riskiness.

Uncertainty in Initial Cash Outflows

In many capital budgeting situations, the initial cost of the project—especially when occurring only at time 0—is assumed to be known with certainty. The idea here is that, in most cases, bids have already been received from vendors, so the initial cost can be predicted with relative precision. However, in some circumstances, there can be substantial uncertainty in initial costs. For example, there can be a great deal of uncertainty in the cost of a building that will not be constructed for several years. Or there can be uncertainty in the cost of a major construction project that will take several years to complete.

When there is uncertainty in initial cost, how should that risk be incorporated into the analysis? If the entire cost (or even the major portion) occurs at time 0, the discount rate is not applied to the cash flow, so the RADR method will not get the job done.

What do you think? Can the CE method be used? Assume that time 0 costs on a project could be $100,000 or $150,000 with equal profitability, so the expected initial cost is $125,000. What is your estimate of the CE cash flow? (Hint: Remember that risk adjustments to cash outflows are the opposite of those applied to inflows.)

The RADR method is implemented as follows:

Key Equation 12.2: Risk-Adjusted Discount Rate (RADR) Implementation Model

Project cost of capital = Corporate cost of capital + Risk adjustment.

Here, the corporate cost of capital is used as the base rate (starting point), and a risk adjustment is applied if the project has non-average risk. For above-average risk projects, the risk premium is added to the base rate, while the risk premium is subtracted for those projects judged to have below-average risk. To illustrate, assume a project having above-average risk is being evaluated. The corporate cost of capital is 10 percent, and the standard adjustment amount is 3 percentage points. With these assumptions, the project cost of capital is 13 percent:

$$\text{Project cost of capital} = \text{Corporate cost of capital} + \text{Risk adjustment}$$
$$= 10\% + 3\% = 13\%.$$

SELF-TEST QUESTIONS

1. How did Ridgeland's managers translate the MRI project's stand-alone risk assessment into a corporate risk assessment?
2. How was risk incorporated into the MRI project decision process?
3. Is the risk adjustment objective or subjective?
4. What is a project cost of capital?

Incorporating Debt Capacity into the Decision Process

Just as different businesses have different optimal capital structures, so do individual projects. In any business, the overall optimal capital structure, which is reflected by the weights used in the corporate cost of capital estimate, is an aggregation of the optimal capital structures of the business's individual projects. However, some projects support only a little debt, while other projects support a high level of debt. The proportion of debt in a project's, or a business's, optimal capital structure is called the project's, or business's, *debt capacity*.

One mistake often made when considering a project's debt capacity is to look at how the project is actually financed. For example, even though Ridgeland may be able to obtain a secured loan for the entire cost of the MRI equipment, the MRI project does not have a debt capacity of 100 percent. The willingness of lenders to furnish 100 percent debt capital for the MRI project is based more on Ridgeland's overall creditworthiness than on the financial merits of the MRI project because all of the hospital's operating cash flow, less interest payments on embedded debt, is available to pay the lender. Think of it this way: Would lenders provide 100 percent financing if Ridgeland were a start-up business and the MRI project was its sole source of income?

The logical question here is whether debt capacity differences should be taken into consideration in the capital budgeting process. In theory, if there are meaningful debt capacity differences between a project and the business, capital structure differentials—as well as risk differentials—should be taken into account in the capital budgeting process. For example, an academic health center might be evaluating two projects: one involves research and development (R&D) of a new surgical procedure, and the other involves building a primary care clinic in a local upscale residential area. The R&D project would have relatively low debt capacity because it has high business risk and no assets suitable as loan collateral. Conversely, the clinic project would have relatively high debt capacity because it has low business risk and involves real estate suitable as collateral.

Incorporating capital structure differentials is mechanically easy. We merely change the weights used to compute the corporate cost of capital to reflect project debt capacity rather than use the standard weights that reflect the business's target capital structure. Projects with higher-than-average debt capacity would use a relatively high value for the weight of debt and a relatively low value for the weight of equity and vice versa. However, a problem arises when attempting to make debt capacity adjustments. We know from chapter 10 that increased debt usage raises capital costs, so both the cost of debt and the cost of equity must increase as more debt financing is used. This dependency of capital costs on capital structure means that as the weights are changed in the cost-of-capital calculation, so should the component costs. However, it is very difficult, if not impossible, to estimate individual project costs of debt and equity that correspond to the project's optimal capital structure. Thus, capital structure adjustments quickly become a somewhat futile guessing game, so most businesses do not make such adjustments unless there are specific benchmark values that can be used for both a project's unique debt capacity and the corresponding capital costs.[7]

SELF-TEST QUESTION

1. Discuss the advantages and disadvantages of incorporating debt capacity differences into the capital budgeting decision process.

Adjusting Cash Outflows for Risk

Although most projects are evaluated on the basis of profitability, some are evaluated solely on the basis of costs. Such evaluations are done when it is impossible to allocate revenues to a particular project or when two competing projects will produce the same revenue stream. For example, suppose that

Ridgeland must choose one of two ways of disposing of its medical waste. There is no question about the necessity of the project, and neither method will affect the hospital's revenue stream. In this situation, the decision will be based on the present value of expected future costs; the method with the lower present value of costs will be chosen.

Exhibit 12.7 lists the projected annual costs associated with each method. A large expenditure would be required at year 0 to upgrade the hospital's current disposal system, but the yearly operating costs would be relatively low. Conversely, if Ridgeland contracts for disposal services with an outside contractor, it will have to pay only $25,000 up front to initiate the contract. However, the annual contract fee would be $200,000 a year. Note that inflation effects are ignored in this illustration to simplify the discussion.

If both methods were judged to have average risk, Ridgeland's corporate cost of capital—10 percent—would be applied to the cash flows to obtain the present value (PV) of costs for each method. Because the PVs of costs for the two waste disposal systems—$784,309 for the in-house system and $783,157 for the contract method—are roughly equal at a 10 percent discount rate, Ridgeland's managers would be indifferent as to which method should be chosen if they were basing the decision on financial considerations only.

However, Ridgeland's managers actually believe that the contract method is much riskier than the in-house method. They know the cost of modifying the current system to the dollar, and they can predict operating costs fairly well. Furthermore, the in-house system's operating costs are under the control of Ridgeland's management. Conversely, if the hospital relies on

EXHIBIT 12.7
Ridgeland Community Hospital: Waste Disposal Analysis

	Cash Flows	
Year	*In-House System*	*Outside Contract*
0	($500,000)	($ 25,000)
1	(75,000)	(200,000)
2	(75,000)	(200,000)
3	(75,000)	(200,000)
4	(75,000)	(200,000)
5	(75,000)	(200,000)
Present value of costs at a discount rate of:		
10%	($784,309)	($ 783,157)
14%	–	($ 711,616)
6%	–	($ 867,473)

the contractor for waste disposal, it more or less will have to continue the contract because it will lose in-house capability. Because the contractor was willing to guarantee the price only for the first year, perhaps the bid was low-balled and large price increases will occur in future years. The two methods have about the same PV of costs when both are considered to have average risk—so which method should be chosen if the contract method is judged to have high risk? Clearly, if the costs are the same under a common discount rate, the lower-risk in-house project should be chosen.

Now, try to incorporate this intuitive differential risk conclusion into the quantitative analysis. Conventional wisdom is to increase the corporate cost of capital for high-risk projects, so the contract cash flows would be discounted using a project cost of capital of 14 percent, which is the rate that Ridgeland applies to high-risk projects. However, at a 14 percent discount rate, the contract method has a PV of costs of only $711,616, which is about $70,000 lower than that for the in-house method. If the discount rate on the contract method's cash flows were increased to 20 percent, an even greater amount, it would appear to be $161,000 cheaper than the in-house method. Thus, the riskier the contract method is judged to be, the better it looks.

Something is obviously wrong here! For a cash outflow to be penalized for higher-than-average risk, it must have a higher present value, not a lower one. Therefore, a cash outflow that has higher-than-average risk must be evaluated with a lower-than-average cost of capital. Recognizing this, Ridgeland's managers applied a 10% − 4% = 6% discount rate to the high-risk contract method's cash flows. The result is a PV of costs for the contract method of $867,473, which is about $83,000 more than the PV of costs for the average-risk in-house method.

The appropriate risk adjustment for cash outflows is also applicable in other situations. For example, the city of Detroit offered Ann Arbor Health Care Inc. the opportunity to use a city-owned building in a blighted area for a walk-in clinic. The city offered to pay to refurbish the building, and all profits made by the clinic would accrue to Ann Arbor. However, after ten years, Ann Arbor would have to buy the building from the city at the then-current market value. The market value estimate that Ann Arbor used in its analysis was $2 million, but the realized cost could be much greater, or much less, depending on the economic condition of the neighborhood at that time. The project's other cash flows were of average risk, but this single outflow was high risk, so Ann Arbor lowered the discount rate that it applied to this one cash flow. This action created a higher present value for the $2 million cost (outflow) and hence lowered the project's NPV.

The bottom line here is that risk adjustment for cash outflows is the opposite of adjustment for cash inflows. When cash outflows are being evaluated, higher risk calls for a lower discount rate.[8]

SELF-TEST QUESTIONS

1. Why are some projects evaluated on the basis of present value of costs?
2. Is there any difference between the risk adjustments applied to cash inflows and cash outflows? Explain your answer.
3. Can differential risk adjustments be made to single cash flows, or must the same adjustment be made to all of a project's cash flows?

Real (Managerial) Options

According to traditional capital budgeting analysis techniques, a project's NPV is the present value of its expected future cash flows when discounted at an opportunity cost rate that reflects the riskiness of those flows. However, as discussed in chapter 11 in the section on strategic value, such valuations generally do not incorporate the value inherent in additional actions that the business can take only if the project is accepted. In other words, traditional capital budgeting can be likened to playing roulette: A bet is made (the project is accepted) and the wheel is spun, but nothing can be done to influence the outcome of the game. In reality, capital projects are more like draw poker: Chance does play a role, but the players can influence the final result by discarding the right cards and assessing the other players' actions.

The opportunities that managers have to change a project in response to changing conditions or to build on a project are called *real*, or *managerial*, *options*. These terms denote that such options arise from investments in real, rather than financial, assets and that the options are available to managers of businesses as opposed to individual investors. To illustrate the concept of real options, we introduce decision tree analysis.

Although risk analysis is an integral part of capital budgeting, managers are at least as concerned (or maybe more concerned) about managing risk than they are about measuring it. One way of managing risk is to structure large projects as a series of decision points that provide the opportunity to reevaluate decisions as additional information becomes available, and possibly to **cancel**—or once it begins, to **abandon**—the project if events take a turn for the worse.

Projects that are structured as a series of decision points over time are evaluated using *decision trees.* For example, suppose Medical Equipment International (MEI) is considering the production of a new and innovative intensive care monitoring system. The net investment for this project is broken down into three stages, as set forth in exhibit 12.8. If the go-ahead is given for stage 1 (year 0), the firm will conduct a $500,000 study of the market potential for the new monitoring system, which will take about one year. If the results of the study are unfavorable, the project will be canceled, but if the results are favorable, MEI will (at year 1) spend $1 million to design and fabricate several prototype systems. These systems will then be tested at two hospitals, and MEI will base its decision to proceed with full-scale production on their medical staffs' reactions to them.

If their reactions are positive, MEI will establish a production line for the monitoring systems at one of its plants at a net cost of $10 million. If this stage is reached, MEI's managers estimate that the project will generate net cash flows over the following four years that will depend on the vitality of the hospital sector at that time and the overall performance of the system.

A decision tree such as the one in exhibit 12.8 often is used to analyze such multistage, or sequential, decisions. Here, for simplicity, let's assume that one year goes by between decisions. Each circle represents a decision point or stage. The dollar value to the left of each decision point represents the net investment required to go forward at that decision point, and the cash flows under the $t = 3$ to $t = 6$ headings represent the cash inflows that would occur if the project is carried to completion. Each diagonal line represents the beginning of a branch of the decision tree, and each carries a probability that MEI's managers estimate on the basis of the information available to them today. For example, management estimates that there is a probability of 0.8 that the initial study will produce favorable results, which would lead to the expenditure of $1 million at stage 2, and a 0.2 probability that the initial study will produce unfavorable results, which would lead to cancellation after stage 1.

The joint probabilities shown in exhibit 12.8 give the probability of occurrence of each final outcome—that is, the probability of moving completely along each branch. Each joint probability is obtained by multiplying together all the probabilities along a particular branch. For example, if stage 1 is undertaken, the probability that MEI will move through stages 2 and 3 and that a strong demand will produce $10 million in net cash flows in each of the next four years is $0.8 \times 0.6 \times 0.3 = 0.144 = 14.4\%$.

The NPV of each final outcome is also given in exhibit 12.8. MEI has a corporate cost of capital of 11.5 percent, and its management assumes initially that all projects have average risk. For example, the NPV of the top branch (the most favorable outcome) is about $15,250 (in thousands of dollars):

EXHIBIT 12.8
Decision Tree Analysis (in thousands of dollars)

Time: $t = 0$	$t = 1$	$t = 2$	$t = 3$	$t = 4$	$t = 5$	$t = 6$	Joint Probability	NPV	Product: Prob. × NPV
			0.3 — $10,000	$10,000	$10,000	$10,000	0.144	$15,250	$ 2,196
		0.6 — ($10,000) — (3)	0.4 — $ 4,000	$ 4,000	$ 4,000	$ 4,000	0.192	436	84
	0.8 — ($1,000) — (2)		0.3 — $ 2,000	$ 2,000	($ 2,000)	($ 2,000)	0.144	(14,379)	(2,701)
($500) — (1)		0.4 — Stop					0.320	(1,397)	(447)
	0.2 — Stop						0.200	(500)	(100)
							1.000	Expected NPV =	($ 338)
								σ_{NPV} =	$7,991

$$
\begin{aligned}
\text{NPV} &= -\$500 - \frac{\$1{,}000}{(1.115)^1} - \frac{\$10{,}000}{(1.115)^2} + \frac{\$10{,}000}{(1.115)^3} + \frac{\$10{,}000}{(1.115)^4} \\
&\quad + \frac{\$10{,}000}{(1.115)^5} + \frac{\$10{,}000}{(1.115)^6} \\
&= \$15{,}250.
\end{aligned}
$$

Other NPVs are calculated similarly.

The last column in exhibit 12.8 indicates the product of the NPV for each branch and the joint probability that that branch will occur; the sum of the NPV products is the expected NPV of the project. Considering the expectations set forth in exhibit 12.8, and assuming a cost of capital of 11.5 percent, we determine that the monitoring equipment project's expected NPV is –$338,000.

Because the expected NPV is negative, it appears that this project would be unprofitable and hence should be rejected by MEI unless other considerations prevail. However, this initial judgment may not be correct. MEI must now consider whether this project is more, less, or about as risky as the firm's average project. The expected NPV is a negative $338,000, and the standard deviation of NPV is $7,991,000, so the coefficient of variation of NPV is $7,991,000 ÷ $338,000 = 23.6, which is quite large. (Note that the negative sign for NPV does not enter into the calculation.) The value for the coefficient of variation suggests that the project is highly risky in terms of stand-alone risk. Note also that there is a 0.144 + 0.320 + 0.200 = 0.664 = 66.4% probability of incurring a loss. On the basis of these findings, the project appears to be unacceptable financially unless it has some embedded real options that will increase its value or reduce its risk.

The Real Option of Abandonment

On the web at: *ache.org/HAP/PinkSong8e*

Abandonment, which is discussed in chapter 11 in connection with estimating a project's economic life, is one type of real option that many projects possess. For an illustration of this real option's impact, suppose that MEI is not contractually bound to continue the project once production has begun. Thus, if sales are poor during year 3 ($t = 3$), if MEI experiences a cash flow loss of $2 million, and if similar results are expected for the remaining three years, MEI can abandon the project at the end of year 3 rather than continue to suffer losses. In this situation, low first-year sales signify that the monitoring equipment is not selling well, so future sales will also be poor, and MEI can act on this new information when it becomes available.

MEI's ability to abandon the project changes the branch of the decision tree that contains the series of $2 million losses in exhibit 12.8. It now appears as follows (in thousands of dollars):

		Joint Probability	NPV	Product: Prob. × NPV
③ 0.3 ($2,000) ④	Stop	0.144	($10,883)	($1,567)

Changing this branch to reflect abandonment eliminates the $2 million cash losses in years 4, 5, and 6 and thus causes the NPV for the branch to be higher, although still negative. This change increases the project's expected NPV from –$338,000 to about $166,000 and lowers the project's standard deviation from $7,991,000 to $7,157,000. Thus, the abandonment real option changes the project's expected NPV from negative to positive and also lowers its stand-alone risk as measured either by standard deviation or by coefficient of variation of NPV.

We can use the data just developed to estimate the value of the abandonment option. The NPV with the abandonment option is $166,000, while the NPV without this option is –$338,000, so the value of the real option is $166,000 – (–$338,000) = $504,000. However, this value understates the true value of the option because the ability to abandon the project also lowers the riskiness of the project. With lower risk, the difference between the two NPVs is greater than that calculated, although the added value of risk reduction would be relatively small in this illustration as well as difficult to quantify with confidence. Because of this and similar complications, discounted cash flow techniques (when they can be used to value real options) generally will not produce an accurate estimate of the option's value.

Here are some additional points to note concerning decision tree analysis and abandonment:

- Managers can reduce project risk if they can structure the decision process to include several decision points rather than just one. If MEI were to make a total commitment to the monitoring equipment project at $t = 0$ and sign contracts that would require completion of the project, it might save some money and accelerate the project, but doing so would substantially increase the project's riskiness.
- Once production or service begins, a business's ability to abandon a project can dramatically reduce the project's risk.
- The cost of abandonment generally is reduced if the firm has alternative uses for the project's assets. If MEI can convert the

abandoned monitoring equipment production line to a different, more productive use, the cost of abandonment would be reduced and the monitoring equipment project would become more attractive.

Finally, note that capital budgeting is a dynamic process. Virtually all inputs to a capital budgeting decision change over time, and firms must periodically review both their expenditure plans and their ongoing projects. In the MEI example, conditions might change between decision points 1 and 2; if they do, this new information should be used to revise the probability and cash flow estimates. If a capital budgeting decision can be structured with multiple decision points, including abandonment, and if the firm's managers have the fortitude to admit when a project is not working out as initially planned, risks can be reduced and expected profitability can be increased.

Other Real Options

The MEI monitoring system project demonstrates that the real option of abandonment can add value to a project. In addition to abandonment, there are many other types of real options.

Flexibility Options

The *flexibility option* allows managers to switch inputs between alternative production or service processes. For example, by training clinical personnel to perform multiple tasks, individuals hired for a new service can potentially be used productively in other parts of the business. Thus, labor costs associated with the new service can be easily reduced if demand estimates are not met. This flexibility option reduces costs in poor utilization scenarios and hence increases the value of the project.

Capacity Options

The *capacity option* allows businesses to manage their productive capacity in response to changing market conditions. If a project can be structured so that its operations can be reduced or suspended if warranted rather than completely shut down, the value of the project increases. The option to expand new services from a relatively small scale to a large scale also adds value.

New Service Options

It is easy to envision a situation in which a negative NPV project is accepted because embedded in it is an option to add complementary services or successive "generations of services." A managed care organization's first move into a new geographic area and the introduction of transplant services at a hospital are two examples. In such situations, the first project may not be profitable, but it can lead to additional opportunities that are.

Timing Options

In our examples thus far, new projects brought with them embedded real options that could be exercised in the future and hence added value to the project. *Timing options* can be somewhat different, in that in some circumstances they involve extinguishing existing real options. Timing options were first analyzed in situations involving natural resources, such as when to harvest a forested area or how much oil to pump out of a well. By harvesting or pumping now, the project can produce immediate cash flows, but doing so eliminates the opportunity to obtain future cash flows from the same resource.

On the web at: *ache.org/HAP/PinkSong8e*

Of most interest to healthcare businesses is the *option to delay*, which is another type of timing option. If a project can be postponed, it might be more valuable in the future because, for example, managed care power is diminishing, technology is advancing, or information that will decrease the project's risk is expected to become available. Of course, the option to delay is valuable only if it is worth more than the costs of delaying, which include time value of money costs, costs associated with competitor actions, and patient satisfaction costs. Thus, in general, the option to delay is most valuable to businesses that have proprietary technology or some other barrier to entry that lessens the costs associated with postponement.

Valuation of Projects That Have Real Options

In general, the true value of a project with real options can be thought of as the discounted cash flow (DCF) NPV plus the value of the real options:

$$\text{True NPV} = \text{DCF NPV} + \text{Value of real options.}$$

In most healthcare situations, a dollar value cannot be placed on any real options associated with a project. However, managers should still think about the value of many projects in terms of this equation. Here are some points to consider:

- Real options can add considerable value to many projects, so failure to consider such options leads to downward-biased NPVs and thus to systematic underinvestment.
- In general, the longer a real option lasts before it must be "exercised," the more valuable it is. For example, suppose the real option is to expand into related services, such as expanding rehabilitative services into sports medicine services. The longer the expansion can be delayed and still retain its value, the more valuable the option.
- The more volatile the value of the underlying source of the real option, the more valuable the option. Thus, the more return volatility there is

in the return on sports medicine services, the greater the value of a real option to expand into such services.

- The higher the cost of capital (the higher the general level of interest rates), the more valuable the real option. This point is not intuitive, but we explain the rationale in chapter 18 (available online) in our discussion of stock options.

SELF-TEST QUESTIONS

1. How can the possibility of abandonment affect a project's profitability and stand-alone risk?
2. What are the costs and benefits of structuring large capital budgeting decisions in stages rather than in a single decision?
3. Why might DCF valuation underestimate the true value of a project?
4. What are some different types of real options?
5. How does the presence of real options influence capital budgeting decisions?

An Overview of the Capital Budgeting Decision Process

The discussion of capital budgeting thus far has focused on how managers evaluate individual projects. For capital planning purposes, healthcare managers also need to forecast the total number of projects that will be undertaken and the dollar amount of capital needed to fund these projects. The list of projects to be undertaken is called the ***capital budget***, and the optimal selection of new projects is called the ***optimal capital budget***.

While every healthcare provider estimates its optimal capital budget in its own way, some procedures are common to all businesses. We use the procedures followed by CALFIRST Health System to illustrate the process:

- The chief financial officer (CFO) estimates the system's corporate cost of capital. As discussed in chapter 9, this estimate depends on market conditions, the business risk of CALFIRST's assets in the aggregate, and the systemwide optimal capital structure.
- The CFO then scales the corporate cost of capital up or down to reflect the unique risk and capital structure features of each division. Assume that CALFIRST has three divisions: LRD (low-risk division), ARD (average-risk division), and HRD (high-risk division).

- Managers in each of the divisions evaluate the riskiness of the proposed projects to their divisions by categorizing each project as LRP (low-risk project), ARP (average-risk project), or HRP (high-risk project). These project risk classifications are based on the riskiness of each project relative to the other projects in the division, not to the system in the aggregate.
- Each project is then assigned a project cost of capital that is based on the divisional cost of capital and the project's relative riskiness. As discussed previously, this project cost of capital is then used to discount the project's expected net cash flows. From a financial standpoint, all projects with positive NPVs are acceptable, while those with negative NPVs should be rejected. Subjective factors are also considered, and these factors may prompt a decision that differs from the one established solely on the basis of financial considerations.

Exhibit 12.9 summarizes CALFIRST's overall capital budgeting process. Here, the corporate cost of capital, 10 percent, is adjusted upward to 14 percent in the HRD and downward to 8 percent in the LRD. The same adjustment—4 percentage points upward for HRPs and 2 percentage points downward for LRPs—is applied to differential risk projects in each division. The end result is a range of project costs of capital in CALFIRST that runs from 18 percent for HRPs in the HRD to 6 percent for LRPs in the LRD.

The result is a financial analysis process that incorporates each project's debt capacity, at least at the divisional level, and riskiness. However, managers also must consider other possible risk factors that may not have been included in the quantitative analysis. For example, could the project being evaluated significantly increase the business's liability exposure? Conversely, does the project have any real option value, social value, or other attributes that could affect its profitability or riskiness? Such additional factors must be considered, at least subjectively, before a final decision can be made. (A framework for considering multiple decision factors—the project scoring approach—is discussed in chapter 11.) Typically, if the project involves new products or services and is large (in capital requirements) relative to the size of the business's average project, the additional subjective factors will be important to the final decision; one large mistake can bankrupt a firm, so "bet-the-firm" decisions are not made lightly. On the other hand, a decision on a small replacement project would be made mostly on the basis of numerical analysis.

Ultimately, capital budgeting decisions require an analysis of a mix of objective and subjective factors such as risk, debt capacity, profitability, medical staff (patient) needs, real option value, and social value. The process is not precise, and often there is a temptation to ignore one or more important factors because they are so nebulous and difficult to measure. Despite this

EXHIBIT 12.9 CALFIRST: Divisional and Project Costs of Capital

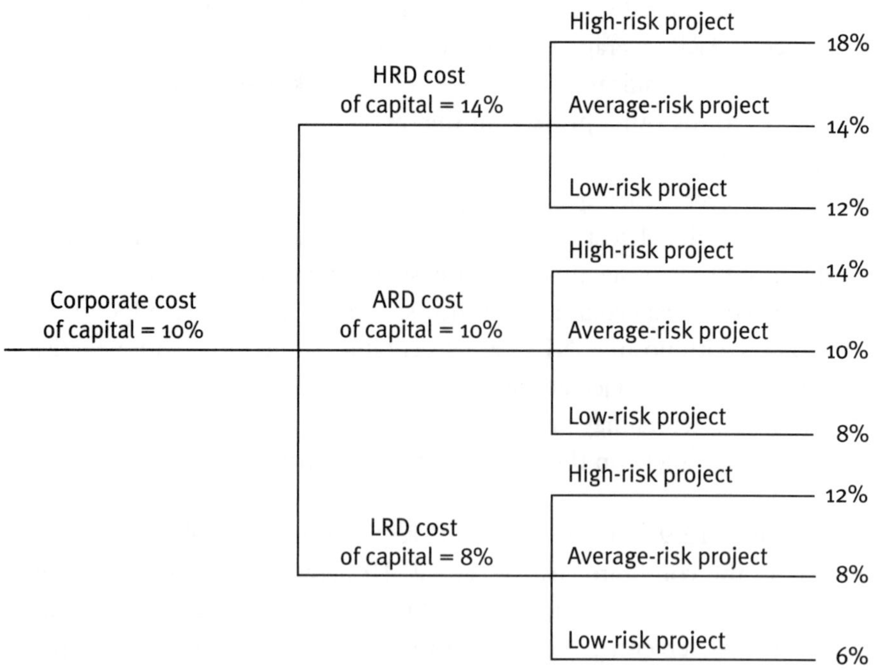

imprecision and subjectivity, a project's risk, as well as its other attributes, should be assessed and incorporated into the capital budgeting decision process.

SELF-TEST QUESTIONS

1. Describe a typical capital budgeting decision process.
2. Are decisions made solely on the basis of quantitative factors? Explain your answer.

Capital Rationing

Standard capital budgeting procedures assume that businesses can raise virtually unlimited amounts of capital to meet capital budgeting needs. Presumably, as long as a business is investing the funds in profitable (i.e., positive NPV) projects, it should be able to raise the debt and equity needed to fund all such projects. In addition, standard capital budgeting procedures assume that a business raises the capital needed to finance its optimal capital budget roughly in accordance with its target capital structure and at an average cost equal to the estimated corporate cost of capital.

This picture of a business's capital financing and capital investment process is probably appropriate for large investor-owned firms in most situations. However, not-for-profit firms and small investor-owned businesses typically do not have unlimited access to capital. Their ability to raise equity capital often is limited, and their debt capital is constrained to the amount supported by the equity capital base. Thus, such businesses will likely face periods in which the capital needed for investment in worthwhile new projects will exceed the amount of capital available. This situation is called *capital rationing*.

If capital rationing exists (i.e., a business has more acceptable projects than capital), from a financial perspective the business should accept the set of capital projects that maximizes aggregate NPV and still meets the capital constraint. This approach can be called "getting the most bang for the buck" because it picks projects that have the most positive impact on the business's financial condition.

Another ROI measure—the *profitability index (PI)*—is useful in a capital rationing situation. The PI is defined as the PV of cash inflows divided by the PV of cash outflows. Thus, for Ridgeland's MRI project discussed earlier in the chapter, PI = \$2,582,493 ÷ \$2,500,000 = 1.03. The PI measures a project's dollars of profitability per dollar of investment, all on a PV basis. The MRI project promises three cents of profit for every dollar invested, which indicates it is not very profitable. (The PI of 1.03 is before adjusting for risk. After adjusting for risk, the project's PI is less than 1.00, indicating that the project is unprofitable.) In a capital rationing situation, the optimal capital budget is determined by first listing all profitable projects in descending order of PI. Then, projects are selected from the top of the list downward until the capital available is used up.

Of course, in healthcare businesses, priority may be assigned to some low or even negative NPV projects, which is fine as long as these projects are offset by the selection of profitable projects, which would prevent the low-profitability priority projects from eroding the business's financial condition.

SELF-TEST QUESTIONS

1. What is capital rationing?
2. From a financial perspective, how are projects chosen when capital rationing exists?
3. What is the profitability index, and why is it useful in a capital rationing situation?

Chapter Key Concepts

This chapter discussed project risk definition, assessment, and incorporation. Here are its key concepts:

- There are three *types of project risk*: (1) stand-alone risk, (2) corporate risk, and (3) market risk.
- A project's *stand-alone risk* is the risk the project would have if it were the sole project of a not-for-profit firm. It is measured by the variability of profitability, generally by the *standard deviation* or *coefficient of variation* of NPV. Stand-alone risk often is used as a proxy for corporate and market risk because (1) corporate and market risk are often impossible to measure and (2) the three types of risk are usually highly correlated.
- *Corporate risk* reflects a project's contribution to the overall riskiness of the business. Corporate risk ignores stockholder diversification and is relevant to not-for-profit firms.
- *Market risk* reflects the contribution of a project to the overall riskiness of the owners' well-diversified investment portfolios. In theory, market risk is relevant to investor-owned firms, but many people argue that corporate risk is also relevant to owners, especially the owners and managers of small businesses, and it is certainly relevant to a business's other stakeholders.
- Three quantitative techniques are commonly used to *assess a project's stand-alone risk*: (1) sensitivity analysis, (2) scenario analysis, and (3) Monte Carlo simulation.
- *Sensitivity analysis* shows how much a project's profitability—for example, as measured by NPV—changes in response to a given change in an input variable such as volume, other things held constant.
- *Scenario analysis* defines a project's best, most likely, and worst possible outcomes and then uses these data to measure its stand-alone risk.
- Whereas scenario analysis focuses on only a few possible outcomes, *Monte Carlo simulation* uses continuous distributions to reflect the uncertainty inherent in a project's component cash flows. The result is a probability distribution of NPV, or IRR, that provides a great deal of information about the project's riskiness.

(continued)

(continued from previous page)

- In addition to quantitative risk assessment techniques, the *qualitative approach* uses the answers to yes-or-no questions to assess project risk.
- Projects that require capital outlays in stages over time often are evaluated using *decision trees*. The branches of the tree represent different outcomes, and, when subjective probabilities are assigned to the outcomes, the tree provides the profitability distribution for the project.
- In addition to the DCF-calculated NPV, some projects have additional value in the form of embedded *real (managerial) options*.
- One type of real option is the ability to *abandon* a project once operations have begun. This option can both increase a project's dollar return and decrease its riskiness and thus has a twofold positive effect on value.
- There are two methods for incorporating project risk into the capital budgeting decision process: (1) the *certainty equivalent (CE) method*, which adjusts a project's expected cash flows to reflect project risk, and (2) the *risk-adjusted discount rate (RADR) method*, which deals with differential risk by changing the cost of capital.
- Projects are generally classified as *high risk*, *average risk*, or *low risk* on the basis of their stand-alone risk assessment. High-risk projects are evaluated at a discount rate greater than the firm's corporate cost of capital, average-risk projects are evaluated at the corporate cost of capital, and low-risk projects are evaluated at a rate less than the corporate cost of capital. In a business with divisions, the risk-adjustment process often takes place at the divisional level.
- In the evaluation of *risky cash outflows*, the risk adjustment process is reversed—that is, lower rates are used to discount more risky cash flows.
- Ultimately, capital budgeting decisions require an analysis of a mix of *objective and subjective factors* such as risk, debt capacity, profitability, medical staff needs, real option value, and social value. The process is not precise, but good managers do their best to ensure that none of the relevant factors are ignored.

(continued)

(continued from previous page)

- In a *capital rationing* situation, the business has more profitable projects than investment capital. In such cases, the profitability index (PI) is a useful measure of profitability (ROI).

This concludes our discussion of capital budgeting. In chapters 13 and 14, we discuss financial and operating analyses and financial forecasting.

Chapter Models, Problems, and Minicases

The following ancillary resources in spreadsheet format are available for this chapter:

- A chapter model that shows how to perform many of the calculations described in the chapter
- Problems that test your ability to perform the calculations
- A minicase that is more complicated than the problems and tests your ability to perform the calculations in preparation for a case

These resources can be accessed online at ache.org/HAP/PinkSong8e.

Selected Cases

Our discussion of capital budgeting is now complete. Several cases in *Cases in Healthcare Finance*, sixth edition, can be used at this point:

- Case 19: Jones Memorial Hospital, which focuses on a capital investment decision that involves use of alternative technologies
- Case 20: Coral Bay Hospital, which focuses on a "bread and butter" capital budgeting analysis of a proposed ambulatory surgery center
- Case 21: National Rehabilitation Centers, which requires a staged entry (decision tree) analysis
- Case 22: Northwest Suburban Health System, which involves a make-or-buy analysis regarding a health system's printing services

Selected Bibliography

Brown, B. 2016. "Using Business Intelligence to Bring Financial Challenges into Focus." *Healthcare Financial Management* 70 (8): 54–63.

Gapenski, L. C. 1992. "Project Risk Definition and Measurement in a Not-for-Profit Setting." *Health Services Management* (November): 216–24.

Hill, L. E. 2016. "Pioneering a Rolling Forecast." *Healthcare Financial Management* 70 (11): 58–62.

Kolman, C. M. 2017. "Transforming Healthcare Analytics to Manage Costs." *Healthcare Financial Management* 71 (6): 28–33.

Moore, K. D., and D. Coddington. 2016. "Integrating Health Care's Many Levels of Thinking." *Healthcare Financial Management* 70 (10): 80–81.

Ratliff, D., and E. A. Jordahl. 2018. "Finding Reality in a Cloud of Possibility." *Healthcare Financial Management* 72 (3): 68–69.

Skinner, J., R. Higbea, D. Buer, and C. Horvath. 2018. "Using Predictive Analytics to Align ED Staffing Resources with Patient Demand." *Healthcare Financial Management* 72 (2): 56–61.

Selected Websites

The following websites pertain to the content of this chapter:

- Several spreadsheet add-on software packages that perform Monte Carlo simulation are available. A demonstration version of one, called @RISK, can be downloaded from www.palisade.com/trials.asp.
- Similarly, a free trial download of decision tree software Precision Tree is available from the same website at www.palisade.com/precisiontree. As discussed in the chapter, it can be used to make decisions that generate consequences in multiple stages.

Notes

1. The three types of risk relevant to capital budgeting decisions are first discussed in chapter 5. A review of the applicable sections may be beneficial to some readers.
2. For an algebraic presentation of the relationships between the three types of risk, see Gapenski, L. C. 1992. "Project Risk Definition and

Measurement in a Not-for-Profit Setting." *Health Services Management* (November): 216–24.

3. Spreadsheet programs have Data Table functions that automatically perform sensitivity analyses. After the table is roughed in, the spreadsheet automatically calculates and records a project's NPV, or some other value, in the appropriate cells in the table. This feature is explained in the chapter 12 model, which can be accessed online at ache.org/HAP/PinkSong8e.
4. *Skewness* measures the degree of symmetry of a distribution. A skewness of zero indicates a symmetric distribution, positive skewness indicates a distribution that is skewed to the right (its right tail is longer than its left), and negative skewness indicates a distribution that is skewed to the left (its left tail is longer than its right). The absolute value of the number indicates the degree of skewness—the larger the number, the more skewed the distribution.
5. Economists use utility theory to explain how individuals make choices among risky alternatives.
6. The risk-free rate does not incorporate the tax advantage of debt financing, so such benefits to taxable firms should be incorporated directly into the cash flows when the CE method is used. Alternatively, the discount rate can be determined using the corporate cost-of-capital formula, but with the risk-free rate in place of the costs of debt and equity. The discount rate calculated in this way is the risk-free rate with the tax advantage included, so it can be applied to the CE cash flows without tax adjustments.
7. Debt capacity adjustments are often made in *project financing*. In this type of financing, lenders provide debt capital solely on the basis of the earnings power of the project because they have limited or no recourse against the business's other cash flows. In this situation, there is a readily identifiable cost of debt and debt capacity for the project.
8. What happens when the cash flows being discounted include both inflows and outflows so that the proper risk adjustment is not obvious? The solution is to try an adjustment and see what happens. For example, if the corporate cost of capital is 10 percent and the mixed cash flow project is judged to have high risk, discount the cash flows at 14 percent. If the NPV of the project increases, the adjustment clearly is wrong because an adjustment for high risk should penalize the project. Thus, the correct adjustment is to decrease the cost of capital—say, to 6 percent.

Integrative Application

The Problem

Zachary Taylor Managed Care (ZTMC) is considering expanding into the Atlanta market. The company is a comprehensive managed care organization and has discovered that several large employers in the area are highly dissatisfied with their current managed care organizations. ZTMC estimates that getting into the Atlanta market will require an initial capital investment of $150 million that will have an estimated life of ten years. However, there is substantial uncertainty around the size of the managed care market, what share of the managed care market ZTMC will be able to attract, the unit price that can be charged, the unit variable utilization cost, and the annual fixed costs. ZTMC uses straight-line depreciation, has a corporate cost of capital of 10 percent, and pays taxes at a rate of 30 percent. Management has prepared the following forecast:

	Pessimistic	*Expected*	*Optimistic*
Market size	900,000	1,000,000	1,100,000
Market share	4%	10%	16%
Unit price	$ 3,500	$ 3,750	$ 3,800
Unit variable cost	$ 3,600	$ 3,000	$ 2,750
Fixed cost	$40,000,000	$30,000,000	$20,000,000

What source of uncertainty in the capital investment decision should ZTMC be most concerned about?

The Analysis

The first step is to calculate the estimated net cash flow from the investment.

	Annual Cash Flow (in millions of dollars)
1. Revenue: (1,000,000 market size × 10% market share × = $3,750 unit price)	= $375.00
2. Variable cost: (1,000,000 market size × 10% market share × $3,750 unit vc)	= $300.00
3. Fixed cost	$ 30.00

4. Depreciation:	($150,000,000 ÷ 10-year life)	= $ 15.00
5. Pretax profit:	(Lines 1 – 2 – 3 – 4)	= $ 30.00
6. Tax:	(Line 5) × 30%	= $ 9.00
7. Net profit:	(Lines 5 – 6)	= $ 21.00
8. Operating cash flow:	(Lines 4 + 7)	= $ 36.00
The expected NPV of the investment is = – PV (10%, 10, $36) + ($150) million.		= $ 71.20

Now, suppose the market size is 900,000 instead of the expected 1,000,000 (and all else remains the same). The estimated net cash flow from the investment becomes:

		Annual Cash Flow (in millions of dollars)
1. Revenue: (900,000 market size × 10% market share × $3,750 unit price)		= $337.50
2. Variable cost: (900,000 market size × 10% market share × $3,750 unit vc)		= $270.00
3. Fixed cost		$ 30.00
4. Depreciation:	($150,000,000 ÷ 10-year life)	= $ 15.00
5. Pretax profit:	(Lines 1 – 2 – 3 – 4)	= $ 22.50
6. Tax:	(Line 5) × 30%	= $ 6.75
7. Net profit:	(Lines 5 – 6)	= $ 15.75
8. Operating cash flow:	(Lines 4 + 7)	= $ 30.75
The expected NPV of the investment becomes = PV (10%, 10, $30.75) + ($150) = $38.95 million.		

Changing one variable at a time and recalculating NPV produces the following table of expected NPVs:

	Net Present Value		
	Pessimistic	*Expected*	*Optimistic*
Market size	$ 38.95	$71.20	$103.46
Market share	($122.35)	$71.20	$264.76
Unit price	($ 36.33)	$71.20	$ 92.71
Unit variable cost	($186.87)	$71.20	$178.73
Fixed cost	$ 28.19	$71.20	$ 114.22

The table shows that the sources of uncertainty that ZTMC should be most concerned about are market share and unit variable cost (and unit price, to a lesser extent). If market share is 4 percent instead of the expected 10 percent or if unit variable costs are $3,600 instead of the expected $3,000, expansion into the Atlanta market could produce very large negative NPVs to ZTMC.

The Decision

ZTMC decided to focus on (1) marketing—that is, approaching employers to ensure the expected market share—and (2) cost control—that is, using Lean and Six Sigma techniques to ensure that services are provided efficiently. ■

PART

VI

FINANCIAL CONDITION ANALYSIS AND FORECASTING

In part VI, we change our focus from capital acquisition and allocation decisions to financial condition analysis and forecasting. Of all the elements needed to effectively manage a healthcare organization's financial performance, perhaps the two most important are (1) understanding the business's current financial condition and (2) having a financial road map in place to move the business into the future.

The material in part VI is divided into two chapters. Chapter 13 discusses the tools used to assess a business's financial condition. Much of this chapter is devoted to ratio analysis, which is the primary technique used in financial condition assessment. Chapter 14 covers the basic techniques used to forecast a business's financial future with a focus on forecasting a business's financial statements. Using the tools discussed in chapter 13, managers can then examine the forecasted statements to assess the financial attractiveness of alternative business strategies.

CHAPTER

13

FINANCIAL CONDITION ANALYSIS

Learning Objectives

After studying this chapter, readers should be able to

- explain the purposes of financial statement and operating indicator analyses,
- apply the primary techniques used in financial statement and operating indicator analyses,
- illustrate the problems associated with financial statement and operating indicator analyses,
- explain the economic-value-added model and its relevance to healthcare businesses,
- describe how key performance indicators and dashboards can be used to monitor financial condition, and
- use basic financial condition analyses to assess the financial performance of a business.

Introduction

Financial condition analysis is of vital concern to healthcare managers, security analysts, equity investors, and lenders. The purposes of such analyses are to assess the financial condition of a business and, perhaps more important, to identify the operating factors that led to that condition. In general, financial condition analysis comprises three pieces. ***Financial statement analysis*** focuses on the data contained in a firm's financial statements, such as revenues, operating costs, accounts receivable, and total assets. ***Operating indicator analysis*** focuses on operating factors, such as occupancy (census), patient mix, length of stay, and labor productivity. Finally, other analysis techniques—such as economic value added (EVA)—provide supplementary information about a business's financial condition.

In this chapter, we discuss several techniques used to extract information from a firm's financial statements (and elsewhere) and combine it in a form that helps managers make judgments about a business's financial condition and the operational factors that led to that condition. Often, the end result of such analyses is a list of a business's strengths and weaknesses and, one hopes, a plan to correct any weaknesses identified. In addition, we discuss related topics, such as the problems inherent in such analyses. For the most part, financial condition analysis is applied to historical data, so judgments made on the basis of this analysis reflect the results of past managerial decisions. However, the more interesting question is what the business will do in the future. Therefore, managers invariably use the analyses discussed in this chapter to help predict and plan for the future, which is the subject of chapter 14.

You will discover that financial condition analysis generates a great deal of data. A significant problem in assessing financial condition is presenting the results in a simple, easy-to-monitor format. Thus, we close the chapter with some ideas about data presentation.

Financial Reporting in the Health Services Sector

Financial reporting in all industries follows standards set forth by the accounting profession, called *generally accepted accounting principles (GAAP)*. The purpose of such standards is to ensure, to the extent possible, that financial information reported to outsiders is consistent across businesses and presented in a manner that facilitates interpretation and judgments. Because the health services field has many unique features, including a high proportion of not-for-profit businesses, there are many organizations involved in setting reporting standards. Although the detail of establishing accounting standards is beyond the scope of this text, note that such standards are constantly being reviewed and modified as necessary to reflect changing economic conditions.

Accounting standards require businesses to prepare several *financial statements*, including three basic types: (1) *income statement*, (2) *balance sheet*, and (3) *statement of cash flows*. Taken together, these statements provide an accounting picture of the firm's operations and its financial position. Detailed data are

New Bad Debt Accounting Standards

Beginning in 2018 (for public entities) and 2019 (for nonpublic entities), the classification and reporting of bad debt losses will change under the GAAP. A new revenue recognition standard will require that hospitals and other healthcare providers consider both explicit and implicit price concessions when reporting net revenue. As discussed in earlier paragraphs, under existing GAAP, discounts, allowances, and charity care are subtracted from revenue before it is reported on the income statement. These deductions are defined as explicit price concessions under the new standard. However, many of the bad debt losses that are currently reported as revenue deductions under existing GAAP will be defined as implicit price concessions under the new standard and will be treated differently.

For example, a patient may owe the hospital a copayment of $800 for services provided. Historical experience with similar patients, or a credit assessment performed on a specific patient, may

(continued)

provided for the two or three most recent periods; plus, brief historical summaries of key operating statistics for longer periods are often included.

Depending on size and ownership, a business's financial statements usually are made available to interested outside parties. Most large businesses prepare an *annual report*, which provides financial statements and a written description of the business's operating results during the past year, along with a discussion of developments that will affect its future operations. In addition, large investor-owned corporations must file even more detailed reports on an annual basis (a 10-K) and a quarterly basis (a 10-Q) with the Securities and Exchange Commission (SEC). Finally, many larger firms publish *statistical supplements*, which include financial statement data and key ratios from the past ten years or so. These reports—and similar reports that may be filed with state regulatory agencies—are often available from online sources, including the business itself.

Exhibit 13.1 contains simplified forms of the 2017 and 2018 income statements (also called *statements of operations* or *statements of revenues and expenses*) for Bayside Memorial Hospital, a 450-bed, not-for-profit, acute care hospital. Although a hospital is being used to illustrate financial condition analysis techniques, such techniques can be applied to any health services setting. Bayside had an excess of revenues over expenses, or net income, of $8,572,000 in 2018. Of course, being not-for-profit, the hospital paid no dividends, so it retained all of its net income. When looking at an income statement, we can get a rough idea of the organization's cash flow, which is approximately equal to its net income plus any noncash expenses. In 2018, Bayside's cash flow was $8,572,000 in

(continued from previous page)

suggest that the patient will not pay the $800. Under current GAAP, the $800 copayment is classified as bad debt loss and is recorded as a revenue deduction on the income statement. However, under the new revenue recognition standard, the $800 copayment would be considered an implicit price concession and would be treated similarly to charity care and discounts and allowances. In other words, the $800 would be deducted from patient service revenue before it is reported on the income statement. Only unanticipated nonpayments, such as those associated with a patient bankruptcy, will be considered bad debt losses, and these will be recorded as an operating expense rather than a revenue deduction. The net result is an expected decline in the total amount of bad debt losses that appear as such on the income statements of healthcare providers.

Some observers are concerned that the new revenue recognition standard will affect how hospitals report their community benefits. Although the Internal Revenue Service (IRS) does not include bad debt in its definition of community benefits, some hospitals include bad debt and charity care in Medicaid or Medicare underpayment calculations. There is also a concern that the change could affect hospitals' justification for tax-exempt status because tax-exempt hospitals report bad debt on their IRS Form 990—reported bad debt would be lower under the new standards. However, it is possible that many hospitals may simply sidestep the change by simply exchanging the term "bad debt" with "implicit price discounts" or "implicit price concession," terms that mean virtually the same thing. Although implicit price concession is not a required disclosure, many not-for-profit health systems will likely disclose this amount in footnotes of their financial statements and for their community benefit reporting (Bannow 2018).

EXHIBIT 13.1
Bayside Memorial Hospital Statements of Operations (Income Statements) Years Ended December 31, 2018 and 2017 (in thousands of dollars)

	2018	2017
Revenues:		
Patient service revenue	$106,502	$ 95,398
Less: Provision for bad debts	3,328	3,469
Net patient service	$103,174	$ 91,929
Premium revenue	5,232	4,622
Other revenue	3,3644	6,014
Total operating revenues	$112,050	$102,565
Expenses:		
Nursing services	$ 58,285	$ 56,752
Dietary services	5,424	4,718
General services	13,198	11,655
Administrative services	11,427	11,585
Employee health and welfare	10,250	10,705
Malpractice insurance	1,320	1,204
Depreciation	4,130	4,025
Interest expense	1,542	1,521
Total expenses	$105,576	$102,165
Operating income	$ 6,474	$ 400
Nonoperating income	2,098	1,995
Net income	$ 8,572	$ 2,395

net income plus $4,130,000 in depreciation expense, for a total estimated net cash flow of $12,702,000. Depreciation does not really **provide** funds; it is simply a noncash charge added back to net income to obtain an estimate of the business's net cash flow. Later in this section, we will discuss the statement of cash flows, which provides better insight into Bayside.

Note that the income statement reports on transactions **over a period**—for example, during fiscal year 2018. (Bayside's fiscal year coincides with the calendar year.) The balance sheet, which we discuss next, may be thought of as a snapshot of the firm's asset, liability, and equity position **at a single point in time**—for example, on December 31, 2018.

Balance Sheet

Exhibit 13.2 contains Bayside's 2017 and 2018 balance sheets. Although the assets are stated in terms of dollars, only the amount of cash in the checking account represents actual money. We see that Bayside could, if it liquidated its cash equivalents and short-term investment securities, write checks at the end of 2018 for a total of $6,263,000 (versus total current liabilities of

EXHIBIT 13.2
Bayside Memorial Hospital Balance Sheets December 31, 2018 and 2017 (in thousands of dollars)

	2018	2017
Cash and equivalents	$ 2,263	$ 3,095
Short-term investments	4,000	2,000
Net patient accounts receivable	21,840	20,738
Inventories	3,177	2,982
Total current assets	$ 31,280	$ 28,815
Gross property and equipment	$145,158	$140,865
Accumulated depreciation	25,160	21,030
Net property and equipment	$119,998	$119,835
Total assets	$151,278	$148,650
Accounts payable	$ 4,707	$ 5,145
Accrued expenses	5,650	5,421
Notes payable	2,975	6,237
Total current liabilities	$ 13,332	$ 16,803
Long-term debt	$ 28,750	$ 30,900
Finance lease obligations	1,832	2,155
Total long-term liabilities	$ 30,582	$ 33,055
Net assets (equity)	$107,364	$ 98,792
Total liabilities and net assets	$151,278	$148,650

$13,332,000 due during 2018). The noncash current assets will presumably be converted to cash within a year, but they do not represent cash on hand.

The claims against assets are of two types: (1) liabilities, or money the firm owes, and (2) equity, also called ***net assets*** or ***fund capital***.[1] Equity is a residual, so for 2018,

Assets	–	Liabilities	=	Equity, or
$151,278,000	–	($13,332,000 + $30,582,000)	=	$107,364,000.

Liabilities consist of $13,332,000 of current liabilities plus $30,582,000 of long-term liabilities. If assets decline in value—suppose some of Bayside's fixed assets were sold at less than book value—liabilities remain constant, so the value of the equity capital declines.

A business's equity account is built up over time by retentions (retained earnings). In 2018, Bayside's income statement reported a net income of $8,572,000. As a not-for-profit organization, none of the net income can be paid out in dividends, so the entire amount must be retained in the business.

Barring any asset sales or revaluations, Bayside's equity account should increase from year to year by the amount of net income. Thus,

2018 Equity balance	=	2017 Equity balance	+	2018 Net income, or
\$107,364,000	=	\$98,792,000	+	\$8,572,000.

Note that accumulated depreciation reported on the balance sheet is a *contra asset* account; that is, it is subtracted from gross property and equipment, so the larger a firm's accumulated depreciation, all else the same, the smaller its total assets. However, as noted earlier, the larger the amount of depreciation in any year, the greater the business's cash flow because depreciation is a noncash expense. Accumulated depreciation on the balance sheet increases each year by the amount of depreciation expense reported on the income statement. For example:

2018 accumulated depreciation	=	2017 accumulated depreciation	+	2018 depreciation expense, or
\$25,160,000	=	\$21,030,000	+	\$4,130,000.

Statement of Cash Flows

The statement of cash flows can be thought of as an income statement that has been converted from accrual accounting to cash accounting. In essence, the statement of cash flows reports where a business gets its cash and what it does with that cash.

The statement is organized into three main sections: (1) cash flow from operating activities, (2) cash flow from investing activities, and (3) cash flow from financing activities. In addition, there is a short section that reconciles the net cash flow reported on the statement with the change in the cash reported on the balance sheet.

Exhibit 13.3 contains Bayside's statement of cash flows, which focuses on the sources and uses of overall cash flow, for 2018. In the statement, cash coming into the hospital (inflows) is shown as positive numbers, while cash being spent (outflows) is shown as negative numbers (shown in parentheses). The top part lists cash generated by and used in operations. For Bayside, operations provided \$9,098,000 in net cash flow. The income statement reported \$6,474,000 in operating income and \$4,130,000 in depreciation, for \$10,604,000 in operating cash flow. But as part of its operations, Bayside invested \$1,297,000 in current assets (receivables and inventories) and lost \$209,000 in spontaneous liabilities (payables and accruals). The end result—*net cash flow from operations*—was \$10,604,000 – \$1,297,000 – \$209,000 = \$9,098,000.

EXHIBIT 13.3 Bayside Memorial Hospital Statement of Cash Flows Year Ended December 31, 2019 (in thousands of dollars)

Cash flows from operating activities:	
Operating income	$ 6,474
Adjustments:	
Depreciation	4,130
Increase in accounts receivable	(1,102)
Increase in inventories	(195)
Decrease in accounts payable	(438)
Increase in accrued expenses	229
Net cash flow from operations	$ 9,098
Cash flows from investing activities:	
Investment in property and equipment	($ 4,293)
Investment in short-term securities	(2,000)
Net cash flow from investing	($ 6,293)
Cash flows from financing activities:	
Nonoperating income	$ 2,098
Repayment of long-term debt	(2,150)
Repayment of notes payable	(3,262)
Finance lease principal repayment	(323)
Net cash flow from financing	($ 3,637)
Net increase (decrease) in cash and equivalents	($ 832)
Beginning cash and equivalents	$ 3,095
Ending cash and equivalents	$ 2,263

The next section of the statement of cash flows focuses on investments in fixed assets (property and equipment) and in financial assets (securities). As noted in the statement, Bayside spent $4,293,000 on capital expenditures in 2018 and invested $2,000,000 in short-term securities, for a net cash outflow from investing of $6,293,000.

Bayside's financing activities, as shown in the third section, highlight the fact that the hospital received $2,098,000 in nonoperating income (unrestricted contributions and investment income) and used cash to pay off previously incurred long-term debt, short-term debt, and finance lease obligations. The net effect of the hospital's financing activities was a *net cash outflow from financing* of $3,637,000.

When the three major sections are totaled, Bayside had a $9,098,000 – $6,293,000 – $3,637,000 = $832,000 *net decrease in cash* (i.e., net cash outflow) during 2018. The bottom of exhibit 13.3 reconciles the net cash flow with the ending cash balance shown on the balance sheet. Bayside began 2018 with \$3,095,000 in cash and equivalents, experienced a net cash outflow of \$832,000 during the year, and ended the year with \$3,095,000 – \$832,000 = \$2,263,000 in its cash and equivalents account, as verified by the value reported in exhibit 13.2.

Bayside's statement of cash flows shows nothing unusual or alarming. It does show that the hospital's operations are inherently profitable (generated a positive cash flow), at least in 2018. Had the statement shown an operating cash drain, Bayside's managers would have had something to worry about; if it continued, such a drain could bleed the hospital to death. The statement of cash flows also provides information about Bayside's financing and fixed-asset-investing activities for the year that is easy to interpret. For example, Bayside's cash flow from operations was used primarily to purchase new fixed assets, invest in short-term securities, and pay off notes payable and long-term debt. Such uses of operating cash flow do not raise red flags regarding the hospital's financial actions. In fact, Bayside's ability to both increase securities investments and pay off debt while adding new fixed assets indicates that 2018 was a very good year financially.

Managers and investors must pay close attention to the statement of cash flows. Financial condition is driven by cash flows, and the statement provides a good picture of the annual cash flows generated by the business.[2] An examination of exhibit 13.3 or, better yet, a series of such tables for the last five years and for five years into the future would give Bayside's managers and creditors an idea of whether the hospital's operations are self-sustaining; that is, does the business generate the cash flows necessary to pay its expenses, including those associated with raising capital? Although the statement of cash flows is filled with valuable information, the bottom line tells little about the business's financial condition because operating losses can be covered by financing transactions such as borrowing or selling new common stock (if investor owned), at least in the short run.

Notes to the Financial Statements

The notes to the financial statements often contain information that can significantly affect a business's financial condition. For healthcare providers, these notes contain information on the firm's pension plan, its malpractice insurance, the amount of charity care it provides, the types of debt financing it uses, its accounting policies, and so forth. Clearly, the information contained in the notes to the financial statements has a bearing on the business's financial condition, and it should be considered, either directly or indirectly, in any financial statement analysis. To professional analysts, the notes are especially vital. Indeed, they occasionally use the notes information to recast financial statements before they even begin an analysis.

SELF-TEST QUESTIONS

1. What governs financial reporting requirements in health services?
2. Briefly describe these three basic financial statements: (1) income statement, (2) balance sheet, and (3) statement of cash flows.
3. What type of information does each type of statement provide?
4. What is the difference between net income and cash flow, and which is more meaningful to a firm's financial condition?
5. What types of information are contained in the notes to a business's financial statements?

Financial Statement Analysis

The first step in most financial condition analyses is to examine the business's financial statements. Financial statement analysis involves a number of techniques that extract information contained in a business's financial statements and then combine it in a form that helps managers make judgments about the firm's financial condition. In the next sections, we discuss some common analytical techniques along with some problems inherent in such analyses.

SELF-TEST QUESTION

1. What is financial statement analysis?

Ratio Analysis

Although a business's income statement and balance sheet contain a wealth of financial information, it is often difficult to make meaningful judgments about financial performance by merely examining the raw data. For example, one managed care plan may have $5,248,760 in long-term debt and interest charges of $419,900, while another may have $52,647,980 in debt and interest charges of $3,948,600. The true burden of these debts, and each managed care plan's ability to pay the interest and principal due on them, cannot be easily assessed without additional comparisons, such as those provided by *ratio analysis*. In essence, ratio analysis combines data from the balance sheet and the income statement to create single numbers whose financial significance is easily interpreted (i.e., numbers that measure various aspects of financial performance). In the case of debt and interest payments, ratios can be constructed that relate each plan's debt to its assets and the interest it pays to the income it has available for payment.

Generally, ratios are grouped into four major categories to make them easier to interpret: profitability, liquidity, debt management, and asset management. We use the data presented in exhibits 13.1 and 13.2 to calculate an illustrative sampling of financial ratios for 2018 for Bayside Memorial Hospital. To help in interpretation, the ratios are compared to hospital peer group average ratios. Note that, in an actual analysis, many more ratios are calculated and analyzed. Also, the ratios used in an analysis depend on the type of healthcare provider being analyzed. Some ratios are more meaningful for hospitals, managed care organizations, group practices, and so on. Here, a hospital is used to illustrate ratio analysis.

To assess their relative performance, many healthcare organizations compare their financial ratios to average values of ratios for similar organizations. For example, Optum annually publishes the *Almanac of Financial and Operating Indicators*, which provides five-year trend information on more than 70 financial ratios for hospitals. The ratios are reported for various peer groups because meaningful comparisons require "apples-to-apples" comparisons. Financial performance and condition can vary substantially among hospitals of different size, geographic location, teaching status, ownership, payment method, and other characteristics. For example, small rural hospitals tend to be less profitable, treat a higher percentage of Medicare and Medicaid patients, and have less cash than urban hospitals. If a small rural hospital wants to assess its financial performance, comparing its financial ratios to those of other small rural hospitals would be meaningful—comparison to an academic medical center would not be realistic or helpful. Therefore, the comparative data in this chapter are termed "peer group averages" to denote average values of ratios for hospitals similar to Bayside Memorial Hospital. The stated peer group averages are for illustrative use only and are not reflective of actual performance for any hospital group. Also note that, in accordance with standard practice, we call the comparative data *averages*, but in reality they are *median* values. Median values are better for comparisons because they are not biased by extremely high or low values in the data set.

How Many Ratios Are Enough?

In our discussion of financial statement ratio analysis, we include 14 ratios that are commonly used to help interpret financial statement data. Although that may seem like a lot of ratios, our discussion just scratches the surface. Without too much additional work, you could probably compile a list of 50 financial ratios. Yet studies have shown that about 90 percent of the information contained in financial statements can be uncovered using about ten carefully selected ratios.

How many ratios do you think are enough? Does it matter how the ratios are selected? Is there a cost to using more ratios than necessary?

Profitability Ratios

Profitability is the net result of a large number of managerial policies and decisions, so ***profitability ratios*** are one measure of a business's aggregate financial performance.

Total Margin

The ***total margin***—often called the ***total profit margin*** or just ***profit margin***—is defined as net income divided by total revenues:

Key Equation 13.1: Total Margin

$$\text{Total margin} = \frac{\text{Net income}}{\text{Total revenues}} = \frac{\$8{,}572}{\$114{,}148} = 0.075 = 7.5\%.$$

Peer group average = 5.0%

Note that total revenues are defined here as total operating revenues plus nonoperating income, so Total revenues = $112,050 + $2,098 = $114,148. Bayside's total margin of 7.5 percent shows that the hospital makes 7.5 cents on every dollar of total revenues. The total margin measures the organization's ability to control expenses. With all else the same, the higher the total margin, the lower the expenses relative to revenues. Bayside's total margin is above the peer group average of 5.0 percent, which indicates good expense control. How good? The sector data source also reports quartiles; for total margin, the upper quartile was 8.4 percent, which means that 25 percent of hospitals had total margins higher than 8.4 percent. Thus, though Bayside's total margin was better than average, it was not as good as the top hospitals' total margins.

Bayside's relatively high total margin may mean that the hospital's gross charges are relatively high, its allowances are relatively low, its costs are relatively low, it has relatively high other (nonoperating) income, or some combination of these factors. A thorough operating indicator analysis would help pinpoint the cause, or causes, of Bayside's high total margin.

Operating Margin

Another useful margin measure is the ***operating margin***, defined as operating income divided by patient-related (operating) revenues:

Key Equation 13.2: Operating Margin

$$\text{Operating margin} = \frac{\text{Operating income}}{\text{Total operating revenues}} = \frac{\$6{,}474}{\$112{,}050} = 0.058 = 5.8\%.$$

Peer group average = 3.5%.

The advantage of this margin measure is it focuses on the primary business line of the enterprise. Thus, it removes the influence of nonoperating income, which often is transitory and more related to stock and bond market conditions than to core operations.

Like total margin, Bayside's operating margin is above the peer group average (5.8 percent vs. 3.5 percent). This is good news because it shows that Bayside is earning its money the "old-fashioned way"—by having profitable operations.

Return on Assets

The ratio of net income to total assets measures the *return on total assets*, usually just called *return on assets (ROA)*:

Key Equation 13.3: Return on Assets

$$\text{Return on assets} = \frac{\text{Net income}}{\text{Total assets}} = \frac{\$8{,}572}{\$151{,}278} = 0.057 = 5.7\%.$$

Peer group average = 4.8%.

Bayside's 5.7 percent ROA (each dollar of total assets generated 5.7 cents in profit) is well above the 4.8 percent peer group average. ROA tells managers how productively, in a financial sense, a business is using its assets. The higher the ROA, the greater the net income on each dollar invested in assets and, hence, the more productive the assets. ROA measures a firm's ability to both control expenses, as expressed by the total margin, and use its assets to generate revenue.

Return on Equity

The ratio of net income to total equity (net assets) measures the *return on equity (ROE)*:

Key Equation 13.4: Return on Equity

$$\text{Return on equity} = \frac{\text{Net income}}{\text{Total equity}} = \frac{\$8{,}572}{\$107{,}364} = 0.080 = 8.0\%.$$

Peer group average = 8.4%.

Bayside's 8.0 percent ROE is slightly below the 8.4 percent peer group average. The hospital was able to generate 8.0 cents of income on each dollar of equity investment, while the average hospital produced 8.4 cents. ROE is especially meaningful for investor-owned businesses because owners use ROE to determine how well the business's managers are using owner-supplied capital. In not-for-profit businesses such as Bayside, boards of trustees and managers use ROE to determine how well, in financial terms, its community-supplied capital is being used.

Bayside's 2018 margin measures and ROA were above the peer group average, yet the hospital's ROE is below the average. As we will show in our discussion of Du Pont analysis later in the chapter, this inconsistency results from Bayside's relatively low use of debt financing.

Liquidity Ratios

One of most managers' first concerns, and a major concern of a firm's creditors, is the business's ***liquidity***. Will the business be able to meet its cash obligations as they become due? Bayside has debts totaling more than \$13 million (its current liabilities) that must be paid off within the coming year. Will the hospital be able to make these payments? A full liquidity analysis requires examination of a hospital's cash budget, which we discuss in chapter 15. However, by relating the amount of cash and other current assets to current obligations, ratio analysis provides a quick, easy-to-use, very rough measure of liquidity.

Current Ratio

The ***current ratio*** is calculated by dividing current assets by current liabilities:

Key Equation 13.5: Current Ratio

$$\text{Current ratio} = \frac{\text{Current assets}}{\text{Current liabilities}} = \frac{\$31{,}280}{\$13{,}332} = 2.3.$$

Peer group average = 2.0.

The current ratio tells managers that the liquidation of Bayside's current assets at book value would provide \$2.30 of cash for every \$1 of current liabilities. If a business is beginning to have financial difficulty, it will start paying its accounts payable more slowly, building up short-term bank loans (notes payable), and so on. If these current liabilities increase faster than current assets, the current ratio will fall, and trouble can result. Because the current ratio is an indicator of the extent to which short-term claims are covered by assets that are expected to be converted to cash in the near term, it is one commonly used measure of liquidity.

Bayside's current ratio is slightly above the peer group average. Because current assets should be converted to cash in the near future, it is highly probable that these assets could be liquidated at close to their stated values. With a current ratio of 2.3, the hospital can liquidate current assets at only 43 percent of book value and still pay off current creditors in full. (To determine the minimum proportion of current assets that must be converted to cash to meet current obligations, divide the number 1 by the current ratio. For Bayside, 1 ÷ 2.35 = 0.426, or 42.6 percent. This proportion is confirmed by noting that 0.426 × \$31,280,000 = \$13,332,000, the amount of current liabilities.) Note that the peer group average is not a magic number that all businesses should strive to achieve. In fact, some very well managed businesses will be above the average, while other good firms will be below it. However, if a firm's ratios are far removed from the average, its managers should be concerned about why this difference exists. Peer group averages will be discussed in detail later in the chapter.

Days-Cash-on-Hand Ratio

The current ratio measures liquidity on the basis of balance sheet accounts (in economic parlance, *stocks*) as opposed to income statement items (*flows*). However, the true measure of a business's liquidity is whether it can meet its payments as they become due, so liquidity is more related to cash flows than it is to assets and liabilities. Thus, the ***days-cash-on-hand ratio*** is a better measure of liquidity than the current ratio is.

Key Equation 13.6: Days-Cash-on-Hand Ratio

$$\text{Days cash on hand} = \frac{\text{Cash and equivalents} + \text{Short-term investments}}{(\text{Expenses} - \text{Depreciation}) \div 365}$$

$$= \frac{\$2{,}263 + \$4{,}000}{(\$105{,}576 - \$4{,}130) \div 365} = \frac{\$6{,}263}{\$277.93} = 22.5 \text{ days.}$$

Peer group average = 205.0 days.

The denominator of the equation estimates average daily cash expenses by stripping out noncash expenses (depreciation) from reported total expenses. The numerator is the cash and securities available to make those cash payments. Because Bayside's days cash on hand is much lower than the peer group average, its liquidity position as measured by this metric is worse than that of the average hospital.

For Bayside, the two measures of liquidity—current ratio and days cash on hand—conflict with each other. Perhaps the average hospital has a greater proportion of cash and marketable securities in its current assets than Bayside. Perhaps Bayside had an extraordinary need for cash in 2017 and 2018. More analysis would be required to make a supportable judgment concerning Bayside's liquidity position. Remember, though, that the cash budget is the primary tool managers use to assess liquidity.

Also keep in mind that a large days cash on hand could indicate that an organization is not effectively managing its cash resources. For example, large cash and near-cash reserves might be better used by investing in longer-term securities with higher returns. On the other hand, amassing cash and short-term investments to meet an expected near-term obligation might be prudent cash management.

Debt Management (Capital Structure) Ratios

The extent to which a firm uses debt financing, or *financial leverage*, is an important measure of financial performance for several reasons. First, by raising funds through debt, owners of for-profit businesses can maintain control with a limited investment. In not-for-profit corporations, the use of debt financing enables the organization to provide more services than it could if it were solely financed with contributed and earned capital. Next, creditors look to owner-supplied funds to provide a margin of safety; if the owners have provided only a small proportion of total financing, the risks of the enterprise are borne mainly by its creditors. Finally, if the business earns more on investments financed with borrowed funds than it pays in interest, the ROE capital is magnified, or leveraged up.

Two types of ratios are used to assess debt management:

1. Balance sheet data are used to determine the extent to which borrowed funds have been used to finance assets. Such ratios are called *capitalization ratios.*
2. Income statement data are used to determine the extent to which fixed financial charges are covered by reported profits. Such ratios are called *coverage ratios.*

The two sets of ratios are complementary, so most financial statement analyses examine both types.

Capitalization Ratio 1: Total Debt to Total Assets (Debt Ratio)

The ratio of total debt to total assets, generally called the *debt ratio*, measures the percentage of total funds provided by creditors:

Key Equation 13.7: Debt Ratio

$$\text{Debt ratio} = \frac{\text{Total debt}}{\text{Total assets}} = \frac{\$43,914}{\$145,797} = 0.290, \text{ or } 29.0\%.$$

Peer group average = 42.3%.

In this definition, debt is defined as all debt and includes current liabilities, long-term debt, and capital lease obligations—everything but equity. However, this ratio has many variations, all of which use different definitions of debt. Creditors prefer low debt ratios because the lower the ratio, the greater the cushion against creditors' losses in the event of bankruptcy and liquidation. Conversely, owners of for-profit businesses may seek high leverage either to leverage up returns or because selling new stock would mean giving up some degree of control. In not-for-profit corporations, managers may seek high leverage to offer more services.

Bayside's debt ratio is 29.0 percent, meaning its creditors have supplied just under one-third of the firm's total financing. Put another way, each dollar of assets was financed with 29 cents of debt and, consequently, 71 cents of equity. (The *equity ratio* is 1 – Debt ratio, so Bayside's equity ratio is 71.0 percent.) Because the average debt ratio in the peer group is more than 40 percent, Bayside uses significantly less debt than the average hospital does. The low debt ratio indicates that the hospital would find it relatively easy to borrow additional funds, presumably at favorable rates.

Capitalization Ratio 2: Debt-to-Equity Ratio

Another commonly used capitalization ratio is the *debt-to-equity ratio*. The debt ratio and debt-to-equity ratios are transformations of each other and hence provide the same information, but with a slightly different twist:

Key Equation 13.8: Debt-to-Equity Ratio

$$\text{Debt-to-equity ratio} = \frac{\text{Total debt}}{\text{Total equity assets}} = \frac{\$43,914}{\$107,364} = 0.409\text{, or } 40.9\%.$$

Peer group average = 73.3%.

This ratio tells analysts that Bayside's creditors have contributed 40.9 cents for each dollar of equity capital, while the sector average is 73.3 cents per dollar. Both the debt ratio and debt-to-equity ratio increase as the proportion of a business's use of debt financing increases, but the debt ratio rises linearly and approaches a limit of 100 percent, while the debt-to-equity ratio rises exponentially and approaches infinity.

Lenders in particular prefer the debt-to-equity ratio to the debt ratio because it tells them how much capital creditors have provided to the business per dollar of equity capital. The higher this ratio, the riskier the creditors' position.

Coverage Ratio 1: Times-Interest-Earned Ratio

The *times-interest-earned (TIE) ratio* is calculated by dividing earnings before interest and taxes (EBIT) by the interest charges. EBIT is used in the numerator because it represents the amount of income available to pay interest expense. For Bayside, a not-for-profit business, which does not pay taxes, EBIT = Net income + Interest expense.

Key Equation 13.9: TIE Ratio

$$\text{TIE ratio} = \frac{\text{EBIT}}{\text{Interest expense}} = \frac{\$8,572 + \$1,542}{\$1,542} = \frac{\$10,114}{\$1,542} = 6.6.$$

Peer group average = 4.0.

The TIE ratio measures the number of dollars of income available to pay each dollar of interest expense. In essence, it is an indicator of the extent to which income can decline before the business's earnings are less than its annual interest costs. If the business fails to pay interest, its creditors can bring legal action, which could result in bankruptcy.

Bayside's interest is covered 6.6 times, so it has $6.60 of accounting income to pay each dollar of interest expense. Because the peer group average TIE ratio is four times, the hospital is covering its interest charges by a relatively high margin of safety. Thus, the TIE ratio reinforces the previous conclusion based on the capitalization ratios—namely, that the hospital is using a very modest amount of debt financing and hence could easily expand its use if necessary to support operations.

Coverage ratios are often better measures of a firm's debt utilization than capitalization ratios because coverage ratios discriminate between low-interest-rate debt and high-interest-rate debt. For example, a group practice might have $10 million of 4 percent debt on its balance sheet, while another might have $10 million of 8 percent debt. If both practices have the same income and assets, both would have the same debt ratio. However, the group paying 4 percent interest would have lower interest charges and hence would be in a better financial condition than the group paying 8 percent. This difference in financial condition is captured by the TIE ratio.

Coverage Ratio 2: Cash-Flow-Coverage Ratio

Although the TIE ratio is easy to calculate, it has two major deficiencies. First, leasing has become widespread in recent years, which imposes a fixed charge similar to interest expense. Also, many debt contracts require that principal payments be made over the life of the loan, rather than only at maturity. Thus, most businesses must meet fixed financial charges other than interest payments. Second, the TIE ratio ignores the fact that accounting income, whether measured by EBIT or net income, does not indicate the actual cash flow available to meet fixed charge payments. These deficiencies are corrected in the *cash-flow-coverage (CFC) ratio*, which shows the amount by which cash flow covers fixed financial requirements. Note that although not shown directly on Bayside's financial statements, the hospital had $1,368,000 of lease payments and $2 million of debt principal repayments in 2018.

Key Equation 13.10: CFC Ratio

$$\text{CFC ratio} = \frac{\text{EBIT} + \text{Lease payments} + \text{Depreciation expense}}{\text{Interest expense} + \text{Lease payments} + \text{Debt principal} \div (1 - \text{T})}$$

$$= \frac{\$10{,}114 + \$1{,}368 + \$4{,}130}{\$1{,}542 + \$1{,}368 + \$2{,}000 \div (1 - 0)} = \frac{\$15{,}612}{\$4{,}910} = 3.2.$$

Peer group average = 2.3%.

What is the purpose of the (1 – T) term applied to the debt principal? Investor-owned firms must *gross up* the debt principal repayments by dividing by 1 – T to recognize that principal payments are made with after-tax dollars. In other words, taxes must be paid on each revenue dollar before those funds are available to make principal payments. Because the numerator of the equation contains pretax dollars, for consistency the denominator must also contain pretax dollars.

Like its TIE ratio, Bayside's CFC ratio exceeds the peer group average, which indicates that Bayside is better than the average hospital at covering its total fixed payments with cash flow. This fact should be reassuring both to creditors and management and reinforces the view that Bayside has untapped debt capacity.

Asset Management (Activity) Ratios

The next group of ratios, the *asset management*, or *activity, ratios*, is designed to measure how effectively a business's assets are being managed. These ratios help to answer whether the total amounts of each type of asset as reported on the balance sheet seem reasonable, too high, or too low relative to current operating levels. Bayside and other hospitals must borrow or raise equity capital to acquire assets. If they have too many assets, their capital costs will be too high and their profits will be depressed. Conversely, if assets are too low, they may lose profitable patient volume or not be able to offer vital services.

Fixed-Asset-Turnover Ratio

The *fixed-asset-turnover ratio*, also called the *fixed-asset-utilization ratio*, measures the usage of property and equipment. It is the ratio of total revenues to net fixed assets:

Key Equation 13.11: Fixed-Asset-Turnover Ratio

$$\text{Fixed asset turnover} = \frac{\text{Total revenues}}{\text{Net fixed assets}} = \frac{\$114{,}148}{\$119{,}998} = 0.95.$$

Peer group average = 2.2.

Note that total revenues are defined here as all revenues, including nonoperating income, so Total revenues = \$112,050 + \$2,098 = \$114,148. Also, net fixed assets are listed on the balance sheet as net property and equipment.

Bayside's ratio of 0.95 indicates that each dollar of fixed assets generated 95 cents in revenue. This value compares poorly with the peer group average of 2.2 times, which indicates that Bayside is not using its fixed assets as productively as the average hospital. (The lower quartile value for the sector is 1.8; thus, Bayside falls well into the bottom 25 percent of all hospitals in its fixed asset utilization.)

Before condemning Bayside's management for poor performance, it should be pointed out that a major problem exists with the use of the fixed-asset-turnover ratio for comparative purposes. Recall that all assets, except cash and accounts receivable, reflect historical costs rather than current value. Inflation and depreciation have caused the values of many assets that were purchased in the past to be seriously understated. Therefore, if an old hospital that had acquired much of its property and equipment years ago is compared with a new hospital with the same physical assets, the old hospital (because of its much lower book value of assets) would report a much higher fixed-asset-turnover ratio. Such a difference is more reflective of the inability of financial statements to deal with inflation than of any inefficiency on the part of the new hospital's managers.

Total-Asset-Turnover Ratio

The *total-asset-turnover ratio* measures the turnover, or utilization, of all of the firm's assets. It is calculated by dividing total revenues by total assets:

Key Equation 13.12: Total-Asset-Turnover Ratio

$$\text{Total asset turnover} = \frac{\text{Total revenues}}{\text{Total assets}} = \frac{\$114{,}148}{\$151{,}278} = 0.75.$$

Peer group average = 0.97.

Again, note that total revenues are defined here as all revenues, including nonoperating income, so Total revenues = \$112,050 + \$2,098 = \$114,148. The total-asset-turnover ratio tells us that each dollar of total assets generated 75 cents in total revenue. Bayside's total-asset-turnover ratio is below the peer group average but not as far below as its fixed-asset-turnover ratio. Thus, relative to the sector, the hospital is using its current assets better than it is using its fixed assets. Such judgments can be confirmed by examining Bayside's current asset turnover. Bayside's 2018 current-asset-turnover ratio (Total revenues ÷ Total current assets) is 3.6, compared to the peer group average of 3.4, so the hospital is slightly above average in its utilization of current assets.

Days in Patient Accounts Receivable

Days in patient accounts receivable is used to measure effectiveness in managing receivables. This measure of financial performance, which is sometimes classified as a liquidity ratio rather than an asset management ratio, has many names, including *days in receivables*, *average collection period*, and *days sales outstanding*. It is computed by dividing net patient accounts receivable by average daily patient revenue to find the number of days it takes an organization, on average, to collect its receivables:

Key Equation 13.13: Days in Patient Accounts Receivable

$$\text{Days in patient accounts receivable} = \frac{\text{Net patient accounts receivable}}{\text{Net patient service revenue} \div 365}$$

$$= \frac{\$21{,}840}{\$103{,}174 \div 365} = \frac{\$21{,}840}{\$282.67} = 77.3 \text{ days.}$$

Peer group average = 64.0 days.

In the calculation for Bayside, premium revenue has not been included because such revenue is collected before services are provided and hence does not affect receivables. Because information on credit sales generally is not available from a business's financial statements, the assumption that all sales are on credit is typically used. Although most hospital services are provided on credit because of the third-party-payer system, other healthcare businesses might have a much lower proportion of credit sales than do hospitals. As the proportion of cash sales increases, the days in accounts receivable measure loses its usefulness. Also, note that it would be better to use average receivables in the calculation, either by finding average monthly receivables or by adding beginning and end-of-year receivables and then dividing by two.

Bayside is not doing as well as the average hospital in collecting its receivables. It is important that businesses collect their receivables as soon as possible. Clearly, Bayside's managers should strive to increase the hospital's performance in this key area.

Average Age of Plant

The *average age of plant* is a rough measure of the average age in years of a business's fixed assets:

Key Equation 13.14: Average Age of Plant

$$\text{Average age of plant} = \frac{\text{Accumulated depreciation}}{\text{Depreciation expense}} = \frac{\$25{,}160}{\$4{,}130} = 6.1 \text{ years.}$$

Peer group average = 9.1.

Bayside's physical assets are newer than those of the average hospital. Thus, the hospital offers more up-to-date facilities than average and hence will probably have lower capital expenditures in the near future. On the other hand, Bayside's net fixed asset valuation will be relatively high, which, as pointed out earlier, biases the hospital's fixed-asset-turnover and total-asset-turnover ratios downward. This fact raises serious questions about the validity of the turnover ratios calculated previously.

Comparative and Trend Analyses

On the web at: *ache.org/HAP/PinkSong8e*

When conducting ratio analysis, the value of a particular ratio, in the absence of other information, reveals almost nothing about financial condition. For example, if a nursing home business has a current ratio of 2.5, it is virtually impossible to say whether its liquidity position condition is good or bad. Additional data are needed to interpret the value of this ratio. In the discussion of Bayside's ratios, the focus was on *comparative analysis*—that is, the hospital's ratios were compared to the average ratios for the sector. Another useful ratio analysis tool is *trend analysis*, which analyzes the trend of a single ratio over time. Trend analysis provides clues about whether a business's financial condition is improving, holding constant, or deteriorating.

It is easy to combine comparative and trend analyses in a single graph, such as the one shown in exhibit 13.4. Here, Bayside's ROE (the solid line) and peer group average ROE data (the dashed lines) are plotted for the past five years. The graph shows that the hospital's ROE has been declining faster than the peer group average from 2014 through 2017 but exceeded the peer group average in 2018. Other ratios can be analyzed in a similar manner.

SELF-TEST QUESTIONS

1. What is the purpose of ratio analysis?
2. What are two ratios that measure profitability?
3. What are two ratios that measure liquidity?
4. What are two ratios that measure debt management?
5. What are two ratios that measure asset management?
6. How can comparative and trend analyses be used to interpret ratio results?

Tying the Ratios Together: Du Pont Analysis

On the web at: *ache.org/HAP/PinkSong8e*

A complete ratio analysis provides a great deal of information about a business's financial condition, but it does not provide an overview or tie any of the ratios together. *Du Pont analysis* provides an overview of a business's financial condition and helps managers and investors understand the relationships among several ratios. Essentially, Du Pont analysis—so named because managers at

EXHIBIT 13.4 Bayside Memorial Hospital: ROE Analysis, 2014–2018

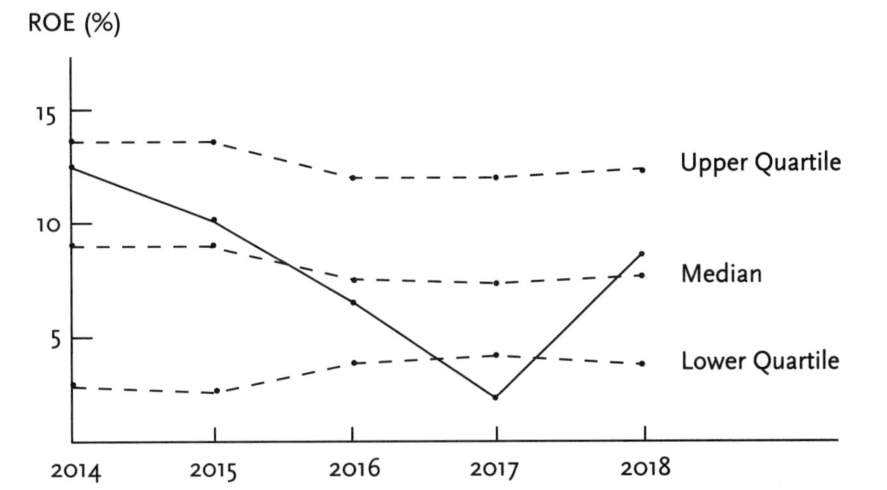

Year	*Bayside (%)*	*Lower Quartile (%)*	*Median (%)*	*Upper Quartile (%)*
2014	12.5	2.6	8.6	13.3
2015	10.0	2.5	8.6	13.3
2016	6.7	2.8	7.2	12.1
2017	2.4	4.1	7.2	12.1
2018	8.0	3.8	7.4	12.3

the Du Pont Company developed it—combines basic financial ratios in a way that provides valuable insights into a firm's financial condition. The analysis decomposes ROE (which is one of the most important measures of a business's profitability) into the product of three other ratios, each of which has an important economic interpretation. The result is the *Du Pont equation*:

Key Equations 13.15 and 13.16: Du Pont Equation

ROE = Total margin × Total asset turnover × Equity multiplier.

ROE = Return on assets × Equity multiplier.

Note that the Du Pont equation actually has two forms. One form (equation 13.15) has three factors on the right side of the equation, while the other recognizes that the product of the total margin and total asset turnover is ROA. By combining these ratios, the second form (equation 13.16) has only two factors on the right side.

The mathematical validity of the Du Pont equation can easily be seen by expressing it in ratio form:

$$\frac{\text{Net income}}{\text{Total equity}} = \frac{\text{Net income}}{\text{Total revenues}} \times \frac{\text{Total revenues}}{\text{Total assets}} \times \frac{\text{Total assets}}{\text{Total equity}}$$

$$= \frac{\text{Net income}}{\text{Total assets}} \times \frac{\text{Total assets}}{\text{Total equity}}$$

By canceling like terms in the numerator and denominator, we see that the left side of the equation is equal to the right side. Here, we use Bayside's 2018 data to illustrate the Du Pont equation:

$$\frac{\$8,572}{\$107,364} = \frac{\$8,572}{\$114,148} \times \frac{\$114,148}{\$151,278} \times \frac{\$151,278}{\$107,364}$$

$$8.0\% = 7.5\% \times 0.75 \times 1.4$$

$$= 5.6\% \times 1.4.$$

Bayside's 2018 total margin was 7.5 percent, so the hospital made 7.5 cents profit on each dollar of total revenue. Furthermore, assets were turned over, or created revenues, 0.75 times during the year, so the hospital earned a return of 7.5% × 0.75 = 5.6% on its assets. This value for ROA is roughly the same as that calculated previously in the ratio analysis section. (Because we are carrying the calculations to only two significant places, rounding differences occur.)

If the hospital used only equity financing, its 5.6 percent ROA would equal its ROE. However, creditors supplied 29 percent of Bayside's capital, while the equityholders (i.e., the community) supplied the rest. Because the 5.6 percent ROA belongs exclusively to the suppliers of equity capital, which makes up only 71 percent of total capital, Bayside's ROE is higher than 5.6 percent. Specifically, ROA must be multiplied by the ***equity multiplier***, which shows the amount of assets working for each dollar of equity capital, to obtain the ROE of 8.0 percent. This 8.0 percent ROE can be calculated directly: ROE = Net income ÷ Total equity = \$8,572 ÷ \$107,364 = 8.0%. However, the Du Pont equation shows how total margin, which measures expense control; total asset turnover, which measures asset utilization; and financial leverage, which measures debt utilization, interact to determine ROE.

Bayside's managers use the Du Pont equation to suggest how to improve the hospital's financial performance. To influence the profit margin (i.e., expense control), the hospital's marketing staff can study the effects of raising charges (or lowering them to increase volume), moving into new services or markets with higher margins, entering into new contracts with managed care plans, and so on. Furthermore, management accountants can study the expense items and, while working with department heads and clinical staff, seek ways to reduce costs.

Regarding total asset turnover (i.e., asset utilization), Bayside's analysts, while working with both clinical and marketing staffs, can investigate ways of reducing investments in various types of assets. Finally, the hospital's financial staff can analyze the effects of alternative financing strategies on the equity multiplier (i.e., debt utilization), seeking to hold down interest expenses and the risks of debt while still using debt to leverage up ROE.

The Du Pont equation provides a useful comparison between a business's performance as measured by ROE and the performance of an average hospital. For example, here is the comparative analysis for 2014:

Bayside:	ROE	=	7.5%	×	0.75	×	1.4
		=		5.6%		×	1.4 = 8.0%.
Peer group average:	ROE	=	5.0%	×	0.97	×	1.7
		=		4.8%		×	1.7 = 8.4%.

The Du Pont analysis tells managers and creditors that Bayside has a significantly higher profit margin, and thus better control over expenses, than does the average hospital. However, the average hospital has a better total asset turnover, so Bayside is getting below-average utilization from its assets. Despite the average hospital's advantage in asset utilization, Bayside's superior expense control outweighs its utilization disadvantage because its ROA of 5.6 percent is higher than the peer group average ROA of 4.8 percent. Finally, the average hospital has offset Bayside's advantage in ROA by using more financial leverage, although Bayside's lower use of debt financing decreases its financial risk. The end result is that Bayside receives somewhat less return on its equity capital than does the average hospital.

One potential problem with Du Pont and ratio analyses applied to not-for-profit organizations, especially hospitals, is that a large portion of their net income may come from nonoperating sources rather than from operations. If the nonoperating income is highly variable and unpredictable, ROE and the ratios (as previously defined) may be a poor measure of the hospital's inherent profitability. All applicable ratios, as well as the Du Pont analysis, can be recast to focus on operations by using net operating revenue in lieu of total revenues and operating income in lieu of net income.

SELF-TEST QUESTIONS

1. Explain how the Du Pont equation combines several ratios to obtain an overview of a business's financial condition.
2. Why may a focus on operating revenue and operating income be preferable to a focus on total revenues and net income?

Operating Indicator Analysis

Operating indicator analysis goes one step beyond financial statement analysis by examining operating variables to explain a business's financial condition. Like the financial ratios, *operating indicators* are typically grouped into major categories to make interpretation easier. For hospitals, the most commonly used categories are

- profit indicators,
- price indicators,
- volume (utilization) indicators,
- length-of-stay indicators,
- intensity-of-service indicators,
- efficiency indicators, and
- unit cost indicators.

Because of the large number of operating indicators used in a typical analysis, the indicators cannot be discussed in detail here. However, to give you an appreciation for this type of analysis, we will discuss seven commonly used hospital operating indicators—one from each category. Note that most of the data needed to calculate operating indicators are not contained in a firm's financial statements. More complete data are required for this type of analysis.

Profit per Discharge

Profit per discharge, a profit indicator, provides a measure of the amount of profit on inpatient services earned per discharge. Note that this measure is "raw" in the sense that it is not adjusted for case mix, which we discuss later, or local wage conditions. Often, operating indicators are calculated in both raw and adjusted forms. In 2018, Bayside's managerial accounting system reported $87,740,000 of inpatient service revenue, $84,865,000 of inpatient costs, and 18,281 patient discharges. Thus, Bayside's profit per discharge was $157:

Key Equation 13.17: Profit per Discharge

$$\text{Profit per discharge} = \frac{\text{Inpatient profit}}{\text{Total discharges}} = \frac{\$87{,}740{,}000 - \$84{,}865{,}000}{18{,}281}$$

$$= \frac{\$2{,}875{,}000}{18{,}281} = \$157.$$

Peer group average = $73.

Compared to the peer group average, Bayside's inpatient services are more than twice as profitable. It is not uncommon in today's tight reimbursement environment for hospitals to lose money (as measured by accounting profit) on inpatient services. In fact, with a peer group average profit per discharge of only $73, half of the hospitals are making less than $73, which indicates that a significant percentage of hospitals are losing money on inpatient services. Most, however, make up the losses with profits from other services or from nonoperating income.

Net Price per Discharge

Net price per discharge, which is one of many price indicators, measures the average inpatient revenue collected on each discharge. Based on the data presented in the discussion of the profit-per-discharge indicator, Bayside's net price per discharge for 2018 was $4,800:

Key Equation 13.18: Net Price per Discharge

$$\text{Net price per discharge} = \frac{\text{Net inpatient revenue}}{\text{Total discharges}} = \frac{\$87{,}740{,}000}{18{,}281} = \$4{,}800.$$

Peer group average = $5,056.

Bayside collects less per discharge than the average hospital; however, we have already seen that Bayside makes a profit of $157 on each discharge, so its inpatient services cost structure must be proportionally even lower than the peer group average. Bayside's ability to make a profit on each discharge could be attributed to a lower-than-average case mix, which measures the average intensity of services provided, or to an aggressive cost management program.

Occupancy Rate (Percentage)

Occupancy rate, one of many volume indicators, measures the utilization of a hospital's licensed beds and hence fixed assets. Because overhead costs are incurred on all assets whether used or not, higher occupancy spreads fixed costs over more patients and hence increases per patient profitability. Based on 95,061 inpatient days in 2018, Bayside's occupancy rate was 57.9 percent:

Key Equation 13.19: Occupancy Rate

$$\text{Occupancy rate} = \frac{\text{Inpatient days}}{(\text{Number of licensed beds} \times 365)} = \frac{95{,}061}{450 \times 365} = 57.9\%.$$

Peer group average = 45.4%.

Bayside has a higher occupancy rate than does the average hospital and hence is using its inpatient fixed assets more productively. Note that this conclusion contradicts the financial statement analysis interpretation of the hospital's 2018 fixed-asset-turnover ratio. While that ratio is affected by inflation, accounting convention, and the amount of assets devoted to other functions, the occupancy rate is not. Hence, it is a superior measure of pure asset utilization, at least regarding inpatient utilization. On this basis, Bayside's managers appear to be doing a good job, relative to the sector, of using the hospital's inpatient fixed assets. This measure can also be applied to staffed beds. In Bayside's case, the two measures of capacity are the same, but some hospitals have fewer staffed beds than licensed beds.

Average Length of Stay

Average length of stay (ALOS), or just *length of stay (LOS)*, is the number of days an average inpatient is hospitalized with each admission. ALOS and an alternative version adjusted for case mix are the sole LOS indicators. Bayside's 2018 LOS was 5.2 days:

Key Equation 13.20: Average Length of Stay

$$\text{LOS} = \frac{\text{Inpatient days}}{\text{Total discharges}} = \frac{95{,}061}{18{,}281} = 5.2 \text{ days.}$$

Peer group average = 4.7 days.

On average, Bayside keeps its patients in the hospital slightly longer than the average hospital does. In general, that longer stay is considered to have a negative impact on inpatient profitability because most hospitals have a reimbursement mix heavily weighted toward prospective (episodic) payment. With payment fixed per discharge, lower LOS typically leads to lower costs and hence higher profitability.

All Patient Case-Mix Index

The *all patient case-mix index* is one of several intensity-of-service indicators. The concept of measuring case mix was first applied to Medicare patients; hence, many hospitals calculate both a Medicare case-mix index and an all patient case-mix index. Case mix is based on diagnosis; diagnoses requiring more complex treatments are assigned a higher value. The idea is to be able to differentiate (on average) between hospitals that provide relatively simple, and hence low-cost, services from those that provide highly complex and costly services. Case-mix values assigned to diagnoses are periodically recalibrated, with the intent of forcing the average hospital to have a case-mix index of 1.0. In general, case mix is related to size because large hospitals typically offer a more complex set of services than do small hospitals. Furthermore, case-mix values tend to be high at teaching hospitals (greater than 1.5) because the most complex cases often are transferred to such hospitals.

Bayside's all patient case-mix index was 1.12 for 2018, which is slightly below the peer group average of 1.15. Thus, the patients that Bayside admits to the hospital require about the same intensity of services that patients at the average hospital require, which tells us that inpatient revenues and costs are not influenced by having a patient mix that is either relatively simple to treat or relatively complex.

Inpatient FTEs per Occupied Bed

The number of *inpatient full-time equivalents (FTEs) per occupied bed* is a measure of workforce productivity and hence is an efficiency indicator. The lower the number, the more productive the workforce. When the focus is on inpatient productivity, inpatient FTEs are used. The measure can also be adapted to outpatient productivity. Needless to say, there are many situations in a hospital setting in which it is difficult to allocate FTEs to the type of service provided. With an inpatient workforce of 1,251 FTEs, Bayside's inpatient FTEs per occupied bed was 4.8 in 2018:

Key Equation 13.21: Inpatient FTEs per Occupied Bed

$$\text{Inpatient FTEs per occupied bed} = \frac{\text{Inpatient FTEs}}{\text{Average daily census}}$$

$$= \frac{1{,}251}{0.579 \times 450} = \frac{1{,}251}{260.55} = 4.8.$$

Peer group average = 5.6.

Note that the average daily census—the number of patients hospitalized on an average day—was calculated by multiplying Bayside's occupancy rate (57.9 percent = 0.579) by the number of licensed beds (450). With higher-than-average labor productivity, coupled with better fixed-asset utilization, it is no surprise that Bayside's inpatient services are more profitable than those of the average hospital.

Salary per FTE

Salary per FTE, one of the unit cost indicators, provides a simple measure of the relative cost of the largest resource item used in the hospital sector—labor. With total salaries of \$83,038,613 in 2019 and 2,681 total FTEs, Bayside's salary per FTE in 2018 was \$30,973:

Key Equation 13.22: Salary per FTE

$$\text{Salary per FTE} = \frac{\text{Total salaries}}{\text{Total FTEs}} = \frac{\$83{,}038{,}613}{2{,}681} = \$30{,}973.$$

Peer group average = \$32,987.

Now, we can see that Bayside's above-average profitability is enhanced by both worker productivity and control over wages and benefits.

In a full operating indicator analysis, many more indicators would be examined in an attempt to identify the operating strengths and weaknesses that underlie a business's financial condition. Although operating indicator analysis has been illustrated using the hospital sector, the concepts can be applied to any healthcare business, although the indicators would differ. Also, operating indicators are interpreted in the same way as financial ratios (i.e., by performing comparative and trend analyses).

SELF-TEST QUESTIONS

1. What is the difference between financial statement analysis and operating indicator analysis?
2. Why is operating indicator analysis important?
3. Describe four indicators that are commonly used in operating indicator analysis.

Limitations of Financial Statement and Operating Indicator Analyses

While financial statement and operating indicator analyses can provide a great deal of useful information concerning a business's operations and financial condition, such analyses have limitations that necessitate care and judgment. This section highlights the more important problem areas:

- Many large healthcare organizations operate a number of different subsidiaries in different lines of business, and in such cases, it is difficult to develop meaningful comparative data. For example, a large integrated system may offer inpatient, outpatient, long-term care, home health care, and hospice services. This problem tends to make financial statement and operating indicator analyses more useful to providers with a single service line than to large, diversified health systems.
- Most businesses want to be better than average, although half will be above and half will be below average. Merely attaining average performance is not necessarily good. However, as discussed earlier, compilers of sector data often report ratios in quartiles or other percentiles. Also, it is useful for managers to compare their businesses not only with the peer group average but also with their leading competitors and the top businesses in the sector. In the end, it is extremely important that senior managers establish their own standards of performance and ensure that all other managers are aware of these goals and are taking actions on a daily basis to achieve them; that is the purpose of the financial planning and control process.
- Making generalizations about whether a particular ratio or indicator is good or bad is often difficult. For example, a high current ratio may show a strong liquidity position (which is good) or an excessive amount of receivables (which is bad). Similarly, a high asset turnover

ratio may denote that a business either uses its assets efficiently or is undercapitalized and cannot afford to buy enough assets.

- Businesses often have some ratios and indicators that look good and others that look bad, which make the firm's financial position—strong or weak—difficult to determine. For this reason, significant judgment is required when analyzing financial and operating indicator performance. Several methodologies have been proposed to reduce the information contained in a financial statement analysis to a single value and hence make interpretation much easier. One such method is *multiple discriminant analysis*, which attempts to place businesses into two groups on the basis (likely versus unlikely) of their probabilities of going bankrupt. Another method combines ratios selected judgmentally into a composite index, which is then compared to the peer group average. Yet another method—economic value analysis—is discussed in the next section. The distillation of the wide variety of information contained in a business's financial statements into a single measure of financial condition is a very difficult endeavor, and hence no method has been widely accepted and used in healthcare.
- Different accounting practices can distort financial statement ratio comparisons. For example, businesses can use different accounting conventions to value cost of goods sold and ending inventories. Or, businesses can use different fiscal years that, when coupled with seasonal factors, can make ratios appear quite different even when the underlying fundamentals are similar. Other accounting practices, such as those related to leases, can also create distortions.
- Inflation effects can distort a business's balance sheets and income statements. Numerous reporting methods have been proposed to adjust accounting statements for inflation, but no consensus has been reached on these methods or on the practical usefulness of the resulting data. Nevertheless, accounting standards encourage—but do not require—businesses to disclose supplementary data to reflect the impact of general inflation. Inflation effects tend to make ratio comparisons over time for a given business, and across businesses at any point in time, less reliable than would be the case in the absence of inflation.

SELF-TEST QUESTIONS

1. Briefly describe some of the problems encountered when performing financial statement analysis and operating indicator analysis.
2. Explain how inflation effects created problems in the Bayside illustration.

Economic Value Added

Up to this point, we have used different techniques to evaluate the financial condition of a business. In many situations, it is useful to have a single measure that provides information on both financial condition and managerial performance. That measure is *economic value added (EVA)*, which focuses on managerial effectiveness in a given year. EVA was developed and popularized by the consulting firm of Stern Stewart and Company. To find EVA, we use the following basic formula:

Key Equation 13.23: Economic Value Added

$$\begin{aligned}\text{EVA} &= \text{Net operating profit after taxes (NOPAT)}\\ &\quad - (\text{Total capital} \times \text{Corporate cost of capital}).\end{aligned}$$

In the EVA equation, NOPAT can be thought of as revenues minus all operating costs, including taxes (if applicable) but excluding interest expense. It is actually calculated as EBIT × (1 − T). Total capital is the sum of the book values of interest-bearing debt and equity, while the corporate cost of capital is the business's cost of financing. In essence, EVA measures the dollar profit in excess of the economic dollar cost of creating that profit. Because the calculation of EVA does not require market value data, it can be applied to both for-profit and not-for-profit businesses. To illustrate the EVA concept, consider Bayside's 2018 EVA. The hospital had $8,572,000 of net income and $1,542,000 in interest expense, for NOPAT of $10,114,000. Its investor-supplied capital was $2,975,000 in notes payable, $30,582,000 in long-term debt and capital lease obligations, and $107,364,000 in equity, for total capital of $140,921,000. Assuming a 7 percent corporate cost of capital, Bayside's 2018 EVA was $249,530:

$$\begin{aligned}\text{EVA} &= \$10{,}114{,}000 - (\$140{,}921{,}000 \times 0.07)\\ &= \$10{,}114{,}000 - \$9{,}864{,}470\\ &= \$249{,}530.\end{aligned}$$

Bayside's EVA of $249,530 tells its managers that the hospital generated a positive economic income in 2018. In essence, it needed $140,921,000 in investor-supplied capital to generate $10,114,000 in operating profit. The $140,921,000 in capital required to support operations had an overall cost of 7 percent, so the dollar cost to obtain the capital was $9,864,470. Because operations earned more in economic profit than it cost to generate that profit, the hospital had positive economic income (EVA).

EVA is an estimate of a business's true economic profit for the year, and it differs substantially from accounting profitability measures such as net income. EVA represents the residual income that remains after **all costs**—including the opportunity cost of the employed equity capital—have been recognized. Conversely, accounting profit is formulated without imposing a charge for equity capital. EVA depends on both operating efficiency and balance sheet management: Without operating efficiency, profits will be low; without efficient balance sheet management, there will be too many assets and hence too much capital, which results in higher-than-necessary dollar capital costs.

For investor-owned businesses, a direct link exists between EVA and the value of the business—that is, the higher the EVA, the greater the value to owners. EVA can be applied to divisions as well as to entire businesses, and the cost of capital should reflect the risk and capital structure of the business unit, whether it is the aggregate business or an operating division.

For not-for-profit corporations, equity (community) capital is a scarce resource that must be managed well to ensure the financial viability of the organization and hence its ability to continue to perform its stated mission. The higher the EVA in any year, the better the job managers are doing in creating value for the community. Of course, EVA measures only economic value; any social value created by the equity capital is ignored and hence must be subjectively considered.

In practice, the calculation of EVA is much more complex than presented here because many accounting issues must be addressed properly when estimating a firm's NOPAT. Nevertheless, the brief discussion here illustrates that a business's true economic profitability depends on both income statement profitability and effective use of balance sheet assets. Specifically, EVA is improved by (1) increasing revenues and decreasing costs and hence increasing NOPAT, (2) decreasing the amount of assets used to create the NOPAT, and (3) decreasing the business's cost of capital. Of course, all of this is easier said than done, and there are potential negative consequences associated with these actions. Still, the EVA model provides a good (but perhaps overly simple) road map to financial excellence.

SELF-TEST QUESTIONS

1. What is EVA, and how is it measured?
2. Why is EVA a better measure of financial performance than are accounting measures such as earnings per share and return on equity?
3. What does EVA tell managers about how to achieve good financial performance?

Benchmarking

Ratio analysis, as well as other financial condition evaluation techniques, requires comparisons to enable managers to make meaningful judgments. In the previous examination of selected financial ratios and operating indicators, Bayside's ratios were compared to peer group average ratios. However, like most businesses, Bayside's managers go one step further—they compare their ratios not only to peer group averages but also to sector leaders and primary competitors. The technique of comparing ratios against selected standards is called ***benchmarking***, while the comparative ratios are called ***benchmarks***. Bayside's managers benchmark against peer group averages; against National/GFB Healthcare and Pennant Hospitals, which are two leading for-profit hospital businesses; and against Woodbridge Memorial Hospital and St. Anthony's, which are Bayside's primary local competitors.

For example, consider how Bayside's analysts present total margin data to the firm's board of trustees:

	2018		2017
National/GFB	9.8%	National/GFB	9.6%
Sector top quartile	*8.4*	*Sector top quartile*	*8.0*
St. Anthony's	8.0	St. Anthony's	7.9
Bayside	**7.5**	Pennant Hospitals	5.0
Sector median	*5.0*	*Sector median*	*4.7*
Pennant Hospitals	4.8	**Bayside**	**2.3**
Sector lower quartile	*1.8*	*Sector lower quartile*	*2.1*
Woodbridge Memorial	0.5	Woodbridge Memorial	(1.3)

Benchmarking permits Bayside's managers to easily see where the firm stands relative to its competition in any given year and over time. As the data show, Bayside was roughly in the middle of the pack in 2018 with respect to its primary competitors and two large investor-owned hospital chains, although its performance was better than that of the average hospital. Its 2017 performance was significantly worse, so it improved substantially from 2017 to 2018. Although benchmarking is illustrated with one ratio, other ratios can be analyzed similarly. Also, for presentation purposes, charts (which are color coded for ease of recognition and interpretation) are often used in benchmarking analyses.

All benchmarking analyses require comparative data, and the relevant data depend on the type of organization. For example, hospitals need comparative data on organizations that are similar in bed size, teaching affiliation, specialty, and geographic location. Information is available from a number of sources, including commercial suppliers, federal and state governmental agencies, and various trade groups. Each of these data suppliers uses a somewhat different set of ratios designed to meet its own needs. Thus, the comparative data source selected dictates the ratios that will be used in the analysis. Also, there are minor and sometimes major differences in ratio definitions between data sources; for example, one source may use a 365-day year while another uses a 360-day year, or one source might use operating values as opposed to total values when constructing ratios. It is very important to know the specific definitions used in the comparative data because definitional differences between the ratios being calculated and the comparative ratios can lead to erroneous interpretations and conclusions. Thus, the first task in a benchmarking analysis is to identify the comparative data set and the ratios to be used. The next step is to make sure that the ratio definitions used in the analysis match those from the comparative data set.

SELF-TEST QUESTIONS

1. What is benchmarking?
2. Why is it important to be familiar with the comparative data set?

Key Performance Indicators and Dashboards

Financial statements and operating indicator data are usually created on an annual and quarterly (or even monthly) basis. Financial condition analyses produced from this information may include literally hundreds of ***metrics*** (ratios and other measures). Although annual and quarterly financial condition analyses are almost always performed, managers need to monitor financial condition on a more regular basis so that problem areas can be identified and corrective action can be taken in a timely manner. However, performing financial condition analyses—say, on a weekly basis—with a large number of metrics would lead to data overload.

To help solve the data overload and timeliness problems, many healthcare businesses use ***key performance indicators (KPIs)*** and ***dashboards***. KPIs are a limited number of financial (and nonfinancial) metrics that measure performance critical to the operational success of an organization. In essence, they assess the current state of the business, measure progress toward organizational goals, and prompt managerial action to correct deficiencies. The KPIs chosen by any business depend on the line of business and its mission, objectives, and goals. In addition, KPIs usually differ by timing. For example, a hospital might have a daily KPI of number of net admissions (admissions minus discharges), while the corresponding quarterly and annual KPI might be occupancy rate. Clearly, the number of KPIs used must be kept to a minimum so managers can focus on the most important aspects of financial and operating performance.

Dashboards are a common way to present an organization's KPIs. The term stems from an automobile's dashboard, which presents key information (e.g., speed, engine temperature, oil pressure) about the car's performance. Often, the KPIs are shown as gauges. The basic idea is to enable managers to monitor the business's most important financial metrics on a regular basis (daily for some metrics) in a form that is easy to read and interpret.

SELF-TEST QUESTIONS

1. What is a KPI? A dashboard?
2. How are KPIs and dashboards used in financial condition analysis?

Chapter Key Concepts

In this chapter, we present the techniques used by managers and investors to assess a business's financial condition. The focus was financial condition as reflected in a business's financial statements, although operating data were also introduced to explain financial performance. Here are its key concepts:

- *Financial statement analysis*, which is the primary method used to assess a business's financial condition, focuses on the data contained in a business's financial statements. *Operating indicator analysis* provides insights into why a firm is in a strong or weak financial condition.
- *Ratio analysis* reveals the relative strengths and weaknesses of a firm as compared to other firms in the same industry and shows whether the firm's position has been improving or deteriorating over time.
- The *Du Pont equation* indicates how the total margin, the total-asset-turnover ratio, and the use of debt interact to determine

(continued)

(continued from previous page)

the rate of return on equity. It provides a good overview of a business's financial performance.
- *Liquidity ratios* indicate the business's ability to meet its short-term obligations.
- *Asset management ratios* measure how effectively managers are using the business's assets.
- *Debt management ratios* reveal the extent to which the firm is financed with debt and the extent to which operating cash flows cover debt service and other fixed-charge requirements.
- *Profitability ratios* show the combined effects of liquidity, asset management, and debt management on operating results.
- Ratios are analyzed using *comparative analysis*, in which a firm's ratios are compared with peer group averages, or those of another firm, and *trend analysis*, in which a firm's ratios are examined over time.
- Financial statement analysis is hampered by some serious problems, including *development of comparative data*, *interpretation of results*, and *inflation effects.*
- *Economic value added (EVA)* is a financial performance measure that focuses directly on management's ability to create value. EVA can be used to assess the economic performance of any business, regardless of ownership.
- *Benchmarking* is the process of comparing the performance of a particular firm with a group of benchmark firms—often, industry leaders and primary competitors.
- *Key performance indicators (KPIs)* are a limited number of *metrics* that focus on measures that are most important to the fulfillment of an organization's mission. Often, KPIs are presented in a format that resembles a *dashboard.*

Although financial condition analysis obviously has its limitations, when used with care it can provide a clear picture of a healthcare business's financial condition as well as identify operating factors that contribute to that condition.

Chapter Models, Problems, and Minicases

The following ancillary resources in spreadsheet format are available for this chapter:

- A chapter model that shows how to perform many of the calculations described in the chapter
- Problems that test your ability to perform the calculations
- A minicase that is more complicated than the problems and tests your ability to perform the calculations in preparation for a case

These resources can be accessed online at ache.org/HAP/PinkSong8e.

Selected Cases

Two cases in *Cases in Healthcare Finance*, sixth edition, are applicable to this chapter:

- Case 23: Commonwealth Health Plans, which has the same focus but applies it to a health maintenance organization (HMO)
- Case 24: River Community Hospital (A), which focuses on conducting financial and operating analyses in a hospital setting
- If time permits, both cases should be assigned because they illustrate how sector-specific factors affect financial statement and operating indicator analyses.

Reference

Bannow, T. 2018. "New Bad Debt Accounting Standards Likely to Remake Community Benefit Reporting." *Modern Healthcare*. Published March 17. www.modernhealthcare.com/article/20180317/NEWS/180319904/new-bad-debt-accounting-standards-likely-to-remake-community-benefit-reporting.

Selected Bibliography

Brown, B. 2016. "Using Business Intelligence to Bring Financial Challenges into Focus." *Healthcare Financial Management* 70 (8): 54–63.

Conner, B. 2017. "The New Revenue Recognition Standard: Where Organizations Stand." *Healthcare Financial Management* 71 (10): 30–33.

———. 2017. "Whatever Happened to Charity Care in Financial Statements?" *Healthcare Financial Management* 71 (1): 30–32.

Rohloff. R. 2017. "Creating a Better Healthcare Analysis Paradigm." *Healthcare Financial Management* 71 (11): 106–7.

Selivanoff, P. 2017. "Taking Control of Pay-for-Performance Contracts." *Healthcare Financial Management* 71 (8): 58–65.

Selected Websites

The following websites pertain to the content of this chapter:

- One of the best ways to access corporate SEC filings by publicly traded investor-owned companies is by using EDGAR, the SEC data access system; see www.sec.gov/edgar.shtml.
- To learn more about EVA, see www.evadimensions.com.
- The American Hospital Directory has summary information, including financial data, on a large number of hospitals. Go to www.ahd.com and click on Free Hospital Profiles.
- The Cleverley & Associates website contains information on the financial data products it sells; see www.cleverleyassociates.com.
- The Decision Resource Group is the largest compiler and seller of HMO data. For more information on their range of publications, see https://decisionresourcesgroup.com/.

Notes

1. One can divide liabilities into (a) interest-bearing debt owed to specific firms or individuals and (b) non-interest-bearing debt owed to suppliers; employees; and, in the case of taxable firms, governments. We do not make this distinction, so the terms *debt* and *liabilities* are used synonymously. Also, note that an investor-owned firm would show common equity rather than net assets on its balance sheet.
2. Takeover specialists in investment banking firms always focus on an organization's cash flows. To them, cash flows are the primary determinant of a business's value. We have more to say about this subject in chapter 16.

Integrative Application

The Problem

Jenna Ito has recently applied for the position of administrator of Palm Valley Nursing Home and has been invited for an interview. Because Jenna wants to be well prepared for the interview, she compiled the following 2014 financial data for Palm Valley with the intent of performing a rough financial condition analysis:

Total revenue	$3,269,404
Net income	$ 57,881
Total assets	$2,502,992
Total equity	$ 357,842

Also, she identified the following peer group average data:

Total margin	3.5%
Total asset turnover	1.5
Equity multiplier	2.5
Return on equity	13.1%

Her goal is to use Du Pont analysis to make some judgments about Palm Valley's financial condition.

The Analysis

ROE = Total margin × Total asset turnover × Equity multiplier

$$\frac{\text{Net income}}{\text{Total equity}} = \frac{\text{Net income}}{\text{Total revenue}} \times \frac{\text{Total revenue}}{\text{Total assets}} \times \frac{\text{Total assets}}{\text{Total equity}}$$

$$= \frac{\$57{,}881}{\$357{,}842} = \frac{\$57{,}881}{\$3{,}269{,}404} \times \frac{\$369{,}404}{\$2{,}502{,}992} \times \frac{\$2{,}502{,}992}{\$357{,}842}$$

$$16.2\% = 1.8\% \times 1.3 \times 7.0$$

$$= 2.3\% \times 7.0.$$

Here is the sector Du Pont equation:

$$13.1\% = 3.5\% \times 1.5 \times 2.5$$
$$= 5.3\% \times 2.5.$$

The Decision

Here are her conclusions. Palm Valley is not doing as well as the average nursing home in both expense control and asset utilization, as reflected by its ROA of 2.3 percent (vs. 5.3 percent for the sector). More specifically, Palm Valley's expense control as measured by profit margin was roughly half as good as the sector (1.8 percent versus 3.5 percent), while its asset utilization as measured by total asset turnover was somewhat below par (1.3 versus 1.5). Nevertheless, it is using very high (perhaps dangerously so) financial leverage, which produces an equity multiplier (7.0 vs. 2.5), and hence ROE (16.2 percent versus 13.1 percent), that is well above the peer group average. ■

CHAPTER

14

FINANCIAL FORECASTING

Learning Objectives

After studying this chapter, readers should be able to

- describe in general terms the overall planning process for businesses,
- use the constant growth method to forecast a business's financial statements, and
- discuss the various methods used to forecast income statement items and balance sheet accounts.

Introduction

In chapter 13, we saw how managers conduct analyses to assess a business's financial condition. Now, we consider the planning actions managers can take to exploit a business's strengths and overcome its weaknesses as they seek to meet its goals and objectives. Healthcare managers are vitally concerned with a business's projected financial statements and with the effects of alternative operating policies on these statements. An analysis of such effects is the key ingredient of financial planning. However, a good financial plan cannot by itself ensure that a business will meet its goals; the plan must be backed up by a financial control system, both to make sure that the plan is carried out properly and to facilitate rapid adjustments if economic and operating conditions change from those built into the plan.

Strategic Planning

Financial plans, which are founded on financial forecasts, are developed in the framework of the business's overall *strategic plan*. Thus, we begin our discussion with an overview of strategic planning. Note that strategic planning in healthcare organizations is an important and complex managerial responsibility, and most schools offer entire courses on the subject. Our purpose here is to acquaint you with some basic concepts directly related to financial forecasting.

Mission Statement

An important part of any strategic plan is the ***mission statement***, which defines the overall purpose of the organization. The mission can be defined specifically or in general terms. For example, an investor-owned medical equipment manufacturer might state that its corporate mission is "to increase the intrinsic value of the firm's common stock." Another might say that its mission is "to maximize the growth rate of earnings and dividends per share while minimizing risk." Yet another might state that its principal goal is "to provide state-of-the-art diagnostic systems at the lowest attainable cost in order to maximize benefits to our customers, employees, and stockholders."

The mission statements of not-for-profit businesses are normally stated in different terms, although competition in the health services sector forces all businesses, regardless of ownership, to operate in a manner consistent with financial viability. For an example of a not-for-profit mission statement, consider the mission statement of Bayside Memorial Hospital, a not-for-profit acute care hospital:

> Bayside Memorial Hospital, along with its medical staff, is a recognized, innovative healthcare leader dedicated to meeting the needs of the community. We strive to be the best comprehensive healthcare provider in our service area through our commitment to excellence.

This mission statement provides Bayside's managers with an overall framework for development of the hospital's goals and objectives.[1]

Corporate Goals

The mission statement contains the general philosophy and approach of the organization, but it does not provide managers with specific operational goals. ***Corporate goals*** set forth specific achievements for management to attain. Corporate goals generally are qualitative in nature, such as "keeping the firm's research and development efforts at the cutting edge of the industry." Multiple goals are established and revised over time as conditions change.

Bayside divides its corporate goals into five major areas:

1. **Quality and customer satisfaction**
   - To make quality performance the goal of each employee
   - To be recognized by our patients as the provider of choice in our market area

   - To identify and resolve areas of patient dissatisfaction as rapidly as possible
2. **Medical staff relations**
   - To identify and develop timely channels of communication among all members of the medical staff, management, and board of directors
   - To respond in a timely manner to all medical staff concerns brought to the attention of management
   - To make Bayside a more desirable location to practice medicine
   - To develop strategies to enhance the mutual commitment of the medical staff, administration, and board of directors for the benefit of the hospital's stakeholders
   - To provide the highest-quality, most cost-effective medical care through a collaborative effort of the medical staff, administration, and board of directors
3. **Human resources management**
   - To be recognized as the customer service leader in our market area
   - To develop and manage human resources to make Bayside the most attractive work location in our market area
4. **Financial performance**
   - To maintain a financial condition that permits us to be highly competitive in our market area
   - To develop the systems necessary to identify inpatient and outpatient costs by unit of service
5. **Health systems management**
   - To be a leader in applied technology based on patient needs
   - To establish new services and programs in response to patient needs
   - To be at the forefront of electronic health record technology

Of course, these goals occasionally conflict. When they do, Bayside's senior managers have to make judgments regarding which takes precedence.

Corporate Objectives

Once a business has defined its mission and goals, it must develop specific objectives designed to help it achieve its stated goals. *Corporate objectives* are generally quantitative in nature. For example, they may specify a target market share, a target return on equity, a target earnings per share growth rate, or a target economic value added. Furthermore, the extent to which corporate objectives are met is commonly used as a basis for managers' compensation. To illustrate corporate objectives, consider Bayside's financial performance goal of maintaining a financial condition that permits the hospital to be highly competitive in its market area. These objectives are tied to that goal in 2019:

- To exceed the hospital's current 5.8 percent operating margin by 2022
- To exceed the hospital's current 7.5 percent total margin by 2022
- To increase the hospital's debt ratio to the range of 35 percent to 40 percent by 2024
- To maintain the hospital's liquidity as measured by the current ratio in the range of 2.0 to 2.5
- To increase fixed asset utilization as measured by the fixed-asset-turnover ratio to 1.5 by 2024

Corporate objectives give managers precise targets to shoot for. These objectives must support the organization's mission and goals and must be chosen carefully so that they are challenging yet attainable.

SELF-TEST QUESTIONS

1. Briefly describe the nature and use of the following corporate planning tools:
   a. Mission
   b. Goals
   c. Objectives
2. Why do financial planners need to be familiar with the business's strategic plan?

Operational Planning

Whereas strategic planning provides general guidance along with specific goals and objectives, operational planning provides a road map for executing a business's strategic plan. The key document in operational planning is the business's *operating plan*, which contains the detailed guidance necessary to meet corporate objectives. Operating plans can be developed for any time horizon. Most firms use a five-year horizon, so the term *five-year plan* has become common. In a five-year plan, the plans are most detailed for the first year, and each succeeding year's plan becomes less specific.

To get a better feel for operational planning, consider exhibit 14.1, which contains Bayside's annual planning schedule. This schedule shows that, for Bayside and most other organizations, the planning process is essentially continuous. Next, exhibit 14.2 outlines the key elements of the hospital's five-year plan, including an expanded section for finance. A full outline would require several pages, but the outline given provides some insight into the format and content of a five-year plan.

For Bayside, much of the planning function takes place at the department level, with technical assistance from the marketing, planning, and financial staffs. Larger businesses with divisions begin the planning process at the divisional level. Each division has its own mission and goals as well as objectives designed to support its goals, and these plans are consolidated to form the corporate plan. A common practice in many health systems is using these plans as a way to measure managers' success during the year; these plans typically take the form of a balanced scorecard, which is a tool that aligns high-level strategy with day-to-day operations measured by key performance indicators.

EXHIBIT 14.1 Bayside Memorial Hospital: Annual Planning Schedule

Months	*Action*
April–May	Marketing department analyzes national and local economic factors likely to influence Bayside's patient volume and reimbursement rates. At this time, a preliminary volume forecast is prepared for each service line.
June –July	Operating departments prepare new project (capital budgeting) requirements as well as operating-cost estimates on the basis of the preliminary volume forecast.
August–September	Financial analysts evaluate proposed capital expenditures and department operating plans. Preliminary forecasted financial statements and cash budgets are prepared with emphasis on Bayside's sources and uses of funds and on forecasted financial condition.
October–November	All previous input is reviewed, and the planning, financial, and departmental staffs draft the hospital's five-year plan. Any new information developed during the planning process "feeds back" into earlier actions.
December	The hospital's executive committee approves the five-year plan and submits it to the board of directors for final approval.

EXHIBIT 14.2 Bayside Memorial Hospital: Partial Five-Year Plan Outline

Chapter 1 Organizational mission and goals
Chapter 2 Organizational objectives
Chapter 3 Projected business environment
Chapter 4 Organizational strategies
Chapter 5 Summary of projected business results
Chapter 6 Service line plans
Chapter 7 Functional area plans

A. Marketing
B. Operations
C. Finance
    1. Current financial condition analysis
    2. Capital investments and financing
        a. Capital budget
        b. Financial plan
    3. Financial operations
        a. Overall policy
        b. Cash budget
        c. Cash and marketable securities management
        d. Inventory management
        e. Revenue cycle management
        f. Short-term financing
        g. Long-term financing
    4. Budgeting and control (first year only)
        a. Revenue budget
        b. Expense budge
        c. Operating budget
        d. Control procedures
    5. Financial forecast
        a. Pro forma financial statements
        b. Projected financial condition analysis

SELF-TEST QUESTIONS

1. What is the purpose of a business's operating plan?
2. What is the most common time horizon for operating plans?
3. Briefly describe the contents of a typical operating plan.

Financial Planning

One of the key elements of operational planning is financial planning, which includes financial forecasting, the focus of this chapter.

The financial planning process can be broken down into the following five steps:

1. Create sets of forecasted financial statements to analyze the effects of alternative operating assumptions on the firm's financial condition. These statements can also be used to monitor operations after the plan has been finalized and put into effect. Rapid awareness of deviations from plans is essential to a good control system, and such a system is essential to organizational success in a changing world.
2. Determine the specific financial requirements needed to support each alternative set of operating assumptions. These financial requirements must include funds for new facilities and renovations as well as for inventory and receivables buildups, for research and educational programs, and for major marketing campaigns.
3. Forecast the financing sources to be used over the next five years to support each alternative set of operating assumptions. This forecast involves estimating the funds that will be generated internally (primarily retentions) as well as those that must be obtained from external sources (primarily contributions and debt financing). Any constraints on operating plans imposed by financial limitations should be incorporated into the plans; examples include expected market conditions or restrictions in debt covenants that limit the availability of new debt financing.
4. Assess the projected financial implications of each alternative set of operating assumptions, including feasibility. To accomplish this, financial condition analysis (as described in chapter 13) is applied—but now to forecasted data as opposed to historical data.
5. Choose the operating alternative that will best meet the organization's goals and objectives. The assumptions inherent in this alternative provide the basis for the firm's base case *financial plan*, which constitutes chapter 7.c of Bayside's operating (five-year) plan (see exhibit 14.2). The most critical part of the financial plan is based on forecasted financial statements, but the plan also contains guidance relative to accounting procedures and other financial functions.

Although our focus in this section is on financial planning, note that it is equally (or more) important to monitor the financial status of the business over time to make sure that the plan chosen is working out as expected. Of course, procedures must be in place for adjusting the base case plan if the forecasted economic conditions do not materialize. For example, if Bayside's forecast on Medicare and Medicaid reimbursement used to develop the base case five-year plan proves to be too high or too low, the correct amounts must be recognized and reflected in operational and financial plans as rapidly as possible.

SELF-TEST QUESTION

1. What are the five steps of the financial planning process?

Revenue Forecasts

On the web at: *ache.org/HAP/PinkSong8e*

The starting point, and most critical element, in the financial forecast is the *revenue forecast*. The reason revenue forecasts play such an important role is that all other elements of the financial forecast stem from the revenue forecast. If the revenue projection is erroneous, the rest of the financial forecast will be suspect.

Revenue forecasts can be done in two ways: from the top or from the bottom. When businesses forecast from the top, they examine historical trends in aggregate (organizational) revenues and use them as the basis for forecasting future revenues. When businesses forecast from the bottom, they forecast revenues for individual services and then aggregate them to create the organizational forecast. Most large organizations use both methods and resolve inconsistencies as the last step in the process. In this way, the best possible forecasts are made.

Forecasting from the Top

When businesses forecast from the top, the revenue forecast generally starts with a review of organizational revenues over the past five to ten years, often expressed in graph form such as that in exhibit 14.3. The first part of the graph shows actual total operating revenues for Bayside from 2014 through 2018. Over these five years (four growth periods), total operating revenues (net patient service revenue plus premium revenue plus other revenue) grew from \$86,477,000 to \$112,050,000, or at a compound annual growth rate of 6.7 percent. Alternatively, a time-series regression can be applied to total operating revenue. We used a spreadsheet to perform a log-linear regression on all five years of operating revenue data, for a resulting annual growth rate of 6.9 percent.[2] However, Bayside's revenue growth rate accelerated in the second half of the historical period, primarily as a result of new capacity added in 2016. Furthermore, a new, aggressive marketing program was instituted in late 2017 that resulted in a growth rate in operating revenues in 2018 of more than 11 percent.

On the basis of the recent trends in operating revenues, anticipated service introductions, and forecasts of local competition and reimbursement

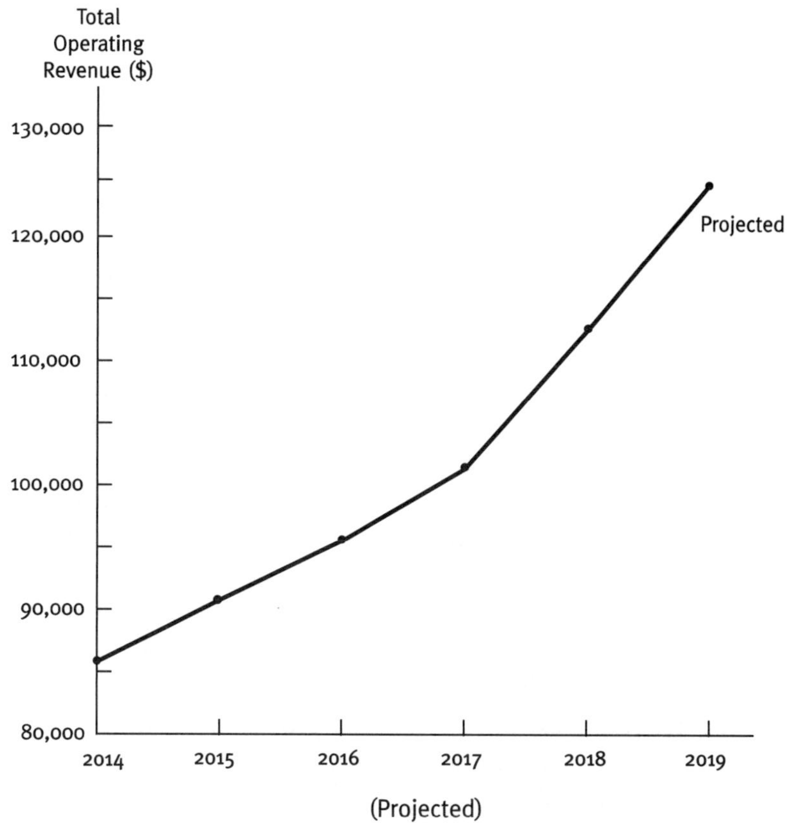

EXHIBIT 14.3
Bayside Memorial Hospital: Historical and Projected Revenues (in thousands of dollars)

Year	*Total Operating Revenue*
2014	$ 86,477
2015	90,568
2016	95,351
2017	102,015
2018	112,050
2019	(projected) 124,376

trends, Bayside's planning group projects a growth rate of 11 percent for 2019, which produces a total operating revenue forecast of $124,376,000.

It is **very important** to recognize that the operating revenue forecast is driven by two elements: changes in volume (utilization) and changes in reimbursement rates. Whereas volume changes tend to have a large impact on facilities and staffing requirements and hence costs, reimbursement rate changes, unless they are either substantial or come as a result of a changing payer mix, do not have much of an effect on operating variables such as facilities and labor requirements. Thus, it is important for managers to recognize whether operating revenue changes are a result of changes in volume, which indicates that the business is experiencing real changes in patient services, or a result of reimbursement effects, which may have little or no impact on operations.

If Bayside's volume forecast is off the mark, the consequences can be serious. First, if the market for a particular service expands more than Bayside has expected and planned for, the hospital will not be able to meet its patients' needs. Potential customers will end up going elsewhere for services, and Bayside will lose market share and perhaps miss a major opportunity. On the other hand, if its projections are overly optimistic, Bayside could end up with too much capacity, which means excess facilities, equipment, inventory, and staff. This excess would mean low turnover ratios, high costs of labor and depreciation, and possibly layoffs. All of these factors would result in low profitability, which could degrade the hospital's ability to compete in the future. If Bayside had financed the unneeded expansion primarily with debt, its problems would, of course, be compounded. Thus, an accurate volume forecast is critical to the well-being of any healthcare provider.

Finally, note that the operating revenue forecast, like virtually any forecast, is actually the expected value of a probability distribution of possible revenues. Because any forecast is subject to a greater or lesser degree of uncertainty, for financial forecasting purposes we are often just as interested in the degree of uncertainty inherent in the forecast (e.g., its standard deviation) as we are in the expected value.

Forecasting from the Bottom

To begin forecasting operating revenue from the bottom, Bayside divides its services into four major groups: (1) inpatient, (2) outpatient, (3) ancillary, and (4) other. Each of these categories is broken down into individual services; for example, neurosurgery is one of the services that is part of the overall inpatient services revenue forecast.

Next, the level of population growth and disease trends are forecasted; for example, analysts predict the population growth in the hospital's service area and any disease patterns that will affect the number of neurosurgeries performed. For an illustration, consider the data obtained from a state health agency, which show that 523 neurosurgeries were performed in Bayside's service area in 2018. With a service area population of 756,508 in 2018, the neurosurgery rate in the service area was 69.1 per 100,000 people. With a population forecast of 788,700 for 2019, Bayside's managers predict that $(788{,}700 \div 100{,}000) \times 69.1 = 545$ neurosurgeries will be performed in its service area.

Bayside's managers then look at the competitive environment. They consider such factors as the hospital's inpatient and outpatient capacities, its competitors' capacities, and new services or service improvements that Bayside or its competitors might institute. For example, Bayside performed 127 neurosurgeries in 2018, so it had 24.3 percent of the neurosurgery market in that year. With an additional neurosurgeon now on the staff, increased marketing, and new managed care contracts, the hospital expects to increase its market share to 30 percent. Thus, Bayside's forecast for neurosurgeries in 2019 is $0.30 \times 545 = 164$.

Bayside's managers then consider the impact of the hospital's pricing strategy and reimbursement trends on the demand for services. For example, does the hospital have plans to raise neurosurgery charges to boost profit margins or to lower charges to gain market share and use excess capacity? Any potential impact of such pricing changes on neurosurgery volume must be worked into the forecasts. Because Bayside has reimbursement and utilization data on its neurosurgeries, it can easily convert the estimate of the number of procedures into a revenue estimate. The end result is a utilization and revenue forecast for neurosurgeries.

Bayside creates a volume and revenue forecast for each individual service and then aggregates these forecasts by service group. Independently, the hospital forecasts operating revenues by service group using the procedures discussed in the previous section. The aggregate forecast based on individual service forecasts is then compared with the service group forecasts.

Differences are reconciled, and the resultant revenue forecast for the hospital is then compared with the from-the-top forecast described earlier. Further refinement is often necessary, but the end result is a total operating revenue forecast for the hospital, broken down by major groups and by individual services.

SELF-TEST QUESTIONS

1. What are two approaches to the total operating revenue forecast?
2. Discuss some factors that must be considered when developing an operating revenue forecast.
3. Why is it necessary for planners to distinguish between volume changes and reimbursement changes?

Creating Forecasted Financial Statements

The revenue forecast provides a starting point from which to create a business's projected financial statements, which sometimes are called *pro forma financial statements*, or just *pro formas*. Many techniques are used to create the pro formas, most of which are too complex or too detailed to discuss here. Thus, we focus more on concepts than on providing a cookbook approach to financial statement forecasting. We begin by discussing a conceptual framework for financial statement forecasting. Then, we consider some issues inherent in the forecasting process.

SELF-TEST QUESTION

1. What is the starting point from which forecasted financial statements are created?

Constant Growth Forecasting

On the web at: *ache.org/HAP/PinkSong8e*

The *constant growth method*—also called the *percentage of revenues method* or, more commonly, *percentage of sales* method—is a simple technique for creating pro forma financial statements. Although this method has limited value in practice, it provides an excellent introduction to the forecasting process and lays the groundwork for understanding the more complex methods used in practice.

Assumptions

The constant growth method is based on two assumptions: (1) most income statement items and balance sheet accounts are tied directly to revenues, and (2) the current levels of most income statement items and balance sheet accounts are optimal for the current volume of services provided. The basic premise is that as revenues increase or decrease, so will most income statement items and balance sheet accounts. Furthermore, the changes in items and accounts will be **proportional** to the change in revenues. Given this premise, we assume that most income statement items and balance sheet accounts will grow at the same rate—the rate of revenue growth.

Of course, revenue changes can be a result of either volume changes or reimbursement rate changes, which typically are driven by inflation. In most situations, revenue changes are a result of both factors. For example, Bayside's 11 percent increase in total operating revenues projected for 2019 might be a result of a projected 6 percent increase in the volume of services provided and a 5 percent inflationary increase in reimbursement rates. Because many of the income statement items and balance sheet accounts are affected by volume and inflation changes, many financial statement variables would be expected to also increase by 11 percent. Variables that are tied to only volume or inflation would be expected to increase at a lower 6 percent or 5 percent rate. However, the constant growth method illustration that follows assumes that all financial statement variables related to revenues are influenced by both volume and inflationary changes.

Illustration

We illustrate the constant growth method with Bayside, whose 2018 financial statements are given in column 1 of exhibits 14.4 and 14.5. We explain the other columns of these tables when we discuss the forecast for 2019.

To begin the process, we assume (contrary to fact) that Bayside operated its fixed assets (property and equipment) at full capacity to support the $112,050,000 in total operating revenue in 2018—that is, the hospital had no excess beds or outpatient facilities.[3] Because we are assuming no excess capacity, if volume is to increase in 2019, Bayside will need to increase its fixed assets along with its current assets.

If, as projected, Bayside's total operating revenue increases to $124,376,000, what will its pro forma 2019 income statement and balance sheet look like, and how much external financing will the hospital require to support operations in 2019? The first step in using the constant growth method to forecast the business's financial statements is to identify income statement items and balance sheet accounts that are assumed to vary directly with revenues. For illustrative purposes, the increased operating revenue forecast for 2019 is expected to bring corresponding increases in all of the income statement items except interest expense—that is, operating costs and administrative expenses are assumed to be tied directly to total operating revenue, but interest expense is a function of financing decisions. Furthermore, nonoperating income is also assumed to grow at the same rate.

Under such naive assumptions, the 2019 first-pass forecasted (or pro forma) income statement is constructed as follows:

- Place the forecasted constant growth rate—11.0 percent—in column 2 of exhibit 14.4 for all items expected to increase with revenues. Items calculated in the forecasted income statement (such as total operating costs) and items not expected to increase proportionally with revenues (such as interest expense) have "NA" (not applicable) in column 2.
- Forecast the 2019 first-pass pro forma amounts by multiplying each applicable 2018 value by the growth rate. For example, the 2019 forecast for nursing services expenses is $58,285,000 × 1.11 = $64,696,000. Note that we generated the forecast with a spreadsheet model, so some of the amounts shown in the financial statements may be slightly different from those obtained by using a calculator. Also, note that the format of the income statement was modified slightly from that used in chapter 13 to place all of the revenue (income) items at the top of the statement.

EXHIBIT 14.4
Bayside Memorial Hospital: Historical and Projected Income Statements (in thousands of dollars)

			2019 Projections		
	2018 *(1)*	*Growth Rate (%)* *(2)*	*First Pass* *(3)*	*Second Pass* *(4)*	*Third Pass* *(5)*
Total operating revenue	$112,050	11.0%	$124,376	$124,376	$124,376
Nonoperating income	2,098	11.0	2,329	2,329	2,329
Total revenues	$ 114,148	NA	$126,704	$126,704	$126,704
Expenses:					
Nursing services	$ 58,285	11.0	$ 64,696	$ 64,696	$ 64,696
Dietary services	5,424	11.0	6,021	6,021	6,021
General services	13,198	11.0	14,650	14,650	14,650
Administrative services	11,427	11.0	12,684	12,684	12,684
Employee health and welfare	10,250	11.0	11,378	11,378	11,378
Malpractice insurance	1,320	11.0	1,465	1,465	1,465
Depreciation	4,130	11.0	4,584	4,584	4,584
Interest expense	1,542	NA	1,542	1,820	1,842
Total expenses	$105,576	NA	$117,020	$117,297	$117,320
Net income	$ 8,572	NA	$ 9,685	$ 9,407	$ 9,385

EXHIBIT 14.5

Bayside Memorial Hospital: Historical and Projected Balance Sheets (in thousands of dollars)

			2019 Projections		
	2018 (1)	*Growth Rate (%)* (2)	*First Pass* (3)	*Second Pass* (4)	*Third Pass* (5)
Cash	$ 2,263	11.0	$ 2,512	$ 2,512	$ 2,512
Short-term investments	4,000	11.0	4,440	4,440	4,440
Accounts receivable	21,840	11.0	24,242	24,242	24,242
Inventories	3,177	11.0	3,526	3,526	3,526
Total current assets	$ 31,280	NA	$ 34,721	$ 34,721	$ 34,721
Gross property and equipment	$145,158	11.0	$161,125	$161,125	$161,125
Accumulated depreciation	25,160	NA	29,744	29,744	29,744
Net property and equipment	$119,998	NA	$131,381	$131,381	$131,381
Total assets	$151,278	NA	$166,102	$166,102	$166,102
Accounts payable	$ 4,707	11.0	$ 5,225	$ 5,225	$ 5,225
Accrued expenses	5,650	11.0	6,272	6,272	6,272
Notes payable	2,975	11.0	3,302	3,302	3,302
Current portion of long-term debt	2,150	11.0	2,387	2,387	2,387
Total current liabilities	$ 13,332	NA	$ 14,799	$ 14,799	$ 14,799
Long-term debt	$ 28,750	NA	$ 28,750	$ 32,221	$ 32,499
Capital lease obligations	1,832	11.0	2,034	2,034	2,034
Total long-term liabilities	$ 30,582	NA	$ 30,784	$ 34,255	$ 34,533
Net assets (equity)	$107,364	NA	$117,049	$116,771	$116,749
Total liabilities and net assets	$151,278	NA	$162,631	$165,824	$166,080

- Some items marked NA, such as interest expense, are carried over into 2019 at their 2018 values. We know that the interest expense in 2019 will be larger than in 2018 if Bayside has to borrow additional funds, but we cannot predict the amount of interest increase until the first-pass financial statements have been completed. The remaining income statement items marked NA, such as total expenses, are calculated by adding or subtracting other forecasted items.
- When the first-pass income statement is completed (column 3 in exhibit 14.4), we see that the projected net income is $9,685,000. Note that an 11 percent increase in net income would be $8,572,000 × 1.11 = $9,515,000. The forecasted amount is somewhat greater than an 11 percent increase because interest expense was held at its 2018 level.

Let's turn to the balance sheet. Because we assumed that Bayside was operating at full capacity in 2018, fixed assets as well as current assets must increase if revenues are to increase. More cash will be needed for transactions, receivables will be higher, additional inventory must be stocked, new facilities must be added, and so on.[4]

To construct the first-pass pro forma balance sheet contained in column 3 in exhibit 14.5, we proceed as follows:

- All balance sheet accounts that are expected to increase with revenues are forecasted in the same way as in the income statement. For example, consider the cash account. The 2019 forecast is created by multiplying the 2018 value by the growth rate, so $2,263,000 × 1.11 = $2,512,000, which is shown in column 3 of exhibit 14.5.
- The forecasted 2019 depreciation expense from the income statement is added to the 2018 accumulated depreciation account on the balance sheet to obtain the 2019 accumulated depreciation forecast: $4,584,000 + $25,160,000 = $29,744,000.
- The long-term debt value **initially** is held at its 2018 value—$28,750,000. However, as explained in the next section, we assume that any external financing required in 2019 will be obtained by issuing more long-term debt. Alternatively, any excess funds generated would be used to retire long-term debt. In effect, long-term debt is the "plug" variable in this illustration. It will be adjusted in the second and third passes to make the balance sheet balance.
- To forecast the equity amount, add the net income projected for 2019, all of which must be retained in the business, to the 2018 balance sheet equity amount: $9,685,000 + $107,364,000 = $117,049,000.

Finally, fill in the missing values in column 3 by adding or subtracting as necessary.

The projected 2019 asset accounts sum to $166,102,000. This sum is less than an 11 percent increase because accumulated depreciation, which is a contra (negative) asset account, increased by about 18 percent. Thus, to support a revenue increase of 11 percent, Bayside must increase its assets from $151,278,000 to $166,102,000. The projected liability and equity accounts sum to $162,631,000. Again, this sum is less than an 11 percent increase because (1) long-term debt was held at its 2018 level and (2) the equity account increased by less than 11 percent.

At this point, the balance sheet **does not balance**: Assets total $166,102,000, while only $162,631,000 of liabilities and equity is projected. Thus, we have a shortfall, or *external financing requirement*, of $3,471,000. This amount will have to be raised externally by bank borrowings and selling securities. The organization could also change operating variables—such as charges (revenues) or expenses—to generate more net income and hence more retained earnings.

The External Financing Plan

Assuming no change in operating variables, Bayside can use short-term notes payable, long-term debt, increased solicitations (contributions), or a combination of these sources to make up the $3,471,000 shortfall. Ordinarily, Bayside would base this choice on its target capital structure, the relative costs of different types of securities, maturity matching considerations, its ability to increase contributions above the forecasted level, and so on. The decision as to how this shortfall will be financed is called the *external financing plan*.

Our simplistic forecast assumes that Bayside will raise the required external funds by issuing additional long-term debt. Because Bayside is financing permanent assets, its use of long-term debt to meet external financing needs indicates that it is taking the matching approach to its debt maturity structure (see chapter 10). However, the use of additional debt capital will change the first approximation income statement for 2019 as set forth in column 3 of exhibit 14.4 because more debt will lead to higher interest expense. Bayside's managers are forecasting that new long-term debt will carry an interest rate of 8 percent. Thus, $3,471,000 of new long-term debt will increase the interest expense projected for 2019 by 0.08 × $3,471,000 = $278,000.

The projected income statement and balance sheet, including *financing feedback* effects, are shown in column 4 (second pass) of exhibits 14.4 and 14.5. We see that although $3,471,000 was added to Bayside's liabilities, the hospital is still \$166,102,000 – \$165,824,000 = \$278,000 short in meeting its external financing requirement. This new, but much smaller, shortfall is a result of the added interest expense; \$278,000 of new interest expense decreases net income by a like amount. Hence, the equity balance falls to \$117,049,000 – \$278,000 = \$116,771,000.

The process can be repeated yet again by adding an additional \$278,000 of external (long-term debt) financing to create a third-pass income statement and balance sheet. As shown in column 5 (third pass) of exhibits 14.4 and 14.5, the projected equity balance would be further reduced by additional interest requirements, but the balance sheet would be closer to being in balance because more long-term debt would be added to the liabilities side. Successive iterations would continue to reduce the discrepancy. If the budget process were computerized, an exact solution could be quickly reached. Even if the process is stopped after just a few iterations, the projected statements would generally be very close to being in balance. They would certainly be close enough for practical purposes, given the large element of uncertainty inherent in the projections themselves.

The base case pro forma financial statements, along with the corresponding financial condition analysis discussed in chapter 13, are then reviewed by Bayside's executive committee for consistency with the hospital's financial objectives. Generally, the committee will make changes to the initial assumptions that will result in a new set of pro forma financial statements, which are then analyzed and reviewed until the forecast is finalized.

The forecasting process undertaken by Ann Arbor Health Care, a for-profit hospital, is similar to that performed by Bayside. The only real difference is that a for-profit business uses stock rather than fund financing. This fact presents three complications. First, Ann Arbor may pay dividends, so net income must be reduced by the forecasted dividend payment to find the amount of capital that is retained in the firm and, hence, flows to the balance sheet. Second, Ann Arbor has the option of issuing common stock to meet its external financing needs. Third, the financing feedback effect must be expanded to include the additional dividend payments, if required, on any new common stock issued.

Finally, note that forecasted financial statements must be checked for internal consistency; that is, accumulated depreciation on the balance sheet must be consistent with the depreciation expense shown on the income statement, and the equity reported on the balance sheet must be consistent with the retentions shown on the income statement. It is imperative that pro forma statements recognize the dependencies between the income statement items and balance sheet accounts.

SELF-TEST QUESTIONS

1. Briefly describe the mechanics of the constant growth forecasting method.
2. Why is the external financing plan so important in the planning process?
3. Do you think most healthcare businesses use the constant growth method to develop pro forma financial statements, or do you think they use some other methodology?

Factors That Influence the External Financing Requirement

The external financing requirement is one of the key pieces of information gleaned from the forecasted financial statements. If the business is unable to fund this requirement, it must alter its plans for the future. The six factors that have the greatest influence on the external financing requirement are (1) projected revenue growth rate, (2) capacity utilization, (3) capital intensity, (4) profitability, (5) dividend policy (for investor-owned businesses), and (6) ability to attract contribution capital (for not-for-profit firms). In this section, we discuss each of these factors in detail.

The faster Bayside's revenues are forecasted to grow, the greater the external financing need. The reasoning here is that increases in revenues normally require increases in assets because growing revenues typically imply growing volumes or inflationary pressures. If revenues are not projected to grow, no new assets will be needed, but any projected asset increases require financing of some type. Some of the required financing will come from spontaneously generated liabilities, such as accruals. Also, assuming a positive profit margin (and for investor-owned firms, a payout ratio of less than 100 percent), the firm will generate some retained earnings.

Sustainable Growth Rate

The maximum growth rate that a business can sustain without requiring external financing is called the *sustainable growth rate*. In Bayside's case, this rate is 8.6 percent, which we estimated using a spreadsheet forecasting model by finding the revenue growth rate that Bayside could achieve with no external financing. At growth rates of 8.6 percent or less, Bayside will need no external financing; all required funds can be obtained by spontaneous increases in current liability accounts plus retained earnings, and the hospital will even generate surplus capital. However, if Bayside's projected revenue growth rate is 8.7 percent or greater, it must seek outside financing, and the greater the projected growth rate, the greater its external financing requirement will be. Although there are formulas that can be used to estimate the sustainable growth rate, it is easier (and potentially more accurate) to use the financial forecasting model for this purpose.

If the revenue growth rate is low enough, spontaneously generated funds plus retained earnings will be sufficient to support the asset growth. However, if the growth rate exceeds a certain level, external financing will be needed. If management foresees difficulties in raising this capital—perhaps because it has no more debt capacity—then the feasibility of the firm's expansion plans may have to be reconsidered.

Capacity Utilization

In determining Bayside's external financing requirement for 2019, we assumed that the hospital's fixed assets were being fully used. Thus, any significant increase in revenues would require an increase in fixed assets. What would happen if Bayside had been operating its fixed assets at less than full capacity? Assume that Bayside's managers consider 90 percent occupancy to be full capacity. Because the hospital had 57.9 percent occupancy in 2018, it was operating at 57.9 ÷ 90 = 64% of capacity. Under this condition, fixed assets could remain constant until revenues reach the level at which fixed assets are being fully used. This level is defined as *capacity sales* and is calculated as follows:

Key Equation 14.1: Capacity Sales

$$\text{Utilization rate (\% of capacity)} = \frac{\text{Actual revenue}}{\text{Capacity sales}},$$

so

$$\text{Capacity sales} = \frac{\text{Actual revenue}}{\text{Utilization rate}}.$$

Because Bayside had been operating at 64 percent of capacity, its capacity sales **without any new fixed assets** would be $112,050,000 ÷ 0.64 = $175,078,125. In reality, Bayside can easily increase its operating revenue to $124,376,000 with no increase in fixed assets. Thus, its external financing requirement would decrease by $161,125,000 – $145,158,000 = $15,967,000 (the projected increase in gross property and equipment), and when Bayside's actual utilization rate is considered, its forecast would show surplus capital in 2019.

Capital Intensity

The amount of assets required per dollar of sales (total assets/sales) is often called the *capital intensity ratio*, which is the reciprocal of the total-asset-turnover ratio. Capital intensity has a major effect on the amount of external capital required to support any level of sales growth. If the capital intensity ratio is low, such as for home health care businesses, revenues can grow rapidly without using much outside capital. However, if the firm is capital intensive, such as a hospital, even a small growth in volume might require a great deal of outside capital if the firm is operating at full capacity.

Profitability

Profitability is also an important determinant of external financing requirements—the higher the profit margin, the lower the external financing requirement, other factors held constant. Bayside's profit (total) margin in 2018 was 7.5 percent. Suppose its profit margin increased to 10 percent through higher reimbursements and better expense control. This increase would cause net income—and hence retained earnings—to increase, which in turn would decrease Bayside's need for external financing.

Dividend Policy

For investor-owned firms, dividend policy also affects external capital requirements. If Ann Arbor foresees difficulties in raising external capital when it forecasts its 2019 financial statements, it might want to consider a reduction in its dividend payout ratio. However, before making this decision, management should consider the possible negative effects of a dividend cut on stock price.

Ability to Attract Contribution Capital

One of the major sources of equity financing for not-for-profit businesses is contribution capital. Unrestricted contributions are listed as revenues on the income statement in the year they become available for use in the organization; hence, they increase forecasted equity and decrease the need for external financing. Clearly, organizations that are able to raise large amounts of charitable contributions are able to grow without using as much external debt financing as organizations that obtain few contributions. For this reason, many organizations operate an affiliated foundation, whose sole purpose is to raise funds for the organization through events and funding campaigns. Note that the earnings on some restricted contributions (endowments) typically are also available to help fund a business's asset growth.

SELF-TEST QUESTION

1. How do the following factors affect the external financing requirement?
   a. Projected revenue growth rate
   b. Capacity utilization
   c. Capital intensity
   d. Profitability
   e. Dividend policy (for investor-owned firms)
   f. Ability to attract contribution capital (for not-for-profit firms)

Problems with the Constant Growth Method

For the constant growth method to produce accurate forecasts, each item and account that is assumed to grow with revenues must increase at the same rate as revenues. Unfortunately, such a situation rarely exists. Here are some of the problems with the constant growth approach that are encountered in real-world forecasting.

Price-Driven Revenue Growth

Earlier we emphasized that revenue growth can occur as a result of volume or pricing (reimbursement) changes. If revenue growth occurs solely as a result of reimbursement rate changes that were **not** caused by inflation, there will be no direct impact on some income statement items (e.g., labor expenses) or on some balance sheet items (e.g., inventories, payables, fixed asset requirements). Because the constant growth method ties most items and accounts directly to dollar revenues, it can produce misleading forecasts when non-inflationary reimbursement rate changes—rather than volume changes—are driving the revenue forecast.

Of course, if the reimbursement changes were made because of inflation effects, there will likely be an inflationary impact on costs. However, in most cases, the effect of inflation will not be neutral—that is, the impact will differ across items and accounts.

Economies of Scale

There are economies of scale in the use of many kinds of assets, and when they occur, the asset growth rates are less than volume growth rates. For example, healthcare businesses typically need to maintain base stocks of different inventory items, even when volume levels are low. As volume expands, so do inventories. But inventories tend to grow less rapidly than volume does, so the use of a constant growth rate would overstate the amount of inventory required.

Lumpy Assets

In many industries, practical considerations dictate that a business must add fixed assets in large, discrete units. For example, in the hospital field, it is not economically feasible to add, say, five beds, so when hospitals expand capacity, they typically do so in relatively large increments. When capacity volume is reached, even a small increase in volume would require a hospital to significantly increase its fixed assets, so a small projected volume increase can bring with it a very large increase in fixed asset requirements.

Suboptimal Relationships

All of the asset projections in a forecast should be based on target, or optimal, relationships between revenues and assets, not on the relationships that actually exist. For example, in 2018 Bayside had $3,177,000 in inventories. Our constant growth forecast projected inventories of $3,526,000 in 2015. The projection assumed that the current inventory level was optimal for the actual revenues realized. However, if the 2018 inventory level was suboptimal—say, too large—it might be possible to grow revenues by 11 percent with no increase in inventories. Conversely, if the inventory level was too small in 2018, the actual level of inventories required in 2019 would be greater than the forecast.

If any of the problems noted here are encountered in practice (and many of them are), the simple constant growth method should not be used. Rather, other techniques must be used to forecast asset and liability levels and the resulting external financing requirement. Some of these methods are discussed in the following section.

SELF-TEST QUESTIONS

1. Describe several conditions under which the constant growth method can produce questionable results.
2. Do these conditions often exist in real-world forecasting?

Real-World Forecasting

We have emphasized that the constant growth method is not used in actual forecasting situations. The overall approach of first forecasting the firm's income statement, then its balance sheet, then its external financing requirement, and so on, is used, but techniques other than constant growth are used to forecast the specific income statement items and balance sheet accounts. In this section, we discuss four forecasting techniques commonly used in practice: (1) simple linear regression, (2) curvilinear regression, (3) multiple regression, and (4) specific item forecasting.

Simple Linear Regression

Simple linear regression often is used to estimate asset requirements. For example, consider Bayside's inventories and total operating revenue over the past five years and the regression plot shown in exhibit 14.6. The estimated regression equation, as found using a spreadsheet, is as follows (in thousands of dollars):

$$\text{Inventories} = \$1{,}372 + (0.0160 \times \text{Total operating revenue}).$$

The plotted points are close to the regression line. In fact, the correlation coefficient between inventories and sales is +0.99, which indicates that there is a strong linear relationship between these two variables. Why might this be the case for Bayside? According to the *economic ordering quantity* (EOQ) model (discussed in chapter 15), inventories should increase with the square root of revenues, which will cause the regression to be nonlinear (the true regression line would rise at a decreasing rate). However, Bayside has greatly expanded its number of service lines over the past decade, and the base stocks associated with these new services have caused inventories to increase. Also, inflation has had a similar impact on revenues and inventory levels. These three influences—(1) economies of scale in existing services, (2) base stocks for new services, and (3) inflationary effects—offset each other, and the result is the observed linear relationship between inventories and sales.

We can use the estimated relationship between inventories and revenues to forecast the 2015 inventory level. Because 2015 total operating revenue is projected at $124,376,000, 2015 inventories should be $3,362,000:

$$\begin{aligned}\text{Inventories} &= \$1{,}372 + (0.0160 \times \$124{,}376)\\ &= \$1{,}372 + \$1{,}990\\ &= \$3{,}362.\end{aligned}$$

This forecast is $3,526,000 − $3,362,000 = $164,000 less than our earlier forecast based on the constant growth method. The difference occurs because the constant growth method assumes that the ratio of inventories to revenues remains constant—or, in other words, the regression line passes

EXHIBIT 14.6 Bayside Memorial Hospital: Linear Regression on Inventories (in thousands of dollars)

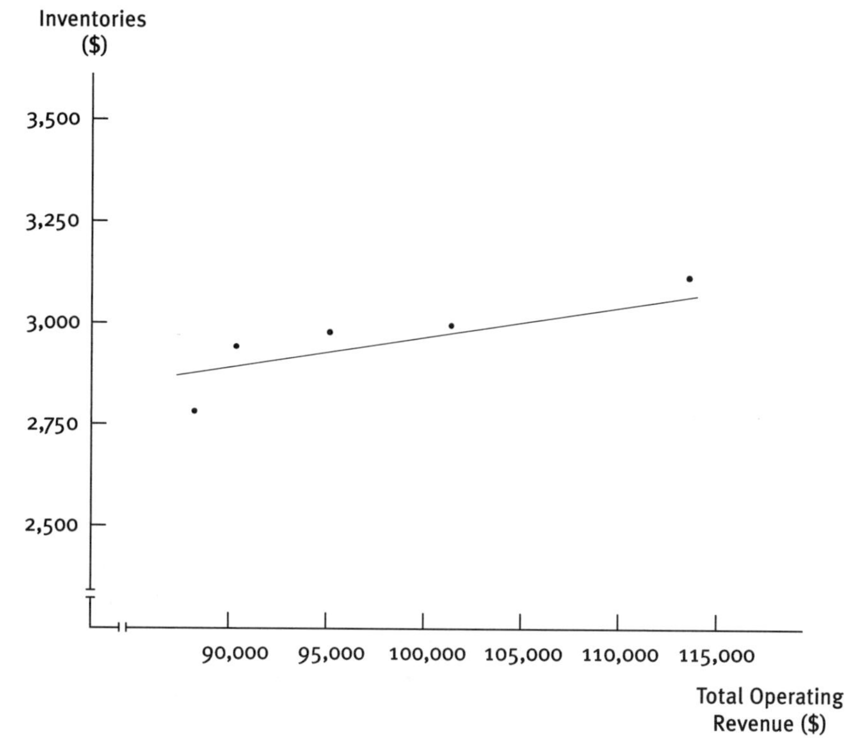

Year	*Total Operating Revenue*	*Inventories*
2014	$86,477	$2,752
2015	90,568	2,838
2016	95,351	2,896
2017	102,015	2,981
2018	112,050	3,177

Inventories = $1,372 + (0.0160 × Total operating revenue).

Note: Table values were calculated on a spreadsheet; rounding differences will occur if a calculator is used.

through the origin. However, as seen in exhibit 14.6, the ratio actually declines because the inventory regression line does not pass through the origin.

We can run linear regressions on all the items on the income statement and all the accounts on the balance sheet that need to be forecasted to determine items and accounts that produce a high correlation (i.e., have a strong linear relationship) and therefore may be forecasted using this technique. Then, we can use these relationships in exhibits 14.4 and 14.5 in place of the constant growth rates to create new pro forma financial statements based on linear regressions.

Curvilinear Regression

Simple linear regression is based on the assumption that a straight-line relationship exists between a particular variable and revenues, or some other variable. Although linear relationships between financial statement variables and revenue frequently do exist, these relationships often assume other forms. For example, if the EOQ relationship had dominated the inventory–revenue relationship, the correct plot of inventory versus revenue would be a concave curve rather than the straight line shown in exhibit 14.6. If we forecasted the inventory level needed to support revenue growth using a linear relationship, our forecast would be too high.

In their databases, healthcare businesses have historical data in the aggregate and by division, service line, and so on. They also have or can easily obtain certain types of data for other firms in the sector. These data can be analyzed using software based on advanced statistical techniques (1) to determine whether a relationship is curvilinear or linear and (2) to estimate the curvilinear relationship, should one exist. Once the best-fit relationship has been estimated, it can be used to project future levels of items such as inventories, given the revenue forecast. Often, a plot of the data will suggest a nonlinear relationship. The data—inventories in this case—can then be converted to logarithms if the regression points appear to slope downward or raised to a power if the slope of the points seems to be increasing. The graphics capabilities of spreadsheets can be used to identify nonlinear relationships.

Multiple Regression

If the relationship between a variable (such as inventories) and revenues is such that the individual points are widely scattered about the regression line (i.e., the correlation coefficient is low) but a curvilinear relationship does not appear to exist, there is a good chance that factors in addition to revenue affect the level of that variable. For example, inventory levels might be a function of both revenue level and the number of different services offered (or products sold). In this case, we would obtain the best forecast for inventory level by using multiple regression techniques to regress inventories against both revenue and the number of services offered. The projected inventories would then be based on forecasts of number of services in addition to total revenue. Most computer installations now have complete regression software packages that make multiple and curvilinear regression techniques easy to apply. Many spreadsheet programs can perform multiple regression analysis as well.

Specific Item Forecasting

Another technique often most useful in practice is to develop a specific model for each income statement item and balance sheet account that must be forecasted. For example, salaries can be projected using payroll records and expected salary increases, receivables can be forecasted by using the payments pattern approach, gross fixed assets can be forecasted on the basis of the firm's capital budget, and depreciation can be forecasted on the basis of the firm's aggregate depreciation schedule. (We discuss the payments pattern approach to receivables management in chapter 15.) Of course, projected volume typically remains an important element behind each of these specific item forecasts.

Specific item forecasting is especially useful when revenues and costs are affected by different forces and hence are expected to grow at different rates. In today's healthcare environment, this is probably the rule rather than the exception.

Comparison of Forecasting Methods

The constant growth method assumes that most financial statement variables are directly related to revenue. It is the easiest approach to use, but its forecasts are often of questionable value. Simple linear regression differs from the constant growth method in that regression does not assume a constant relationship to revenue. Use of this technique can improve the forecasts of many financial statement variables. Note, too, that curvilinear and multiple regression techniques can provide especially accurate forecasts when relationships either (1) are not linear or (2) depend on other variables in addition to sales. Finally, specific item forecasting based on other decision models related to a specific line item can be used.

As we move down the list of forecasting methods, accuracy may or may not increase, but the costs of creating the forecasts are sure to increase. The need to employ more complicated, and consequently more costly, methods varies from situation to situation. As in all situations, the costs of using more refined techniques must be balanced against the benefits obtained. Unfortunately, there is no assurance that the use of more sophisticated forecasting methods will produce better forecasts. Furthermore, more complicated forecasting methods often hide the assumptions inherent in the forecast. As with much of healthcare financial management, judgment and common sense are necessities in this process.

SELF-TEST QUESTIONS

1. Identify several techniques that can be used instead of constant growth forecasting.
2. Which techniques do you think produce the most accurate forecasts? Which techniques do you think are the most costly to use?

Use of Financial Forecasting Models in Practice

In practice, almost all healthcare businesses use some type of financial forecasting model. Such models are used to show the effects of different volume and reimbursement rates, different relationships between volume and operating assets, and even different assumptions about reimbursement rates and input costs (e.g., labor, materials). Plans are then made regarding fulfillment of any projected external financing requirements—through short-term bank loans; selling long-term bonds; or, in the case of investor-owned firms, selling new common stock. Pro forma balance sheets, income statements, and statements of cash flows are generated under the different financing plans, and key risk/return ratios (e.g., current ratio, debt-to-assets assets ratio, times-interest-earned ratio, return on assets, return on equity) are calculated.

Depending on how these projections look, management may need to modify the initial forecast assumptions. For example, management might conclude that the projected volume growth rate must be cut because external financing requirements exceed the firm's ability to raise money, or management might decide to raise more funds internally, if possible. Alternatively, the firm might investigate service processes that require fewer fixed assets, or it might consider the possibility of contracting out some services rather than offering them in-house.

The most important benefit of a financial forecasting model is the ability to estimate the effects of changing both basic assumptions and specific financial policies. The forecasting process can be repeated over and over, each time creating a new scenario that changes one or more of the basic operating assumptions inherent in the model. For example, what if there is a significant reduction in Medicare reimbursement rates? What if a large managed care contract is lost to a competitor? What if nurses strike during the coming year? What if a competitor opens a new outpatient surgery center? Changes in basic assumptions about Medicare reimbursement, labor costs, or competitors' actions have a significant effect on volume, reimbursement rates, cost relationships, profit margins, and so on. Using a forecasting model, managers can quickly develop forecasts to match numerous scenarios, although the forecasts are only as good as the managers' ability to predict the impact of each scenario on key forecasting parameters.

Managers can also use forecasting models to assess the impact of changes to financial variables, such as changing the source of external financing or interest rate forecasts. This ability is a powerful tool in preparing for the future. Unfortunately, the analysis can encompass many combinations of operating assumptions and financial policies, so a large number of different sets of pro forma financial statements can easily be created. As a result, a great deal of managerial insight is required to evaluate the alternative forecast results.

One way to reduce the number of possible scenarios is to perform a sensitivity analysis to determine the effect of each assumption; assumptions that have little effect on the key financial condition ratios need not be changed from their base case levels. Another approach to reducing the number of scenarios is to perform a Monte Carlo simulation analysis. For example, instead of specifying volume, reimbursement levels, labor costs, and so on at discrete levels, probability distributions can be specified. The key results would then be presented as distributions rather than point estimates.[5]

SELF-TEST QUESTION

1. Why do computerized forecasting models play such an important role in corporate management?

Financial Controls

Financial forecasting and planning are vital to corporate success, but planning is for naught unless the business has a control system that both (1) ensures implementation of the planned policies and (2) provides timely information that permits operational adjustments if the assumed market conditions change. In a financial control system, the key question is not "how is the firm doing in 2019 compared to 2018?" Rather, it is "how is the firm doing in 2019 in comparison to the forecasts, and if results differ from those expected, what can we do to get back on track?"

The basic tools of financial control are budgets and forecasted financial statements. These documents set forth expected performance; hence, they express management's targets. These targets are compared to actual corporate performance—on a daily, weekly, or monthly basis—to determine the *variances*, which in this context are the differences between realized values and target values. Thus, the control system identifies areas in which performance is not meeting target levels. If a business's actual results are better than its targets, we might conclude that its managers are doing a great job, but it could also mean that the targets were set too low and, thus, should be raised in the future. Conversely, failure to meet the financial targets could mean that market conditions are changing, that some managers are not performing up to par, or that the targets were set initially at unrealistic, unattainable levels. In any event, some action should be taken, and, if the situation is deteriorating rapidly, taken quickly. By focusing on variances, managers can "manage by exception," concentrating on operations most in need of improvement.

Entire textbooks have been written on financial controls. Here, we want to emphasize that financial controls are as critical to financial performance as are financial planning and forecasting. Also note that financial control systems are not costless. Thus, control system costs must be balanced against the savings the system aims to produce.

SELF-TEST QUESTIONS

1. What are the purposes of a financial control system?
2. What basic financial control tools do businesses use, and how do they work?

Chapter Key Concepts

This chapter describes how firms forecast their financial statements and estimate their future financing requirements. Here are its key concepts:

- The primary planning documents are *strategic plans*, *operating plans*, and *financial plans*.
- *Financial forecasting* generally begins with a forecast of the firm's revenues, in terms of both volume and reimbursement rates, for some future period.
- *Pro forma*, or *projected*, *financial statements* are developed to estimate a business's future financial condition and external financing requirements.
- The *constant growth method* of forecasting financial statements is based on the assumptions that (1) most income statement items and balance sheet accounts vary directly with revenues

(continued)

(continued from previous page)

and (2) the business's income statement items and balance sheet accounts are optimal for its current level of revenues.

- A business can determine its *external financing requirement* by estimating the amount of assets necessary to support the forecasted level of revenues and then subtracting from that amount the forecasted total claims. The business can then plan to raise the necessary funds through bank borrowing, by issuing securities, or both.
- Additional external capital means additional interest and dividends, which lowers the amount of forecasted retained earnings. Thus, raising external funds creates a *financing feedback* effect that must be incorporated into the forecasting process.
- Six factors have the greatest impact on the external financing requirement:

  1. The higher a firm's *projected revenue growth rate*, the greater its need for external financing.
  2. The greater the *capacity utilization*, the greater the organization's need for external financing.
  3. The greater the *capital intensity*, the greater the need for external capital.
  4. The higher the *profitability*, the lower the need for external capital.
  5. The larger a for-profit business's *dividend policy*, the greater its need for external funds.
  6. Finally, the greater a not-for-profit firm's *ability to attract contribution capital*, the smaller its need for external capital.

- The constant growth method typically is inadequate to deal with real-world situations such as *price-driven revenue growth*, *economies of scale*, *lumpy assets*, and *suboptimal relationships.*
- *Simple linear regression*, *curvilinear regression*, *multiple regression*, and *specific item forecasting* techniques can be used to forecast asset requirements when the constant growth method is not appropriate.
- Businesses use *financial planning models* to forecast their financial statements and external financing needs.
- *Financial controls* should be an integral part of a firm's planning system.

(continued)

(continued from previous page)

The type of forecasting described in this chapter is important for several reasons. First, if the projected operating results are unsatisfactory, management can go back to the drawing board, reformulate its plans, and develop more reasonable targets for the coming year. Second, it is possible that the funds required to meet the forecast simply cannot be obtained; if so, it is better to know this in advance and to scale back the projected level of operations than to suddenly run out of cash and have operations grind to a halt. Third, even if the required funds can be raised, it is desirable to plan for their acquisition well in advance.

Chapter Models, Problems, and Minicases

The following ancillary resources in spreadsheet format are available for this chapter:

- A chapter model that shows how to perform many of the calculations described in the chapter
- Problems that test your ability to perform the calculations
- A minicase that is more complicated than the problems and tests your ability to perform the calculations in preparation for a case

These resources can be accessed online at ache.org/HAP/PinkSong8e.

Selected Case

One case in *Cases in Healthcare Finance*, sixth edition, is applicable to this chapter: case 25: River Community Hospital (B), which focuses on the creation of pro forma financial statements in a hospital setting. (This case is best used as a follow-up to case 1, which is a financial statement analysis of the same hospital.)

Selected Bibliography

Hill, L. E. 2016. "Pioneering a Rolling Forecast." *Healthcare Financial Management* 70 (11): 58–62.

Kolman, C. M. 2017. "Transforming Healthcare Analytics to Manage Costs." *Healthcare Financial Management* 71 (6): 28–33.

Moore, K. D., and D. Coddington. 2016. "Integrating Health Care's Many Levels of Thinking." *Healthcare Financial Management* 70 (10): 80–81.

Skinner, J., R. Higbea, D. Buer, and C. Horvath. 2018. "Using Predictive Analytics to Align ED Staffing Resources with Patient Demand." *Healthcare Financial Management* 72 (2): 56–61.

Selected Websites

The following websites pertain to the content of this chapter:

- For information on the Institute of Business Forecasting & Planning (IBF), see www.ibf.org.
- For a great deal of valuable information on forecasting, see www.forecastingprinciples.com.

Notes

1. Many businesses have one or two statements that complement the mission statement. A *vision statement* focuses on what the business aspires to be, rather than on what it is today. A *values statement* lists the core priorities that define the organization's culture.
2. In a log-linear regression, the operating revenue amounts are converted to natural logarithms and regressed against time. The slope coefficient of the regression line, which is 0.0669 = 6.69% in this case, is the **continuous** growth rate over the five-year period. The continuous growth rate is converted to a **compound annual** growth rate as follows:

$$e^{0.0669} - 1 \approx 6.9\%.$$

3. This assumption does not imply that Bayside's 2019 occupancy rate was 100 percent. A hospital is operating at **full** capacity when its average occupancy is somewhere between 80 percent and 90 percent. A few times during the year, a hospital may operate at 100 percent capacity, but most hospital managers prefer to maintain a reserve capacity to meet emergency situations.
4. Some assets, such as short-term investments, are not tied directly to operations and hence would not vary directly with revenues. In

fact, Bayside can reduce its short-term investments to zero, thereby reducing any external financing requirements. However, the naive methodology applied here assumes that most balance sheet accounts would automatically increase with revenues.

5. This is a good time to mention the basic axiom of computer modeling: GIGO (which means "garbage in, garbage out"). Stated another way, the output of a financial model is no better than the assumptions and inputs used to construct it, so when you build models, proceed with caution. Note, though, that one advantage of computer modeling is that it brings the key assumptions out into the open, where their realism can be examined. One strong advocate of models made this statement: "Critics of our models generally attack our assumptions, but they forget that, in their own forecasts, they simply assume the answer."

Integrative Application

The Problem

Chapel Hill Orthopedics (CHO) is a large for-profit group practice that specializes in treating sports injuries. Here are its latest financial statements:

2018 Income Statement (in thousands of dollars)

Revenues	$18,000
Operating costs	15,263
EBIT	$ 2,737
Interest	1,017
EBT	$ 1,720
Taxes (30%)	516
Net income	$ 1,204
Dividends (60%)	$ 722
Addition to retained earnings	$ 482

EBIT: earnings before interest and taxes; EBT: earnings before taxes

2018 Balance Sheet (in thousands of dollars)

Cash	$ 1,800	Accounts payable	$ 5,200
Receivables	5,400	Notes payable	1,400
Inventories	8,600	Accruals	800
Total current assets	$15,800	Total current liabilities	$ 7,400
Net fixed assets	10,600	Long-term debt	5,000
		Common stock	2,000
		Retained earnings	12,000
Total assets	$26,400	Total liabilities and equity	$26,400

The best revenue growth estimate for 2019 is 10 percent. Also, any external financing required will be obtained by adding new short-term debt (notes payable) having an interest rate of 8 percent. Fixed assets (property and equipment) are being used at 80 percent of capacity. CHO's managers must now forecast its financial statements for 2019 to estimate the practice's external financing requirement. It has a line of credit with a local bank that is capped at

$2,000,000, of which CHO has already used $1,400,000. The primary purpose of the forecast is to determine whether the credit line is adequate for 2019. Will the practice have to seek additional financing sources?

The Analysis

First, note that Capacity sales (revenues) = 2018 revenue ÷ Utilization rate = $18,000,000 ÷ 0.80 = $22,500,000. Because growth is expected to be 10 percent, 2019 revenues = $18,000,000 × 1.10 = $19,800,000, which is far less than capacity sales of $22,500,000. Thus, CHO can attain the new revenue level without the requirement for additional property and equipment (net fixed assets).

Forecasted Income Statement for 2019 (in thousands of dollars)

	2018	*Growth %*	*1st Pass*	*2nd Pass*	*3rd Pass*
Revenues	$18,000	10%	$19,800	$19,800	$19,800
Operating costs	15,263	10%	16,789	16,789	16,789
EBIT	$ 2,737				
Interest	1,017	NA	1,017	1,051	1,051
EBT	$ 1,720		$ 1,994	$ 1,960	$ 1,959
Taxes (30%)	516		598	588	588
Net income	$ 1,204		$ 1,396	$ 1,372	$ 1,371
Dividends (60%)	$ 722		$ 837	$ 823	$ 822
Addition to RE	$ 482		$ 558	$ 549	$ 549

EBIT: earnings before interest and taxes; EBT: earnings before taxes; RE: retained earnings

Forecasted Balance Sheet for 2019
(in thousands of dollars)

	2018	*Growth (%)*	*1st Pass*	*2nd Pass*	*3rd Pass*
Cash	$ 1,800	10	$ 1,980	$ 1,980	$ 1,980
Receivables	5,400	10	5,940	5,940	5,940
Inventories	8,600	10	9,460	9,460	9,460
Total current assets	$15,800		$17,380	$17,380	$17,380
Net fixed assets	10,600	NA	10,600	10,600	10,600
Total assets	$26,400		$27,980	$27,980	$27,980
Accounts payable	$ 5,200	10	$ 5,720	$ 5,720	$ 5,720
Notes payable	1,400	NA	1,400	1,822	1,831
Accruals	800	10	880	880	880
Total current liabilities	$ 7,400		$ 8,000	$ 8,422	$ 8,431
Long-term debt	5,000	NA	5,000	5,000	5,000
Common stock	2,000	NA	2,000	2,000	2,000
Retained earnings	12,000		12,558	12,549	12,549
Total liabilities and equity	$26,400		$27,558	$27,971	$27,980
External financing requirement			$422	$9	$0
Added interest expense			$34	$1	$0

Note the following points:

1. We know that the interest expense in 2019 will be larger than in 2018 if CHO has to borrow additional funds, but we cannot predict the amount of increase until the first pass is completed.
2. Because any financing required is borrowed as notes payable at an interest rate of 8 percent, notes payable is the "plug" variable that will be adjusted in the second and third passes to make the balance sheet balance.
3. Long-term debt and common stock remain at their 2018 levels because those financing sources will not be used to obtain any needed capital.
4. After the first-pass forecast, interest expense is $1,017 from 2018; notes payable is $1,400 from 2018; retained earnings is $12,000 plus additions

of \$558 for a total of \$12,558; and the external financing requirement is total assets of \$27,980 minus total liabilities and equity of \$27,558, which amounts to \$422. Finally, \$422 in added short-term debt (notes payable) having an 8 percent interest rate will result in $\$422 \times 0.08 = \$34$ in added interest in the second pass. (Note that the solution was created on a spreadsheet that carries calculations to 15 significant digits, so rounding differences occur in the solution data presented here.)

5. After the second pass, interest expense is \$1,017 from the first pass plus added interest expense of \$34 from the new notes payable, for a total of \$1,051. This added expense reduces the net income by \$24 and the addition to retained earnings by \$9, which adds that amount to the external financing requirement, thus requiring additional notes payable and interest expense.
6. After the third pass, total assets equal total liabilities and equity and the external financing requirement is zero.

The Decision

The forecast for 2019 predicts a total external financing requirement of \$422,000 + \$9,000 = \$431,000, which increases the notes payable amount to \$1,400,000 + \$431,000 = \$1,831,000. Because the current line of credit is capped at \$2,000,000, it appears that it will be sufficient for 2019. However, note that, like all forecasts, there is uncertainty in the results—perhaps a great deal of uncertainty. Thus, CHO's managers decided to renegotiate the line of credit with a \$2,500,000 maximum to ensure that funds will be available in the event the actual need for external financing exceeds the forecast amount. ■

PART VII

OTHER TOPICS

In parts I through VI, the chapters focused on the environment, basic financial management concepts, capital acquisition and allocation, and financial analysis and forecasting. In the two chapters of part VII, we discuss topics that do not mesh well with the previous coverage.

Chapter 15 focuses on managing the revenue cycle, as well as other short-term assets (e.g., cash and inventories) and liabilities (e.g., payables), which are essential activities in all health services organizations. Chapter 16 discusses business combinations (e.g., mergers, acquisitions, joint ventures) and the valuation of entire businesses (as opposed to individual projects).

In addition to the chapters in the text, two supplemental chapters are available online. Chapter 17 describes how for-profit businesses return capital to owners, while chapter 18 discusses the management of risks inherent in financial transactions. The supplemental chapters can be accessed online at ache.org/HAP/PinkSong8e.

CHAPTER

15

REVENUE CYCLE AND CURRENT ACCOUNTS MANAGEMENT

Learning Objectives

After studying this chapter, readers should be able to

- discuss in general terms how businesses manage cash and marketable securities,
- construct and use a cash budget,
- explain the revenue cycle and the key issues involved in its management,
- discuss some important elements of supply chain management, and
- measure the cost-of-trade credit and determine when costly trade credit is preferable to other short-term debt sources.

Introduction

In the discussion of healthcare financial management leading up to this chapter, the general focus has been on long-term strategic decisions. Another important element of healthcare finance involves the management of short-term (current) accounts, such as cash, receivables, inventories, and payables. In corporate finance, the management of current assets accounts is commonly called *working capital management*.

How important is current accounts management? The average hospital has almost 10 percent of its balance sheet assets in cash and short-term investments (marketable securities), plus almost 15 percent in accounts receivable. In addition, not-for-profit hospitals have another 20 percent of their assets invested in long-term financial assets, which are often called *funded depreciation* because the account is funded by depreciation cash flow that is being accumulated to replace old and obsolete fixed assets. Thus, hospitals, on average, have close to half of their assets invested in accounts that require management techniques discussed in this chapter. In addition to discussing

> **Working Capital**
>
> The term *working capital* originated in the 1700s in the United States when Yankee peddlers were the main source of goods for many farmers in remote areas of the Northeast. These merchants loaded up their wagons with goods and set off on a regular route to peddle their wares. According to the economic definitions of capital (assets) versus labor, the peddler's horse and wagon constituted the business's fixed capital, while the merchandise was called *working capital* because it was what was sold, or turned over, to produce a profit.

the management of short-term assets, this chapter covers two short-term liabilities: accruals and trade credit. Although accruals and trade credit are sources of short-term financing as opposed to assets, they typically are considered to be part of working capital (current accounts) management.

In general, the goal of current accounts management is to support the operations of the business at the lowest possible cost. The implementation of current accounts management principles depends on the size and nature of the healthcare business. For example, current accounts management in a large hospital differs significantly from that in a small home health agency. Thus, this chapter focuses on basic concepts only.

Cash Management

All businesses need *cash*—which includes both actual cash and funds held in commercial checking accounts—to pay for labor, materials, and supplies; to buy fixed assets; to pay taxes; to service debt; and so on. However, cash earns no return and hence is classified as a *nonearning asset*. (Except for proprietorships that meet certain qualifications, banks are prohibited by law from paying interest on commercial checking accounts.) Although cash earns no return, every dollar on the asset side of the balance sheet, including dollars of cash, must be financed; that is, there must be a corresponding dollar on the liabilities and equity side of the balance sheet. Because each dollar of financing has either a direct or an indirect (opportunity) cost, the goal of cash management is to minimize the amount of cash on hand but at the same time have sufficient cash to support operations.

Synchronizing Cash Flow

If an individual receives income once per year, he would probably put it in the bank, draw down the account during the year as cash is needed, and have an average balance over the year equal to about half the annual income. If an individual receives income monthly instead of once per year, she would proceed similarly, but the average balance would be much smaller. If the individual could arrange to receive income daily and to pay for rent, food, and other charges on a daily basis and is confident of the forecasted inflows and outflows, she could, at least in theory, hold a zero cash balance.

The same situation applies to businesses. By improving cash flow forecasts and taking steps to match cash receipts with required cash outflows, businesses can reduce their cash balances to a minimum. Recognizing this point, some firms bill customers on a regular billing cycle that matches their own outflows throughout the month. This system improves the *synchronization of cash flows*, which in turn enables a business to reduce its cash balances, decrease its bank loans, lower interest expenses, and boost profits.

Managing Float

A well-run business has more money in its checking account than the balance shown in its checkbook. *Net float*, or just *float*, is defined as the difference between the balance shown in the bank's records and the balance in the business's checkbook. Alternatively, float can be calculated as the sum of the business's two component floats: disbursement and collections.

For an illustration of net float and its components, assume that, on average, Gainesville Primary Care writes checks in the amount of $5,000 each day. Furthermore, it takes six days for these checks to be mailed, delivered, deposited, and cleared and for the amounts to be deducted from the clinic's bank account. This delay will cause the clinic's checkbook to show a balance that is 6 × $5,000 = $30,000 less than the balance on the bank's records. Because the clinic's actual balance at the bank is $30,000 greater than the amount shown in its checkbook, the clinic has a positive $30,000 *disbursement float*.

Now assume that the clinic receives checks in the amount of $5,000 daily, but it loses four days while they are being deposited and cleared. This difference will result in 4 × $5,000 = $20,000 of *collections float*. Because of the delay in depositing and clearing checks, the clinic's balance at the bank is $20,000 less than that in its checkbook, which means a negative collections float of $20,000.

The clinic's net float, which is the sum of the positive $30,000 disbursement float and negative $20,000 collections float, is $10,000. On average, the clinic's balance at the bank is $10,000 larger than the balance in its checkbook. If a business's own collections and clearing process is more efficient than that of the recipients of its checks, the business will have a positive float. Some businesses are so good at managing float that they carry a negative checkbook balance but have a positive balance at the bank. For example, one medical equipment manufacturer stated that its bank records show an average cash balance of about $200,000, while its own book balance is **minus** $200,000—it has $400,000 of net float.

A firm's net float is a function of its ability to speed up collections on checks received and slow down collections on checks written. Efficient businesses go to great lengths to speed up the processing of incoming checks, thus putting the funds to work faster, and they try to stretch their own payments out as long as possible (without engaging in unethical or illegal practices).

A 2018 Federal Reserve payment study (Gerdes, Greene, and Liu. 2019) found that the number of checks decreased by 3.6 percent from 2015 to 2016 and decreased by 4.8 percent from 2016 to 2017. However, many people still pay their healthcare expenses by check, particularly elderly and low-income patients, who tend to cosume a large quantity of healthcare services. Therefore, checks will likely be with us for the foreseeable future, and well-run businesses continue to recognize the value inherent in float.

Accelerating Collections

Managers have searched for ways to collect receivables more quickly since the day credit transactions began. Although cash collection is the responsibility of a firm's managers, the speed with which checks are cleared depends on the banking system. Several techniques are used to speed up collections and send funds where they are needed, but the three most popular are lockbox services, concentration banking, and electronic claims processing. Following are some points to note about lockbox services and concentration banking. We will discuss electronic claims processing later in this chapter.

Lockboxes are one of the oldest cash management tools, and virtually all banks that offer cash management services offer lockbox services. In a lockbox system, incoming checks are sent to post office boxes rather than to corporate headquarters. For example, Health SouthWest, a regional HMO (health maintenance organization) headquartered in Oklahoma City, has its Texas members send their payments to a box in Dallas, its New Mexico members send their checks to Albuquerque, and so on, rather than have all checks sent to Oklahoma City. Several times per day, a local bank collects the contents of each lockbox and deposits the checks into the firm's local account. The bank then provides the HMO with daily records of the receipts collected in a format that updates the firm's receivables accounts—usually electronic data transmission.

A lockbox system reduces the time required for a business to receive incoming checks, deposit them, and clear them through the banking system so that the funds become available for use quickly. This time reduction occurs because mail time and check collection time are both reduced if the lockbox is located in the geographic area where the customer (check writer) is located. For businesses whose customers are spread over a large geographic area, lockbox services can often increase the availability of funds by one to four days over the regular system.

Lockbox systems, although efficient in speeding up collections, spread the business's cash among many banks. The primary purpose of *concentration banking* is to mobilize funds from decentralized receiving locations—whether they are lockboxes or decentralized firm locations—into one or more central cash pools. In a typical concentration system, the firm's collection banks record deposits received each day. On the basis of disbursement needs, funds are then transferred from these collection points to a concentration bank. Concentration accounts enable businesses to take maximum advantage of economies of scale in cash management and investment. Health SouthWest uses an Oklahoma City bank as its concentration bank. The HMO cash manager uses this pool for short-term investing or reallocation among its other banks.

Electronic systems make concentration banking easy. The *Automated Clearing House (ACH)* is a communication network that sends data from one financial institution to another. Instead of using paper checks, the ACH creates electronic files that place all transactions for a particular bank on a single file and then send it to that bank. Some banks send and receive their data on tapes, while most link to the ACH electronically. In addition to the ACH, the *Fedwire* is used to move large sums between banks. Between the two systems, trillions of dollars are efficiently moved among banks on a daily basis.

Controlling Disbursements

Accelerated collections are one side of float; control of fund outflows is the other. Efficient cash management can result only if both inflows and outflows are effectively controlled.

No single action controls disbursements more effectively than *payables centralization*. Such centralization enables the firm's managers to evaluate the payments coming due for the entire business and to meet these needs in an organized and controlled manner. Centralized disbursement also enables more efficient monitoring of payables and float balances. However, centralized disbursement does have a downside—centralized offices may have difficulty making all payments promptly, which can create ill will with suppliers and disqualify the business from receiving prompt-payment discounts.

Zero-balance accounts (ZBAs) are special disbursement accounts that have a zero-dollar balance on which checks are written. Typically, a firm establishes several ZBAs in the concentration bank and funds them from a *master account*. As checks are presented to a ZBA for payment, funds are automatically transferred from the master account. If the master account goes negative, it is replenished by borrowing from the bank against a line of credit or by selling some securities from the firm's marketable securities portfolio. ZBAs simplify the control of disbursements and cash balances and hence reduce the amount of idle (i.e., non-interest-bearing) cash.

Whereas ZBAs are typically established at concentration banks, *controlled disbursement accounts* can be set up at any bank. In fact, controlled disbursement accounts were initially used only in relatively remote banks, so this technique was originally called *remote disbursement.* The basic technique is simple: Controlled disbursement accounts are not funded until the day's checks are presented against the account. The key to controlled disbursement is the ability of the bank that has the account to report the total amount of checks received for clearance each day by 11 a.m., Eastern Standard Time. This early notification gives a firm's managers sufficient time to wire funds to the controlled disbursement account to cover the checks presented for payment and to invest excess cash at midday, when money market trading is at a peak.

Matching the Costs and Benefits of Cash Management

Although the techniques discussed earlier can reduce cash balance requirements, implementing these procedures is not a costless operation. How far should a business go in making its cash operations more efficient? As a general rule, a business should incur these expenses only as long as the marginal returns exceed the marginal costs.

The value of careful cash management depends on the opportunity costs of funds invested in cash, which in turn depend on the current rate of interest. For example, in the early 1980s, with interest rates at relatively high levels, businesses were devoting a great deal of care to cash management. Today, with interest rates much lower, cash management is less valuable. Clearly, larger businesses with larger cash balances can better afford (than can smaller firms) to hire the personnel necessary to maintain tight control over their cash positions. Cash management is one element of business operations in which economies of scale are present. Banks also have placed considerable emphasis on developing and marketing cash management services. Because of scale economies in cash management operations, smaller businesses generally find bank-supplied services to be less costly than operating in-house cash management systems.

Creating the Cash Budget

In chapters 13 and 14, our discussion of financial planning and forecasting focused on a business's financial statements. However, financial statements, which are prepared infrequently and in accordance with accounting standards, do not provide complete and timely information about a business's cash position. This situation is corrected by the *cash budget.*

To create a cash budget, managers forecast fixed asset and inventory requirements, along with the times such payments must be made. This information is combined with projections about delays in collecting accounts receivable, wage payment dates, interest payment dates, and so on to produce a report showing the organization's projected cash inflows and outflows over some specified period. Generally, businesses use a monthly cash budget forecasted over the coming year, plus a more detailed daily or weekly cash budget for the coming month. The monthly cash budget is used for liquidity planning purposes, and the daily or weekly budget is used for actual cash control.

Cash budget creation does not require the application of a complex set of accounting rules. Rather, all the entries in a cash budget represent the actual movement of cash into or out of the organization. Exhibit 15.1 contains a monthly cash budget that covers six months of 2019 for Mission County Homecare, a small, for-profit home health care business. Mission's cash budget, which is broken down into four sections, is typical, although there is a great deal of variation in formats used by different organizations.

The first section of the cash budget contains the *collections worksheet*, which translates the billing for services provided into cash revenues. Because of its location in a summer resort area, Mission's patient volume (and hence billings) peak in July. However, like most health services organizations, Mission rarely collects when services are provided. What is relevant from a cash budget perspective is not when services are provided or when billings occur but rather when cash is collected. On the basis of previous experience, Mission's managers know that most collections occur 30–60 days after billing. In fact, Mission's managers have a collections table that they use to forecast, with some precision, the timing of collections. This table was used to convert the billings shown in line 1 of exhibit 15.1 into the collection amounts shown in lines 2 and 3.

The next section of Mission's cash budget is the *supplies worksheet*, which accounts for timing differences between supply order and purchase. Mission's patient volume forecasts, which are used to predict the billing amounts shown in line 1, are also used to forecast the supplies (primarily medical) needed to support patient services. Mission orders these supplies and receives them one month before they are expected to be used, as shown in line 4. However, Mission's suppliers do not demand immediate payment. Rather, Mission has, on average, 30 days to pay for supplies after it receives them. Thus, the actual payment occurs one month after purchase, as shown in line 5.

The third section combines data from the collections and supplies worksheets with other projected cash outflows to show the *net cash gain (loss)* for each month. Cash from collections is shown in line 6. Lines 7 through 12 list cash payments that Mission expects to make during each

EXHIBIT 15.1

Mission Homecare: May Through October Cash Budget

	Mar	*Apr*	*May*	*Jun*	*Jul*	*Aug*	*Sep*	*Oct*
Collections Worksheet:								
1. Billed charges	$50,000	$50,000	$100,000	$150,000	$200,000	$100,000	$100,000	$50,000
2. Collections:								
a. Within 30 days			19,600	29,400	39,200	19,600	19,600	9,800
b. 30–60 days			35,000	70,000	105,000	140,000	70,000	70,000
c. 60–90 days			5,000	5,000	10,000	15,000	20,000	10,000
3. Total collections			$59,600	$104,400	$154,200	$174,600	$109,600	$ 89,800
Supplies Worksheet:								
4. Amount of supplies ordered			$15,000	$ 20,000	$ 10,000	$ 10,000	$ 5,000	$ 5,000
5. Payments made for supplies			$10,000	$ 15,000	$ 20,000	$ 10,000	$ 10,000	$ 5,000
Net Cash Gain (Loss):								
6. Total collections (from line 3)			$59,600	$104,400	$154,200	$174,600	$109,600	$ 89,800
7. Total purchases (from line 5)			$10,000	$ 15,000	$ 20,000	$ 10,000	$ 10,000	$ 5,000
8. Wages and salaries			60,000	70,000	80,000	60,000	60,000	60,000
9. Rent			2,500	2,500	2,500	2,500	2,500	2,500
10. Other expenses			1,000	1,500	2,000	1,000	1,000	500
11. Taxes				20,000			20,000	
12. Payment for capital assets						50,000		
13. Total payments			$73,500	$109,000	$104,500	$123,500	$ 93,500	$ 68,000
14. Net cash gain (loss)			($13,900)	($ 4,600)	$ 49,700	$ 51,100	$ 16,100	$ 21,800
Borrowing/Surplus Summary:								
15. Cash at beginning with no borrowing			$15,000	$ 1,100	($ 3,500)	$ 46,200	$ 97,300	$113,400
16. Cash at end with no borrowing			$ 1,100	($ 3,500)	$ 46,200	$ 97300	$113,400	$135,200
17. Target cash balance			10,000	10,000	10,000	10,000	10,000	10,000
18. Cumulative surplus cash (loan balance)			($ 8,900)	($ 13,500)	$ 36,200	$ 87,300	$103,400	$125,200

month, including payments for supplies. Then all payments are summed, and the total is shown in line 13. The difference between expected cash receipts and cash payments, line 6 minus line 13, is the net cash gain or loss during the month, which is shown in line 14. For May, there is a forecasted net cash outflow of $13,900 (the parentheses indicate a negative cash flow [or loss]).

Although line 14 contains the meat of the cash budget, the final section (the borrowing/surplus summary) extends the basic budget data to show Mission's forecasted cash position for each month. Line 15 shows the forecasted cash on hand at the beginning of each month, assuming no borrowing takes place. Mission is expected to enter the budget period—the beginning of May—with $15,000 of cash on hand. For each succeeding month, the value in line 15 is the value shown in line 16 for the previous month. The values in line 16, which are obtained by adding lines 14 and 15, show the cash on hand at the end of each month, assuming no borrowing takes place. For May, Mission expects a cash loss of $13,900 on top of a starting balance of $15,000, for an ending cash balance of $1,100, in the absence of borrowing. This amount is the cash on hand at the beginning of June, with no borrowing amount, shown in line 15.

Note that Mission's target cash balance (i.e., the amount it wants on hand at the beginning of each month) is $10,000, which is shown in line 17. The target cash balance is subtracted from the forecasted cash at the end, with no borrowing amount, to determine the firm's borrowing requirements (shown in parentheses) or surplus cash (shown without parentheses). Because Mission expects to have only $1,100 at the end of May, as shown in line 16, it will have to borrow $10,000 – $1,100 = $8,900 to bring the cash account up to the target balance of $10,000. Assuming Mission does borrow this amount, the total loan outstanding will be $8,900 at the end of May. (The assumption is that Mission will not have any loans outstanding on May 1 because the beginning cash balance exceeds the firm's target balance.)

The cumulative cash surplus or required loan balance is shown in line 18; a positive value indicates a cash surplus, while a negative value indicates a loan requirement. The surplus cash or loan requirement shown in line 18 is a **cumulative amount**. Thus, Mission is projected to borrow $8,900 in May; it has a cash shortfall during June of $4,600, as reported in line 14, so its total loan requirement projected for the end of June is $8,900 + $4,600 = $13,500, as shown in line 18.

The same procedures are followed in subsequent months. Patient volume and billings are projected to peak in July, accompanied by increased payments for supplies, wages, and other items. However, collections are projected to increase by a greater amount than costs, and Mission expects a $49,700 net cash inflow during July. This amount is sufficient to pay off the cumulative loan of $13,500 and have a $36,200 cash surplus on hand at the end of the month.

Patient volume, and the resulting operating costs, are expected to fall sharply in August, but collections will be the highest of any month because they will reflect the high June and July billings. As a result, Mission would normally be forecasting a healthy $101,100 net cash gain during the month. However, the firm expects to make a cash payment of $50,000 to purchase a new computer system during August, so the forecasted net cash gain is reduced to $51,100. This net gain adds to the surplus, so August is projected to end with $87,300 in surplus cash. If all goes according to the forecast, later cash surpluses will enable Mission to end this budget period with a surplus of $125,200.

Mission's managers use the cash budget for liquidity planning purposes. For example, the cash budget in exhibit 15.1 indicates that Mission will need to obtain $13,500 in total to get through May and June. Thus, if the firm has no marketable securities to convert to cash, it will have to arrange for some type of financing to cover this period. Furthermore, the budget indicates a $125,200 cash surplus at the end of October. Mission's managers will have to consider how these funds can be best used. Perhaps the money should be paid out to owners as dividends or bonuses, used for fixed asset acquisitions, or temporarily invested in marketable securities for later use in the business. They will make this decision on the basis of Mission's overall financial plan.

This brief illustration shows the mechanics and managerial value of the cash budget. However, before concluding this discussion, several additional points need to be made. First, if cash inflows and outflows are not uniform during the month, a monthly cash budget can seriously understate a business's peak financing requirements. The data in exhibit 15.1 show the situation expected on the last day of each month, but on any given day during the month it could be different. If all payments had to be made on the fifth of each month but collections came in uniformly throughout the month, Mission would need to borrow cash to cover within-month shortages. For example, August's $123,500 cash payments may be made before Mission receives the full $174,600 in collections. In this situation, Mission would have to obtain some amount of cash to cover shortfalls in August, even though the end-of-month cash flow after all collections have been received is positive. In this case, Mission would have to prepare a weekly or daily cash budget to indicate such borrowing needs.

Second, because the cash budget is a forecast, all the values in the table are "expected" values. If actual patient volume, collection times, supply purchases, wage rates, and so on differ from forecasted levels, the projected cash deficits and surpluses will be incorrect. Thus, there is a reasonable chance that Mission may end up needing to obtain a larger amount of funds than is indicated in line 18. Because of the uncertainty of the forecasts, spreadsheet programs are particularly well suited for constructing and analyzing cash budgets. For example, Mission's managers can change any assumption (e.g., projected monthly volume, time third-party payers take to pay), and the program will automatically recalculate the cash budget. This assumption would show Mission's managers exactly how the firm's cash position would change under alternative operating assumptions. Typically, such an analysis is used to determine how large a credit line is needed to cover temporary cash shortages.[1] In Mission's case, such an analysis indicated that a $20,000 line is sufficient.

SELF-TEST QUESTIONS

1. What is float, and how do businesses use it to increase cash management efficiency?
2. What are some methods that businesses can use to accelerate receipts? To control disbursements?
3. How should cash management actions be evaluated?
4. Considering all the information in projected financial statements, why do organizations need a cash budget?
5. Do managers need to have extensive knowledge of accounting principles to create a cash budget?
6. In your view, what is the most important line of the cash budget?

Marketable Securities Management

Many businesses hold portfolios of temporary financial investments historically called *marketable securities*. On the balance sheet, such securities are labeled *short-term investments*. Typically, such investments are held as a substitute for cash balances. Thus, although discussed in separate sections, cash and marketable securities management cannot be separated in practice because management of one implies management of the other. In addition to marketable securities, which are held to meet short-term needs, many providers also hold portfolios of securities that will be used for long-term as opposed to short-term purposes. These portfolios will be discussed in the chapter supplement.

Rationale for Holding Marketable Securities

Most businesses hold marketable securities in lieu of larger cash balances and liquidate some of the securities periodically as needed to increase the cash account (when outflows exceed inflows). In addition, most businesses also rely on bank credit lines to meet unforeseen needs, but they may still hold marketable securities to guard against a possible shortage of bank credit. Of course, the motivation to hold marketable securities instead of cash is the ability to convert a nonearning asset into an earning asset. Even if the yield on marketable securities is low, it is clearly more than the zero yield on cash holdings.

In addition to being held as a substitute for cash, marketable securities are used to accumulate funds to meet large payments anticipated in the near term. Thus, funds might be accumulated in marketable securities to pay for an expected liability settlement or to make a tax payment that is coming due. The key here is that marketable securities are carried either to account for uncertainty in cash flows or to fund a known short-term need.

Criteria for Selecting Marketable Securities

In general, the key characteristics sought in marketable securities investments are safety and liquidity. Thus, most healthcare managers are willing to give up some return to ensure that funds are available, in the amounts expected, when needed.

Large businesses that have large amounts of surplus cash often directly own Treasury bills, commercial paper (i.e., an unsecured, short-term debt instrument issued by a corporation, typically for the financing of accounts payable and inventories and meeting short-term liabilities), negotiable certificates of deposit, and even Euromarket securities (i.e., dollar-denominated loans held outside the United States). Such securities, which are highly liquid and free of interest rate and default risk, are known as ***cash equivalents***. In addition, large taxable firms often hold floating-rate preferred stock because of its 70 percent dividend exclusion from federal income taxes. Conversely, smaller businesses are more likely to invest with a bank or in a money market or preferred stock mutual fund because a small business's volume of investment does not warrant hiring specialists to manage the marketable securities portfolio. Small businesses often use a mutual fund and then literally write checks on the fund to bolster the cash account as the need arises.[2] Interest rates on mutual funds are somewhat lower than rates on direct investments of equivalent risk because of management fees. However, for smaller firms, net returns may be higher on mutual funds because no in-house management expense is incurred.

In a typical marketable securities portfolio mix, the average hospital holds roughly 10 percent domestic stocks and bonds and about 90 percent cash equivalents. Clearly, hospital managers are willing to sacrifice return for safety when securities are chosen for **short-term** purposes.

SELF-TEST QUESTIONS

1. Why do businesses hold marketable securities?
2. What are some securities that are commonly held as marketable securities?
3. Why are these securities preferred?

Revenue Cycle Management

One of the hottest topics in healthcare finance today, especially among hospitals, is revenue cycle management. Its importance stems from the fact that most healthcare providers do not get paid at the same time services are rendered. Thus, providers incur cash costs for facilities, supplies, and labor but do not receive immediate payment to cover those costs. In fact, hospitals and medical practices have to wait about 50 days, on average, to collect from third-party payers.

Generally, the *revenue cycle* is defined as the set of recurring business activities and related information processing necessary to bill for and collect the revenues due for services provided. More pragmatically, the revenue cycle at provider organizations should ensure that patients are properly categorized by payment obligation, that correct and timely billing takes place, and that the correct payment is promptly received.

Revenue Cycle Activities

Revenue cycle activities, or functions, can be broken down into four phases on the basis of when they occur: (1) those that occur before the service is provided, (2) those that occur simultaneously with the service, (3) those that occur afterward, and (4) those that are continuous. Here are some examples of revenue cycle activities listed by phase.[3]

Before-Service Activities

- *Preservice insurance verification.* The insurance status of the patient is identified immediately after the outpatient visit (or inpatient stay) is scheduled to ensure that the patient actually has the insurance indicated when the appointment was made.
- *Precertification or prior authorization (if necessary).* If the insurance verification indicates that the payer requires *precertification*, it should be done immediately. Without precertification for services that require it, the provider runs the risk of having the claim (bill) denied even though the services were provided.

- *Preservice patient financial counseling.* The patient should be counseled regarding the payer's and patient's payment responsibilities. It is not fair to present a large bill to an unsuspecting patient after the service is rendered.

At-Service Activities

- *Time-of-service insurance verification.* The patient's insurance status should be reverified with both the patient and the payer at time of service to ensure that no changes have occurred since the initial verification.
- *Service documentation or claims production.* The services to be provided should be documented in a way that facilitates correct claims submission. The documentation process should ensure that (1) the services provided are coded in accordance with the payer's claim system, (2) the code reflects the highest legitimate reimbursement amount, and (3) the claim is formatted in accordance with payer guidelines and contains all required information.

After-Service Activities

- *Claims submission.* The claim should be submitted to the payer as quickly as possible after the service is rendered. However, speed should not take precedence over accuracy because incomplete and inaccurate billing accounts for a large proportion of late payments.
- *Third-party follow-up.* If payment is not received within 30 days, a reminder should be sent.
- *Denials management. Claims denial* by third-party payers is one of the major impediments to timely reimbursement. Typically, most denials are caused by improper precertification and incomplete or erroneous claims submission. Prompt claims resubmission is essential to good revenue cycle management.
- *Payment receipt and posting.* When the reimbursement is received, it must be properly deposited and credited. This activity ends the revenue cycle.

Continuous Activities

- *Monitoring.* Once revenue cycle activities are identified and timing goals are set for each activity, the provider should implement a system of metrics (key indicators) to ensure that these goals are being met.
- *Review and improvement.* The key indicators monitoring the revenue cycle must be continuouly reviewed and any deficiencies corrected.

The revenue cycle requires constant attention because the external factors that influence the cycle are constantly changing. Also, problems (typically called *deficiencies*) that occur at any point in the cycle tend to have ripple effects; that is, a problem that occurs early in the cycle can create additional problems at later points in the cycle. For example, failure to obtain required precertification can lead to claim denial, which at best means delayed payment and at worst means no payment.

The ability of healthcare providers to convert services rendered into cash is critical to their financial performance. Problems in the revenue cycle lead to lost and late payments, both of which degrade provider revenues and hence financial condition. You can think of the provider as furnishing to the payer an interest-free loan that covers the costs of the services rendered. The faster the loan is repaid, the better for the lender (provider).

Monitoring Revenue Cycle Performance

The ultimate goal of revenue cycle management is to convert services provided into cash. Thus, a provider's patient accounts receivable plays a key role in assessing performance. The total amount of accounts receivable outstanding at any given time is determined by two factors: (1) the volume of services provided and (2) the average length of time between services and collections. For example, suppose Home Infusion, Inc., a home health care business, begins operations on January 1 and on the first day starts to provide services to patients billed at $1,000 each day. For simplicity, assume that all patients have the same insurance, that it takes Home Infusion two days to submit patients' bills, and that it takes the insurer another 18 days to make the payments. Thus, it takes 20 days from delivery of service to receipt of payment.

At the end of the first day, Home Infusion's accounts receivable will be $1,000; they will rise to $2,000 by the end of the second day; by January 20, they will rise to $20,000. On January 21, another $1,000 will be added to receivables, but, assuming that the insurer pays the full amount for services provided 20 days earlier, payments for services provided on January 1 will reduce receivables by $1,000, so total accounts receivable will remain constant at $20,000. If either patient volume or the collection period changes, the amount in accounts receivable will change.

What is the cost implication of carrying $20,000 in receivables? The $20,000 on the left side of the balance sheet must be financed by a like amount on the right side. Home Infusion uses a bank loan to finance its receivables, which has an interest rate of 8 percent. Thus, over a year, the firm must pay the bank $0.08 \times \$20,000 = \$1,600$ in interest to carry its receivables balance. The cost associated with carrying other current assets can be thought of in a similar way.[4]

Monitoring Overall Performance

If a sale is made for cash, the profit is definitely earned, but if the sale is on credit, the profit is not actually earned until the account is collected. If the account is never collected, the profit is never earned. Thus, healthcare managers must closely monitor receivables to ensure that they are being collected in a timely manner and to uncover any deterioration in the "quality" of receivables. Early detection can help managers take corrective action before the situation has a significant negative impact on the organization's financial condition.

The common approach to monitoring revenue cycle performance, both in the aggregate and by specific activity, is by using metrics. Generically, a *metric* is a single quantitative indicator—usually a ratio—that can be used to measure the performance of some process. The primary purpose of metrics is to monitor performance and aid in the identification of corrective action plans if performance is subpar. In this section, we discuss two metrics that monitor overall revenue cycle performance: average collection period and aging schedule.

Suppose Adolph Weiss & Sons, a manufacturer of surgical instruments, manufactures and sells 200,000 instruments per year at an average sales price of $198 each. Furthermore, assume that all sales are on credit, with terms of 2/10, net 30; this means that customers must pay within 30 days, but they receive a 2 percent discount if they pay within ten days. Finally, assume that 70 percent of the firm's customers take discounts and pay on day 10, while the other 30 percent pay on day 30.

Weiss's *average collection period (ACP)*, generally called *days in patient accounts receivable* in provider organizations, is 16 days:

Key Equation 15.1: Average Collection Period

ACP = (Percent of customers who take discount × Day on which they pay) + (Percent of customers who do no take discount × Day on which they pay).

$$ACP = (0.7 \times 10 \text{ days}) + (0.3 \times 30 \text{ days}) = 16 \text{ days}.$$

The ACP is a measure of the **average** length of time it takes Weiss's customers to pay off their credit purchases. It is often compared to the industry-average ACP. For example, if all surgical instrument manufacturers sell on the same credit terms, and if the industry-average ACP is 25 days versus Weiss's 16-day ACP, Weiss either has a higher percentage of discount customers or has a credit department that is exceptionally good at ensuring prompt payment.

The ACP can also be compared to the firm's own credit terms. For example, suppose Weiss's ACP has been 35 days versus its 2/10, net 30 credit terms. A 35-day ACP indicates that some customers have been taking more than 30 days to pay their bills. In fact, if some customers have been paying within ten days to take advantage of the discount, the others would, on average, have to have been taking much longer than 35 days. One way to check this possibility is to use an aging schedule, which we describe in the next section.

If you know both the accounts receivable balance and average daily credit sales, the ACP can be calculated in an alternative way. Weiss's *average daily sales (ADS)*, assuming a 360-day year, is $110,000:

Key Equation 15.2: Average Daily Sales

$$\text{ADS} = \frac{\text{Annual sales}}{360} = \frac{\text{Units sold} \times \text{Sales price}}{360} = \frac{200{,}000 \times \$198}{360}$$
$$= \frac{\$39{,}600{,}000}{360} = \$110{,}000.$$

If the firm had made cash as well as credit sales, the analysis would focus on credit sales only, and the calculated amount would have been average daily *credit* sales.

Weiss has an accounts receivable balance of $1,760,000, so its ACP, calculated in the alternative way, is also 16 days:

Key Equation 15.3: Average Collection Period (Alternative Calculation)

$$\text{ACP} = \frac{\text{Receivables}}{\text{ADS}} = \frac{\$1{,}760{,}000}{\$110{,}000} = 16 \text{ days.}$$

An *aging schedule* breaks down a firm's receivables by age of account. Exhibit 15.2 contains the December 31, 2018, aging schedules of two surgical instrument manufacturers—Weiss and Cutright. Both firms offer the same credit terms—2/10, net 30—and both show the same total receivables balance. However, Weiss's aging schedule indicates that all of its customers pay on time: 70 percent pay on day 10, while 30 percent pay on day 30. Cutright's schedule, which is more typical, shows that many of its customers are not abiding by its credit terms: 27 percent of its receivables are more than 30 days past due, even though Cutright's credit terms call for full payment by day 30.

Aging schedules cannot be constructed from the type of summary data that are reported in a business's financial statements; they must be developed

EXHIBIT 15.2
Aging Schedules for Two Firms

	Weiss		Cutright	
Age of Account (Days)	*Value of Account*	*Percentage of Total Value*	*Value of Account*	*Percentage of Total Value*
0–10	$1,232,000	70%	$ 825,000	47%
11–30	528,000	30	460,000	26
31–45	0	0	265,000	15
46–60	0	0	179,000	10
Over 60	0	0	31,000	2
Total	$1,760,000	100%	$1,760,000	100%

from the accounts receivable ledger. However, well-run businesses have computerized accounts receivable records. Thus, they can easily determine the age of each invoice, sort electronically by age categories, and generate an aging schedule.

A key managerial decision as it relates to aging accounts receivable is calculating an allowance for doubtful accounts. Allowance for doubtful accounts is a contra asset on the balance sheet and is used as an estimate of collections on receivables that will not be received. Managers who can accurately predict the actual bad debt on receivables will be able to better understand their organization's financial situation and make more informed managerial decisions.

Monitoring Specific Revenue Cycle Activities

Of course, overall revenue cycle performance is a function of how well the specific revenue cycle activities are performed. Here are five metrics, of many, that are commonly used to measure the performance of specific revenue cycle activities:

1. **Cost to collect**. This metric is used to measure the overall cost-effectiveness of an organization's revenue cycle management. It is defined as Total revenue cycle costs ÷ Total amount collected. The idea here is that it makes no sense to spend $1.50 to collect $1.
2. **Point-of-service collection rate**. This metric is defined as Point-of-service collections ÷ Total patient collections. Its purpose is to measure what percentage of the monies owed by patients is collected when the service is rendered. Clearly, the more money that is collected at time of service, the better. Collection when the patient is at the facility saves the cost of billing and ensures that the payment is made.

3. **Initial denial rate**. This metric, which is a broad measure of billing efficiency, is defined as Number of initial claims denied ÷ Number of claims submitted. Here, the higher the metric value, the greater the cost of collecting payments due from insurers. Denials increase revenue cycle costs in three ways. First, denials require additional work, and hence cost, at the billing organization. Second, denials delay the receipt of payment, which increases the cost of carrying the receivables balance. Third, if the denial is permanent, the claim is never paid and the cost of service is borne by the provider.
4. **Registration quality score**. This metric measures the effectiveness of the patient registration process. It is defined as Number of correct patient demographic and insurance data elements at registration ÷ Total number of data elements. A high score indicates good upfront patient data collection and prevents downstream revenue cycle defects.
5. **Charge lag days**. This metric measures the time it takes from the day a service is provided to the day a bill is sent to the payer (patient or insurer). It is defined as Total days between service and billing ÷ Number of bills. Note this definition gives the average lag days over some period. The metric could also be calculated by payer (patient, Medicaid, or others). Clearly, on average, the faster that bills are generated and sent, the quicker the collection.

Before we end our discussion of specific metrics, it is useful to consider this question: What makes a good metric? First and foremost, metrics are supposed to measure process performance. So good metric design starts with defining what the fundamental purpose is for the process being assessed. Only after having defined the process purpose can a discussion begin about measuring performance. In the case of the revenue cycle, the fundamental purpose can be defined as identifying the correct amount "owed" to the organization for services rendered and converting that amount into cash.

Second, recognize that metrics are used to provide the organizational focus to ensure that resources are aimed at the correct activities. To further this concept, selected metrics, coupled with associated goals, are used to define incentive pay plans to motivate staff to achieve the desired results. With these goals in mind, here are several characteristics of good metrics:

- Metrics must directly measure the degree of "success" of the process purpose.
- Metrics must be measurable and quantitative.
- Metrics must be objective and precise.
- Metrics must be measureable over time.

- Metrics should be easily defined and understood by all affected managers and staff.

While the performance monitoring objective of metrics is apparent to most individuals, the human component evades many. Metrics play a major role not only in motivating staff to work better but also in communicating organizational goals and objectives. In high-performing organizations, managers and staff have a sense of purpose related to their daily activities, and metrics play a fundamental role in communicating how this purpose is achieved.

Unique Problems Faced by Healthcare Providers

Although the general principles of revenue cycle management discussed up to this point are applicable to all businesses, healthcare providers face some unique problems. The most obvious problem is the billing complexity created by the third-party payer system. For example, rather than having to deal with a single billing system that applies to all customers, providers have to deal with the rules and regulations of many different governmental and private insurers that use different payment methodologies. Thus, providers have to maintain large staffs of specialists who report to a *patient accounts manager*.

For an illustration of the problem, consider exhibit 15.3, which contains the receivables mix for the hospital sector. There are multiple payers in many of the categories listed in the exhibit, so the actual number of different payers can easily run into the hundreds or thousands.

Exhibit 15.4 provides information on how long it takes hospitals to collect receivables. Because of the large number of payers and the complexities involved in billing and follow-up actions, hospitals clearly have a great deal of difficulty collecting bills in a timely manner. On average,

EXHIBIT 15.3
Hospital Sector's Receivables Mix

Payer	*Percentage of Total Accounts Receivable*
Medicare	30.9%
Managed care	22.5
Self-pay	13.2
Medicaid	13.1
Commercial insurers	11.6
Other	8.7
	100.0%

Source: Data from *Hospital Accounts Receivable Analysis* (2015).

EXHIBIT 15.4
Hospital Sector's Aggregate Aging Schedule

Age of Account (Days)	*Percentage of Total Accounts Receivable*
0–30	50.4%
31–60	16.5
61–90	9.7
91–120	6.3
Over 120	19.8
	100.0%

Source: Data from *Hospital Accounts Receivable Analysis* (2015).

it takes about 50 days to collect a receivable. However, this number has decreased in recent years as hospital managers have become increasingly aware of the costs associated with carrying receivables and as automated systems have made the collections process more efficient. Despite the positive trend, about 33 percent of receivables still were more than 60 days old. In addition, the American Hospital Association (2019) estimates the cost of uncompensated care (hospital care provided for which no payment was received from patient or insurer) to be about $38.4 billion, or 4.2 percent of total expenses in 2017.

To help providers collect from managed care plans in a timely fashion, many states have enacted laws that mandate prompt payment. For example, New York State requires that all undisputed claims by providers be paid by plans within 45 days of receipt. If prompt payment is not made, fines are assessed.

SELF-TEST QUESTIONS

1. What is the revenue cycle?
2. What four phases make up the cycle?
3. Why is proper management of the revenue cycle critical to the financial performance of healthcare providers?
4. Explain how a firm's receivables balance is built up over time and why there are costs associated with carrying receivables.
5. Briefly discuss two metrics used to monitor overall revenue cycle performance.
6. What are some of the unique problems healthcare providers face in revenue cycle management?

Supply Chain Management

Inventories are an essential part of virtually all business operations. As is the case with accounts receivable, inventory levels depend heavily on patient volume and hence revenues. However, whereas receivables build up after services have been provided, inventories must be acquired beforehand. This difference is critical, and the necessity of forecasting volume before establishing target inventory levels makes inventory management a difficult task. Also, because errors in inventory levels can lead to either catastrophic consequences for patients or excessive carrying costs, inventory management in health services organizations is as important as it is difficult.

The overall management of inventory, including purchasing, transportation, storage, and use or disposal, is called *supply chain management* or *materials management.* Proper supply chain management requires close coordination among the marketing, purchasing, patient services, and finance departments. The patient services departments are generally the first to spot changes in volume. These changes must be worked into the business's purchasing and operating schedules, and the financial manager must arrange any financing that will be needed to support the inventory buildup. Improper communication among departments, poor volume forecasts, or both can lead to disaster.

The key to cost-effective supply chain management is information technology. *Inventory control systems* start with an inventory count in system memory and, as withdrawals are made, the system records them and revises the inventory balance. When the order point is reached, the system automatically places an order, and when the order is received, the system increases the recorded balance.

A good supply chain management system must be dynamic. A large provider may stock thousands of different items of inventory. Increased or decreased use of these items may have no correlation to an increase or decrease in aggregate utilization of services. As the usage rate for an individual item begins to rise or fall, the supply chain manager must adjust its balance to avoid running short or ending up with an obsolete item. If the change in the usage rate appears to be permanent, the *base inventory* level should be recomputed, the *safety stock* should be reconsidered, and the computer model used in the control process should be reprogrammed.

One inventory control method commonly used today in all fields, including health services, is the *just in time (JIT)* system. The use of just-in-time systems among providers may be illustrated by the following example. At one time, a large hospital maintained a 25,000-square-foot warehouse to hold its medical supplies. However, as cost pressures mounted, the hospital closed its warehouse and sold the inventory to a major hospital supplier.

The JIT streamlining process began with daily deliveries to the hospital's loading dock but soon expanded to a *stockless inventory* system. Now, the supplier fills orders in exact (sometimes small) quantities and delivers them directly to the hospital's departments, including the operating rooms and nursing floors. The hospital's managers estimate that the stockless system has saved about $1.5 million per year since it was instituted, including $350,000 from staff reductions and $650,000 from inventory reductions. In addition, the hospital has converted space that was previously used for storage to patient care and other cash-generating uses. The suppliers that offer stockless inventory systems typically add a 3 percent to 5 percent service fee, but many hospitals still can realize savings on total inventory costs.

The stockless inventory concept has its own set of problems. The main concern is that a *stock-out*, which occurs when an inventory item is not in stock, will cause a serious problem. "We walk very carefully and slowly because we can't afford a glitch," said a spokesperson for the supplier. "The first morning that an operating room doesn't open, we have a problem." Some hospital managers are concerned that such systems create too much dependence on a single supplier and that the cost savings will disappear as prices increase.

As stockless inventory systems become more prevalent in hospitals, more and more hospitals are relying on outside contractors who assume both inventory management and supplier roles. In effect, hospitals are beginning to outsource supply chain management. For example, some hospitals are experimenting with an inventory management program known as *point-of-service distribution*, which is one generation ahead of stockless systems. Under point-of-service programs, the supplier delivers supplies, intravenous solutions, medical forms, and so on to the supply rooms. The supplier owns the products in the supply rooms until the hospital uses them, at which time the hospital pays for the items.

In addition to reducing inventories, outside supply chain managers often are better than their in-house counterparts at ferreting out waste. For example, an outside manager found that one hospital

The GS1 System of Standards

Founded in 1977, GS1 is an international not-for-profit organization dedicated to the improvement of supply chain efficiency. GS1's primary activity is the development of the GS1 System, a series of standards composed of four key elements: (1) barcodes, which are used to automatically identify items; (2) eCom, which creates standardized business inventory messaging data; (3) Global Data Synchronization, which allows multiple businesses to have consistent inventory data; and (4) EPCglobal, which establishes a system that uses radio frequency chips to track items across the entire supply chain.

In the US healthcare sector, many companies—from manufacturers to distributors to end users such as hospitals—are actively supporting the adoption of GS1 Standards. The goals of the companies involved include enhanced patient safety, improved supply chain management, enhanced drug control, and better connectivity to electronic health records.

was spending $600 on products used in a single open-heart surgery, while another was spending only $420. Because there was no meaningful difference in the procedure or outcomes, the hospital was able to change the type of medical supplies used in the surgery and pocket the difference.

In an even more advanced form of inventory management, some hospitals negotiate with suppliers to furnish materials on the basis of how much medical care is delivered, rather than according to the type and number of products used. In such agreements, providers pay suppliers a set fee for each unit of patient service provided—for example, $125 for each case-mix-adjusted patient day. Under this type of system, a hospital ties its supply expenditures to its revenues, which, for the most part and at least for now, are tied to the number of units of patient service. The end of the evolution of inventory management techniques for healthcare providers is expected to be some form of capitated payment; providers will pay suppliers a previously established fee regardless of actual future patient volume and hence regardless of the amount of materials actually consumed.

SELF-TEST QUESTIONS

1. Why is good supply chain management important to a business's success?
2. Describe some recent trends in supply chain management by healthcare providers.

Current Liability Management

At this point in the chapter, we conclude our discussion of current asset management and turn our attention to two current liability accounts: (1) accruals and (2) accounts payable or trade credit. Although these accounts are liabilities and hence a source of financing to businesses, they are considered to be part of working capital (short-term account) management. Thus, accounts payable and accruals management are discussed in this chapter rather than in chapter 6 (Debt Financing).

Accruals

Businesses generally pay employees on a weekly, biweekly, or monthly basis, though wages are actually earned on a daily basis. Similarly, the business's estimated income taxes (if applicable), Social Security and income taxes withheld from employee payrolls, and sales taxes collected are generally paid on a weekly, monthly, or quarterly basis, though the obligations are created on a daily basis. The wages and taxes that a business owes because of these timing differentials are listed on the balance sheet as *accruals*. It is important to recognize that these accruals are different from accruals created as part of managerial accounting practices.

Accruals increase automatically, or **spontaneously**, as a business's operations expand. Furthermore, this type of short-term debt is free in the sense that no explicit interest is paid on accruals. For these two reasons, accruals are an important source of short-term financing for businesses, especially those that are growing rapidly. However, a business cannot ordinarily control the amount of accruals on its balance sheet because the timing of wage payments is set by economic forces and industry custom, and tax payment dates are established by law. Because accruals represent "free" financing, businesses should use all the accrual financing they can obtain, but managers have little control over the levels of such accounts.

Accounts Payable (Trade Credit)

On the web at: *ache.org/HAP/PinkSong8e*

Healthcare businesses often make purchases from other firms on credit. Such debt is recorded on the balance sheet as an *account payable*. Accounts payable, or *trade credit*, is the largest single category of short-term debt for many businesses. Because small businesses typically do not qualify for financing from other sources, they rely heavily on trade credit.

Like accruals, trade credit is a spontaneous source of financing in the sense that it arises from ordinary business transactions. For example, suppose that a hospital purchases an average of $2,000 of medical supplies per day on terms of net 30, which means that the hospital must pay for goods 30 days after the invoice date. On average, the hospital will owe 30 × $2,000 = $60,000 to its suppliers, assuming that the hospital's managers act rationally and do not pay before the credit is due. If the hospital's volume and consequently its purchases were to double, its accounts payable would also double to $120,000. Simply by growing, the hospital would spontaneously generate an additional $60,000 of financing. Similarly, if the terms under which it bought supplies were extended from 30 days to 40 days, the hospital's accounts payable would increase from $60,000 to $80,000. Thus, both greater volume and a longer credit period generate additional financing for a business.

Firms that sell on credit have a *credit policy* that includes certain *terms of credit*. For example, Lake Michigan Medical Supply Company sells on terms of 2/10, net 30, which means the buyer receives a 2 percent discount if payment is made within ten days of the invoice date. If the discount is not taken, the full invoice amount is due and payable within 30 days. Suppose that East Chicago Health System, Inc., buys an average of $12 million of medical and surgical supplies from Lake Michigan each year, less a 2 percent discount, for net purchases of $11,760,000 ÷ 360 = $32,666.67 per day. For the sake of simplicity, suppose that Lake Michigan is East Chicago Health's only supplier. If East Chicago Health takes the discount (pays at the end of the tenth day), its payables will average 10 × $32,666.67 = $326,667; thus, East Chicago Health will, on average, be receiving $326,667 of credit from Lake Michigan, its only supplier.

Suppose now that East Chicago Health's managers decide not to take the discount. What effect will this decision have on the system's financial condition? First, East Chicago Health will begin paying invoices in 30 days, so its accounts payable will increase to 30 × $32,666.67 = $980,000. Lake Michigan will now be supplying East Chicago Health with $980,000 – $326,667 = $653,333 of **additional** trade credit. The health system can use this additional credit to pay off bank loans, expand inventories, increase fixed assets, build up its cash account, or even increase its own accounts receivable.

Note that we used $32,666.67 for average daily sales, which is based on the discounted price of the surgical supplies, **regardless of whether** East Chicago Health takes the discount. In general, businesses treat the discounted price of supplies as the "true" cost when reporting expenses on the income statement. If the business does not take the discount, the cost difference is reported separately on the income statement as an expense called *discounts lost*. Thus, we used the discounted price to reflect the cost of the supplies in both instances.

East Chicago Health's additional credit from Lake Michigan has a cost: It is forgoing a 2 percent discount on its $12 million of purchases, so its costs will rise by $240,000 per year. Dividing this $240,000 dollar cost by the amount of additional credit provides the implicit approximate percentage cost of the added trade credit:

$$\text{Approximate percentage cost} = \$240{,}000 \div \$653{,}333 = 36.7\%.$$

Assuming that East Chicago Health can borrow from its bank or from other sources at an interest rate lower than 36.7 percent, it should not expand its payables by forgoing discounts.

The following equation can be used to calculate the approximate annual percentage cost of forgoing discounts:

Key Equation 15.4: Approximate Annual Percentage Cost

$$\text{Approximate percentage cost} = \frac{\text{Discount percentage}}{100 - \text{Discount percentage}} \times \frac{360}{\text{Days credit received} - \text{Discount period}}.$$

The numerator of the first term (Discount percentage) is the cost per dollar of credit, while the denominator in this term (100 – Discount percentage) represents the funds made available by not taking the discount. Thus, the first term is the periodic cost rate of the trade credit. In this example, East Chicago Health must spend \$2 to gain \$98 of credit, for a cost rate of 2 ÷ 98 = 0.0204 = 2.04%. The second term shows how many times each year this cost is incurred; in this example, 360 ÷ (30 – 10) = 360 ÷ 20 = 18 times. If we put the two terms together, the approximate cost of forgoing the discount when the terms are 2/10, net 30, is computed as follows:

$$\text{Approximate \% cost} = \frac{2}{98} \times \frac{360}{20} = 0.204 \times 18$$
$$= 0.367 = 36.7\%.$$

The cost of trade credit can be reduced by paying late—that is, by paying beyond the date that the credit terms allow. Such a strategy is called *stretching*. If East Chicago Health System can get away with paying Lake Michigan in 60 days rather than in the specified 30, the effective credit period would become 60 – 10 = 50 days, and the approximate cost would drop from 36.7 percent to (2 ÷ 98) × (360 ÷ 50) = 14.7%. In recessionary periods, businesses may be able to get away with late payments to suppliers, but they will also suffer a variety of problems associated with stretching accounts payable and being branded a slow payer.

On the basis of the preceding discussion, it is clear that trade credit consists of two components:

1. *Free trade credit* is credit received during the discount period.
2. *Costly trade credit* is credit in excess of the free credit. The cost of this credit is implied because it is obtained only if the discount is forgone.

From a finance perspective, managers should view trade credit in this way. First, the actual price of supplies is the discounted price—that is, the price that would be paid on a cash purchase. Any credit that can be taken without an increase in price is free credit that should be taken. Second, if the discounted price is the actual price, the additional amount that must be paid if the discount is not taken is, in reality, a *finance charge* for additional credit. A business should take the additional credit only if the finance charge is less than the cost of alternative credit sources.

In the example, East Chicago Health should take the \$326,667 of free credit offered by Lake Michigan. Free credit is good credit. However, the cost rate of the additional \$653,333 of costly trade credit is approximately 37 percent. The health system has access to bank loans at a 9.5 percent rate, so it does not take the additional credit. Under the terms of trade found in most industries, the costly component involves a relatively high percentage cost, so stronger firms avoid using it.

SELF-TEST QUESTIONS

1. What is meant by the term *spontaneous financing*?
2. What are accruals, and what should a business's policy be regarding the use of accrual financing?
3. What is trade credit?
4. What is the difference between free and costly trade credit?
5. How should businesses determine the amount of trade credit they should use?

Chapter Key Concepts

This chapter examines short-term accounts management, including accruals and trade credit. Here are its key concepts:

- The essence of *short-term accounts management* is to support the business's operations at the lowest possible cost.
- The *primary goal of cash management* is to reduce the amount of cash held to the minimum necessary to conduct business.
- *Cash management techniques* generally can be broken down into four categories: (1) *synchronizing cash flows*, (2) *managing float*, (3) *accelerating collections*, and (4) *controlling disbursements.*
- *Lockboxes* are used to accelerate collections. A *concentration banking system* consolidates the collections into a centralized pool that can be managed more efficiently than a large number of individual accounts.
- Three techniques for controlling disbursements are (1) *payables centralization*, (2) *zero-balance accounts*, and (3) *controlled disbursement accounts.*
- The implementation of a sophisticated cash management system is costly, and all cash management actions must be evaluated to ensure that the benefits exceed the costs.
- Firms can reduce their cash balances by holding *marketable securities*, which serve as both a *substitute for cash* and a

(continued)

(continued from previous page)

temporary investment for funds that will be needed in the near future. Safety is the primary consideration when selecting marketable securities.

- *Cash budgets*, which forecast future cash inflow and outflows, are key to good cash and marketable securities management.
- The *revenue cycle* includes all activities associated with billing and collections for services provided.
- The revenue cycle can be broken down into these activity categories, depending on when they occur: (1) *before-service* activities, (2) *at-service* activities, (3) *after-service* activities, and (4) *continuous* activities.
- When a firm sells goods to a customer on credit, an *account receivable* is created.
- Businesses use *average collection period (ACP)* and *aging schedules* to monitor overall revenue cycle performance.
- In the revenue cycle, specific activities (functions) are monitored using an extensive set of metrics, each designed to provide information about the effectiveness of that activity.
- Proper *supply chain (inventory) management* requires close coordination among the marketing, purchasing, patient services, and finance departments as well as a sophisticated information technology system. Because the cost of holding inventory can be high and the consequences of stock-outs severe, supply chain management is important in health services organizations.
- *Just-in-time (JIT)* systems, including *stockless inventory* systems, are used to minimize inventory costs and, simultaneously, improve operations.
- *Accruals* are a source of short-term financing that result from the buildup of wages and taxes due. Because they are a costless source of financing, businesses should take all the accruals they can get.
- *Accounts payable*, or *trade credit*, is a source of short-term financing that stems from buying supplies on credit.
- Businesses should take all of the *free trade credit* available but should take *costly trade credit* only if the implied cost is less than that on other sources of short-term credit.

(continued)

(continued from previous page)

Our discussion of the revenue cycle and current accounts management has been brief. However, the concepts covered should give you at least some appreciation for the issues involved. For additional information, see any of references listed in the Selected Bibliography section.

Chapter Models, Problems, and Minicases

The following ancillary resources in spreadsheet format are available for this chapter:

- A chapter model that shows how to perform many of the calculations described in the chapter
- Problems that test your ability to perform the calculations
- A minicase that is more complicated than the problems and tests your ability to perform the calculations in preparation for a case

These resources can be accessed online at ache.org/HAP/PinkSong8e.

Selected Cases

Three cases in *Cases in Healthcare Finance*, sixth edition, are applicable to this chapter:

- Case 27: Foster Pharmaceuticals, which focuses on the basic concepts of receivables management
- Case 28: Clarinda Community Hospital, which covers inventory management with emphasis on the economic ordering quantity model
- Case 29: Milwaukee Regional Health System, which focuses on revenue cycle management

References

American Hospital Association. 2019. *Uncompensated Hospital Care Cost Fact Sheet.* Published January. www.aha.org/system/files/2019-01/uncompensated-care-fact-sheet-jan-2019.pdf.

Gerdes, G., C. Greene, and X. Liu. 2019. "The Federal Reserve Payments Study: 2018 Annual Supplement." Federal Reserve System. Updated January 18. www.federalreserve.gov/paymentsystems/2018-December-The-Federal-Reserve-Payments-Study.htm.

Hospital Accounts Receivable Analysis. 2015. Vol. 30 (1): 51–68.

Selected Bibliography

Baker, K. B. 2016. "Aligning Systems for Improved Revenue Cycle Performance." *Healthcare Financial Management* 70 (9): 44–51.

Burns, W., and A. Harmon. 2016. "Reducing Administrative Write-Offs Through Improved Denial Management." *Healthcare Financial Management* 70 (7): 30–33.

Healthcare Financial Management Association. 2018. "Transforming Accounts Payable: Opportunities, Challenges, and Next Steps." *hfm.* Published August 1. www.hfma.org/Content.aspx?id=61336.

———. 2016. "Leveraging Data Analytics to Improve the Revenue Cycle." *hfm.* Published August 1. www.hfma.org/RevCycleAnalytics.

———. 2016. "Transforming the Disbursement Cycle: Four Steps for Selecting a Diversified Payment Strategy." *hfm.* Published June 1. www.hfma.org/Content.aspx?id=48250.

Jordahl, E. A., and D. Ratliff. 2017. "Refocus Treasury Functions for Continued High Volatility." *Healthcare Financial Management* 71 (7): 54–56.

Melling, J. 2017. "Preparing for Value-Based Payment: Fundamental Change That Encompasses the Revenue Cycle." *Healthcare Financial Management* 71 (5): 60–66.

Saharia, D. 2016. "Revenue Cycle Leakage: 5 Red Flags Indicating Major Inefficiencies." *Healthcare Financial Management* 70 (9): 60–64.

Selected Websites

The following websites pertain to the content of this chapter:

- To learn more about the cash management services offered by large banks, see www.wellsfargo.com/com/treasury-management.
- For more information about the automated clearing house (ACH) network, see the Nacha website at www.nacha.org.
- For more information on the revenue cycle, see the Healthcare Financial Management Association website at www.hfma.org. Click on Browse by Topic and then Revenue Cycle.

- To learn more about supply chain management, see the Council of Supply Chain Management Professionals website at http://cscmp.org.

Notes

1. A *credit line* is an agreement between a borrower and a financial institution that obligates the institution to furnish credit over some period—typically a year—up to the agreed amount. The borrower may use some, all, or none of the credit line. Usually, borrowers must pay an up-front fee—called a *commitment fee*—for the credit guarantee.
2. Money market mutual funds cannot be used as a replacement for commercial checking accounts because the number of checks that can be written against such funds normally is limited to just a few per month.
3. Note that there is not a single universally accepted description of revenue cycle activities. Different professional organizations tend to include somewhat different sets of activities. Still, the basic premise remains the same: Revenue cycle management encompasses the information systems, policies, and methodologies used to review patients' and insurers' financial obligations, document services provided, translate the services into appropriate billing amounts, issue invoices, and collect the correct payments—all in a timely manner.
4. More precisely, the full amount of the receivables account does **not** require financing. The cash costs associated with providing the services that produce the $20,000 in revenues do need to be financed, but the profit component does not. For example, assume that Home Infusion has cash costs of $800 associated with each day's revenues of $1,000. If so, 20 days of receivables would actually require only 20 × $800 = $16,000 in financing. The remaining $4,000 of receivables, which represent profits, would be offset on the balance sheet by increasing the retained earnings (equity) account by a like amount.

Integrative Application

The Problem

Jamestown Medical Practice (JMP) has annual net patient services revenues of $14,400,000, primarily provided by two major third-party payers along with a few self-payers. The self-pay patients contribute 10 percent of net revenues, while the two third-party payers contribute 45 percent each. The receivables are financed using a loan from a local bank with an interest rate of 8 percent. JMP's patient accounts manager estimates the following payment patterns:

Table A

	Pay on Day 30 (%)	*Pay on Day 60 (%)*	*Pay on Day 90 (%)*	*Charity Care (%)*
Self-pay	25	70		5
Payer A		60	40	
Payer B		40	60	

JMP is considering outsourcing its receivables management function to a company that specializes in providing such services to medical practices. The receivables management vendor guarantees that they can reduce the days in accounts receivable to 50, roughly the average for medical practices. The cost for these services would be a contract initiation fee of $250,000 and an annual payment of $100,000. In addition, JMP would be able to reduce its financial staff by one FTE, resulting in an annual savings of $60,000. JMP's managers must decide whether to accept the outsourcing proposal.

The Analysis

To begin, convert table A to reflect the percentage of JMP's total net receivables collected on each day:

Table B

	Pay on Day 30 (%)	Pay on Day 60 (%)	Pay on Day 90 (%)	Total (%)
Self-pay	2.6	7.4		10.0
Payer A		27.0	18.0	45.0
Payer B		18.0	27.0	45.0
Total	2.6%	52.4%	45.0%	100.0%

Note that, to create table B, the percentages in table A are adjusted to reflect (1) the proportion that each payer contributes to the receivables balance and (2) the fact that the 5 percent charity care amount does not flow to (net) receivables because it is never expected to be collected.

Using these collection percentages, the days in patient accounts receivable, or average collection period (ACP), is 72.7 days:

$$\begin{aligned} \text{ACP} &= (0.026 \times 30 \text{ days}) + (0.524 \times 60 \text{ days}) + (0.450 \times 90 \text{ days}) \\ &= 72.7 \text{ days.} \end{aligned}$$

With $14,400,000 in net patient service revenues, JMP's average daily sales (ADS) are $14,400,000 ÷ 360 = $40,000, which leads to a receivables balance of $2,908,000:

$$\begin{aligned} \text{Receivables balance} &= \text{ADS} \times \text{ACP} \\ &= \$40{,}000 \times 72.7 \text{ days} \\ &= \$2{,}908{,}000. \end{aligned}$$

Finally, with a cost of carrying receivables of 8 percent, the dollar cost is $232,640.

$$\begin{aligned} \text{Dollar cost} &= \text{Receivables balance} \times \text{Percent cost} \\ &= \$2{,}908{,}000 \times 0.08 \\ &= \$232{,}640. \end{aligned}$$

If the ACP is reduced to 50 days, then the receivables balance would be reduced to $2,000,000 and the annual carrying cost would fall to $160,000:

$$\begin{aligned} \text{Receivables balance} &= \$40{,}000 \times 50.0 \\ &= \$2{,}000{,}000. \end{aligned}$$

$$\text{Dollar cost} = \$2{,}000{,}000 \times 0.08$$
$$= \$160{,}000.$$

The Decision

With a reduction in receivables of $2,908,000 – $2,000,000 = $908,000, the annual carrying cost savings is 0.08 × $908,000 = $72,640. (Alternatively, from above, $232,640 – $160,000 = $72,640.) At the same time, JMP would save $60,000 in labor expense, for a total benefit of $72,640 + $60,000 = $132,640. Because the annual cost of the outsourcing is $100,000, the annual net benefit is $132,640 – $100,000 = $32,640.

But what about the initiation fee of $250,000? When the receivables balance is reduced, JMP will receive a one-time cash inflow of $908,000, part of which could be used to pay the initiation fee. Thus, the numerical analysis indicates that the vendor's proposal should be accepted. Still, many qualitative factors—such as loss of control—must be considered before the final decision is made. ■

CHAPTER

16

BUSINESS COMBINATIONS AND VALUATION

Learning Objectives

After studying this chapter, readers should be able to

- discuss the history of merger activity in the United States,
- describe the most popular motives for mergers and judge their validity,
- value businesses using the discounted cash flow and market multiple approaches,
- discuss the unique problems that arise when small businesses are being valued and when not-for-profit businesses are acquired by investor-owned businesses, and
- describe some corporate alliances that fall short of true mergers.

Introduction

Most of the growth in health services organizations occurs through internal expansion; that is, a business's existing operations grow through normal capital budgeting activities. However, the most dramatic examples of growth result from business combinations, including mergers, acquisitions, and corporate alliances. For some purposes, it is necessary to distinguish between mergers and acquisitions, but those distinctions are more legal in nature and do not affect the fundamental business and financial considerations involved. Thus, we generally will refer to all combinations in which a single entity is formed from two or more existing businesses as a *merger*.

We begin our discussion of business combinations with some general background information. Later, we will focus on business combinations in the health services sector, including the factors that must be considered when investor-owned and not-for-profit businesses merge. In addition, we will discuss business valuation, a key element in any business combination analysis.

Level of Merger Activity

Before the 1990s, mergers in the health services sector were neither as frequent nor as large as mergers in most other industries. First, the health services sector—at least in its current form—is relatively new, not having fully developed until after World War II. Second, the motivations that fueled the wave of the 1980s only partially applied to health services, so the sector was not one of the major participants in that wave, although there were some spectacular mergers between for-profit hospital chains. However, the wave of mergers in the health services sector in the 1990s was strong; the record for the greatest number of deals was set in 1996. The number of mergers declined substantially between the mid-1990s and 2003. The Balanced Budget Act of 1997 placed significant restrictions on the growth of Medicare reimbursement rates, which lessened the value of many healthcare providers—primarily nursing home, rehabilitation, and home health care businesses.

Exhibit 16.1, which reports the number of deals, provides some sense of recent levels of merger activity in the health services sector. After the 2008 financial crisis, the number of financially distressed organizations increased substantially. Operating margins fell because of lower patient volume and payer-mix deterioration. Capital needs for new and updated equipment and facilities, more employed physicians, implementation of information technology, and service-line growth were beyond what many organizations could afford. Some of these organizations came to the sober realization that they could not survive without a partner. As a result, a new wave of healthcare mergers and acquisitions—similar to the first wave in the 1990s—began and continues to this day. Some mergers and acquisitions will seek consolidation in current markets, while others will seek growth in adjacent and more distant markets in which investment makes sense from a financial and strategic perspective.

Here are two examples of recent healthcare mergers:

1. In 2018, HCA (www.hcahealthcare.com) announced its intention to acquire Mission Health for $1.5 billion. This acquisition represented a unique situation because HCA, a for-profit company, acquired a not-for-profit healthcare system that has a state-sanctioned monopoly in the western part of North Carolina. As a result, the acquisition has a number of additional provisions—for example, not selling any rehabilitation or acute-care hospitals for 10 years and a commitment to spend a minimum of $430 million in capital expenditures over five years. This is an excellent example of the usual nature of mergers and acquisitions in the healthcare space.

EXHIBIT 16.1
Merger Activity in the Health Services Sector: 2007–2016

Sector	*2007*	*2008*	*2009*	*2010*	*2011*	*2012*	*2013*	*2014*	*2015*	*2016*
Hospitals	58	60	52	75	92	94	86	99	102	90
Behavioral health	13	14	11	7	13	17	18	24	40	41
Home health	49	47	42	41	29	35	39	70	51	55
Labs, MRI, dialysis	54	41	30	39	29	45	34	33	52	41
Long-term care	127	96	75	103	172	188	237	302	359	337
Managed care	28	16	15	13	20	27	14	22	45	21
Physician groups	41	53	41	60	108	68	59	60	100	119
Rehabilitation	16	27	11	12	14	18	13	19	33	40
Other	110	123	78	91	86	121	124	136	171	196
Total	496	477	355	441	563	613	624	765	953	940

Source: Phillips (2017).

2. In 2013, Tenet Healthcare Corporation of Dallas (www.tenethealth.com) acquired Vanguard Health Systems of Nashville, increasing Tenet's size from 49 to 79 hospitals. Tenet paid $21 for each share of Vanguard outstanding, for a total acquisition price of about $1.8 billion. According to observers, Tenet's national sprawl and Vanguard's concentrated presence have combined to provide the new enterprise with more opportunities to concentrate on specific markets and to expand its focus on outpatient care, which is trending upward while inpatient care dwindles.

SELF-TEST QUESTIONS

1. Are mergers in the health services sector increasing or decreasing? Explain your answer.
2. Describe one recent merger in the healthcare sector.

Motives for Mergers: The Good, the Bad, and the Ugly

In the previous section, we presented some factors that fueled merger waves in the past. In this section, we take a more detailed look at some of the motives behind business mergers and present some views regarding the validity of these motives.

Synergy

From an economic perspective, the best motivation for a merger is to increase the value of the combined enterprise. If firms A and B merge to form firm C, and if C's value exceeds the summed values of A and B taken separately, *synergy* is said to exist. When synergy drives a merger, value is created and society benefits. Furthermore, such a merger can be beneficial to both A's and B's stockholders if the firms are investor owned.

Synergistic effects can arise from four sources:

1. **Operating economies**. Operating economies result from economies of scale in management, marketing, contracting, operations, or distribution, including mergers that better position a business strategically.
2. **Financial economies**. Financial economies can result in lower transaction costs and better access to capital markets.
3. **Differential efficiency**. When differential efficiency is involved, inefficient management is replaced by new management that uses the business's assets more productively.
4. **Increased market power**. Increased market power (reduced competition) can create synergistic effects by increasing the contracting clout of the enterprise.

Operating and financial economies are socially desirable for both investor-owned and not-for-profit businesses, as are mergers that increase managerial efficiency. To some extent, increased market power can also be beneficial to society, such as the savings that result when major insurers pay for healthcare services. However, too much market power can turn into monopoly or monopsony power, which can be harmful to society and hence is undesirable and illegal. (*Monopsony* power arises when there is a single buyer, so healthcare insurers can, at least in theory, become monopsonies.)

Availability of Excess Cash

Mergers are an easy—perhaps too easy—way for managers to get rid of excess cash. If a business has a shortage of internal opportunities in which to invest its cash flow, it can (1) increase its dividend or repurchase stock, if investor owned; (2) invest in marketable securities; or (3) purchase another business. Marketable securities often are a good temporary parking place for money, but in general the rate of return on such securities is lower than the return on real-asset investments.

Although there is nothing inherently wrong with using excess cash to buy other firms, the acquisition must create value to be economically worthwhile. Business enlargement may benefit managers, but it does not necessarily benefit stockholders or society. If the return on a potential acquisition is not as high as the opportunity cost of the capital used, the capital should be used for other purposes. If the business is investor owned, the capital should be returned to the firm's investors; if the firm is not for profit, the capital should be used to retire debt or invested temporarily in securities until better uses are found.

Purchase of Assets at Less than Replacement Cost

Sometimes a business will be touted as a possible acquisition candidate because the cost of replacing its assets is considerably greater than its market value. For example, suppose that a small, rural hospital can be acquired for $15 million, while the cost to construct a similar hospital from the ground up is $30 million. One might be tempted to say that the hospital is a "good buy" because it can be bought for less than its replacement value.

However, the true economic value of any business should be based on its earning power, which sets the value of its assets. The real question, then, is not whether the hospital can be acquired for less than its replacement cost but whether it can be acquired for less than its *economic value*, which is a function of the cash flows that the hospital is expected to produce in the future. If the rural hospital's earning power sets it at a value of $20 million, it is a good buy at $15 million, but this conclusion is based on economic, not replacement, value. (Note that not-for-profit hospitals often have social [noneconomic] value that might increase their overall value, especially to acquiring not-for-profit organizations.)

Diversification

Managers often claim that diversification into other lines of business is a reason for mergers. They contend that diversification helps stabilize the business's earnings stream and thus benefits its owners. Stabilization of earnings is certainly beneficial to managers, employees, suppliers, customers, and other stakeholders, but its value is less certain from the standpoint of stockholders. If a stockholder is worried about the variability of a firm's earnings, he can diversify more easily than the firm. Why should firms A and B merge to stabilize earnings when a stockholder in firm A can sell half of his stock in A and then use the proceeds to purchase stock in firm B?

Also, if a stockholder is concerned about the relative performance of different industry segments, she can solve the problem more easily through portfolio diversification than can managers through mergers. For example, assume that a stockholder who holds primarily hospital stocks is concerned that the increased purchasing power of managed care plans will erode hospital profits, and hence value, over time. It is easier for the stockholder to purchase a managed care company's stock than it is for hospitals to diversify into managed care.

Of course, in some situations, mergers for diversification do make sense from a stockholder's perspective. For example, if you were the owner and manager of a closely held business, it might be nearly impossible for you to sell part of your ownership interest to diversify because you would dilute your ownership and perhaps also generate a large capital gains tax liability. In this case, a diversification merger might be the best way to achieve personal diversification. Also, as mentioned earlier, diversification mergers that better position businesses to deal with future events are worthwhile because such mergers can create operating synergies.

Even though diversification without synergy does not benefit shareholders directly, it clearly benefits a firm's other stakeholders. Thus, diversification-motivated mergers can be beneficial to not-for-profit businesses. Furthermore, stockholders can obtain indirect benefits from diversification because reduction of the firm's risk to managers, creditors, suppliers, customers, and the like can have positive implications for the owners of the business.

Personal Incentives

Economists like to think that business decisions are based solely on economic considerations. However, some business decisions are based more on managers' personal motivations than on economic analyses. Many people—business leaders included—like power, and more power is attached to running a larger business than a smaller one. Obviously, no executive would ever admit that their ego was the primary reason behind a merger, but knowledgeable observers are convinced that egos do play a prominent role in many mergers. Executive salaries, prestige, and perquisites are also highly correlated with the firm's size—the bigger the firm, the higher the executive benefits. This factor may also play a role in the aggressive acquisition programs of some corporations.

Managers' personal incentives as a basis for mergers illustrate the *agency problem*—a conflict between managers' motives and what is best for the business. Of course, it is not wrong for executives to feel good about increasing the size of their firms or to receive a better compensation package as a result of growth through mergers, provided that the mergers make economic sense.

Breakup Value

In general, firms are valued on the basis of the assumption that they will continue to operate. However, if the value of a business is greater when it is broken into pieces and sold than when it remains intact, the relevant value is its *breakup value*. Takeover specialists identify such businesses, buy them, sell off the pieces, and make a profit. Although this rationale is not common in health services acquisitions, mergers do occur occasionally because of breakup value.

SELF-TEST QUESTIONS

1. Define synergy. Is synergy a valid rationale for mergers?
2. Describe several situations that might produce synergistic gains in the health services sector.
3. Suppose your firm can purchase another firm for only half of its replacement value. Would this opportunity be sufficient justification for the acquisition?
4. Discuss the merits of diversification as a rationale for mergers.
5. Can managers' personal incentives motivate mergers? Explain your answer.
6. How can breakup value motivate mergers?

Types of Mergers

Economists have traditionally classified mergers into three primary categories:

1. **Horizontal**. A *horizontal merger* occurs when one firm combines with another in its line of business—for example, when one hospital acquires another or one home health care business merges with a second. The 2013 acquisition of Vanguard Health Systems by Tenet Healthcare described in a previous section is an example of a horizontal merger. The merger was a horizontal merger because both businesses were in the hospital management sector.
2. **Vertical**. A *vertical merger* occurs when a firm merges with a supplier or when one type of provider acquires another. An example of a vertical merger is a drug manufacturer's acquisition of a pharmaceutical distribution firm, such as Eli Lilly's (www.lilly.com) acquisition of PCS Health Systems. Another example is a hospital's acquisition of a medical practice, such as Milwaukee-based Aurora Health Care's (www.aurorahealthcare.org) acquisition of a 43-employee medical group in northern Illinois.
3. **Conglomerate**. A *conglomerate merger* occurs when unrelated enterprises combine. Because most health services organizations are in related business lines, mergers between such firms are rarely classified as conglomerate.

Realization of operating economies and anticompetitive effects are partly dependent on the type of merger involved. Vertical and horizontal mergers generally produce the greatest synergistic operating benefits, but they are also most likely to be attacked by federal or state authorities as anticompetitive. In any event, these economic classifications are useful when analyzing the feasibility of a prospective merger.

SELF-TEST QUESTIONS

1. What are the three primary economic classifications of mergers?
2. Briefly describe the characteristics of each classification.

Hostile Versus Friendly Takeovers

In the majority of merger situations, a business (the *acquirer*) simply decides to buy another firm (the *target*), negotiates a price with the target firm's management, and acquires the firm. Occasionally, the acquired firm will initiate the action, but it is much more common for a firm to seek acquisitions than to seek to be acquired.

Once an acquiring entity has identified a possible target, it must (1) establish a suitable price, or range of prices, and (2) tentatively set the terms of payment. Will it offer cash, its own common stock, bonds, or a mix of securities? Next, the acquiring firm's managers must decide how to approach the target firm's managers. If the acquirer believes that the target's management will support the merger, it will simply propose a merger and try to work out suitable terms. If the two management groups reach an agreement, they will issue statements indicating that they approve the merger and, if the firms are investor owned, recommend that stockholders agree to the merger. Generally, the stockholders of acquiring firms must merely vote to approve the merger, but the stockholders of target firms are asked to *tender*, or send in, their shares to a designated financial institution along with a signed power of attorney that transfers ownership of the shares to the acquiring firm. The target firm's stockholders then receive the specified payment—be it common stock of the acquiring firm (in which case, the target firm's stockholders become stockholders of the acquiring firm), cash, bonds, or some mix of cash and securities. This type of merger is called a *friendly merger*, or a *friendly tender offer*.

The 2004 acquisition of WellPoint Health Networks by Anthem (www.anthem.com) typifies a friendly merger. First, the boards of directors of the two firms announced that agreement on the merger had been reached. Then, the merger was approved by shareholders of both firms, by the Department of Justice, and by the states in which the businesses operated. Note, however, that a great deal of negotiation between state regulators and the two companies was required before the acquisition was finally completed.

Often, however, the target firm's management resists the merger. Perhaps the managers feel that the price offered for the stock is too low, or perhaps the business simply wants to retain its autonomy. In either case, the acquiring firm's offer is said to be hostile rather than friendly, and the acquiring firm must make a direct appeal to the target firm's stockholders. In a *hostile merger*, the acquiring firm will again make a tender offer and again ask the stockholders of the target firm to tender their shares in exchange for the offered price. This time, though, the target firm's managers will urge stockholders not to tender their shares, generally stating that the price offered (cash, bonds, or stocks in the acquiring firm) is too low.

Although many *hostile takeover* bids fail, most eventually succeed. It is difficult to defend against a hostile takeover attempt if the bidder has a large amount of resources that it is willing to spend on the battle. In such situations, the acquiring firm can offer enough cash to shareholders to overcome even the most adamant managerial resistance.

SELF-TEST QUESTIONS

1. What is the difference between a hostile merger and a friendly merger?
2. Describe the mechanics of a typical friendly takeover and of a typical hostile takeover.

Mergers Involving Not-for-Profit Businesses

One of the unique aspects of the health services sector is the large proportion of not-for-profit firms. In general, the concepts presented thus far in the chapter are applicable to both for-profit and not-for-profit businesses. Furthermore, the merger of two not-for-profit firms generally does not require special consideration. However, the acquisition of a not-for-profit firm by an investor-owned business can present two significant problems.

The first major problem is posed by the *charitable trust doctrine.* This doctrine, which was established in English common law and has been adopted by most states, holds that assets used for charitable purposes must be held in trust. The doctrine shaped the state incorporation laws for not-for-profit firms, which require that assets being used for charitable purposes be used for such purposes in perpetuity (forever). The implication of this doctrine is that the proceeds from the sale of a not-for-profit corporation to an investor-owned business must continue to be used for charitable purposes.

Charitable trust laws place two requirements on the board of trustees of a target not-for-profit business. First, the trustees must ensure that the acquisition price reflects the full fair (market) value of the assets being acquired. This assurance is normally obtained by getting the opinion of an investment banker specializing in mergers and acquisitions. Alternately, they can employ a professional appraiser. Second, the trustees must ensure that the acquisition proceeds continue to be used for charitable purposes. When a not-for-profit firm sells only a portion of its assets, no problem arises. The acquisition price is paid to a not-for-profit organization that continues to exist, so the funds continue to be used for charitable purposes. However, when a stand-alone entity is acquired, that not-for-profit organization ceases to exist. Thus, a new charitable entity must be created to administer the proceeds from the sale. The usual vehicle for continuing the charitable purpose of the not-for-profit corporation is the tax-exempt *foundation*.

More than 200 foundations have been spawned by the sales of not-for-profit businesses to investor-owned firms, primarily in the hospital industry and primarily as a result of acquisitions by large investor-owned chains. Note, however, that foundations have also been created by sales of health maintenance organizations and other not-for-profit healthcare businesses. For an illustration of the foundation concept, consider the Ottumwa Regional Legacy Foundation (www.orlf.org), which was created in 2010 when Iowa-based not-for-profit Ottumwa Regional Health Center was acquired by Tennessee-based for-profit RegionalCare Hospital Partners (www.regionalcare.net). The foundation, which has distributed more than $17 million in grants to date, has a mission of improving the health, education, and vitality of the Ottumwa area (Legacy Foundation 2019). By law, at least 5 percent of assets of charitable foundations must be distributed each year.

Although merger-related foundations are clearly doing a substantial amount of good work with their vast amounts of assets—estimated at roughly $20 billion—they have their critics. Most of the criticism stems from the close relationships that many foundations have with the for-profit providers that created them. Indeed, some foundations—instead of being funded entirely with cash—have ownership interests in the for-profit acquirer, a situation that can easily prompt conflicts of interest. One not-for-profit foundation even lost its tax-exempt status because it squandered millions of dollars on overpriced clinics, excessive compensation, and extravagant spending on personal items for managers and employees. Not-for-profit hospitals usually are constrained by competitive forces, whereas the burden of oversight at charitable foundations falls completely on the board of trustees.

Many states have passed laws in recent years to ensure that hospital conversions are subject to full public scrutiny and oversight. For example, Georgia's law requires not-for-profit hospitals that are being sold or merged to file with the state attorney general's office, regardless of whether the merger is with a for-profit or a not-for-profit business. Such filings, which become public information, must include the merger plan plus any financial gain that would accrue to board members, physicians, or managers. Furthermore, the state has the power to hold public hearings to determine whether the buyer is paying fair market value for the target hospital.

The second major problem, in addition to that posed by charitable trust requirements, involves the tax-exempt, or municipal, debt that not-for-profit targets typically carry. Such debt is issued for the sole purpose of funding property and equipment owned by not-for-profit corporations. Furthermore, such debt usually has restrictive covenants that constrain the provider from merger activity that would lower the creditworthiness of the bonds or negatively affect the bonds' tax-exempt status.

To somewhat ease the conversion problems associated with municipal debt, many not-for-profit providers now include the so-called *Columbia clause* in their municipal bond indentures. In most indentures, the issuing hospital lists the circumstances under which the bonds may be redeemed before maturity. The Columbia clause allows bonds to be redeemed in the instance of a sale, lease, or joint venture with a for-profit firm involving a facility that had been financed with tax-exempt debt. Before placing such clauses in municipal bond indentures, hospitals selling to for-profit entities had to obtain private-letter rulings from the Internal Revenue Service (IRS) to retire the bonds or make a tender offer to bondholders, and both of these mechanisms are relatively expensive compared to a call triggered by the clause.

Clearly, the restrictions on mergers involving not-for-profit firms and for-profit firms make such activities more complicated than mergers involving only for-profits or only not-for-profits. Nevertheless, these kinds of mergers do occur.

SELF-TEST QUESTIONS

1. What is the charitable trust doctrine, and what impact does it have on for-profit acquisitions of not-for-profit firms?
2. What unique problems arise in the acquisition of a not-for-profit business by an investor-owned business as a result of outstanding municipal debt?

Business Valuation

Businesses are valued for many purposes, including acquisitions, divestitures, and estate tax assessments. Our discussion here focuses on valuation for acquisition purposes, but the basic principles of valuation are applicable to all purposes. A key point to remember throughout this discussion is that **business valuation is an imprecise process**. The best that can be done, even by professional *appraisers* who conduct these valuations on a regular basis, is to attain a reasonable valuation, as opposed to a precise one.

Many different approaches can be used to value businesses, but we confine our discussion to the two most commonly used in the health services industry: (1) discounted cash flow and (2) market multiple. However, regardless of the valuation approach, it is crucial to recognize two factors that affect acquisition valuations. First, the business being valued typically will not continue to operate as a separate entity but will become part of the acquiring business's portfolio of assets. Thus, any changes in ownership form or operations that will occur as a result of the proposed acquisition and affect the value of the target business must be considered in the analysis. Second, the goal of merger valuation is to set the value of the target business's equity, or ownership position, because a business is acquired from its owners, not from its creditors. Thus, although we use the phrase "business valuation," the ultimate goal is to value the equity stake in the business rather than its total value.

Discounted Cash Flow Approach

On the web at: *ache.org/HAP/PinkSong8e*

The *discounted cash flow (DCF)* approach to valuing a business involves the application of traditional capital budgeting procedures to an entire business rather than to a single project. To apply this approach, we need two key items: (1) a set of pro forma statements that contain the incremental cash flows expected to result from the merger and (2) a discount rate, or cost of capital, to apply to these cash flows. There are two primary methods of DCF analysis: (1) the free operating cash flow method and (2) the free cash flow to equityholders method. The methods differ in how the cash flows and discount rate are formulated.

The development of accurate postmerger cash flow forecasts is the most important step in the DCF approach. In a pure *financial merger*—a merger in which no synergies are expected—the incremental postmerger cash flows are simply the expected cash flows of the target firm if it were to continue to operate independently. However, even in this situation, the cash flows of a healthcare provider may be difficult to forecast because the industry is changing so rapidly. In an *operational merger*—a merger in which operations are to be integrated—the acquiring firm usually intends to change the target's operations to achieve better results, so forecasting future cash flows is even more complex.

Exhibit 16.2 contains projected profit and loss (P&L) statements for Doctors' Hospital, an investor-owned hospital that is being evaluated as a possible acquisition by United Health Services Corporation (UHSC), a large integrated healthcare business. These statements are formatted similar to income statements, but they (1) focus on cash flows rather than on accounting income and (2) do not have to conform to generally accepted accounting principles (GAAP). The projected data are for the postmerger period, so all synergistic effects have been included in the estimates. Doctors' currently uses 50 percent debt, and if it were acquired, UHSC would maintain Doctors' debt ratio at 50 percent. Doctors' has a 30 percent marginal tax rate.

Line 1 of exhibit 16.2 contains the forecast for Doctors's net revenues, including patient services revenue and other revenue. Note that all contractual allowances and other adjustments to charges, including collection delays, have been considered, so line 1 contains actual cash revenues. Note also that any change in the hospital's stand-alone forecasted revenues resulting from synergies have been incorporated into the line 1 amounts. Lines 2 and 3 contain the cash expense forecasts, while line 4 lists depreciation, a noncash expense. Again, the expense amounts pertain to Doctors's operations if the merger takes place, so savings resulting from efficiencies are included. Line 5—which is line 1 minus lines 2, 3, and 4—contains the EBIT projection for each year.

In the P&L forecasts, interest expense is shown in line 6. Note that line 6 includes both interest on Doctors's existing debt and interest on any

EXHIBIT 16.2
Doctors' Hospital: Projected Profit and Loss Statements and Retention Estimates (in millions of dollars)

	2019	*2020*	*2021*	*2022*	*2023*
1. Net revenues	$105.0	$126.0	$151.0	$174.0	$191.0
2. Patient services expenses	80.0	94.0	111.0	127.0	137.0
3. Other expenses	9.0	12.0	13.0	16.0	16.0
4. Depreciation	8.0	8.0	9.0	9.0	10.0
5. EBIT	$ 8.0	$ 12.0	$ 18.0	$ 22.0	$ 28.0
6. Interest	4.0	4.0	5.0	5.0	6.0
7. EBT	$ 4.0	$ 8.0	$ 13.0	$ 17.0	$ 22.0
8. Taxes (30 percent)	1.2	2.4	3.9	5.1	6.6
9. Net profit	$ 2.8	$ 5.6	$ 9.1	$ 11.9	$ 15.4
10. Estimated retentions	$ 4.0	$ 4.0	$ 7.0	$ 9.0	$ 12.0

Note: EBIT = earnings before interest and taxes; EBT = earnings before taxes

new debt expected to be issued to help fund future growth. Line 7 contains the EBT, and line 8 lists the taxes that would be incurred at a 30 percent marginal rate, which is the rate that would be applied to the combined enterprise. Line 9 lists each year's profit or loss. Finally, because some of Doctors's assets are expected to wear out or become obsolete, and because UHSC plans to expand the hospital if the acquisition occurs, some equity funds must be retained and reinvested in the subsidiary to pay for asset replacement and growth. These retentions, which are not available for transfer from the hospital to the UHSC parent, are shown in line 10.

The postmerger cash flows attributable to the target firm are extremely difficult to estimate, but in a friendly merger, the acquiring firm would send a team of dozens of accountants, financial analysts, engineers, and so forth to the target firm to go over its books, set values on assets such as real estate, estimate required maintenance expenditures, and the like. This work would be done as part of a due diligence analysis, which we discuss in a later section.

Exhibit 16.3 provides relevant cost of capital data for Doctors'. These data are used to set the discount rates in the DCF valuations.

Free Operating Cash Flow Method

On the web at: *ache.org/HAP/PinkSong8e*

As its name implies, the *free operating cash flow* method focuses on operating cash flows, which creates a value estimate for the entire business. Remember that operating cash flows do not recognize financial expenses, so debt payments are not subtracted when operating flows are constructed. Because our ultimate goal is to value the equity position in a business, the value of the debt financing must be stripped out after the overall business has been valued.

Free operating cash flow is defined as net operating profit after taxes (NOPAT) and is calculated as (EBIT × [1 − T]) plus noncash expenses

EXHIBIT 16.3 Doctors' Hospital: Selected Cost-of-Capital Data and Calculations

Cost of equity	18.2%
Cost of debt	12.0%
Proportion of debt financing	0.50
Proportion of equity financing	0.50
Tax rate	30.0%

$$\begin{aligned} \text{CCC} &= [w_d \times R(R_d) \times (1 - T)] + [w_e \times R(R_e)] \\ &= [0.50 \times 12.0\% \times (1 - 0.30)] + [0.50 \times 18.2\%] \\ &= 4.2\% + 9.1\% = 13.3\%. \end{aligned}$$

Note: See chapter 9 for a discussion of the corporate cost of capital.

(depreciation) less the portion of the operating cash flow needed for reinvestment in the business. Exhibit 16.4 uses the data contained in exhibit 16.2 to forecast the free operating cash flows for Doctors'. In merger valuations using the free operating cash flow method, the term *free* means cash flows available to the enterprise after all expenses—including asset replacement costs and costs supporting growth—have been taken into account.

Now, because the cash flows in exhibit 16.4 are operating cash flows—like the cash flows in a conventional capital budgeting analysis—the appropriate discount rate is the corporate cost of capital. Should it be UHSC's corporate cost of capital? No. The cost of capital must reflect the riskiness of the cash flows being discounted, so the appropriate rate (which was estimated in exhibit 16.3 to be 13.3 percent) is that for Doctors'. At this discount rate, the present value of the free operating cash flows shown in exhibit 16.4—discounted back to the end of 2018 (the beginning of 2019)—is $46.9 million. (If the merger will affect the riskiness of the cash flows being discounted, an adjustment must be made to the target's corporate cost of capital to reflect this change.)

Note that we have projected only five years of cash flows; UHSC would likely operate Doctors' for many years—perhaps 30 or more. If the free operating cash flows given in exhibit 16.4 are assumed to grow at a constant rate after 2023, the constant growth model can be used to estimate Doctors's *terminal value*. (The constant growth model was first introduced in chapter 7 in connection with stock valuation.) Assuming a constant 5 percent growth rate in free operating cash flow forever, the terminal value is estimated to be $222.7 million:

$$\text{Terminal value} = \frac{\text{2023 Cash flow} \times (1 + \text{Growth rate})}{\text{Corporate cost of capital} - \text{Growth rate}}$$

$$= \frac{\$17.6 \times 1.05}{0.133 - 0.05} = \frac{\$18.48}{0.083}$$

$$= \$222.7 \text{ million.}$$

EXHIBIT 16.4
Doctors' Hospital: Selected Cost-of-Capital Data and Calculations (in millions of dollars

	2019	*2020*	*2021*	*2022*	*2023*
1. NOPAT (EBIT × (1 – T))	$5.6	$ 8.4	$12.6	$15.4	$19.6
2. Plus depreciation	8.0	8.0	9.0	9.0	10.0
3. Less total retentions	4.0	4.0	7.0	9.0	12.0
4. Free operating cash flow	$9.6	$12.4	$14.6	$15.4	$17.6

The terminal value of Doctors', which represents the value at the end of 2023 of all cash flows beyond 2023, is $119.3 million when discounted back to 2018 at the 13.3 percent corporate cost of capital.

The final estimate of the total value of Doctors' to UHSC is $46.9 + $119.3 = $166.2 million. However, Doctors' has outstanding debt that has a current market value of $55.7 million, so the ownership (equity) value of the hospital is $166.2 – $55.7 = $110.5 million.

Free Cash Flow to Equityholders Method

On the web at: *ache.org/HAP/PinkSong8e*

The *free cash flow to equityholders* method—also called the *equity residual* method—focuses solely on the cash flows that would be available to UHSC's stockholders, which are developed in exhibit 16.5. Note that the starting cash flow in exhibit 16.5 is net profit as opposed to NOPAT, which was used in the net operating cash flow method, so interest expense is deducted when the cash flows are constructed. Also, because asset replacement and additions are assumed to be financed at the optimal capital structure, 50 percent of the retentions represent debt financing. Thus, the values in exhibit 16.5, which represent the amount of equity financing retained for reinvestment in the business, are only half of the amounts used in the net operating cash flow method.

Because the cash flows shown in line 4 of exhibit 16.5 are equity flows (as opposed to operating flows), they should be discounted at the cost of equity rather than at the corporate cost of capital. Furthermore, the cost of equity used must reflect the riskiness of the free cash flows in the exhibit, so the discount rate is more closely aligned with the cost of equity of Doctors' than with the cost of equity of either UHSC or the consolidated enterprise.

As before, the current value of Doctors' to UHSC is the present value of the free cash flows given in exhibit 16.5 plus the terminal value, all discounted at the 18.2 percent cost of equity. The present value of the cash flows in exhibit 16.5 is $41.4 million. The terminal value (calculated in a manner similar to the way it was calculated in the free operating cash flow method) is $154.3 million, and its present value is $66.9 million. Thus, the equity value of Doctors' is $41.4 + $66.9 = $108.3 million.

EXHIBIT 16.5 Doctors' Hospital: Projected Free Cash Flow to Equityholders (in millions of dollars)

	2019	*2020*	*2021*	*2022*	*2023*
1. Net profit	$2.8	$ 5.6	$ 9.1	$11.9	$15.4
2. Plus depreciation	8.0	8.0	9.0	9.0	10.0
3. Less equity retentions	2.0	2.0	3.5	4.5	6.0
4. Free cash flow to equityholders	$8.8	$11.6	$14.6	$16.4	$19.4

Of course, we "cooked the books" to ensure that the value came out to be close under both of the DCF methods. Still, in real-world valuations, the two methods would produce relatively close results if the assumptions are consistent, so either can be used.

Note that the final value estimate of Doctors' probably would be higher than the DCF value. The reason is that the DCF method values only the **operations** of the business. Thus, $108.3 million represents the value of all of the business's assets that support operations. Many businesses hold some nonoperating assets, such as marketable securities holdings, in excess of that required for operations or hold real estate that will not be needed in the foreseeable future to support operations. The overall value of a business is the sum of its *operational value*, as estimated by the DCF method, plus the market values of any nonoperating assets. In this example, we assume that Doctors' does not have material nonoperating assets, so a reasonable estimate of its value is $100 million.

Obviously, UHSC would try to buy Doctors' at as low a price as possible, while Doctors' owners would hold out for the highest possible price. The final price is determined by negotiation, and the stronger negotiator will capture most of the incremental value. The larger the synergistic benefits, the more room for bargaining and the higher the probability that the merger will actually be consummated. We will have more to say about setting the bid price in a later section.

Although we do not illustrate it here, UHSC would perform a risk analysis on the cash flows in both exhibit 16.4 and exhibit 16.5, just as it does on any set of capital budgeting flows. Generally, scenario analysis and Monte Carlo simulation would be used to give UHSC's management some feel for the risks involved with the acquisition and resulting range of valuations. In the illustration, as with many healthcare mergers, the target firm is investor owned but not publicly traded, so it is not possible to obtain a market beta on Doctors' stock. However, we can obtain market betas of the stocks of the major investor-owned hospital chains, and these values can be used to help estimate the capital costs given in exhibit 16.3.

Market Multiple Analysis

On the web at: *ache.org/HAP/PinkSong8e*

Another method of valuing a business is *market multiple analysis*, which applies a market-determined multiple to some proxy for value—typically some measure of revenues or earnings. As in the DCF valuation approach, the basic premise here is that the value of any business depends on the cash flows that the business produces. The DCF approach applies this premise in a precise manner, while market multiple analysis is more ad hoc.

For example, suppose that in recent hospital mergers, acquirers have been willing to pay six times the EBITDA of the target. *EBITDA*—earnings before interest, taxes, depreciation, and amortization—is one of the more common proxies for value used in market multiple analyses. To estimate the value of Doctors' using this method, note that its 2019 EBITDA estimate is $8 million in EBIT plus $8 million in depreciation, or $16 million. If we multiply EBITDA by the market multiple 6, we obtain a value of $96 million for Doctors'. Because equity multiples are typically used in these analyses, the resulting value is the equity, or ownership, value of the business.

For an illustration of another, less direct value proxy, consider the nursing home industry. In recent years, prices paid for nursing home acquisitions have ranged from $80,000 to $120,000 per bed, for an average of roughly $100,000. Thus, using number of beds as the proxy for value, a nursing home with 50 beds would be valued at 50 × $100,000 = $5 million.

Asset-Based Valuation Approaches

We have discussed two methods of business valuation: discounted cash flow and market multiple. But several other methods can also be used, including asset-based valuation, which has three different approaches. All asset-based valuation approaches look to the balance sheet for answers, but the values used for the asset and liability accounts differ for each approach.

- **Book value.** Book value is merely the value of the equity account on the business's balance sheet. Note that, according to GAAP, balance sheet asset values typically reflect historical costs reduced by book depreciation, when applicable.
- **Liquidation value.** Liquidation value is the amount that remains if the assets of the business were quickly sold, without taking the time to obtain full market value, and then the proceeds are used to pay off the business's liabilities.
- **Fair market value.** In this approach, the values of the business's assets and liabilities are first adjusted to reflect their fair market values. Then, the liability values are subtracted from the asset values to obtain the valuation estimate.

What is your opinion of asset-based valuation? Do you think there are some situations in which asset-based valuation may be superior to either the discounted cash flow approach or market multiple analysis?

Comparison of the Two Methods

Clearly, the valuation of a business can be considered only a rough estimate. Although the DCF approach has strong theoretical support, one has to be concerned over the validity of the estimated cash flows, growth rates, and discount rates applied to those flows. Just a little variation in any of these estimates can create large differences in estimated value.

Market multiple analysis is more ad hoc, but its proponents argue that a proxy estimate for a single year—such as that measured by EBITDA—is more likely to be accurate than a multiple-year cash flow forecast. Furthermore, market multiple analysis sidesteps the problems of having to estimate a terminal value and discount rate. Of course, market multiple analysis has problems of its own. One concern is the comparability between the business being analyzed and the firm (or firms) that set the market multiple. Another concern is how well one year, or even an average of several years, of EBITDA captures the value of a business that will be operated for many years into the future and whose EBITDA could soar as a result of merger-related synergies.

The bottom line is that there are problems with both methods. In general, business valuations should use both the DCF approach and market multiple analysis as well as other available methods. Then, a great deal of judgment must be applied to reconcile any valuation differences that occur.

SELF-TEST QUESTIONS

1. Briefly describe two approaches commonly used to value acquisition candidates.
2. What are some problems that occur when valuing target firms?
3. Which approach do you believe to be best? Explain your answer.

Unique Problems in Valuing Small Businesses

As demonstrated in our discussion, the valuation of potential takeover candidates is a difficult task, even when the target is a large, publicly traded firm. One of the primary difficulties in the process is estimating the right market *capitalization rate*, which is either the discount rate in the DCF approach or the market multiple in market multiple analysis. When the target is a small, privately owned firm—say, a medical practice—the influence of additional factors such as the ones described in the following list might necessitate modification of a rate based on the analysis of large publicly traded firms:

- **Geographic and business line diversification**. Capitalization rates based on large business transactions typically involve businesses that have geographic and business line diversification. If the transaction behind the valuation does not have the same diversification benefits, the capitalization rates may need to be adjusted. For example, the acquisition of one hospital by a large national chain places the target in a large diversified portfolio of hospitals. The same acquisition by a neighboring stand-alone hospital lacks such a diversification benefit. This fact makes the acquisition riskier for the neighbor than for the national chain and hence calls for a higher discount rate or a lower market multiple. Of course, there may be more synergies inherent in merging with the neighbor, which would show up in the valuation as higher cash flow forecasts. Still, the added risk needs to be considered in the valuation process.
- **Owners' diversification**. When a large, publicly traded firm makes an acquisition, the target business is being added to the well-diversified

personal investment portfolios of the acquiring firm's stockholders. Thus, the owners see only market risk in the transaction, as opposed to corporate risk. When mergers take place between smaller businesses or when the acquirer is a not-for-profit business, market risk is not relevant. Thus, the portfolio benefit associated with owners' personal diversification is not applicable, so the riskiness inherent in the transaction may increase.

- **Liquidity (marketability)**. The ownership of a small business lacks liquidity (marketability), which lowers its value relative to the stock of a large firm that is publicly traded. In effect, a liquidity premium should be assessed when valuing small businesses to raise the discount rate used in the DCF approach and lower the multiple used in market multiple analysis. The purpose of all three of these adjustments is to lower the value of the target firm. It is difficult to judge how much lower the value should be because of lack of diversification or liquidity, but it has been suggested that the loss of value is large—as high as 50 percent or more.
- **Control**. Another factor that often arises in valuing closely held businesses is control. The ability to control a business is important, and, as such, it has value. For example, assume that a business valued at $100,000 has three owners—one with 50.2 percent of the stock and two each with 24.9 percent. The value of the stock owned by the controlling stockholder is worth more than the proportionate amount—that is, it is worth more than $50,200, perhaps a great deal more. Similarly, the stock of each of the minority stockholders is worth less than $24,900, which is their proportionate share. The value of *control interests*—as opposed to *minority interests*—must be taken into account when assessing value, especially when less than 100 percent of the stock of the target firm is to be acquired. Furthermore, control issues need to be considered when setting the terms of the acquisition offer.
- **Cash flows of medical practices**. Smaller medical practices typically use a modified cash basis accounting methodology. Furthermore, at the end of each year, any net income generated in excess of that required for retentions is paid out to the owner and physicians as bonuses. To determine the true cash flows that would accrue to an acquirer, the statements must be recast with the bonuses "backed out." The assumption, of course, is that in the absence of bonuses physicians would be willing to work as hard in the future as they do today.

The effects of the factors described here clearly make the valuation of small businesses more difficult than the valuation of large businesses, primarily because of the difficulties in estimating the correct capitalization rate but also because of cash flow forecasting problems. In general, the rates estimated from the data of large businesses must be adjusted to reflect the risk and liquidity factors unique to small businesses. (See chapter 9 for a discussion of the cost of capital to small businesses.)

SELF-TEST QUESTION

1. What unique considerations arise when valuing small, privately held businesses?

Setting the Bid Price

Assume that after a thorough valuation, UHSC concludes that Doctors' is worth $100 million. Furthermore, assume that Doctors' has one million shares of stock outstanding and that some shares sold recently in a private sale at $80 a share. The hospital's total market value is assumed to be $80 million. With an estimated value of $100 million to UHSC, it can offer as much as $100 per share for Doctors' without diluting the value of its own stock.

Exhibit 16.6 illustrates the situation facing UHSC's managers as they set the bid price. The $100 per share maximum offer price is shown as a point on the horizontal axis, which plots bid price. If UHSC pays less—say, $95 a share—its stockholders will gain $5 per share, or $5 million in total, from the merger. On the other hand, if UHSC pays more than $100 per share, its stockholders will lose value. The line that shows the impact of the per share bid price on UHSC's stockholders is a 45-degree downward-sloping line that cuts the *x*-axis at $100. The distance between this diagonal line and the *x*-axis is the amount that UHSC's stockholders will gain, or lose, for each share of Doctors' acquired. The situation facing Doctors' shareholders is depicted by a 45-degree upward-sloping line that crosses the *x*-axis at $80. If the hospital is acquired for more than $80 per share, its shareholders will gain value, but shareholders will lose value if the price is less than $80 per share.

Note that there is a bid price range between $80 and $100 in which the shareholders of both UHSC and Doctors' would benefit from the merger. The range exists because the merger has synergistic benefits that can be divided between the two groups of stockholders. The greater the synergistic benefits, the greater the range of feasible bid prices and the greater the chance that the merger will be consummated.

The issue of how to divide the synergistic benefit is critically important in any merger transaction. Obviously, both parties will want to gain as much as possible. If Doctors' owners knew the maximum price that UHSC

EXHIBIT 16.6
Evaluating the Takeover Bid

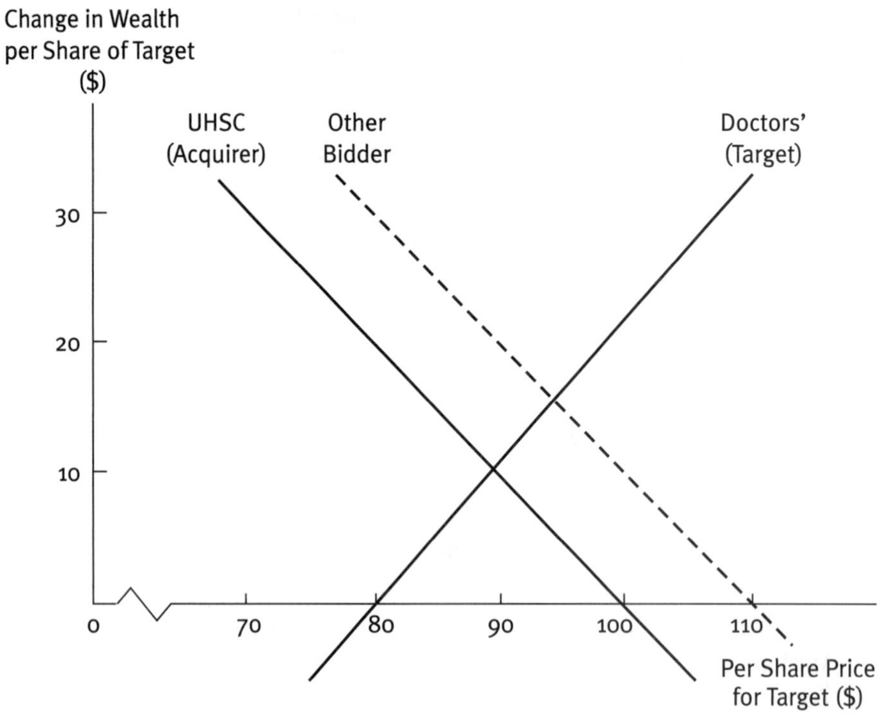

is willing to pay—$100—they would hold out for that price. UHSC, on the other hand, will try to acquire the hospital at a price as close to $80 per share as possible. Where in the $80 to $100 range should UHSC set its initial bid? The answer depends on a number of factors, including whether UHSC will pay with cash or securities, whether the managers of UHSC or Doctors' have the better negotiating skills, and whether another bidder is likely to enter the picture.

The likelihood of a bidding war for Doctors' is influential in setting the initial bid. Suppose that no other bidder is likely. In this situation, UHSC might make a relatively low take-it-or-leave-it offer, and Doctors' owners might take it because some gain is better than no gain. On the other hand, assume that Doctors' is in a unique position that makes it attractive to several competing health systems. Now, when UHSC announces its bid, other bidders may enter the fray, and the final price will likely be close to $100 per share. Perhaps another potential acquirer can achieve even greater synergies with Doctors' than can UHSC, as shown in exhibit 16.6 by the dashed line labeled "Other Bidder." If so, the bid price could increase to more than $100, in which case UHSC should drop out of the bidding.

UHSC would, of course, want to keep secret its maximum bid, and it would plan its bidding strategy carefully and consistently according to the situation. If UHSC thought that other bidders would emerge or that Doctors' owners would resist a bid, UHSC might decide to make a high ***preemptive***, or ***knockout***, ***bid*** in hopes of scaring off competing bids, eliminating any resistance to the merger, or both. On the other hand, if no other bidders were expected, UHSC might make a lowball bid in hopes of "stealing" the hospital.

Another factor that influences the initial bid is the employment and control situation. First, consider the sale of a small, owner-managed firm to a larger concern. The owner–manager may be anxious to retain a high-status position, and he may also have developed a close relationship with the firm's employees and thus be concerned about keeping operating control of the organization after the merger. These points are often stressed during merger negotiations. When a large, publicly owned firm merges with another firm, the acquired firm's management is also worried about its postmerger position. If the acquiring firm agrees to retain the acquired firm's management, it may be willing to support the merger and recommend its acceptance to the firm's stockholders. If the acquired firm's management will be removed, it will probably resist the merger.

SELF-TEST QUESTIONS

1. How does the amount of potential synergistic benefits affect the likelihood that a merger will be consummated?
2. What are some factors that influence the starting and final bid prices?

Structuring the Takeover Bid

If the acquiring firm is investor owned, its offer to target shareholders can take the form of cash, equity securities (stock) of the acquiring firm, debt securities (bonds) of the acquiring firm, or a combination of the three. The structure of the bid is extremely important because it affects (1) the capital structure of the postmerger firm, (2) the tax treatment of the acquiring firm and the target's stockholders, (3) the ability of the target firm's stockholders to reap the rewards of future merger-related gains, and (4) the types of federal and state regulations to which the acquiring firm will be subjected. In this section, we focus on how taxes and regulation influence the structure of acquiring firms' offers.

The form of payment offered to the target's shareholders determines the personal tax treatment of the target's stockholders. Target shareholders do not have to pay taxes on the transaction if they maintain a substantial equity position in the combined firm. According to the IRS, a ***substantial equity position*** means at least 50 percent of the payment to target shareholders must be in shares (either common or preferred) of the acquiring firm. In such nontaxable offers, target shareholders do not realize capital gains or losses until the equity securities they receive in the takeover are sold. However, capital gains must be taken and treated as income in the transaction year if cash, debt securities, or a combination of the two make up more than 50 percent of an offer.

All else equal, target stockholders prefer nontaxable offers, especially when they believe that the combined firm will perform well, because they can (1) benefit from the continuing good performance of the combined firm and (2) postpone the realization of capital gains and payment of taxes. Most target shareholders are thus willing to sell their stock for a lower price in a nontaxable offer than in a taxable offer. As a result, one might expect nontaxable bids to dominate; however, other factors are at work. If a firm pays more than book value for a target firm's assets in a taxable merger, it can write up those assets, depreciate the marked-up value for tax purposes, and thus lower the postmerger firm's taxes vis-à-vis the combined amount of taxes the two firms would have each paid separately. However, if the acquiring firm writes up the target firm's assets for tax purposes, the target firm must pay capital gains taxes in the year the merger occurs. (These taxes can be avoided if the acquiring firm elects not to write up acquired assets and depreciates them on their old basis.)

Securities laws also affect the construction of an offer. As we discussed in chapter 7, the Securities and Exchange Commission (SEC) has oversight over the issuance of new securities, including stock or debt issued in connection with a merger. Therefore, whenever a corporation bids for control of another firm through the exchange of equity or debt securities, the entire process must take place under the scrutiny of the SEC. The time required for such reviews allows target management to implement defensive tactics and allows other firms to make competing offers. As a result, most hostile tender offers are for cash rather than securities.

SELF-TEST QUESTIONS

1. What are some alternative ways of structuring takeover bids?
2. How do taxes influence the payment structure?
3. How do securities laws affect the payment structure?

Due Diligence Analysis

One of the most important aspects of a merger is *due diligence analysis*. In generic terms, due diligence is the level of judgment, care, and prudence that a person would be reasonably expected to achieve before taking some action. The term *due diligence* first came into common use as a result of the United States Securities Act of 1933. This act included a defense, referred to as the *due diligence defense*, which could be used by securities dealers when accused of inadequate disclosure to investors of material information with respect to the purchase of securities. As long as brokers exercised due diligence in their investigation into the company whose securities they were selling and then disclosed to the investor what they found, brokers would not be held liable for nondisclosure of information that was not discovered in the process of that investigation. The dealer community quickly adopted, as standard practice, due diligence analysis of any securities offerings in which dealers were involved. Originally, the term was limited to public offerings of securities investments, but over time it has come to be associated with investigations of mergers and acquisitions as well.

The primary purposes of a merger due diligence analysis are (1) to uncover issues that would prevent the acquirer from pursuing the acquisition and (2) to provide the acquirer with insights into the day-to-day operations of the target firm so that an appropriate transaction can take place. The acquirer must take a uniform, disciplined approach to due diligence analysis to minimize the risk of overlooking issues that are key to a successful acquisition.

Due diligence analysis normally takes place after the acquiring and target firms have signed a letter of intent but before the terms of the transaction have been completed. It is normally carried out by a team that has been specially assembled for the task. Typically, the team includes one or two top executives and specialists from applicable staffs such as finance, legal, medical, nursing, personnel, risk management, and engineering. The team may consist entirely of personnel from the acquiring firm, or it may include consultants in addition to the in-house members.

The due diligence team gathers and analyzes information about the acquisition. The end result is a report that summarizes the team's findings and makes recommendations as to whether to proceed with the acquisition and, if so, how the deal should be structured. The time required to conduct a due diligence analysis varies according to the number of individuals on the team, the nature of the acquisition, and the accessibility of information. Generally, however, due diligence analyses take about 60 days to 90 days, so acquirers must allow sufficient time for due diligence analysis when developing merger timetables.

A thorough due diligence analysis is a necessary component of the acquisition process. In addition to protecting the acquirer against a poor acquisition, it can foster a relationship between the acquiring and target firms' management that not only facilitates successful negotiations but, more important, can also lead to a successful merger.

SELF-TEST QUESTIONS

1. What is due diligence analysis?
2. Why is due diligence analysis so important in the merger process?

Corporate Alliances

Mergers are one way for two firms to join forces, but many firms are striking cooperative deals called *corporate alliances* that do not integrate the two entities as thoroughly as merging would. Whereas mergers combine all of the assets of the firms involved—as well as managerial and technical expertise—to create a single surviving business entity, alliances create new entities that focus on specific business lines that have the most potential for synergies. These alliances take many forms—from straightforward marketing agreements to joint ownership of world-scale operations.

A common form of corporate alliance is the *joint venture*, in which parts of firms join to achieve specific, limited objectives. A joint venture is controlled by a management team consisting of representatives of the two, or more, parent firms. Joint ventures are becoming more prevalent in the health services industry as it strives to consolidate both insurance and provider functions. For example, Select Medical Corporation (www.selectmedical.com), UC San Diego Health (https://health.ucsd.edu) and Vibra Healthcare (www.vibrahealthcare.com) recently announced the formation of two joint ventures to serve San Diego and its surrounding communities. Under the agreements, one joint venture will operate a critical illness recovery hospital, also known as long-term acute care, and the other will operate an inpatient rehabilitation hospital. As part of the joint ventures, Vibra Healthcare contributed its existing Vibra Hospital of San Diego, maintaining majority ownership. Select Medical serves as the new operating manager of the hospital and has been renamed Select Specialty Hospital—San Diego (Select Medical 2018).

Another example is the 2014 creation of GSK Consumer Healthcare (www.gsk.com/en-gb/about-us/consumer-healthcare), a joint venture of

GlaxoSmithKline (www.gsk.com) and Novartis (www.novartis.com), two major pharmaceutical companies. As the name implies, Glaxo will control the business with 63.5 percent ownership and 7 of the 11 directors. The joint venture—with sales of roughly $11 billion—combines the two company's over-the-counter and food supplement businesses. With this venture, the two companies are looking to add scale to better compete with larger consumer-focused rivals as well as reduce costs by as much as $650 million annually.

A joint venture analysis is similar to a merger analysis, except that there are multiple classes of equity investors (partners), each having its own set of cash flows and risk. The financial attractiveness of the venture to each partner is assessed by breaking down the overall cash flows to the venture into individual partner distributions. Then, each partner's cash flows are discounted at a cost of equity that reflects the unique risk faced by that partner. In effect, each partner conducts its own capital budgeting analysis to determine whether the venture is in its best interest.

For an example of an alliance other than a joint venture, consider the BJC Collaborative (www.bjc.org), which is a nonownership agreement among four not-for-profit health systems (i.e., BJC HealthCare, St. Luke's Health System, Cox-Health, Memorial Health System) owning 30 hospitals located primarily in Missouri. The agreement aims to reduce costs for the four systems by allowing coordination of purchases and hence realizing economies of scale. The collaborative will not have a physical location or its own employees but will be managed by "operating committees" representing the leadership teams from each system.

SELF-TEST QUESTIONS

1. What is the difference between a merger and a corporate alliance?
2. What is a joint venture? Give some reasons why joint ventures may be advantageous to the parties involved.

Goodwill

We close this chapter by briefly discussing the accounting concept of goodwill, which recognizes that the price paid for an acquired business is usually greater than its book value. In such situations, balance sheet asset values are increased, or written up, to recognize that the assets are worth more than their book values. The balance sheet is rebalanced by adding the dollar amount of the asset write-up to the book value of equity to obtain a new equity value called the ***net asset value***. Then, if the purchase price exceeds the net asset value, this excess is placed on the balance sheet of the combined enterprise in an asset account called ***goodwill***. The theory is that the business being acquired has some intangible asset, such as a trademark or consumer (patient) loyalty, that creates value that exceeds the value of the business's tangible assets.

For example, assume that Big Hospital is acquiring Small Hospital (SH) for $20 million. SH's premerger balance sheet has $10 million in liabilities and $10 million in equity. Furthermore, SH's total assets will be written up from $20 million to $25 million. The result is a net asset value for SH of $10 million + $5 million = $15 million. Now, with a purchase price of $20 million versus a net asset value of $15 million, the merger will create $5 million in goodwill that will appear on the asset side of the combined balance sheet.

What happens to goodwill? Under old accounting guidelines, it was written off over 40 years, so $5 million ÷ 40 = $125,000 in goodwill amortization expense would have appeared on the combined income statement for the next 40 years. Under current guidelines, goodwill "sits" on the balance sheet until some event occurs that reduces (impairs) its value. An organization's auditors are required to test the goodwill annually for impairment to ensure that the value of the asset has not decreased over time. Then the entire amount—or some portion thereof—is written off. Because it is not a cash expense, the expensing of goodwill does not affect a business's cash flow, but it does lower reported income and earnings per share.

Note that goodwill is a residual of the merger valuation rather than a component—that is, often you will hear someone ask, "Where is the premium for goodwill?" Any amount paid for goodwill must stem from the valuation process described previously. If this process does not identify a value that exceeds the balance sheet net asset value, the business has no goodwill, or at least none that raises its value above that stated on the balance sheet.

SELF-TEST QUESTION

1. Describe the concept of goodwill.

Chapter Key Concepts

This chapter examines mergers and acquisitions, including business valuation. Here are its key concepts:

- A *merger* occurs when two firms combine to form a single firm.
- In most mergers, one firm (the *acquirer*) initiates action to take over another (the *target*).
- The primary *motives* for mergers are (1) synergy, (2) excess cash, (3) purchase of assets for less than replacement cost, (4) diversification, (5) personal incentives, and (6) breakup value.
- A *horizontal* merger occurs when two firms in the same line of business combine. A *vertical* merger is the combination of a firm with one of its customers or suppliers. A *conglomerate* merger occurs when firms in totally different industries combine.
- In a *friendly merger*, the managers of both firms approve the merger, whereas in a *hostile merger*, the target firm's management opposes the merger.
- *Merger analysis* consists of three tasks: (1) valuing the target firm, (2) setting the bid price, and (3) structuring the bid.
- Two approaches are most commonly used to *value businesses*: (1) discounted cash flow (DCF) approach and (2) market multiple analysis.
- The DCF approach has two variations: (1) the *free operating cash flow method* focuses on operating cash flows, which are available to distribute to both debt and equity investors, and (2) the *free cash flow to equityholders method* focuses on cash flows available solely to equityholders.
- *Market multiple analysis* selects some proxy for value—such as earnings before interest, taxes, depreciation, and amortization (EBITDA)—and multiplies it by a multiple derived from recent merger transactions.
- The *DCF approach* has the strongest theoretical basis, but its inputs—projected cash flows and discount rate—are difficult to estimate. Market multiple analysis is somewhat ad hoc, but it requires a much simpler set of inputs.

(continued)

(continued from previous page)

- The valuation of *small businesses* is complicated by several factors, including (1) lack of geographic and business line diversification, (2) lack of owners' diversification, (3) and lack of liquidity.
- Potential acquirers undertake *due diligence analysis* (1) to uncover issues that would prevent the acquirer from pursuing the acquisition and (2) to gain insight into the day-to-day operations of the target firm so that an appropriate transaction can take place.
- Mergers are one way for two firms to join forces, but many firms are striking cooperative deals—called *corporate alliances*—that fall short of merging. A *joint venture*, which is one of the more popular forms, is a corporate alliance in which two or more firms combine some of their resources to achieve a specific, limited objective.
- Unique problems arise when not-for-profit firms are involved in mergers with for-profit firms. Two are most significant: (1) A *charitable foundation* must be created from the merger proceeds, and (2) all *tax-exempt debt* must be refunded.
- *Goodwill*, a balance sheet asset account, is created when a business is acquired for more than its *net asset value*.

This concludes our discussion of business combinations and valuation as well as the chapters of the book itself. Note that there are two online chapters that accompany this book: chapter 17 (Distributions to Owners: Bonuses, Dividends, and Repurchases) and chapter 18 (Financial Risk Management).

Chapter Models, Problems, and Minicases

The following ancillary resources in spreadsheet format are available for this chapter:

- A chapter model that shows how to perform many of the calculations described in the chapter
- Problems that test your ability to perform the calculations
- A minicase that is more complicated than the problems and tests your ability to perform the calculations in preparation for a case

These resources can be accessed online at ache.org/HAP/PinkSong8e.

Selected Cases

Three cases in *Cases in Healthcare Finance*, sixth edition, are applicable to this chapter:

- Case 30: St. Benedict's Teaching Hospital, which focuses on the valuation and acquisition of one hospital by another
- Case 31: Beachside Health Partners, which examines the feasibility of a proposed joint venture
- Case 32: Bedford Clinics, which focuses on the valuation of a medical practice

References

Legacy Foundation. 2019. "Financial Information." Accessed June 20. www.orlf.org/meet-your-foundation/financial-information.

Phillips, L. 2017. "Health Care M&A Deal Volume in 2016 Beats 2015, According to HealthCareMandA.com." Irving Levin Associates. Published January 16. https://products.levinassociates.com/aboutus/press-releases/pr1701healthcare.

Select Medical. 2018. "Select Medical, UC San Diego Health and Vibra Healthcare Form Two Post-acute Joint Ventures to Serve Southern California." PR Newswire. Published October 17. www.prnewswire.com/news-releases/select-medical-uc-san-diego-health-and-vibra-healthcare-form-two-post-acute-joint-ventures-to-serve-southern-california-300732671.html.

Selected Bibliography

Abrams, M. N., and M. J. Kuckenreuther. 2017. "The Independence Question." *Healthcare Financial Management* 71 (12): 30–33.

Gelineau, S., and R. Green. 2017. "How to Perform a 'Stress Test' on a Proposed Merger or Partnership." *Healthcare Financial Management* 71 (12): 50–56.

Grauman, D. M., D. Bangs, and S. Looby. 2017. "Using Due Diligence to Optimize Post-transaction Benefits." *Healthcare Financial Management* 71 (11): 68–74.

Jordahl, E. A., and M. Robbins. 2018. "Merging Treasury Functions to Optimize Strategic Value." *Healthcare Financial Management* 72 (8): 60–62.

Klar, B. 2018. "Health System Integration: Prescription for Success." *Healthcare Financial Management* 72 (5): 56–60.

Walker, E. W., and J. W. Petty. 1986."Chapter 13." In *Financial Management of the Small Firm*. Upper Saddle River, NJ: Prentice-Hall.

Wilensky, G. R. 2018. "The Continued Move to Greater Integration and Consolidation." *Healthcare Financial Management* 72 (1): 26–27.

Zall, R. J. 2016. "Managing Risk in Today's Healthcare M&A Transaction." *Healthcare Financial Management* 70 (4): 56–64.

Selected Websites

The following websites pertain to the content of this chapter:

- To learn more about merger activity in the health services industry, see the Irving Levin Associates website at www.levinassociates.com.
- For more information on due diligence analysis, see the Healthcare Financial Management Association (HFMA) paper at www.hfma.org/Content.aspx?id=56578.

Integrative Application

The Problem

Assume that Naylor Hospital Corporation (NHC), a large for-profit chain, is conducting a due diligence analysis on the potential acquisition of Brentville Hospital, a stand-alone for-profit hospital. One of the essential aspects of the analysis is to place a value on the target hospital and recommend an initial bid price. The following relevant data have been assembled for performing the valuation:

Brentville Hospital: Profit and Loss Statements and Equity Reinvestment Requirements, Assuming the Acquisition Takes Place (in millions of dollars)

	2019	*2020*	*2021*	*2022*	*2023*
Net revenues	$225.0	$240.0	$250.0	$260.0	$275.0
Cash expenses	200.0	205.0	210.0	215.0	225.0
Depreciation	11.0	12.0	13.0	14.0	15.0
Earnings before interest and taxes (EBIT)	$ 14.0	$ 23.0	$ 27.0	$ 31.0	$ 35.0
Interest expense	8.0	9.0	9.0	10.0	10.0
Earnings before taxes (EBT)	$ 6.0	$ 14.0	$ 18.0	$ 21.0	$ 25.0
Taxes (30 percent)	1.8	4.2	5.4	6.3	7.5
Net profit	$ 4.2	$ 9.8	$ 12.6	$ 14.7	$ 17.5
Equity reinvestment requirements	$ 6.0	$ 6.0	$ 6.0	$ 6.0	$ 6.0

Miscellaneous Data

Brentville Hospital cost of equity	16.0%
Brentville Hospital long-term growth rate	
Best case	6.0%
Most likely case	4.0%
Worst case	2.0%
Average EBITDA market multiple	5.2
Brentville number of shares outstanding	10,000,000
Current price per share	$10.00

The Analysis

The first task in the DCF method is to develop the free equity cash flows (in millions):

	2019	2020	2021	2022	2023
Net revenues	$4.2	$ 9.8	$12.6	$14.7	$ 17.5
Plus: Depreciation	11.0	12.0	13.0	14.0	15.0
Less: Equity reinvestment	6.0	6.0	6.0	6.0	6.0
Free equity operating cash flow	$9.2	$15.8	$19.6	$22.7	$ 26.5
Terminal value					229.7
Free equity cash flow	$9.2	$15.8	$19.6	$22.7	$256.2

Note that the terminal value was estimated using the constant growth model with the most likely growth rate forecast of 4 percent:

$$\text{Terminal value} = (\$26.5 \times 1.04) \div (0.16 - 0.04) = \$229.7.$$

Because these are equity cash flows, the appropriate discount rate is Brentville's 16 percent cost of equity. The present (end of 2018, beginning of 2019) value of this cash flow stream, when discounted at 16 percent, is $193.4 million.

In the best case, using a long-term growth rate estimate of 6 percent, the equity value increases to $221.7 million. Conversely, a drop in the growth rate to 2 percent (the worst case) decreases the equity value to $173.2 million. The point here is that the DCF-estimated value of any business is highly dependent on the assumed long-term growth rate. Any errors in the growth rate estimate can lead to large errors in the value estimate.

Now, let's apply market multiple analysis. Brentville's 2019 EBITDA is $25.0 million:

$$\text{EBITDA} = \text{EBIT} + \text{Depreciation expense} = \$14.0 + \$11.0 = \$25.0.$$

With a market multiple of 5.2, the value estimate is 5.2 × $25.0 = $130.0 million. Assuming that the synergistic effects of the acquisition are not fully realized until 2020, it might be useful to repeat the market multiple estimate for that year: 5.2 × $35.0 = $182.0 million.

Here is a recap of the value estimates (in millions):

DCF method best case	$221.7

DCF method most likely case	$193.4
DCF method worst case	$173.2
Market multiple analysis (2019)	$130.0
Market multiple analysis (2020)	$182.0

The Decision

After reviewing the relevant data, NHC's managers decided to make an all-cash offer of $19.00 per share for Brentville's stock, which results in a total price of $19.00 × 10,000,000 shares outstanding = $190 million. This offer price is based on the most likely DCF value of $193.4 million coupled with the average market multiple value of $130 million. Because many of Brentville's shareholders are physicians that staff the hospital, NHC did not want to create ill will by offering a lowball bid. Furthermore, by offering a premium of more than 50 percent above the current stock price, NHC feels confident that the offer will be accepted with minimum pushback. Finally, with a potential value of $221.7 million (DCF best case) or $182.0 million (2020 market multiple), NHC's shareholders would also benefit from the acquisition. ■

GLOSSARY

Abandonment value. The value of a project if discontinued before the end of its economic life.

Account payable. A balance sheet current liability account created when supplies are received from a vendor but payment has not yet been made.

Account receivable. A balance sheet current asset created when a service is performed but payment has not been received.

Accountable care organization (ACO). A provider organization characterized by a reimbursement model that ties payments to quality metrics and reductions in the total cost of care.

Accounting rate of return (ARR). A capital budgeting metric generally defined as the average dollar return over the life of the project divided by the average investment.

Accrual. A balance sheet liability account created when obligations such as taxes or wages are created but payment has not yet been made.

Acquiring company. A business that seeks to acquire another business.

Adverse selection. The greater incentive to purchase insurance among individuals or businesses that are more likely to have claims.

Agency problem. The problem that arises when an individual (or group)—called the *principal*—hires another individual (or group)—called the *agent*—to perform a service and then delegates decision-making authority to the agent.

Aging schedule. A table that expresses a business's accounts receivable in terms of how long each account has been outstanding.

Alternative minimum tax (AMT). A provision of the federal tax code that requires profit-earning businesses (or individuals) to pay a minimum amount of income tax regardless of the amounts of certain deductions.

Ambulatory payment classification (APC). A set of patient procedures that forms the basis for Medicare reimbursement for hospital outpatient services.

Amortization schedule. A table that breaks down the fixed payment of an installment (amortized) loan into its principal and interest components.

Amortized (installment) loan. A loan that is repaid in equal periodic amounts that include both principal and interest payments.

Annual percentage rate (APR). The stated annual interest rate when compounding occurs more frequently than annually; calculated by multiplying the periodic rate by the number of compounding periods per year. See *effective annual rate (EAR).*

Annual report. A report issued annually by a corporation to its stockholders (or stakeholders) that contains descriptive information and historical financial statements.

Annuity. A series of payments of a fixed amount for a specified number of equal periods.

Annuity due. An annuity whose payments occur at the beginning of each period. See *ordinary (regular) annuity.*

Arbitrage. The simultaneous buying and selling of an identical item in different markets at different prices. This practice enables the arbitrageur—the person or business engaged in arbitrage—to earn a risk-free return.

Asset management ratios. Financial statement analysis ratios that measure how effectively a firm is managing its assets.

Asymmetric information. A situation in contracting where one party has more or better information than the other.

Average collection period (ACP). The average length of time a business takes to collect its receivables. Also called *days sales outstanding (DSO)* and *days in patient accounts receivable.*

Average length of stay (ALOS). The average time a patient spends in an inpatient setting per admission. Also called *length of stay (LOS).*

Balance sheet. A financial statement that lists a business's assets, liabilities, and equity (fund capital).

Base case. In financial analysis, the scenario that is expected to occur as opposed to other scenarios that might occur.

Benchmarking. The comparison of performance factors, such as financial ratios, of one company against those of other companies and industry averages. Also called *comparative analysis.*

Beta coefficient (β). A measure of the risk of one asset relative to the risk of a collection of assets. Often, *beta* refers to the risk of a stock relative to the risk of the overall market as measured by some stock index. See *characteristic line.*

Bond. Long-term debt issued by a business or government unit and generally sold to a large number of individual investors. See *term loan.*

Bond indenture. The loan agreement between the bond issuer and bondholders that spells out the terms of the bond.

Book depreciation. Depreciation calculated according to generally accepted accounting principles (GAAP). See *depreciation.*

Book value. The values of a business's assets, liabilities, and equity as reported on the balance sheet as opposed to the values determined by the marketplace.

Breakeven analysis. An analysis performed to estimate the value required of a single variable for the business (or investment) to either break even (have zero profit) or achieve some profit target (economic breakeven).

Breakup value. The value of a business if its assets are sold off separately.

Build-up method. A method for estimating the cost of equity for a small business that starts with an estimate for a large, publicly traded proxy business and then adds risk premiums to account for risk differentials between large and small businesses.

Bundled (global) reimbursement (pricing). A reimbursement methodology that provides a single payment for an episode of care that involves multiple procedures and multiple providers.

Business risk. The risk inherent in the operations of a business if it uses zero debt (or preferred stock) financing.

Call risk premium (CRP). The premium added to the risk-free rate to account for call risk when estimating a bond's required rate of return.

Callable bond. A bond that has a call provision.

Capital. The funds used to finance a business.

Capital asset pricing model (CAPM). An equilibrium model that specifies the relationship between a stock's value and its market risk as measured by beta. See *security market line (SML).*

Capital budget. A plan (budget) that outlines a company's future expected expenditures on new fixed assets (land, facilities, equipment).

Capital budgeting. The process of analyzing and choosing new fixed assets.

Capital gain (loss). The profit (loss) from the sale of certain assets at more (less) than their purchase price.

Capital gains yield. The percentage of capital gain (loss), usually applied to stocks and bonds.

Capital intensity. The amount of assets required per dollar of sales (revenues), which is the reciprocal of the total-asset-turnover ratio.

Capital market. The financial markets for long-term capital (usually stocks and long-term debt). See *money market.*

Capital rationing. The placement of limitations on new investments in situations in which a business has more attractive investment opportunities than it has capital to invest.

Capital structure. The structure of the liabilities and equity section of a business's balance sheet, often expressed as the percentage of debt financing.

Capitalizing. The process of listing a long-term asset on the balance sheet and then depreciating its cost over time; applies to purchased assets and some leased assets.

Capitation. A reimbursement methodology based on the number of covered lives as opposed to the amount of services provided. See *fee-for-service.*

Case-mix index. A measure of inpatient service intensity calculated by averaging the patient diagnosis-related group (DRG) weights.

Cash budget. A schedule that lists a business's expected cash inflows, outflows, and net cash flows for some future period.

Cash discount. The amount by which a seller is willing to reduce the price for cash payment.

Census. The number of hospital inpatients.

Characteristic line. The simple linear regression line created by plotting individual investment returns on the *y*-axis and portfolio returns on the *x*-axis. The slope of the characteristic line is the investment's beta coefficient. Also called *market characteristic line.*

Charge-based reimbursement. A reimbursement methodology based on charges (chargemaster prices).

Chargemaster. The official list of a provider's charges (prices) for goods and services rendered.

Charitable trust doctrine. A legal doctrine that holds that assets created for a charitable purpose must be used for such a purpose in perpetuity.

Closely held corporation. A corporation, typically small, whose stock is held by a small number of individuals and not publicly traded.

Coefficient of variation. A statistical measure of an investment's stand-alone risk, calculated by dividing the standard deviation of returns by the expected return.

Coinsurance. The amount paid for medical services by a patient, as opposed to the insurer, typically expressed as a percentage of the amount charged—for example, 20 percent of the cost of each outpatient visit.

Combination lease. A lease that contains features of both an operating lease and a financial lease.

Commercial paper. Unsecured short-term promissory notes (debt) issued by large, financially sound businesses.

Community rating. Premiums based on the health status of the entire community as opposed to the characteristics of one group or individual.

Comparative analysis. The comparison of one business's key financial and operating indicators with those of comparable businesses or averages. Also called *benchmarking.*

Compounding. The process of finding the future value of a lump sum, annuity, or series of unequal cash flows. See *discounting.*

Conglomerate merger. A merger of businesses that operate in unrelated lines.

Constant growth method. A valuation model that assumes the investment value will grow at a constant rate in perpetuity.

Consumer-directed health plans (CDHPs). Insurance plans that use financial incentives to influence consumer (patient) behavior.

Convertible bond. A bond that can be exchanged at the option of the bondholder for shares of stock of the issuing firm at a fixed price.

Corporate alliance. A cooperative venture between two businesses that is smaller in scope than a merger.

Corporate bond. Debt issued by for-profit businesses, as opposed to government or tax-exempt (municipal) bonds.

Corporate cost of capital (CCC). The discount rate (opportunity cost of capital) that reflects the overall (average) risk of the entire business. See *divisional cost of capital* and *project cost of capital.*

Corporate goals. Specific aims, including financial, that an organization strives to attain. Generally, corporate goals are qualitative in nature. See *corporate objectives.*

Corporate objectives. Quantitative targets that an organization sets to meet its corporate goals.

Corporate risk. A type of portfolio risk; the portion of the riskiness of a business project that cannot be diversified away by holding the project as part of the business's portfolio of projects. See *market risk.*

Corporation. A legal business entity that is separate and distinct from its owners (or community) and managers.

Correlation. The tendency of two variables to move together.

Correlation coefficient. A standardized measure of correlation that ranges from −1 (variables move perfectly opposite to one another) to +1 (variables move in perfect synchronization).

Cost-based reimbursement. A reimbursement methodology based on the costs incurred in providing services.

Costly trade credit. Credit taken by a company from a vendor in excess of the free trade credit.

Cost of capital. A generic term for the cost of a business's financing. See *corporate cost of capital.*

Cost of debt. The return required (interest rate) on a business's debt financing; a component of the cost of capital.

Cost of equity. The return required on the equity investment in a business; a component of the cost of capital.

Coupon (interest) rate. The stated annual rate of interest on a bond, which is equal to the coupon payment divided by the par value.

Coupon payment. The dollar amount of annual interest on a bond.

Coverage ratio. A debt management ratio that reports the amount of funds available to meet a fixed payment obligation per dollar of obligation. There are many different coverage ratios, depending on the definition of "funds available."

Credit policy. A business's rules and regulations regarding granting credit and collecting from buyers that take the credit.

Credit rating. Rating assigned by a rating agency, such as Standard & Poor's or Moody's, that measures the probability of default on a debt issue.

Current (bond) yield. The annual coupon payment divided by the current bond price.

Current ratio. A liquidity ratio, calculated by dividing total current assets by total current liabilities, that measures the number of dollars of current assets available to pay each dollar of current liabilities.

Dashboard. A format for presenting a business's key performance indicators that resembles the dashboard of an automobile. Dashboards are designed to allow managers to quickly assess the financial or operational performance of the organization.

Days-cash-on-hand ratio. The number of days that a business can meet its cash obligations with only its current cash balance.

Days in patient accounts receivable. The average length of time a provider takes to collect its receivables. Also called *days sales outstanding (DSO)* and *average collection period (ACP).*

Days sales outstanding. The average length of time a business takes to collect its receivables. Also called *average collection period (ACP)* and *days in patient accounts receivable.*

Debenture. An unsecured bond.

Debt capacity. The amount of debt in a business's optimal (target) capital structure.

Debt ratio. A debt utilization ratio that measures the proportion of debt (versus equity) financing; typically defined as total debt (liabilities) divided by total assets.

Debt service requirements. The total amount of principal and interest that has to be paid on an issue either in each year or over the entire life of the issue.

Debt-to-equity ratio. A debt utilization ratio that measures the dollars of debt financing for each dollar of equity financing; typically defined as total debt divided by total equity.

Decision tree. A form of scenario analysis that incorporates multiple decision points over time. The end result resembles a tree on its side with branches extending to the right.

Deductible. The dollar amount that must be spent on healthcare services before benefits are paid by the third-party payer—for example, $2,000 per year.

Default. Failure by a borrower to make a promised interest or principal repayment.

Default risk. The risk that a borrower will not pay the interest (or repay principal) as specified in the loan agreement.

Default risk premium (DRP). The premium that creditors demand (added to the basic interest rate) for bearing default risk. The greater the default risk, the higher the default risk premium.

Demographic approach. An approach to premium setting that focuses on the demographics (primarily age and gender) of the covered population.

Depreciation. A noncash charge against earnings on the income statement that reflects the wear-and-tear on a business's fixed assets. See *book depreciation* and *Modified Accelerated Cost Recovery System (MACRS).*

Derivative. A security whose value stems from the value of another asset—for example, futures and options.

Diagnosis-related group (DRG). A numerical code for a single patient diagnosis. Medicare reimbursement of hospital inpatient services was initially based on DRGs. See *Medicare Serverity Diagnosis-Related Groups (MS-DRGs).*

Discounted cash flow (DCF) analysis. The use of time-value-of-money techniques to value investments.

Discounted payback (period). The number of years it takes for a business to recover its investment in a project when time value of money is considered. See *payback (period).*

Discounting. The process of finding the present value of a lump sum, annuity, or series of unequal cash flows. See *compounding.*

Diversifiable risk. The portion of the risk of an investment that can be eliminated by holding the investment as part of a diversified portfolio. See *portfolio risk.*

Dividend. The periodic payment made to owners of common and preferred stocks.

Dividend reinvestment plan (DRIP). A plan under which the dividends paid to a stockholder are automatically reinvested in the company's common stock.

Dividend yield. The annual dividend divided by current stock price.

Divisional cost of capital. The discount rate (opportunity cost of capital) that reflects the unique riskiness of a division in a corporation. See *corporate cost of capital* and *project cost of capital.*

Due diligence analysis. The process of research and analysis that takes place before making an investment, moving forward with a merger, or forming a business alliance.

Du Pont analysis. A financial statement analysis tool that decomposes return on equity into either (1) three components: profit margin, total asset turnover, and equity multiplier, or (2) two components: return on assets and equity multiplier.

Duration. A measure of the maturity of a debt security that considers both the interest payments and the return of principal; in essence, the weighted average maturity of the security.

EBITDA. A common measure of earnings used in business valuation; defined as earnings before interest, taxes, depreciation, and amortization.

Economic life. The number of years that maximizes the value (net present value) of a project.

Economic value added (EVA). A measure of the economic profitability of a business that considers all costs, including the cost of equity.

Economies of scale. Cost advantages that arise when the ratio of assets (or costs) to sales decreases as sales increase (the business grows). The end result is lower costs per unit as volume grows.

Effective annual rate (EAR). The interest rate that, under annual compounding, produces the same future value as that produced by more frequent compounding. See *annual percentage rate (APR).*

Effective tax rate. The tax rate on the next dollar of income, including all applicable taxes.

Efficient markets hypothesis. The theory that states that (1) stocks are always in equilibrium and (2) it is impossible for investors to consistently earn excess returns (beat the market).

Employee stock ownership plan (ESOP). A retirement plan in which employees own the stock of the employing company.

Equilibrium. In an efficient market, the premise that prices instantaneously move toward equilibrium between supply and demand.

Equivalent annual annuity. A technique for comparing the profitability of competing projects that have different lives. See *replacement chain.*

Exercise price. In options, the price at which the underlying security can be purchased (call option) or sold (put option); also called *strike price.*

Expected rate of return. The return expected on an investment when the purchase is made. See *realized rate of return.*

Expected value. In statistics, the probability-weighted value of a numerical distribution; otherwise, the value for an uncertain variable that is anticipated to occur.

External financing plan. An organization's plan for meeting its external financing requirements.

External financing requirement. The dollar amount needed to meet a capital budget in excess of the amount of internal funding (retained earnings).

Fee-for-service. A reimbursement methodology in which a payment is made each time a service is provided. See *capitation.*

Finance lease. A lease agreement that has a term (life) approximately equal to the expected useful life of the leased asset. See *operating lease.*

Financial asset. A security, such as a stock or bond, that represents a claim on a business's cash flows. See *real asset.*

Financial distress costs. The direct and indirect costs associated with the probability of business bankruptcy. These costs play a key role in the trade-off theory of capital structure.

Financial future. A contract that secures the purchase or sale of a financial asset at some time in the future at a fixed price.

Financial intermediary. A business that buys securities with funds it obtains by issuing its own securities; examples include commercial banks and mutual funds.

Financial leverage. The use of fixed-cost financing, such as debt and preferred stock.

Financial merger. A merger in which the companies will continue to be operated as separate entities. See *operational merger.*

Financial plan. The portion of the operating plan that focuses on the finance function.

Financial risk. Generically, the risk that the return on an investment will be less than expected; in a capital structure context, the additional risk placed on the business's owners (or community) when debt (or preferred stock) financing is used.

Financial statements. The accounting statements required under generally accepted accounting principles (GAAP). The three primary statements are the income statement, balance sheet, and statement of cash flows.

Financial statement analysis. The process of using data contained in a business's financial statements to make judgments about financial condition.

Fixed-asset-turnover (utilization) ratio. The ratio of revenues to net fixed assets. It measures the ability of fixed assets to generate revenues.

Fixed-rate debt. Debt on which the interest rate is fixed for its entire life. See *floating-rate debt.*

Float. The difference between the balance shown on the bank's books and the balance shown on the business's (or individual's) checkbook.

Floating-rate debt. Debt on which interest payments are linked to the rate on some other debt (or index). As the index goes up and down, so does the interest rate on the floating-rate debt. See *fixed-rate debt.*

Flotation cost. The administrative costs associated with issuing new securities, such as legal, accounting, and investment banker's fees; sometimes called *issuance cost.*

Free cash flow. The cash flow available for distribution from a business or project after all costs have been considered, including investments in fixed assets.

Free trade credit. The amount of supplier-issued credit that has no explicit cost attached; in other words, credit received during the discount period.

Friendly merger. A merger supported by the management of the target company. See *hostile merger (takeover).*

Full-time equivalent (FTE). The number of full-time employees a staff equates to, including full-time, part-time, and contracted employees; calculated by totaling the number of hours paid to all employees over a given period and dividing by the number of hours a full-time employee would regularly work in that period.

Fund capital. Equity capital in a not-for-profit corporation. Also called *equity* and *net assets.*

Future value (Fv). The end amount of an investment of a lump sum, annuity, or uneven cash flow stream. See *present value (Pv).*

Going public. The initial sale of stock to the general public by a closely held corporation. See *initial public offering (IPO).*

Goodwill. An accounting term for the amount paid in a business acquisition that exceeds the net asset value of the target business.

Guideline lease. A lease contract that meets Internal Revenue Service requirements for a genuine lease, allowing the lessee to deduct the full amount of the lease payment from taxable income.

Health insurance exchange (HIE). An organized marketplace, established by a governmental unit, for the purchase of health insurance.

Health reimbursement arrangement (HRA). An account established by employers for the purpose of paying the out-of-pocket medical expenses of employees. Also called *health reimbursement account.*

Health savings account (HSA). A savings account established by individuals for the purpose of paying out-of-pocket medical expenses.

Hedging. A transaction undertaken to lower the risk caused by price fluctuations in financial and real assets, such as input commodities and interest rates.

High-deductible health plan (HDHP). A health insurance plan with lower premiums and higher deductibles than a traditional health plan; usually paired with a *health savings account (HSA).*

Historical (embedded) cost. In cost of capital, the average cost of a business's existing capital. See *marginal cost.*

Holding company. A corporation formed for the sole purpose of owning other companies.

Horizontal merger. A merger between two companies in the same line of business.

Hostile merger (takeover). A merger (takeover) that occurs despite the resistance of the target firm's management. See *friendly merger.*

Hurdle rate. The minimum required rate of return on an investment. Also called *opportunity cost rate.*

Incentive compensation plans. Compensation plans that create incentives for business managers to act in the best interests of owners.

Income statement. A financial statement that summarizes a business's revenues, expenses, and profitability.

Incremental cash flow. A cash flow produced solely by a project being evaluated, and hence one that should be included in the project analysis. See *nonincremental cash flow.*

Indenture. A legal document that spells out the rights and obligations of bondholders and the issuing corporation; in other words, the loan agreement for a bond.

Index rate. An interest rate that is used as the basis for setting other rates.

Inflation premium (IP). The premium that debt investors add to the base interest rate to compensate for inflation.

Initial public offering (IPO). The initial sale of stock to the general public by a closely held corporation. See *going public.*

Inpatient prospective payment system (IPPS). The reimbursement system used by Medicare to pay for inpatient hospital services.

Integrated delivery system. A single organization that offers a broad range of healthcare services in a unified manner.

Interest rate risk. The riskiness to current debtholders that stems from interest rate changes. See *price risk* and *reinvestment rate risk.*

Internal rate of return (IRR). A project return-on-investment (ROI) measure that focuses on percentage rate of return. See *net present value (NPV).*

Inverted yield curve. A yield curve that slopes downward. See *normal yield curve.*

Investment banker. An intermediary between businesses that want to raise capital and the investors who supply the capital.

Investment horizon. The expected holding period for an investment.

Investor-owned business. A for-profit business whose capital is supplied by owners (stockholders, in the case of corporations). See *not-for-profit/nonprofit corporation.*

Issuance cost. The administrative costs associated with selling (issuing) new securities, such as legal, accounting, and investment banker's fees; sometimes called *flotation cost.*

Joint venture. The combination of parts of two different companies to accomplish a specific, limited objective.

Junk bond. A bond that has a rating of BB or lower.

Key performance indicator (KPI). A financial or operating indicator metric that management considers critical to the business's financial performance.

Law of large numbers. A statistical concept that states that the standard deviation of a large number of identical independent probability distributions is much smaller than the standard deviation of only one of the distributions.

Length of stay (LOS). The average time a patient spends in an inpatient setting per admission. Also called *average length of stay (ALOS).*

Lessee. In a lease agreement, the party that uses the leased asset and makes the rental payments. See *lessor.*

Lessor. In a lease agreement, the party that owns the leased asset and receives the rental payments. See *lessee.*

Leveraged lease. A lease in which the lessor borrows a portion of the purchase price to buy the leased asset.

Liquid asset. An asset that can be quickly converted to cash at its fair market value.

Liquidity. A business's ability to meet its cash obligations as they become due.

Liquidity premium (LP). The premium that debt investors add to the base interest rate to compensate for lack of liquidity.

Long-term debt. Debt that has a maturity of more than one year.

Lumpy assets. Fixed assets that cannot be acquired smoothly as demand grows but rather must be added in large increments—for example, hospital beds.

Managerial options. Options inherent in projects that give managers an opportunity to create additional value. For example, a project to build a small outpatient surgery center creates a managerial option to expand the center if patient demand increases. Also called *real options.*

Marginal cost. In cost of capital, the cost of the next dollar of capital raised. See *historical (embedded) cost.*

Marginal tax rate. The tax rate that applies to the next dollar of income.

Market multiple analysis. A technique for valuing a business that applies a market-determined multiple to some proxy for value, such as net income.

Market portfolio. A portfolio that contains all publicly traded stocks; often proxied by some market index, such as the S&P 500.

Market risk. The portion of the risk of a stock investment that cannot be eliminated by holding the stock as part of a diversified portfolio; also, the portion of the riskiness of a business project that cannot be diversified away by holding the stock of the company as part of a diversified portfolio. See *corporate risk.*

Market risk premium (RP_M). The difference between the expected rate of return on the market portfolio and the risk-free rate; in other words, the premium above the risk-free rate that stock investors require to bear average risk.

Market value. The values of a business's assets, liabilities, and equity as determined by the marketplace, as opposed to the values listed on the balance sheet.

Marketable securities. Securities held in lieu of cash; typically safe, short-term securities, such as Treasury bills.

Materials management. The management of the procurement, storage, and utilization of supply inventories; also called *supply chain management.*

Maturity. The amount of time until a loan matures (must be repaid).

Maturity date. The date on which the principal amount of a loan must be repaid.

Medicaid. A federal and state government health insurance program that provides benefits to low-income individuals.

Medicare. A federal government health insurance program that provides benefits primarily to individuals aged 65 or older.

Medicare severity diagnosis-related groups (MS–DRGs). The diagnosis coding system used by Medicare to determine hospital inpatient reimbursement. It adds severity indicators to the original DRG coding system.

Merger. The combination of two entire businesses into a single entity.

Miller model. A capital structure theory model that introduces the effects of personal taxes to the Modigliani and Miller (MM) model.

Mission statement. A statement that defines the overall purpose of an organization.

Modified Accelerated Cost Recovery System (MACRS). The system specified by the Internal Revenue Service for calculation of depreciation for tax purposes. See *depreciation.*

Modified internal rate of return (MIRR). A project return-on-investment (ROI) measure similar to IRR but based on a different reinvestment rate assumption. See *internal rate of return (IRR).*

Modigliani and Miller (MM) model. A capital structure theory model that defines the relationship between the use of debt financing and firm value. The model has two variants: one with zero taxes and one with corporate taxes. See *Miller model.*

Money market. The financial markets for debt securities that have maturities of one year or less. See *capital market.*

Monte Carlo simulation. A computerized risk analysis technique that uses continuous distributions as the uncertain input variables.

Moral hazard. The risk that insured individuals or businesses will purposely take destructive actions or fewer precautions simply because they are covered by insurance and as a result will more likely file a claim.

Mortgage bond. A bond, issued by a business, that pledges real property (land and buildings) as collateral.

MS–DRGs. See *Medicare severity diagnosis-related groups.*

Municipal bond (muni). A tax-exempt bond issued by a governmental entity, such as a healthcare financing authority. See *corporate bond.*

Mutual fund. A company that sells shares and uses the proceeds to buy securities.

Net advantage to leasing (NAL). The discounted cash flow dollar value of a lease to the lessee as opposed to financing with debt; similar to *net present value* (NPV).

Net cash flow. The actual amount of cash generated by a business or project; for businesses, can be approximated by the sum of net income and noncash expenses (typically depreciation).

Net operating profit after taxes (NOPAT). The profit a business would generate if it had no debt; generally defined as earnings before interest and taxes (EBIT) multiplied by (1 – Tax rate).

Net present social value (NPSV). A project's social value on a present value basis; added to the financial NPV to find a project's total value.

Net present value (NPV). A project return-on-investment (ROI) measure that focuses on expected dollar return. See *internal rate of return (IRR).*

Net working capital. A liquidity measure equal to current assets minus current liabilities. See *working capital.*

Nonearning asset. An asset that does not generate revenues; primarily cash held in commercial checking accounts.

Nonincremental cash flow. A cash flow that is not produced solely from a project being evaluated. Nonincremental cash flows are not included in a project analysis. See *incremental cash flow.*

Nonnormal cash flows. Project cash flows that contain one or more outflows after the inflows have begun. See *normal cash flows.*

Normal cash flows. Project cash flows in which all of the outflows occur before all of the inflows. See *nonnormal cash flows.*

Normal yield curve. A yield curve that slopes upward. See *inverted yield curve.*

Notes payable. A current liability account created when a business takes out a short-term loan, defined as a loan with a maturity of one year or less.

Not-for-profit/nonprofit corporation. A corporation that has a charitable purpose, is tax exempt, and has no owners. See *investor-owned business.*

Occupancy rate. The percentage of hospital beds occupied.

Off-balance-sheet financing. Debt financing that does not appear on a business's balance sheet—for example, under current generally accepted accounting principles (GAAP), short-term (operating) leases.

Operating indicator. A ratio that focuses on operating data rather than on financial data.

Operating lease. A lease whose term is much shorter than the expected life of the asset being leased. See *finance lease.*

Operating leverage. The degree to which a business uses fixed (versus variable) costs. The greater the operating leverage, the greater the impact of revenue changes on net income.

Operating margin. Net operating income divided by total operating revenues. It is a measure of the amount of operating profit per dollar of operating revenues and hence focuses on the core activities of a business. See *profit (total) margin.*

Operating plan. An organizational road map for the future, typically for five years.

Operational merger. A merger in which the operations of two companies are combined into a single entity.

Opportunity cost. The cost associated with alternative uses of the same asset. For example, if land is used for one project, it is no longer available for other uses, so an opportunity cost arises.

Opportunity cost principle. The idea that a financially sound investment must earn at least as much as can be earned on alternative investments of similar risk.

Opportunity cost rate. The rate of return expected on alternative investments similar in risk to an investment being evaluated. Also called *hurdle rate.*

Optimal capital budget. The list of projects to be undertaken that maximizes total (aggregate) net present value. If there are no capital constraints, the optimal capital budget is all projects that have a return greater than their cost of capital.

Optimal capital structure. (1) The mix of debt and equity financing that management believes to be appropriate for the business. It is generally based on both quantitative and qualitative factors and becomes the business's target capital structure. (2) In theory, the capital structure that maximizes the value of the business.

Ordinary income. Income generated by working (or by business operations) as opposed to capital gains income, which is created passively by selling an investment for more than its purchase price.

Ordinary (regular) annuity. An annuity whose payments occur at the end of each period. See *annuity due.*

Original issue discount bond. A bond that sells for less than its par value.

Outlier payment. A separate payment made by an insurer to a provider to account for patients who have exceptionally high costs.

Outpatient prospective payment system (OPPS). The reimbursement system used by Medicare to pay for outpatient services provided by a hospital.

Outstanding bond. A bond that has been issued and is currently held (and available for trading) by bond investors.

Over-the-counter (OTC) market. The marketplace where stocks that are not listed on an exchange are traded.

Par value. The face (nominal) value of a security. The par value of a debt security is the amount to be repaid at maturity.

Partnership. An unincorporated business entity created by two or more individuals.

Patient Protection and Affordable Care Act (ACA). The legislation enacted on March 23, 2010, designed to provide all US citizens and legal residents with access to affordable health insurance, to reduce healthcare costs, and to improve care and quality.

Pay for performance (P4P). A reimbursement method that requires providers to meet specified performance goals, usually involving costs and quality. Also called *value-based purchasing (VBP).*

Payback (period). The number of years it takes a business to recover its investment in a project, without considering the time value of money. See *discounted payback (period).*

Payment (PMT). In time value of money, the dollar amount of an annuity cash flow.

Per diem. A reimbursement methodology that pays a set amount for each inpatient day.

Per member per month (PMPM). A form of payment to providers used by insurers under capitated reimbursement. Payment consists of a fixed monthly amount for each covered life (member).

Percentage of sales method. A technique for forecasting financial statements that is based on the assumption that most income statement items and balance sheet accounts are tied directly (proportionately) to sales (revenues).

Periodic rate. In time value of money (discounted cash flow analysis), the interest rate per period—for example, 2 percent quarterly interest, which equals an 8 percent stated (annual) rate. See *effective annual rate (EAR).*

Permanent current assets (working capital). The dollar amount of current assets that is permanent in nature.

Perpetuity. A debt security that has no stated maturity.

Physical life. The useful life of capital assets (such as diagnostic equipment) as opposed to economic life, which maximizes financial value.

Poison pill. A provision in a company's charter that makes it an unattractive hostile-takeover target—for example, a provision that allows existing stockholders to buy more stock at a low price if a hostile takeover occurs.

Pooling of losses. Losses spread over a large group of individuals rather than borne solely by one individual.

Portfolio. A number of individual investments held collectively.

Portfolio risk. The riskiness of an individual investment when it is held as part of a large portfolio as opposed to held in isolation. There are two types of portfolio risk: corporate risk and market risk. See ***stand-alone risk***, ***corporate risk***, and ***market risk***.

Postaudit. The feedback process in which the performance of projects previously accepted is reviewed and necessary actions are taken.

Preemptive right. The right that gives current shareholders the opportunity to purchase any newly issued shares (in proportion to their current holdings) before they are offered to the general public.

Preferred stock. A hybrid security issued by for-profit corporations that has characteristics of both debt and equity.

Premium tier. A category of employee health insurance coverage. For example, a two-tier system might offer individual and family coverage.

Present value (Pv). The beginning amount of an investment of a lump sum, an annuity, or an uneven cash flow stream. See ***future value (Fv)***.

Price risk. The risk that rising interest rates will lower the values of outstanding debt. See ***interest rate risk***.

Price risk premium (PRP). The premium that debt investors add to the base interest rate to compensate for bearing price risk (the risk of value loss resulting from increasing interest rates).

Primary market. The market in which newly issued securities are sold for the first time. See ***secondary market***.

Principal. The amount borrowed.

Private placement. The sale of newly issued securities to a single investor or small group of investors. Private placements cost less, and may be accomplished more quickly, than public offerings. See ***public offering***.

Probability distribution. All possible outcomes of a random event along with their probabilities of occurrence—for example, the probability distribution of rates of return on a proposed project.

Profit (total) margin. Net income divided by total revenues; measures the amount of total profit per dollar of total revenues. See ***operating margin***.

Profitability index (PI). A project return-on-investment (ROI) measure defined as the present value of cash inflows divided by the present value of outflows. It measures the number of dollars of inflow per dollar of outflow (on a present value basis)—"bang for the buck."

Profitability ratios. A group of ratios that measures different dimensions of profitability and hence the combined effects of operational decisions.

Pro forma. As applied to financial statements, a statement constructed on the basis of assumptions that differ from generally accepted accounting principles (GAAP). The term is also used to indicate forecasted financial statements.

Project cost of capital. The discount rate (opportunity cost rate) that reflects the unique riskiness of a project. See *corporate cost of capital (CCC)* and *divisional cost of capital.*

Project scoring. An approach to project assessment that considers both financial and nonfinancial factors.

Proprietorship. A simple form of business owned by an individual. Also called *sole proprietorship.*

Prospective payment. A reimbursement methodology that is established beforehand by the third-party payer and, in theory, is not related to costs or charges.

Provider. An organization that provides healthcare services (treats patients).

Proxy. A document giving one person authority to act for another—typically, the power to vote on shares of common stock.

Proxy fight. An attempt to take control of a corporation by soliciting the votes (proxies) of current shareholders.

Public offering. The sale of newly issued securities to the general public through an investment banker. See *private placement.*

Publicly held corporation. A corporation whose shares are held by the general public as opposed to closely (privately) held, in which case the shares are held by a small number of individuals—usually the managers.

Pure play approach. A method for estimating a small business's cost of equity by using the cost of equity of a similar large, publicly traded business (pure play) as a proxy.

Qualitative risk assessment. A process for assessing project risk that focuses on qualitative issues as opposed to profit variability.

Rate of return. The percentage return on an investment (as opposed to the dollar return).

Ratio analysis. The process of creating and analyzing ratios; applied to financial statement data to assess financial condition and to operating data to assess causes.

Real asset. Property—such as land, buildings, and equipment—used to create a business's cash flows. See *financial asset.*

Real options. Options inherent in projects that give managers an opportunity to create additional value. For example, a project to build a small outpatient surgery center creates a real option to expand the center if patient demand increases. Also called *managerial options.*

Real rate of return. The rate of return on an investment, net of inflation effects.

Real risk-free rate (RRF). The rate of interest on a riskless investment in the absence of inflation.

Realized rate of return. The return actually achieved on an investment when it is sold. See *expected rate of return.*

Reinvestment rate risk. The risk that falling interest rates will reduce the returns earned on the reinvestment of debt interest payments (and perhaps principal repayments). See *interest rate risk.*

Replacement chain. A technique for comparing the profitability of competing projects that have different lives. See *equivalent annual annuity.*

Required rate of return. The minimum rate of return required on an investment, considering its riskiness. Also called *hurdle rate.*

Reserve borrowing capacity. The business practice of using less than the true optimal amount of debt to ensure easy access to new debt at reasonable interest rates regardless of circumstances.

Residual value. The estimated market value of a leased asset at the end of the lease.

Restrictive covenant. A provision in a bond indenture (loan agreement) that protects the interests of bondholders by restricting the actions of management.

Retained earnings. The portion of net income retained within the business as opposed to paid out as dividends. Not-for-profit corporations must retain all earnings.

Return on assets (ROA). Net income divided by the book value of total assets; measures the dollars of earnings per dollar of book asset investment.

Return on equity (ROE). Net income divided by the book value of equity; measures the dollars of earnings per dollar of book equity investment.

Return on investment (ROI). The financial gain from an investment; may be measured in percentage terms (rate of return) or dollar terms (net present value).

Revenue cycle. The set of recurring activities and related information processing required to document, bill for, and collect for services provided.

Rights offering. The mechanism by which new common stock is offered to existing shareholders. Each stockholder receives an option (right) to buy a specific number of new shares at a given price.

Risk-adjusted discount rate (RADR). A discount rate that accounts for the specific riskiness of the investment being analyzed.

Risk aversion. The tendency of individuals and businesses to dislike risk. The implication of risk aversion is that riskier investments must offer higher expected rates of return to be acceptable.

Risk management. Management of the risks encountered by a business, which includes minimization of the occurrence of adverse events and the costs associated with an event if it occurs.

Risk/return trade-off. In efficient markets, the premise that higher returns can be obtained only by assuming greater risk.

S corporation. A corporation with a limited number of stockholders that is taxed as a proprietorship or partnership.

Sale and leaseback. A type of lease transaction in which an owned asset is sold to another party but simultaneously leased back. The seller receives the purchase price of the asset but now is obligated to make lease payments to the new owner.

Salvage value. The expected market value of an asset (project) at the end of its useful life.

Scenario analysis. A project risk analysis technique that assesses how best- and worst-case scenarios affect profitability.

Secondary market. The market in which previously issued securities are sold.

Secured loan. A loan backed by collateral, often inventories or receivables.

Securities and Exchange Commission (SEC). The government agency that oversees the sale of securities and the operations of securities exchanges.

Security market line (SML). The portion of the capital asset pricing model that specifies the relationship between market risk and required rate of return.

Sensitivity analysis. A project analysis technique that assesses how changes in single input variables, such as utilization, affect profitability.

Serial issue. A type of bond issue in which there are multiple maturity dates.

Short-term debt. Debt that has a maturity of one year or less.

Social value. The nonfinancial value created when not-for-profit organizations provide services for which they are not paid.

Stand-alone risk. The riskiness of an investment held in isolation as opposed to held as part of a portfolio. See *portfolio risk.*

Standard deviation (σ). A statistical measure of the variability of probability distribution equal to the square root of the variance.

Stated (nominal) interest rate. The interest rate stated in a debt contract; does not reflect the effect of compounding that occurs more frequently than annually. See *effective annual rate (EAR).*

Statement of cash flows. A financial statement that focuses on the cash flows that come into and go out of a business.

Statistical supplement. A section sometimes included in an annual report that provides a business's key financial metrics for the last ten (or so) years.

Strategic value. The value of a proposed project that stems not from forecasted cash flows but from the potential that the project brings for future follow-on projects.

Stretching. The practice of paying receivables late.

Subordinated debenture. A debt security that, in the event of bankruptcy, has a claim on assets below (subordinate to) other debt.

Sunk cost. A cost that has already occurred or is irrevocably committed; nonincremental to project analyses and hence should not be included.

Supply chain management. Management of the procurement, storage, and utilization of supply inventories. Also called *materials management.*

Synchronization of cash flows. A cash management technique that matches the receipt of cash inflows to the pattern of expected cash outflows.

Synergy. A feature sought in mergers in which the merged entity is worth more than the sum of the individual businesses.

Takeover. The taking of control of a business by an outside individual (or group), often against the wishes of its management.

Target capital structure. The capital structure (mix of debt and equity) that a company strives to achieve and maintain over time; generally the same as *optimal capital structure.*

Tax book value. The value of a business asset according to tax laws; generally calculated as the acquisition price less total tax depreciation taken.

Tax-exempt lease. A special type of lease-like arrangement that treats the implied interest portion of the lease payment to the lessor as tax-exempt income.

Tender offer. A means of acquiring a firm without gaining approval from the target's management. Stockholders are asked to sell (tender) their shares directly to the acquiring company (or investor group).

Term loan. Long-term debt obtained from a financial institution. See *bond.*

Term structure. The relationship between yield to maturity and term to maturity for debt of a single risk class—for example, Treasury securities. See *yield curve.*

Terminal value. The estimated value of a project at the end of its expected life.

Terms of credit. The statement of terms that extends credit to a buyer. For example, "2/10, net 30" means that a 2 percent discount is offered if the buyer pays in 10 days. If the discount is not taken, the full amount of the invoice is due in 30 days.

Third-party payer. An entity, other than the patient, that pays for healthcare services; examples include commercial insurance companies and government programs such as Medicare.

Time line. A graphical representation of time and cash flows; may be an actual line or cells on a spreadsheet.

Times-interest-earned (TIE) ratio. Earnings before interest and taxes divided by interest charges; measures the number of times a business's interest expense is covered by earnings available to pay that expense.

Total-asset-turnover (utilization) ratio. Total revenues divided by total assets; measures the amount of revenue generated by each dollar of total assets.

Total net present value (TNPV). The combined value of a project's conventional NPV and the value created by the opportunity to lease (rather than buy) the asset. Alternatively, a project's conventional NPV plus the present value of any social value created.

Trade credit. The credit offered to businesses by suppliers (vendors) when credit terms are offered. See *account payable.*

Trade-off model. A capital structure model that hypothesizes that a business's optimal capital structure balances the costs and benefits associated with debt financing.

Trend analysis. A ratio analysis technique that examines the value of a ratio over time to see whether it is improving or deteriorating. See *comparative analysis.*

Trustee. An individual or institution, typically a bank, that represents the interests of bondholders.

Underwriting. The process of selling new securities through an investment banker.

Unrelated business income (UBI). Income earned by a not-for-profit business that is not related to the charitable mission of the organization and hence is taxable.

Value-based purchasing (VBP). A provider reimbursement system in which some portion of the payments is tied to performance as measured by quality or costs. Also called *pay for performance (P4P).*

Values statement. Statement listing the core priorities that define the organization's culture.

Variance (σ2). A statistical measure of the variability of a probability distribution. Standard deviation is the square root of variance.

Vertical merger. A merger between an upstream company and a downstream company—for example, a hospital that acquires a medical practice.

Vision statement. Statement of what the business aspires to be in the future, rather than what it is today.

Working capital. A business's short-term (current) assets. See *net working capital.*

Yield curve. A plot of the term structure of interest rates (yield to maturity versus term to maturity). See *term structure.*

Yield to call (YTC). The expected rate of return on a debt security if it is held until it is called.

Yield to maturity (YTM). The expected rate of return on a debt security if it is held until maturity.

Zero-balance accounts (ZBAs). Bank accounts held by businesses to help control disbursements. Funds are placed in such accounts in the amounts needed to just cover daily outflow requirements, so the ending balance each evening is zero.

Zero-coupon bond. A bond that pays no interest. It is bought at a discount from par value, so its return comes solely from price appreciation.

Zero-sum game. A situation wherein the gains of one party are exactly matched by the losses of another party. Leasing is a zero-sum game when the economics of the lease are the same to both the lessee and the lessor.

APPENDIX: KEY FORMULAS IN CHAPTERS

Chapter 4

Key Equation 4.1: Future Value of a Lump Sum

$$Fv_N = Pv \times (1 + I)^N.$$

Key Equation 4.2: Present Value of a Lump Sum

$$\text{Compounding: } Fv_N = Pv \times (1 + I)^N.$$

$$\text{Discounting: } Pv = \frac{Fv_N}{(1 + I)^N}.$$

Key Equation 4.3: Present Value of a Perpetuity

$$Pv\ (\text{Perpetuity}) = \frac{\text{Payment}}{\text{Interest rate}} = \frac{\text{PMT}}{\text{Interest rate}}.$$

Key Equation 4.4: Effective Annual Rate

The EAR can be determined, if given the stated rate and number of compounding periods per year, by using this equation:

$$\text{Effective annual rate (EAR)} = (1 + I_{\text{Stated}} \div M)^{M} - 1.0.$$

Here, I_{Stated} is the stated (nominal or annual) interest rate and M is the number of compounding periods per year. Note that the term $I_{\text{Stated}} \div M$ is the **periodic** interest rate, so the EAR equation can be restated as follows:

$$\text{Effective annual rate (EAR)} = (1 + \text{Periodic rate})^{M} - 1.0.$$

Chapter 5

Key Equation 5.1: Expected Value of a Return Distribution

$$\begin{aligned} E(R) = {} & (\text{Probability of return 1} \times \text{Return 1}) \\ & + (\text{Probability of return 2} \times \text{Return 2}) \\ & + (\text{Probability of return 3} \times \text{Return 3}) \text{ and so on.} \end{aligned}$$

Key Equation 5.2: Variance of an Expected Return Distribution

$$\begin{aligned} \text{Variance} = {} & (\text{Probability of return 1} \times [\text{Rate of return 1} - E(R)]^2) \\ & + (\text{Probability of return 2} \times [\text{Rate of return 2} - E(R)]^2) \text{ and so on.} \end{aligned}$$

Key Equation 5.3: Standard Deviation of an Expected Return Distribution

$$\text{Standard deviation} = \text{Square root of variance.}$$

Key Equation 5.4: Return of a Historical Return Distribution

$$r_T = \frac{(r_1 + r_2 + \ldots r_t)}{T}.$$

Key Equation 5.5: Standard Deviation of a Historical Return Distribution

$$S = \sqrt{\frac{(r_1 - r_T)^2 + (r_2 - r_T)^2 + \ldots + (r_t - r_T)^2}{T - 1}}.$$

Key Equation 5.6: Return on a Portfolio

$R_{Portfolio} = (w_1 \times R_1) + (w_2 \times R_2) + (w_3 \times R_3)$ and so on, where w_1 is the proportion of investment 1 in the overall portfolio and R_1 is the rate of return on investment 1, and so on.

Key Equation 5.7: Diversifiable Versus Market Risk

Stand-alone risk = Diversifiable risk + Market risk.

Key Equation 5.8: Beta

$$b_i = (\sigma_i \div \sigma_m) \times r_{im},$$

where

σ_i = standard deviation of stock i's returns,

σ_m = standard deviation of the market's returns, and

r_{im} = correlation coefficient between stock i's returns and the market's returns.

Key Equation 5.9 Portfolio Beta

$$b_{Portfolio} = (w_1 \times b_1) + (w_2 \times b_2) + (w_3 \times b_3) + (w_i \times b_i) \text{ and so on.}$$

Key Equation 5.10: Security Market Line (SML)

Required return on stock i = Risk-free rate + Risk premium for stock i

Required return on stock i = Risk-free rate + (Beta of stock i) × (Market risk premium)

$$R(R_i) = RF + (R[R_M] - RF) \times b_i$$
$$= RF + (RP_M \times b_i).$$

Chapter 6

Key Equation 6.1: Current Yield on a Bond

Current yield = Annual coupon payment ÷ Beginning price.

Key Equation 6.2: Capital Gains Yield on a Bond

Capital gains yield = Annual capital gain (or loss) ÷ Beginning price.

Key Equation 6.3: Rate of Return (Total Yield) on a Bond

Rate of return (Total yield) = Total dollar return ÷ Beginning price, or

Total yield = Current yield + Capital gains yield.

Chapter 7

Key Equation 7.1: Constant Growth Model (Valuation)

$$E(P_0) = \frac{D_0 \times [1 + E(g)]}{R(R_S) - E(g)} = \frac{E(D_1)}{R(R_S) - E(g)}.$$

Key Equation 7.2: Security Market Line (SML)

$$R(R_{MHS}) = RF + [R(R_M) - RF] \times b_{MHS}.$$

Key Equation 7.3: Constant Growth Model (Rate of Return)

$$E(R_s) = \frac{D_0 \times [1 + E(g)]}{P_0} + E(g) = \frac{E(D_1)}{P_0} + E(g).$$

Chapter 8

Key Equation 8.1: Net Advantage to Leasing (NAL)

NAL = PV cost of leasing – PV cost of owning.

Key Equation 8.2: Adjusted NPV

Adjusted NPV = NPV + NAL.

Chapter 9

Key Equation 9.1: After-Tax Cost of Debt

$$\text{After-tax cost of debt} = R(R_d) \times (1 - T).$$

Key Equation 9.2: Security Market Line of the Capital Asset Pricing Model

$$R(R_e) = RF + [R(R_M) - RF] \times b_i$$
$$= RF + (RP_M \times b_i).$$

Key Equation 9.3: Constant Growth Dividend Valuation Model

$$E(R_e) = \frac{D_0 \times [1 + E(g)]}{P_0} + E(g) = \frac{E(D_1)}{P_0} + E(g).$$

Key Equation 9.4: Debt Cost Plus Risk Premium Model

$$R(R_e) = R(R_d) + \text{Risk premium}.$$

Key Equation 9.5: Corporate Cost of Capital

$$CCC = [w_{ed} \times R(R_d) \times (1 - T)] + [w_e \times R(R_e)].$$

Chapter 10

Key Equation 10.1: Value of a Firm Assuming No Taxes

$$V_L = V_U = \frac{EBIT}{CCC} = \frac{EBIT}{R(R_{eU})}.$$

Key Equation 10.2: Cost of Equity to a Levered Firm Assuming No Taxes

$$R(R_{eL}) = R(R_{eU}) + \text{Risk premium} =$$
$$R(R_{eU}) + \{[R(R_{eU}) - R(R_d)] \times (D \div E)\}.$$

Key Equation 10.3: Value of a Levered Firm with Corporate Taxes

$$V_L = V_U + (T \times D).$$

Key Equation 10.4: Value of Unlevered Firm with Corporate Taxes

$$E = V_U = \frac{EBIT \times (1 - T)}{R(R_{eU})}.$$

Key Equation 10.5: Cost of Equity to a Levered Firm with Corporate Taxes

$$R(R_{eL}) = R(R_{eU}) + \text{Risk premium}$$
$$= R(R_{eU}) + \{[R(R_{eU}) - R(R_d)] \times (1 - T) \times (D \div E)\}.$$

Key Equation 10.6: Value of Unlevered Firm with Corporate and Personal Taxes

$$V_U = \frac{EBIT \times (1 - T_C) \times (1 - T_e)}{R(R_{eU})(1 - T_e)}.$$

Key Equation 10.7: Value of a Levered Firm with Corporate and Personal Taxes

$$V_L = V_U + \left\{\left[1 - \frac{(1 - T_c) \times (1 - T_e)}{1 - T_d}\right] \times D\right\}.$$

Key Equation 10.8: Value of a Levered Firm with Financial Distress

$$V_L = V_U + (T \times D) - \text{PV of expected financial distress costs.}$$

Chapter 11

Key Equation 11.1: Net Present Social Value Model

$$\text{TNPV} = \text{NPV} + \text{NPSV}.$$

Chapter 12

Key Equation 12.1: Risk-Adjusted Discount Rate (RADR) Theoretical Model

$$\text{Project cost of capital} = \text{Risk-free rate} + \text{Risk premium}.$$

Key Equation 12.2: Risk-Adjusted Discount Rate (RADR) Implementation Model

$$\text{Project cost of capital} = \text{Corporate cost of capital} + \text{Risk adjustment}.$$

Chapter 13

Key Equation 13.1: Total Margin

$$\text{Total margin} = \frac{\text{Net income}}{\text{Total revenues}}.$$

Key Equation 13.2: Operating Margin

$$\text{Operating margin} = \frac{\text{Operating income}}{\text{Total operating revenues}}.$$

Key Equation 13.3: Return on Assets

$$\text{Return on assets} = \frac{\text{Net income}}{\text{Total assets}}.$$

Key Equation 13.4: Return on Equity

$$\text{Return on equity} = \frac{\text{Net income}}{\text{Total equity}}.$$

Key Equation 13.5: Current Ratio

$$\text{Current ratio} = \frac{\text{Current assets}}{\text{Current liabilities}}.$$

Key Equation 13.6: Days-Cash-on-Hand Ratio

$$\text{Days cash on hand} = \frac{\text{Cash and equivalents} + \text{Short-term investments}}{(\text{Expenses} - \text{Depreciation}) \div 365}.$$

Key Equation 13.7: Debt Ratio

$$\text{Debt ratio} = \frac{\text{Total debt}}{\text{Total assets}}.$$

Key Equation 13.8: Debt-to-Equity Ratio

$$\text{Debt-to-equity ratio} = \frac{\text{Total debt}}{\text{Total equity assets}}.$$

Key Equation 13.9: TIE Ratio

$$\text{TIE ratio} = \frac{\text{EBIT}}{\text{Interest expense}}.$$

Key Equation 13.10: CFC Ratio

$$\text{CFC ratio} = \frac{\text{EBIT} + \text{Lease payments} + \text{Depreciation expense}}{\text{Interest expense} + \text{Lease payments} = + \text{Debt principal} \div (1 - \text{T})}.$$

Key Equation 13.11: Fixed-Asset-Turnover Ratio

$$\text{Fixed asset turnover} = \frac{\text{Total revenues}}{\text{Net fixed assets}}.$$

Key Equation 13.12: Total-Asset-Turnover Ratio

$$\text{Total asset turnover} = \frac{\text{Total revenues}}{\text{Total assets}}.$$

Key Equation 13.13: Days in Patient Accounts Receivable

$$\text{Days in patient accounts receivable} = \frac{\text{Net patient accounts receivable}}{\text{Net patient service revenue} \div 365}.$$

Key Equation 13.14: Average Age of Plant

$$\text{Average age of plant} = \frac{\text{Accumulated depreciation}}{\text{Depreciation expense}}.$$

Key Equations 13.15 and 13.16: Du Pont Equation

$$\text{ROE} = \text{Total margin} \times \text{Total asset turnover} \times \text{Equity multiplier.}$$

$$\text{ROE} = \text{Return on assets} \times \text{Equity multiplier.}$$

Key Equation 13.17: Profit per Discharge

$$\text{Profit per discharge} = \frac{\text{Inpatient profit}}{\text{Total discharges}}.$$

Key Equation 13.18: Net Price per Discharge

$$\text{Net price per discharge} = \frac{\text{Net inpatient revenue}}{\text{Total discharges}}.$$

Key Equation 13.19: Occupancy Rate

$$\text{Occupancy rate} = \frac{\text{Inpatient days}}{(\text{Number of licensed beds} \times 365)} .$$

Key Equation 13.20: Average Length of Stay

$$\text{LOS} = \frac{\text{Inpatient days}}{\text{Total discharges}} .$$

Key Equation 13.21: Inpatient FTEs per Occupied Bed

$$\text{Inpatient FTEs per occupied bed} = \frac{\text{Inpatient FTEs}}{\text{Average daily census}} .$$

Key Equation 13.22: Salary per FTE

$$\text{Salary per FTE} = \frac{\text{Total salaries}}{\text{Total FTEs}} .$$

Key Equation 13.23: Economic Value Added

$$\begin{aligned}\text{EVA} = {} & \text{Net operating profit after taxes (NOPAT)} \\ & - (\text{Total capital} \times \text{Corporate cost of capital}).\end{aligned}$$

Chapter 14

Key Equation 14.1: Capacity Sales

$$\text{Utilization rate (\% of capacity)} = \frac{\text{Actual revenue}}{\text{Capacity sales}},$$

so

$$\text{Capacity sales} = \frac{\text{Actual revenue}}{\text{Utilization rate}}.$$

Chapter 15

Key Equation 15.1: Average Collection Period

$$\text{ACP} = (\text{Percent of customers who take discount} \times \text{Day on which they pay}) + (\text{percent of customers who do no take discount} \times \text{Day on which they pay}).$$

Key Equation 15.2: Average Daily Sales

$$\text{ADS} = \frac{\text{Annual sales}}{360} = \frac{\text{Units sold} \times \text{Sales price}}{360}.$$

Key Equation 15.3: Average Collection Period (Alternative Calculation)

$$\text{ACP} = \frac{\text{Receivables}}{\text{ADS}}.$$

Key Equation 15.4: Approximate Annual Percentage Cost

$$\text{Approximate percentage cost} = \frac{\text{Discount percentage}}{100 - \text{Discount percentage}} \times \frac{360}{\text{Days credit received} - \text{Discount period}}.$$

INDEX

Note: Italicized page locators refer to exhibits.

ABOUT THE AUTHORS

George H. Pink, PhD, is the Humana Distinguished Professor in the Department of Health Policy and Management, Gillings School of Global Public Health, at the University of North Carolina at Chapel Hill and is a senior research fellow at the Cecil G. Sheps Center for Health Services Research at the university. Prior to receiving a doctorate in corporate finance, he spent ten years in health services management, planning, and consulting. Dr. Pink teaches courses in healthcare finance and is involved in several large research projects, including studies of hospital financial performance. In the past 30 years, he has served on the boards and committees of more than 100 hospitals and other healthcare organizations. He has written more than 80 peer-reviewed articles and has made more than 200 presentations in 10 countries.

Paula H. Song, PhD, is associate professor and director of the residential master's program in the Department of Health Policy and Management, Gillings School of Global Public Health, at the University of North Carolina at Chapel Hill, and is a research fellow at the Cecil G. Sheps Center for Health Services Research at the university. Dr. Song's research and teaching interests cover areas such as healthcare financial management, investment strategies in not-for-profit hospitals, payment reform, and business case evaluation for health initiatives. Dr. Song received a doctorate in health services organization and policy, as well as a master's in health services administration and applied economics, from the University of Michigan, Ann Arbor.

Remembering Louis C. Gapenski, PhD

This tribute is reprinted with permission from the *Journal of Healthcare Finance.*

In the field of health care finance, one need not look far to see the impact of Louis "Lou" C. Gapenski, PhD. When he passed away on April 20, 2016, we all lost a gifted scholar, writer, teacher, mentor, and friend. After retiring from the Marine Corps as a Lieutenant Colonel in 1979, Lou earned both an

MBA and a PhD in Finance and Economics from the University of Florida. He spent his academic career as a faculty member in the College of Public Health and Health Professions' Department of Health Services Research, Management, and Policy at the University of Florida. If Lou had not decided to embark on this second career, the field of health care finance would not be the same.

By traditional academic metrics, Lou was a successful scholar: many peer-reviewed articles, other publications and book reviews, and presentations at academic and professional conferences. His scholarship offered some of the earliest applications of standard corporate finance theory to healthcare issues, examining topics such as capital structure decisions and financial risk, capital investment methods and return on investment measures, determinants of hospital profitability, and the importance of non-patient revenues to hospitals. A cited reference analysis of his work in healthcare and management using the Web of Science showed the breadth of his influence. His findings have been cited in both peer-reviewed and professional gray literature involving over 200 different authors or co-authors, many of whose names are well-known in the field of health care finance today. These authors represented almost 100 different colleges and universities and close to 20 provider, consulting, or government organizations in 19 different countries.

However, Lou was best known for his compendium of best-selling textbooks on corporate finance and healthcare financial management. His collaboration with Eugene Brigham produced a textbook factory: Lou was a coauthor of five editions of *Financial Management: Theory and Practice* (translated into Bulgarian, Chinese, French, Indonesian, Italian, Portuguese, and Spanish), six editions of *Intermediate Financial Management*, and five editions of *Cases in Financial Management*. In the early 1990s, Lou turned his attention to the nascent discipline of healthcare financial management, being among the first to argue that the theory and application of corporate finance was both relevant and necessary to the training of healthcare managers. Over the next twenty-five years, Lou authored seven editions of *Understanding Healthcare Financial Management*, five editions of *Cases in Healthcare Finance*, six editions of *Healthcare Finance: An Introduction to Accounting and Financial Management*, and two editions of *Fundamentals of Healthcare Finance*. By any standard, this was an extraordinary level of textbook productivity and was a constant source of amazement and curiosity among his colleagues. Lou was once asked "How do you manage to write so many textbooks?" to which he replied "When I get up in the morning, I tell myself that Chapter 1 has to be finished by the end of the day, and then I sit down and do it." We always suspected that his career in the Marines was excellent preparation for the self-discipline required to write textbooks.

Lou's textbooks and casebook in health care finance were novel and innovative in that they offered the rigorous finance training commonly found in business schools, but using language and context that would speak to those whose passion was health care. In all of Lou's work, his commitment to teaching and learning was evident. In planning for new textbooks or new editions of existing books, Lou would reach out to colleagues, students, and individuals working in the field, seeking input on how to improve his books and the associated ancillary learning materials. He was eager to receive feedback, and he worked tirelessly to implement the recommendations of those around him. His creativity was apparent in the new features offered in each edition, and the stories and examples he included to engage students and draw them into the subject matter. When Lou originally approached us about becoming co-authors, we had no idea how much we would learn from him about writing textbooks—assessment of learning needs, clear exposition of complex concepts and calculations, development of ancillary learning materials, as well as the business of publishing itself. Better than anyone we knew, Lou understood how to write a good textbook.

Lou has received abundant praise from students for his uncanny ability to clearly explain the most complex or theoretical concepts, and appreciation for his use of humor and stories to create interest and motivate discussion. His talent for teaching carried over into the classroom, where he implemented innovative case-based teaching methods and was recognized for excellence through nineteen teaching awards. He was also regularly asked to teach courses in other programs both in the US and globally, and to conduct seminars at provider organizations, including the Mayo Clinic. His work has touched thousands of students and professionals, and his books are undoubtedly on the reference shelves of healthcare leaders everywhere.

While his professional contributions are evident, Lou will also be remembered for his outstanding character. In spreading the sad news of his passing with colleagues throughout the country, it was not uncommon to hear comments such as, "Lou was one of a kind" or "There will never be another like Lou." He was witty, generous, and extraordinarily kind. Lou was a selfless mentor to those around him—quick to provide opportunities, and reluctant to take any of the credit. He was also genuinely interested in getting to know the people with whom he worked. He took the time to develop meaningful and lasting relationships, and he gratefully acknowledged the contributions of all of his partners, colleagues, and collaborators. Along with his wife Jane, Lou generously sponsored lunches, student events, conferences, scholarships and an endowed professorship. Jane was often seen with Lou at healthcare finance–related events, and they were true partners, both with an enduring commitment to his life's work.

With the passing of Lou Gapenski, the field of health care finance has lost a great leader and a champion. However, his memory and his legacy will live on in his scholarship, his textbooks, the students he trained, the leaders he inspired, and the colleagues whose lives he impacted for the better. This issue of the *Journal of Healthcare Finance* is dedicated to Lou's memory, and his influence can be seen throughout the work in the pages that follow.

Kristin L. Reiter, PhD, Professor
George H. Pink, PhD, Humana Distinguished Professor

Department of Health Policy and Management
Gillings School of Global Public Health
The University of North Carolina at Chapel Hill
1104H McGavran-Greenberg Hall, Campus Box 7411
Chapel Hill, North Carolina 27599-7411